http://routledgesw.com//washburn/engage/video to see *each* of these videos which are included within *each* of the web-based **cases**.

- Exercises at the end of each chapter provide you with the means to insure that your students can *demonstrate their mastery* of the theoretical frameworks, skills, and core competencies of generalist social work practice as presented *not just* in the text, but in the free web-based **cases** and **videos** as well.

- A wealth of **instructor-only resources** also available at www.routledgesw .com/practice provide: **full-text readings** that link to the concepts presented in each of the chapters; a complete bank of objective and essay-type **test items, all linked to current CSWE EPAS standards; PowerPoint presentations** to help students master key concepts; **a sample syllabus**; annotated **links to a treasure trove of social work assets on the Internet**; and a forum inviting all instructors using texts in the *New Directions in Social Work* series to communicate with each other, and share ideas to improve teaching and learning.

- A clear focus on generalist social work practice, informed by the authors' decades of real-world practice experience, at *all* levels of engagement and intervention.

"I am excited at the prospect of Routledge publishing this book. The approach is a needed contemporary response to current introductory practice books. The integration of theoretical perspectives and case examples will truly help bring to life the core competencies for generalist social work practice. In particular, the companion website provides an innovative and accessible means of letting students "play" and "try on" different components of practice in a creative and modern way. It is an essential first read on what generalist social work practice entails and would be great in an introductory social work practice class."

—Leslie K. Hasche, Ph.D, Social Work

Routledge
Taylor & Francis Group

www.routledgesw.com

THE UNIVERSITY OF
WINCHESTER

Alice A. Lieberman, The University of Kansas, Series Editor

An authentic breakthrough in social work education

New Directions in Social Work is an innovative, integrated series of texts, website, and interactive cases for generalist courses in the social work curriculum at both undergraduate and graduate levels. Instructors will find everything they need to build a comprehensive course that allows students to meet course outcomes, with these unique features:

- All texts, interactive cases, and test materials are linked to the 2008 CSWE Policy and Accreditation Standards (EPAS).

- **One web portal** with easy access for instructors and students from any computer—no codes, no CDs, no restrictions. Go to www.routledgesw.com and discover.

- **The series is flexible** and can be easily adapted for use in online distance-learning courses as well as hybrid and bricks-and-mortar courses.

- Each text and the website can be used individually or as an entire series to meet the needs of any social work program.

TITLES IN THE SERIES

Social Work and Social Welfare: An Invitation, Second Edition by Marla Berg-Weger
Human Behavior and the Social Environment, Second Edition by Anissa Taun Rogers
Research for Effective Social Work Practice, Second Edition by Judy L. Krysik and Jerry Finn
Social Policy for Effective Practice: A Strengths Approach, Second Edition by Rosemary K. Chapin
Contemporary Social Work Practice, Second Edition by Julie Birkenmaier, Marla Berg-Weger, and Marty Dewees

The Practice of Generalist Social Work

Second Edition
by Julie Birkenmaier and Marla Berg-Weger,
Saint Louis University, and Marty Dewees,
University of Vermont

To access the innovative digital materials integral to this text and completely FREE to your students, go to www.routledgesw.com/practice

In this book and companion custom website you will find:

- Complete coverage of the range of social work generalist practice within the framework of **planned change, encompassing engagement, assessment, intervention, and evaluation and termination**—for work with **individuals, families, groups, organizations, and communities**. This edition features expanded coverage of practicum with families, groups, organizations, and communities.

- Consistent and in-depth use of key theoretical perspectives and case examples to demonstrate essential knowledge, values, and skills for generalist social work practice. But the text does not overwhelm the student reader with a plethora of nuances of intervention and other skills that will occur in a variety of practice settings and roles. *Instead, this book presents clearly the core competencies for general social work practice.*

- Three *unique*, in-depth, interactive, easy-to-access **cases**, which students can easily reach from *any* computer, provide a **"learning by doing" format unavailable with any other text(s)**. Your students will have an advantage unlike any other they will experience in their social work education. Go to www.routledgesw.com/cases to see each of these **cases** on the free website.

- In addition, *three new and original* (to this text) **streaming videos** that relate to specific competencies and skills discussed in the book at the three client system levels—one each for individuals and families, groups, communities. The videos depict social workers demonstrating skills discussed in the chapters, and offer instructors numerous possibilities for classroom instruction. Go to http://routledgesw.com//sanchez/engage/video, http://routledgesw.com//riverton/engage/video, and

The Practice of Generalist Social Work

Second Edition

Julie Birkenmaier
Saint Louis University

Marla Berg-Weger
Saint Louis University

Marty Dewees
University of Vermont

Routledge
Taylor & Francis Group

NEW YORK AND LONDON

First published 2011
by Routledge
711 Third Avenue, New York, NY 10017

Simultaneously published in the UK
by Routledge
2 Park Square, Milton Park, Abingdon, Oxon OX14 4RN

Routledge is an imprint of the Taylor & Francis Group, an informa business

Typeset in Stone Serif by RefineCatch Limited, Bungay, Suffolk
Printed and bound in the United States of America on acid-free paper by Edwards Brothers, Inc.

Library of Congress Cataloging in Publication Data
A catalog record has been requested for this book

ISBN13: 978–0–415–87457–1 (hbk)
ISBN13: 978–0–415–87336–9 (pbk)
ISBN13: 978–0–203–82946–2 (ebk)

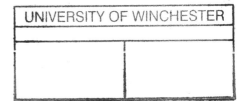

SUSTAINABLE FORESTRY INITIATIVE

Certified Fiber Sourcing

www.sfiprogram.org

BRIEF CONTENTS

Preface xxviii

About the Authors xxxvi

CHAPTER 1   *Understanding Social Work Practice*   1

CHAPTER 2   *Applying Values and Ethics to Practice*   35

CHAPTER 3   *Individual Engagement: Relationship Skills for Practice at All Levels*   61

CHAPTER 4   *Assessing and Planning with Individuals: Deepening the Dialogue*   96

CHAPTER 5   *Intervening in Context: Initiation, Intervention, Termination, and Evaluation*   154

CHAPTER 6   *The Family: Engagement and Assessment*   203

CHAPTER 7   *Intervening with Families: Initiation, Termination, and Evaluation*   243

CHAPTER 8   *Social Work Practice with Groups: Engagement, Assessment, and Planning*   272

CHAPTER 9   *Social Work Practice with Groups: Intervention, Termination, and Evaluation*   305

CHAPTER 10   *Social Work Practice with Communities: Engagement and Assessment*   339

CHAPTER 11   *Social Work Practice with Communities: Intervention, Termination, and Evaluation*   375

CHAPTER 12   *Social Work Practice with Organizations: Engagement, Assessment, and Planning*   403

CHAPTER 13   *Social Work Practice with Organizations: Intervention, Termination, and Evaluation   430*

References   R–1

Credits   C–1

Glossary/Index   I–1

DETAILED CONTENTS

Preface   xxviii

About the Authors   xxxvi

CHAPTER 1   *Understanding Social Work Practice   1*

Purpose of Social Work   2

Practicing Social Work   2

Social Work Competencies   4

Knowledge, Values, and Skills   4

Knowledge   4

Values   5

Skills   6

Types of Client Groupings   6

Practice Framework   7

Engagement   7

Assessment and Planning   8

Intervention   9

Termination   9

Evaluation   9

Licensure of Social Work   10

Tensions in Social Work   11

Clinical and Nonclinical Approaches   11

Developmental Socialization and Resocialization   12

Integrating Approaches for Clinical and Indirect (Macro) Practice   13

Social Control and Social Change   15

Change and Acceptance   16

Adjustment and Challenge   16

Experts and Shared Power   17

Minimization of Distance   18

Global Citizenship and the Local Community   18

Factors Promoting Globalization   19

Perspectives on the Conceptualizations of the Social Work Profession   21

Importance of Self-Knowledge   21

Theoretical Perspectives for Social Work Practice   23

Ecosystems Perspective   24

Social Justice Perspective   24

Human Rights Perspective   25

The Strengths Perspective   26

Principles of the Strengths Perspective   26

Postmodern Perspective and the Social Construction Approach   27

Social Construction   27

Deconstruction   28

Critical Social Construction   30

Complementary Aspects of the Theoretical Perspectives   30

Straight Talk about the Translation of Perspectives into Practice   31

Conclusion   31

Main Points   32

Exercises   33

CHAPTER 2   *Applying Values and Ethics to Practice   35*

A Brief History of Social Work Ethics   36

Professional Codes of Ethics   37

The NASW Code of Ethics   37

International Federation of Social Workers Ethical Statement   38

Limits of Ethical Codes   39

The Role of Context   41

Risk Taking and Creativity   41

Diversity   43

Ethics and the Law   45

Parallels between Ethics and the Law   45

Conflicts between Ethics and the Law   46

   Duty to Report: Child Protection   46

   Duty to Report: Adult Protection   47

   Duty to Protect: Threats of Violence   47

Collaboration between Ethics and the Law   48

Dilemmas and Critical Processes   49

   The Distinction between Value Conflicts and Ethical Dilemmas   49

   The Ethical Principles Screen   50

   Models for Resolution of Ethical Dilemmas   51

   Representative Examples of Practice Dilemmas   52

      Dual Relationships   52

      Responsibility to the Larger Society and Client Well-Being   54

      Paternalism and Client Self-Determination   55

Straight Talk about Expectations and Standards in a Litigious World   56

   Thoughtful Practice in a Postmodern World   57

   Risk Management in a Litigious World   57

Conclusion   58

Main Points   58

Exercises   59

CHAPTER 3   *Individual Engagement: Relationship Skills for Practice at All Levels   61*

Hearing the Client's Situation and Perspective   62

   Core Relationship Qualities   64

      Warmth   64

      Empathy   64

      Genuineness   65

      Unconditional Positive Regard   65

   Specific Skills for the Dialogue   65

      Preparing to Listen   65

      Diversity Considerations   67

   Specific Interviewing Skills   67

Discovery-Oriented Questions   67

Silence   67

Following Responses   69

Paraphrasing   69

Clarifying   69

Summarizing   70

Direct, Closed Questions   70

Open-Ended Questions   71

Indirect Questions   71

Empathic Communication   72

Avoiding Communication Pitfalls   73

Jargon   73

Leading Questions   73

Excessive Questioning   74

Multiple Questions   74

Irrelevant Questions   74

Integrating the Core Qualities and Skills in Dialogue and Interviewing   75

Articulating Purpose: Social Worker Role and Agenda   75

Moving from Spotting Deficiency to Recognizing Strengths   76

Skills and Methods   77

Mirroring   77

Contextualizing   78

Self-Disclosure   78

Accompaniment   79

Reinforcement and Celebration   79

Logistics and Activities   79

Recognizing and Articulating Power   80

Sources of Power   81

Agency Resources   81

Expert Knowledge   81

Interpersonal Power   81

Legitimate Power   82

Power in Client Lives: Jasmine Johnson   82

Jasmine's Situation   82

Jasmine and Power Relationships   82

Jasmine and the Social Worker   83

Jasmine Johnson: Conclusions   85

Viewing the Client System Situation and Perspective from Social Justice
and Human Rights Perspectives   85

Full Participation in Culture   86

Strategies and Skills for Promoting Social Justice and Human Rights   86

Straight Talk about the Relationship: Interpersonal Perspectives   88

Confidentiality   88

Privacy   89

Ongoing Evaluation   90

Conclusion   91

Main Points   91

Exercises   92

CHAPTER 4   *Assessing and Planning with Individuals: Deepening
the Dialogue   96*

A Brief History of Assessment   98

Where Does the Client Want to Go?   99

Implications of Theoretical Perspectives   99

Classic Theories   100

Psychoanalytic Theory   100

Attachment Theory   100

Cognitive Theory   101

Contemporary Theoretical Perspectives   101

The Strengths Perspective   102

Narrative Theory   103

Solution-Focused Approach   105

Theory and Evidence Matters   106

Implications of Diversity in Assessment   108

Cultural Humility   109

Culturally Competent Practice Behaviors   109

Connecting with the Spiritual Aspects of the Client System　110

Global Connections　111

Skills for Assessment and Planning　112

Strengths Perspective　112

Narrative Theory　112

Solution-Focused Approach　114

Developing a Shared Vision　115

Support for the Client's Goals and Dreams　116

Setting Goals　117

Contracting　118

Honest Responding　118

When Confrontation Is Necessary　119

When Alternatives Are Necessary　120

Using Mapping Skills to Enhance the Dialogue　120

Genograms　121

Ecomaps　122

Skills for Assessing Resources　123

Formal and Informal Resources　123

Assessment When Resources Are Available or Unavailable　125

Social Action When Resources Are Inadequate　126

Planning　126

Straight Talk about Assessment and Planning: The Agency, the Client, and the Social Worker　129

The Agency Perspective　130

Administrative Tasks　130

Documentation　131

The Client Perspective　135

Involuntary, Mandated, and Nonvoluntary Clients　135

Challenges in Working with Involuntary Clients　137

Engagement with Involuntary Clients　137

Legal Issues　139

Opportunities in Working with Involuntary Client Systems　139

Individual Scenarios　139

Power Issues　140

Violence   140

   Safety in Social Work Practice   141

      Skills for Working with Clients Who Are Angry   142

      What Agencies Can Do   142

Crisis Intervention   144

Suicide   145

The Social Worker Perspective: The Social Worker as a Whole Person   146

   Painful Events   146

      Personal Triggers   147

   Self-Care   147

      Sustaining Ethical Practice in the Face of Challenges   149

Conclusion   150

Main Points   151

Exercises   152

CHAPTER 5   *Intervening in Context: Initiation, Intervention, Termination, and Evaluation   154*

Supporting Clients' Strengths in Developing Interventions   155

   Strengths-Based Perspectives and Intervention   156

      Acting in Context   156

      Capitalizing on Strengths   157

   Narrative Intervention   157

   Solution-Focused Intervention   158

   Strengths-Oriented Practice Skills and Behaviors   158

      Supporting Diversity   159

Supporting Clients' Environments   159

   Principles for Taking Environments into Account   159

      The Social Worker Should Be Accountable to the Client System   159

      The Social Worker Should Follow the Demands of the Client Task   160

      The Social Worker Should Maximize the Potential Supports in the Client System's Environment   161

      The Social Worker Should Proceed from the Assumption of "Least Contest"   161

The Social Worker Must Help the Client Deconstruct Oppressive Cultural Discourse and Reinterpret Experience from Alternative Perspectives   161

The Social Worker Should Identify, Reinforce, and/or Increase the Client System's Repertoire of Strategic Behavior for Minimizing Pain and Maximizing Positive Outcomes and Satisfaction   162

Social Workers Should Apply the Principles to Themselves   162

Environment-Sensitive Processes and Skills   162

Providing Information   163

Refocusing and Confronting   163

Interpreting Client Behavior   165

Mapping as an Intervention Strategy   165

Traditional Social Work Roles in Contemporary Social Work Practice   166

Case Manager   167

Common Components of Case Management   167

Counselor   168

Broker   168

Brokering Functions and Context   168

Building and Maintaining Networks for Brokering   169

Making the Match in Brokering   170

Mediator   170

Finding Common Ground   170

Walking through It   171

Educator   172

Developing Client Skills   172

Working with the Public   173

Client Advocate   173

Case Advocacy   174

Cause Advocacy   174

Legislative Advocacy   174

Thoughts about Power and Advocacy   175

Collaborator   175

Putting It All Together   177

Empowerment Practice   177

Straight Talk about Interventions: Unexpected Events and Ongoing
    Evaluation   180

Supporting Clients' Strengths in Termination and Evaluation   181

Endings and Termination   182

Planning the Process: Overview   182

    Negotiating the Timing   183

    Reviewing the Agreement for Work   184

    Processing Successes and Shortcomings   184

    Making and Clarifying Plans   185

    Sharing Responses to Endings   186

    Respecting Cultural Consistency   187

Straight Talk about Termination and Endings   188

Formal Evaluations   189

Priorities in Evaluation   189

Quantitative and Empirical Processes: Evidence-Based Practice   190

    Single-Subject Design   190

    Goal Attainment Scaling   191

    Other Forms of Evaluation   194

    Postmodern Views of Evaluation   194

Qualitative and Reflective Processes   195

    Case Studies   195

    Explorations of Compatibility with Theoretical Perspectives   196

    Explorations of Quality of Relationship   197

Straight Talk about Evaluation and Reclaiming Our Knowledge   197

Conclusion   199

Main Points   199

Exercises   200

CHAPTER 6   *The Family: Engagement and Assessment   203*

Familiar Perspectives and Some Alternatives   204

Historical Antecedents for Family Social Work   205

Family as a Functioning Unit   207

Family as a System   208

   Change in One Component   208

   Subsystems and Boundaries   209

     Family Norms   209

  Implications of Family Systems Theory for Generalist Practice   210

   Family Structure   211

   Intergenerational Patterns   212

The Contemporary Context for Family Work   213

  Grandparents Rearing Grandchildren   213

  Gay, Lesbian, Bisexual, and Transgender Parents   214

  Single Parent Families   216

  Families of Multiple Racial and Ethnic Heritages   218

  Families Including Persons with Disabilities   218

  Blended Families   221

  International Families   222

Contemporary Trends and Skills for Engagement and Assessment with
Families   225

  Narrative Theory in Family Engagement and Assessment   225

   Thickening the Story   226

   Externalizing Problems   227

   Unearthing the Broader Context   227

  Solution-Focused Family Work   227

   Environmental Focus   229

  Constructionist and Social Justice Approaches to Family Social Work   230

   Critical Constructionist Emphasis   230

   Social Justice Emphasis   231

  Generalist Practice Skills Guidelines for Family Engagement and Assessment   231

   Mapping: A Family Assessment and Planning Tool   232

Straight Talk about Family Social Work Practice   236

Conclusion   238

Main Points   239

Exercises   240

CHAPTER 7   *Intervening with Families: Initiation, Termination, and Evaluation   243*

Theoretical Approaches to Intervening with Families   244

Strengths and Empowerment Perspectives and Family Interventions   246

Narrative Theory and Family Interventions   249

Solution-Focused Family Interventions   250

Contemporary Trends and Skills for Intervening with Families   252

Reframing   254

Perspectival Questions   255

Family Group Conferencing   256

Motivational Interviewing   256

Re-enactments   257

Mapping as an Intervention   258

Ending Work with Family Constellations   259

Endings with Strength and Empowerment   259

Endings in Narrative-Focused Work   260

Endings in Solution-Focused Work   260

Evaluation of Social Work Practice with Families   261

Strengths-Based Measures for Families   262

Straight Talk about Family Intervention, Termination, and Evaluation   267

Conclusion   268

Main Points   268

Exercises   269

CHAPTER 8   *Social Work Practice with Groups: Engagement, Assessment, and Planning   272*

Groups: The Source of Community   273

Group as a Natural Orientation   274

Implications of Cultural and Global Connections for Social Work Practice   274

Historical and Contemporary Contexts for Group Work   275

Dimensions of Social Work Practice with Groups   278

Types, Forms, and Functions of Groups   278

Group Work Logistics   284

Theoretical Approaches to Engagement and Assessment with Groups   285

Narrative Approach in Group Engagement and Assessment   285

Solution-Focused Approach in Group Engagement and Assessment   286

Contemporary Trends and Skills for the Beginning Phases of Group Work: Engagement and Assessment   287

Pre-group Planning   288

Need   288

Purpose   290

Composition, Eligibility, and Appropriateness   290

Structure   291

Content   291

Agency Context   291

Social Context   291

Pre-group Contact   291

Contacting Prospective Group Members   292

Engagement   292

Assessment and Planning   295

Straight Talk about Group Engagement and Assessment   296

Conclusion   302

Main Points   302

Exercises   303

CHAPTER 9   *Social Work Practice with Groups: Intervention, Termination, and Evaluation   305*

Interface: Social Justice, Diversity, and Human Rights   306

Theoretical Approaches to Intervening with Groups   307

Strengths and Empowerment Perspectives on Group Intervention   307

Narrative Theory and Group Interventions   308

Solution-Focused Group Interventions   309

Developmental Models   310

Boston Model   310

Relational Model   313

Contemporary Trends and Skills for the Middle Phase of Group Work:
Intervention   314

Social Work Group Interventions   315

Constructionist Groups for Women Experiencing Intimate Partner
Violence   316

Restorative Justice Groups for Combating Crime   317

Social Work Skills for Group Interventions   318

Leadership   318

Communication   319

Problem Solving   321

Management of Group Function and Process   322

Social Worker Roles   322

Group Member Roles   323

Contemporary Trends and Skills for the Ending Phase of Group Work:
Termination and Evaluation   325

Social Work Group Endings   325

Endings in Group Work with Strengths and Empowerment   326

Endings in Narrative-Focused Group Work   326

Endings in Solution-Focused Group Work   327

Skills for Social Work Group Terminations   327

Ending the Relationship between Group Members and Social Worker   328

Ending the Relationships among Group Members   329

Ending the Group Itself   330

Evaluation of Social Work Practice with Groups   331

Straight Talk about Group Intervention, Termination, and Evaluation   336

Conclusion   336

Main Points   337

Exercises   337

CHAPTER 10   *Social Work Practice with Communities: Engagement and
Assessment   339*

Familiar Perspectives and Some Alternatives   340

Community Practice and Generalist Practice   341

Definitions and Types of Community   342

  Communities of Locality   342

  Communities of Identity   342

  Personal Communities   343

Community Functions   343

Understanding a Community   344

  Community as a Social System   344

  Community as an Ecological System   345

  Center for Power and Conflict   345

    Power Dependency Theory   346

    Conflict Theory   346

    Resource Mobilization Theory   346

  Contemporary Perspectives for Community Practice   347

    Strengths, Empowerment, and Resiliency Perspectives   347

    Community in a Postmodern Perspective   347

Engagement and Assessment of Communities   348

  Engagement of Communities   348

  Assessment Process   349

  Comprehensive Community-Based Analysis   349

    Physical Setting   349

    History   349

    Demographics of the Population   349

    Economic System   349

    Political System   350

    Social Characteristics   350

    Human Service System   350

    Values, Beliefs, Traditions   350

    Evidence of Oppression and Discrimination   350

  Community Needs Assessment   351

    Using Evidence-Based Practice in Community Practice   352

    Community Needs Assessment Process   352

    Sources of Data   353

      Observation   353

Participant Observation   353

Service Statistics and Previous Studies   353

Use of Census Data   354

Administrative Data   354

Other Data   354

Mapping of Data   354

Interviews with Key Informants   355

Focus Groups   357

Community Forum   357

Survey Data   359

Determining Your Assessment Approach   359

Assessing Specific Population Needs and Social Problems   362

Mapping Community Assets   363

Skills for Community-Based Participatory Research   367

Contemporary Trends Impacting Community Practice   368

The World as a Community   369

Global Interdependence: Implications for U.S. Practice   369

Approaches for a Global Community   370

Straight Talk about Community Practice   371

Conclusion   372

Main Points   372

Exercises   373

CHAPTER 11   *Social Work Practice with Communities: Intervention,
Termination, and Evaluation   375*

Social Work Theory and Models for Community Intervention   376

Planning/Policy   378

Community Capacity Development   378

Social Advocacy   379

Blending Models   379

Planning/Policy Can Be Utilized with Community Capacity Development   379

Planning/Policy Can Be Utilized with Social Advocacy   380

Community Capacity Development Can Be Combined with Planning/
Policy   380

Community Capacity Development Can Be Combined with Social
Advocacy   381

Social Advocacy Can Be Mixed with Planning/Policy   381

Social Advocacy Can Be Combined with Community Capacity
Development   382

Contemporary Trends and Skills for the Middle Phase of Community Work:
Intervention   382

Community Social and Economic Development   382

Community Development Skills   383

Community Development Programs   384

Asset-Based Community Development   388

Community Organizing   389

Community Organizing Skills   390

A Generalist Approach to Community Intervention   391

Global Approaches for Community Social Work Practice   392

International Social Work Community Development   393

Globalization and Community Organizing in Social Work Practice   394

Contemporary Trends and Skills for the Ending Phase of Community Social
Work: Termination and Evaluation   397

Community Social Work Practice Endings   397

Endings in Community Practice Utilizing Strengths and Empowerment   398

Evaluation of Social Work Practice with Communities   399

Straight Talk about Community Intervention, Termination, and Evaluation   400

Conclusion   401

Main Points   401

Exercises   402

CHAPTER 12   *Social Work Practice with Organizations: Engagement, Assessment,
and Planning   403*

Understanding Organizations   404

Organization as a Social System   404

Contemporary Theories and Organizations   405

Dimensions of Organizations   405

Purpose   405

    Organizations Sanctioned by Law   405

    Organizations with Service Goals   406

    Organizations Arising from Social Movements   406

Structures of Governance   406

    Bureaucracies   407

    Project Teams   408

    Functional Structures   408

Internal Power Relations   409

    Traditional Authority   409

    Charismatic Authority   409

    Rational/Legal Authority   409

Intersections among Dimensions of Organizations   410

Social Work Practice in Host Settings   410

    Guest Status   411

    Interprofessional Teams   412

Engagement and Assessment of Organizations   412

Engagement of Organizations   413

Assessment of Organizations   413

Elements of an Internal Assessment   414

    Legal Basis   415

    Mission Statement   415

    By-laws   415

    History   415

    Administrative Structure and Management Style   416

    Structure of Programs, Services, and Activities   416

    Organizational Culture   416

    Physical Surroundings   416

    Public Relations   418

    Language   418

    Procedures   418

    Social Justice/Diversity Factors   420

Personnel Policies and Procedures   422

Resources (i.e., Financial, Technical and Personnel)   422

Elements of an External Assessment   422

Relationship with Funders and Potential Funders   422

Relationship with Clients   423

Relationship with Organizations in Network (i.e., Referrals and Coalitions)   423

Relationships with Political Figures   423

Organizational Engagement and Assessment and Generalist Practice   423

Skills for Engagement and Assessment with Organizations   424

Straight Talk about Practice within Organizations   426

Conclusion   427

Main Points   427

Exercises   428

CHAPTER 13   *Social Work Practice with Organizations: Intervention, Termination, and Evaluation   430*

Approaches, Perspectives, and Models for Interventions with Organizations   432

Self-Learning Model   432

Systems Model   433

Power and Politics Model   434

Postmodern Approaches   434

Social Constructionist Approach   435

Framework for Organizational Change   435

Gathering Allies and Creating a Change Work Group   435

Considerations for the Development of Feasible Solutions for Organizational Change   437

Change Proposal Form   439

Selecting an Organizational Change Strategy   440

Change Strategies   442

Contemporary Tactics and Skills for Interventions with Organizations   443

Implementation Skills   443

Capacity Building   444

Education   444

Persuasion   444

Mass Media Appeals   444

Bargaining and Negotiation   445

Group Actions   445

Ethic and Change Tactics   446

Implementing Organizational Change   448

Implementation Structure   449

Gantt Chart   450

Challenges to Implementation   450

Change Participant Affects   451

Generality of the Change   451

Organizational Supports   451

Termination and Evaluation of Change in Organizations   451

Evaluation of Social Work Practice with Organizations   452

Types of Evaluation   453

Structure of Evaluation   453

Logic Model   454

Information and Data Sources   454

Roles in Evaluation   455

Straight Talk about Organizational Life   456

Conclusion   457

Main Points   457

Exercises   458

References   R–1

Credits   C–1

Glossary/Index   I–1

PREFACE

Our new edition of *The Practice of Generalist Social Work* provides detailed coverage of the knowledge, skills, values, competencies, and practice behaviors needed for contemporary generalist social work practice. Using a strengths-based perspective, students are provided with a comprehensive overview of the major areas relevant for social work practice, including: theoretical frameworks; values and ethics; expanded coverage of communication skills for all client systems; and extensive coverage of practice with all client systems through all phases of the change process. *The Practice of Generalist Social Work* offers a comprehensive discussion of practice with individuals, families, groups, communities, and organizations within the concepts of planned change, encompassing engagement, assessment, intervention, and evaluation, and termination. Students have the opportunity to learn about generalist practice through in-depth case studies, examples, and exercises integrated throughout the text.

ORGANIZATION OF THE BOOK

The following paragraphs serve to briefly introduce each of the chapters included in this book with emphasis on the updated content.

Chapter 1

Understanding Social Work Practice   provides an overview of social work practice by grounding students in the purpose of social work, social work competencies, types of client grouping, and the practice framework of engagement, assessment, intervention, termination, and evaluation. A discussion of the licensure of social work, and the tensions in social work, provides students with real-world information about the profession. Students are also introduced to major theoretical perspectives for social work practice, including the ecosystems, social justice, human rights, strengths, and postmodern perspectives.

Chapter 2

In contrast to a straightforward overview of values and ethics, **Applying Values and Ethics to Practice**   provides a brief history of social work ethics and the NASW *Code of Ethics* (2008), then contrasts the *Code of Ethics* with the International Federation of Social Workers' Ethical Statement, and also discusses the limits of ethical codes. A discussion of the intersection of ethics and the law gives students information about the interplay between the two, followed by a discussion of ethical dilemmas and processes for resolving them. Extensive discussion about common practice dilemmas gives students exposure to situations that they may encounter in practice, followed by an emphasis on risk management.

Chapter 3

Individual Engagement: Relationship Skills for Practice at All Levels   provides students with the characteristics of core relationships qualities, as well as a description of the specific skills for dialogue with clients at all system levels, including coverage of common communication pitfalls. As the helping relationship includes the dimension of power, the chapter provides extensive coverage of sources of power within relationships, and provides guidance on the use of power through a case study of "Jasmine and the Social Worker." Students are also provided with strategies and skills for promoting social justice and human rights within helping relationships.

Chapter 4

Assessing and Planning with Individuals: Deepening the Dialogue   includes a focus on the assessment and planning process within the global environment in which modern-day social workers live and practice. The chapter begins with a discussion of the history of assessment and then moves to an overview of theoretical approaches to social work practice, both classic and contemporary (strengths, narrative, and solution-focused). The application of evidence-based practice approaches is highlighted. The need for practice knowledge and behaviors in the area of diversity within the assessment and planning phases emphasizes the need for cultural competence. The chapter concludes with a discussion of the relevant skills and practice behaviors in the assessment and planning phases of the intervention process.

Chapter 5

Intervening in Context: Initiation, Intervention, Termination, and Evaluation introduces students to key areas of social work practice that will impact virtually every dimension of their professional lives. With an emphasis on theoretical perspectives, students learn to apply various intervention, termination, and evaluation practice behaviors. Traditional and contemporary social work roles are highlighted and discussed. Interventions with individuals are also framed within an empowerment practice approach. Framed within theoretical perspectives for understanding diversity, students are offered an overview of the skills required to be a culturally competent social work practitioner.

Chapter 6

The Family: Engagement and Assessment The chapter begins with a history of social work practice with families, grounded within a systems framework. Theoretical perspectives, including narrative and solution-focused, are discussed within the context of the engagement and assessment phases of interventions with families. Students encounter a broad range of family constellations as they read about contemporary family social work. Practice behaviors and skills are presented for achieving engagement and assessment with families.

Chapter 7

Intervening with Families: Initiation, Termination, and Evaluation conceptualizes generalist social work practice interventions with families. Continuing with the theoretical perspectives discussed in Chapter 6, this chapter develops interventions with families using strengths and empowerment, narrative, and solution-focused approaches. Skills and practice behaviors for intervening, terminating, and evaluating family-focused interventions are discussed in detail.

Chapter 8

Social Work Practice with Groups: Engagement, Assessment, and Planning provides students with up-to-date perspectives on social work practice with groups. The chapter opens with an overview of the role of groups within our communities and profession followed by a historical and contemporary perspective on the use of groups for change. The dimensions of group practice are presented within the framework of theoretical perspectives (i.e., narrative and solution-focused). Planning for group interventions, including the engagement and assessment of group members, is emphasized from a practice behaviors perspective.

Chapter 9

Social Work Practice with Groups: Intervention, Termination, and Evaluation Developing and implementing interventions with various types of groups is the emphasis of this chapter. Continuing the framing of skills and techniques within theoretical perspectives, interventions with groups are introduced using the

strengths, narrative, and solution-focused frameworks. Models for group intervention are described along with an in-depth examination of the roles, skills, and practice behaviors required for carrying out a group-level intervention. Termination and
evaluation of group interventions are also covered.

Chapter 10

Social Work Practice with Communities: Engagement and Assessment   introduces
students to the concept of community. The chapter defines and discusses types and
functions of communities. Students learn about various theoretical perspectives,
including contemporary perspectives for community practice. Engagement and
assessment concepts, including community-based analysis, evidence-based practice,
and community needs assessments, are extensively discussed. Community practice
skills are thoroughly covered, as are the implications of global interdependence for
community practice in the United States.

Chapter 11

Social Work Practice with Communities: Intervention, Termination, and Evaluation
builds on the engagement and assessment content of Chapter 10 to present
strategies and techniques for community practice. Using the insights gained about
practice at the individual, family, and group levels, this chapter expands the
students' awareness of social work practice with communities through a discussion
of today's trends and skills for intervention, including community social and
economic development, and community organizing. Included in this discussion is
coverage of international community practice. Students also learn the knowledge
and skills needed for termination and evaluation of community practice.

Chapter 12

Social Work Practice with Organizations: Engagement, Assessment, and Planning
covers a challenging client system for beginning practitioners—the organization.
Students learn a wealth of practical and theoretical aspects of organizations, including a discussion about the purpose and structure of organizations, power relations
within organizations, and social work within host organizational settings. The
chapter provides discussion about the elements of an internal assessment of
organizations, to include organizational culture, and external assessments as well.

Chapter 13

Social Work Practice with Organizations: Intervention, Termination, and Evaluation
uses the foundation built in Chapter 12 to discuss approaches, perspectives, and
models for intervening with organizations. This chapter provides extensive coverage

of the relationship between theoretical perspectives and organizational change, as well as a practical framework for thinking about generating change and the needed knowledge for a social work generalist in this endeavour. Termination and evaluation of change efforts within organizations, including a discussion about the role of the generalist practitioner in this process, help students see their potential role in a change effort with organizations.

INTERACTIVE CASES

The website www.routledgesw.com/cases presents three unique, in-depth, interactive, fictional cases with dynamic characters and real-life situations that students can easily access from any computer and that provide a "learning by doing" format unavailable with any other text. Your students will have an advantage unlike any other they will experience in their social work education. Each of the interactive cases uses text, graphics, and video to help students learn about planned change, encompassing engagement, assessment, intervention, evaluation, and termination at all levels of practice. The "My Notebook" feature allows students to take and save notes, type in written responses to tasks, and share their work with classmates and instructors by email. Through the interactive cases, you can integrate the skills-based videos, and classroom discussions by acquainting your students with:

The Sanchez family   a Latino family of 10, who have numerous strengths, but are faced with a variety of challenges. Students will have the opportunity to experience the phases of the social work intervention, grapple with ethical dilemmas, and identify strategies for addressing issues of diversity.

Riverton   a small midwest city in which the social worker lives and works. The social worker identifies an issue that presents her community with a challenge. Students and instructors can work together to develop strategies for engaging, assessment, and intervening with the citizens of the social worker's neighborhood.

Carla Washburn   a 74-year-old woman who is facing numerous physical and emotional challenges. Students and instructors can collaborate to plan and implement the phases of social work practice, develop cultural competency, and learn about the impact of stages of life development on social work practice.

Skill Based Videos   originally written and produced for this text are embedded within *EACH of the three web-based CASES just mentioned (Sanchez Family, Riverton, and Carla Washburn). These videos engage students in developing demonstrated practice skills and behaviors and include text transcripts for use by all students.*

ADDITIONAL INSTRUCTOR SUPPORT MATERIALS AVAILABLE ON THE WEBSITE

If you are an instructor, you can go to www.routledgesw.com/practice. Click on the "create account/log-in" button within the brown square on the page which is labelled "Access Instructor Resources for this Text." Within 24 hours, you will be given a log-in and password that will provide you with access to high quality support material you are free to use whether you teach a conventional "bricks-and-mortar course" or an online course, or a hybrid between the two, using your school's course management system. The materials that are available free for your use include the following:

- EPAS MAPS BY COMPETENCIES AND/OR COURSE OBJECTIVES

  Available either in PDF or Word downloads, these maps enable you, the instructor, to see how the 2008 CSWE Policy and Accreditation Standards are met by the printed text and companion website materials.

- SUGGESTED COURSE SYLLABI

  Generalist practice courses vary in length and coverage. Some schools offer a two-semester sequence, others require three semesters or perhaps more. A variety of suggested syllabi are offered on our website allowing you, the instructor, to tailor this text and its wealth of web-based materials to your school's and your course's exact specifications. The syllabi are available in PDF or Word downloads.

- FREE COMPANION READINGS

  Some generalist practice courses are offered at the BSW level, others at the MSW level and any given practice course may vary considerably in depth and detail from another. To provide even further useful content for the course, we have also included 31 additional scholarly articles from the practice literature to accompany our text. They are available for download onto your course management system from our website. We have also created a bank of objective quizzes for instructors to use that apply to *each* of these readings.

- TESTBANK AND ANSWER KEY

  An additional bank of objective and open-ended short answer and essay questions are available, together with answer keys, for each chapter of the text and associated web-based case materials. These tests are formatted in WORD and also in RESPONDUS for maximum ease of use in online course environments.

- ANNOTATED WEB LINKS AND ACTIVITIES

  The internet is a great potential source of terrific stimulus materials for the classroom, but it takes a tremendous amount of work to sift through the volume of information potentially available and select only those materials that truly assist teaching and learning in generalist social work practice courses. We have done "our version" of that legwork and have made our annotated list of links and ideas for teaching available to you on our website.

- POWERPOINT PRESENTATIONS

  Organized on a text chapter-by-chapter basis, we have created special PPT presentations on subject matter and concepts that, in our teaching experience, have proven difficult for students to grasp. As with all our materials, these can easily be edited and adapted by you so they more perfectly suit your specific, unique teaching needs.

- CHAPTER SUMMARIES

  We include these especially for instructors teaching online courses where data on instruction suggest they are most helpful.

IN SUM

We have written this book with the purpose of providing you and your students with the information needed to learn the knowledge, skills, values, competencies, and practice behaviors that are required for a competent and effective generalist social work practice. The multiple options for supporting your teaching of this content are intended to help you address the diverse range of student learning styles and needs. The design of this text and the instructor support materials are aimed at optimizing the experiential options for learning about generalist practice. We hope this book and the support materials will be of help to you and your students as they embark on their social work practice.

ACKNOWLEDGEMENTS

We would like to thank the many colleagues who helped to make this book possible. To Alice Lieberman, we are grateful for your innovation and vision that has resulted in this series and the web-based supplements that bring the material alive. We appreciate the camaraderie and support of the authors of the other books in this series—Rosemary Chapin, Anissa Rogers, Judy Kryzik, and Jerry Finn. A special thank you to Anissa Rogers and Shannon Cooper-Sadlo whose creativity makes the exercises, test questions, and PowerPoint slides enticing and easy to use. We want to thank the group who participated in the production of the video vignettes: actors John Abram, Patti Rosenthal, Beverly Sporleder, Sabrina Tyuse, Kristi Sobbe, Myrtis Spender, Phil Minden, Katie Terrell, and Shannon Cooper-Sadlo and videographers Tom Meuser and Elizabeth Yaeger. Thanks to student assistants Erin Moriarity and Hannah Shanks for their help with research and editing. We also want to thank:

Megan Query of Butler University
Chrystal Barranti of California State University, Sacramento
Keva Miller of Portland State University
Sally Booth of Rivier College
Shannon Mokoro of Salem State University
Felix Amato of Salem State University
Nancy Gonchar of The College of New Rochelle
Pam Clary of Missouri Western University
Joseph Pickard of University of Missouri, St. Louis
Leslie Hasche of Kansas University

for their reviews of the book as it was evolving. Finally, we are most appreciative to the staff of Routledge for their support and encouragement for making this book a reality. It takes a village. . . .

ABOUT THE AUTHORS

Julie Birkenmaier is an Associate Professor in the School of Social Work at Saint Louis University, Missouri. Dr. Birkenmaier's practice experience includes community organizing, community development, and nonprofit administration. Her research and writing focuses on community development, financial capability, financial credit, and asset development. With Marla Berg-Weger, she also co-authored the textbook, *The Practicum Companion for Social Work: Integrating Class and Field Work* (3rd edition).

Marla Berg-Weger is a Professor in the School of Social Work at Saint Louis University, Missouri. Dr. Berg-Weger holds social work degrees at the bachelor's, master's, and doctoral levels. Her social work practice experience includes public social welfare services, domestic violence services, mental health, medical social work, and gerontological social work. Her research and writing focuses on gerontological social work and social work practice. She is the author of *Social Work and Social Welfare: An Invitation* (2nd edition). With Julie Birkenmaier, she co-authored the textbook, *The Practicum Companion for Social Work: Integrating Class and Field Work* (3rd edition). She is the Past President of the Association of Gerontology in Social Work and currently serves as the Chair of the *Journal of Gerontological Social Work* Editorial Board Executive Committee and is a fellow in the Gerontological Society of America.

Marty Dewees, Associate Professor Emerita of the University of Vermont, made her way into social work through counseling and then focused on mental health work at the state psychiatric facility. Her inclusion on the faculty at the University of Vermont provided the impetus for looking at social work practice through the lenses of human rights, social justice, strengths, and social construction. These are reflected in her previous publications and in the first edition of this book.

CHAPTER 1

Understanding Social Work Practice

Debbie, Joan, Marcy, and Kate felt as if the whole cosmos had just opened up for them. As a group they had already shared their experiences as women who had experienced intimate partner violence. Their social worker had explained how they could use their stories to help educate children in schools about violence at home. Their collective power felt liberating to them.

Harry, an 11-year-old orphaned child in Southeast Asia, hung on every word the community development worker uttered. She spoke of human rights that he had in his workplace. He had never imagined that he had any rights.

At their annual meeting, the neighborhood association expressed gratitude for the work of the community social worker. Her efforts, along with her colleagues', had resulted in neighbors who were more connected to job opportunities, teens involved in working for a new community park, and additional city funding made available to the neighborhood by local elected officials.

Key Questions for Chapter 1

(1) How can I prepare to engage, assess, intervene, and evaluate with client systems (EPAS 2.1.10(a)–(d))?

(2) How do you define the practice of social work?

(3) How does theory relate to social work practice?

WELCOME TO THE WORLD OF SOCIAL WORK PRACTICE. This world is sometimes exhilarating, sometimes frustrating, and sometimes heartbreaking. It is nearly always challenging, offers a deep sense of purpose, and once you have entered it, you may find it impossible to imagine doing any other kind of work.

This chapter introduces you to the practice of social work. The chapter examines the professional competence that the social worker brings to her or his work and the way in which the mission of the profession has been framed. Described are a number of ways to think about social work practice, types of client groupings and processes, tensions in social work, a brief account of the way the profession has dealt with theory, and the contemporary practice commitments that underlie this book. The brief vignettes you have just read describe only a few of the many types of social work practice and client systems.

PURPOSE OF SOCIAL WORK

What is social work trying to accomplish? The primary mission of social work, according to the National Association of Social Workers (NASW) *Code of Ethics* is "to enhance human well-being and help meet the basic human needs of all people, with particular attention to the needs and empowerment of people who are vulnerable, oppressed, and living in poverty" (2008). This mission can be narrowly defined as tied to a particular type of system (e.g., mental health, correction, and child welfare). Alternatively, the mission can be defined as tied to a specific method (e.g., behavioral or cognitive change), a particular problem-solving process or the elimination of a problem-focus (e.g., through the strengths perspective). The mission can also be defined as trying to achieve goals, such as adaptation, sobriety, or a clean criminal record. Although these end points are real examples of social work purpose, they are embedded in the deeper and broader mission. The purpose of social work is expressed generally and somewhat vaguely in the *Code of Ethics*, and therefore leaves much open to interpretation. Tensions, therefore, have arisen within the profession about the identity of the profession, some of which are discussed below.

PRACTICING SOCIAL WORK

Social work practice can be conceptualized in several different ways, including: (1) type of practice or range of practice settings; (2) set of activities; (3) set of roles; (4) set of competencies and practice behaviors; (5) types of client grouping; (6) practice framework; (7) a profession that is licensed by states; (8) by purpose (as mentioned above); and (9) by the tensions experienced in the profession. Self-knowledge is also a critical component of effective practice. These concepts are described below, and some are described in depth in this chapter.

Generalist social work practice, included in the curricula of undergraduate social work programs and in the foundation coursework in social work graduate programs, is aimed at preparing students to work with a range of systems, from direct, one-to-one practice to group-level practice to local and global community development work and work in international settings. Advanced social work practice, taught in the concentration curriculum of graduate school, focuses on more specialized practice, such as social work within a medical setting, family therapy, and administration of social service organizations. The range of generalist and advanced practice settings includes psychiatric facilities, schools, community organizations, family service organizations, legislatures, correctional settings, and a host of others.

Social work practice is also framed as a set of activities. Often these activities are associated with particular agencies and the functions they carry out in the community. Examples of these include: (1) advocating for policy change regarding the rights of older adults to services from an area agency on aging; (2) facilitating an empowerment group in a domestic violence program, such as the group in which Debbie, Joan, Marcy, and Kate belong; (3) mentoring students in a neighborhood school; (4) developing a psycho-educational group in a mental health agency; (5) supporting families in an emergency housing shelter; (6) implementing human rights policies in another culture by learning a new language and traveling to another part of the world to assist children like Harry; (7) advocating with public officials, companies, and corporations; (8) working with a group of adolescents; and (9) fundraising from government and foundation sources to assist in the empowerment of disadvantaged neighborhoods.

Another way to look at generalist social work practice emphasizes the roles that a social worker utilizes with client systems that define the relationship between the two. In the helping process, the generalist social worker working in direct practice with individuals may take on the role of *case manager* (i.e., assisting clients to assess for, arrange, and coordinate needed goods and services), *counselor* (i.e., providing suggestions to assist clients to reach their goals), *broker* (i.e., referring clients to appropriate needed goods and services), *mediator* (i.e., assisting two parties to mutually resolve a dispute), *educator* (i.e., providing relevant information to client systems), and *client advocate* (i.e., working with or on behalf of a client to obtain goods and services). Some definitions of role relationships are driven largely by theoretical perspectives. These roles are discussed in great detail in Chapter 5. All social worker functions are associated with roles that clarify the nature of the interaction between a social worker and the client system. These roles are fluid, and can change from interaction to interaction, and even within interactions. The roles define responsibilities for both the client system and the social worker. Social work practice involves a wide variety of roles because social work is involved in the breadth of human experience.

Social work is a complex and multi-faceted profession, with practitioners engaged in a wide variety of activities. Other than type of settings, activities, and roles, social work practice can also be described by social work competencies and practice behaviors, types of client grouping, practice frameworks, as a licensed profession, and by the purpose of social work. These various ways of defining and describing the profession are discussed in the following section.

SOCIAL WORK COMPETENCIES

Generalist social work practitioners bring a set of competencies and practice behaviors to serve client systems. These competencies, or ". . . measureable practice behaviors that are comprised of knowledge, values and skills" (Council on Social Work Education (CSWE), 2008, p. 3), are defined by the Council on Social Work Education's Educational Policy and Accreditation Standards (EPAS) to guide social work education, and therefore influence social work practice. The 10 competencies define practice elements, as well as address the practice structure of engagement, assessment, intervention, and termination and evaluation. Each competency consists of several descriptive practice behaviors that social workers should competently be able to demonstrate in practice settings. These competencies are comprised of knowledge, values, and skills, and are the attributes that social workers bring to the interaction with the client system of individuals, families, groups, organizations, and communities.

Knowledge, Values, and Skills

The trio of knowledge, values, and skills is often considered the core of social work education and training. As an integrated whole, these elements can be considered as the tools that a practitioner brings to the work, as they reflect personal aspects and attributes acquired by, and some scholars think inherent to, the social worker. Each is necessary for effective service delivery.

Knowledge Facts and research findings comprise professional **knowledge** along with broader topics such as intuition and cultural awareness. A practice-based example may include the need for social workers to know facts, histories, theories, and trends about human development, policy, research, and practice, which are often combined and labeled "biopsychosocial" knowledge. Knowledge of a variety of theories of human behavior and the social environment is central to generalist social work practice. This knowledge is needed to understand normal (or expected) behavior for an adolescent under stress, or the likely dynamics in an agency when a policy change is initiated from the administration. This arena also assumes that the knowledge required is largely agreed upon and that it is attainable through study, discussion, research experimentation, and related activities. According to the EPAS competencies, social workers should also know the history of social work, the value base and ethical standards of the profession, and the history and current structures of social policies and services (CSWE, 2008). Knowledge may also include your experience of utilizing theory and ideas, and even the knowledge emanating from the first-hand experience of seasoned practitioners, or "practice wisdom." This form of practice knowledge may elude traditional empirical measurement, an ongoing challenge both in the field and in social work education. This practice knowledge is the integration of knowledge learned "on the job" with knowledge from other sources, such as prior education and continuing education. Practice wisdom is an invaluable part of social work practice.

Two other areas that are critical areas of knowledge are culture and spirituality. First, social workers must understand the broad ways in which a culture's structure and values may create or enhance privilege and power for certain groups in society, and to eliminate the influence of personal biases and values in working with diverse clients (Council on Social Work Education, 2008). **Cultural competence** refers to the "process by which individuals and systems respond respectfully and effectively to people of all cultures, languages, classes, races, ethnic backgrounds, religions, and other diversity factors in a manner that recognizes, affirms, and values the worth of individuals, families, and communities, and protects and preserves the dignity of each" ("Indicators for the Achievement of the NASW Standards for Cultural Competence in Social Work Practice," 2008). The notion of spirituality as another form of knowledge has been recently added to models of both human development and social work education. Spirituality is integrally connected with culture and therefore gives practitioners access to knowledge about important dimensions of their clients. For example, recognizing a Navajo child's spiritual affirmation of harmony may help a social worker understand the child's reluctance to engage in aggressive competition in school. In some areas of practice, such as end of life, a biopsychosocial-spiritual model is being utilized to serve the needs of clients as whole persons (Sulmasy, 2002).

Values Social work has always strongly identified itself as a profession of **values**, which are strongly held beliefs about preferred conditions of life. The values of the social work profession articulate several key elements, such as (1) the inherent worth of people; (2) the need for open and honest communication to build relationships; and (3) respect for the unique characteristics of diverse populations (to name just a few of the values of the social work profession). Although the social work profession has clearly stated values, you may hear spirited discussion about the ways in which these values are implemented in practice. Consideration of values and ethics will present many challenges to social workers, and will often look different in complicated practice contexts from the way they do in isolation. Through the professional organization, the National Association of Social Workers (NASW), the profession has developed a *Code of Ethics* (NASW, 2008) that plays a significant role in sorting out complex situations in which values are at issue. While values, as beliefs, guide professional thinking about behavior and judgments about conduct, **ethics** are the rules, or prescriptions, for behavior that reflect those values. For example, one of the cardinal values held by the social work profession is that all human life is worthy. From that value arises the ethical principle that human life should be protected in social work practice, which means that social workers actively try to prevent any harm that might occur to another person. Ethical dilemmas arise when ethical principles conflict, such as the case when trying to prevent harm to one person puts another at risk. The National Association of Social Workers *Code of*

Ethics was developed to clarify the principles of ethical practice. The role of values provides critical criteria for the ways in which the profession shapes itself and the professional rules of conduct.

Skills   The third element that the social worker brings to the professional work is **skills,** or the implementation of the knowledge, theoretical perspectives, and values the social worker brings to her or his work with client systems. Social workers need a wide range of skills, from traditional communication skills and individual assessment skills, to skills in working with families, groups, communities, and organizations. The range of skills will be discussed in subsequent chapters of this book, and the skills mentioned in the EPAS core competencies (CSWE, 2008) will be emphasized.

Types of Client Groupings

Competencies to practice social work may be viewed within the context of client groupings. Social workers work with individuals, couples, families of all types, groups, communities, and organizations, both domestically and internationally. These client groups often overlap, as in the need for group work within community practice, and the need to engage in community work to assist families. These groupings define the constellation of the service beneficiaries involved in the interaction. The more recent expansion of global awareness has resulted in the inclusion of international and global social work, extending the arena in which social work practice is both relevant and critical. Social work education frequently uses this organizational scheme in the layout of its curriculum by specific course content or emphasis. A brief discussion is found here, with a detailed discussed following in later chapters of the book.

- *Individual work, family work, or casework:* This face-to-face focus, or **individual work, family work,** or **casework,** spans all fields of practice, populations, and settings. Casework may include working with an adolescent struggling with sexuality issues, a mother concerned with her child's development, an older adult who is facing an inability to care for himself, or a five-year-old who does not pay attention in school. The nature of the work will be heavily influenced by the agency's purpose, the practice perspective, the personal characteristics of the client (individual or family), and your skills and theoretical perspective. Cultural context, social and political influences, and current community concerns will also affect client relationships.

- *Group work:* Social workers frequently practice with **groups.** The focus of group work may be on helping the group members make individual changes, the group as a whole make changes, or for the group to make changes in the environment. **Group-level social work practice** is conceptually social, and embodies the relationship emphasis of the profession. Group work can be a powerful tool for change, and has similarities and differences in the many different practice settings and contexts within which it is implemented. Social work with groups is one of the most distinctive practices of the profession.

- *Community practice:* The method of practice known as **community practice** usually involves a common locality, such as a city neighborhood, small town, or rural area. Beyond locality, however, *community* also refers to a common concern, interest, or identification. For example, you might consider yourself a member of a hometown as well as a community of gay men or Jewish women or people of Irish descent. Social work practice has historical work in community practice, and aspires toward inclusive participation of community citizens in addressing their self-defined concerns.

- *International work:* An emerging focus of practice is **international social work.** The social work profession is increasingly integrating a global, transnational perspective of local issues, such as employment, homelessness or HIV/AIDS, into the professional knowledge and response to local issues, to provide a full account for the challenges faced by client systems.

This organizational scheme based on client groupings contains a number of underlying assumptions rooted in culture about social work skill development. For example, many U.S. social workers agree that one-to-one practice work is the natural starting place for social work practice, and other types of practice refer back to one-to-one methods. However, in other cultures in which family or community is the major organizing structure or reference point, this assumption may not fit. Although the distinctions between types of groupings continue to be a useful way of thinking about social work, generalist practice emphasizes an integration of knowledge and skills across all system levels and sizes.

Practice Framework

The practice framework provides a view of social work practice related to the process of the work. The practice framework most commonly used in social work describes the activities of the social worker and the client system as they together proceed through relatively standard phases. Although these phases are described here in a linear progression, the social worker and client frequently loop back and forth between phases as is needed. The phases described below are more fully discussed relative to client systems in subsequent chapters.

Engagement   Building a relationship among the social worker, the client, and the client's environment is referred to as **engagement**. Successful engagement involves establishing a degree of trust and a sense that the work ahead will be helpful to the client system and professionally rewarding and satisfying to the social worker.

Engaging a client system requires effective communication and engagement skills with individuals, as well as establishing significant and collaborative connections with the client system's environment and the relevant service systems that will impact your work and the client's goals. For example, your client has asked for your help in negotiating and advocating within the public school system in which her child with disabilities is being educated. You carefully develop a relationship with her so that you may understand the issues and her experiences. You will also need to engage with the client's network (in this case the school system), to learn about the system constraints and challenges, in order to be effective in facilitating a more productive relationship between your client and the school.

Without a successful engagement, the effectiveness or helpfulness of the work that follows may be compromised or more challenging. Engagement may not be effective for a variety of reasons. For instance, the client may lose investment in a process due to a lack of significant meaningful connection to the work, or the critical network contacts in the environment may not perceive their role as appreciated or understood fully. In the situation just described, if the school staff think that you have failed to understand the difficulties of providing extensive services with shrinking resources, they may actually become less willing to work on improving their relationship with your client.

Assessment and Planning   Generally, **assessment** encompasses recognition of the parameters of the practice situation and the way in which the participant(s) is(are) affected. The client's goals are central to the process of assessment and planning for an intervention. Through mutual exploration of the issues, the client and social worker decide the best ways to address the client's goals. Assessment focuses on the analysis of the major area for work; the aspects of the client environment that can offer support for a solution; the client knowledge, skills, and values that can be applied to the situation; and ways in which the client can meet her or his goals.

The social worker's theoretical perspective guides the selection of assessment styles and planning approaches. The overall mission of the agency also plays an important, perhaps defining role in the activity. For example, the assessments conducted in foster care agencies may vary, but they are all likely to be focused on children and parenting, rather than vocational development or personal growth counseling.

Planning is an integral part of the assessment process. Developing the plan will require the client and social worker to assess or evaluate the options, the resources, the barriers, client preferences, and the agreed-upon goals, along with the established methods of achieving them. The plan should also include consideration of the less-than-obvious or unexpected outcomes of reaching a goal. For example, a social worker may assist a couple in adopting a child for whom they provided foster care. Another child in the family may have accepted the temporary nature of the foster care arrangement but suddenly feels threatened by the permanency of foster care turning into an adoption. The complexity of human emotion frequently appears in unexpected places and times in social work practice.

Intervention   The next stage in this sequence, **intervention** refers to the action— the doing of the work that will enable the client and the practitioner to accomplish the goals decided upon in the assessment. Generalist practice interventions vary widely, from helping an older adult tenants' union organize a rent strike to helping a family receiving Medicaid benefits receive health care for an ill child. Intervention is the joint activity of the client system and the social worker. In some cases, the intervention may involve the social worker listening to and reflecting on the client's situation, helping the client think about the situation and her or his role in it, and facilitating an opportunity to create a different, more preferable situation. The intervention process is also influenced by the theoretical and/or practice perspective of the social worker. In some practice models, the social worker is very active in determining the client's best interests and initiating action to achieve a specific outcome. In other models, the planning and intervention is a more collaborative process with shared responsibility for actions, and together deciding on the best course. As with other aspects of practice, the type, level, and focus of the intervention vary widely.

Termination   Ending with client systems, or **termination**, is a long-standing area of focus for social workers. Many clients have experienced abrupt, sometimes violent or completely disconcerting endings to relationships or arrangements; therefore, the profession is committed to facilitating appropriate and effective termination with client systems. In general, the termination process includes reviewing the work and accomplishments, discussing the development of the working relationship, and planning the future to sustain the changes that have been achieved. To many social workers, termination is one of the most difficult as well as one of the most important aspects of the work. Those who want to focus more on the future sometimes call it "consolidation" or "graduation."

Evaluation   Although many social workers are pressed for time to complete other tasks, present and future clients benefit from **evaluation** to determine the effectiveness of the practice intervention. The social work *Code of Ethics* (NASW, 2008) mandates social workers engage in and utilize research to improve practice, which can include program evaluation and research on individual effectiveness. CSWE accreditation guidelines require social workers to "engage in research-informed practice and practice-informed research" (CSWE, 2008, EPAS, 2.1.6). At the same time, the profession has put increasing emphasis on evidence-based practice, defined as "an educational and practice paradigm that includes a series of pre-determined steps aimed at helping practitioners and agency administrators identify, select, and implement efficacious interventions for clients" (Jensen & Howard,

2008). Use of evidence-based practice facilitates the integration of research findings, client values and preferences, practitioner knowledge and expertise, and other factors to make practice, policy, and research decisions.

Research on practice may involve evaluation tools that assess the progress of a program, and may provide encouragement for a reflective approach by individual workers on the quality of their work. Others see an important link between research activities and effective client advocacy. For example, if you want to advocate for persons who are homeless by demonstrating that existing services are inadequate or are not directed effectively, an understanding of the demographics of the homeless population, the number of homeless, and their background (among other things) is imperative.

There are many kinds of evaluation, including quantitative, qualitative, subjective, objective, **formative** (during the work), **summative** (at the end of the work), self-report, reflection, and standardized tests. The prevailing trend within the various funding and accountability arrangements associated with social work practice is to require more evaluative activity both to demonstrate effectiveness and to justify continued or increased financial support for practice initiatives and policy programs.

Licensure of Social Work

Another way to conceptualize social work is as a helping profession that is licensed by states to protect the public. Social work, as a profession, is regulated within and by all 50 states, the District of Columbia, Puerto Rico, the Virgin Islands, and 10 Canadian provinces. Regulation protects the public by establishing; (1) the qualifications that a professional must possess; (2) a means of holding professionals accountable; and (3) a system for the public to make complaints against incompetent or unethical practitioners and have them investigated and adjudicated. Today, there are almost 400,000 licensed social workers practicing in the United States and Canada (Randall & DeAngelis, 2008).

The social work profession has four types of licensure available: BSW (usually upon graduation); MSW (one type upon graduation, and a second type, independent, after two years of supervised general experience); and clinical (after two years of supervised clinical experience). Most jurisdictions license social workers at two or more of these categories. While the requirements vary from jurisdiction to jurisdiction, the general requirements for licensure are a specific level of education, supervised experience by a social worker, and demonstration of knowledge and minimum competence by passing an exam, providing references, and demonstrating evidence of good moral character. Some locales require more than two years of supervised clinical experience, or proof of a minimum number of hours in a clinical field placement, or proof of specific clinical coursework. After licensure, many states require that licensed social workers complete ongoing professional continuing education units (CEUs) through professional workshops or conferences that provide skills training for new situations, new populations, and new ways of thinking about the work (Randall & DeAngelis, 2008).

Tensions in Social Work

Almost since its inception, the social work profession has been challenged by a set of tensions that have sometimes seemed to obscure the identity of the profession. The most significant tensions (discussed below) are those that strongly shape the identity of the social work profession and the way in which social workers practice. They are:

- Whether to promote a clinical or nonclinical approach to working with clients

- The extent to which social workers exercise social control or promote social change

- The extent to which social workers promote change or acceptance of their clients

- The struggle between encouraging clients to adjust to their circumstances or challenge their circumstances

- Whether social workers promote their expert position or share power with their clients

- The adjustment to globalization by the profession

Clinical and Nonclinical Approaches   Yet another tension that underlies social work practice involves the question of whether practitioners should focus primarily on clinical or nonclinical work. The word *clinical* has many meanings, and can represent a code for a medically based private practice model that involves such concepts as diagnosis and managed care. *Clinical* can be associated with cold, calculated, stiff, or impersonal interchanges that are driven by the expert and received by the patient.

In this book, **clinical work** is considered to encompass social work with individuals, groups, and/or families that is not only **direct practice**, or **direct work** (face-to-face) but also designed to change behaviors, solve problems, or resolve emotional or psychological issues (Grant, 2008). For example, clinical work can include intervening individually with a young woman to address her self-harming behavior, facilitating a series of groups for children who have experienced the death of a parent, and assisting a family to redefine the communication patterns among the three generations of its members. Clinical work can extend into many practice arenas such as physical and mental health, substance abuse treatment, school social work, gerontological social work, and some child welfare work. Some state social work licenses define clinical work explicitly and require a master's degree. Additional or different credentials may be required to work in some areas (for example, an addictions certificate for substance abuse work).

Nonclinical work usually implies that the work addresses the environment. Macro, or indirect, practice addresses social problems in community, institutional, and society systems. Nonclinical, or macro, practice social workers, achieve social change through neighborhood organizing, community planning, locality development, public education, policy development, administration, and social action. Nonclinical work can also include social work that is political or focused on social reform efforts. These efforts involve such activities as working for improved institutional responses or changing or supporting laws, policies, and social structures relating to various dimensions of diversity, such as class, gender, ability, and cultural ethnicity. This field of work, **policy practice**, focuses specifically on ensuring that policies are more responsive to client needs and rights. Nonclinical work focuses less on the internal dynamics of an individual's experience and more on opportunity and change in the environment. While tension can exist between clinical and nonclinical work, thoughtful and principled efforts can connect the approaches. For example, clinical social workers can identify and communicate client needs to administrators and other nonclinical social workers, so that policy practice efforts are appropriately channeled to the client needs that are the most significant. In another example, clinical social workers can be involved in and refer clients to neighborhood organizing efforts to make social connections with others concerned about similar topics. The following discussion considers some dimensions of this tension.

Developmental Socialization and Resocialization   The late Harry Specht, a social work policy educator, distinguished between "developmental socialization" and "resocialization" (Specht, 1990). Specht defined **developmental socialization** as the attempt, through providing support, information, and opportunities, to help people enhance their environments by making the most of their roles. Developmental socialization also involves confronting obstacles such as abuse or oppression that impede people's attempts to make the most of their roles. Developmental socialization was the natural domain of social work, and is basically nonclinical. In contrast, Specht defined **resocialization** as the attempt to help people with feelings and inner perceptions that relate primarily to the self. Specht purported that psychotherapeutic approaches associated with psychology and psychiatry, rather than social work, should deal with such issues. Significantly, Specht argued that social work had been seduced from its original mission by clinical psychotherapy, which many people characterize as a higher-status activity. As an advocate for an emphasis on the social environment, rather than inner psychological life, Specht called for social work to build its professional core in public, rather than private, services and institutions and to replace all its clinical training with adult education, community work, and group work. His last major co-written publication was tellingly called *Unfaithful Angels: How Social Work Has Abandoned Its Mission* (Haynes, 1998).

Many social workers are heavily committed to the kind of work that Specht rejects as inappropriate. These practitioners view social work as providing useful perspectives for dealing with clinical, interactional, interpersonal, and sometimes intrapersonal issues. Many practitioners view these perspectives as appropriate tools in the realms of individual counseling, family intervention, and a host of other areas that might be called clinical, or therapeutic. This location of social work's appropriate domain has been a prevalent controversy since Mary Richmond's day. In more recent times, some social workers who are committed to environmental or structural intervention have seen the movement to license social workers as a negative continuation of the move into professionalism, which in this context usually means individual psychotherapy and, often, private-pay practice.

The perceived polarity between clinical and nonclinical practice is an obstacle in contemporary social work. You have already seen that the *Code of Ethics* (NASW, 2008) requires that social workers engage in work that supports socially equitable allocations of opportunity, which by definition is environmental and political. When clinical practice focuses entirely on individual issues and ignores or excludes the nonclinical work of advocacy and power analysis inherent in the pursuit of social justice, it comes into conflict with the *Code*. The proximity of some clinical practice settings (such as mental health and substance abuse) to the health care delivery world and its requirements for individualized, de-contextualized labels of pathology, sometimes discourages or diverts social workers from entering into social justice pursuits.

Integrating Approaches for Clinical and Indirect (Macro) Practice The debate between an individual, clinical focus and a nonclinical, or macro, environmental focus can be reconciled through integrating approaches. For example, Gitterman and Germain (2008b) argue that social work professionals must be prepared to work with all types of client systems, as situations require. Many methods and skills are common across all client systems. The historical loyalties to both the individual and to the macro advocacy pursuits to match client needs with environmental resources are a strength of the profession. The Educational Policy and Accreditation Standards (EPAS) (CSWE, 2008) for social work education underscore the commitment of social work to work with all client systems, with competencies and practice behaviors that require mastery of knowledge, skills, and values across all client systems.

There are many contemporary and generally complementary efforts to connect clinical practice with social justice issues. One approach expands the definition of clinical work to include "case management, advocacy, teamwork, mediation, and prevention roles, as well as therapeutic and counseling roles" (Swenson, 1998, p. 527). The clinician also uses self-reflection to consider her or his privilege. This in turn addresses the worker's accountability to clients, clearly an important component of a social justice approach.

A second approach to integrating approaches lies in the use of theory, perspectives, and approaches that guide social work practitioner approaches to working with client systems. For example, a generalist, **empowerment** perspective (discussed further below) also bridges the clinical and indirect practice tension. Within this perspective, social work practice is both clinical and indirect, and is at the intersection of private troubles and public issues. According to the empowerment perspective, social work utilizes an integrated view of humans in the context of their physical and social environments. Social workers using the empowerment perspective seek to promote a mutually beneficial interaction between individuals and society (Parsons, 2008). **Narrative** approaches (discussed in more detail in Chapters 4 and 6) provide an example of the way in which the issue of clinical practice and nonclinical pursuit of social justice occurs. A narrative approach to working with client focuses on empowerment, collaboration, and viewing problems in social context. A narrative-oriented practitioner addresses the societal injustices individuals and families encounter in the client intervention (Kelly, 2008). The issues that individuals and families bring to the work are always put into the contextual arena of the social and power relations in the client's experience. Although narrative approaches began in family therapy work, narrative approaches have also been applied to work at the individual, group, and community levels (Kelly, 2008). The use of the concept of **social construction** also blurs the distinction between clinical and nonclinical work. Social construction emphasizes the power of agency, a person's ability to affect her or his own circumstances that human beings exercise in creating their social locations. For example, looking at "human actors as co-constructors of, not just interactors within, their social environments" (Kondrat, 2002, p. 435) allows for human agency. In this view, people shape their environments, which in turn (or recursively) influence them. For example, you are a member of a community, and as such, you respond to other members of the community. However, you also take a part in creating your community, a process that goes beyond simply reacting to various individuals. By focusing on the client as co-constructor of the environment, this approach blurs the distinction between clinical work with the person and nonclinical work with the environment. Finally, a highly integrative model bridges individual, clinical work and environmental practice concerns through the use of **deconstruction** (Vodde & Gallant, 2002). In this conceptualization, the social worker moves from helping the client conquer the internal ramifications of the problem (such as clinical depression) to helping the client connect with others who are experiencing the same kind of oppression but resist it. Georgia's story will help demonstrate many of these points about deconstruction.

Georgia is a 25-year-old woman from the southern United States. She has come to a large city in the Midwest to see a different world and another part of the country. Very early in her stay, she met and fell in love with Tom, a native to the

Midwest. Georgia and Tom developed a serious relationship, and Georgia moved into his apartment when she discovered that she was pregnant. From that time on, things did not go well for Georgia. Tom began to resent her interest in the coming birth, and at times he was verbally abusive, insulting her southern background and degrading every personal aspect he could find wrong with her. He then started to be physically rough with her when they had any difference of opinion. Eventually he began to shove her into the wall, slap her, and kick at her belly. Georgia was disillusioned and frightened both for her own safety and that of her child. She could not understand how she had failed Tom, or what she had done to become so disgusting to him, or how she had become so hard for him to be around.

When Georgia finally believed she could no longer manage this situation, she contacted a local women's shelter. She was devastated. By this time she believed herself to be entirely worthless and thoroughly unlovable due to Tom's labeling her as ugly and stupid. Georgia was at a very low point and was fearful for her future.

Georgia's social worker, over time and with the use of her professional skills, helped her to see that Tom's battering was not a function of her personality or unworthiness but rather of his own impulses. Therefore, Tom, and not Georgia, was responsible for Tom's abusive behavior. With support, Georgia began to regain her sense of worth and resilience and to feel stronger about her own capacities. Gradually she felt less in need of intense work on her esteem. She began to explore how our society supports violence. She met with other women at the shelter and joined in their resistance to societal violence through advocating for education in the schools and providing personal testimonies to groups of women who requested them.

This work empowered Georgia by enabling her to take control of her own emotions while addressing an environmental issue in a meaningful manner. The scenario presented here demonstrates the integrated approaches described earlier that address both clinical issues and social justice concerns. The approach spans the inner psychological turmoil that Georgia experienced as it began to become more political, and facilitates Georgia's role in influencing her environment. In this way the work has gone from an individual clinical focus to a nonclinical, integrated political focus without sacrificing either, as each supports the other.

Social Control and Social Change   Social work operates within, and is supported by, the same society that is the object of change efforts. Some of the regulatory bodies in which social workers practice, such as child protection, criminal justice, and mental health, carry an authoritative sanction for social control. In some circumstances this control appears to be at odds with the commitment of the social work profession to social change, a process in which social workers attempt to alter basic social structures. The two functions, control and change, are not inherently irreconcilable, but the ways in which they play out in their respective practice arenas tend to make them appear incompatible at times.

Change and Acceptance   Another related tension involves the degree to which the goal of social work is change, either in individual or environmental, or acceptance of the client's current status as "good enough." As you would expect, the particular circumstances and settings associated with each situation strongly influence the social worker's approach to this issue. In fact, although the pull between acceptance and change occupies a place in the historical tensions of the profession, it may prove to be so contextually influenced that it will never be fully put to rest as long as individuals continue to evaluate social contexts, based on their own idiosyncrasies, in different ways.

Adjustment and Challenge   The dilemma of helping people to adjust to their circumstances or helping people challenge their circumstances is another historical tension in social work. This question must be answered in context according to factors relating to social justice. For example, many practitioners might support a female client who feels angry, distressed, and overburdened in a marital relationship and struggles with the sociological realities of contemporary families. These realities might include the expectations of partners, employers, and society at large that most mothers, even those working full time outside the home, should assume more responsibility than fathers for child care and home life. In this situation the social worker would offer support to bolster the client's existing coping mechanisms rather than facilitating a change in the basic self.

The social worker (who could possibly see herself in the same scenario) may offer suggestions for child care respite, recreation, or self-care that would help mitigate the client's sense of injustice in the arrangement, but not address an overall change in a significant or structural way, while other clients and practitioners would respond differently. They may not be willing to wait until parenting and homemaking become more equitable but instead demand or at least work for substantial change, both within the marriage and in the larger society. The possible stances that either client or practitioners take are not polarized but can be thought of as situated on a continuum, meaning that both the client and social worker may wish for large-scale social change, and both may believe that they need personally to make peace with the current reality of an individual situation.

The question becomes: are their respective positions compatible enough so they can agree on the goal of the work? If the social worker has a strong position that the client needs to change the situation, and the client really wants to learn to accept the situation, setting mutually agreeable goals will be challenging. There may be situations in which the tension of adjustment or challenge involves a significant concern for personal safety of an adult. The response to such a situation is not clear cut. You may suggest that to overcome this relationship stress, the client can work through its internal dynamics in couples counseling or other interpersonal work rather than through overt activism. Others may suggest that practitioners need to respond to any available opening for services, even if a woman cannot or will not separate from her partner. This is a controversial issue, in part because of the differences of opinion about what is tolerable, and the larger or political ramifications of inequitable relationships.

Experts and Shared Power The relationship between the ideas of expertise and shared power creates a particularly contemporary tension within the social work profession. The history and development of both the educational and professional systems in U.S. culture have revolved around the idea of expertise, or **expert knowledge**. Social workers are educated and socialized in professional programs to become respected members of a profession in which there are others with the same or similar expertise. In contrast, the idea of **shared power** is relatively recent in professional culture and challenges the claims of expert power. In shared power, the individual is the expert on her or his life, culture, dreams, experience, and goals. This creates a mandate in the work for social work practitioners to assume power only over limited activities in which they are trained while the client retains the power to direct the work. For example, if you are working in a college setting as an advocate for an African American student who experienced discrimination in housing options on campus, you may claim expertise on the process of advocacy, but your client would retain control regarding those issues that require your focus and the goals to be met through the advocacy. In this way, the power is shared.

Shifting your views of your expertise and interest in sharing power may not come easily; the U.S. population is socialized to value expertise, thus, we may interpret our own value and contributions through the lens of expertise. Given the competition that can develop between complex specialization on the one hand and client empowerment on the other, this tension is likely to persist. Some clients may want social workers to be the expert on their lives and relationships in the same way people want their dentist to be an expert on dental care.

Like much of U.S. culture, the social work profession has been caught up in the status and seeming legitimacy of being scientific and thus tends to take on the same metaphors of expertise. Social workers have spent decades trying to "prove" the effectiveness of their interventions, and have fought for professional prestige through this "expert" label. However, social workers have come to recognize that the expertise on the experience of any particular relationship, oppression, or phenomenological event belongs to the person who has lived it, and social workers can honor this wisdom by sharing power within the professional relationship. In the contemporary world, many strong client voices in the realm of human service interchanges, situations, and relationships have made it known that adopting the role of expert is not necessarily helpful, particularly when it obscures their own ownership or participation in the work. Social workers recognize the disillusionment and anger in people, such as people with disabilities, women, and people of color, who have experienced service systems that rely on expertise as humiliating, insulting, or patronizing. The development of many contemporary social work perspectives reflects this reality in their deliberate attempt to reduce the centrality of expertise and to substitute an enhanced commitment to partnership, or shared power.

Minimization of Distance   Such theoretical perspectives as the strengths perspective, nearly all feminist approaches, and empowerment approaches make a conscious effort to minimize the rigid boundaries of expertise between social worker and client. The client is seen as the expert on her or his life, whereas the social worker is seen as skilled in various arenas that will help the client get to a client-defined destination. This shift is played out in practice approaches that involve visiting clients' homes or meeting in community facilities like coffee shops and public parks. These approaches emphasize client comfort in familiar surroundings, in contrast to the 50-minute clinical hour in the agency office, which tends to send a message of worker authority and increased distance between social worker and client.

This trend toward more fluid relationships represents a deliberate shift in thinking and a transformation of values. For some theoreticians, the shift signals a new way to respect the experiences and views of people who previously had never been listened to closely. For others it is a critical response to a power analysis that results in the elimination of abusive or oppressive authority relationships. In broader terms, this shift to a more egalitarian relationship affirms the right of the client to enter into a relationship of shared power in which the assets of both the client and the worker are recognized, valued, and taken into account. Accordingly, in this conception, one person does not have power over the other; rather, a collective power is facilitated through sharing.

One of many Native American views of shared power has much to offer contemporary practitioners (Lowery & Mattaini, 2001). This approach conceptualizes shared power as shared responsibility allocated according to the particular strengths of each participant. It does not mean equality of responsibility, but recognizes that skill levels differ and emphasizes the worth of all contributions. Social workers are responsible for maintaining professional ethics, and clients are responsible for making changes in their lives. For example, in a situation of client substance abuse, social workers would ask questions such as, "How does your drinking affect your children?" rather than making a statement such as, "You need to quit drinking" (p. 116). The relationship created by this approach discourages hierarchies in the client–worker relationship and encourages a sense of joint investment in both the process and the results.

Global Citizenship and the Local Community   The final tension considered here, between local and global investments of effort, is more relevant for social work practitioners today than it has ever been. Traditionally, U.S. social workers have carried out most of their activities in local or neighborhood contexts and have regarded global developments as remote. The social and cultural history, geography, and resource wealth of the United States have all contributed to national and professional insularity. The tendency to judge U.S. culture as preferable is shaped by and reflected in such devaluing language as "third world" or "underdeveloped" that is almost exclusively based on the U.S.-defined dimensions of economy in any given culture. Traditional Western markers are primarily limited to economic assets that are important for all people but are not the totality of life for any person.

Globalization is a process that consists of the creation and consciousness of global interdependencies and exchanges (Steger, 2003), and consists of a complex of economic, social, and technological processes that have resulted in the formation of a single world community in which we are all citizens. The essence of globalization is the flow of information, ideas, knowledge, technology, capital, labor, artifacts, and cultural norms and values across national borders (Kaplinsky, 2005). The impact of global occurrences, such as refugee migration movements, have a direct and compelling influence on the environment and practice of social work at home and require workers to develop new skills and devise new perspectives. Social problems such as HIV/AIDS, homelessness, neglect and exploitation of children, poverty, violence, health and aging issues, and epidemic infections are worldwide issues that impact all nations (Sowers & Rowe, 2009).

The process of globalization facilitates the recognition of the signs of U.S. economic dominance. For example, the availability of Coca-Cola in Bangkok or the presence of Pizza Huts in Manila are signals that the U.S. economy dominates many world markets. The **outsourcing** of many U.S. jobs to countries in which much cheaper labor can be located has resulted in high rates of unemployment domestically as well as exploitation abroad. Yet many U.S.- and other Western-based companies are thriving. These dimensions of globalization are part of the reality of expanding international trade in the **Global South** (Payne & Askeland, 2008), which is a respectful term for the nations of the southern hemisphere ("third world" or "developing" countries).

Factors Promoting Globalization International financial institutions, such as the World Bank, the International Monetary Fund (IMF), and the World Trade Organization (WTO) have promoted and facilitated globalization, which has been accompanied with significant challenges and questions. These organizations were originally instituted to promote economic stability and growth and to help individual countries as they experience economic crises, but the strategies they have adopted to achieve these objectives have been problematic and counterproductive. Many question the policies of these international financial institutions, as they have disproportionately benefited wealthy people around the world, failed to address concerns about the environment from worldwide development, led to abuses in human rights, and provided significant setbacks to those promoting social justice. Globalization agreements and efforts have not incorporated regard for employment creation, expanded or improved health, or educational or social services for the poor, or promoted progressive land reform. Decision-making within these international financial institutions is not an open process and lacks transparency (Kaplinsky, 2005; Steger, 2003; Stiglitz, 2002; The World Commission on the Social

Dimension of Globalization, 2004; United Nations, Department of Economic and Social Affairs, 2005).

As an example, the WTO has been the primary promoter of free trade policies. Although free trade policies were ostensibly designed to encourage the development of market economies, the policies often require receiving nations to accept particular conditions thought to foster trade and economic growth, including privatization of resources and restrictions on imports and exports, as well as cutbacks in many social programs such as health, education, and housing and income assistance. In many cases these conditions have had the effect of abolishing welfare entitlement programs and social safety nets, debilitating local economies, altering or eliminating substantial aspects of indigenous ways of life, and eroding the autonomy of national governments. In their place, large multinational corporations have been free to build enormous industries whose purposes relate entirely to profit, with little regard to environmental or other concerns. Globalization policies have been associated with a substantial increase in worldwide poverty, misery, violence, HIV/AIDS cases, drug addiction, and economic stratification (to name a few), as well as the exploitation of the land and other important environmental resources (Payne & Askeland, 2008).

In such a context, social work as a profession must develop models of understanding that are global in context. For example, social workers in domestic settings must prepare to work with diverse populations, including immigrants and refugees, in this country, and to gain knowledge of non-Western ideas and perceptions. Rather than focus on strictly clinical work, social workers in international settings may also be called to assist with economic and social change to change situations of economic inequality and poverty (Payne & Askeland, 2008). While globalization provides both challenges and opportunities for social work, social workers can advocate and work toward a process of globalization that has a strong social dimension, ". . . is fair, inclusive, and participatory; that respects human dignity and human rights; that is democratically governed; and that offers tangible benefits to all people in all countries and not just the fortunate few" (Khinduka, 2008).

At the individual practitioner level, a social work commitment to reciprocity, interdependence, human rights, and social justice in practice is one way to incorporate globalization within practice. Social workers must be familiar with global events through media sources, as well as the ways in which events that occur within the U.S. impact individuals within other countries and other nations. The implications of globalization for social work practice are likely to increase in number and in impact (Finn & Jacobson, 2003). Ironically, increased localization has been one of the important responses to globalization (Payne & Askeland, 2008) as people seek local alternatives that are appropriate for their particular circumstances. Social work, therefore, must focus on both global and local perspectives and make meaningful connections between global inequities and domestic social justice issues that will discourage any artificial local/global polarity (Polack, 2004), as well as initiate educational and political initiatives to ensure respect for human rights, democratic decision making, environmental protection, and meaningful benefits to local populations.

Perspectives on the Conceptualizations of the Social Work Profession   Although each of these conceptualizations of social work practice discussed above provides a useful way of thinking about social work practice, and highlights a dimension of the work, each also has its limitations. To use them for the best interests of the client system, the models must be used flexibly. For example, knowledge, values, and skills can overlap, and over-focusing on one dimension, such as factual knowledge, may lead practitioners to apply knowledge without adequate consideration of the appropriate skill level and social work values. The integration of many kinds of knowledge, values, and skills as applied through competencies is the goal of social work education. Likewise, dividing the work into constituent groups of beneficiaries may suggest that the background, values, and skills necessary for each kind of practice vary more significantly than the reality of practice.

Generalist social work practice requires that the social worker be proficient at all levels of client groupings, as the competencies can be applied to all system levels. The similarities far surpass their differences; work in any of them is grounded in the practitioner's consistent set of values, theoretical perspectives, and goals. Similarly, a social worker does not build a relationship, then cease utilizing engagement skills (i.e., become "all business") because she or he has moved on to the assessment phase. Like all relationships, the professional connection between social worker and client must be attended to, nurtured, and encouraged to grow throughout the time of their work together, or it will wither. Likewise, assessment occurs throughout the course of the work, beginning with the first interaction and continuing through the last. The phases of helping are highly connected, with special emphasis paid to one phase at any given time during the work. The tensions discussed in social work, while useful, may fall short of describing the full, day-to-day realities of social work practice within specific practice settings and with specific populations. Therefore, while the structures are helpful, flexibility in the application is important.

Importance of Self-Knowledge   To practice competently, social workers must have a clear understanding of themselves, including biases and the ways in which the biases may influence practice. One type of bias that can impact practice is bias about socioeconomic class. For example, you may notice that you respond differently to people who are living in poverty than to persons who are considered socioeconomically middle-class. To grow in cultural competence, you can explore the reasons for such a difference, to possibly include that you learned as a child that "poor people" are somehow less worthy than affluent people, or that they are not hardworking. Your family and/or the wider culture may have supported these views. To uncover your biases, you can ponder the following questions: How do the previously mentioned views clash with the view that persons living in poverty are resilient in the face of debilitating exploitation through no shortcomings of their own? How is your view implemented in your practice? Are you less empathic, energetic, or invested when you work with persons living in poverty? Are you less likely to advocate or seek out resources? Do you have an opinion about a client that is a "truth" in your mind, or do you treat it as one interpretation out of many possible interpretations?

Practice decisions are shaped by our experiences, motivations, values, attitudes, and a host of other factors. Sometimes practitioners are unaware of the influences on practice decision. Therefore, social workers need to continually explore the ways in which their values are prioritized and the patterns they develop in making decisions and exhibiting practice behaviors. This exploration may include recognizing idiosyncratic approaches, quick responses, and patterns of reaction. Are you patient and likely to stand by your client, even when things do not go well? Are you quick to assume someone is judging you or wants to bring you harm? Are you likely to blow off steam or sulk when you are rebuffed? Do you assume that you are competent to deal with any crisis? Are you inclined to address an interpersonal problem privately and quietly? Are you more likely to "sound off" in a meeting? All of us have idiosyncratic ways of dealing with relationships, stresses, and social interactions that are personality variations. Social workers must recognize their behavioral patterns, understand how they impact their work, and identify those responses that, if changed, would help them to practice with a higher degree of competency and skill.

Culture has a strong influence on social work practitioner biases. For example, culture may impact practitioner beliefs and attitudes about a situation in which an adolescent's choice of vocation may clash with the family's ideas about suitable professions. In another example, cultural bias may influence a practitioner belief that, in social relationships, participants are equal and all should speak out honestly about tension in the relationship. These two examples are part of mainstream U.S. culture, and are cultural variants that are not necessarily shared by all people and therefore do not represent a universal truth. The emphasis on individual drive and ambition as well as equality and forthrightness are Western beliefs, and clash with other cultures. In another example, an Asian client, who is 20 years older than a practitioner, may relate in very formal terms with the practitioner and appear reluctant to share details about her family life, even though she has been referred for parent support. Rather than labeling her "resistant" or "closed," the practitioner can recognize potential bias in the perspective applied about such relationships and style and evaluate the "fit" of the practitioner and client perspectives.

The emphasis on our own biases and assumptions is closely related to values and how these values influence our ideas of ethical practices. These constructs are critical to social work practice. The next chapter will deal more explicitly with the ideas and contexts relating to values and ethical frameworks and the emphases placed on them in social work practice.

THEORETICAL PERSPECTIVES FOR SOCIAL WORK PRACTICE

Social work has a long history of adopting, adapting, formulating, and integrating various theoretical perspectives to guide its work. A **theory** is an explanation of some event or phenomenon. Theories usually have clear principles and propositions that provide a framework for predicting events and a body of empirically based evidence to support it. Theory assists social workers by providing the flexibility to see client systems and social problems from many points of view, anticipating outcomes of different interventions, and in applying the results to future situations (McNutt & Floersch, 2008). Theories can bring order and coherence to practice situations so that activities are based on a logical assessment of the fit between a client system situation and the assertions of the theory. Theories relating to the social world tend to evolve and adjust in order to fit new, developing ideas or to accommodate further evidence that adds to or is contradictory to their claims. Consequently, some theories are discarded when they are no longer acceptable to the professional community (for example, theories asserting that some races are superior to others) or when they are unable to be grounded in reliable research. Other theories evolve to incorporate additional refinements or methods, such as the contemporary interpretations of Freud's 19th-century psychoanalytic theory.

A **perspective** is a view, or lens, through which to observe and interpret the world. A perspective is generally less structured than theory but is similar in that it is often based on values and beliefs about the nature of the world or people. For example, a belief that people are generally good is a perspective that will guide practice and interpretations of client system situations. In that way the ideas behind theory and perspective are similar. In social work practice, the terms **theory** and **perspective** are often viewed as synonymous and may also be called **theoretical perspectives.** These three terms are used interchangeably throughout this book.

The theoretical positions of the social work profession have received important contributions from biology, ecology, sociology, anthropology, psychology, and many of the humanities and human service professions. More recently, social work scholars have expanded the development of the profession's own understandings of practice to create theories specific to the provision of social work services. Some of these theories focus on psychosocial systems, problem-solving, ecological/ecosystems, and empowerment, as they represent uniquely social work emphases on the interface between a person and her or his environment.

Theories are important to the social work profession, as they are driven by values. The ways in which social workers select, implement, and evaluate a theory or theoretical perspective will be highly influenced by their value orientations. For example, creating an alliance with a client that results in complete dependence on the social worker could be the result of an adherence to a theory that supports "reparenting," because the theory allows for directing the client's activities toward the goal of carrying out the will of the social worker. On the other hand, utilizing a theory in which autonomy and self-determination are prioritized will result in a different outcome. The role of theory in this scenario would be critical in directing the work of the practitioner.

This book presents five practice perspectives that guide the focus and are central to the content. They are: (1) the ecosystems perspective; (2) the social justice perspective; (3) the human rights perspective; (4) the strengths perspective; and (5) postmodern perspective approaches, including critical social construction, narrative theory, and solution-focused interventions. Other perspectives are included in subsequent chapters as they relate to specific levels of practice. Some of these perspectives have a longstanding history within social work education and practice (such as social justice), and others are more contemporary (such as postmodern approaches).

Ecosystems Perspective

Using concepts from systems theory and ecology, the ecosystems perspective is a well-used framework for generalist practice. This perspective examines the exchanges between individuals, families, groups, and communities and their environment. Systems theory utilizes constructs to organize complex activity in the social environment, while ecology seeks to explain how people adapt to and influence their environment. Taken together, these two concepts describe the functioning and adaptation of human systems in a dynamic interchange with each other. Interactions or transactions between the two help explain how people influence their environment, and vice versa. The ecosystems perspective is very useful for social work practice, as it encourages increasing the degree to which people and their environments fit one another. Increasing the degree of fit between the two can lead the social worker toward direct services with individuals, families, and groups to mobilize and draw on personal and environmental resources for effective coping. Increasing the degree of fit between human needs and environment can also lead the social worker to influence the client system's social and physical environment to adequately address human needs. Influencing the environment can include working to *influence organizations* to develop more responsive policies and programs, as well as working to influence legislation, regulation, and implementation of laws (Gitterman & Germain, 2008a).

Social Justice Perspective

Social justice refers to the manner in which society distributes resources among its members, including material goods and social benefits, rights, and protections. Although there are various theories of social justice regarding the criteria for the distribution of wealth, the profession of social work generally accepts an egalitarian focus that is concerned with the fair distribution of both material and nonmaterial resources (Rawls, 1971) and equal access for all people (Reichert, 2003). From this perspective, developing or distributing social and natural resources based on political or social power rather than social justice or human need is unacceptable

(Saleebey, 2009). The social justice perspective has important implications for social workers and their practice as it requires a response to much of the injustice that is status quo in our society.

As required by the National Association of Social Workers *Code of Ethics* (NASW, 2008), social workers invest a significant amount of time and effort in championing individual, group and community rights, working toward more effective institutional responses, and influencing major social policy shifts. Social work is, therefore, a political profession. Social workers identify individual, family, group, and community needs, and seek to address the areas of injustice that have a negative impact on people. For example, if a social worker is working at the community level with a group of older adults who have been wrongfully denied access to services or government support programs, it is the social worker's responsibility to confront that injustice either directly or indirectly by utilizing community resources to address the issue. The issue can be addressed individually, or if the problem rests in policy or procedures, at the group-level.

Human Rights Perspective

The United Nations describes **human rights** as those rights that are inherent in our nature and without which we cannot live as human beings. Human rights and fundamental freedoms allow us to fully develop and use our human qualities, our intelligence, our talents and our conscience, and to satisfy our spiritual and other needs. They are basic for mankind's increasing demand for a life in which the inherent dignity and worth of each human being will receive respect and protection. (United Nations, 1987)

The principle of human rights offers a powerful and comprehensive framework for social work practice; it not only recognizes needs but strives to satisfy those needs (Reichert, 2003). The human rights perspective provides a moral grounding for social work practice and reflects an ongoing commitment to the belief that all people should have basic rights and access to the broad benefits of their societies. Many social workers evaluate their practice based on its contribution to an environment in which universal human rights are honored.

Contemporary perspectives on human rights emphasize the social understandings of our commonality rather than the rigid assertions about specific human rights. Accordingly, human rights can be viewed as socially constructed, reflecting differing contexts, ideas, and cultures (Gil, 1998). Ife (2000) likewise suggests that the human rights discourse should de-emphasize the focus on legalistic, Western views of entitlements in favor of a more reflective dialogue among the world's peoples. This dialogue would center on exploring the meaning of human existence, and how humans want to recognize our interdependence, protect our futures, and safeguard our survival in the current and future global era. This focus is consistent with social work's emphasis on community, quality of relationship, and concern for the future of the world's inhabitants. It also recognizes the dynamic nature of living one's principles, such as those inherent in human rights, as they continuously evolve to remain meaningful.

Despite the limited support of the United States for economic, social, and cultural rights through world bodies, human rights have the potential to occupy a central place in social work practice and can provide a focal point in the evolution of people's understanding of their place on this planet. Viewed as a set of dynamic principles that can provide a substantive contribution to guidelines on international relations as well as community-based practice, human rights constitutes a vital focus for work with people. Social work as a profession can take up the lead started by many of our global colleagues in making human rights a central discourse and in exploring its relevance more thoroughly to our everyday work.

The Strengths Perspective

An increasingly widespread approach in social work practice, the **strengths perspective** is explicit in its emphasis on affirming and working with the strengths found both in people seeking help and in their environments. Like human rights practice, this perspective emphasizes basic dignity and the resilience of people in overcoming challenging obstacles. Contemporary advocates have established some significant breaks with social workers' historical and cultural tendency to focus their work and energies on problems and pathology (Kim, 2008a).

Principles of the Strengths Perspective   Saleebey (2009) identified six key principles for the strengths perspective (pp. 15–19):

1. *Every individual, group, family, and community has strengths.* Social workers must view their clients as competent and possessing skills and strengths which may not be initially visible. In addition, clients may have family and community resources that need to be explored and utilized.

2. *Trauma and abuse, illness and struggle may be injurious, but they may also be sources of challenge and opportunity.* Clients can not only overcome very difficult situations, but also learn new skills and develop positive protective factors. Individuals exposed to a variety of trauma are not always helpless victims or damaged beyond repair.

3. *Assume that you do not know the upper limits of the capacity to grow and change, and take individual, group, and community aspirations seriously.* Too often professional "experts" hinder their clients' potential for growth by viewing clients' identified goals as unrealistic. Instead, social workers need to set high expectations for their clients so that the clients believe they can recover and that their hopes are tangible.

4. *We best serve clients by collaborating with them.* Playing the role of expert or professional with all the answers does not allow social workers to appreciate

their clients' strengths and resources. The strengths perspective emphasizes collaboration between the social worker and the client.

5. *Every environment is full of resources.* Every community, regardless of how impoverished or disadvantaged, has something to offer in terms of knowledge, support, mentorship, and tangible resources. These resources go beyond the general social service agencies in the communities and can serve as a great resource for clients.

6. *Caring, caretaking, and context.* Strength perspective recognizes the importance of community and inclusion of all its members in society and working for social justice. This is built on the basic premise that caring for each other is a basic form of civic participation.

Although these key principles may evolve and be refined, the focus of the strengths perspective is on clients' personal assets along with their environmental resources rather than on their pathology and limitations is a core element. Using the strengths perspective, social work interventions are centered on helping the client system to achieve their goals, affirming and developing values and commitments, and making and finding membership in or as a community. The strengths perspective does not preclude the need to validate the suffering and pain of the client system (i.e., the physical, emotional, or existential) nor the seriousness of the situation or distress. Rather, the strengths perspective seeks to acknowledge clients' expertise regarding their own lives and to focus on their resilience and capacities to survive and to confront such seemingly overwhelming obstacles.

Postmodern Perspective and the Social Construction Approach

A contemporary perspective that questions the way in which knowledge is attained and valued, and distinguishes belief from truth, comes under the broad heading of **postmodernism.** Postmodern approaches invite examination of the cultural assumptions that underlie many of the arrangements of power and politics, and it tends to be critical of assumptions or theories that claim absolute or authoritative truth. To illustrate, the contention that "all people in the United States can get ahead if they work hard enough; therefore, all poor people are lazy" is an example of an assumption or belief that is asserted as truth. Postmodernism invites people to challenge the truth of such claims (Logan, Rasheed, & Rasheed, 2008).

Social Construction   A useful postmodern perspective for understanding the social realities of the lives of the people served by social workers, **social construction** suggests that people construct reality based on experiences in the social world, which occur within the context of culture, society, history, and language. Practicing from this perspective means that rather than being a product of an objective external world, or the result of the individual mind, social realities are actually beliefs formed through social interchanges (usually starting with the family) that regulate learning to make sense of things and, often, to form judgments. For example, when children experience people as good-hearted and the world as a kind place throughout their youth, this social experience informs their adult belief that the world is a relatively decent place. On the other hand, when their social experiences tell them that the world is full of evil, hurtful people, their view of reality is often very different. This observation of how people decide the nature of their world is meaningful for social workers when they work with people who have lived in a different reality than one then they experienced (Lee & Greene, 2009).

Noticing your social location in this way is consistent with postmodernism and social construction. Recognizing that a person's reality is based on her or his perceptions and experiences in the social world and that there can be more than one reality of an experience because each person perceives the world differently and has different experiences is one way to implement postmodernism and social construction. Social workers, using these approaches, approach clients from their realities, rather than the reality of the practitioner. For example, if a client appears to have little ambition to financially support themselves or to participate in civic life, an understanding of the reality of the client's culture and environment may help you to understand the realities of institutionalized racism that may leave clients bitter and non-participatory, with little vision of what their life might be. Recognition of this postmodern principle of multiple realities impacts the purpose of practice and may expand one's practice to advocate for or take up the causes of people who have little power. In practice, postmodernism and social construction require acknowledgment of the practitioner's boundaries and allow practitioners to enter the world of the client system.

Deconstruction   Constructionist thinking opens the way to explore particular beliefs, such as that the world is a kind place, through a process of taking those beliefs apart to examine the way they developed, or **deconstruction**. Through the process of deconstruction, you can explore the factors that helped these beliefs to develop and determine those ideas that had power and dominated. The following is an example of both social construction and deconstruction.

For many years in the 20th century it was a "reality" that adults with severe disabilities were neither capable of negotiating nor entitled to engage in adult relationships, particularly sexual ones. Institutions and community-based facilities worked diligently to prevent relationships and sometimes even kept couples with disabilities from being together alone in the same room. That particular social understanding and sense of reality contributed to the infamous practice of eugenics, which sought to eliminate the reproduction of people who were seen as genetically deficient.

As advocates for the rights of persons with disabilities began to deconstruct and debunk the assumptions of the social construction that supported this callous practice, eugenics became less acceptable. Some of the many assumptions made in this reality follow:

- People with severe disabilities are like children who should not enter into adult relationships.

- People with severe disabilities are not adequate as human beings and should not have children.

- People with severe disabilities are not entitled to define their needs or desires.

- People with severe disabilities do not have the capacity for love.

Although these assumptions are by no means extinct now, they are situated in a specific economic, historical, and cultural setting that is no longer dominant. The concept of contextual setting, or **social location**, refers to the time, place, and prevailing ideas or discourse that influence standards, particularly about what is considered "right." All ideas emerge from within a context that includes attitudes or beliefs, and ideas must be recognized as contextual rather than as absolute, moral truths for all situations and contexts (Kelley, 2009). Consider, for example, a new social worker who is judged and silenced if she or he counters the so-called truth regarding persons with disabilities and, based on human rights or social justice concerns, objects to such social restrictions. You might consider those beliefs or customs that are so strongly held in your own community or agency that deviance from them has significant professional or personal consequences and is interpreted morally.

Questions that expose the attitudes and beliefs that underlie ideas often have the effect of creating opportunities and visions for people. Using social construction, social workers are likely to question arrangements that bring harm to people and to be suspicious or wary of presumed expertise that denies people their own experience. For example, a social worker may advocate for an older adult whose acute medical distress is being dismissed by a physician as insignificant. The social worker, with support from a supervisor or others, may even need to challenge the adequacy of the medical care offered to the client. In this way, the social worker refutes the idea that any particular set of assumptions or positions cannot be challenged, and operates on the idea that all beliefs, ideas, and arrangements can be respectfully questioned.

Consistent with postmodernism are narrative and solution-focused interventions (Kelley, 2008). **Narrative theory** guides practitioners to utilize "stories" to understand the lived experience of clients. Conversational in nature, this approach involves helping clients make sense of the meanings they give to events in their lives. A narrative is the thread that binds disparate events together. Stories involve events linked together in a time sequence and have a plot. Narrative approaches view problems as separate from people, and people possess the qualities and skills needed to change their relationship with the problem(s) they are facing in life (Morgan, 2000).

In contrast, a **solution-focused** approach invites clients to explore and determine the concrete change desired in their lives and the resources and strengths clients possess to make the change occur. Using a solution-focused approach, clients identify a specific goal that they believe will make their lives better in some fashion, and to attach specific strengths to a plan to reach that goal. Often clients are asked to think about an exception, times in which the challenge did not exist, and to identify the condition under which the challenge did not exist, as indicators of potential ways to address the problem. For example, if a child is struggling to focus in school, a discussion of the exceptions to this situation, or conditions under which the child is ever able to focus on schoolwork, may shed light on the factors on which to focus. Is the child able to focus early in the school day? When seated with specific classmates or away from specific classmates?

Critical Social Construction   The *critical* in **critical social construction** is derived from a contemporary analysis of power, which recognizes that any social group can shape its beliefs to its own benefit at the expense of other groups. The critical dimension then allows the social worker to question power arrangements, especially if many people's voices have been silenced or "subjugated" (Hartman, 1994) and those who were able to arrange such systems as slavery had the power to **privilege** themselves, while oppressing others. In this way the privileged group not only benefits from but also perpetuates the privilege by using their power to assert their beliefs, which come to be regarded as truth. Although many groups today who benefit from privilege would not consciously choose such advantage if presented with a choice, such groups as whites, heterosexuals, Christians and those who are able bodied benefit from privilege (Diller, 2007; Swigonski, 1996).

Critical social construction can be utilized in social work practice through critical viewing of power relations and dominance of specific beliefs that result, which especially impacts non-privileged groups with whom social workers often work. This critical viewing has significant repercussions for social work practice, which will be addressed throughout the book.

Complementary Aspects of the Theoretical Perspectives

Each of the five perspectives—ecosystems, social justice, human rights, the strengths perspective, and the postmodern perspectives—offers the social worker unique and sometimes complex challenges. In many respects they complement each other by placing a slightly different emphasis on the work that fits well with the other views. The strengths perspective, for example, is used in the service of bringing social justice to people who have experienced inequities. Human rights, in turn, may be seen as the moral grounding for undertaking justice-oriented work. The constructionist ideas regarding the influence of historical and cultural standpoints allow the social worker to question previously unexamined ideas and approaches that marginalize people and characterize them as pathological or undeserving. Taken together these perspectives provide a comprehensive and compelling approach to social work.

STRAIGHT TALK ABOUT THE TRANSLATION OF PERSPECTIVES INTO PRACTICE

The relevance of theoretical perspectives to actual practice situations has always raised questions from students and social work educators. Some of the frameworks and perspectives may seem abstract or far removed from client systems, such as a destitute older adult, or a politically active group of adults with psychiatric disabilities. On the other hand, when perspectives reflect and honor the experience of people and fit the situation, they can be a critical guide to social work practice. For example, using the strengths perspective may mean focusing on the support networks and clean-up efforts of a struggling, poverty-stricken neighborhood to focus on the capabilities and assets, rather than focusing on the dilapidated housing, trash, and abandoned cars that line the streets. While utilizing the frameworks and perspectives and integrating theory and practice can be very challenging, the frameworks and perspectives offer guides and a foundation for social work practice.

CONCLUSION

This chapter has presented several different perspectives with which to view social work practice. Social work practice is defined in the following ways: (1) by type of practice or range of practice settings; (2) as a set of activities; (3) as a set of roles; (4) as a set of competencies and practice behaviors; (5) by types of client grouping; (6) by practice frameworks; (7) as a licensed profession; (8) by purpose; and (9) by the tensions experienced in the profession. Self-knowledge is also a critical component of effective social work practice.

Exploring social work practice through this array of methods allows for many interpretations and emphases, some of which will be discussed in subsequent chapters. Coverage of the tensions experienced by the profession allows you to consider the profession in its ongoing concerns and have a sense of reference and context. Also discussed were five explicit theoretical perspectives, and you were encouraged to use them flexibly to offer an empowering and liberating approach to people who have lived their lives in the margin of society. Although the challenge of translating these approaches into ethical, sustainable, effective social work competencies will always be present in your practice, it will also sustain your growth. Building on this frame, Chapter 2 will delve into the role these values and ethics play in social work practice.

MAIN POINTS

- Social work practice can be conceptualized in at least nine different ways, to include by type of practice or range of practice settings, by the activities of the profession, as a set of roles, and as a licensed profession.

- Tensions that persist in contemporary practice include those between social control and social change, acceptance and change, clinical and nonclinical perspectives, experts and shared power, and global citizenship and the local community.

- Effective social work practice requires questioning your own assumptions, understanding the impact they have on your work, and framing your methods.

- Theoretical perspectives play a significant role in guiding practice activities. The five perspectives, or frames, presented in this book are ecosystem perspective, the social justice perspective, the human rights perspective, the strengths perspective, and postmodern approaches, such as critical social constructionism, narrative and solution-focused.

- The ecosystems perspective provides a frame for generalist practice, and examines the fit between individuals and their environment.

- The social justice perspective addresses the manner in which resources are allocated.

- Guided by the United Nations Universal Declaration of Human Rights, the human rights perspective is a frame that encompasses the conviction that all people have civil, political, social, economic, and cultural rights simply because they are human beings.

- The strengths perspective is a practice approach that highlights and works with individual, family, group, and community resilience and assets, honoring the client system's goals and dreams, and asserts that all communities possess resources.

- Critical social constructionism is a contemporary, postmodern frame based on the assertion that social truths are agreed-upon beliefs shaped in a common history and culture and perpetuated through assumptions, language, and stories. It also notes the power arrangements responsible for the prevalence of such truths.

- The translation of perspectives into practice is challenging and necessary for effective social work to maintain its mission, integrity, and consistency.

EXERCISES

1. Go to www.routledgesw.com/cases and explore the Sanchez family interactive case study by reviewing the introduction and the tasks of each of the four phases. Click on the "Start this Case" button (under the Engage Tab), and complete Tasks #1, 2, and 3.

2. After completing Exercise #1, imagine that you are working with the Sanchez family as a social worker employed by the U.S. Bureau of Citizenship and Immigration Service. You are assigned to Celia and Hector Sanchez as they receive their permanent resident cards, or "green cards," which authorize them to live and work legally in the U.S. Your role is to help them understand their new rights and responsibilities. What knowledge, values, and skills do you think would be particularly important for your work with the couple? Identify at least one *specific* area of knowledge, one value, and one skill. What challenges might result from emphasizing one (i.e., knowledge, value, or skill) over the other two?

3. After completing Exercise #1 and #2, consider the social justice issues involved in the family's permanent resident status and the ways in which the issues are related to human rights. Respond to the following:
   a. From your knowledge of human rights and the Sanchez family, identify two human rights that apply particularly to Hector and Celia as immigrants.
   b. How might you expect that having a green card would impact the family?

4. Consider the consequences of different social work practice discourses, and respond to the following:
   a. Describe the ways in which a social work discourse of strengths differs from a discourse of pathology when applied to the Sanchez family.
   b. Describe the way in which the strengths-based social worker would approach the family. How would you describe the professional relationship? How would you describe the focus of the work? Be as specific as possible.

5. Go to www.routledgesw.com/cases. Click on the Sanchez family, then "Start this Case," then review the case file for Emilia Sanchez (including Client History, Client Concerns, and Goals for the Client). Click on "Mapping this Case" (under "Case Study Tools"). Explore Emilia's relationship with her relatives by reviewing the family genogram. Also review Emilia's ecomap, and interaction matrix (under "Case Study Tools"). Answer Emilia's critical thinking questions.

6. After completing Exercise #5, consider the following case, which occurs prior to the time depicted on the website:

   You are employed as a hospital social worker, and have been assigned to Emilia Sanchez. Emilia is 24 years old and has just given birth to Joey. She used crack cocaine during her pregnancy, and Joey tested positive for the drug. A child protection social worker assigned to the case believes that Joey will likely be taken into the custody of the state, and probably placed with Celia and Hector, who have already indicated their willingness to take him as a foster child. As Emilia's social worker, your specific responsibility is to work with her on a plan to address her substance abuse and to adjust to the placement of Joey in foster care with her parents. You have been told by the nursing staff that she has just had an angry outburst and is now quietly sullen. You are currently heading to her hospital room.

   a. What do you notice about your own responses to the information you have received about Emilia? How will they influence your attitude about her? How will your attitude influence your work with her?

   b. What are you thinking as you walk to her room to meet with her? What emotions, if any, are you bringing with you?

   c. From the information you have at this point, what areas of strengths can see in Emilia?

   d. Balancing the safety of the child with the rights of the parent, would you suggest that Emilia have interaction with Joey while in foster care? If so, under what circumstances?

   e. You are anticipating that Emilia will be sullen when you first meet with her. What will you say to her? If she later expresses anger at the situation, what might you say then? What might be the next step in this situation?

7. Write a two paragraph reflection journal entry to answer the question, "Why do I want to be in the helping profession?"

8. Reflect on three concerns that you have about being an effective helper. How can those also be strengths? (For example, Concern: "I am afraid that I will become too attached to my clients." Strength: "I am capable of developing strong relationships.")

CHAPTER 2

Applying Values and Ethics to Practice

Deeply earnest and thoughtful people stand on shaky footing with the public.

Johann Wolfgang von Goethe

Key Questions for Chapter 2

(1) How can I identify as a professional social worker and conduct myself accordingly (EPAS 2.1.1)?

(2) How can I apply social work ethical principles to guide my professional practice (EPAS 2.1.2)?

(3) How can I apply critical thinking to inform and communicate professional judgments (2.1.3)?

(4) How can I advance human rights and social and economic justice through my professional practice (EPAS 2.1.5)?

CONSIDER THE DEGREE TO WHICH YOU AGREE WITH the following statements related to social work practice:

- Persons who choose to smoke cigarettes or cigars, chew tobacco, or drink excessive amounts of alcohol are responsible for resolving and paying for their own health problems related to their use of tobacco or alcohol, since the risks of this behavior are widely known.

- Under some conditions, physical discipline of children is acceptable.

- Children who are sexually abused should never be returned to the residence of the person who perpetrated the abuse.

- Social workers who agree to the terms of agency employment do not have the right to criticize agency practices.

- Most homeless persons want to live out on the streets.

- Under particular circumstances, suicide is an acceptable strategy.

- All world citizens, regardless of what they have done, deserve to be free from hunger.

- Persons who test HIV-positive should be tattooed on the heel so that potential sexual partners can take safety precautions.

- Perpetrators and victims of crime are equally justified in receiving social work services.

Social work is a value-laden profession. While social workers may not agree about all values, the importance of professional values is central to the practice of social work.

Values are best defined as beliefs, while *ethics* are defined as the rules of conduct that embody those beliefs. This chapter focuses particularly on the social work professional ethics that are informed by social work values. Ethical codes and their application to practice in various contexts are explored. The relationship between ethics and the law, and the ways in which social workers manage challenging ethical conflicts and dilemmas, are discussed.

A BRIEF HISTORY OF SOCIAL WORK ETHICS

At the inception of the profession, social workers were more concerned about the morals of clients than about the conduct of individual social workers or of the profession (Reamer, 2006). In the early 20th century, the emphasis on social reform shifted to address social problems, such as those related to health, employment, and poverty (Reamer, 2008). By the late 1940s and early 1950s, social workers made a variety of attempts to develop an official, written code, or document that articulated the current, collective thinking of the profession. In 1947, the American Association of Social Workers (a predecessor of the current National Association of Social Workers) adopted the profession's first formal code that established guidelines and standards for its ethical conduct (Reamer, 2006). The National Association of Social Workers adopted the first formal code of ethics in 1960 (Reamer, 2008).

The second period of the development of social work ethics occurred in the late 1970s and early 1980s. Advances in biotechnology (relating to such phenomena as organ and bone marrow transplants and genetic manipulation) launched the introduction of bioethics in medical settings. These developments were especially influential in sensitizing social workers (and other human service workers) to the importance of their own values and the relationship between their values and their professional decisions. Professional concern surfaced regarding the process of decision-making, decisions about the appropriate decision-makers, as well as the outcome of decisions. Due to medical advances, choices were being made about those persons who received a liver transplant, had access to genetic information, and had the right to choose to die. Other societal phenomena such as developments in computer technology, globalized ecopolitics, and the surge of interest in human rights also shaped and intensified the concern for values in ethical practice (Reamer, 2008).

In recent times, social work ethics have been concerned with **risk management**. Ethical standards are utilized to guide conduct with a concern for liability risk and professional malpractice. A body of literature has been developed to provide risk-management strategies to protect clients and prevent ethics problems (Reamer, 2008). In sum, the social work profession has attempted to develop standards to guide workers, prioritize principles, affirm its values, and distinguish parameters that define the profession's responsibilities. The social work *Code of Ethics* (NASW, 2008) (referred to hereafter as "*Code of Ethics*") reflects the social work profession's views on appropriate social work conduct with clients, with one another, and with respect to organizations, the profession itself, and society at large.

PROFESSIONAL CODES OF ETHICS

The social work *Code of Ethics* (2008) is a comprehensive code of ethical standards and guidelines that serves to: (1) affirm social work as a legitimate profession; (2) provide guidance for a wide variety of practice circumstances; and (3) explicate the standards through which the public may hold the profession accountable. Social work practitioners generally appreciate the structure to ethical practice provided by the *Code of Ethics* in today's increasing complex practice situations.

Groups of professionals with the social work profession have developed other codes of ethics directed at the promotion of ethical practice, including (Reamer, 2008):

- National Association for Black Social Workers Clinical Social Work Federation

- International Federation of Social Workers (IFSW)

- Canadian Association of Social Workers

The *Code of Ethics* is the most widely known and utilized of the codes. This chapter will briefly review the *Code of Ethics*, discuss the *Code of Ethics* as a tool of practice, and highlight the most recent IFSW code, due to the relevance of this code to practice in a global context.

The NASW *Code of Ethics*

The *Code of Ethics* is built around six core values from the preamble, which match six broad ethical principles, as shown in Exhibit 2.1. The core values represent a mix of

EXHIBIT 2.1	CORE VALUES	ETHICAL PRINCIPLES
The Foundation of the Social Work Perspective	*Service*	Social workers' primary goal is to help people in need and to address social problems.
	Social justice	Social workers challenge social injustice.
	Dignity and worth of the person	Social workers respect the inherent dignity and worth of the person.
	Importance of human relationships	Social workers recognize the central importance of human relationships.
	Integrity	Social workers behave in a trustworthy manner.
	Competence	Social workers practice within their areas of competence and develop and enhance their professional expertise.

the worker's activities, skills, principles, character, and attitudes, and they relate integrally to the *Code of Ethics* in its specifics. The heart of the *Code of Ethics*, which is the ethical standards, follows the six principles. These cover and are organized according to the following six relationship categories or standards:

1. Social workers' ethical responsibilities to clients.

2. Social workers' ethical responsibilities to colleagues.

3. Social workers' ethical responsibilities in practice settings.

4. Social workers' ethical responsibilities as professionals.

5. Social workers' ethical responsibilities to the social work profession.

6. Social workers' ethical responsibilities to the broader society.

Within each of these categories the *Code of Ethics* contains from two (category five) to 16 standards (category one), along with varying subcategories, to total 155 standards. These standards explain the appropriate conduct for social workers. Social workers may deviate from these expected norms when appropriate ethical justification is available (Barsky, 2010). The standards present both the rules and the hopes of the profession.

International Federation of Social Workers Ethical Statement

The International Federation of Social Workers (IFSW), a worldwide professional organization of social work organizations and individuals, documents its position on ethical practice in a statement that reflects concerns that are similar but not identical to the NASW *Code*. The IFSW document, *Ethics in Social Work: Statement of Principles ("Statement of Principles")* was approved at the General Meetings of the International Federation of Social Workers and the International Association of Schools of Social Work in Australia in October 2004. This document contains a more explicit and pervasive emphasis on human rights than does the NASW's *Code of Ethics*, as reflected in the following language (IFSW & IASSW, 2004, para. 3):

> *Definition of Social Work: The social work profession promotes social change, problem-solving in human relationships, and the empowerment and liberation of people to enhance well-being. Utilising theories of human behaviour and social systems, social work intervenes at the points where people interact with their environments. Principles of human rights and social justice are fundamental to social work.*

As a federation, IFSW assumes that member organizations, including the National Association of Social Workers (NASW), adhere to the standards in the *Statement of Principles*. Therefore, a comparison between the *Code of Ethics* and the *Statement of Principles* reveals some of the different emphasis of the U.S. and international ethical practice. The following section of the *Statement of Principles* highlights seven international conventions that form "common standards of achievement and recognise rights that are accepted by the global community" (IFSW & IASSW, 2004, para. 4). These include the Universal Declaration of Human Rights (1948), the International Covenant on Civil and Political Rights (1965), and the International Covenant on Economic, Social, and Cultural Rights (1965), as well as some conventions that the U.S. has not yet ratified.

The next two sections in the IFSW statement, on human rights and social justice, are the equivalent of the first two principles in the *Code of Ethics*. These equate human rights with human dignity and address social work's commitment to them. The full text of the Principles is shown in Box 2.1. The broad value base reflected in these statements is similar to the *Code of Ethics*. However, the Universal Declaration of Human Rights, which is central to the IFSW statement, includes emphases on a global (rather than national) perspective and on the importance of economic, social, and cultural rights for all people.

Limits of Ethical Codes

Although the *Code of Ethics* offers helpful guidance to social work practitioners wrestling with difficult ethical practice situations, all codes present a conundrum to practitioners due to their general nature, can be difficult to interpret, and may offer unrealistic guidance given the specifics of the worker's practice (Strom-Gottfried, 2008). Issues of context, risk taking and creativity, and diversity also provide challenges to ethical codes.

B O X 2 . 1

*Final Proposal
for New IFSW
Ethical
Document,
2004*

Human rights and human dignity: Social work is based on respect for the inherent worth and dignity of all people, and the rights that follow from this. Social workers should uphold and defend each person's physical, psychological, emotional, and spiritual integrity and well-being. This means:

1. Respecting the right to self-determination—social workers should respect people's rights to make their own choices and decisions, irrespective of their values and life choices, providing this does not threaten the rights and interests of others.

2. Promoting the right to participation—social workers should promote the full involvement and participation of people using their services in ways that enable them to be empowered in all aspects of decisions and actions affecting their lives.

3. Treating each person as a whole—social workers should be concerned with the whole person, within the family and the community, and should seek to recognise all aspects of a person's life.

4. Identifying and developing strengths—social workers should focus on the strengths of all individuals, groups and communities and thus promote their empowerment.

Social justice: Social workers have a responsibility to promote social justice, in relation to society generally, and in relation to the people with whom they work. This means:

1. Challenging negative discrimination—social workers have a responsibility to challenge negative discrimination on the basis of irrelevant characteristics such as ability, age, culture, gender or sex, marital status, political opinions, skin color or other physical characteristics, sexual orientation, or spiritual beliefs.

2. Recognizing diversity—social workers should recognize and respect the racial and cultural diversity of societies in which they practice, taking account of individual, family, group, and community differences.

3. Distributing resources equitably—social workers should ensure that resources at their disposal are distributed fairly, according to need.

4. Challenging unjust policies and practices—social workers have a duty to bring to the attention of policy makers, politicians and the general public situations where resources are inadequate or where policies and practices are unfair or harmful.

5. Working in solidarity—social workers have an obligation to challenge social conditions that contribute to social exclusion, stigmatization or subjugation, and to work towards an inclusive society.

Source: IFSW & IASSW, 2004

The Role of Context   Rather than being made in isolation or in the abstract, ethical decisions are made within a practice context, which may shape the decision-making process in subtle ways. For example, if a social worker is unaware of attributing negative qualities to a client because of missed appointments, the social worker may believe that the client does not want services, is not able to take full advantage of scarce resources, or that the client is not deserving of such resources. If the social worker is in a position to choose the clients who have access to a limited service, she or he may disqualify the client without further reflection. On the one hand, this could be viewed as using good judgment as the social worker is seeking to maximize the effectiveness of the scarce service. On the other hand, the decision reflects a decision-making process that is not transparent, that is influenced by one interpretation of client behavior, and is perhaps inaccurate. For example, if the client did not have reliable transportation to appointments, an unstable home life, or a medically needy child, the decision-making process may have resulted in a different outcome. Such judgments may not only be inaccurate but also present an ethical question relating to the professional discretion and impartial judgment that the *Code of Ethics* requires. Therefore, an ethical code provides guidance that is decontexualized.

Professionals must be aware of the influence of their perspectives as important influences in making ethical decisions that involve professional judgment (Barsky, 2010). Thoughtful social workers frequently come to the conclusion of "it depends" (Strom-Gottfried, 2003) when ethical questions confront them, in recognition of the importance of the surrounding circumstances, social location, and current pressures. It also suggests the value of a "dialogic process" (Strom-Gottfried, 2003), which engages all the parties (or positions) involved in an ethical question in an in-depth conversation regarding their thinking, the implications of varying choices, and an analysis of their values. For example, many health care facilities have committees that review situations that involve ethical questions, and make a decision based on their discussion. In other situations, social workers engage in a discussion with a knowledgeable colleague or supervisor about a situation, and arrive at a decision through dialogue (also discussed later in this chapter).

Risk Taking and Creativity   Another concern regarding the rigid interpretation of ethical rules relates to the potential for oversimplification. Social workers may rely on the *Code of Ethics* to avoid using their creativity and professional judgment, based on their interpretation of the *Code of Ethics*. Using critical thinking to inform professional judgment is a valuable component of social work practice and some-times requires some risk taking (Strom-Gottfried, 2008). Witkin (2000) suggests that hypercautious adherence to a formal authority can discourage creative, responsive relationships on the part of the practitioner and can also lead a practitioner to over-look (or not notice) alternative responses to a situation.

The following case vignette illustrates this idea: A school social worker named Cora, in strict adherence to the ethical principle of practicing only within her area of competency (Code Standard 4.01a), at first declined to see a young student who clearly was struggling with the abuse of a variety of substances. Cora felt thoroughly competent to work with adolescents regarding developmental issues, but she was not educated to treat those struggling with substance abuse, so she decided it would be unethical to work with the student. The student, however, was in great need of assistance and was ready to work on the problem, and had no other obvious or realistic options for services in the rural community. The substance use issue was intertwined with other challenges related to growing up in difficult circumstances, and developmental issues were involved. When the student asked her to reconsider, Cora decided to discuss the matter with a social work colleague. The colleague reminded Cora that she had many skills and much experience that would directly benefit the student. For example, she was knowledgeable regarding adolescent development, had competent relationship skills with adolescents, and was committed to a hopeful, resilience-based perspective regarding people. In addition, Cora's colleague advised that she might find a resource in her former supervisor, who had become certified in the area of substance abuse treatment. Cora contacted the former supervisor, who was interested in the scenario and recommended available training for Cora, as well as a nearby clinician who could be contacted for ongoing supervision for Cora.

Substance abuse in school populations is common, yet a potentially life-changing issue for youth. Cora was able to advocate with the school administration to successfully negotiate for time and reimbursement to obtain the training that would allow her to better serve her individual clients, and the school population in general. Cora was creative and willing to explore options in response to important needs, and her client(s) were likely to receive competent services from an experienced worker who sought both training and supervision. There is some risk in Cora's assumption of the role of providing substance abuse treatment; however, taking on the issue is more closely aligned with social work's values than denying help to the student.

Strict and nonreflective adherence to a standard code can help preserve the current social order, which may be in direct conflict with the profession's commitment to confront social injustice and oppression (Witkin, 2000). If the student's family in the example was limited financially and belonged to an ethnic population that experienced oppression, the student would likely experience more barriers to receiving needed services than students in other families without these characteristics. Therefore, the student's access to needed resources would be constricted, a situation of social injustice. Cora's commitment to responding to the student's need and attempting to provide services can be seen as serving social work's obligation to confront injustices.

While Cora made a decision using the *Code of Ethics*, colleague advice, and critical thinking, not everyone may agree that her solution was the best solution. For example, advocates for diversity empowerment might view Cora's effort as perpetuating social injustice because the situation involves ethnically diverse people receiving substandard services through noncredentialed workers. While there may be different, well-informed opinions about the best course of action in this situation, a too-narrow interpretation of the *Code of Ethics* that precludes critical thinking and creativity should be avoided. The resolution of issues like this is seldom easy and frequently overlooks some worthwhile concerns. Social work practitioners are encouraged to consider the *Code of Ethics*, and engage in a dialogic process with a colleague for a full exploration of the issues. The process of making such decisions contributes to the ongoing dynamics of the profession's overall ethical stance.

Diversity A postmodern recognition of diversity and multiple realities raises another concern about the use of codes. Universal codes meant to apply to everyone in all situations can fail to address the experiential contexts of both social workers and clients, or to recognize differences among people and cultures. For example, the ethical mandate for **confidentiality**, which refers to the social worker's obligation to keep information about clients from becoming public in any way, is often regarded as absolutely critical in maintaining a professional relationship. However, a universal application of confidentiality as an ethical mandate may present an obstacle in cultures less individualistic than that in the U.S., in which the community may be both the reference point and a rich source of resources that may assist individual clients. In such communities, maintaining confidentiality can be experienced as secretive, alienating, divisive, and harmful.

Over a decade ago, Briskman and Noble (1999) suggested that an ethical model is needed that is more affirming of difference. One possibility is to develop multiple codes, grounded in client-based and service delivery schemes. For example, the authors cite an organization that works to prevent and treat sexual assault in Melbourne, Australia, that shapes its code based on the perspective that sexual assault is a violation of human rights (p. 64). This is an example of a specific code tailored to the organization's commitments to a particular client population. Another way to recognize difference is to develop constituency-based codes based on specific concerns, such as tolerance for sexual orientation in the schools. In this case, norms would be developed with specific reference to the issues raised by gay, lesbian, bisexual, transgendered, and questioning groups. The development of specialized codes for different groups departs from the universal application of the U.S. and Canadian codes.

In some cases a **bicultural code of practice** may be desirable. For example, the New Zealand Association of Social Work currently uses a Bicultural Code that reflects an effort to deal justly with its native Maori people through recognition of the independence guaranteed to them in a treaty negotiated in 1840. The historical emphasis on the Maori people's independence has led New Zealander social workers to recognize the contemporary demands that this principle places on their work with Maori people. The code is based on the IFSW code and explicitly requires a bicultural focus for all of New Zealand's social workers. See Exhibit 2.2 for an excerpt from the code.

EXHIBIT 2.2

*Sample
Bicultural
Code of
Practice*

In New Zealand, the Treaty of Waitangi, negotiated in 1840 between the occupying British and the native Maori chiefs, recognized the native Maori people as Tangata Whanua and guaranteed their right to independence. This treaty is an integral part of contemporary ethics in New Zealand social work, and it reflects an active commitment for the promotion of indigenous identity. The following is an excerpt from Section C, the Bicultural Code of the Code of Ethics of the New Zealand Association of Social Work.

Independence

Social work organisations and agencies and individual social workers should acknowledge and support the whanau [here, Maori clients] as the primary source of care and nurturing of their members.

1.2 Social workers are expected to work in ways that recognise the independence of the whanau and its members, by empowering the whanau and its members to handle their own lives and living conditions, and by enabling them to take care of themselves and to develop autonomously and collectively.

1.3 NZASW [New Zealand Association of Social Workers] recognises the right of Maori clients to have a Maori worker. Social work agencies and organisations should ensure that Maori clients have access to Maori workers at all levels, and social workers are expected to open up access to Maori workers. If no Maori worker is available, appropriate referral may be made if the client requests that. During their social work education Maori social workers should receive appropriate training in Maori models and methods.

Liberation through Solidarity

2.1 Social workers should work with agencies and organisations whose policies, procedures and practices are based on the Treaty of Waitangi, and actively and constructively

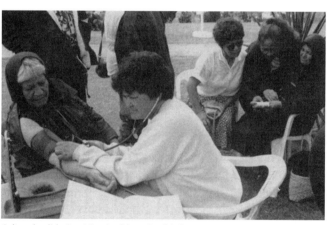

promote change in those agencies and organisations that operate from a monocultural base.

Non Discrimination

3.1 All social workers are expected to participate in Treaty of Waitangi education as part of their entry into social

Cultural solidarity: Maori address health issues.

work and on an ongoing basis. This should include a knowledge and understanding of their own ethnicity and the actual history of Aotearoa New Zealand.

Despite these inherent faults, the NASW *Code of Ethics* provides a valuable structure to the social work profession. The *Code of Ethics* articulates expectations and provides overall guidance about conduct so that social workers have clear expectations and can identify points of departure from the norms. The *Code of Ethics* is value-based and is consistent with many traditional commitments. Like all ethical codes, the *Code of Ethics* has limitations and is framed in consideration of experiences out of the mainstream. As such, the *Code of Ethics* addresses growing concerns for recognition and affirmation of diverse peoples worldwide. Codes are evolving documents that reflect the consensus of the profession at the time of adoption, a consensus that can change as contexts change. Social workers are encouraged to be involved in the professional dialogue about the *Code of Ethics*, and to contribute to the evolution of the document.

ETHICS AND THE LAW

International, federal, state, and local laws have a significant impact on social work practice, and its constant changes create a complex, sometimes bewildering climate in which to practice (Strom-Gottfried, 2008). Ethics and the law are related and sometimes overlap, yet there are clear distinctions between the two. The following discussion highlights parallels and distinctions between social work ethics and the law, as well as the potential for, and benefit of, collaboration between social workers and lawyers.

Parallels between Ethics and the Law

Many parallels exist between social work ethics and the laws that impact practitioners. For example, social workers who make derogatory comments to colleagues about clients who are living in poverty may be accused of actually violating the *Code of Ethics* (Section 1.12), as well as the spirit of the profession by expressing oppressive attitudes. In many states, clients could initiate a complaint with the state licensing board that a social worker has violated the *Code of Ethics*. If the client's culture differed from that of the social worker, a complaint could be added regarding a violation of *Code of Ethics* Section 1.05b, which requires the social worker to understand the function of culture and recognize the strengths of all cultures. State licensing boards can impose sanctions or require various forms of corrective action, such as license suspension or revocation (Reamer, 2008). NASW can also sanction social workers through a process by an ethics committee, and can impose a range of sanctions such as suspension from NASW, mandated supervision or consultation, censure, or others (Reamer, 2008), which includes publication of the names of those sanctioned. While NASW's process is a professional process, rather than a legal process, great professional hardship can ensue for those members sanctioned.

Conflicts between Ethics and the Law

Social workers may experience practice situations in which there is an overt conflict between ethical practice and the law. In the next section, two legal duties are considered: the duty to report and the duty to protect. Both of these legal mandates support ethical practice in many situations, but each also presents social workers with conflicts in particular contexts.

Duty to Report: Child Protection   Social workers operating in the arena of child protection frequently find themselves in a contentious environment. Like many types of helping professionals, social workers have a legal **duty to report** their suspicions of child abuse or neglect to child protection authorities or law enforcement.

A common sequence of events leading to a report of suspected child abuse or neglect begins with a child telling a teacher, school nurse, or another school-related adult that she or he has been abused or neglected. Alternatively, a nurse or doctor may suspect abuse or neglect based on physical signs. In either situation, the professional reports these allegations to the proper authorities. The charges are then investigated by a child protection worker, who often interviews the parents/guardians as well as the child, and makes a determination about whether the charges are substantiated and further action is required. The person making the referral may be convinced that the child is being abused or neglected, but she or he may also suspect that the abuse or neglect is going to be difficult to substantiate. In such a case, reporting the abuse might place the child at much greater risk, because the parent/guardian will learn about the accusation, become angry and take out the anger on the child. Where there is no obvious way to protect the child, the referring professional may be tempted not to obey the reporting law.

A similar situation may occur if the social worker is cynical about the adequacy, timeliness, or effectiveness of the response of the child protection agencies. For example, a social worker who experiences an unreasonably long response time from a child protection agency, due to inadequate department staffing and resources that leads to the inability of the department to collect important information about the abuse, may be reluctant to report again.

Social workers may encounter other practice situations that lead to a determination that compliance with the law may create more harm than good. For example, a social worker may assist a 15-year-old pregnant client to work through her options about the pregnancy. In a discussion with the client, the social worker discovers that the client knows who the father of the baby is, and the father is terribly frightened about the possible reaction of his family to the pregnancy. The client is under 18, and legally a child; therefore, the pregnancy becomes a matter of child abuse and, by law, must be reported. However, the social worker views the reporting possibility as nonproductive: the client claims that the sexual activity was consensual; reporting will not assist the client; the father is under 18 years old; reporting will possibly alienate the baby's father, who might otherwise participate in the decision-making process; and reporting could put the baby's father at risk of a violent reaction from his family.

Duty to Report: Adult Protection   All states have reporting laws for older adults designed to protect them from abuse, neglect, and exploitation; however, each state has its own definition of reportable acts, those responsible for reporting, and the entity that is responsible for accepting the report and investigating (Barsky, 2010). Social workers may experience similar challenges between the law and ethical duties with situations involving suspected abuse of older adults.

Duty to Protect: Threats of Violence   Social workers also have an ethical obligation to protect people from serious, foreseeable, and imminent harm (Barsky, 2010). This ethical and legal responsibility emerged from a court case resulting from a tragic situation. In 1969, Tatiana Tarasoff, a young student at the University of California at Berkeley, had a casual dating relationship with a graduate student from India. He apparently did not understand dating customs in the U.S., and consequently was despondent that Tatiana was simultaneously dating several men. Depressed, he went to a psychologist at the University Health Services and told the psychologist that he intended to kill Tatiana with a gun. The psychologist wrote a letter to the campus police and asked that the graduate student be detained in a psychiatric hospital. The police interviewed the young man but did not feel there was evidence to prove that he was dangerous. The police required him to promise that he would not contact Tatiana. When Tatiana returned from a summer visit abroad, the man stalked her, and finally stabbed her to death. Tatiana's family sued the campus police, the University Health Services, and the Regents of the University of California for failing to warn them that their daughter's life was in danger. The trial court dismissed the case because although there was precedence for notifying the victim, there was no precedence for warning a third party (which, in this situation, would have been Tatiana's parents). The appeals court supported the dismissal, and an appeal was taken to the California Supreme Court, which overturned the dismissal, citing the therapist's responsibility to warn people who have been threatened as Tatiana had been. This was *Tarasoff I* of 1974 and is often thought of as the **Duty to Warn** decision.

This ruling opened the way for the family to sue the police and the therapist. A massive outcry from members of both police and treatment-related groups led to the decision by the California Supreme Court to hear the case again. The 1976 court decision, *Tarasoff II*, stressed that when a therapist has determined that her or his client presents serious danger of violence to another, the therapist must "use reasonable care to protect the intended victim against such danger." The court's position was that the therapist might have to take any of several steps to ensure the safety of the person threatened by the client, and the emphasis was on the **Duty to Protect** rather than the warning emphasized in *Tarasoff I*. Although the Tarasoff decisions were based on the work of a clinical psychologist, social workers, as well as other human service professionals, are subject in most states to the same legal precedents.

Social workers must now carefully consider any threats of violence about which they learn in the course of practice. For example, if a client with a history of violence threatens to "belt" his girlfriend after discharge from a hospital, an assessment of the seriousness of the threat must be completed. Additionally, social workers must practice with consideration of protection against legal charges. A situation of this type is complex, and social workers must respond with several considerations in mind, to include the policy of their employer, the legal obligation of duty to protect, and the *Code of Ethics*. In the case of the Tarsoff decisions, the courts, not the ethics board of the profession, defined the parameters of responsibility.

Practice situations at various client system levels can involve the legal system. U.S. society has become increasingly litigious, and social workers may encounter practice situations with legal questions in policy practice, research, and community practice, as well as in direct practice (Barksy, 2010). For example, a social worker may encounter ethical challenges at the policy level in a situation in which a new adoption law might require adoption workers to provide the "adoption triad" (i.e., birth parents, adoptive parents, and adopted children) with access to all the information regarding the adoption. If a birth mother had been guaranteed confidentiality at the time of the adoption, she, along with her social worker, may be distraught by this sudden breach of the document that she signed, which she considered a binding legal agreement. Another example would be a social worker who is faced with maintaining a city zoning ordinance against the establishment of a group home for those leaving prison that she or he believes is critically needed in the community. Social workers can discover challenges in attempting to practice within the constraints of the law and the *Code of Ethics*.

Collaboration between Ethics and the Law

In the best scenarios, the law and social work professions can work together to empower people whose legal and social rights are frequently violated. There are many examples of this kind of collaboration in joint law and social work degree programs; for example, collaborations occur in legal clinics for refugee and immigrant peoples, and in family law and social work partnerships. In the U.S., the law drives much of the complex social welfare system, as well as the structures for shaping income and benefits distribution. A joint effort between the professions of social work and the law, based on common goals, can benefit a great number of people, with each profession enhancing and enriching the work of the other.

The law also serves as an external pressure on all of the helping professions to hold one another accountable within their professions. The law protects the general public from the possibility that helping professionals can collude to cover up or obscure unethical conduct within their profession. Although the incidence of covering up unethical behavior is relatively low, all professionals may be tempted to minimize the seriousness of any offense raised. Recent child abuse allegations and convictions involving priests from the Roman Catholic Church are tragic reminders of the potential dangers to vulnerable populations of unethical behavior by people in helping professions.

DILEMMAS AND CRITICAL PROCESSES

The complex context of real client system situations often highlights the potential for competition between social work values, and/or between ethical standards in a given situation. This complexity can make it difficult to identify the appropriate ethical decision. In the next section, the distinction between ethical conflicts and dilemmas, the idea of an ethical screen, various models for resolving dilemmas, and some examples of common dilemmas in social work practice are addressed.

The Distinction between Value Conflicts and Ethical Dilemmas

Value conflicts occur when an individual's personal values clash with those of another person or system. Although such conflicts are frequently distressful, the conflicts generally are simple disagreements between two opposing viewpoints. In contrast, an **ethical dilemma** occurs when a person holds two or more values that compete with each other. An ethical dilemma exists when there is no clear single response that satisfies all considerations in a situation, which is a more complicated situation than a value conflict.

Many practice situations involve ethical dilemmas. For example, social workers may learn that their clients are having affairs or using prostitutes, and struggle with the possible contrasting ethical and legal obligations to maintain confidentiality and notify client partners of physical harm. In another example, clients may demonstrate racism toward their social worker, who would then struggle with weighing an ethical mandate against abandoning clients with confidentiality, client self-determination and other ethical obligations. Another situation involving an ethical dilemma is when a relative of a suicidal person asks a social worker to help their relative, but the person has not sought services her/himself.

In all of these situations, no one response is clearly the correct, ethical way to handle the situation. Social workers must struggle with their ethical and legal mandates, consult with colleagues, and engage in other activities to arrive at a decision. In the next section, structures to assist with the decision-making process are discussed.

The Ethical Principles Screen

A useful tool in considering ethical priorities is the **ethical principle screen** (Dolgoff, Loewenberg, & Harrington, 2009). This screen assists in the decision-making process by highlighting the relative significance of values and the likely results of particular decisions. The elements in the screen, listed in Box 2.2, are reflected and prioritized in professional social work values, and are rank ordered so that Principle 1 has the highest priority and Principle 7 the lowest. The screen is constructed to reflect socially constructed priorities that involve values.

The following scenario demonstrates the use of the ethical principle screen. A social worker believes that a child on her caseload is at risk because his father regularly beats him to discipline him. This case clearly reflects Principle 1 regarding

---

BOX 2.2

Elements of the Ethical Principles Screen

- **Principle 1: Protection of Life** This principle refers to guarding against death, starvation, violence, neglect, and any other event or phenomenon that endangers a person's life.

- **Principle 2: Equality and Inequality** This principle reflects a commitment to equal and fair access to services and basic treatment.

- **Principle 3: Freedom and Autonomy** This principle affirms the notion of self-determination and supports people's right to make free choices regarding their lives.

- **Principle 4: Least Harm** This principle supports the idea of protecting people from harm; when harm seems likely in any event, it asserts that people have the right to experience the least amount possible.

- **Principle 5: Quality of Life** This principle confirms that people, families, and communities all have the right to define and pursue the quality of life they desire.

- **Principle 6: Privacy and Confidentiality** This principle supports the right of people to be protected from having their personal information made public. Maintaining confidentiality means the social worker must not share client circumstances, struggles, or decisions without the client's explicit (generally written and signed) permission. Information revealing any identifying characteristics (such as name and physical description) must also be kept confidential.

- **Principle 7: Truthfulness and Full Disclosure** This principle directs social workers to tell clients the full truth of any information pertaining to them, and explain whatever is needed to ensure understanding.

Source: Dolgoff, Loewenberg, & Harrington, 2009

threats of bodily harm. A competing concern is a violation of confidentiality and the continuing trust of the child that is threatened if the abuse is reported. Thus, the case also involves Principle 6. To resolve the dilemma, the ethical questions involved are identified, which are the protection of life versus confidentiality. These questions are prioritized by applying the ethical priorities screen, the priorities are rank ordered. In this situation, the life of the child provides a more urgent and compelling principle to guide actions than does a desire to maintain silence so that the child will continue to trust the social worker.

While not all social workers would agree with the prioritizations of the ethical screen in this situation, the screen offers a tool for decision making. However, the principles address very broad concepts that are subject to interpretation, and their relative evaluation in the real practice world often invites critical thinking skills. In the next section, other models for resolution of ethical dilemmas are discussed.

Models for Resolution of Ethical Dilemmas

Other models for resolution of ethical dilemmas structure decision-making in other ways, reflecting a different ordering of social work values. Two models are briefly described in this section.

Reamer (2005) suggests that social workers follow four steps to enhance the quality of their ethical decision making:

1. Identify the ethical issues, including the social work values and duties that conflict.

2. Identify the individuals, groups, and organizations that are likely to be affected by the ethical decision.

3. Tentatively identify all possible courses of action and the participants involved in each, along with the possible benefits and risks for each.

4. Thoroughly examine the reasons in favor of and opposed to each possible course of action.

5. Consult with colleagues and appropriate experts (i.e., professional colleagues, supervisors, agency administrators, and attorneys).

6. Make the decision and document the decision-making process.

7. Monitor and evaluate the decision.

Strom-Gottfried (2003) adds several options for addressing ethical dilemmas, including researching the literature, consulting formally with established committees, obtaining supervision, and consulting with peers. Strom-Gottfield (2003) also suggests the following strategies for solving ethical dilemmas: (1) consider the "worst case scenario" of each option; (2) consider the principles of least harm, justice, fairness, and the level of publicity that will result; (3) consider clinical and ethical implications; (4) consider the process; and (5) consider barriers to acting on the principal identified power relationships. Each of these approaches is helpful in analyzing the issues involved in any particular dilemma. While Reamer's model is more methodical than Strom-Gottfried's because it prescribes a specific sequence of analysis, the Strom-Gottfried model allows for a creative strategy that can accommodate specifics of the client system situation. Like codes of ethics, neither can provide an infallible result, and flexibility is needed in applying models to the specifics of the individual context.

Representative Examples of Practice Dilemmas

Of the many potential dilemmas, three types that commonly present in the social work practice context can be categorized as dual relationships, professional versus private tensions, and struggles between paternalism and client self-determination. Representative examples of these types of dilemmas are discussed next.

Dual Relationships   Relationships between social workers and clients that exist in addition to and are distinct from their professional contacts create **dual relationships**. Such relationships are often only publically known in extreme circumstances, such as when the worker has a sexual relationship with the client. Sexual relationships, although an egregious affront to the profession, are fairly easy to resolve because the prohibition against them is clear.

Nonsexual dual relationships pose another set of questions that are raised across many kinds of situations. For example, consider the situation of Lara, a new social worker. Lara works in a local community health center with young adults who have been identified as delinquent by legal authorities. Her responsibility is to support their integration into the work-study program that the center sponsors in the community. Lara finds her work interesting and rewarding, and particularly enjoys working with one client, Joe, who is progressing in the program. Lara's 20-year-old sister recently called her to tell her about her new boyfriend. Lara realized that her sister's new boyfriend is her client, Joe.

The dilemma created by this dual relationship is between personal values and professional responsibilities. There are many reasons for Lara to maintain the current situation. Lara enjoys her job, values her work with Joe, and does not want to resign. On the other hand, Lara also wants to participate in her family gatherings, which are likely to include her sister's new boyfriend. The *Code of Ethics*, however, cautions against dual relationships, which includes a professional and a personal relationship. Lara is not free to share the information with her family that Joe is a client, or anything about his situation, due to the ethical mandate about client confidentiality.

Specifically, Section 1.06c of the *Code of Ethics* stresses that social workers should not engage in dual relationships with clients or former clients in which there is a risk of exploitation or potential harm to the client. Reamer (2003) classifies dual relationships as unethical when they

- Interfere with the social worker's exercise of professional discretion.

- Interfere with the social worker's exercise of impartial judgment.

- Exploit clients, colleagues, or third parties to further the social worker's personal interests.

- Harm clients, colleagues, or third parties. (p. 129)

In this scenario, the dual relationship Lara has with Joe has the potential to affect her professional discretion and impartial judgment. For example, if Lara discovers personal information about Joe that suggests he might not be a viable candidate for marriage, Lara may experience difficulty conducting herself in a professional manner.

In some situations, the social worker may have justification for a dual relationship with a client. For example, in rural areas dual relationships may be very difficult to avoid, given the small number of service providers (Barsky, 2010). In a rural area, clients may have worked for a member of a social worker's family, attend the same faith community as a social worker, or be behind the social worker in the checkout line at the local grocery store. In a world characterized by expanding notions of community and multicultural experiences, social workers may find that they are asked to maintain relationships in several domains with others and to perform multiple roles. For example, in some cultures, social workers would risk insulting a family by refusing an invitation to a family dinner party. Social workers working with all types of client system levels struggle with the notion of professional boundaries and dual relationships.

Some social workers reject the notion of rigid boundaries as necessary or desirable. Vodde and Giddings (1997) maintain that some aspects of dual relationships— such as greater connectedness and an increase in the client's self-determination— can actually benefit rather than harm the client. They discuss a specific framework that separates the idea of exploitation into more manageable components and to determine whether a certain aspect is potentially beneficial or hurtful in any particular relationship. The continuum, which appears in Exhibit 2.3, allows the social worker to explore the areas and degrees to which a specific relationship dimension (for example, a social relationship with a client) might benefit or harm a client.

Applying this to the situation described earlier, Lara might evaluate the risk of exploiting Joe rather than empowering him if she were to continue to work with him. Lara might also consider the likelihood of increasing Joe's vulnerability through her knowledge of his past struggles. Some variables, such as control of resources, might not be applicable; unless, of course, Lara favored Joe as a potential

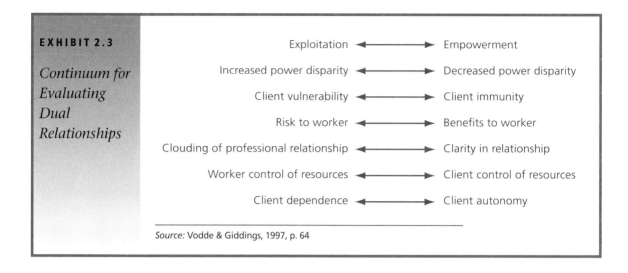

EXHIBIT 2.3

Continuum for Evaluating Dual Relationships

Exploitation ←——————→ Empowerment

Increased power disparity ←——————→ Decreased power disparity

Client vulnerability ←——————→ Client immunity

Risk to worker ←——————→ Benefits to worker

Clouding of professional relationship ←——————→ Clarity in relationship

Worker control of resources ←——————→ Client control of resources

Client dependence ←——————→ Client autonomy

Source: Vodde & Giddings, 1997, p. 64

brother-in-law by allocating an unfair share of resources, such as work stipends. Lara may be at high risk for clouding the professional relationship by working with him while he is dating her sister. Lara will need to evaluate whether the level of risk is too high to continue working with him.

A second framework proposed by Vodde and Giddings (1997) allows the social worker to decide if the dual relationship occurs naturally (with no intention of the social worker) or is contrived (arranged by the social worker for her or his own purposes). The framework also allows the social worker to examine whether the relationship is exploitive (for the worker's benefit), essential (for survival in the community), or enhancing (beneficial to the client). Returning to Lara's situation, although her relationship with Joe is naturally occurring (she did not arrange for the relationship), the dual relationship is neither essential for the community's well-being, nor empowering for Joe. The dual relationship has the potential to be exploitive. Analysis using this framework can be helpful in situations in which dual relationships are impossible to avoid. The framework uses the specific content of the case rather than applying a one-size-fits-all model that simply prohibits all dual relationships.

Responsibility to the Larger Society and Client Well-Being   Relationships that involve child or elder abuse or neglect, exploitation of older adults, and intimate partner violence were once considered private, family issues outside the jurisdiction of the law or of any public sector interest. Through the legal and social welfare systems, the larger society has wrestled with the question of a particular event being a private matter or a public issue that impacts society. While social workers often tend to value the private experience of families to recognize and acknowledge clients' perspectives on their experiences, social workers are also obligated to intervene with the client's environment to the extent that public issues impact and reflect the quality of lives of all citizens. The dilemma in this situation arises when the social worker values both the client's right to privacy and the potential benefit to the community of making the issues public.

As an example of this dilemma, social workers struggle with the extent of their obligation to encourage a survivor of rape to report the incident to the police if the client does not wish to do so (Dombo, 2005). Survivors of rape or sexual assault are often treated poorly by authorities, and are reluctant to pursue legal recourse for a variety of reasons, including: (1) survivors may want to heal and to work on beginning their lives again, and want to avoid dredging up the past through the legal proceedings; (2) survivors may fear rejection by others if their experiences are made public; and (3) survivors may fear that actions of the authorities could retraumatize them by implying that they are the guilty parties. Due to these reasons and more, rape is often underreported. Many social workers encourage reporting, so the crime is reported and appropriate resources can be devoted to the issue. This benefit to society of reporting the crime must be balanced with the experiences and wishes of individual women who have been raped. Attempting to force a woman to report her experience of rape to the authorities may jeopardize her well-being. Striking a balance between promoting the general welfare for the public and honoring the wishes of individuals is very challenging in practice, and must be the result of critical thinking and practice experience. When making decisions, social workers must consider the following questions: What is clearly a public issue and clearly a private issue? Is violence against persons an individual event or a violation of a larger social order as well? Does violence affect the entire community? Does a zealous social worker have the right to raise a public issue that could exploit the client's pain?

Paternalism and Client Self-Determination   Long a cornerstone of the social work profession, **self-determination** is the right of a client system to make choices and exercise control over her or his life. In the *Code of Ethics*, self-determination is listed in Section 1.02, second only to a general commitment to clients. In contrast, **paternalism** refers to a process of interfering with clients' self-determination because the social worker believes she or he has a better understanding than the client of the actions that are in the clients' best interests. Reamer (2006) identifies three different forms of paternalism: (1) withholding information from clients for their own good (for example, not communicating a medical prognosis or the extent of injury in an accident); (2) deliberately lying to clients, which is more overt than withholding information (for example, assuring a distraught family member that a dying client will improve); and (3) intervening to prevent clients' behavior by controlling their physical placement (for example, facilitating involuntary hospitalizations). A paternalistic approach can also be seen in situations where social workers provide too much assistance to clients, who avoid developing their problem-solving skills; or give too many suggestions; or interact in a controlling manner.

Questions about what rights and responsibilities social workers have to interfere in client situations have been debated since the profession began. In some situations, social worker rights and responsibilities are dictated by the law. However, social workers are sometimes asked to make an ethical decision concerning client self-determination without such a clear cut guide, such as intervening with a client who is disorderly or does not adhere to social norms in public, which are issues experienced frequently in the mental health sector. Another example is whether a client should be forced to conform to mainstream standards of cleanliness in a residential setting, or whether a social worker must facilitate the involuntary hospitalization of a person with a mental illness who is not adequate in her or his self-care. In such a case, someone must make a judgment about the standards of "adequate." In another example, some social workers may struggle with the question of whether to intervene with clients who are eating in an unhealthy manner, and who have a health condition that is exacerbated by the eating habits. Situations in which social workers question whether to intervene are questions involving social control and social change, and raise the broader issues about the degree to which U.S. society tolerates eccentricities or even mere differences. Social workers are obliged to "promote the well-being of clients" (Section 1.01 of the *Code of Ethics*), and must decide about the balance between responsible caretaking and excessive interference with client self-determination.

A more subtle variation of this dilemma occurs when the social worker urges clients to engage in activity that the worker values. Reamer (1983) has called this "pseudopaternalism" because the paternalistic interference does not arise out of professional values but from personal self-interest, even if the social worker has good intentions. For example, most social workers would agree that it is consistent with the profession's values to encourage a young person to achieve the highest level of education possible. At the same time, most social workers also value education personally. If a social worker encourages an adolescent with great academic potential to achieve scholastically beyond the goals of her or his family, the social worker could be acting paternalistically if the client is not interested in such achievement. The social worker could be considered to be imposing her or his dreams and goals on the client. In contrast, accepting the adolescent's limited view of life may not be upholding the social worker's commitment to promote an individual's well-being. The issue of client system self-determination versus paternalism occurs frequently in social work practice, and social workers must be constantly alert to this dilemma and make the decisions based on critical thinking.

STRAIGHT TALK ABOUT EXPECTATIONS AND STANDARDS IN A LITIGIOUS WORLD

Many issues concerning ethics and values are complicated by context and are difficult to resolve in real practice situations. Social workers must consider values and ethics thoughtfully throughout their practice career. The following sections consider ethical social work practice in terms of postmodernism and in the context of a litigious environment for professionals. While different, social workers must navigate social work practice with consideration of both perspectives.

Thoughtful Practice in a Postmodern World

The current substance of professional ethical inquiry tends to be focused on ethics enforcement and risk management (Reamer, 2008). Rather than serious client issues, such as poverty, or the collective responsibilities of the social work profession, the *Code of Ethics* and most ethical inquiries are focused on the individual conduct of the practitioner. Social workers, however, can explore other dimensions to enrich the professional discourse about ethical practice. For example, Walz and Ritchie (2000) suggest that Gandhian principles (based on the work of Mahatma Gandhi, an Indian pacifist) could make a valuable contribution to Western thinking about ethical issues in social work practice. These principles include service, social justice, nonviolence, priority to the disadvantaged, and the notion of the heart as unifier of all things. Social workers interested in expanding the notion of ethical practice might examine the degree to which their practice is consistent with nonviolence, maintaining material simplicity, or prioritizing the needs of the disadvantaged.

Risk Management in a Litigious World

Some practice situations require social work practitioners to be concrete and decisive about their actions. U.S. society is increasingly litigious, particularly with regard to the activities of helping professionals. Licensed social workers are obligated by a state regulating body to uphold the *Code of Ethics*, even if practitioners question certain aspects and/or challenge the *Code of Ethics* to encourage change. While an uncommon occurrence, social workers face risks of censure and lawsuits charging malpractice or negligence. Social workers are held accountable for upholding the *Code of Ethics* by the profession through the NASW ethics complaints process, and by the courts through lawsuits and state licensing boards. In a very small number of cases, social workers are also indicted on criminal charges about ethical misconduct (such as an allegation of fraudulent billing) (Reamer, 2008). Strom-Gottfried (2000), in an examination of 781 ethics violations, discovered that boundary violations (with sexual relationships as the most numerous) composed the greatest number of ethics violations (at 254). "Poor practice" (160) was the second, and "Competence" (86) was the third most common violation, with "Record keeping," "Honesty," "Breach of confidentiality," "Informed consent," "Collegial violations," "Billing," and "Conflicts of interest" accounting for the remainder violations.

Social workers are encouraged to take advantage of the knowledge and experiences of other competent and concerned social workers through supervision when wrestling with decisions that have an ethical component. Strategic thinking and planning with another professional, particularly one with more experience in recognizing various perspectives and aspects of the situation, can be an invaluable decision-making aid. Further, receiving input on practice through regular social work supervision can assist in the prevention of inadvertent ethical violations.

Social work practice occurs within a context of reflective, contextual practice in which values are explored and rules about them are challenged, and the litigious structure of absolute rights and wrongs of ethical violations. The ability of social workers to transition from a postmodern perspective to one in which the legal and professional obligations are clear requires that social workers be "bilingual" in a sense. Social workers must be aware of the expectations of the law and the profession, as well as maintaining a person obligation to engage in critical thinking.

CONCLUSION

This chapter has examined many of the moral and value rules by which the profession governs itself. Consistent with the postmodern ideas of challenging taken-for-granted precepts, social workers are encouraged to explore the implications of the profession's values and ethics.

As social workers gain skills in ethical decision-making, increasingly complex ethical dilemmas may be encountered. Although social workers strengthen the profession through active participation in questioning the values and ethics principles, social workers must also understand contemporary concerns about ethical violations, and the need for critical thinking about societal expectations.

MAIN POINTS

- Ethical codes are useful in providing standards of professional conduct, but may also restrict creativity when dealing with different contexts and multiple realities.

- Social workers have an ethical responsibility to contemplate, challenge, and work to change the profession's ethical awareness.

- Social work ethics and the law are different, although they have parallels and offer the potential for interdisciplinary collaboration. Ethics and law can conflict when legal duties, such as the duty to report, come into question in certain contexts.

- Ethical dilemmas arise out of competing values—for example, dilemmas involving dual relationships, privacy versus public issues, and paternalism versus self-determination.

- Social workers need to develop sophistication in risk management practices that protect them from ethical violations by learning from others' experiences and familiarizing themselves with basic legal mandates.

EXERCISES

1. You are a social worker in a psychiatric hospital setting. While most patients are discharged from the hospital setting after only a few days, some patients are able to stay for longer periods of time. Due to the mandate from insurance companies to discharge patients as soon as possible, discharge planning begins as patients are admitted.

    Your client, Bea, was admitted for psychiatric reasons and is terrified to leave the hospital after a stay of over three weeks. Your responsibility is to locate long-term housing and outpatient care for her in the community. As you meet with her one morning, you find her tearfully pleading with you to be allowed to stay longer, as she does not feel able to live independently. You are not sure that she is ready either, although the medical staff state that she is ready for discharge. You feel caught between the demands of your organization and the wishes of Bea.

    a. What three primary values are represented in your thinking about Bea's situation?
    b. Is this an ethical dilemma? Justify your answer.
    c. In what section of the *Code of Ethics* would you look for guidance?
    d. Apply one strategy for resolving ethical dilemmas discussed in the chapter to Bea's situation.
    e. How will you go about resolving this situation?
    f. Compare your response with other students. Do using different strategies lead to different resolutions?

2. After reading the following scenarios, consider these questions:
    a. What is the ethical issue?
    b. What are the values of the client system?
    c. Are they in conflict with your values? Society's?
    d. What strategy would you use for resolving the situation?
    e. What would you do?
    After answering these questions, discuss findings with classmates.

    1. In a public setting over lunch, one of your co-workers begins speaking disparagingly about a challenging client. The co-worker does not use the client's full name.
    2. You are new to the area in which you have taken a job. Your new client, a hairdresser, offers to cut your hair.
    3. You are seeing a couple for marriage counseling. Both parties report that they are committed to remaining in the marriage. While you are out socially, you see the wife holding hands with someone other than her husband.
    4. While out with friends at a restaurant, you notice one of your clients is sitting at the next table.
    5. You are working with a teenage girl in a youth shelter. She reveals to you that she was raped by her neighbor, who is involved with gangs and drugs. She reports

that she told her father and they agreed not to press charges due to fear of retaliation.

6. Your client of six months reveals that he/she has begun to experience romantic feelings for you.

7. One of your clients reports symptoms of a mental illness to you. She reports that she wanders around her neighborhood at night in the winter without appropriate clothing, is hearing voices, and refuses to take her medication or go to the hospital. You are concerned about her safety.

8. You are working with a family in a family preservation program. In the home, the teenage daughter is violent towards her mother. During an altercation, the mother hit the daughter, presumably in self-defense, leaving a mark.

9. You are leaving the agency for another position. On your last day, a client brings you a goodbye gift and asks if you will still call her.

10. You receive an emergency call from your client. He reports to you that he just got fired from his job. He states, "I am not going to let him get away with this. He is going to be sorry. He has not seen the last of me." You know that this client has access to firearms and a history of assault.

11. You receive a call from the spouse of your client. He wants to discuss his wife's case with you. The wife's chart does not contain a release of information.

12. One of your adolescent clients invites you to his graduation and family party.

13. A client's insurance benefits have ended but you feel she needs continued care.

14. You are working with a teenage client. She reports to you that she is having sex with her boyfriend when her parents are not at home. She asks you not to tell her parents, and if you do, that she will feel as though you have betrayed her trust.

3. In a journal entry, reflect on a time when you faced a situation that challenged your personal values. What did you do? Why? How did you decide what to do? What were the results of your decision? If you could re-live the situation, would you handle it differently?

4. Go to www.routledgesw.com/cases and select the Sanchez family case. Review the client history of Celia and Hector Sanchez. Imagine that you are a social worker employed by Our Lady of Guadalupe Church, where the Sanchezes are parishioners. You have noticed that when Celia comes to pick up commodities, she talks about the desperation of her family. When asked about food stamps, she replies that her husband will not allow her to enroll in the program, even though she thinks it would be a good idea, and is considering enrolling despite her husband's wishes, if she could think of a way to do this. You have helped other families access the program, even when one member does not wish to enroll. Should you encourage Celia to use your assistance to enroll? What social work values are involved in this situation? Is it an ethical dilemma? How might you resolve the situation? What might be the implications?

5. Go to www.routledgesw.com/cases and select and become familiar with the Riverton case. Under the "Engage" tab, answer the Critical Thinking Question #1.

Individual Engagement: Relationship Skills for Practice at All Levels

What do I need out of a relationship? What can I give in a relationship? I am no different than any of you out there today. I have the same heart, I have the same feelings, I have the same aches and pains and the same hope and dreams that you do. I have suffered disappointment in relationships, as have you. I have been hurt too, but through all of this I have grown . . .

Resa Hayes, disability activist, in Mackelprang & Salsgiver, 1999, p. 161

Key Questions for Chapter 3

(1) How can I prepare for action with all client systems? (EPAS 2.1.10(a))

(2) What are the key interpersonal skills and techniques that I need to know to work with any client system? (EPAS 2.1.10(a))

(3) What communication mistakes can I avoid?

(4) How do I utilize a social justice and a human rights perspective when working with client systems?

RELATIONSHIP IS AT THE VERY HEART OF SOCIAL WORK PRACTICE. The idea of building relationships with people is probably a major element in your first attraction to the profession and will likely be an abiding component that sustains your commitment. Social work scholars and practitioners have long recognized relationship as a crucial element of the profession's work with all types of client systems. Relationship building, or engagement, is the first step in the professional helping process and leads to the other processes of assessment, intervention, and evaluation.

When you think of relationship, you may first think of the close, careful, one-to-one partnership that characterizes much of direct practice. These relationships, however, rarely stand alone and are usually enhanced and facilitated by effective connections with other players who are significant to the client system. At the individual level, these players can include teachers, landlords, therapists, case managers, clergy, friends, and family, as well as other participants in community services and institutions who help the client to reach her or his goals. Relationship is also as critical in group, family, organization, and community development work as it is in interventions with individuals. At the community level, relationship skills are essential for work with decision-makers, community members, coalition partners and funders. Relationship between cultures may become the single most important dimension of our global well-being in the future. Relationship shapes the connection between the social worker and client system and stimulates the investment in the work they set out to do together.

This chapter explores several aspects of engagement, the process of building relationships across direct and indirect practice settings, and its importance to the overall success of social work practice. In the first section, the importance of listening to the situation and perspective of a client system is examined. A number of specific beginning and interviewing skills and approaches that help the social worker both elicit sharing by the client system and enlist the assistance of others will be presented. This section also includes some skill combinations that are helpful in establishing the connection and setting the stage for a productive effort. Later sections in the chapter view this continuous engagement process through the lenses of strengths-based, social justice, and human rights practice as the perspectives that ground the work.

HEARING THE CLIENT'S SITUATION AND PERSPECTIVE

Probably the most important few moments of a social work relationship occur at the very beginning. Regardless of the focus of your agency or the theoretical perspective you may be using, you first want to hear the client's situation and perspective. The length and the type of listening that you do will vary from practice setting to practice setting and agency to agency. For example, some agencies will expect you to complete a comprehensive psychosocial history that details a client's whole life, which may seem much more focused on the past than on the present. Despite this past focus, you will want to prepare for your intervention work with the client system by carefully listening to them first. As you listen, you might ask yourself the following key questions:

- What brings the client system here today?

- How does the client system describe the situations, and what meaning do these situations have for them?

- What will life look like when the situation is better?

- What are their expectations of me?

- What strengths and talents do they have?

- What do they want to happen in their work with me?

- What can we accomplish together?

Although these may seem like general considerations, they are helpful in establishing the respect and affiliation in the first connections that lead to successful work together. You will want to approach the relationship with genuine curiosity, out of which you may ask questions to help you understand. This understanding helps keep the conversation fresh and honest, as you are less likely to ask questions designed to confirm what you already think. You may yourself have experienced frustration with people who assume they understand your thoughts or situation because they knew a lot about others' thoughts and situations in the same realm. It is challenging to remain open to and hear the story of the person before you if you have made conclusions mid-dialogue, based on information in a textbook or from your experience.

The ability to carefully listen is a critical social work skill because you want to hear the client's situation as she or he has experienced it and be open to the experience of difference. Relationship qualities and listening skills are essential elements that constitute a genuine approach to working with people in general, and as such are just as meaningful for interactions with client family members, community members, and staff in organizations as they are with individual clients.

For example, you may have made a skillful connection with an individual client in that you have heard their situation and perspective, conveyed professional and warm acceptance, generated confidence and hope in a genuine manner, and clarified the tasks upon which you and your client have agreed. If one of those tasks is to help the client locate and secure housing that better suits her needs, you may want or need to work with a reluctant landlord. In such a situation you might perceive the scenario only in the client's terms—that is, you might be inclined to criticize a landlord who resists renting to your client. For this reason, in your beginning contacts with the landlord, you want to use the same relationship qualities and listening skills that you used with your client. That is, you enter the conversation with genuine curiosity and you avoid jumping to conclusions about "slumlords" or accusations of evildoing. You will also want to understand the particular difficulties the landlord has in maintaining rental properties in a profitable manner.

You may also work to avoid stereotyping the landlord or deciding you know all about the rental business because you worked with a difficult landlord in another client situation. Social workers are frequently so invested in the rights of clients that they may be tempted to leap to conclusions regarding perceived adversaries that are based more on eagerness to help the client than on the person's actual responses. In some cases, that person may be the only person or the key person who can assist the client; therefore, a full effort at engaging in an effective relationship is needed. The social worker's role is to be fair, articulate, and open with all the concerned parties. You will need to recognize your own biases and understand the client population. In the next section the core relationship qualities and specific skills for going beyond the initial interchange and establishing a productive dialogue will be explored.

Core Relationship Qualities

In a seminal work that holds true in contemporary social work practice, Carl Rogers (1957) defined the aspects of attitude as prerequisites to forming and maintaining effective professional relationships to include unconditional positive regard and empathy. Later, genuineness and warmth were added as essential items. These core attitudes or conditions are the basis for caring, and assist in forming a positive, non-possessive relationship with a client system.

Warmth   The demonstration of **warmth** is "non-possessive caring" (Shebib, 2003, p. 72). The expression of warmth entails the expression of caring and concern without expectations for the individual or relationship, as well as goodwill by the social worker. Warmth can be demonstrated through such behaviors as attentive and caring facial expressions, soothing tone of voice, and appropriate pacing of verbal interaction. Social workers also show their concern and warmth through extending courtesies, such as making sure that the client system is physically comfortable, offering them something to drink, making eye contact, and offering well-timed, appropriate humor. However, social workers will want to consider ethnic and cultural considerations about the expression of warmth, and offer flexibility in the amount of warmth demonstrated to coincide with the comfort level of the client system.

Empathy   is the "act of perceiving, understanding, experiencing, and responding to the emotional state and ideas of another person" (Barker, 2003, p. 141). **Empathy** is a core condition for all helping relationships, and social workers must develop a capacity for working with feelings, even intense feelings, without changing the subject, offering quick solutions or moving the dialogue to the intellectual level. An empathic attitude is characterized by a willingness to learn about the emotional world of another. Suspending judgment by controlling personal biases, assumptions and reactions is a first step toward adopting empathic attitude. A key element to empathy is the ability to enter into the emotional state of another person without actually feeling the same feelings as the person. For example, if the client has experienced a death in the family, rather than making assumptions about how the client feels and the intensity of the feeling, an empathetic stance toward the client is to attempt to understand the nature and intensity of the client's feelings about the situation. Also important is the ability to make an empathetic response by putting into words the feelings as expressed by the client, as more fully described later in the chapter.

Genuineness   Sincerity and honesty are essential elements of **genuineness**. Developing an effective relationship requires these elements, as well as being unpretentious, acknowledging your limitations, and providing only sincere re-assurances (Barker, 2003). Being authentic, real, and reliable provides the basis for a trusting relationship, which is the core of a helping relationship. Social workers who are genuine provide information that is timely, helpful, and accurate, and avoid hidden agendas and games with client systems (Shebib, 2003).

Unconditional Positive Regard   Each human being is considered to be "of worth whose rights and dignity are to be respected without reservation" (Barker, 2003, p. 445). **Unconditional positive regard** requires acceptance and non-judgmentalness of client systems, regardless of whether a social worker approves or accepts individual or collective client system actions.

While these qualities must exist for a positive relationship, the existence of these qualities does not guarantee that client systems will always interpret these qualities in a positive manner. That is, social workers should expect to be rejected by clients at times, despite their best efforts. For example, clients may interpret empathy as manipulation, and view genuineness as fake. A mature acceptance of the limits of possibilities will help social workers avoid burnout.

Specific Skills for the Dialogue

Communication is complex, and demonstrating specific oral communication skills is important to professional practice. In this section, specific approaches and skills that are useful in the process of purposeful communicating with your client for an interview or another purpose will be examined. The discussion will include nonverbal and verbal communication skills that facilitate a professional relation-ship with clients. Consistent with the strengths approach, the discussion below will emphasize skills used in facilitation of a dialogue with clients (Saleebey, 2009) rather than interviewing skills.

Preparing to Listen   **Attending** is the term used to describe the way in which social workers convey their interest in communicating with clients that, combined with appropriate verbal responses, promotes exploration of ideas and challenges. Attend-ing has verbal and nonverbal components. Attending is expressed through appropriate verbal following, eye contact, posture, and disciplined attention (Barker, 2003).

Prior to meeting with clients, you need to ensure that you have a physical and psychological commitment to a professional conversation in the best interest of the client. This can mean ensuring that any psychological needs you may have do not interfere with your listening to the client system. Additionally, attending means that you fully disengage from prior interactions with others before engaging with a new client system. You also need to mentally prepare yourself to avoid reacting to client system communication in a verbal or nonverbal way that conveys judgment or impatience. Third, ensure that you practice nonverbal behaviors that facilitate dialogue, such as the following:

- Turning your shoulders and legs toward the client.

- Sitting with an open body position, with uncrossed arms and legs.

- Slightly leaning toward the client.

- Smiling and using head nodding to provide positive reinforcement.

- Maintaining eye contact, within the comfort and cultural norms of the client.

- Using responsive facial expressions.

- Speaking in a warm, pleasant tone.

- Giving brief, encouraging comments.

- Avoiding the presence of large objects and heavy furniture between you and the client.

In most cases you will want to sit relatively close to the client. When the client is not upright (i.e., the client is in a hospital bed), the social worker will usually want to minimize the height differential by sitting on a low chair at an angle to empower the client to control the amount of eye contact and full face contact. While these are general guidelines, you will need to alter your nonverbal behaviors to match the comfort level of your client. A facet of the interchange that can be both highly variable and powerful is the degree of eye contact that you maintain with the client. In most cases you will make strong intermittent contact to indicate interest and connection. For clients of almost any culture, eye contact that is too constant and intense may be acutely uncomfortable; to some clients, even minimal amounts may seem intrusive. Individualizing your eye contact to maintain client comfort is an important practice skill.

Other important aspects of client interaction include dress and time of day of meeting. In general, your dress will be guided by the policies of your agency. Some agencies ask their staff to dress formally or "business casual," while others ask that staff match the style of dress of the clients, which may be informal. Clothes that are relatively modest in nature facilitate the interaction focus to be on the client, rather than on the social worker. Social workers work a wide variety of hours (i.e., day, evening, overnight, and weekend), depending on the nature of the work. If meeting clients in a community setting outside of the office, social workers must exercise some flexibility because there is less control over the environment of the interaction than in an office setting. In settings outside of offices, such as in client homes, community centers, and public locations, social workers must maintain professional verbal and nonverbal communication, or work to minimize distractions.

Diversity Considerations Your preparation will include consideration of elements of culture or style—both yours and your client's—to which you need to attend. Supervision, peer consultation, and a general assessment of the particular culture in which you work will be helpful. Weigh whether your dress, posture, and language are appropriate to the person you are working with and the setting in which that work takes place. In general, the goal is to communicate respect for your client and for the nature of the event in which you are accompanying her or him. For example, in most practice contexts do not wear jeans to a courtroom appearance or use "dorm room" slang to the judge. Conversely, you might dress more informally in making an outreach home visit to a client and family. Continually be aware of the customs and contexts of the client system with whom you are working, and work to match the nonverbal behavior of the client.

Specific Interviewing Skills

Discovery-Oriented Questions In general, your role is to hear the client's situation and perspective in the way in which she or he wants to tell it, without making assumptions and filling in information gaps yourself. **Discovery-oriented questions** are designed to invite your client to communicate her or his purposes in communicating with you and to express goals for the relationship. Discovery-oriented questions assist you in getting to know the client, and they can put the client at ease. Such a process may mean waiting a minute after you make welcoming introductions to allow your client an opportunity to begin. If she or he does not take that cue, you can invite her or him with such phrases as, "Where would you like to begin?" or, "Can you tell me what brings you here?" Some clients may be prepared for a much more directive stance on your part, so you may need gently to encourage their ownership of the dialogue.

Silence As you dialogue with a client, moments of silence should be permitted. There are many interpretations of silence, and some people feel more comfortable with silence than others. While some practitioners and clients struggle with their ability to allow silence in a dialogue, you will want to develop a comfort with silence. There are at least six meanings to silence:

1. *The client is thinking.* Some clients need more time than others to gather and organize their thoughts. Allowing time for this helps clients feel empowered, and worthy of the patience of the social worker.

2. *The client is confused.* Your questions may be unclear, or clients are unsure what you expect from them. If you suspect this, you might try asking whether

the client is confused and needs the explanation or question again. Clients may demonstrate confusion or uncertainty during the beginning stages of the relationship or time together.

3. *The client is experiencing uncomfortable thoughts and/or feelings.* Providing silence gives the client time to process pain or anxiety, and consider proceeding further in the discussion. If you think the client is silent because of powerful emotions, you may wish to provide empathy. A statement such as, "I sense that the topic of your daughter's life provokes some strong feelings," provides support for the client and conveys understanding.

4. *The client is working to develop trust with you.* Silence provides clients with a sense of dignity and control over their lives, a way to avoid rejection, and a way to maintain control over the conversation. To move the relationship toward more openness, you could proceed slowly with a discussion of less personal matters, or you might choose to raise the issue of trust directly with clients.

5. *The client is a quiet person.* You might utilize open-ended questions to draw out the client, or, in a supportive manner, discuss her or his silence directly in terms of your working relationship. Consider using other methods for the discussion, as some clients are more expressive when combining an activity with a discussion, journaling or when using the arts.

6. *The client has achieved closure.* If you think this may explain the client's silence, you can ask the client if there is anything else to discuss at the moment.

During silence, you can attend to the silence through the use of eye contact, maintaining your psychological focus on the client, maintaining strong nonverbal focus (i.e., avoid shifting your body, checking your watch, or other means of communicating discomfort), and using self-discipline to minimize external and internal distraction. Conversely, some silences should be broken by the social worker to discern the meaning of the silence or to shift to another topic. Silence during your dialogue can be encouraged to allow for self-reflection and for slowing the pace of the conversation. Use of silence can also lead clients to answer their own questions and discover their own next steps toward a resolution (Shebib, 2003). The appropriate length of silence between the social worker and the client must be determined by the situation and context. If, for example, a client is giving deep thought to a question asked by the social worker, a long silence may be appropriate. Long silences may not be appropriate in settings where the social worker may only have a few minutes with each client, such as some hospital or school settings, or when a client is clearly suicidal or homicidal. Ultimately, professional judgment must be the guide to interpreting and responding to silence.

Following Responses   This type of response gives clients immediate feedback that their message has been heard and understood. This immediate feedback can be conveyed through paraphrasing, summarizing, conveying empathy, and showing attentiveness through short verbal statements and questions such as "Go on," "I see," and "Can you tell me more?" (Barker, 2003). You will use **following responses** to provide only enough response to inspire the client to continue speaking. Providing a more complete response at the time may interrupt the client's direction and distract the client from fully sharing her or his situation and/or perspective.

Paraphrasing   Expressing an idea of the relevant points of the immediate past statement of the client in your own words is **paraphrasing**. When the social worker states the essence of the client statement, clients are assured that the social worker heard and understood them accurately. Paraphrasing can also assist clients to clarify their own thoughts to them (Barker, 2003). After paraphrasing, you can invite the client to correct you if you are mistaken. An invitation to correct can communicate both that you care enough about them to want to accurately understand their situation and perspective, and that you recognize that you may have the wrong understanding of the specific issues at hand. Paraphrasing is presented without judgment and without an attempt to solve any issues. There is no attempt to add meaning to or change the meaning of the client's statement (Shebib, 2003).

> Example:
> Client: *I don't really get what is going on. I mean, I put food on the table, keep a roof over our heads, and try to keep her going to school. I don't understand what her problem is!*
>
> Social Worker: *You are working really hard to provide for her, and cannot understand what your daughter is talking about.*
>
> Client: *Yeah! She is skipping school, running off, and now I am in trouble!*
>
> Social Worker: *In other words, she is not grateful for everything you are doing for her. In fact, she is getting you in hot water with the law.*

To avoid monotony, social workers can use a variety of lead-ins for paraphrasing, to include the following:

> As I understand it . . .
> It sounds a little like . . .
> As I hear it . . .
> The picture I am seeing is . . .

Clarifying   The role of clarifying is closely related to paraphrasing, but the social worker is directly asking for client feedback to clarify a point. **Clarifying** could be used at the end of a paraphrase. For example, the worker might say, "What I understand you to be saying is. . . . Is that right?" Clarification contributes to understanding the uniqueness of the client's message rather than generalizing or framing it in a way that matches your own perceptions. Clarifying increases the accuracy of your assessment while communicating a respect for the complexity of the client. Clarification may be needed at any point in the planned change process, especially to clarify each other's intent, interpretations, and meanings. For example, a client may demonstrate tearfulness or giddiness that you might assume is joy, but the tears may also be a sign of regret, loss, or confusion. Clarifying the meaning of a client's communication is an important component of the work.

Example:

Client: *The last time she ran off, she told me that she was never coming back, and that she hated me. Can you believe that?*

Social Worker: *Did I get this right? You are saying that she refuses to ever come back home?*

Client: *Yeah. What does she think, that she can live at a friend's house forever?*

Summarizing   A summary can provide closure and consensus either after a segment of the session is complete or at the conclusion of the whole session. A summary is a way of confirming your understanding thus far of the client's message and checking the validity of your assumptions. **Summarizing** can also help to establish organization for the entirety of your work together as well as frame the particular interaction. In situations in which the issues evoke significant client emotion, or in which the work is directed at some complex task, summing up the interaction can demonstrate manageability and hopefulness. Summing up can provide both you and your client with a snapshot of the topics discussed thus far, which can help to clarify the future direction of the dialogue. Summarizing can also assist to focus a conversation that wanders off topic.

Examples:

Social Worker to Client: *So far we have talked about your job responsibilities and my responsibilities, and how they overlap. We have discussed this vaguely in prior staff meetings, but no one has really picked up on the idea that this is a problem because we are wasting some time. Do you agree with this?*

Social Worker to Client: *Let me try to sum up our discussion so far. Your daughter has run away many times, and refuses now to come home. As far as you can tell, you have not done anything to cause her to run away and skip school. No one at the school believes that you are trying to fix the problem. Is that a fair summary so far?*

Social Worker to Client: *You have been working to get this street fair organized, but you are really in need of some people from the business community to get involved in the organizing and recruiting phase. Do you agree?*

Direct, Closed Questions   Direct [closed questions] encourage the client to provide factual information in a concise manner, and can be helpful in gaining specifics about behaviors, such as frequency, duration, and intensity. This type of question can be answered "yes" or "no," or with a numerical answer. While such questions do not encourage clients to open up and share, they are useful in certain situations in which precise information is needed. These situations include times when you will need a numerical number to get a sense of the situation, or involve dangerous conduct or some imminent threat of harm that must be dealt with directly in order to ensure safety. An example of a situation in which you would seek concrete information is a situation in which a client is expressing an intention of hurting her- or himself or someone else and you need to know if the client has a real plan to engage in the dangerous behavior (for example, suicide) and the means to carry out the plan (Shebib, 2003).

Examples:

Client: *I have not eaten in quite a while.*

Social Worker: *How many days have it been since you had a meal?*

Community Member: *We had a community organizer working on health care in this neighborhood a while back.*

Social Worker: *For how many years did the organizer work in this neighborhood?*

Open-Ended Questions   **Open-ended questions** are designed to elicit extensive answers (Barker, 2003). While both open- and closed-ended questions are useful for social workers, open-ended questions are especially helpful at the beginning of a dialogue to encourage client systems to share their experiences and perceptions in the manner which is most comfortable to them, and in the way that makes the most sense to them.

Examples:

Client: *My brother and I always fight after school.*

Social Worker: *What are your fights like?*

Community Member: *We are trying to push the drug dealers out of our community.*

Social Worker: *How do the drug dealers affect the neighborhood?*

Indirect Questions   **Indirect questions** are questions phrased as sentences, rather than questions. Indirect questions allow clients the freedom to choose to respond or not, as well as provide flexibility in the type of response. In a conversation, mixing direct and indirect questions can help clients to feel less pressured and avoid monotony in the types of questions asked (Barker, 2003).

Examples:

Client: *I would like to save some money to buy a house some day.*

Social Worker: *I wonder how you would be able to save money, given all of your responsibilities.*

Client: *My teacher is picking on me! She punishes me for things that other kids get away with!*

Social Worker: *Wow! That sounds really upsetting. It must be so hard to try to get your work done in class while you are worrying about your teacher looking over your shoulder all of the time.*

Empathic Communication **Empathic communications** assist client systems to identify and label their feelings, as well as provide the support to process feelings that previously were overwhelming. Social workers must, therefore, gain familiarity with the range of feelings, and become skilled at accepting feelings at face value, rather than placing judgments on feelings or demonstrating disapproval about client feelings (Shebib, 2003). To demonstrate empathy, social workers identify the feelings expressed as well as communicate their understanding of the feelings to the client. Social workers also must be aware of their own emotional state at the start of a relationship, so that the social worker is aware of the potential impact of her or his emotional state on the interaction with the client (Shulman, 2009a).

Three types of empathy are: (a) basic empathy, in which the social worker mirrors clients' statements; (b) inferred empathy, in which the social worker makes guesses about feelings based on clues in clients' statements; and (c) invitational empathy, in which the social worker encourages clients to talk about their feelings. Invitational empathy provides an opening for the clients to talk about feelings, without making a demand to do so (Shebib, 2003).

Example of basic empathy:
Client: *I am ready to kill my daughter. This whole thing is very embarrassing. I have not done anything wrong!*

Social Worker: *So you are angry with your daughter for putting you in this situation where you have to defend yourself.*

Example of inferred empathy:
Client: *My husband tells me that I am no good, and beats me all the time. But last week, he started beating my daughter too!*

Social Worker: *This is a really tough situation. I suspect that you might have been scared at what he might do to her.*

Example of invitational empathy:
Client: *My son died in a fire last week.*

Social Worker: *Oh, I am so sorry for your loss! A lot of people in your situation might feel in shock about their sudden loss.*

A common challenging scenario with beginning social workers and the use of empathic communication is the challenge of working with clients who are older than they are who have had different types of life experiences. For example, a young social worker who does not have children may be working with a mother of several children. If the social worker is asked whether she has any children, the social worker may be tempted to respond defensively by talking about her training, or suggest that they are not here to talk about her background, but instead about the situation with the mother. Instead, this scenario provides the opportunity to utilize inferred empathy by thinking about the likelihood that the client might be wondering about her ability to understand the client's situation. A response of, "No, I do not have any children. Are you wondering whether I am going to be able to understand what it is like for you to raise your children? I am wondering that too, and I am wondering if you will explain it to me so I can understand?" might help to uncover the true concern that underlies the question (Shulman, 2009a).

As mentioned earlier, when clients experience or verbalize emotions, some-times the use of silence is the best response. When you sit with a person who is experiencing powerful emotions and simply wait until that person is ready to speak, you are respecting her or his pace of processing feelings. In a profession characterized by verbal purposefulness, respecting your client's silence can be a challenge. Clients generally experience this process as non-pressuring, accepting, and highly respectful. This silence can be needed at any point in the planned change process (i.e., engagement, assessment, intervention, or termination and evaluation).

Avoiding Communication Pitfalls

Communication is an art and a skill. When dialoguing with client systems, social workers need to keep in mind the possibility of creating communication errors. Some of the more common errors are described below:

Jargon   Social workers, like most professionals, have their own **jargon**, or verbal shortcuts, to describe their activities that can be confusing to clients. Jargon can include abbreviations, distinctive words, and routines. You are encouraged to keep your communication with clients as free from jargon as possible (Shebib, 2003).

> Example of jargon:
> Social Worker: *After the intake process, you will be on level one for a week. Then your DJO will assess you, and decide whether you can go to level two or you need to go back to court.*

Leading Questions   The way in which a question is asked can shape the response. **Leading questions** manipulate client systems to choose the preferred answer. Lead-ing questions can mask the preferred approach of the social worker. Clients who have a need to be liked and/or those who are compliant are especially vulnerable to leading questions (Shebib, 2003).

Example of leading questions:

Social Worker: *Given all that you have tried in the past, don't you think it is time to call the police to get the drug dealers out of the neighborhood?*

Client: *Well, I guess so.*

Social Worker: *Do you want to call now to report what you just saw?*

Excessive Questioning   While questions are an essential part of the helping dialogue, the asking of questions also puts the social worker in control of the dialogue. Client systems can feel resentful of answering questions, which can interfere with the relationship. Utilizing a diversity of responses can avoid a situation where clients feel interrogated. When dialoging with client systems, mixing different types of questions with empathic communication, summarizing, silence, and other types of approaches may help to avoid defensiveness, frustration, avoidance, and other responses that interfere with building a relationship. In those situations in which the social worker must ask many questions, it may be helpful to have a periodic break to check in with the client to convey respect and recognition that the questioning may be taxing (Shebib, 2003).

Example of check-in:

Social Worker: *I have asked a lot of questions of you today. How are you doing so far?*

Multiple Questions   Asking two or more questions at the same time, or **multiple questions**, can be problematic, because the client can become confused. If the questions are complementary, or the second question clarifies or adds to the first question, the multiple questions are not a problem.

Example of complementary multiple questions:

Social Worker: *What happened after the police arrived? What did the police do?*

Irrelevant Questions   Social workers need to have a clear idea of the purpose of the dialogue, and avoid asking **irrelevant questions**, which are questions that do not relate to the topic at hand. While you might be curious about details of situations or perceptions, you must consider the relevancy of the information before asking a question.

Example of irrelevant question:

Client: *My boyfriend broke up with me for the second time this week. He already asked my friend out!*

Social Worker: *How did he tell you that he wanted to break up?*

Integrating the Core Qualities and Skills in Dialogue and Interviewing

Social work practice activates the core qualities and skills through dialogue and interviews. Interviews are "purposeful conversations between social workers and clients . . ." (De Jong, 2008, p. 539). While many skills are important to social work, meta-analysis of controlled research studies indicate that relationship factors may be more important to positive client change than specific practice models utilized. Social workers spend more time in dialogue and interviewing client systems than any other professional activity, including individuals, couples, families, small groups, in supervision, organizational task groups, and with colleagues in other organizations (De Jong, 2008).

ARTICULATING PURPOSE: SOCIAL WORKER ROLE AND AGENDA

In addition to demonstrating the core qualities and basic skills, social workers must be able to articulate the purpose of their involvement with the client. **Transparency** refers to social workers' communication about the intention of their involvement. More specifically, transparency can be defined as the social worker's openness in discussing such issues as "why s/he asked a particular question, [and/or] why s/he pursued one particular direction or 'line' of questioning" (Morgan, 2000, p. 126). This kind of openness can help the client understand the social worker's thought process about the client's situation and address possible obstacles in the working relationship. Transparency helps to remove the mystery from the work and lessen the distance and power difference that may exist between the worker and client. Social workers who are transparent with their clients can, if asked, acknowledge that they are a student who will leave at the end of the year, or are young and have no children, or are not a person of color.

The beginning of the professional relationship is often the most appropriate time to articulate your purpose through a clear, concrete description of roles or job responsibilities, as well as describe the types of activities that are outside of your roles and responsibilities. For example, if you are a court advocate for a family violence shelter, you will want to be clear with your clients about the type of work that you do as an advocate, and that you cannot provide counseling, medication, or other types of services for them or their children.

On a more subtle level, the **overall purpose** of the work should also be transparent and explicit. It is sometimes tempting to engage the client in work on one issue and attempt, somewhat surreptitiously, to work on other issues you may think are more worthy. For example, if you and your client agree to work on the client's troubling relationship with school authorities regarding her child, you will focus on this task without trying to covertly intervene in her parenting style, or her negative relationships with men or any other issue. To maintain a genuine and honest relationship with clients requires that you are open about the jointly agreed-upon direction of the work, the methods you are employing, and the goal of your intervention. If you believe that another construction of the issue is more relevant or that the goals should be different, you should raise this issue early as a tentative point of negotiation about the nature and scope of the work. You would then take your cue from the client's response. Avoiding secret agendas is important to enhance the overall genuineness of the initial engagement, which will make a great deal of difference to the client's sense of being valued and accepted in the relationship.

This respectful stance regarding the client is one way to demonstrate a strengths-based approach. The following section will elaborate on the strengths approach in the engagement process.

MOVING FROM SPOTTING DEFICIENCY TO RECOGNIZING STRENGTHS

A central hallmark of the profession is the **strengths perspective**, or an orientation that emphasizes client systems' resources, capabilities, support systems, and motivations to meet challenges and overcome adversity to achieve well-being (Barker, 2003). The strengths approach to engagement can be challenging due to the need to identify and intervene in practice-based challenges. Social work as a profession developed during the late 1800s, in which moral conversion was a focal point. Poverty was often seen as a reflection of moral deficiency or laziness rather than as a structural failing that places and maintains people in adversity. As professional fields of helping, including psychology, developed more sophisticated and complicated assessment schemes (including the *Diagnostic and Statistical Manual of Mental Disorders DSM IV-TR Fourth Edition,* the first edition of which was published in 1958), the focus on pathology became more pervasive. Although social workers have a long history of recognizing their clients' strengths, this emphasis on pathology, problems, or dysfunction is deeply embedded in the culture and the traditions of the helping professions. An emphasis on pathology also persists in the current social service delivery system. Agencies often offer services around specific types of problems (for example, substance abuse or major mental illnesses), and these problems define the focus of the agency. Given the agency purpose and milieu, developing the ability to focus on strengths when meeting a client may seem like an enormous challenge.

Nevertheless, when there is support for, and commitment to, a departure from illness-based models, social workers can implement strategies based on client strengths rather than deficiencies. For example, an increasingly visible body of literature reflects a different perspective from the various models of deficit, damage, or blame. Much of this literature focuses on **resiliency**, or "the human capacity to deal with crises, stressors, and normal experiences in an emotionally and physically healthy way" (Barker, 2003). Resiliency is an important area of potential strength in client systems, and social workers consider resiliency in assessing the coping skills of their client systems. Most people raised or living in the most daunting of circumstances survive, and sometimes even thrive. Communities can demonstrate resiliency after a traumatic event or natural disaster by processing grief and shock through utilizing the resources of community systems and assets to hold events and rituals, help victims, and demonstrate the ability to cope and function as a community. Resilient client systems can generate strengths and coping capacities even in some of the most oppressive and compromising scenarios.

In the first encounter with a social worker, client systems are often wondering about several aspects of the social worker, such as whether the social worker will be trustworthy, whether the social worker will be understanding or judgmental, and whether the social worker will be able to help. Additionally, clients are often unsure whether they really need or want any assistance (Shulman, 2009a). Strong engagement skills and methods, discussed below, will assist to build an effective professional relationship and overcome these complex challenges to working together. For example, sending a clear nonverbal and verbal message that you will not make negative judgments or try to change the client as a person, but rather will affirm their aspirations and work to make them a reality can help build client trust. Engaging in enjoyable activities together, when possible, and seeking to incorporate humor, joy, and laughter into the helping process is another strengths-based approach. Lastly, being sensitive to cultural factors, honoring diversity, and seeking to assist people in activities and involvements that hold meaning for them will serve you well in a great variety of practice settings (Kisthardt, 2002).

Skills and Methods

Rapp and Goscha (2006) identify a series of methods for building a strengths-based relationship. Beyond exhibiting the core conditions described earlier, they suggest mirroring, contextualizing, self-disclosure, accompaniment, and reinforcement and celebration.

Mirroring   Reflecting the client's talents and capabilities so that the client can see himself or herself from a strengths perspective is called **mirroring.** The worker focuses on these strengths, emphasizing their presence in the client's daily life and stressing their importance. This metaphor is employed to counter the negative reflections many clients have of their own value and worth. While all mirrors distort images to some degree, the social worker uses a mirror that is more positively focused while building the relationship and throughout the work with the client system. For example, if family members identify specific issues that they experience with one another, the social worker might reflect on the care that they are demonstrating for one another by wanting to improve their family functioning, rather than split up the family.

Contextualizing   Social workers use **contextualizing** to put clients' issues into the wider community, society, and/or global context in order to discourage them from blaming themselves for their problems, and encourage them to take environmental and structural roots of their challenges. For example, when landlords discriminate against clients of the mental health system simply because they do not want "those people" to live in their building, some clients blame themselves for somehow being undesirable. In such a situation, the social worker can explore with the clients the effects of stigma in an intolerant society or provide evidence that they are acceptable to other, more positive landlords. In another example, a social worker might point out to a community group experiencing drug dealing and violence that their community is struggling with funding cuts to city social and community services. Rather than blaming themselves completely for their problems, community residents must also consider that their security challenges are at least partly rooted in lack of sufficient city-sponsored security resources and a lack of sufficient job opportunities. The goal of contextualizing is to point out the environmental roots, causes, and contributions of client system challenges, while working with clients to maximize their strengths and take advantage of their opportunities and resources toward addressing their specific challenges.

Self-Disclosure   The extent to which social workers should reveal their feelings, values, and personal information to their clients remains a controversial issue in social work practice and is called **self-disclosure** (Barker, 2003). Rapp and Goscha (2006) point to the inequities of expecting clients to disclose the most personal and profound aspects of their hearts and souls, while professionals sit back and reveal little about themselves. A strengths-based approach, based on normalizing the relationship in genuine ways, calls for some degree of worker self-disclosure to establish trust, validate the quality of the relationship, and model effective ways of managing emotions for the benefit of the client. Although there are no accepted standards governing the amount and nature of the disclosure, social workers should only reveal themselves to clients to assist to achieve a client goal. Social workers should carefully consider the purpose of self-disclosure, and avoid self-disclosure that strictly meets their personal needs and goals, such as for expressing strong feelings about something. For example, the social worker might share a story from her or his life to demonstrate appropriate behavior in a specific situation to meet a client goal of learning this skill, rather than for bragging about how well they handled a certain situation.

While caution should be exercised about self-disclosure, social workers can strive to foster open communication and a caring relationship, which may mean sharing relatively unimportant aspects of one's life routinely with clients, while maintaining a focus on the client. You can, for example, converse with clients by talking about your hobbies and interests, or share information about your familial or parenting status if asked. Social workers are warm and genuine with client systems and avoid strict formality by sharing information about themselves to further the relationship, yet avoid self-disclosure of significant information unless it serves a therapeutic purpose or is designed to achieve a client goal.

Accompaniment   Rapp and Goscha (2006) advocate for accompanying a client in the performance of a task. This can be **accompaniment** in the literal sense of going with a client to court or to a landlord's office, and/or in a metaphorical sense, as in joining the client in her or his journey of change. Rapp and Goscha (2006) acknowledge the concern for dependence on the social worker that can emerge when accompanying clients. Social workers may wonder whether helping a client through a task is serving the best interests of the client in the long run, or whether clients should be encouraged to complete tasks on their own most of the time. The need or desirability for accompaniment should be assessed critically according to the specifics of the situation. Social workers should take into account such aspects of the situation as the emotional, physical, and intellectual capabilities of the client, as well as the working relationship with the client, when making decisions about accompaniment. Social workers should be careful to take cultural considerations into account as well, and avoid making decisions about clients based on *their* cultural or personal sense of the optimal level of independence, especially when the client either does not share or cannot attain their ideal. When literal accompaniment is not appropriate, the metaphor of accompaniment can be vital to the working relationship and resonate with the client long after the work is over.

Reinforcement and Celebration   To carry out a strengths-based approach successfully, the social worker needs to understand the meanings the client attaches to such behaviors as praise or recognition of particular events or accomplishments. **Reinforcement**, a procedure that strengthens the tendency of a response to recur, can assist to build a strong working relationship, but the social worker cannot make assumptions about the client system's view of reinforcement (Barker, 2003). Some expressions of support, for example, can affirm one person and embarrass another. By the same token, indiscriminate praise can be insulting, whereas purposeful, immediate, and specific positive feedback may be highly valued and strengthening. Although nearly everyone wants to feel appreciated, the worker needs to anticipate client responses in a particular context.

Logistics and Activities

Location and arrangements for the first contact convey an important message about the nature of the ongoing work and the assumptions made about the partnership. Accordingly, strengths-based social workers will give the client the choice of the location, day, and time to meet, and offer the option of meeting in a community location, rather than an office setting. Some clients may request that the meeting be held at their home, either because they have small children, they lack transportation, or they are simply more comfortable in this setting. As is true of much of social work, the client's choice of location depends on the nature of the contact, the context of the interaction, concerns regarding confidentiality, and the agency purpose.

The incorporation of activities can also help the client to engage and feel comfortable. Some clients, such as children, adolescents, immigrants, and others, may struggle with sharing aspects of themselves in an office, face-to-face setting, and may be more comfortable in another setting, or talking while engaged in another activity. For this reason, playing basketball with an adolescent, playing a board game with a group of children, or walking in the woods with a client struggling with mental health issues can create an environment that is much less intense (and therefore more tolerable for some clients) than an interview-type meeting in an office.

An interesting variation on this theme is a strategy known as "talking in the idiom of the other" (Middleman & Wood, 1990, p. 66). This approach assumes that some clients will use metaphors in their verbal communications as a way to communicate without exposing the specific details of their own lives until they are ready to do so. The following scenario provides an example: A client whose small business has recently failed asks a social worker if the social worker had ever thought about how long it takes a spider to spin a web and how fast it can be wiped out of the corner with a dust rag. The social worker said that it sounded very demoralizing. The client looked at the social worker with a sad expression on her face and nodded. The social worker said that spider webs were very vulnerable, and the client said that spiders were very vulnerable too. After nodding in agreement, the social worker said that sometimes people were vulnerable, giving her a chance to be more direct if she were ready to be. The client said she should never have allowed herself to get so emotionally invested in the business (Middleman & Wood, 1990).

As you can see, the social worker responds by using the same metaphors that the client suggests, and is sensitive to the client's readiness to be more direct. The purpose of "talking in the idiom of the other" is to respect the client's communications rather than seeing them as a form of resistance. The social worker can use the information conveyed by the client to support the client's efforts to communicate the depth of her or his experience. This strategy honors the client's meaning and validates her or his approach to engagement in the work.

RECOGNIZING AND ARTICULATING POWER

Social work practice almost always involves issues related to power. The relationship of power, or the possession of resources that enable a client system to accomplish a task or to exercise influence and control over others (Barker, 2003), to social work practice may not be readily apparent for to you. You may genuinely want to engage with people in their struggles and help them achieve their goals; you may not immediately see the relevance of a discussion of power. Yet in most instances, the obstacles clients face involve power, and the effective management of power can benefit the client. Power is a component in a variety of social work relationships, from political advocacy to one-to-one counseling. Following is a discussion about various sources of power in the professional relationship.

Sources of Power

There are four sources of power with which social workers engage: agency resources, expert knowledge, interpersonal power, and legitimate power (Hartman, 1994).

Agency Resources   Social service agencies have access to and control over a number of resources. These include **tangible resources**, such as clothing or money for emergency housing, and **intangible resources**, such as individual counseling and education groups. Traditionally, social workers and administrators have allocated resources to client groups or individuals depending upon their evaluation of the fit with agency purposes and funding source(s) guidelines and constraints. However, some contemporary organizations, and even some federal programs, have experimented with arrangements that empower clients to determine and control the resources they receive. For example, an agency that serves children with disabilities might encourage the child's family members to identify the services they need, both within and outside the agency, rather than undergoing an agency-driven assessment in which a professional tells them what they need. By the same token, some Medicaid provisions include a waiver that permits a family member (usually a parent) to act as case manager, thereby coordinating services for the child and eliminating the costs of professional case management. Services that the family chooses and obtains with assistance are called **client-directed resources.** The concepts of power sharing and client-consumer advocacy threaten the notion that social workers and administrators should continue to control the disposition of agency resources. Most agencies struggle with the idea of giving up their authority in this arena.

Expert Knowledge   Many social workers find that some clients see them as possessing **expert knowledge** because they have credentials and experience. Social workers can counter that assumption in part by using the strengths perspective to clearly articulate that clients are the experts on their own lives, and work to develop a partnership with clients that focuses on reaching client-defined goals.

Interpersonal Power   The personal attribute characterized by the ability to build strong relationships, develop rapport, and persuade people is known as **interpersonal power.** Both social workers and clients may have this type of personal power, which is closely related to charisma. Although the social worker's interpersonal power can benefit clients when used to attain resources or access to services, the social worker's interpersonal power can also perpetuate the power imbalance between the client and social worker by diminishing the client's efforts to reclaim power. Social workers must strive to reduce their interpersonal power by establishing more egalitarian relations and genuine collaboration with clients (Hartman, 1994).

Legitimate Power   The term **legitimate power** refers to legal power to perform actions to control the behavior of others. Social workers need to be very careful about this power. The responsibility to protect clients and others (as in cases of child or elder abuse) must be acknowledged, but social workers must also recognize that legitimate power must be exercised very carefully, and have limits. Social workers must be careful not to replicate the power abuses of the past by exercising legitimate power beyond what is absolutely necessary to protect clients. Although social workers may choose to retain their various powers to use for individual, family, group, or community client benefit, they may alternatively try to work to change structures that impact client systems at the policy and organizational levels to empower clients.

Power in Client Lives: Jasmine Johnson

There are many other ways to think about power with clients. One approach focuses on the power relationships with which the client system is struggling that are external to the social worker relationship, either in interpersonal, community, policy, or larger cultural terms. For example, a community may be struggling to convince their local government to allocate and spend city funds on trash pickup in their area. The second involves power issues experienced directly between the social worker and the client. A case vignette about Jasmine Johnson provides examples of the types of power.

Jasmine's Situation   You work in a family support agency. Your client, Jasmine Johnson, is an African American mother who comes to you with a concern about parenting. Her teenage son is difficult to manage behaviorally both at home and, increasingly, at school, and Jasmine is unsure how to deal with him. He often does not seem to respect her authority, and ignores her attempts to discipline him. He is "sassy," talks back, and is occasionally quite rude to her. He ignores the limits she sets, and he does not obey school-night curfews or help with any household chores. Jasmine struggles financially to support him with only sporadic help from his father. Her job pays poorly, carries little status in the work world, and does not provide extra money for either her or her son to enjoy any recreational activities. Overall, Jasmine appears to struggle with low self-esteem.

Jasmine and Power Relationships   At first glance, Jasmine's challenges appear to be strictly personal. Jasmine knows that she does not feel good about herself or her situation, and she assumes she needs to improve at something. You might assume that she needs to address her self-esteem issues, or you might even conclude that she is depressed and needs medical attention. Yet, from another vantage point, it is likely that power, or lack of it, plays an important role in her experience. She is a woman who performs many interpersonal roles (i.e., ex-wife, single mother, daughter, worker, friend, and neighbor) and a member of a cultural group that has experienced pervasive and persistent oppression for more than 300 years in our culture.

These are areas that can be deconstructed and examined (Krumer-Nevo, 2005). Although Jasmine may have interpreted her experiences as signs of her own deficiencies, she has also exhibited remarkable resilience in dealing with disadvantage and oppression. She has managed to survive in trying circumstances that have had a far-reaching political repercussion in her life. If she is to be empowered, she will need to recognize those political events in which her life is embedded. You can bring these events to her consciousness through purposeful (and skillful) articulation.

This does not mean that Jasmine's own sense of her problem is erroneous and that the real problems are racism and sexism. Rather, as a social worker, you want to validate her experience and recognize the meaning she makes of it. However, Jasmine has genuine feelings of inadequacy, and she has experienced the negative side of the power differential. That realization can open many doors. For example, Jasmine may begin to separate her feelings of inadequacy from her sense of identity and start to look at her experiences as a function of her social location. In turn, this new perspective might inspire her to engage in some action, such as forming an informal support group for single, African American mothers. This group can share stories and experiences, provide day care arrangements for one another, or coordinate grocery shopping. Adopting a different outlook also might encourage Jasmine to become a spokesperson for more stringent requirements regarding child support payments or increased benefits for working women with children. The possibilities for Jasmine's roles and activities are endless, and these types of activities may affirm Jasmine's experience even as they are instrumental in changing the quality of life for her and others.

Jasmine and the Social Worker There are nearly always noticeable differences between social workers and clients. As long as the profession sustains the concept of the social worker as the expert, there will be a felt power differential based solely on distinct roles in the social worker-client relationship. There are also likely to be additional differences related to gender, age, race, socio-economic status, and other dimensions of diversity. These differences, if perceived as problems, can complicate the engagement process.

For example, Jasmine may find it challenging to think of social work students or younger workers in general as a genuine source of help to her. Students may come from a different cultural or ethnic background, and they may not have partners or children. They may also seem to her to be so privileged by their race and education that she thinks that they cannot relate to any experiences in her life. Yet, social workers are supposed to be experts, and as such they have some level of power that she may resent, admire, or barely recognize. In most cases, these differences related to worker and client roles or attributes are, at the core, about power and power differences. It is necessary, then, to discuss these differences openly when they get in the way of the work. Simply raising them can open up the whole relationship. For example, in the early stages of the relationship, a social worker working with Jasmine might ask whether she has any hesitation about working together. The social worker might acknowledge that the two of them have experienced different life circumstances in the past and present, and ask that Jasmine be willing to tell her about her background and current life situation so that the social worker can try to help her. Asking the client to share this type of information, and giving the client the opportunity to talk about any hesitations that they may have in working together, provides the client with the opportunity to talk about differences, and the impact they may have on the relationship.

BOX 3.1

Recognizing and Articulating Power

"Look, Mr. Cook, I know you think I'm a nice kid and that you like me," I said.
   "I do like you," he confirmed.
"But you know I'm too young to have experienced what you go through every day!" I said.
   Silence.
   "And you may even figure that a kid like me can't help you."
   Silence.
   "Right?" I continued.
   A nod.
   "But you want to get out of this depression real bad, don't you." I said.
   "I sure do," he said. Then he sighed and added, "I'm probably being foolish.

 You youngsters are right out of school with the latest techniques. I guess I'd just be more comfortable talking to someone closer to my own age. But here I am already talking to you, aren't I? So I guess I already decided to try it out with you."
   I nodded. "How about if anytime you feel uncomfortable, you say so and every time I think you may be a little uncomfortable I'll say so?" I suggested.
   "It's a deal," he said.

Source: Middleman & Wood, p. 163

Jasmine Johnson: Conclusions Situations that involve power differentials are sometimes awkward or even embarrassing to confront, particularly for you as a student or an otherwise humble person. You may understand that the client sees you as having power simply because of your role as a helping person, an employee, or a student. At the same time, you may secretly wonder yourself about the extent to which you can help an exasperated parent who might be of a different race and remote social class, when you might not even be a parent yourself. You may feel some hesitation at working with an oppressed client when you have enjoyed so much privilege. Thus, the concept of power in the relationship can become quite complex and problematic.

When these situations arise, you might hope that the concern will pass or that clients will just trust that you know what you're doing in spite of these differences. Unfortunately, once these issues are perceived as problematic, they will not simply go away. You and your client should confront them directly through open acknowledgment and exploration. Box 3.1 provides an additional case example. In this excerpt, consider the ways in which the worker addresses the issue at hand. What impact do you think this approach will have on the future of the relationship?

This vignette in Box 3.1 conveys an extended message. First, the social worker addresses the immediate obstacle, namely, that the social worker is both much younger than the client and comparatively inexperienced. The social worker also paves the way for ongoing honesty in the relationship by addressing the obstacle openly and directly. The scenario is a relatively complex one in which both participants seem to feel an initial lack of power that is subsequently alleviated by open acknowledgment. Ultimately, the case suggests that there is a broader context for the work than the one-on-one issues that emerge between the social worker and client, leading to recognition of social justice and human rights issues in client stories.

VIEWING THE CLIENT SYSTEM SITUATION AND PERSPECTIVE FROM SOCIAL JUSTICE AND HUMAN RIGHTS PERSPECTIVES

When clients describe a situation that involves hardship or oppression, or is emotionally challenging, social workers use their professional skills and methods to respond to the client. However, social workers are human, and are often personally moved by the situation as well. There is something very powerful about talking directly to an individual who is sharing a powerful story with you. This experience typically creates a personal connection of bonding. In such circumstances, the larger perspectives of social justice and human rights may seem like remote, intellectual concepts in the face of the personal pain that your client is experiencing. Nevertheless, these perspectives provide the rationale for your practice, and they help to connect client system experiences together. The perspectives thus provide an organizing frame for your work so that your practice transcends the parameters of individual emotional responses or simple sympathy and becomes a carefully planned and cohesive activity in response to clear, principled commitments.

Although you will always want to recognize personal pain and respond on a human level, you will also want to go beyond the intensity of the direct relationship and see your client's experiences as social justice and human rights issues as well.

Full Participation in Culture

As discussed previously, work toward social justice is a cornerstone of social work practice and is mandated in the NASW *Code of Ethics* (2008). A number of "isms"—racism, elitism, sexism, heterosexism, ageism, and others—that you have probably already studied reflect the degree of social injustice that is prevalent in our culture. These prejudicial attitudes toward the "other" are generated by our society and suggest a discriminatory standpoint that most social workers find profoundly distasteful. The attitudes also carry concrete repercussions for individuals, families, groups, and communities that take many forms of exclusion, including exclusion from resources and limited class mobility within society. The term "exclusion from society" refers to the process through which people are unable to participate in the benefits of public and cultural resources. This inability can be felt quite literally (for example, when there is no access ramp to the public library for people with disabilities) or more indirectly (for example, when policies and poverty limit public investment in public schools). Clearly, these exclusions are injustices because they represent arbitrary allocation of access to public benefits, and are violations of the principles of human rights. Such exclusion tends to be pervasive and on all levels—individual, organizational, and structural. Box 3.2 examines these three levels of social and cultural exclusion. Considering client situations relative to all three levels is necessary for the practitioner's work to have an impact on larger systems. Although many practitioners see their labors in terms of individual, one-by-one achievements, the collective achievements make a difference in the larger environment. Social workers respond to clients on a personal, one-to-one level while acknowledging and addressing social injustices and human rights violations that exist on a variety of levels.

Strategies and Skills for Promoting Social Justice and Human Rights

Social justice and human rights issues call for well-organized strategies and skill sets that usually fall within the realm of policy practice. The following strategies are particularly applicable in such situations.

- Understanding the repercussions of social injustices on clients, and helping clients understand.

Individual Exclusion

BOX 3.2

During your dialogue, clients may make an explicit reference to the way exclusion has influenced their situation. Individual exclusion refers to the perception of being left out of or barred from participation in interpersonal situations. This situation could include, for example, that your client was a victim of racist harassment by peers in school or was dismissed by teachers as having no future because of her or his ethnicity or ability status. Other clients may not give voice to any strong or concrete sense of their own exclusion or the violation of their human rights but rather describe it as "fate" or the "way things are."

Organizational Exclusion

Like individual exclusion, organizational exclusion, the phenomenon of being prevented from participation in activities by an organization, can be obvious to clients (and others), or obscure. For example, even hiring practices that appear to be fair may actually favor some groups over others through their written or unwritten rules, regulations regarding promotions, or subtle differences in work assignments. In fact, many battles over such efforts as affirmative action arise from a concern for the organizational structures in which unjust practices and advantages have taken hold. For example, given that there is no equality in access to this country's top-rated educational institutions, the organization that automatically hires the candidate with the most prestigious degree—even when the requirements of the job do not mandate it—is engaging in preferential practices that are rooted in injustice.

Just as Jasmine Johnson interpreted her difficulties as individual failings, your clients may not be sensitized to the role that discrimination plays in their place of work. It is important in connecting and engaging with clients to recognize manifestations of organizational exclusion and work with clients regarding the meanings they attach to these life events. In some situations, this alone can be a liberating activity.

Structural Exclusion

Institutionalized arrangements such as poverty tend to maintain and perpetuate themselves. Structural exclusion refers to the interconnecting role of institutions and societal forces in preventing participation or limiting access, such as the connections among poverty, poor schools, limited achievement, limited employment options, restricted housing, poor health care, and shortened life expectancy. Recognizing poverty as a structural problem directly conflicts with presumptions about equal opportunity and the myth that anyone can get ahead. Social workers may need to work with client systems over a period of time before clients and others can begin to see the roots of their personal challenges as stemming from structural exclusion.

- Helping clients gain access to their legal entitlements through social advocacy.

- Convincing legislative bodies to adopt, amend, or repeal laws when such changes would benefit clients.

- Educating the community regarding certain populations, for example, giving a talk on the needs of refugee children or families with disabilities.

- Developing resources (this involves identifying and procuring resources that are needed but do not exist currently).

- Facilitating the redistribution of resources.

- Testifying in court hearings regarding issues that affect clients.

This list is by no means exhaustive, but it suggests the flavor of work focused on systems larger than the individual. These strategies do not negate the importance of individual connections with human beings on a personal level, but enrich the engagement and the worker's understanding in a way that is consistent with the complexities of people in the contemporary world.

STRAIGHT TALK ABOUT THE RELATIONSHIP: INTERPERSONAL PERSPECTIVES

Being transparent, or explicit about your work, means being clear about the restrictions you encounter as a practitioner. A goal of the work is to establish a meaningful and trusting relationship with the client system, and the tasks of discussing constraints or inviting critical evaluation may not seem very appealing. In fact, the social worker may tend to postpone or avoid them altogether. Nevertheless, attending to the boundaries of your role early in the development of the professional relationship, along with confidentiality and maintaining client privacy as discussed below, is important to developing a trusting relationship.

Confidentiality

There are at least three areas in which social workers may be required to break confidentiality, including cases of child abuse/neglect/exploitation, older adult abuse/neglect/exploitation, and when a client threatens harm to another person. First, as mandated reporters, social workers, among many human service professionals, are legally required to report cases of child abuse, neglect, or exploitation. Second, most states have mandated reporting laws for adult protective services for older adults and persons with disabilities. Third, as mentioned in Chapter 2, social workers in many states have a duty to protect as a result of the *Tarasoff II* court ruling. Legal ramifications regarding these reporting requirements may vary somewhat by state or locality; however, social workers must report incidents of abuse, neglect, or exploitation that are witnessed or described to them, and must consider taking steps to ensure the safety of a person threatened by a client.

Depending on the setting of the work, the mandate to break confidentiality can appear to be a significant obstacle to establishing a relationship of trust. For example, you may be concerned that clients will not share any information with you if told that you must call the authorities. Although this concern is legitimate, to represent yourself fairly, you must communicate your responsibility in that area early in the work. Informing clients of the limits of your confidentiality may affect the relationship in unexpected ways. Clients may understand that they need help from authorities. For example, consider the social worker who worked with a woman who struggled with substance abuse and had a difficult time keeping track of her five children, for whom she was the single, caretaking parent. During the sixth meeting, she told the social worker that she felt sure she was grossly neglecting the younger children and that she often struck the oldest child "hard" when he "mouthed off" to her. After discussing this situation, she informed the social worker that she had finally confided the information *because* the social worker was a mandated reporter and she knew she could get help.

While the mandated reporter role in this case produced an unusually fortunate outcome, social workers must be honest with clients about their roles and not assume that an adversarial relationship will evolve simply because of the mandated reporter obligations. Most clients who struggle with caring for their children want to be good parents. Even if the client is guarded about what she or he tells you (which you might expect), you still have significant opportunities to build a relationship. You can address the obstacles to the client's successful parenting (or caretaking for an older adult), model a genuine relationship in which you support the client's parenting competence rather than search to discover deficits, and build the foundation for further work. Adopting this approach does not suggest that the imminent safety of a child or adult should be compromised. Rather, it is a strategy of beginning to work in those countless scenarios in which there is concern but no clear mandate for legal intervention.

Privacy

Implementing client privacy can be challenging for many reasons, to include the problem that actions that some people consider invasive can seem caring to others. When negotiating with clients about the nature and parameters of the work during engagement, you and your client should address the issues of privacy and invasiveness. For example, a client who perceives your care and enthusiasm for the work may get the impression that you want to know everything about her or his life and become an active participant in it. If this is not your intention, you should make the client aware of this. Similarly, in a group setting, you will want to discuss plans for allowing individuals to maintain some information about themselves as private, while sharing pertinent information of their choice with the group. Being straightforward about your involvement and the parameters of privacy is important to avoid the client system feeling disappointed and perhaps even betrayed. For example, if your role involves monitoring of client activities and you have established a mutual, client-driven relationship, you will likely be the initiator in situations that the client may not expect. For instance, if you have suggested that the client call you when she wants to meet again, but you then drop in unannounced "just to see how she's doing" (or to see how the children seem or if they have eaten that day), she may rightly perceive your visit as an invasion of privacy.

On a deeper level, as a practitioner in your particular role and setting, you might consider the extent of privacy to which clients are entitled. For example, in a residential or correctional setting, what is important to know? If your work involves a social control function, do your clients deserve less privacy? How does your agency's purpose affect the degree of privacy granted? These questions all relate to the importance of knowing yourself and the values, skills, and roles that you bring to the setting, and noticing how you (and/or your agency) may or may not be influenced by predominant social norms about the rights (or lack thereof) of clients.

Ongoing Evaluation

All through the engagement process, you have invested your energy and skills in establishing a solid initial connection with your client that will grow as your work together progresses. Another task you must undertake in this early stage, and throughout the work, is evaluation of the effectiveness of your efforts. Relationships can be easily misunderstood. You may be concerned that your client is hesitant to be as open as you would like, or that she or he seems uneasy in some way. Conversely, you may feel wonderful about the productive beginning of a professional relationship. In either case, it is important to find out how your client feels about your relationship and to make any needed changes in your approach that are indicated by your client's feedback. Although you are not likely to use formalized tools at this point, you will want to ask your client about how the work is going. For example, you might ask an individual client whether he or she is comfortable talking about the issues discussed thus far? How does it work for him that you are a Hispanic woman and he is a black man? Is the process of meeting with you similar to, or different from, what he thought it would be? If it's different, how does he feel about it? What can you do to be more supportive or clearer or helpful? For group work, you might ask the group for feedback about your role as facilitator or teacher. At the community level, seeking feedback from individuals and colleagues in the community as well as from committees can elicit important suggestions.

At the individual level, the process of continuously monitoring your work also applies to your engagement with the people who are significant in your client's life. You will want to validate your understanding of their role in helping to achieve your client's goals and to check for any misunderstandings. This strategy will be particularly important in situations that involve contentious feelings, such as the reluctant landlord considered earlier in this chapter. While landlords might assume that you will take sides with your client, you will want to take care not to alienate them from your client's goals.

CONCLUSION

Now that you have explored the importance and various aspects of engagement, or building the relationship in social work practice, you are well prepared to support your connection with your client system as you enter into the assessment arena of the work. Although you are not likely to have addressed all the issues presented here in the first interactions with client system, you have the framework to go beyond the initial connections and respond to an ongoing, dynamic association. You have taken care to anticipate the meaning for the client of your particular work together, and you will find that this dimension grows and is shaped by the nature of your shared activities and experiences.

One further caveat about skills: At first you may feel that thinking about and trying to use them interferes with your spontaneity and/or responsiveness. However, as you use the skills and develop your practice style, you will become much more relaxed in using and personalizing the skills, and develop your own style. While the engagement stage is often thought of as the beginning stage, engagement is a process that will occur throughout your work with client systems. You will continue to notice engagement dynamics, your own growth as a worker in establishing engagement, and how engagement assists your client as the work continues into the assessment, planning, and implementation of the work. In particular, the next step, assessment, will build on the relationship foundation that you build during the engagement phase.

MAIN POINTS

- The social worker's first and probably most important activity in the engagement process is careful listening to the client's situation and perspective. This activity requires the worker to initiate a skilled, purposeful dialogue that nurtures the relationship.

- Negotiating the purpose and direction of the work enhances the trust between the practitioner and client. For this process to be successful, the agenda must be open and must not contain any hidden aspects.

- Using the core relationship qualities of warmth, empathy, genuineness, and unconditional positive regard, along with strong interviewing skills, will assist the social worker to establish a strong, professional working relationship with the client system.

- Respecting the strengths and resilience of the client system has an enormous impact on the work. Respect for strength is critical in establishing the relationship, and must be pervasive throughout the relationship.

- Power and its relationship to social work practice present both obstacles and potential. The various sources of worker power, the power in client lives, and the power between the worker and the client are all part of the relationship. These sources should be recognized and articulated as explicitly as possible.

- Although client stories may appear to be private and are certainly unique, they can always be seen from the perspective of social justice and human rights. This perspective gives the entirety of the work meaning and frames your commitments.

- The worker and client should discuss the issues of confidentiality and privacy openly and directly, even if these topics make them uncomfortable. The client may not welcome some of these constraints on practice, but the worker owes it to her or him to be respectful and clear about them from the beginning.

- Evaluation of the work, including the relationship, should occur at all stages, beginning with engagement.

EXERCISES

1. Go to www.routledgesw.com/cases. Select the Sanchez case and review the Engagement phase on the interactive case study of the Sanchez family and the tasks of that phase. With classmates, discuss the needs of the Sanchez family.
2. After completing Exercise #1, review the Client History, Client Concerns, and Goals for the Client for Alejandro Sanchez. Next, click on the "Explore the Town" (under "Case Study Tools") to review the neighborhood, review Alejandro's Critical Thinking Questions, and explore his Interactional Matrix. Consider the following scenario:

    Alejandro is one of your clients. He presents as melancholy although pleasant and respectful. He says he is "unhappy" and seems to carry with him an existential sort of sadness that relates to his family. He notes on the first interview that his father Hector was also 19 when he came to this country as an undocumented worker.

    With a classmate assuming the role of Alejandro, role-play for 10–15 minutes the scenario that you are meeting Alejandro for the first time. In the session, you attempt to engage Alejandro and begin an assessment. (The classmate who is playing the role of Alejandro should prepare by reviewing his concerns and goals, as well as his strengths.) Other classmates should observe, and consult during the role-play as needed. Afterwards, the entire class can debrief by considering the following questions:

a. Which attending skills were used? Which were not used?

b. Were empathic responses used? What were they? What was most challenging to you about the use of empathy?

c. Was the social worker in the role-play able to validate his feelings of unhappiness, and identify strengths and verbally share those strengths with Alejandro? Were there other strengths that were not mentioned? How can a social worker emphasize a client's strengths when the client is not receptive to hearing them?

d. What was the experience of the student who played the role of Alejandro? Did the student, in character, feel that the social worker demonstrated specific listening skills? Which skills?

e. What elements of Alejandro's experiences reflect social justice and human rights concerns?

3. You are a social worker in a neighborhood community mental health center. You are awaiting the arrival of a new client, Jasmine Johnson (discussed in this chapter), who lives near the center. After you introduce yourself and she relaxes somewhat, she states, "My life is a mess; nothing I ever do is right; sometimes I think I can't go on."

   Using relationship building and interviewing skills, indicate how you would respond to her statement by giving a very brief verbal (one sentence or less if possible) or a behavioral example (if appropriate) if you were:

   1. Attending
   2. Responding nonverbally
   3. Responding with minimal verbalization
   4. Paraphrasing
   5. Clarifying
   6. Summarizing (make any needed assumptions about information provided prior to the statement above)
   What other skills do you think are important for this situation?

4. For these role-playing exercises, create groups of three students so that one is the client, one is the social worker, and one is an observer.

   a. Set a stopwatch for three minutes. The client tells the social worker a peculiar story. The social worker may not speak for three minutes. However, the social worker conveys nonverbally that the client is being heard. At the end of the three minutes, the observer provides feedback to the social worker, and the social worker and client share their perspective on the process. Each student should have the opportunity to play each role.

   b. Set a stopwatch for three minutes. The client will tell the social worker about a serious concern in their life. The social worker reacts in each of the following ways:

1. Disinterested
2. Inappropriate affect (forced smile, blank stare)
3. Distracting behaviors (e.g., foot tapping, excessive gesturing, fidgeting, head nodding)

After three minutes, the client provides feedback regarding the process. Each student should have the opportunity to play each role.

5. Review the following case to prepare for a role-play: Gina is your 16-year-old female client at a local teen drop in center. Gina is usually talkative and outgoing with staff and other participants. Today you notice that Gina is sitting in the corner alone and she looks as though she has been crying. When you approach Gina and inquire about her day she wipes her eyes and says in a quiet voice, "I can't do this anymore. My parents are always fighting and I just can't take it. I am not going back there."

   For the role-playing, create groups of three students so that one is the client, one is the social worker, and one is an observer. Using the above case, the client begins the interview. The observer will buzz the social worker whenever he/she becomes aware of the social worker using the following:
   a. Excessive questions
   b. Closed-ended questions
   c. Jargon
   d. Leading questions
   e. Multiple questions
   f. Irrelevant questions

   Each student should have the opportunity to play each role.

6. Using the case about Gina (provided in Exercise #5), the class instructor will take the role as Gina. Various students fulfill the role as a social worker. Each social worker will demonstrate appropriate skills for the interview. When the helper has a point when he/she feels stuck, s/he may return to the class and the next student begins where the previous student left.

7. The instructor creates flashcards with various interviewing skills. For the role-playing, create groups of three students so that one is the client, one is the social worker, and one is an observer. Using the case of Gina (provided in Exercise #5), during the interaction between Gina and the social worker, the observer randomly presents a card with a skill listed on it to the social worker, who must demonstrate the skill in the interaction. Each student has the opportunity to play each role. After a 10–15 minute role-play, discuss the degree to which the skills were utilized appropriately.

8. Go to www.routledgesw.com/cases and watch the videotaped interview with Emilia and the social worker. While watching the interview, note where in the interview each of the following skills were demonstrated:
   a. Open-ended question
   b. Closed-ended question
   c. Reframing

d. Paraphrasing
e. Attending
f. Nonverbal communication
g. Clarifying
h. Summarizing
i. Empathic communication

What were the strengths of the interview and what could the social worker have done differently?

CHAPTER 4

Assessing and Planning with Individuals: Deepening the Dialogue

Barbara is a sixteen-year-old mother of a baby, is on public assistance, and lives alone in one room. She dropped out of school when she became pregnant, her family and the father of the baby have abandoned her, and her only social contact is a neighbor who works during the day. One afternoon the young mother, lonesome and depressed, went out for an hour and left the baby alone. The baby fell off the bed and cut his head on an object, seriously injuring himself. When Barbara returned home she took him to the hospital, where the doctor in the emergency room, suspecting child abuse (maybe neglect?), referred her to the child welfare agency.

Carol Meyer, 1993, p. 22.

Key Questions for Chapter 4

(1) How can I prepare for assessment with individual client systems? (EPAS 2.1.10(b))

(2) What are the evidence-based theoretical perspectives that I will use to guide my assessment and planning with individual client systems?

(3) What are the skills that I need to have to work with an individual? (EPAS 2.1.10(b))

(4) How can I ensure that I engage in appropriate professional and personal self-care activities?

IN HER CLASSIC 1993 WORK *ASSESSMENT IN SOCIAL WORK PRACTICE*, MEYER notes that the way social workers think about such situations as Barbara's, or the conceptual boundaries they apply to them, includes many dimensions. Consider your conceptual boundaries, as you read about Barbara: What first comes to mind? Do you see her as an unfit mother? As a lonely young woman? What are the major issues you see? What do you want to know more about? Where would an assessment begin?

This chapter considers assessment, the process that looks for the meaning in client situations, orders and prioritizes the relevant factors, and leads to appropriate action. Assessment is a key social work practice skill that encompasses the collection of information about the client system to determine strengths as well as problems (Jordan, 2008, p. 178). The history of assessment, the importance of the client's goals, and approaches and skills through the lenses of theory, diversity, and graphics will be examined as well. Assessment of resources and approaches when resources are inadequate are also explored. The chapter will conclude with a review of the planning process and two areas of challenges.

Consider several questions about Barbara's situation that Meyer (1993) poses: Is hers a

> case of a mother and child, a teenager without any family, a teenager subject to the rules of social institutions? Would one focus on child abuse? Child neglect? Adolescent acting-out? A teen in need of guidance about romantic relationships? A single parent in need of family planning? Loss of family and social supports? Poverty? (p. 22)

The risk in this situation is in taking too narrow a focus that could make Barbara a case focused solely on one dimension rather than another. The task then becomes how to acknowledge the complexity of the situation and at the same time focus with enough specificity to intervene in a helpful way. The assessment process, therefore, attempts to make sense of the particulars within a larger understanding of the client's context. At the same time, the social worker will want to discover Barbara's goals and keep them central to the process.

When you, as the social worker, begin a relationship with Barbara (or someone like her) through the engagement process, you will also consider many of the preceding questions to shape your focus in the case. Highly interconnected with engaging the client system, the assessment and planning process has already begun as you have taken the time to hear Barbara's story and consider its meaning. Putting her story into the context of the social work values of social justice and human rights frames your understanding. As part of your careful listening, you will have some initial idea about the way in which she sees her life, where she wants to go, and how you might help her get there. Perhaps you will also have reservations about the obstacles that seem to be in the way of the goals and priorities held by Barbara, your agency, or even the legal system. Thinking through these issues, including Barbara's strengths, constitutes the assessment process.

A BRIEF HISTORY OF ASSESSMENT

Since Mary Richmond published her pioneer work, *Social Diagnosis*, in 1917, assessment has been considered a critical component of social work practice. Many contemporary social workers still consider assessment to be absolutely central to practice in that it guides the worker's focus and directs the intervention. However, criticism has been raised regarding the language used in assessment and the implications it may carry regarding the worker's expertise. The idea of assessment seems to suggest that the worker has the power to define the client's situation and to impose that definition. A look at how the profession arrived at the word *assessment* may provide some perspective on this debate.

Since Mary Richmond introduced the term into social work practice, *diagnosis* has been a part of the profession's history. However, diagnosis now firmly connotes a medicalized understanding of disease, dysfunction, symptoms, and the authority associated with the declaration of an illness. As the concept of diagnosis is not rooted in a strengths-based perspective, social workers may find it challenging to use the diagnostic term.

Contemporary social workers have adopted the term assessment as representing a more complete understanding of the client's context, one that focuses on strengths and resources as well as challenging areas. Assessment today is also considered a process by which clients can partner with the professional to make informed decisions about the work that can be done together. Client resources include the environment in which the client lives, and the history, culture, and traditions embedded in the life experience of the client system. Treating assessment as an act of client-focused discovery shifts the focus from professional expertise and analysis toward client definitions of the parameters for work. This process is a source of empowerment for clients.

A strengths-based approach is more consistent with the profession's systemic emphasis on the interface between the client and the environment as it occurs in the client context. A strengths-based systemic perspective invites social workers to examine the whole person, whose many dimensions are never recognized in psychiatric diagnosis. Social workers then stress the importance of **dialogue** as a way of looking fully at client situations, considering their significance, hearing what goals clients have, and understanding the ways in which clients believe they can achieve these goals. This larger view of assessment and assumes that the client, rather than the worker, directs the resulting decisions about the substance of the work. In essence, assessment has evolved into an integrative collaboration between the social worker and the client system from which the intervention flows (Jordan, 2008).

WHERE DOES THE CLIENT WANT TO GO?

Having established the importance of dialogue between social worker and client system in the process of gaining a holistic picture of the client's situation, initiating assessment then becomes the next step. Many assessment processes begin with long, detailed social histories. These histories have advantages and disadvantages. On the positive side, asking clients to talk about their life events can reveal important issues, such as their great resilience in the face of childhood abuse, that might not emerge right away but that are important to fully understand the client's situation. On the negative side, long accounts can seem intrusive, irrelevant, or even judgmental to clients as they cover personal aspects of a client's life when, for example, a single parent came only to talk about a child care allowance so she can attend a class. Such histories may also seem to emphasize previous difficulties or situations that the client would prefer to leave in the past. Finally, they can appear to be driven by the worker or agency or even the profession itself, because they seem disconnected and remote from whatever sense of urgency the client brings to the first interaction.

For example, Barbara may find an extensive history-taking process invasive and beside the point, when she is being investigated by child protection services and may be interested only in getting her baby back. At the same time, it is possible to imagine that such a process can reveal aspects of Barbara's life that could assist the social worker in helping her to achieve her goals in her situation through more or better-placed supports. The major requirement in this situation is that you, as the social worker, have effective communication and relationship skills in order to make the client feel comfortable and respected. Whether the history is lengthy or brief, it is critical that the work center on the client's goals. The most detailed, painstaking social history will be of little use if the history, and not the goals of the client system, becomes the driving force of the work.

IMPLICATIONS OF THEORETICAL PERSPECTIVES

Despite efforts to minimize prejudices and personal biases about the client's situation, assessments are not neutral gatherings of the facts. The nature of the facts gathered and questions asked suggests, at the least, your theoretical biases. For every area on which you focus, there are others you do not. For example, if you focus on Barbara's relationship with her baby because you see her as "case of mother and child," and you do not consider her experience as a child herself, you are choosing not to explore an area that could influence the work you do with her. Likewise, if you stress her history of delinquency but not of sexual abuse, you are adopting an approach that will affect the nature of your work with her.

In both scenarios, you take a specific approach that is a result of your judgment about what is both relevant and important. This judgment is usually influenced by many personal attributes (for example, who you are, what you believe about the nature of people, and where you work) and by the type of information you believe helps to make a story understandable. The theoretical perspective and its assumptions will also influence what you consider useful here, as will the context and function of the agency. All of these components shape the kinds of questions you ask and therefore the information you receive. Framed as it is by your perspectives, the client's assumptions, and your own interpretation of a situation, the assessment process is never unbiased.

Classic Theories

The theoretical perspective that the worker adopts strongly influences the assessment, the client–worker relationship, and the subsequent work. The following sections present three classic theories that have throughout the history of the social work profession influenced assessments: psychoanalytic theory, attachment theory, and cognitive theory. The discussion then shifts to an examination of strengths-based assessments and narrative approaches as contemporary alternatives.

Psychoanalytic Theory   Based primarily on the writings of the Austrian physician Sigmund Freud, **psychoanalytic theory** maintains that the unconscious is at the root of human behavior. Freud identified three structures that interact to determine human behavior: the id, ego, and superego. Each structure has a distinct function. The id is the repository of unconscious drives such as sex and aggression. In contrast, the ego is the managerial, rational part of the personality, which mediates between drives and perceived obligations. Finally, the superego serves as judge and conscience.

A social worker who believes that inner, unconscious motives and explanations determine the client's choices would orient an assessment toward interpreting the client's unconscious wishes. For example, if Barbara repeatedly describes herself as a "loser," the worker's assessment would likely be directed toward discovering the rewards and gratification she receives from perpetual failure. These rewards might include more concern from previously disinterested parents or protection from the high expectations of others. The first models of assessment were rooted in psychoanalytic theory, but as psychoanalytic theory gave way to more contemporary models based on evidence, approaches began to shift away from psychoanalytic origins (Jordan, 2008).

Attachment Theory   Looking through another lens, the social worker might first want to address Barbara as both a person who was parented and is now parenting. The assessment might take up a perspective influenced by attachment theory, which is currently the subject of some interest, especially in child protection work. **Attachment theory**, originally proposed by U.S. psychologist John Bowlby (1969), holds that very early bonding occurs between a mother and infant and subsequently plays a critical role in the child's future capacity to provide and sustain opportunities for her or his own children to attach. Most of this bonding activity occurs within the first two years of life, and it creates the foundation for the health of all future relationships.

A social worker who uses attachment theory focuses on Barbara's relationships with her early caregivers and the way in which these relationships may have contributed to her current struggles. An assessment of the attachment between Barbara and her child might include experimental observation to identify behavior patterns both child and mother demonstrate when a stranger is introduced into the scene. In stressing these relationships of parental bonding, the social worker would de-emphasize Barbara's other relationships in the environment.

Cognitive Theory   In contrast to psychoanalytic and attachment theories, if the theory guiding the work emphasizes the importance of **cognitions**, or thoughts, then the worker will see things differently. This approach is consistent with **cognitive theory**, which asserts that thoughts largely shape moods and behaviors. In this approach the focus in assessment is more likely to be on what Barbara thinks about herself, what she subsequently thinks about the way in which she would like to think and act differently to achieve her goals, and the ways in which her thoughts and feelings influence her behavior (Beck, 2005). The cognitive approach assumes that people are thinking beings and if they change their thinking, their emotions will also change. Further, one's feelings influence both specific behaviors and general approaches to life. For example, because Barbara felt depressed, lonely, abandoned, or hopeless, she used poor judgment in leaving her baby. The work with her might involve helping her appreciate her assets more fully, which in turn would help her feel better about herself and lead her to make caretaking choices that would be safer for her baby.

You may find the assumptions in cognitive theory more similar to your own than those of the psychoanalytic perspective or more hopeful than those concerning attachment. Nevertheless, they are still predicated on assumptions that make a significant difference in the way that the worker perceives, relates to, and works with the client. The point is not to reject every theory: We are all guided by theories, formal or not. Rather, the point is to recognize that none of them is "truth" and that you may use a mix of theories to frame your thinking about the approach you will select for working with a client system.

Contemporary Theoretical Perspectives

The three classic theories illustrate the way in which theory can influence social work practice. The following sections describe the implications for assessment approaches and skills of two contemporary approaches, the strengths-based perspective and narrative theory. Like the classic theories, contemporary theoretical approaches influence assessment practice behaviors as the focus is shaped by the worldview inherent in the perspective.

The Strengths Perspective   One of the four major perspectives of this book, the strengths perspective is widely discussed in the literature on assessment. Strengths-based practitioners are likely to uncover client assets, resources, goals, and dreams. A strengths approach also examines the potential of the environment to nurture and support the strengths of individuals. The assessment does not focus on a history of failures but on successes, resources, and goals for the future. The strengths perspective was developed for working with clients receiving mental health services but has since been used with many populations, including families and children, youth at risk, older adults, residents of economically distressed communities, and persons experiencing substance abuse. Saleebey (2009, pp. 104–105) identifies two elements for strengths-based assessments that are useful with all populations:

The social worker meets the client in the struggle: People have real struggles. There can be a fine line between supporting the positive dimension of a client's personality, skills, or accomplishments and denying the client experiences as lasting grief, terror, sorrow, or discouragement. For this reason, it is critical to the relationship that you validate the pain that clients feel. In starting where the client is and listening to the client relate her or his concerns, painful as they may be, it is possible to uncover evidence of potential strengths on which to build.

The social worker stimulates the discourse and narratives of resilience and strength: A narrative approach can be helpful in eliciting the client system's strengths. This "reframing" is dependent on the social worker supplying the words to help the client's strengths, being affirming, and emphasizing possibilities. With supportive questioning—for example, you might ask, "How have you managed with the demands of your kids?"—you can return the focus to client strengths. Even in the face of repeated, entrenched stories of trouble and pain, you can help clients to recognize their inner capacities for survival and learn the language of strengths in order to uncover a small seed of hope.

Another specific approach for assessing strengths incorporates a series of guidelines for the social worker that focus on understanding the client's perceptions regarding the problem situation (Anderson, Cowger, & Snively, 2009). See Box 4.1 to consider these guidelines. In this approach, the assessment includes a two component model in which the worker first explores a series of questions with the client to define the problem situation (Component 1), and then together they identify the relevant strengths and obstacles that the client brings to bear. These strengths and obstacles can be charted on the grid in Component 2 to provide visual representation of the assessment results. See Box 4.2 for the two component model.

Guidelines for a strengths-based assessment include:

BOX 4.1

The Strengths-Based Perspective in Assessment

- Document the client's story.
- Support and validate the story.
- Honor the client's self-determination.
- Give pre-eminence to the client's understanding of the facts.
- Discover what the client needs.
- Discover uniqueness.
- Reach a mutual agreement on the assessment.
- Avoid blame and blaming.
- Assess; but do not get caught up in labels (i.e., diagnoses).

Source: Anderson et al., 2009, pp. 186–188

The assessment process helps clients identify their own strengths, use the resources in their environment, and tell their story about the problem. The approach is also explicitly political in that it recognizes and articulates the power relationships that clients experience and/or in which they participate. In addition, the strengths approach encourages a complex view of the environment as a source of both resources and obstacles. Although this approach seeks to identify obstacles, they are not the primary focus of the assessment.

Narrative Theory   Recall from Chapter 1 that narrative theory, influenced by post-modern thought, focuses on the client's story as the central component in the work. The primary interest for social workers using this approach is in discovering the stories of the people who consult them and in helping them to "re-author" those stories if they wish. A story is defined as consisting of events linked in sequence across time according to a plot (Morgan, 2000, p. 5). Narrative theory is consistent with the mission and values of the social work profession as it "focuses on empowerment, collaboration, and viewing problems in social context" (Kelley, 2008, p. 291). Narrative practitioners also subscribe to a person-centered approach to working with clients that embraces the essentials of social justice, a cultural context and collaboration with and respect for the client system (Kelley, 2008).

Narrative practitioners are interested in helping the consulting person to broaden or "thicken" her or his story. For example, Georgia is a woman who experienced intimate partner violence. Georgia developed a negative self-story response to a pattern of abuse that was perpetrated by her partner. Whereas her story originally was that of a strong and competent young woman, it slowly began to erode, reflecting increasing doubt and finally wholesale dejection as she adopted the persona of an unworthy human being. It became a thin story in that it lacked complexity, reflecting only her self-rejection.

BOX 4.2

Two-Component Model for Assessing Client Strengths

In Anderson, Cowger, and Snively's two-component model for assessing client strengths, Component 1 is a process by which the worker and client define the problem situation and clarify how the client wants the worker to help. Component 2 is a graphic representation of the analysis of the problem defined in Component 1 (i.e., the assessment). It invites the worker and client together to chart strengths and obstacles in each of the four quadrants. Quadrant 2 is highlighted and may contain subcategories relating to cognition, emotion, motivation, coping, and interpersonal.

COMPONENT 1

Defining the Problem Situation: Getting at Why the Client Seeks Assistance

- *Brief summary of the identified problem situation*. This should be in simple language, straightforward, and mutually agreed upon between worker and client.
- *Who* (persons, groups, organization) is involved, including the client(s) seeking assistance?
- *How* or in what way are participants involved?
- *What* happens between the participants before, during, and immediately following activity related to the problem situation?
- *What* meaning does the client ascribe to the problem situation?
- *What* does the client want with regard to the problem situation?
- *What* does the client want/expect by seeking assistance?
- *What* would the client's life be like if problem was resolved?

COMPONENT 2

	Environmental Factors	Help Seeker Factors
Strengths	**Quadrant 3** Social and Political Strengths • Civic engagement • Social networks	**Quadrant 4** Personal and Interpersonal Strengths • Cognition • Emotion • Motivation • Coping • Interpersonal • Physical and physiological
Obstacles	**Quadrant 1** Social and Political Obstacles • Systemic oppression • Legitimization of domination and violence	**Quadrant 2** Personal and Interpersonal Obstacles • Powerlessness • Violation • Intense suffering • Isolation • Secrecy/silence

Adapted from Anderson et al., 2009, p. 192

In addition to seeking a more in-depth story, the social worker recognizes the importance of the broader social context of storytellers' lives. In one sense this is a story just about Georgia and her partner. In a broader sense, however, it is also about a pervasive social phenomenon in this culture that kills thousands of women every year. The work with Georgia is to help her rewrite the thin story of worthlessness to one that more accurately reflects her talents, attractiveness, and competence. The goal of assessment is to discover what alternative story the consulting person wishes to author.

In Barbara's situation, the narrative worker would first want to hear her story. How does she fill the day? What is it like to be mother to this baby? When are the best times? When did her loneliness first interfere with her life? When is she able to conquer it? Who would say she's a good mother?

These are a few of the most basic ideas of narrative theory and how it is used to assess the work to be done. As you can see, narrative theory differs from many of the more classic theoretical perspectives, but is similar in that it emphasizes the story. Narrative approaches are largely driven by the person seeking assistance, although you, as the social worker, contribute your ideas as well. A narrative approach fits well with the strengths perspective as it assumes that people are the experts on their lives and that they have multiple talents, values, beliefs, and skills for improving their lives. The applicability of narrative approaches will be highlighted in Chapters 6–9 in the context of developing interventions with families and groups.

Solution-Focused Approach As introduced in Chapter 1, the solution-focused approach is another example of postmodern-influenced practice in which the client is recognized as the expert on her or his life as well as ways to affect change. Similar to a narrative approach, solution-focused interventions build on a strengths perspective and utilize solution-related language to empower client systems toward self-initiated change (Lee, 2009). Three primary assumptions and principles guide practitioners using this approach: (1) language is the mechanism for clients and social workers to understand the meanings of the client's life and actions; (2) as clients are the experts on their own lives, they have both the resources and the answers that will guide the solutions; (3) clients, not the professionals, function as the "knowers" within the intervention process and are therefore in the best position to create the solutions.

Solutions to the issues that clients bring to the social worker are developed in stages and created utilizing a series of questions. The stages of solution building include: (1) description of the problem; (2) development of well-formed goals; (3) exploration of exceptions; (4) provision of end-of-session feedback; and (5) evaluation of client progress (DeJong & Berg, 2008, pp. 17–18). To be discussed in more depth later in this chapter, the questions posed to the client are aimed at eliciting the client's self-evaluation of the meaning of her or his life events and a futuristic exploration of possibilities.

While similar in their strengths-based orientation, client-centered empowerment approach, and commitment to collaboration, narrative and solution-focused approaches are distinct from each other as well. Proponents of the narrative approach emphasize the importance of "not knowing" and listening for unique outcomes to the client's presenting concerns, while solution-focused adherents delve into the possibility of "exception" questions (i.e., questions aimed at identifying instances in which the problem did not exist) (Kelley, 2008). With their similarities and differences, both approaches can be successfully integrated with each other as well as coupled with other theoretically driven models (e.g., cognitive behavioral interventions) (Kelley, 2008). Combining approaches requires a skillful and knowledgeable practitioner who is competent in the areas being combined.

Theory and Evidence Matters

The contrast between the traditional or classic theories and more contemporary models provides just one example of the ways in which theoretical orientations help to shape and define the assessment processes and skills as well as the roles of the participants. As mentioned, the idea is not that one theory is better than another, but rather that theory matters in assessment and should be consistent with the social worker's basic assumptions and beliefs concerning people.

While theory guides and informs the development of social work practice knowledge and values, social work practitioners can benefit from engaging in the practice of utilizing evidence to determine the appropriate skills, competencies, and behaviors to be applied to the social work intervention. In fact, the Council on Social Work Education (CSWE) Educational Policy and Accreditation Standards (2008) calls for social workers to engage in research-informed practice and practice-informed research. **Evidence-based practice** (EBP) is a process that aids practitioners to "systematically integrate evidence about the efficacy of interventions in clinical decision-making" (Jenson & Howard, 2008, p. 158). Within evidence-based practice context, social workers systematically determine, utilize, and assess interventions based on the consideration and integration of research findings, clinical expertise, client system preferences, values, and presenting issues, and the values and circumstances that will best serve the client system (Thyer, 2009). The five-step process of an evidence-based approach includes: (1) converting practice information needs into answerable questions; (2) locating evidence to answer the questions; (3) appraising the evidence; (4) applying evidence to practice and policy decisions; and (5) evaluating the process of using evidence to guide the practice intervention (Jenson & Howard, 2008).

Utilizing the five-step process evidence-based approach to work with Barbara, where would you begin? Consider the following (Carter & Matthieu, 2010; Jensen & Howard, 2008):

1. Convert practice information into questions about background information, effectiveness of intervention or policy

    - *Information*—Barbara jeopardized her child's safety by leaving him alone.

    - *Question*—What are the risk factors most associated with teenage parent neglect?

- *Information*—Barbara wants to be a good parent.

- *Question*—How can social workers provide assistance to teenage parents at risk of child neglect?

- *Information*—Barbara appears to be experiencing depressive symptoms.

- *Questions*—What assessment tools are most appropriate to assess for depression among teenage parents? What are the most effective intervention strategies to lower depressive symptoms in teenage parents?

2. Locate evidence to answer the questions

- Conduct a search of research and literature on child development, parenting, and assessment of and intervention with depression.

- Consult with social work practitioner(s) who possess(es) knowledge and expertise in the areas of interest and ask for their options of best practices in the areas.

3. Appraise evidence

- Assess the quality of the best available evidence, including the appropriateness of the research design for the question, sponsorship of the research, the similarity of the research subjects to your client system, and other factors.

- Considering the evidence compiled from literature review, your judgment and practitioner discussion and experience, and the client's goals and social context, develop a plan for assessment and intervention.

4. Apply evidence to practice decisions

- Implement assessment and intervention plan.

- Determine the appropriateness of the research methods for the client system situation being explored while maintaining a client-centered approach, cultural humility, and applicability to the practice approach, setting, and client system.

5. Evaluate the process of using evidence to guide practice intervention

- At each step in the change process, conduct an evaluation of the efficacy of the assessment and intervention process. Questions to consider:

  - Was the assessment accurate?

  - Was the intervention effective?

  - Was the information compiled from the literature and practitioner helpful?

- Did ethical questions emerge in the process? How were those resolved?

- What would you have done differently? Why?

The adoption of an evidence-based practice approach can direct the practitioner to information regarding assessment, intervention, and evaluative strategies and other key resources needed to effectively intervene with a client system. Effective interventions also include the use of clinical judgment and skills that are required for competent and ethical social work practice. Each client circumstance must be assessed as the unique situation that it is, encompassing all aspects of the client system.

IMPLICATIONS OF DIVERSITY IN ASSESSMENT

Although theoretical perspectives play a major role in assessment, other lenses are also crucial to recognize. One such lens, the impact of diversity on assessment, can hardly be exaggerated in contemporary social work practice. The implications of keeping diversity considerations central and the approaches and skills this focus implies are critical for competent social work practice. To be a culturally competent practitioner, the emphasis must be on developing a global set of practice behaviors (i.e., knowledge, skills, values, and actions) that prepare you to address both affective and cognitive domains and are measurable so you may evaluate your own practice (Simmons, Diaz, Jackson, & Takahashi, 2008).

Social work as a profession is an institution of culture, affected by the same pressures and forces that influence other aspects of culture. Because of the shifting patterns of diverse populations in U.S. society, social workers must develop appropriate competencies and practice behaviors that are responsive to different cultures. Consider these diversity-related questions as they may impact your ability to competently work with Barbara: (1) What is Barbara's background, including race, ethnicity, family background, religious/spiritual beliefs, and education?; (2) How might Barbara's experiences related to aspects of diversity impact her knowledge of parenting?; (3) How does your background related to diversity impact your knowledge of Barbara's ethnic, racial, and cultural background?; (4) What information do you need to know to work with Barbara in a culturally competent way?; and (5) What culturally competent practice behaviors will be appropriate for working with Barbara?

The theoretical perspectives of the strengths-based social worker, as well as the narrative worker, call upon her or him to develop an approach that affirms individuals' strengths and honors their culture. This point has important repercussions for assessment, particularly in the areas of (1) cultural competence; (2) connecting with the spiritual dimensions of culture; and (3) global connections.

Cultural Humility

The social worker who embraces a systemic, strengths-based perspective engages in an assessment process that includes components of the client system's culture that are meaningful for the client and the world in which she/he lives (NASW, 2007b). Known as **cultural competence** (NASW) or "cultural humility" (Clowes, 2005), this practice behavior is defined as "the process by which individuals and systems respond respectfully and effectively to people of all cultures, languages, classes, races, ethnic backgrounds, religions, and other diversity factors in a manner that recognizes, affirms, and values the worth of individuals, families, and communities and practices and preserves the dignity of each" (NASW, 2007b, p. 10). Cultural competence requires that social workers are aware of their limitations and have respect for the unique culturally defined needs of others. As you have learned, assessment involves discovering what is important to the client system, those cultural influences that shape her or his values, how they have affected the client's experience, and how the client's perspectives differ from the worker's.

Clearly, the worker's ability to approach another culture in this way is predicated upon her or his thorough self-knowledge and knowledge of her or his culture (Schultz, 2004). That is, workers must understand their cultural influences, examine the influences of their own culture on their work, and understand the role culture plays in all of our lives.

The assessment process is contingent on the development of cultural competence so that you, as the social worker, do not simply assess the degree to which your client differs from you. Your understanding of the issues that the client brings and the way they are shaped by culture impacts the way you will perceive the presenting "problem." For example, when your client describes communicating with the spirit of his deceased father, you might wonder if he is demonstrating psychosis or hearing voices, unless you have a clear understanding that this kind of spiritual communication is part of his culture and represents a strong, loving relationship.

Culturally Competent Practice Behaviors

Developing the skills necessary to conduct a culturally competent assessment can take time and significant effort. Social workers need specific skills for culturally competent assessment including the ability to engage in dialogues that focus on gaining insights into the meaning of client system's culture, language, cultural norms and behaviors and, of considerable importance, that these aspects are viewed as strengths on which to build an equally culturally meaningful intervention (NASW, 2007b).

Social workers who adopt a strengths-based culturally competent model of assessment and planning begin the helping relationship by initiating friendly yet purposeful conversations. Rather than focusing on long social histories, the worker may consider some aspect of the client's cultural frame that is puzzling or particularly interesting and ask about it through a "global question." For example, consider the situation you encounter as you are working with your client, Emilia Sanchez (refer to www.routledgesw.com/cases for information), a 24-year-old Mexican-American woman with a history of substance abuse and the mother of a four-year-old, Joey, who lives with her parents, Hector and Celia Sanchez. Joey has lived with his grandparents for most of his four years and, while he knows that Emilia is his mother, he considers Hector and Celia as his parents. Emilia has just learned that Hector and Celia are going to take legal action to officially adopt Joey. She is furious and has come to you for your help in preventing the adoption from going forward. As a culturally competent practitioner, you inquire about Emilia's cultural background and work to understand the impact of her background on her beliefs and current situation. As the client/cultural guide answers your questions, you remain highly attuned to the language she uses and inquire about **cover terms**, which are expressions and phrases that seem to carry more meaning than the literal meaning the words would suggest. For instance, your client might respond to the question about what her family thinks with a comment like, "I don't care what those hypocrites think about me; I will never be the person they want me to be!" In this case the cover terms are "hypocrites" and "person they want me to be," because they seem to have a cultural relevance to how the woman understands her social location.

Although this kind of extensive cultural interviewing may seem somewhat removed from assessing the particular issue that is pressuring the client, attending to and understanding the impact of the client's culture influences the overall effectiveness of the work, especially in those areas that will become barriers if they are ignored. For example, given what you have discovered about Emilia, you will likely make a significant mistake if you begin work by suggesting that the next step is a family conference with her parents.

Connecting with the Spiritual Aspects of the Client System

In recent years the social work profession has placed greater emphasis on the value of helping people define what gives their life purpose and meaning (see, for example, Hodge, 2005a). Insofar as this effort might be seen as a spiritual quest, it can encourage people to find the most sustaining areas of their lives. Such areas of meaning may be found in religious practices, outdoor activities focusing on nature, and in social connections like volunteering in a hospice, to name only a few. They can also be incorporated into both the assessment and action stages of the work in meaningful ways. For example, your client's volunteer work may be identified as evidence of her or his value to the community, which in turn might reduce her or his sense of isolation. Facilitating a client's connection with her or his spiritual side is likely to be a lasting and significant contribution of the social work intervention.

Global Connections

Social workers have the opportunity to work with a diverse and often international client population both in the U.S. and in other countries. Having competencies in internationally focused social work practice with individuals is an important area for social workers in contemporary society. With the number of foreign-born international migrants currently over 12 percent of the U.S. population and growing (Terrazas & Batalova, 2009), social workers may work with individuals who have come to live in the U.S. as non-immigrants (e.g., visitors, students, and temporary workers), legal or non-legal immigrants, or refugees who fled political or religious persecution. At the individual practice level, social workers can work with international migrants in a number of different areas, but the following areas generally encompass many of the interventions social workers will have with international clients: health, mental health, family conflict, language and education, economic well-being, and interethnic relations (Potocky, 2008, p. 445). Social workers can also work with individuals in foreign countries through casework, during times of disaster, and international adoptions (Healy & Hokenstad, 2008).

Whether you are working with individuals in this or another country, you can build on the skills of cultural competence and humility discussed earlier to individualize them for the specific cultural characteristics of the client. A strengths-based approach is particularly appropriate when working with a client who has come to the U.S. If one considers the fortitude and coping skills required for leaving one's country of origin to establish a life in a new country, there will be considerable strengths on which to draw for aiding the client in her or his social and cultural adaptation to the new life.

Working in an international area can be a learning experience for both you and your client. To begin your journey toward becoming a culturally competent practitioner, you must gain cultural awareness first about your own cultural heritage, identity, and belief systems (Lum, 2008). After exploring your own cultural make-up you can then begin to gain knowledge and develop skills to work with an international client system. Learn as much as possible about your client's heritage, but exercise caution about making any assumptions regarding the client's culture, particularly in the areas of beliefs, knowledge of you and your professional value system, language proficiency, familiarity with their new home, or openness to working with a helping professional.

While not presuming to understand the individual client's life experience or goals is important in working with any client system, it is critical with a client who has relocated to a new country. Some clients may have experienced trauma that resulted in their need to flee their country, trauma during relocation, or challenges adjusting to the new culture and environment, or they may have concerns regarding their legal status in their new country. Building rapport and trust is an important element of the social work relationship that may be challenging for a client who is unfamiliar with customs, language, legal issues, or the role of helping professionals.

Approaching the assessment and planning process with a repertoire of strategies will serve both the client and you well. Through research and consultation, arm yourself with culturally appropriate knowledge and skills, be open to learning from the client by asking for the client's help and guidance in understanding her or his culture and experience, and tap into the strengths the client brings.

SKILLS FOR ASSESSMENT AND PLANNING

At this point in the process of assessment, the social worker will begin to form a view of the future that includes the client system's vision and her or his own opinions about how they might engage in its fulfillment. This is the sense of a shared vision between client and social worker. In developing this vision, social workers will help client systems articulate the kinds of changes they want to make. The questions that social workers ask will affirm that change is possible and that it can be shaped in a way that makes the client's life better. Building on the foundation of strengths, narrative, and solution-focused perspectives, skills for assessing and planning with the individual client emphasize a collaborative, client-focused approach. Skills are shared here that highlight each of these approaches, but first, consider the unique aspects of each approach.

Strengths Perspective

Commitment to a being a strengths-based social work practitioner involves beginning the social work intervention from that perspective. Establishing a climate during the engagement, assessment, and planning phases in which client strengths are fully explored and acknowledged creates an environment in which both the social worker and the client can identify the strengths the client brings to the intervention, those resources that can be mobilized, and those that can evolve.

Earlier in this chapter, the elements of a strengths-based assessment were highlighted. Consider now a grouping of specific strengths-based questions that you can ask to engage the client in the assessment process. Saleebey (2009) provides a grouping of questions that are designed to elicit information from the client so that both the client and you can work together to identify strengths in order that they may be transformed into planning for an intervention. Box 4.3 presents the list of eight questions that can provide the basis for an assessment on which you and your client can collaborate on the development of an intervention plan.

Narrative Theory

Identifying and building on client strengths provides the basis of a narrative approach to assessment. Another of the empowerment-based practice approaches,

Survival Questions:

How have you managed to survive this far, given all the challenges you have had to contend with? What have you learned about yourself and your world during your struggles?

Support Questions:

Who are the special people on whom you can depend?
What did they respond to in you?

Exception Questions:

When things were going well in life, what was different?
What parts of your world and your being would you like to recapture?

Possibility Questions:

What are your hopes, visions, and aspirations?
How can I help you achieve those goals?

Esteem Questions:

When people say good things about you, what are they likely to say? When was it that you began to believe that you might achieve some of the things you wanted in life?

Perspective Questions:

What is your perspective on your current situation?
How would you describe your current situation to others?

Change Questions:

What thoughts do you have about ways your situation could change?
What things have worked well for you in the past? How can I help?

Meaning Questions:

What beliefs do you hold above all others? What gives you a sense of purpose? What are the origins of your beliefs?

Adapted from Saleebey, 2009, pp. 102–103.

BOX 4.3

Types of Questions for Discovering Strengths

---

narrative approaches are distinguished from other similar and overlapping approaches (most notably, solution-focused and strengths-based) in the way in which the perceptions of clients are elicited and interpreted. Narrative practitioners first help clients to share their stories, or "deconstruct," and then through expanding and externalizing perceptions and meanings of the client's words, the stories are "reconstructed" to provide a broader, more effective approach to functioning (Kelley, 2008).

Within a narrative framework, the social worker completing the assessment and planning stages of work will engage the client in reconstructing her or his reality into a new reality. Using a series of strategies and questions, the social worker and client together cast new meaning on the client's life in such as way as to empower the client to interact differently within her or his world. Upon gleaning from the client her or his perceptions of current realities, the social worker helps the client to: (1) "externalize" the problem by re-focusing on the outcome rather than the root cause and de-emphasizing problem-saturated stories; (2) discover "exceptions" (i.e., those instances in which the problem or concern did not exist for the client); (3) "re-author" or reconstruct a new reality through mapping of the domain of the issue or problem; and (4) "reinforce" the change by involving others in the client's life and/or sharing the client's change experience to identify unique outcomes (Kelley, 2009; Nichols, 2009). To this end, the social worker poses questions throughout the assessment process that aid the client in reaching her or his desired new reality. Questions are categorized as:

- *Deconstruction questions*—re-focus the issue on an outcome.

- *Opening space questions*—create the possibility for unique outcomes the client may not have considered.

- *Preference questions*—translate the unique outcomes identified through the use of opening space questions into preferred experiences.

- *Story development questions*—move the preference questions to the next stage of change by creating a new reality (or story).

- *Meaning questions*—provide an opportunity for the client to replace negative perceptions with positive interpretations based on strengths identified in the story development.

- *Extending the story into the future*—the client is empowered to see her or himself in future situations. This phase may involve bringing others into the process to support the client as she or he embarks on a new reality.

Solution-Focused Approach

Utilizing overall strategies similar to those described in a narrative-focused assessment and planning process, solution-focused assessment also incorporates a series of specific types of questions to elicit client perception, strengths, resources, and, ultimately, the solution. Starting where the client is, the social worker begins the assessment by asking the client to share her or his concerns, which is then followed by goal-setting. Solution-focused questions can be described as (Lee, 2009, p. 595; Nichols, 2009):

- *Evaluative questions*—the client engages in an evaluation of the "doing, thinking, and feeling" as it relates to the issue that brought her or him to you.

- *Miracle questions*—the client describes a vision of the future in which the problem or concern no longer exists. Miracle questions promote creativity and hopefulness while, at the same time, promote client self-determination and development of planning for concrete and achievable change.

- *Exception questions*—the client considers a time when the problem or concern was not present, thus allowing the client and social worker to identify existing assets and resources which can be clues of strategies that can be used in the present situation.

- *Scaling questions*—the client is asked to consider her or his situation on a continuum from worst (1) to best (10). Quantifying the issues enables the client and social worker to frame goals, provide feedback, monitor progress, change course, and evaluate outcomes.

Drawing on the similarities of the previously described strengths, narrative, and solution-focused approaches, a number of practice skills are common to all three philosophical frameworks. In the following section, several of these practice skills and strategies are highlighted.

Developing a Shared Vision

The term **preferred reality** refers to the client's goal for a changed reality. Preferred reality reflects a postmodern (i.e., client systems are the experts about their lives and situations) and narrative assumption that there are different realities. Long before postmodernism became a common theme in social work theory, however, the profession engaged in efforts to make things different—that is, to work toward a different or preferred reality.

The discussion of the assessment process has emphasized that the social worker's role is to engage in a dialogue with the client about her or his history, goals, and dreams. This process requires the practitioner to work with the client to develop a picture of what could be. Sometimes this process is difficult for clients, who may feel overwhelmed by the obstacles they face and thus find it quite impossible to be hopeful. Even more challenging, clients may be accustomed to seeing their dreams defeated through their long experience in living at the margins of society. In these cases the social worker has an important job in helping the client see that things can be different, that there are other realities, and that the client can work toward one that she or he prefers.

This process of being genuinely hopeful and translating that hopefulness to the client can be challenging to social workers as well. When you hear very painful stories, you feel swallowed up in them. For example, you might have to struggle to be hopeful after hearing about generations of violence or oppression. However, the idea of preferred realities benefits both the social worker and the client because the idea that the client's reality can be different helps to protect both from a hopeless view of the client's situation.

Remember that working toward a preferred reality does not necessarily require a grand sweeping vision of riches where there was poverty or complete harmony where there was vicious violence. As much as anyone might wish for these long-range dreams, they will appear elusive and unrealistic in many contexts if they are not shared by the client. Workers need to start with the client's vision of how things should be different, which may only involve small changes in the client's situation. Clients will often frame this vision in clear, small-scale terms when workers are drawn toward a more grandiose transformation.

Support for the Client's Goals and Dreams

As an illustration of the process of moving toward a preferred reality, consider once again the case of Jasmine Johnson, the single mother whom you met in Chapter 3. Recall that Jasmine is concerned because she has sometimes hit her son "hard" when he talked disrespectfully to her. Jasmine may verbalize a request to you, as a family support social worker, for help in developing another way to respond to him. Although this request might be seen as a relatively concrete goal for behavior change, it might also be thought of as developing a preferred reality because realization of this goal suggests creating a different mother–son relationship, which could have many positive ramifications. Right now Jasmine is asking for help with a behavioral response. Her goal might be simply to avoid child protection charges or to reduce the likelihood that her son will respond violently back to her. Therefore, your work with her might involve exploring her vision of a long-term goal. For example, Jasmine might want to establish a more satisfying emotional connection with the most important person in her life. She may not have allowed that kind of emphasis on feelings to enter into her interpersonal experiences, or she may never have had the time to think that way. It is even possible that she has not known anyone who articulated such a goal or she may simply be disinclined to consider relationships that way. In this scenario, it is important to start with Jasmine's meaning of the situation and then explore it further without imposing your own meanings.

The shared vision in this case will be that Jasmine learns other ways to respond to her son because she has articulated that vision as her concern and because you have agreed that is an appropriate area for work and that you can contribute to it. As you work together toward achieving this vision, other, more encompassing dreams about the possibilities for her relationship with her son might evolve. Your role in this kind of strengths-based assessment strategy is to support her dream, always affirming its potential for fulfillment. In order to help Jasmine's dream become reality, you will need to engage in a process of specifying both her goals and a plan for the two of you to work together. Both of these issues will be examined below.

Setting Goals   The reason for **setting goals** is to emphasize the usefulness of clarity of purpose and the utility for clients of recognizing the difference between central, current, behavioral concerns and the longer view of the dream. As emphasized throughout this chapter, a thorough assessment is key to effective and ultimately successful goal-setting. Specifically, prior to establishing short- and/or long-term goals *with* the client system, the social work intervention includes assessing the level of possible attainment, incorporating resources as well as limitations, and changes needed in order to experience change (Garvin, 2009, p. 309). Depending on the client's goals and needs, work takes on multiple forms. Consider the following goals in the context of your work with Jasmine:

1.   Goals that are discrete (single outcome) or continuous (part of an ongoing plan)—a discrete goal is to respond differently when her son speaks to her in a disrespectful way, while a continuous goal may be to improve her relationship with her son.

2.   Goals that are framed within different aspects of the client system (individual, family, group, or community)—be viewed by others (e.g., family and co-workers) with greater respect.

3.   Goals that are related to various behaviors and behavior changes—get a new job or get her son to speak to her more respectfully.

4.   Goals that are dependent on the individual client or need to involve others (e.g., couple or family)—invite her son to participate in family meetings with the social worker. (Garvin, 2009, p. 310)

Jasmine wants to respond differently to her son when he is disrespectful to her. This goal can be measured in a variety of ways. For example, does Jasmine want to "feel better" about their conversations? Does she want to reduce by half the number of times she is tempted to respond physically to him? Does she want to eliminate those episodes altogether? Does she want him to report that things are better? Clearly, the selection of an appropriate measure should reflect Jasmine's priorities. In starting where the client system is, setting priorities will help Jasmine and the social worker sort through expectations to determine the outcomes that are more critical within a particular time frame. For example, what if Jasmine's son is well behaved two times and then rude once, which provokes her inclination to hit him? Does his positive behavior matter in terms of the goal? Is the goal to change Jasmine's behavior or her son's behavior? As you can see, establishing goals and measuring progress toward achieving them can become complicated. Nevertheless, it is worth the effort to clarify how each party defines the goal of the work and how each one will know when the goal is achieved. Unless you are in clear agreement on an end point, Jasmine may believe you will be there to work on her particular situation until she feels it is "fixed." To avoid misunderstandings, you will want to make sure you have a mutual agreement regarding this issue. Setting goals helps both the client and the social worker evaluate the degree to which they are communicating clearly and have similar expectations, and are making progress. It is also true that agencies and organizations need to understand the purpose and goals of the work, often in concrete, measurable terms. This topic is discussed more thoroughly in Chapter 5 as a function of formal evaluation.

Contracting   The process of **contracting** is one in which the client and worker reach an agreement about what is to happen, who will be responsible, a timeframe, and the priorities. Developing a clear, measurable and achievable contract with the client system can serve to support and empower the client as it emphasizes the client's role in the intervention and recognizes her or his right to self-determination (Rothman, 2009b). Contracts vary greatly depending on practice setting, and they can be formal or informal. A formal contract generally takes the shape of a written document signed by both parties. In contrast, an informal contract can consist simply of a verbal agreement. If a formal contract is used, details should be clarified, including frequency of meetings, goals, individual roles, ways to change the plan, monitoring of progress, and the degree to which each goal needs to be met. Whether formally or informally executed, a contract should include: (1) goals; (2) objectives that emphasize action, timeframe, and strategies for determining success (or failure); and (3) proposed intervention specifying "who" is responsible for "what" aspects of the plan (Rothman, 2009a). Of critical importance to both the social worker and the client is clarity regarding the desired outcomes for the intervention. While the assessment and evaluative components of the social work intervention are dynamic, ongoing, and can change, the social worker and client both will be frustrated and unsuccessful if the goals and the path to achieve those goals are not clearly stated (and re-stated).

Honest Responding

Up to this point you have learned how social workers and clients can identify and work toward a preferred reality. This discussion has emphasized the importance of establishing a shared vision that reflects the client's goals and dreams. However, as a social worker you might find yourself in a situation in which you are inclined to challenge your client's priorities after hearing the story. For example, if your client's overall goal is to avoid being arrested again for selling illegal drugs, you might want to contest that goal as a purpose for work. To you, a more healthful goal might be for the client to abstain from using and selling drugs, or to separate from a drug-using peer group. Conflicts over goals raise many difficult questions for social workers. For example, do you have the right to disagree about the client's priorities? Are you inappropriately pushing your values? At the same time, how can you engage enthusiastically to achieve a goal you really do not approve of? Social workers often struggle with these questions.

Questions that might serve as guidelines here include:

- Are you able to maintain objectivity about the client's goals?

- Do client goals reflect your priorities, values, or cultural practices?

- What are your legal and professional commitments in this situation?

- Will you violate an ethical principle by not addressing the issue, even if the client would rather not deal with it?

- Do you think the client's goals are either unrealistic or not extensive enough?

Although there are no easy solutions in this kind of scenario, you can respond honestly if you "own" your own biases, which might include more belief in the client's potential than the client seems to possess.

When Confrontation Is Necessary You have probably concluded from the preceding discussion that in some situations in which the goal conflict is particularly acute, the worker has to confront the client system directly. To examine how this process can be conducted, return to the Jasmine Johnson case for a moment. Jasmine has requested your help to change the way she responds when her son talks back. However, you have discovered through reliable sources that she is actually beating him regularly. How will this revelation affect the assessment? You may be convinced that you must call the authorities to investigate the serious allegations, with the possible outcome of a temporary separation between Jasmine and her son. This may occur before you can begin to work with her on a different way of relating to him. In this case you may decide that you must establish a new, short-term goal to carry out your professional and legal commitments, and postpone work toward Jasmine's long-term goal. The assessment then moves to an intermediate plateau in which there is a dangerous, or potentially dangerous, situation that requires a more immediate (and ethical) response. You will need to be honest with Jasmine about your understanding of the situation and what you see as your ethical obligations. This process will likely involve some confrontation. In this situation, Jasmine needs to hear that there is an immediate need that must temporarily derail her long-range goals.

You may have noticed in this scenario that any decision to call child welfare authorities, which might lead to a separation between Jasmine and her son, does not necessarily negate her preferred reality of getting along better with him. In fact, a temporary separation may help her achieve this reality. It will be critical in your work with Jasmine to find the common ground and support her dream, even though you must initiate another intervention at the moment. Ideally this respite will improve her chances of working on her original goal after the crisis is past. Your honest dialogue with her will then reassure her that you share her vision and you want to help her work toward it and that you can be trusted to tell the truth.

When Alternatives Are Necessary   In most cases, those persons who come to social workers for assistance are realistic about their goals and dreams. Many clients are keenly aware of the level of change that would be required to realize their vision of a more satisfying life. In other cases, social workers must help people expand their vision of what is possible because they have been discouraged, oppressed, or otherwise have had their vision restricted. In such cases the task is to affirm the client's potential and power in changing her or his life.

Occasionally, however, clients will need assistance in clarifying and articulating their goals and their understanding of the situation. Their goals might seem unrealistic or even grandiose to you. These situations are tricky, particularly for strengths-based social workers. One strategy for responding in this type of situation is to help clients lower their aspirations, that is, to become more realistic. The argument for establishing realistic goals is that to endorse goals that clients cannot achieve is to set them up for failure, which represents a major disservice to them.

At the same time, you are not in the position to determine goals that are realistic or the upper limits of the individual's capacity to growth and change. If social workers are to "hold high our expectations of clients and make allegiance with their hopes, vision, and values" (Saleebey, 2009, p. 17), you should not simply disregard a person's dream as unrealistic. Moreover, many strengths-based social workers insist that clients have the right to fail in the pursuit of their dreams, just like the rest of us. The issue is difficult to resolve and will undoubtedly take on a different look in different contexts.

One option for approaching such a situation is to help clients determine the steps involved in achieving their goals. For example, if you are the high school social worker and your client states that she wants to be a nuclear physicist, you and she can consider together what level of education she would require, what it might cost, and how long it would take. You should not use this kind of step-by-step discussion to discourage her, but rather to provide information that she can consider. You may then help her consider alternatives that could serve as stepping-stones. Breaking down goals into workable and achievable sub-goals, or procedural goals, can aid client systems in developing clarity regarding the practical side of the dream and how far they want to take it. This may or may not alter their enthusiasm, but it is an honest response to a sometimes troubling scenario.

Using Mapping Skills to Enhance the Dialogue

As you have seen, assessment on any level is influenced by your interpretation of the client's story. This interpretation is shaped by both your own and the client's culture, ethnicity, class, gender, sexual orientation, and age, as well as evidence-based theoretical perspectives, practice skills, and professional knowledge and values. Human stories often have many layers, however, and can be difficult to grasp in their complexity. Frequently, a visual picture can make the information more accessible. **Mapping** is a technique that represents complex phenomena visually so that they can be absorbed perceptually rather than linguistically. Two fundamental types of mapping—genograms and ecomaps—are discussed next.

Genograms   Technically a family tree—geneticists call it a pedigree—the **genogram** usually represents three generations and indicates various aspects of the relationships of the individuals included. Exhibit 4.1 presents a sampling of the conventions for indicating these relationships while Exhibit 4.2 provides a genogram completed for the Sanchez family interactive case (see routledgeswhome.com). As you can see from the Sanchez family genogram, when used flexibly, a genogram can portray a broad range of issues and family patterns, such as strained relationships as well as stable marital relationships that can affect individual and family functioning. A review of the family history through the use of a genogram can add important information to the individual assessment, which may inform our work together on a contract. By adding labels to the map that indicate such dimensions as vocational accomplishment or alcohol use, genograms can be used in a more focused way to address a single issue. Patterns can indicate strengths of the family as well.

Genograms should be introduced carefully with client systems that are vulnerable. The memories evoked and the visual nature of a genogram can result in more intense emotions (for example, a sense of loss or regret) than mere words can. For example, a couple who review a genogram may become so distraught at the memory of a relative who died by suicide that each may abruptly and separately leave their meeting with a social worker.

People in a genogram are represented by the following symbols:
- Males = □ (occasionally represented by the medical symbol of ♂)
- Females = O (occasionally represented by the medical symbol of ♀)
- Unborn or aborted children are triangles (△)
- X through a person symbol indicates death (usually accompanied by age or year of death)

Relationships are represented by the following symbols:
- Strong, solid black line = strong, positive relationship _____
- Dotted line = tenuous relationship - - - - - - - - -
- Railroad track line = contentious or strained /-/-/-/-/-/-/-/-/-/
- Slanting vertical lines = separation or divorce (on marriage line) //
- Circle enclosing people indicates household
- Arrows along connecting lines indicate the flow of energy, reciprocity ↔

EXHIBIT 4.1

Genogram Symbols

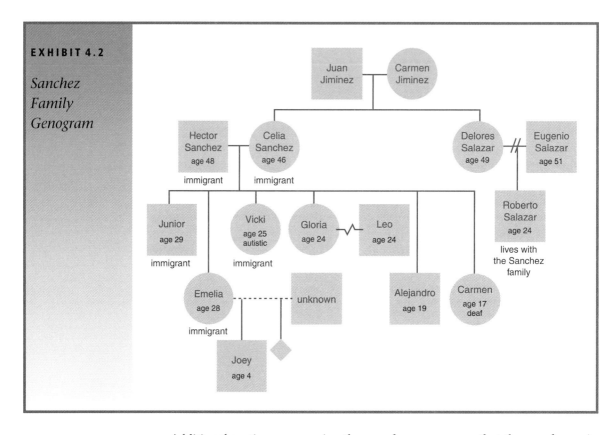

Additional cautions concerning the use of genograms are that they are frozen in time (that is, they represent relationships at the moment of the map's creation), and that they are sometimes subject to privileged interpretation, making it important to remember that the map represents one person's perception. Most importantly, they may seem deterministic, especially when they exhibit family patterns. For example, if a multigenerational exploration reveals that all or nearly all young male members on one side of a family have had major substance use problems, it may be tempting to see such a pattern as inevitable. When discussing the genogram, the social worker can give clients hope and the assurance that they can change. Therefore, family pattern exploration should never suggest that people are doomed by their familial history. Rather, a family history provides context and can help you locate your most effective intervention points.

Ecomaps   A diagrammatic representation of the client's world that illustrates the client's levels of connection to such institutions as schools, religious centers or spiritual practices, the workplace, extended family, friends, and recreation is known as an **ecomap**. An ecomap helps clients to make sense of their experience by showing them how their day-to-day world looks and the resources and strengths that exist within that world. Ecomaps can also focus on a particular aspect of the client's life. For example, a social worker who is involved with children with special health needs can use an ecomap of medical and social supports relating to the child's health status to help shape the intervention. Some ecomaps include a miniature genogram.

Like all mapping techniques, the ecomap enables your client to explore patterns of everyday living that may or may not be initially accessible in verbal form. For example, your client may complain about being lonely and estranged from his community. An ecomap could reveal that he has very few supports in the community—no satisfying work life, only one friend, no spiritual connections, and no outlet for recreation. Such a diagram would suggest that you expand your dialogue with him into these areas. Here, as always, it is important not to interpret and make conclusions directly from the map without exploring the meaning of the indicators with the client. Consider the Sanchez family ecomap as depicted in Exhibit 4.3 (refer to the Sanchez family case at routledgeswhome.com for more information). Can you identify the strengths, resources and areas for potential intervention that you see present in this ecomap? In reviewing the ecomap, you will note that there is a stressful relationship reported between Celia and Emilia, with Celia perceiving that the relationship is not reciprocal (i.e., Celia is devoting more energy to the relationship than she is receiving from the relationship). To fully understand the meaning of that statement, you, as the social worker, can invite Celia to share with you the reasons behind the statement, her emotional response to the relationship, and the implications of her feelings for her relationship with Emilia and others in the family.

Social workers occasionally use a sequence of ecomaps to evaluate the effectiveness and progress (or lack) of the work. For example, if the client mentioned above who is experiencing loneliness wants to expand his social world but feels fearful of that prospect, your work with him might be to develop safe connections, which could be indicated on subsequent ecomaps.

SKILLS FOR ASSESSING RESOURCES

By developing individual skills, such as creating a shared vision, becoming culturally competent and mapping, social workers can work toward an effective assessment. Nevertheless, even the most skilled workers can rarely provide all the assistance that a client needs. Workers should also familiarize themselves with resources that are available in the larger environment. There are several dimensions to assessing resources that are useful in reaching client goals, from their type and source to their availability.

Formal and Informal Resources

External, structured opportunities for assistance, which usually take the form of services, are **formal resources**. Training in parent education, financial assistance,

EXHIBIT 4.3

Sanchez Family EcoMap

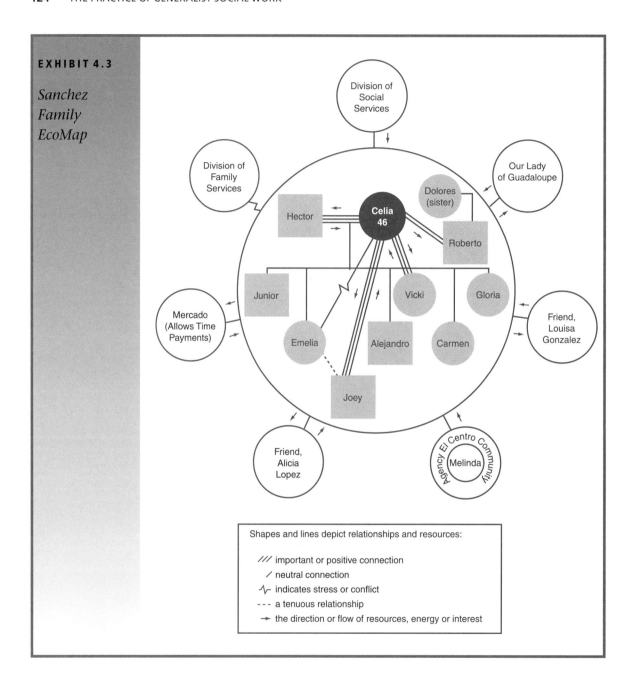

Shapes and lines depict relationships and resources:

/// important or positive connection
/ neutral connection
-√- indicates stress or conflict
- - - a tenuous relationship
→ the direction or flow of resources, energy or interest

caregiver respite, and support groups for children in schools are all examples of the hundreds of services you might be able to name that are helpful to clients.

Not all resources are formal, however. **Informal resources** may be people, your own creativity, or naturally occurring social networks, like church groups, friends, or families. The informal, internal, or community-based assets can also be mobilized to better serve client systems. Within the practice context, natural helping networks, such as those available from individuals, groups, families, and communities, can be the most important. These resources may endure long past the time that formal resources are involved with a client system. For example, many children benefit from regular contact with an older child who befriends them, understands their troubles, or is just supportive of their abilities. An older adult may benefit from creating networks of friends that are similar age through attendance at a senior center or through volunteer work. It is not necessary in all such situations to hire someone or obtain a service. Some of the most meaningful relationships emerge from informal contexts of community life.

Assessment When Resources Are Available or Unavailable

Your familiarity with both formal and informal resources is an enormous benefit to your client system. Simply locating resources is not adequate. Rather, you also need to know enough about the client system and the resources to estimate the fit and likelihood of a successful interaction between them. For example, your client asks you, as a family support worker, for help in managing an ill infant, and you concur that some supports would help her become more like the effective parent she wants to be. In particular, you might recommend some regular time away from the demands of the child and also some assistance in managing the child's challenging behaviors. You would probably then explore the availability of both formal and informal resources that could stabilize the situation. For example, you could investigate formal parent support programs, focusing on the collaborative capacity of the trainers, as well as informal parent support resources such as a child care cooperative and family and friends, and include consideration of concrete issues such as cost and schedule.

Unfortunately, even the more careful social workers cannot locate necessary resources in all situations. In fact, most have had the experience of looking for a particular way to help a client and finding that it does not exist. Even in these situations, you are not powerless. You have at least two options when adequate resources are not available: You can advocate for a change in formal resources, policies, or programs that are not responding adequately (for example, an older adult day center), or you can create resources where none have been developed. For example, you might assist single parents in a housing complex to organize a network of child care where none existed, or help a community write a grant proposal to fund summer youth employment for neighborhood teens.

These points suggest that workers do not simply accept, for example, that an uncooperative agency does not respond appropriately to their client, or this housing project has no child care facilities. Social workers need to remain hopeful and energetic in identifying and developing resources but must also be realistic and careful not to promise more than they can reasonably deliver. In a client's world, where many promises may have been broken, social workers need to maintain trust through an honest approach about the possibilities.

Social Action When Resources Are Inadequate

Many of the cases in which the resources you think necessary are inadequate, nonexistent, or discriminatory are clearly political situations that call for policy practice approaches. Action on behalf of clients is one possible response to an unjust situation. **Social action** is a policy practice method in which the social worker generally aims to shift power structures in order to change an institutional response. The efforts come in many forms and may involve varying degrees of confrontation. For example, if the public health department is slow to investigate a situation of child lead poisoning at a local school, you might assist your individual client through their formal grievance process, and/or organize a protest with other concerned parents if the health department does not respond to the initial inquiry. Both the actions on behalf of one client and on behalf of many clients are forms of social action. However, the latter is clearly more confrontational than the former. In situations in which this kind of action is contemplated, the assessment will take on the additional dimension of an analysis of the actions that actually should or will happen, who will do it, and what the potential consequences will be. In addition, the assessment must address the client's interest in, and capacity to engage in, the action indicated. The social worker must be completely honest and sensitive to the possible consequences of political action for the client or the client's family. In many ways this last requirement can be considered a dimension of ethics. Read how this might play out in the tenants' story in Box 4.4.

Despite the risks that may be involved, when an understanding is truly reached in partnership, few experiences are more positive or powerful than a successful social action based in client–worker advocacy. Even if the results are somewhat less than hoped for, the process itself can be remarkably empowering for both social worker and client.

Although this scenario expands into the phase of intervention, it points up the importance of assessment throughout the client relationship. The assessment drives the action stage of the work, and therefore, must also address the very action inherent in it.

PLANNING

When you and your client have developed a shared vision and specified the goals, means, and end points you envision for the work, you will have addressed the components of a solid, detailed plan. This section will revisit these briefly and then consider the potential impact of two insidious influences—oppression and the emotional impact of change—on the planning process in particular and on the assessment in general.

In a privately run, not-for-profit housing project in a midsize city, there are several families with young children and some with elderly grandparents. In the past, the housing was kept in marginally acceptable repair, but the residents stayed there because the rent is fixed and relatively low. A change in ownership leads to a distinct deterioration in maintenance, adequate and timely repairs, and the amount of heat allotted to each apartment. Toilets are clogged, rats are visible in the basement, and lead-based paint is beginning to crumble from the walls. The residents are unsure how they can respond to this deteriorating situation so they request that you, as a social worker from the city's housing authority, advocate for them. After discussing the situation with client spokespeople and then asking each client for approval, you sponsor a meeting for residents with the landlord's representatives. Although you have been careful to hear the landlord's side and have used your best engagement skills, the meeting results in a deadlock, and no progress is made.

BOX 4.4

Social Action: The Tenants' Story

Convinced that you have exhausted all of the available approaches, you consult with peers who affirm your position. At that point you consider the possibility of organizing your tenants to withhold their rent. You feel for many reasons that this is an appropriate and effective strategy to elicit a more satisfactory response from the landlord. At the same time, however, you know from prior experience that this particular landlord has a history of retaliation against complaining tenants.

You fully recognize the need to collaborate with tenants about the potential plan of withholding their rent. There is some hesitation among them because they too are concerned with the likely consequences of riling a powerful landlord who could throw them out. Some of the residents are people of color, and they are especially concerned with the availability and accessibility of other housing.

Let's consider the following ways the story might play out:

- *Plotline A:* You are so convincing that this is the way to deal with the problem that you are able to engage the tenants in a full-blown movement to withhold their rent. Your clients nervously await the landlord's response.

- *Plotline B:* You hear those who have specific concerns and play out alternative responses. You locate other sources of housing, and you identify legal advocates for those interested in pursuing new housing. You arrange for press coverage and obtain the full support of your agency and supervisor in taking this action.

Social Action: The Moral of the Story

You may fill in the ending of this story. It could be empowering or disastrous or a lot of things in between. The point is that when others live the results of your advocacy attempts, they need to have all the available information about possible consequences, the likelihood of certain outcomes, and the opportunity to choose which path they want to take. You, as the social worker, need to be very clear about who will pay the price of any repercussions. Because the "who" is often the client, the client should enter into such an agreement only when she or he clearly understands the risks and is motivated to follow through with the action consequences. Can you identify an alternative Plotline C?

The key components that influence the concrete plan for work include:

- Setting and prioritizing goals

- Identifying methods of reaching goals

- Developing a clear understanding of responsibilities

- Setting time frames

- Recognizing when an alternative plan is necessary

- Identifying resources

- Identifying an end point for the work

Incorporating these elements into a plan can enhance the client's understanding of what will happen and how she or he will experience the process. These components have been negotiated as an ongoing feature of your work together and constitute the mutually developed plan.

Although the ideal is that workers and clients collaborate to plan the process, even the most careful approaches cannot account for all of the potential obstacles that might arise. Many clients face real disabilities. They may have emotional, cognitive, or physical challenges that make it almost impossible for them to participate in planning. Although social workers should never minimize these obstacles, they need to work directly with the client to the greatest extent possible, while bearing in mind that many clients who have experienced lifelong challenges have never been considered as adequate participants in service provision planning. Consequently, clients may be hesitant or even afraid to participate, even though they have the ability to make substantial contributions. Many others who have experienced racial or ethnic oppression will find it difficult to trust the process of mutual assessment and planning.

The transgression of excluding clients from this process has generated two negative consequences. First, service providers have often lost, dismissed, or ignored helpful information that only the person experiencing the context could provide. Second, many of these clients have internalized this kind of oppression and actually have come to believe that they have no right or capacity to participate. The **internalization of oppression**—the process by which individuals come to believe that the external judgments are valid, thus resulting in a devaluing of one's self—is one of the most sinister aspects in the oppression and domination dynamic (Van Soest, 2008) and clearly undermines the spirit of human rights.

Another component of assessment and planning that social workers must keep in mind relates to the impact of emotions. In their zeal to develop a plan, address the issues, mobilize the resources, and engage the contract, social workers may sometimes forget that certain elements of the work are not as visible or as easy to categorize as others. By the time social workers have listened to the story and established a preferred reality, they will probably have heard and felt a lot of the emotional content that is related to the client's experience. They may not as easily, however, recognize the power that complicated feelings about change can generate.

For example, whole families are systems that can be organized around one member's addiction to alcohol. In some families, everyone knows how to respond if Dad is drunk and has passed out on the couch. John, the eldest son, may be the one to carry him to bed; everyone else might ignore Dad, step around him, and pretend his drinking does not happen. Mom takes this opportunity to make decisions about the family finances that Dad has always made. The specific patterns may not be as important as the idea of changing them. Although Mom has come to your agency to get help with Dad's addiction problem because it is obviously destroying his health, their marriage, and their family life, the social worker must be aware that there is a cost to change. Mom may feel uniquely competent when she is so clearly needed to make major decisions, or John may take great pride in being able to manage the chaos. Again, the patterns are not as important as the disruption of them. If Dad successfully withdraws from alcohol, Mom may actually have some regrets because she will have to develop a new role when her husband is more present. John may lose his place as competent caretaker, and all members of the family will need to relate to Dad and each other differently. This need for renegotiating family roles can have some disturbing emotional consequences.

Although there is a risk of over-interpretation, any change that the client is genuinely seeking is embedded in a social context and therefore can generate a powerful emotional response. A change in one part of the system has the potential to change the entire system. This response may take the form of reluctance to engage in ongoing collaboration or hesitation when making progress on specific goals. In such cases, consider engaging in a dialogue that goes beyond the technical or mechanical processes of goal setting and contracting. Specifically, it will be helpful to explore the meaning of the change itself in terms of emotional and logistical outcomes as well as the impact of the change on roles, functioning, and patterns.

STRAIGHT TALK ABOUT ASSESSMENT AND PLANNING: THE AGENCY, THE CLIENT, AND THE SOCIAL WORKER

You have seen that several agency, client system, and professional issues influence your work with clients. From those perspectives, the following discussion will address a range of issues that you will likely encounter as a social worker. Having insights in advance of such encounters can arm you with the knowledge and skills to respond competently and ethically.

The Agency Perspective

From the agency perspective, work methods, schedules, length of the work, documentation, and agency resources used in work all need to be recognized and discussed openly with the client. For example, you need to provide information to the client regarding your schedule, appropriate ways to contact you, ways in which you will be documenting your interactions with her or him, and agency resources that are or are not available to her or him. The social worker needs to inform clients about their work processes from the beginning of the engagement so that there is no confusion or frustration as the relationship evolves.

Administrative Tasks   With an increasing emphasis being placed on brief, effective, and accountable treatment for individuals, families, and groups, managed care organizations (MCOs) have influenced the assessment and planning process in significant ways (Hopson & Wodarski, 2009). You may be required to complete your assessment, planning, intervention, termination, and evaluation processes within a limited time frame. Standardized, rapid assessment measurement tools have become a mechanism for practitioners to complete assessments in a short period of time while maintaining optimal accuracy. In order to work within the current service delivery environment, your agency may opt to utilize a rapid assessment process. With numerous rapid assessment instruments (RAIs) available to choose from, the key is to ensure the instrument relates to the issues being presented by the client system and has been empirically validated with that population (Hopson & Wodarski, 2009). Utilizing any assessment tool on a population for which the instrument has not been shown to be effective can produce misleading outcomes in the areas of age, gender, race, ethnicity, and culture.

Other formalities about which to inform the client relate to administrative tasks or financial coverage. For example, if you are required to submit monthly reports to the court, you should discuss this stipulation with your client. Even when clients are not happy with such an idea, they are likely to respect your communicating such information from the outset of the relationship. For another example, if your client will have to file a Medicaid application in order to continue working with you, explain the need for action as early as possible. For many clients, filing for financial assistance for services may be challenging, because it may mean to them that they are admitting defeat, disability, or helplessness. Being sensitive to your client's perspective about the meaning of these aspects of your work together is important.

Another mandate that is becoming increasingly prevalent in community agencies is the requirement for diagnosis as part of the assessment and planning process. As discussed earlier, many institutions now demand a *DSM* diagnosis in order to bill for third-party payment. This mandate can provide uncomfortable moments for social workers who believe strongly in helping clients to identify and use their strengths. The attempt to provide a psychiatric diagnosis requires a focus on deficiencies and can create a stigma. For example, a school social worker who is providing support to a five-year-old whose parents are addicted to heroin may struggle with diagnosing the child with an "adjustment disorder," which will then appear in school records, label the child for years to come, and may be transmitted to other institutions.

Obviously, if your agency requires social workers to make or utilize diagnoses, then you need to consider your feelings on this issue before you accept a position. Practicum students are not likely to formulate diagnoses, but the use of diagnosis inevitably categorizes clients, which can impact the working environment of a setting and some may object to working in such a setting. Others may find the process tolerable as long as it facilitates service provision. Still others may find the use of diagnosis helpful because they are able to use evidence-based practice to provide the best possible service to clients for their challenges, and collaborate easily with non-social work colleagues who also use the *DSM*. Ethical conduct obliges all social workers to inform their clients when a diagnosis is required to access services. The client can then decide if she or he wants to participate in that exchange. For some clients and social workers the diagnostic process may seem a small price to pay for receiving appropriate services and possibly medication, whereas for others, the benefits do not outweigh the costs involved in using the *DSM* with clients.

Documentation   Recording information about your work with client systems is both universal and unique. Social work encounters are recorded in virtually every setting, but the requirements and formats are typically unique to the setting. Social work documentation begins with the first encounter and continues through each phase of the planned change experience. Documentation is important for social work practitioners as recording information from the engagement, assessment, intervention, and termination and evaluation encounters serves a number of key functions, including accountability, supervisory and administrative purposes, practice enhancements, reimbursement, and planning (Kagle, 2008).

Despite the need to learn the agency's preferred method for documentation, there are basic components that are likely to be found in the recordings developed by social workers. Kagle and Kopels (2008, pp. 38–40) suggests the following structure for creating a written record of the social work intervention:

1.   opening summary;

2.   data gathering and social history;

3.   assessment;

4.   decisions and actions resulting from initial assessment;

5.   service planning, including service options and purpose, goals, and plans of service;

6.   interim notes;

7. special materials (e.g., forms, consents, emergencies, and service reviews); and

8. closing summary.

The opening summary portion of the documentation encompasses the engagement phase of your intervention. Information that is typically included in an opening summary relates to the client's demographic characteristics (i.e., name, gender, address, contact information, birth/age, family composition, employment, insurance coverage, etc.), reason for requesting or receiving services, and eligibility status. The assessment portion of the client record should specifically include the social worker's observations and descriptions, sources of the information, criteria used in making the judgments (e.g., formalized measures and information from past history with the agency or referring entity), and inferences and appraisals (Kagle & Kopels, 2008). This may be an appropriate place to record perceptions of strengths, resources, needs, cultural factors, and risks related to services that may be delivered.

While formats are agency- or program-dependent, there are elements of social work recording that are common across the profession. Most agencies have a structured format for documenting client encounters or meetings, conducting an intake or eligibility interview, completing a social history, and a treatment/intervention plan. Examples of information to include in client records of these three documentation activities are presented here: (1) Box 4.5 provides an example of information to obtain in a client assessment; (2) Box 4.6 includes examples of information to

---

BOX 4.5

Information to Include in a Client Assessment

Demographic Data:
- Name
- Contact information
- Legal status
- All persons participating in assessment
- Presenting need
- Living situation (level of stability and safety)
- Social environment (level of activity, satisfaction, and relationships with others)
- Cultural environment (client satisfaction and view on helping-seeking, and cultural view of help-seeking)
- Religion/spirituality (statement of beliefs and levels of activity and satisfaction)
- Military experience (branch, time in service, discharge status, coping with experience, and view of experience)
- Childhood (supportive, strengths, and significant events, including trauma)
- Family (composition—parents, siblings, spouse/significant other(s), children, and others; level of support; and family history of mental illness)

- Sexual history (activity level, orientation, satisfaction, and concerns)
- Trauma history (physical, sexual, and/or emotional abuse or neglect and experience with perpetrator(s))
- Financial/employment circumstances (employment status, satisfaction, financial stability, areas of concern or change)
- Educational history (highest level achieved, performance, goals, and challenges)
- Legal needs (arrest/conviction history and current legal status)
- Substance use/abuse (history of addictive behaviors—alcohol, drugs, gambling, sexual, or other). Addiction screen (questions include: (1) Have you ever felt you should cut down on your drinking/drug use? (2) Have people annoyed you by criticizing your drinking/drug use? (3) Have you ever felt bad or guilty about your drinking/drug abuse? (4) Have you ever had a drink/used first thing in the morning or to steady your nerves or to get rid of a hangover (eye-opener))?

BOX 4.5
continued

History of Emotional/Behavioral Functioning:
For each of the following areas, gather information regarding: current status (current, previous, or denies history); description of behavior; onset and duration; and frequency

- Self-mutilation
- Hallucinations
- Delusions or paranoia
- Mood swings
- Recurrent or intrusive recollections of past events
- Lack of interest or pleasure
- Feelings of sadness, hopelessness, isolation or withdrawal
- Decreased concentration, energy, or motivation
- Anxiety
- Crying spells
- Appetite changes
- Sleep changes
- Inability to function at school or work
- Inability to control thoughts or behaviors (impulses)
- Irritability or agitation
- Reckless behavior, fighting, or fire setting
- Stealing, shoplifting, or lying
- Cruelty to animals
- Aggression

BOX 4.5
continued

Behavioral Health Treatment History:
- Date
- Program or facility
- Provider
- Response to treatment

Mental Status Exam:
- Attention (rate on scale of: good, fair, easily distracted, or highly distractible; and describe behavior)
- Affect (rate on scale of: appropriate, labile, expansive, constrictive, or blunted; and describe behavior)
- Mood (rate on scale of: normal, depressed, anxious, or euphoric; and describe behavior)
- Appearance (rate on scale of: well groomed, disheveled, bizarre, or inappropriate; and describe behavior)
- Motor activity (rate on scale of: calm, hyperactive, agitated, tremors, tics, or muscle spasms; and describe behavior)
- Thought process (rate on scale of: intact, circumstantial, tangential, flight of ideas, or loose associations; and describe behavior)
- Thought content (note: normal, grandiose, phobic, reality, organization, worthless, obsessive, compulsion, guilt, delusional, paranoid, ideas of reference, and hallucinations; and describe behavior)
- Memory (note: normal, recent (good or impaired), past (good or impaired); and describe behavior)
- Intellect (note: normal, above, below, or poor abstraction; and describe behavior)
- Orientation (note: person, place, situation, and time; and describe behavior)
- Judgment and Insight (rate on scale of: good, fair, or poor; and describe behavior)
- Current providers (including psychiatrist, primary care physician, therapist, caseworker, etc.)
- Community resources being used (including support groups, religious, spiritual, other)
- Client goal(s) for treatment
- Summary of social worker's observations and impressions

Adapted from St. Anthony's Medical Center, St. Louis, Missouri

Suicide Risk Assessment:

- Name, date, and time of assessment
- Clinical assessment (include current suicidal thoughts, obsessions with death or indications of putting one's affairs in order, even with no specific plan). If yes to any items, follow-up questions include: is there a plan, is the plan lethal, is there potential access to plan?
- Frequency of thoughts
- Intensity of thought (rate on scale of: (1) no pressure to (5) high pressure)
- Risk level (rate on scale of: negligible, mild, moderate, or severe)

Harm to Others Assessment:

- Name, date, and time of assessment
- Clinical assessment (current thoughts of harming another person). If yes, follow-up questions include: is there a plan, is there a target/victim, and is there potential access to plan?
- Frequency of thoughts
- Intensity of thought (rate on scale of: (1) no pressure to (5) high pressure; and describe plan and victim)
- Risk level (rate on scale of: negligible, mild, moderate, or severe)
- Notify physician
- Complete duty to warn protocol

Adapted from St. Anthony's Medical Center, St. Louis, Missouri

BOX 4.6

Information to Include in Assessment of Suicide Risk and Harm to Others

include in a suicide risk and harm to others assessment; and (3) Box 4.7 is an example of information to include in a treatment/intervention plan (adapted from St. Anthony's Medical Center, St. Louis, Missouri).

The Client Perspective

Just as agency issues can present challenges for the social worker, there are client situations that can prove to be difficult to address in the assessment phase of work. Client issues that require specialized practice skills can include working with client system situations that involve: involuntary, mandated, and nonvoluntary clients; violent situations, including suicidal clients; and the need for crisis intervention skills.

Involuntary, Mandated, and Nonvoluntary Clients   When you first considered social work practice, you may have assumed that people would come to you because

BOX 4.7

Information to Include in a Treatment/ Intervention Plan

Intervention/Treatment Plan:

- Preliminary assessment/diagnosis
- Preliminary plan for intervention/treatment (to be developed at first visit)
- Interventions for emergency/safety need
- Other interventions needed
- Needs (include date, identified need, status (active, inactive, deferred, or referred), and reason for deferral or referral)
- Strengths
- Facilitating factors for intervention/treatment
- Limitations
- Barriers to intervention/treatment
- Other care providers/referrals and purpose (including plan for service co-ordination)
- Plan for family involvement (note if client opts for no family involvement)
- Termination criteria/plan
- Planned frequency and duration of intervention/treatment

Adapted from St. Anthony's Medical Center, St. Louis, Missouri

they wanted your services and believed in the possibility, at least, that you would be helpful. The principles of self-determination and working toward the preferred reality seem counter to coercion, and some social workers question the appropriateness of this kind of practice. Yet, because of the constant tension between social work as an agent of social control and an agent of change, a significant proportion of clients (in some settings, *all clients*) are involuntary.

Involuntary has several different meanings. In some sense, all clients are involuntary in that few are happy to experience the issues that bring them to services. Certainly those people who seek public sector welfare services are likely to be involuntary in that way. Thus, the distinction between voluntary and involuntary is not always clear cut, but three ways of distinguishing this type of client are accepted in the profession.

Clients are considered to be **involuntary** if they have been compelled to receive services but do not seek them out, including mandated and nonvoluntary client systems (Barker, 2003). **Mandated clients** are typically required by an authority (e.g., legal system, employer, etc.) to receive services in order, for example, to reclaim children, escape criminal charges, or sometimes avoid institutionalization. Such mandates occur most often in the systems of care that are heavily shaped and sanctioned by the law in the first place, such as child protection, mental health, and criminal justice. **Nonvoluntary clients** are not formally or legally obliged to participate in services but are pressured into receiving them. For example, persons with substance abuse issues may be "strongly encouraged" by their employers to seek help, or a parent "takes" an adolescent to family counseling. In these situations the client is in some way persuaded that she or he needs to get services in order, for example, to keep the peace or remain married or stay employed.

There are many patterns of engagement within these scenarios, some of which are not predictable. For example, some angry mandated clients become convinced that they can benefit from genuine involvement, whereas others simply wait out their time. Nonvoluntary clients may simply go through the motions to satisfy someone else, or they may work for real change. The whole notion of involuntary clients presents several challenges as well as opportunities for workers.

Challenges in Working with Involuntary Clients   For many social workers, both students and more seasoned practitioners, the idea of working with a client who does not want to be there is uncomfortable, if not daunting. In some cases, the issues relate to the interface the social worker needs to maintain with the mandating agency, which may seem rigid or overly authoritarian. In others, workers might feel distaste for the behavioral conduct associated with the involuntary client (for example, relating to child abuse, criminal activity, or substance abuse). In still others, social workers are unsure how to build a relationship in such circumstances. These are understandable concerns, but they put many more limits on the situation than are necessary. Engagement issues in involuntary work can provide opportunities as well.

ENGAGEMENT WITH INVOLUNTARY CLIENTS   Being well prepared for your first visit with a client who is involuntary is the first step. First, prepare *yourself*. In general, you can expect that your client may be angry, hostile, or fearful. If you are assaulted by spiteful or even hateful remarks at the beginning of a meeting, you can feel surprised and hurt, so it is helpful to know how you may react and to think ahead about how to respond.

Involuntary clients often take on a perception that they need nothing you have to offer and they may have a valid reason for believing what they believe (DeJong & Berg, 2008). As a result, they do not truly engage with you. Although this seems challenging, it can actually assist you in refraining from taking any angry remarks personally, because the client is not engaged and makes few role demands on you. Another way to prepare for the resentment and negativity of some involuntary clients is to place yourself in their position. Remember the times you have felt coerced, invisible, unrecognized, or ignored. You can connect with some part of that scenario that can make you more empathic and help you to understand the client's disinclination to trust anyone, including you.

Not all clients, of course, will barge in with this level of antagonism. Some will be overly polite or seem controlled as if you will not be able to touch them in any way. Some may actually view meeting with you as an opportunity to think about making changes. Since the tendency may be to decide the client is resistant before you start the work, consider remaining as "unknowing" as you can. In any case, the most helpful approach is to listen, as it is in any client situation, to the story. Find out how the client sees the situation. Ask about how things could have been different, respect the client's reality without challenging it, and assume the client has both strengths and competence in spite of the current predicament. Find out what is important to the client and how she or he wants things to change. This is often an excellent situation for questions that probe for the client's perspective because they can reveal that there is more to the client than the involuntary situation and that she or he is not just "bad," or a personified crime—for example, "a B & E" (breaking and entering) or a "shoplifter." If the adolescent who is substance-using feels like a "loser" and worthless, you might ask, "What would your best friend say is your greatest strength?" or, "What would your favorite teacher say you're good at?" (DeJong & Berg, 2008). For more on useful approaches with involuntary clients, see Box 4.8.

In most cases of mandated services, you will have some externally structured pattern for your work. This can be a set number of sessions (such as 12) or a

---

BOX 4.8

Involuntary Clients

Guidelines for Interviewing Involuntary Clients

- Assume you will be interviewing someone who probably will start out not wanting anything you might have to offer.
- Assume the client has good reason to think and act as he or she does.
- Suspend your judgment and agree with the client's perceptions that stand behind his or her cautious, protective posture.
- Listen for who and what are important to the client, including when the client is angry and critical.
- When clients are openly angry or critical, ask what the offending person or agency could have done differently to be more useful to them.
- Be sure to ask for the client's perception of what is in his or her best interest; that is, ask for what the client might want.
- Listen for and reflect the client's use of language.
- Bring the client's context into the interview by asking relationship questions.
- Respectfully provide information about any nonnegotiable requirements and immediately ask for the client's perceptions regarding these.
- Always stay "not knowing" (i.e., social worker's focus is on the client's frame of reference, not her or his own).

Source: De Jong & Berg, 2008, p. 176

curriculum to follow. You may need to explain this to your client in order to encourage the engagement process. One of the major ways you can assist your client is to give her or him as much control as possible by emphasizing any choices that are real (for example, you may be able to meet once or twice a week, on Tuesdays or Fridays) and by being as clear as possible regarding requirements. If the court requires you to notify authorities if your client misses a single session, inform her or him of that. Consider that mandated clients typically feel as if control and choice have been taken away from them, and stay attuned to those issues. You will want to provide all the information you can about the contingencies as a respectful gesture of recognition.

LEGAL ISSUES   In spite of your best efforts to engage your client, mandated or not, you may find yourself having to take a position regarding the best interests of the client system, including children and older adults. This position can become difficult when you have been trying to respect the individual's situation and work with the goals and wishes expressed by the client. For example, do not decide prematurely that the single parent in a child protection scenario is not ready to have her children back or that your older adult client cannot live safely in the community. You want to keep working toward the goals of the client system to arrive at a point at which her or his preferred reality can be realized.

Nevertheless, there are times when you may have to take a conscience-driven stand that may seem to work against the client system. In such cases, inform the client(s) before any court hearing or other meeting. Avoid any surprises for your client that would further violate trust. For example, initiating an honest dialogue (e.g., "this is the way I see it") conveys respect even if the client does not agree with the assessment. Another way to help the client understand the perspective of others is to ask perspectival questions, such as "What do you think the judge might think about the times when you left the baby alone?" (DeJong & Berg, 2008).

Opportunities in Working with Involuntary Client Systems   Although involuntary situations challenge both the professional and the client and few social workers would say these are ideal scenarios, they are seldom disastrous. Such interactions can present the opportunity to engage people who might never undertake any change without being forced into seeking services. These challenges also present social workers with an opportunity to practice their most cherished social work skills. By hearing and respecting clients' perceptions, assuming they can grow, and believing that their situation is workable, you have an opportunity to engage them in ways that can potentially transform their lives.

INDIVIDUAL SCENARIOS   Consider the man who was adjudicated by the court as a perpetrator of domestic violence, but because he also had a substantial history as a client of mental health services and had just been discharged from a psychiatric hospital, you were asked by your supervisor to meet with him individually. This departure from the agency's standard intervention (which was group work for men) was made on the grounds that the client would not respond well in the potential confrontation of a group. He was painfully embarrassed at being singled out as inappropriate for a group process, angry that he was treated like a "common criminal," and exceedingly hostile about meeting with you.

Using a basic approach of respect, a willingness to hear him out, and a position of wanting to understand his life, you can connect with him after several sessions. He then confided that he had never had the opportunity to talk about the challenging issues in his family and that he felt humiliated and stigmatized in receiving mental health services. By the end of the twelve mandated sessions, he wanted to engage in further work, and he had come to believe that he could change his violent behaviors by responding differently to the stresses he felt. This is an example of the way people can respond to an affirming approach that recognizes their strengths even in light of the fact that the client was not being initially involved in the decision regarding the treatment approach which may have placed limits on his capacity to participate.

POWER ISSUES   There is a clear association with power, specifically coercive power, in any kind of involuntary and especially mandated service. Regardless of the relationship or work that transpires, you have considerable power in determining the course of the client's life. In these situations, you need to recognize the power you have, be as comfortable with it as possible, articulate your understanding of the power to your client system and elicit the client's understanding. Transparency about power creates a rich opportunity to demonstrate your genuineness and trustworthiness to clients, and enables the opportunity to discuss power and its meaning to your client. You are presented with an opportunity to struggle with the tension between your role as a person of social control and your role as a person who assists client system who are caught in social control.

Focusing on power provides a context for discussing with your clients her or his goals and strategies for accomplishing desired and realistic outcomes. For the client, the goal might be as simple as getting authorities "off my back," or it may involve much more complex efforts to change a system that she or he experiences as oppressive. For example, the woman trying to regain custody of her children who has to see you, get clean, get a job, and find a home with no instrumental supports might, for example, want to join with others in an empowerment-focused approach to influence the system in helping her meet her mandates.

Violence   None of us can remain oblivious to the increasing violence in our culture. Violence looms in almost every newspaper, television news story, and on all too many urban street corners and rural crossroads across the country and beyond. From the wars waged overseas to the high school horrors executed in quiet heartland towns, violence is expressed in ideological as well as interpersonal terms, and is a common theme everywhere. Social workers are frequently in the position of working with the effects of a violent culture and are not immune from direct exposure to violent threats in the workplace. The escalation of violence in our lives has become an insidious component of contemporary experience and should be addressed on personal, agency, and policy levels.

Safety in Social Work Practice   Although it can be comforting to think of violent acts, particularly those related to social work practice, as discrete, chance occurrences, there is often a difficult-to-deny connection between violence and many historical, political, and cultural processes that reflect a cycle of escalation. Violence in any setting breeds negative, destructive attitudes and relationships that are reinforced by periodic eruptions in social contexts, but social workers must be knowledgeable about and prepared for violence within any practice setting. School bullying, interracial taunting, and sexual harassment are just a few pervasive examples that are translated into interpersonal persecution that may occur in social work practice. Occasionally these situations escalate into physical violence on an interpersonal or social level, as witnessed by isolated attacks, school murders, or race-related altercations. Some people resort to violence to get their basic needs met, and our society struggles to eliminate the barriers that prevent people from doing so.

As evidenced by the NASW-issued policy statement calling for the development of organizational policies to address employee safety, the social work profession has shown commitment to minimizing violence in the workplace (NASW, 2009–2012b). Social workers can observe the growing disparities between rich and poor in the United States, consider the wider political components that seem to spur people to hate one another, and renew their efforts to work for a just society. Building on the profession's systemic perspective, social workers can address racist and economic policies of welfare reform that punish people of color and maintain poverty, and can analyze, for example, legal approaches to limiting weapons, their commitment to antiviolence principles, and their positions on war. All of these issues are at the heart of people's lives and as such are in the realm of social justice-oriented social work practice from the most local to the most global levels.

Considering that practitioners are very likely to work with persons who are the most affected by the quality of this cultural fabric, it is not surprising that, as symbols of the dominant culture and agents of social control, social workers are increasingly the objects of violence themselves (Jayartne, Croxton, & Mattison, 2004). As early as 1995, Newhill documented that "physical and emotional violence by clients toward social workers is increasing in all settings" (1995, p. 631). A recent survey of NASW members (Whitaker & Arrington, 2008) details specific areas of incidence and risk. Forty-two percent of social workers working in mental health services identify violence as a safety concern, while 43 percent of mental health social workers and 30 percent of social workers working in child welfare settings have actually experienced violence from adult clients in the workplace. Unfortunately, the trend toward violence against human service workers is not abating as workers report being subjected to physical assault, and "all workers were routinely subjected to psychological aggression" (Shields & Kiser, 2003, p. 13), such as outbursts of anger, profanity, or intimidation. As startling as these reports are, social workers can work together to ensure preparedness.

SKILLS FOR WORKING WITH CLIENTS WHO ARE ANGRY   As an individual social worker in a context of potential violence, you can take reasonable precautions based on common sense and effective communication. See Box 4.9 to consider these strategies. Possibly the single most useful tool for working with a client who is angry or hostile is empathy. Using your knowledge of basic social work engagement skills, you can also speak in a calm, quiet, and impartial manner while maintaining a physical and non-threatening distance (Burry, 2002). Empathic responses to clients demonstrate that you recognize they are upset, would like to understand the reasons for their distress, and want to assist them. In turn, such responses can defuse the anger of persons who are inclined to strike out at the world for causing them to suffer. In addition to this overall compassionate stance, you will want to observe the following:

- Recognize your own tension. Be alert for feelings of defensiveness, and prepare yourself to avoid returning angry or hostile comments.

- Acknowledge the client's strengths as you listen, and include them in your responses when they can be heard as genuine (rather than patronizing).

- Focus on positive and current alternatives that are realistic and open to the client.

- Avoid moralizing or lecturing, no matter how destructive you think the client's conduct has been.

- When necessary, focus on keeping your own control rather than on the client's anger.

WHAT AGENCIES CAN DO   In situations of potential violence, agencies need to assume some of the responsibility to avert danger. Employers can recognize and validate the hazards to which workers are exposed, so that they will report their experiences openly. Policies for handling incidents should be clear and worker focused. Opportunities for processing and group consultation should be frequent and responsive. Preparation for workers entering possibly dangerous situations and debriefing for those who have experienced aggressive or violent clients should be standard practice and should not require that the worker initiate a formal request. Larger agencies should consider establishing a management team to address violence specifically and should offer training on physical safety and verbal de-escalation procedures that meet worker needs and interests. The majority of social workers surveyed by NASW believe their employers appropriately respond to issues of safety in the workplace (Whitaker & Arrington, 2008). Feeling safe in one's place

BOX 4.9

Violence

What Social Workers Can Do in the Context of Violence

- Always inform your client of the time you expect to make a home visit. Keep to that schedule as closely as possible. This is not only respectful, but you are more likely to be safe if you don't surprise anyone with your appearance.

- Consult with others (especially a supervisor) before entering a situation you think may be dangerous. If your client has a history of violence and is highly stressed or is known to have firearms or other weapons, do not make a home visit or an office visit after hours without talking it over with others who may have more experience and can consult with you about your decision.

- When you leave the office to make home visits, always inform someone about your schedule. Check by phone in worrisome (or all) situations.

- Pay attention to your surroundings. If you are on a home visit and you hear fighting or crying from outside the residence, reassess the timing of your visit. If there is activity that seems suspicious and/or is not what you expected, avoid confrontation.

- Do not put yourself physically in a position to be trapped in a potentially violent client's home. Keep a clear path to the door, so you can leave quickly if necessary.

- Make connections with the local police if you work in a dangerous neighborhood, or with local shop owners or residents in rural areas. Alert them of your plans when circumstances warrant and to the extent that confidentiality permits. Know when police should accompany you, and do not hesitate to ask them when appropriate.

- Do not challenge an angry client with rebuttals or consequences. A calm, kind, and reflective presentation can encourage de-escalation.

- If you sense that something is wrong and you are at risk, even if you can't tell exactly what it is, leave. There is time for analysis later, and if you overreacted, you can explore that in a safe environment.

- Report incidents of any kind to your supervisor, or use an agency-designated process if there is one. This both helps you work through your own reactions and skills and facilitates the agency's effective response to its workers.

- Recognize your own tension. Be alert for feelings of defensiveness, and prepare yourself to avoid returning angry or hostile comments.

- Acknowledge the client's strengths as you listen, and include them in your responses when they can be heard as genuine (rather than patronizing).

- Focus on positive and current alternatives that are realistic and open to the client.

- Avoid moralizing or lecturing, no matter how destructive you think the client's conduct has been.

- When necessary, focus on keeping your own control rather than on the client's anger.

of work is just one aspect of the social worker as an effective practitioner. Read on about issues of self-care and ethical practice.

Crisis Intervention   Crises are an expected part of the social work professional's practice life; therefore all social workers must develop competencies for responding to the wide range of crises that will present themselves. Events occur in individuals' lives that bring them to social workers as mandated, involuntary, frightened, or hysterical clients. While a life crisis may be the trigger that brings the client system to the social worker, each crisis is uniquely experienced by the client system and should not be considered routine. Crises occur when an intense and stressful event creates disruption in one's life that cannot be resolved using one's usual coping mechanisms, the precipitating event is perceived as meaningful or threatening, or the individual experiences fear, tension, confusion, and/or subjective discomfort following a period of disequilibrium (Roberts, 2008; 2005, p. 13).

Regardless of the origins of the crisis (i.e., forces over which the client has no control or the result of a poor life choice by the client), the trauma felt by the client can be real and devastating. The social worker's ability to quickly and accurately conduct an assessment can support and empower the client in her/his response to the crisis situation. Crisis situations provide the opportunity for the client system (and the social worker) to grow and change, but it is incumbent on the social worker to have a repertoire of practice behaviors that can help the client view what is likely perceived to be a painful experience as the opportunity to strengthen her/his coping skills and possibly even quality of life.

Social workers can benefit from having a theoretically and evidence-based model for responding to crises. Two models that lend themselves particularly well to assessing and intervening in crisis situations are Roberts' seven-stage model of crisis and solution-focused approach (Roberts, 2005; 2008). Roberts' (2005; 2008) model emphasizes the importance of assessment in the ability to facilitate an effective intervention plan. Specifically, initiating a rapid and timely response to the client's crisis is a critical first step in working with the client's situation. In reviewing the seven stages of crisis intervention presented here, note the prominent role that assessment plays in the professional's response both in the initial steps and throughout the intervention (Eaton & Roberts, 2009, pp. 210–212):

1.   Plan and conduct a crisis assessment including lethality, dangerousness to self or others, and immediate psychosocial needs.

2.   Rapidly establish rapport and the therapeutic relationship.

3.   Identify the issues pertinent to the client and any precipitants to the client's crisis contact.

4.   Deal with feelings and emotions by effectively using active listening skills.

5.   Generate and explore alternatives by identifying the strengths of the client as well as previous successful coping mechanisms.

6.   Implement the action plan.

7.   Establish a follow-up plan and agreement.

Through its emphasis on strengths, solutions, the present and future (versus the past), and short-term intervention, the solution-focused approach is applicable to crisis intervention. Blending well with Roberts' model described here, a solution-based assessment and intervention hones in on the assumption that crisis provides the opportunity for clients to embark on changes; in particular, changes they may have been reluctant or unable to make previously (Roberts, 2005).

Suicide   Whether it is the client who is threatening or has attempted to intentionally take her/his life, the family coping with the suicidal death of a loved one, or the client experiencing depression who you fear is at risk for suicide, the social worker is faced with a situation of an individual or a group in crisis. Just as with the other forms of client crises, social workers are ethically bound to identify and assess clients who may be at risk for suicide and take appropriate actions to prevent suicidal attempts.

As with the previous discussion regarding crisis intervention, the key to effectiveness is rapid and timely assessment. An important first step in preventing a suicide attempt or completion is a suicide risk assessment (Freedenthal, 2008). A suicide risk assessment includes questions focused on any thoughts the client may be having about death and suicide. The social worker then inquires if the client has developed a plan, a time frame, and a means for carrying out the suicide. The social worker must then assess the lethality of the client's plan. For example, does the client have access to the means of suicide that she/he has stated will be used, is the plan well formulated, or does the client talk about giving away her/his possessions? These indicators can be evidence that the client is serious about ending her or his life. Also of importance is the client or family history with suicide attempts.

Of critical importance for the social worker is knowledge of agency and legal procedures for immediately and appropriately responding to suicidal ideations, threats, or attempts. Mobilizing an emergency response to bring the client to safety is imperative. Responses may include negotiating a contract in which the client agrees not to attempt suicide, involving members of the client's support network or community, facilitating the prescription of antidepressant medication, and/or seeking hospitalization for the client. Regardless of your response, a thorough and immediate assessment is critically important for your client.

An ethical issue that may arise is the ethical commitment the social work professional makes to honor the client system's right to self-determination as the highest priority in most situations. However, while advocating for the client's ability to determine her or his own actions is a social work value, preserving life takes priority in the case of threatened or attempted suicide (Freedenthal, 2008). In the practice context, this means that the social worker intervenes to prevent any threat of suicide by contacting authorities or negotiating a no-suicide contract.

The Social Worker Perspective: The Social Worker as a Whole Person

Just as it is necessary to be attuned to safety issues, social workers must be sensitized to their own physical and emotional health. As you have seen, several areas of challenge in social work practice might lead to increasing discouragement and ultimately to the emotional and physical exhaustion associated with burnout (Nissly, Barak, & Levin, 2005). Working with client systems who experience oppression and trying to help with inadequate resources, engaging involuntary clients who may challenge your capacities, confronting a violent culture and avoiding its direct expression against you, coping with the bureaucratic tensions of managed care—all of these may seem to confound and certainly challenge your best intentions in the practice of social work. Social workers report that the lack of time to complete job tasks is the major stressor, followed by heavy workloads and working with difficult and challenging client situations (Arrington, 2008). When added to the pressure that can be induced by organizational policies and practices (discussed in Chapters 10 and 11), social workers can experience frustration and alienation day after day if effective self-care strategies are not developed.

Therefore, it is important to address two phenomena that are difficult to manage: the incidence of painful events and the occurrence of personal triggers. Social workers need self-care strategies for dealing with the stresses that lead to **secondary trauma**, **burnout**, and **compassion fatigue**. Secondary trauma can occur when helping professions react to pain experienced by client systems, while burnout is a stressful response to the work. When both secondary trauma and burnout occur, the social worker may be experiencing compassion fatigue (Wharton, 2008).

Painful Events   Although most of social work practice deals with struggles experienced by client systems, and does so as a routine dimension of the territory, many (probably most) practitioners at one time or another experience a particularly jolting event that shakes their confidence and makes them question their capacity or commitment. This event often takes on the character of crisis—for example, a client suicide, a murder, an unspeakable case of child abuse, or an annihilating fire, to name a few. Such events can be experienced as trauma that splits the worker's world wide open, taking a generally well-balanced human being off guard. As these occurrences reflect a departure from the social worker's usual ability to cope, she or he may be reluctant to recognize or acknowledge an unusual reaction. Ignoring the signs can be dangerous for the social worker's own stability and ability to bounce back. Social workers need to allow themselves to be human in this profession, and the experience of overload, contrary to negative connotations, can reflect the traits of a caring, human person.

When isolated situations such as these occur, the social worker should seek and receive as much support as possible. Time away from work, debriefing sessions, or a shift in responsibility may be indicated. The social worker's response should be normalized (i.e., assurance given that her or his response is appropriate to the situation). With appropriate supports and adequate time, most workers will work through such situations and return to their practice as committed as they were before.

Personal Triggers   In a related but distinctive scenario, the social worker may have some unresolved or not-quite-resolved personal issues that affect her or his capacity to carry out the work of the agency. For example, a worker who experienced an abusive father in childhood may harbor a great deal of rage. While anger may be understandable and normal, it can be a serious problem if, for example, the worker verbally or physically attacks a client who may be suspected of child abuse. In such cases the agency response is likely to be different from that for a painful event. The event is more likely to become a supervisory issue that is addressed administratively or with corrective action. Here, the social worker can engage in a process (i.e., therapy or education) to effectively change her or his behavior. An extreme reaction can be a difficult experience for someone who is committed to the profession and has the capacity to make a solid contribution. The intensity of the trigger situation can lead a worker to assess herself or himself as inadequate and not suited to the profession.

As all helping professionals likely have areas that can be triggered, this phenomenon can be normalized to the extent possible. The social worker's behavior is not acceptable and will need to change. While no professional can claim perfect balance, social workers are obligated to identify and respond to those triggers that may impact personal and professional well-being.

Self-Care   In carrying out the work of the profession, social workers need to learn to care for themselves, even as they care for clients. As in the case of safety, the profession, through a policy statement, has deemed self-care a priority for all social workers from students to individuals to administrators (NASW, 2009–2012b). Although this process will take on different dimensions in different people, strategies that may prove useful include:

- *Learn to use yourself as a resource:* Knowing your own responses, biases, and limits in various processes of your work is a first step in self-care. Self-awareness is critical not only in ethical, culturally sensitive practice but also in taking care of yourself. Appreciating your strengths and accepting your vulnerabilities will help you make good practice connections with clients as well as avoid expecting too much of yourself, which frequently leads to feeling disheartened. In the face of extensive client need, you may expect to save the world and inspire clients to love you while you do it. When you know that about yourself, you can laugh at your own grandiosity, let go of the need for all clients to like you, and continue to strive for competent practice.

- *Understand shared power:* Within a model of planned change that includes engagement, assessment, intervention, and termination/evaluation, the use of the strengths perspective assumes that clients have the ability to control their lives and do not need you to do it for them. Such an approach carries an unexpected benefit of reducing the pressure to be all-knowing and all-delivering, a stance that can be burdensome to clients and professionals as well as harmful to clients. In essence, you do not have to assume responsibility for clients' behaviors; you cannot be responsible for any behavior other than your own.

- *Focus on practical goals:* Related to the impulse to rid the world of all evil, you will always be disappointed and will continue to fail. When you concentrate on the strengths clients have to achieve their own goals and when you stress social justice and human rights in ways the client can relate to, you are more likely to see joint successes more frequently. This in turn will bolster your commitment.

- *Find your own systems for support:* Social workers understand the importance of support for clients but may forget its value to themselves. Support, in and outside of the workplace, is critical for the connectedness discussed throughout this book. Developing a group of peers at work can be helpful and enjoyable. Such a collective can function as a peer supervisory/support network or a strictly social group. Friends outside of work and family are also critical. Spiritual support in the way of religious affiliation or a more informal connection with the dimensions that seem most important in life can help put the occasional but inevitable disappointments and frustrations of the work into a perspective that helps keep you from feeling overwhelmed.

- *Live healthy:* Social work jobs are demanding physically and emotionally. Ensuring that you are caring for your physical health through exercise, adequate sleep, and balanced nutrition is critically important as well (Wharton, 2008).

Although social work will never be an easy job, it need not be overwhelming. Recalling the joys and connections of working with people can fill out the compensation side of the balance sheet. Taking control of your own reactions and caring for yourself will enhance your capacities to stay committed.

Just as social workers emphasize the whole client person in context, they need to think of themselves as whole people, too. This means that they are not just workers. Like clients, they are children, partners, bicycle racers, amateur politicians, musicians, parents, belly dancers, and artists. They are good in some roles and need work in others. They may connect well with involuntary clients and yet steer away from children or older adults. They may be stimulated by institutional settings or find them hopelessly oppressive. They may need to work on how to change urban agency policies effectively or thrive in rural locations where the sole agency has no walls and policy is an on-the-go venture.

Workers may also be subject to restrictions related to social justice themselves. Their human rights may be violated daily, and it is likely that they—although inadvertently—violate those of others daily. Their identities are privileged in some contexts and devalued in others. When you see yourself as a whole human, belonging in a context, you will be more likely to engage in your human work with enthusiasm and vigor.

Sustaining Ethical Practice in the Face of Challenges   Social workers are bound by the *Code of Ethics* (NASW, 2008) to care for oneself and practice ethically in spite of setbacks and situations that do not go as planned; to keep growing in response to new ideas, perceptions, and client-informed experience; and to keep a vision of what ethical social work practice can be and how you can contribute. The ethical aspects of practice can become obscured by the struggles workers experience. Just as practitioners need to guard against rationalizing funding cuts or avoiding client contact, they need to keep the ethical considerations of omission as much in mind as those of commission. For example, not working for active reform of harmful systems (omission) is as neglectful as committing an outright violation of the *Code of Ethics*. If workers increasingly withdraw, defending themselves against the challenges of dehumanizing contexts, they can slowly lose the spirit of ethical practice without even realizing it.

One of the most effective ways to negotiate troubling practice contexts is to engage fully in a positive, supportive supervisory relationship (Smith, 2005), in which both the supervisor and the social worker can grow. As the social worker, you can contribute to that relationship by bringing something to the process; supervision is not a commodity that is given to you (or done to you), but rather it is an interactive relationship. The term *supervision* conjures up images of a hierarchy. Literally interpreted as "watching from above," it suggests an authoritarian relationship in which one member judges and corrects the other. Fortunately, social work supervision is not limited to that configuration, in spite of the inevitable evaluative nature of the term.

Supervision, then, in all its forms—individual, group, ad hoc, formal case, and peer—has the potential to contribute a great deal to sustaining ethical practice in challenging contexts. Hearing others' beliefs about the issues involved in a challenging practice situation, for example, can expand your thinking and help you work through the places in which you are immobilized or perplexed. Such a dialogic process encompasses a genuine interchange regarding the values and ethics of a case situation. Effective, collaborative supervision can provide technical support, in that it has the potential to increase and improve your practice responses; and emotional support, in that it reduces isolation and increases hopefulness. See Box 4.10 for tips on effectively engaging in supervision.

CONCLUSION

In an effort to help you experience the contemporary climate, this chapter has addressed a range of practice behaviors related to assessment (including the very idea of assessment) along with a variety of difficult and challenging issues that exist in social work practice today. Clearly, the process of assessment involves a major combination of efforts and tools. While there are literally hundreds of instruments that social workers can use depending on the practice setting, type of client served, and the range of issues, your agency will use a few selected instruments that are consistent with the mission and focus of the agency's services.

Assessment is viewed as an integrated activity that arises out of an effective engagement with the client system and progresses into the action-oriented phase of the work. The tone and focus should be consistent with the practice process as a whole. Finally, assessment continues throughout the practice process, sometimes

BOX 4.10 *Tips for Using Supervision Effectively*	• Be prepared for each session by reviewing your work and identifying the issues you want to discuss. • Demonstrate a genuine eagerness about learning more and expanding your knowledge and experience base in practice. • Take responsibility for your work, your thinking, and your reactions. • Trust in so far as possible in the supervisory relationship so that you do not need to cover mistakes or deny any struggles you have with the work. • Assume a willingness to take thoughtful risks. • Understand the parameters of your work and the expectations your agency/supervisor has of you. • Respect the difference between the focus of supervision (how an issue affects your work) and the focus of psychotherapy (how an issue affects your emotional life). • Remain open and non-defensive if/when your supervisor suggests you do things differently. • Demonstrate a respectful and professional approach to relationships with all colleagues, including your supervisor.

shifting the work slightly and sometimes significantly. It is a fluid activity that fits into an ever-evolving integrated whole.

MAIN POINTS

- Assessment involves dialogue to discover the goals and aspirations of the client system.

- The theoretical perspective used by the social worker has significant implications for the assessment and the intervention. Five theories discussed in this chapter are psychoanalytic, attachment, cognitive, strengths-based perspective, and narrative.

- The social worker develops a shared vision with the client system by respecting the client's preferred reality and responding honestly to it.

- Mapping is a useful addition to verbal assessment. Two types of maps that are widely used within the profession are genograms and ecomaps.

- Assessment evaluates the types of resources, both formal and informal, that the client and the client's environment can bring to bear.

- When resources are not present or adequate or available to client systems, workers need to respond appropriately, possibly with social action.

- Assessment and planning move from a shared vision to specific details regarding the intervention. Internalized oppression and the emotional impact of change can influence the entire assessment process and the client's capacity for participation in planning.

- Social workers are ethically bound to be clear and honest with clients about specific agency constraints and requirements that will influence the client's experience of the work.

- The phenomenon of involuntary/mandated/nonvoluntary clients creates challenges for social workers that can be met effectively if framed adequately and met with a basic approach of respect and willingness to listen to the client.

- Violence is a pervasive quality in U.S. culture and influences both the work of the social work practitioner and the potential for her or his personal safety. Workers can engage in social justice-oriented practice to try and minimize societal violence, and they and their agencies can develop skills and policies to deal with situations of potential violence associated with clients.

- Secondary trauma, burnout, and compassion fatigue reflect physical and emotional exhaustion in a complex practice context; it may arise out of painful events and personal triggers and can be mitigated through appropriate agency and social worker response.

- Several aspects of holistic self-care can carry you through difficult moments and are consistent with ethical practice. As in your work with clients, think of yourself as a whole person, with strengths and vulnerabilities and a need for your own systems of support.

- Effective supervision is a useful interactive relationship for negotiating difficult practice contexts.

EXERCISES

1. Go to www.routledgesw.com/cases and review the case file for Emilia Sanchez, including the genogram and ecomap of the family for both its content and form. Click on the Assess tab and view the tasks you will need to complete. To prepare for this exercise, also review "Focus on Strengths" in the Values Inventory.

   Using Emilia as the anchor family member, develop two genograms. The first should reflect her relationships prior to age 14 and the second should be an "update" to her current age of 24. Include as much information as possible while ensuring that the drawing is informative and clear. After completing the first genogram and before completing the second, develop an ecomap that represents your interpretation of the systems and networks supporting Emilia's "change" (her involvement in drugs) that might have led to her estrangement from her family.

   In class, partner with another student and exchange the three drawings. Are they similar? In what respects do they differ? What information is particularly helpful? What facets of Emilia's life are the most effectively represented in a social mapping format? Which ones are the most challenging?

2. Go to www.routledgesw.com/cases and review Emilia's video vignette. After viewing the vignette, complete the following exercise.

   Emilia Sanchez has come to you for help because she has decided she must conquer her substance addiction. Emilia's long history of substance abuse, her family's outrage regarding the out-of-wedlock birth of her son Joey, and the following abortion of another child resulted in her feeling discouraged. Specifically, she is doubtful about her ability to make a place for herself in the family again and to make the changes she wants to make. Using the strengths perspective the social worker can identify and assess Emilia's strengths. Respond to the following:

   a. What was the most challenging aspect of identifying the strengths of someone who has had the number of challenges experienced by Emilia?

    b. How do you as the social worker encourage Emilia to recognize her strengths?

    c. Identify the strengths pointed out by the social worker in the vignette.

3. Go to www.routledgesw.com/cases and review the case of Carla Washburn. Click on Phase 2: Assess the Client System. Review the goals for this phase and complete Tasks 1, 2, and 3.

4. To begin the process of developing engagement and assessment practice behaviors, complete the following role-playing exercise. Begin by partnering with two other students.

    Using Confrontation: Engage in brief re-enactments of the following scenarios with each student assuming the role of the social worker, the client, or the observer. Utilize the engagement and assessment practice behaviors highlighted in this chapter to role-play the beginning phases of work with clients in these situations. Upon completion of the role-play, each member of the triad will provide balanced feedback regarding the others' performance of skills. Select from the following list of potential client scenarios:

    a. Client sporadically attends scheduled sessions.

    b. Client reports that when she was angry with her 10-year-old son at the mall she spanked him in public.

    c. Client is having difficulty obtaining employment. You recognize that the client's style of dress and hygiene may be a concern for employers.

    d. Client continues to use language that you find offensive.

    e. Your colleague is not completing tasks and you are experiencing negative consequences.

5. Review and discuss with other students the following situations. Evaluate your level of comfort in them. What makes you comfortable or uncomfortable? Be specific. Upon completion of the discussion, brainstorm with other students strategies for maintaining your safety.

    a. Conducting a home visit

    b. Working after dark at your agency

    c. Driving a client to an appointment

    d. Working with young males (if you are female) or females (if you are male)

    e. Working with individuals with mental illness

    f. Working with individuals with substance abuse issues

    g. Having an initial meeting with a client who is unknown to you

    h. Working with a client with a criminal record

6. In writing, reflect on situations in which you have been involved that resulted in a confrontation between you and another person. If you cannot recall such a situation, remember a situation in which confrontation may have been appropriate, but did not occur. Imagine in that situation that you were confronted by a caring individual in your life. What was your reaction to being confronted? How did you receive feedback? How do you give feedback? What is your level of comfort ability with confronting others? What were the benefits to being confronted?

CHAPTER 5

Intervening in Context: Initiation, Intervention, Termination, and Evaluation

Where after all, do human rights begin? In small places, close to home—so close and so small that they cannot be seen on any map of the world. Yet, they're the world of individual persons: the neighborhood he lives in; the school or college he attends; the factory, farm, or office where he works.

Eleanor Roosevelt (1958)

Key Questions for Chapter 5

(1) How can I prepare for intervening with individual client systems? (EPAS 2.1.10(c))

(2) How can I utilize the strengths-based perspective to guide the development of intervention, termination, and evaluation strategies with individuals?

(3) What are the social work roles that enable me to effectively intervene, terminate, and evaluate with individuals? (EPAS 2.1.10(c))

(4) How do I determine the appropriate evaluation tool(s) for use with interventions with individual client systems? (EPAS 2.1.10(d))

THE EMPHASIS IN THIS BOOK IS ON THE CONTEXT OF the social work intervention as it shapes the meaning of experience for clients and for social workers. In this chapter, the concept of "context" is integrated into all aspects of practice. Context both shapes what you do and likewise is shaped by what you do. Whether you are working with a person recently diagnosed with a chronic illness, an adult child who is experiencing stress from caring for an aging parent, or an immigrant who is seeking U.S. citizenship, you interact with the choices and capacities of individuals, the systems in which people are embedded, and the accessibility of existing and potential resources. All of these dimensions contribute to the totality of the social work practice context.

Accordingly, there are multiple ways to intervene in any issue or problematic situation. Viewed through a critical constructionist lens (i.e., knowledge is not transmitted, but created, acquired, processed, and relative) (Barker, 2003, p. 93), a useful, direct intervention for one person will not necessarily meet the needs of another person in a similar situation. For example, a single woman with a six-month-old baby may identify job training and finding suitable child care as the goal of the intervention. In contrast, another woman in seemingly the same circumstances may need assistance with locating housing, handling roller-coaster emotions, and keeping a safe environment for her infant. Yet another single mother will need intensive advocacy efforts in order to deal with discriminatory practices in her employment. Social workers must expect differences and advocate against the one-size-fits-all interventions that are sometimes considered optimal by social service organizations and/or public policy.

In recognition of individuals' unique circumstances, you will locate the starting point of your work on the most pressing issue, as defined by each client system. This decision should reflect the priorities for action that are agreed upon in the assessment and planning phase. Each client is the chief negotiator of her or his journey, therefore the work will first assume and then reflect the strengths and capacities to be successful in that journey. From this starting point, the chapter examines the generalist practice competencies and practice behaviors of supporting client strengths within client environments. A variety of social work roles and methods that support client–worker relationships will be explored, including strengths, narrative, and solution-focused approaches. A case example illustrates a unifying theoretical perspective that bridges the work with clients' strengths and environments from the perspectives of social justice, human rights, strengths, and critical social construction. As do social work interventions, this chapter will end with a discussion of termination and evaluation of the planned change intervention, focusing specifically on strengths-based strategies for empowering the client system to maintain the change that has been achieved.

SUPPORTING CLIENTS' STRENGTHS IN DEVELOPING INTERVENTIONS

Through its theoretical lens, the strengths perspective offers a focused, committed effort for identifying, expanding, and sustaining the resilience and assets that client systems bring to their interface with the world. Using a strengths-based method suggests that the worker will not only seek out and identify client strengths in the assessment (see Chapter 4) but will also support and maximize them throughout the working relationship. For many practitioners this effort will be the major focus of the work. The strengths-based approach views supporting clients as central to the worker's action. Social workers may need to remind themselves of the client's strengths and centrality as our culture, even for the most strengths-oriented practitioners, focuses on "what needs fixing." Strengths, like all human dimensions, need recognition, validation, and nourishment to remain vital. The following discussion will highlight intervention from the perspectives of strengths, narrative, and solution-focused approaches.

Strengths-Based Perspectives and Intervention

Consider two principles of the strengths-based approach as they apply to the practice context and the action of intervention. Saleebey (2009, pp. 104–105) identifies these as follows:

- *The social worker acts in context:* Through listening for the strengths as the client shares her or his concerns, the client's competencies become apparent. These competencies can then become the focus of the assessment and intervention process and they frame the goals to be achieved in the intervention. This "project" results from the social worker and the client system collaborating to identify the strengths and plan of action.

- *The social worker can work with the client system to move toward normalizing and capitalizing on one's strengths:* The product of a strengths-based assessment is the intervention in which the articulated strengths and resources are brought together, normalized, and shared with others.

Acting in Context The social worker's activity centers on helping the client system use the strengths she or he is beginning to recognize, as well as those already discovered, and to link them with her or his goals and dreams. That kind of effort might lead, for example, to social worker support for more independence or more assertiveness than a client has previously been comfortable in demonstrating.

Consider the situation of the client who has experienced trouble interacting with her landlords and now feels that she cannot negotiate a lease arrangement. The social worker can help her consider the advantages of establishing a positive rental history as they work together to identify appropriate options. The social worker can also encourage her to recognize her capacity to understand the business-focused details of renting and to negotiate for certain options. This endeavor involves some risk-taking to stretch beyond her usual comfort zone to initiate change, but the action also offers an unusual opportunity to decide and act on her own. When the venture is successful—for example, the client negotiates a lease and bargains for a rental rebate in exchange for her painting the living room walls—the client experiences the benefit of adding another competency to her growing list.

Conversely, when the effort does not go as planned, she becomes more aware of the specific areas in which she wants to direct her energies to make changes.

Capitalizing on Strengths   To focus on strengths is the consolidation step in which the social worker and client together recognize the successes they have had in establishing and stabilizing the client's competencies. Keeping with the same example, assume that the client found an apartment she likes at a rate she can afford. The social worker would then affirm the skills she demonstrated, encourage her to generalize those particular skills into other arenas, and support her ability to generate new skills. The social worker can also help the client recognize that she is building useful relationships in the community. For example, when she has established a record of reliability in paying her rent on time and maintaining her apartment, her landlord is likely to become a resource if she needs a reference for a job or wants to find a larger apartment across town. The social worker's effort at education, advocacy, and support for the client's capacity to develop a network that links her accomplishments to her goals is critical for the consolidation of her growth. By normalizing the task, in this case, of securing housing, the social worker not only demonstrates the client's capacities, but also reinforces the availability of community resources, and establishes that disengagement, or ending the work, is appropriate. The ultimate normalization is the client's continued development and the recognition that she or he can successfully manage the everyday tasks of living.

Narrative Intervention

Building on the deconstruction of client perceptions that occurred in the assessment process, a narrative-oriented intervention remains focused on the client, her or his strengths, and the meaning that is assigned to current and future realities. Questions posed by the social worker to the client play a central role in the development and implementation of a narrative-based intervention. As opposed to eliciting information and interpretation, intervention stage questioning is aimed at helping the client to move toward implementing changes in order to reach the previously stated goal. Return to Chapter 4 for a review of narrative-focused questioning strategies.

Once the original concern or issue is deconstructed and a plan is conceived, the social worker continues to utilize strategies (i.e., questions) intended to externalize the client from *being* the problem to having a relationship *with* the problem (Nichols, 2009). As the intervention is underway, the social worker continues to help the client view herself or himself from a position of strength and working toward the re-authoring of the original issue that was presented. Upon achieving success, the client can be invited to work on celebrating and sharing her or his new perceptions by inviting persons who are important to her or him (from the past or present) to hear about the changes. As with many interventions, the path from beginning to end may not be linear. The client-centered nature of a narrative approach may require both the client and the social worker to return periodically to the early discussions of the problem and reconstruct them in light of new insights that unfold throughout the intervention.

Solution-Focused Intervention

Utilizing a solution-focused approach to the social work intervention provides the client and the social worker with a clear-cut strategy for arriving at the client's goals in a relatively brief, time-limited manner. As you recall from the discussion in Chapter 4 on solution-focused assessment and planning, the client engages in a self-evaluative process (evaluative questions) to learn how she or he views the situation that is being addressed. The client has also envisioned times when the problem did not (exception questions) and will not (miracle questions) exist, thus lending insight into possible strategies for resolving the problem utilizing the client's existing and created strengths and resources. In the intervention phase of change, these questions continue to be important as reminders of the goal and connections to the client's past and future life.

Also used in the assessment and planning phases, scaling questions continue to be a critical aspect of the solution-focused intervention. Prompting the client to regularly assign a numeric value to a particular issue, experience, or behavior can empower her or him to continue to engage in self-evaluation and mutual feedback with you (Lee, 2009). While this practice strategy is evaluative in terms of progress (or lack of), it can also serve to motivate the client and inspire confidence that change can, in fact, be a reality. Being able to acknowledge small, concrete gains can be a powerful motivator for continued work (for both client and social worker).

Due to the emphasis on concrete solutions, the solution-focused intervention can be impactful for the client. As a social worker utilizing this approach, as the sole approach or in concert with another intervention model (as discussed in Chapter 4), your attention will be directed toward maintaining the client's motivation and focus on solutions and change along with reinforcing your respect and confidence in the client's capacity for reaching the desired outcome (Lee, 2009).

Strengths-Oriented Practice Skills and Behaviors

When used effectively, many classic social work practice skills and behaviors can affirm client strengths and support their underlying position in the work. For example, the familiar "reflection of empathy" has remained a time-honored practice behavior because it mirrors the respect and regard for human beings that is inherent in social work. The practice skills and behaviors discussed in the following sections have also earned their place in social work practice history as consistent with the profession's commitments to social justice and respect and dignity for the client system.

Supporting Diversity   As discussed in Chapter 3, a client's cultural background is viewed as a potential source of strength rather than an obstacle or deficit. An appropriate practice behavior is thus to use the traditions or aspects of your client's culture that nourish and give meaning to life. For example, many cultures demonstrate far greater respect for authority or the wisdom of age than U.S. culture has traditionally done. When you work with clients from such a culture, learning the practice behaviors that will support those values is critical as they are assets and can be incorporated as such into the intervention phase of your work. Although you should always confer with your clients regarding your actions, remain especially sensitized to the "fit" of your approach with your client's culturally influenced sense of propriety. Would it be appropriate, for instance, to encourage the client from such a culture to participate in a rent strike aimed at a prominent elder statesman who owns the property, if such an action would likely become highly adversarial?

SUPPORTING CLIENTS' ENVIRONMENTS

Having confirmed the importance of recognizing and supporting client strengths and cultural influences in the intervention process, we will focus now on identifying and intensifying the strengths of the environments in which clients live. This dual emphasis on person and environment is consistent with the traditions of the social work profession. Accordingly, social workers often direct their efforts toward making the environments in which their clients live more responsive to client needs. This approach looks to the institutions and policies outside of the client rather than viewing the client's difficulties as a symptom of inner pathology. In maintaining this focus on improving environmental response, the work reflects an underlying commitment to a social justice framework. In the process, clients are assumed to possess the capacity both to identify their difficulties and to participate in the work necessary to alleviate them.

Principles for Taking Environments into Account

In a classic application of a systemic intervention that embraces the environment in which the client system lives, Wood and Tully (2006) identify six major principles. Consistent with the basic tenets of the social work profession, these principles strongly emphasize a social justice orientation. The principles are reviewed in detail.

The Social Worker Should Be Accountable to the Client System   In being accountable to the client system, the social worker responds to the client's perception of the problem or situation. If, for example, an individual client is experiencing substantial difficulty in accessing certain public assistance benefits because he does not speak English fluently, the social worker will direct energies to addressing that need. Strategies may include arranging for an interpreter, requesting an agency worker who is fluent in the client's native language, or simply accompanying the client to advocate for appropriate and equitable treatment.

The Social Worker Should Follow the Demands of the Client Task Creating a "Frame of Reference" is a strategy for conceptualizing the demands of the client task (Wood & Tully, 2006). The Frame of Reference can be illustrated through a quadrant diagram covering the parameters of the social worker's tasks (see Exhibit 5.1). This scheme suggests that practitioners may (A) work with client systems on their own behalf, (B) work with client systems on behalf of themselves and others like them, (C) work with others (nonclients) on behalf of client systems, and (D) work with others (nonclients) on behalf of categories of persons at risk. The principle of following the demands of the client stresses that the social worker will look beyond the individual client in order to see if there are others in the same situation. If so, the worker needs to adapt by moving from one quadrant to another or functioning in multiple quadrants.

To learn how the Frame of Reference works, consider the case of a social work practitioner who is working with the mother of a child with disabilities who has no viable transportation to school. The social worker, with the mother's agreement, can locate a driver, or a person to accompany the child on the regular school bus, or request extended school hours so that the mother can pick up the child after work (working with a client on behalf of the client, Quadrant A). However, if the social worker discovers that there are four other children with disabilities in the school who lack adequate transportation, she or he, still working with the mother, might organize and coordinate a team of drivers for all five children in the school (working with the client on behalf of the client and others like her, Quadrant B). If the social worker's efforts were directed at enlisting the aid of a community group to help locate and fund a small van that could hold six children, the work would fall in a different quadrant (working with others out of concern for specific clients, Quadrant

EXHIBIT 5.1	INTENDED BENEFICIARY		
Frame of Reference for Structural Approach to Social Work Tasks	FOCUS OF INTERVENTION	SINGLE	MULTIPLE
	Clients	Work with clients on their own behalf **Quadrant A**	Work with clients on behalf of themselves and others like them **Quadrant B**
	Others	Work with others (nonclients) on behalf of clients **Quadrant C**	Work with others, such as (nonclients), on behalf of a category of persons at risk **Quadrant D**

Adapted from Wood & Tully, 2006

C). Finally, if the worker proposes statewide transportation funding to the legislature on behalf of a category of clients—in this case, children with disabilities—the work falls into Quadrant D, working with others on behalf of a category of clients. Although the worker's efforts may vary, move from one quadrant to another, and operate simultaneously, the work is always performed on the behalf of clients.

The Social Worker Should Maximize the Potential Supports in the Client System's Environment This generic principle requires the social worker to identify, access, and, where necessary, modify or even create the supports that a client system needs. These supports might include such resources as temporary housing for a family who is homeless, hospice services for a family dealing with an older member's imminent death, and child care services for a young mother who is employed outside her home. Chapter 3 discussed this aspect of resource development; it remains a central focus for this work phase as well.

The Social Worker Should Proceed from the Assumption of "Least Contest" This tenet holds that the social worker should use the minimal amount of pressure that is required to meet a client's need. For example, a social worker can explore the availability of affordable child care for a client before pressuring the mayor to initiate a city-sponsored child care system. If these early attempts fail, and there is no adequate, affordable child care, the social worker can "up the ante" and begin to mobilize an effort to facilitate change at the community level.

In a different situation, the "least contest" approach might encourage the social work practitioner to contact another service before engaging in advocacy. For example, a practitioner working with a young woman who was not accepted into a local parent support group might make a referral to a different group. If a series of appropriate referrals does not yield the desired results, the worker can consider other approaches of greater contest, such as advocating with the person who organized the original group.

The Social Worker Must Help the Client Deconstruct Oppressive Cultural Discourse and Reinterpret Experience from Alternative Perspectives Embracing this principle guides the social worker and client to discuss the larger cultural and societal issues that impact the ways in which the client experiences the world. Exploring the oppression, discrimination, and/or violence that may be a part of the client's life experience can help the client gain insight into the origins of these negative forces and construct alternative perspectives. Creating a different view of one's self can free the individual to develop a new, healthier perspective on themselves, others, and their current life situation. Consider the older adult refugee who recently came to the U.S. with her large extended family after fleeing her country of origin and living for several years in a refugee camp. This client brings with her a lifetime of oppression and discrimination and she and her family have been victims of violence in their home country. As a social worker working with this client, your role can be to help her to create a new perspective on the world in which she now lives. By examining her previous life experiences within the context of her new life, you can work with her to develop an alternative to the life of fear and dread that she previously knew.

The Social Worker Should Identify, Reinforce, and/or Increase the Client System's Repertoire of Strategic Behavior for Minimizing Pain and Maximizing Positive Outcomes and Satisfaction   Also known as the "minimax" principle, this principle cautions the social worker against holding the client responsible for a lack of community responsiveness in the development of resources or support. The principle recognizes, however, that the client may need assistance in developing behaviors that are likely to elicit cooperation from the community. For example, clients who have been excluded from the community on various levels might present as eager to the point of aggressiveness, and demonstrate a lack of interest in using a grievance process of an organization. This group of clients will likely improve their chances of being accepted if they curb their enthusiasm somewhat, by speaking in a softer voice and initially using a grievance process, for example.

In applying this principle, social workers are reminded that our culture has led many people to blame themselves for various acts of violence or oppression that they have experienced at the hands of others. Therefore, it is important that social workers, as well as client systems, do not attribute difficulties in accessing resources to our/their own failures. Social workers whose clients have adopted this perspective can employ consciousness-raising techniques to challenge these beliefs and transform personal issues such as child abuse and violence against women into political issues. Returning to the earlier example of the older adult woman who has recently arrived in the U.S., a focus of your work with her can be directed to examining the violence that she experienced in her home country. Within the social work intervention, you can help her to recognize that the perpetrators of the violence were responsible for the violence and, despite the pain and guilt she suffers, she and her family are not responsible. Freeing the client from the guilt can aid her in maximizing her opportunity to create a new life with her family in the U.S.

Social Workers Should Apply the Principles to Themselves   Social workers can consistently sustain competent and effective practice through utilizing appropriate principles in work with client systems. Accordingly, social workers make clear, accountable service and/or therapeutic contracts and explore common practice issues with other social workers. Social workers are also encouraged to apply the principles to their work in agency settings.

Environment-Sensitive Processes and Skills

The groups of skills and behaviors discussed earlier can also be applied to the environment when relevant to supporting clients' effective use of environmental supports. Following is a discussion of practice behaviors that can be utilized with the individual client situation within the context of the environment in which the client lives.

Providing Information   Client systems often want, need, and ask for information about the environment, which may be their most valuable resource. You may be uneasy that you will over-influence decisions or be too directive or create dependency. While such concerns are legitimate, they also can be managed. When you consider that information in our society is clearly linked to power, you may become less reluctant to provide it to clients. The challenge with providing information arises when it is confused with advice or is strongly one-sided. This concern becomes more difficult to mitigate with the understanding that you are never able to have all the information related to a particular situation or circumstance. Still, you can offer what you know as a simple proposition, always framed by the limits of your knowledge. Consider again the situation of the older adult refugee with whom you are working on creating a new and healthier perspective. She is concerned about the impact of the previously experienced violence on the younger female members. She is aware that you have been working with her daughter and granddaughters. She has asked you to share the information that you know about her daughter and granddaughters and to direct them to not discuss their experiences with anyone. While you are sensitive to her concerns, you are ethically bound not to share information about other clients without their consent. Moreover, your commitment to practicing social work in an ethical manner would not allow you to advise any client system in their beliefs or behaviors.

Be clear that you do not hold any expectations about what clients do with the information. Information is typically not yours to be given away only with certain restrictions. For example, if you are a social worker working in the field of child welfare helping a young couple to learn more effective methods to care for their three-year-old who has recently been diagnosed with autism, you may want to generate a compilation of resources you think would be helpful to the parents. You may believe that they would benefit from respite services because you suspect it will be helpful for the mother to develop some trust in a caretaker outside of the family. Therefore, you provide her with the names of several agencies that provide respite services. When she does not follow up on this information, you may become frustrated or even irritated. In this case, your "information" was interpreted by the client as "advice," and the mother is not at a point where she is able to or agrees to act on the information in the way you assumed she would. This simple example illustrates the problematic nature of an investment in giving information. Fortunately, you can process this kind of situation with the client so that your agenda becomes transparent and the client is free to accept or reject it.

Refocusing and Confronting   Bringing the client back to the original focus of the work is known as **refocusing** and can span several possible directions, including two discussed here: referring back to purpose and confronting clients' beliefs, plans, and/or behavior. Social workers frequently use refocusing to assist clients in taking advantage of the potential in their environments.

When clients begin to digress into arenas other than the agreed upon focus area of your work (based on the previously developed contract), a simple reference to the original agreements regarding the focus of the work during the action phase of the work is sometimes all that is necessary. Occasionally the client (or the social worker) will simply become distracted by other compelling issues. Although such diversion is understandable, you are responsible for using your time with the client productively.

In other situations, the client may not carry out the plan or contract as agreed because the plan is not truly embraced by the client as a priority, is proving uncomfortable, or the client is unable to implement the plan for some reason. For example, your client, Jane, established a plan to seek counseling because she had been sexually abused and was experiencing many painful memories. However, initiating that kind of contact involved breaking the culturally and family imposed rule of conduct that she should never discuss anything so personal with an outsider. She finds the effort to initiate this counseling more difficult than she had imagined. An alternative to refocusing is to confront her very gently, even though she may simply need more informal support and acknowledgment from you to manage the unanticipated struggle. You may say to Jane, "Help me to understand your concerns about talking about your painful memories with an outsider." This development might also signal that the plan is not working for Jane and is not likely to lead to the outcome previously anticipated. In situations like these you need to return to the goals, review the client's experience, and make changes as necessary.

Significantly, clients often perceive gentle confrontation of their behavior as not only helpful but supportive. If the social worker carefully contrasts what a client said she or he would do with what she or he actually did, the client might experience this activity as respectful because it affirms her or his capacity to meet the agreed-upon commitments. Such a process must be carried out sensitively, of course, to prevent the client from experiencing the confrontation as hostile and argumentative. Confrontation is certainly not the first approach to use in working with clients in such situations; rather, referring to purpose (refocusing) should be tried first. When it is used selectively and sensitively, however, gentle confrontation can convey hope and respect.

There will be situations, however, in which a digression from the intended focus of your work with the client system is warranted. You will be called upon to exercise your professional judgment to be able to recognize when a digression warrants a new focus. Returning to the example of Jane, should Jane present to your office with an eviction notice in her hand, the focus of your work related to her addressing the prior sexual abuse would be placed on hold until she could resolve her housing crisis.

Interpreting Client Behavior Interpretation refers to the social worker's making sense of the client's behavior in ways the client may not perceive or acknowledge. The goal of interpretation is to inspire the client to consider her or his situation in a new or different way. From a social constructionist view, interpreting can be one of the most challenging practice skills to master.

You may ascribe a different meaning to a client's behavior than the client. Still, there may be a place for interpreting when you are careful to test it out with clients and when you acknowledge that the meaning you take from the situation is only one possibility. Again, returning to the earlier example of Jane, you might, in helping her to use her environmental supports, say "It seems to me as if you do not feel ready to take on the kind of work that this type of counseling is likely to be. Is that correct?"

Although many of us have encountered situations in which the thoughts of others about our behavior were helpful, having others interpret our experience can also be frustrating and alienating, particularly when the interpretation seems judgmental or "expert" (as if someone else possesses the secret of understanding our behavior). Interpreting is a widely applicable process but one that should be used tentatively, checked for accuracy with the client, and with the use of ongoing supervision.

Mapping as an Intervention Strategy Recall from the discussion in Chapter 4 that incorporating the family and community system within which the client lives is an important aspect of the assessment phase of the social work intervention. Just as mapping the client's family constellation and current living and relationships profile can be a useful strategy for assessment, the same visual depictions of the client's environment can become a component of the intervention itself. As you know, the genogram is a tool used to enable the client system to gain insights into her or his family history and patterns of a wide array of behaviors and issues, including physical and mental health, substance use and abuse, relationship patterns, and estrangements. Ecomaps, on the other hand, provide a visual depiction of the client's current life situation, including relationships, resources, and assets.

In the development and implementation of the intervention, the same information gathered from both of these tools in the assessment phase can be incorporated into the client's goals and action steps for facilitating behavior and life changes. For example, consider the client who identifies in the course of completing her genogram a multi-generational pattern of intimate partner violence directed toward the women in her family. She has also experienced violence in her own relationships. Understanding the pattern of the abuse can aid your client in understanding the nature of her previous relationships and strategies she can take to enable herself to seek out healthier relationships. The genogram can later be used to help the client determine if the pattern is broken.

In the assessment phase of your work with client systems, the ecomap aids the client in identifying strengths, directionality of her or his energy and benefits, and areas for change. While this information is important for developing the intervention plan, the ecomap can be used as a visioning tool to enable the client to view her or his life after the intervention is implemented. Specific behavior and life changes can be determined as a result of the client's new perspective on her or his current life. Previously unrecognized resources can be mobilized, unhealthy behaviors can be addressed, and dysfunctional relationships can be targeted for change. The ecomap thus becomes a "work in progress" and serves as a mechanism for monitoring progress and outcomes.

TRADITIONAL SOCIAL WORK ROLES IN CONTEMPORARY SOCIAL WORK PRACTICE

In thinking about the preceding descriptions of social work skills and behaviors, consider the specific roles that workers assume in order to support client strengths and environments. As introduced in Chapter 1, social workers engage in specific practice behaviors associated with specific roles that can be isolated, highlighted, and deconstructed. The following discussion will focus on the assumptions that underlie these roles and the ways they are actualized in the context of social work practice. Specifically, these roles are:

- Case manager

- Counselor

- Broker

- Mediator

- Educator

- Client advocate

- Collaborator

Together they represent much of social work's activity across the dimensions of supporting both client strengths and client environments.

These five roles are not mutually exclusive. Rather, there is considerable overlap among them—for example, educating the legislature regarding the needs of foster children may also pave the way for a future effort at advocacy for this group. Such a blending and overlapping of social work roles is common in social work practice, and it can be helpful to be clear about the roles in which you are undertaking with particular practice behaviors. For example, if you were to assume an educator role in presenting useful and relatively unbiased information about adults who have experienced psychiatric hospitalization, you would want to be clear whether you were going to additionally utilize a client advocate role to advocate for a particular treatment. While education and advocacy are often interlinked, it is important to be clear when you are advocating for a client system and when you are providing education about the client system.

Case Manager

A classic view of **case management** is defined as "a procedure to plan, seek, and monitor services from different social agencies and staff on behalf of a client" (Barker, 2003, p. 58). Clients with multiple challenges and needs particularly benefit from case management. For example, a client with a serious mental health issue, a back injury, and a housing issue may be in need of medication, a referral to vocational rehabilitation, and a referral to a housing resource. This client may be an appropriate candidate for case management. **Case managers** not only coordinate these services but are also responsible for monitoring the responsiveness of services to clients by holding providers accountable, ensuring client participation, and collaborating with others to raise awareness of unmet needs. As mentioned, a case manager may also collaborate with others to advocate for and build needed resources in a community.

Common Components of Case Management   While there are multiple case management models, steps that are typically included are: (1) accessing the client system by ensuring eligible persons are informed of available services; (2) assessing client system's needs and strengths; (3) developing a plan for intervention; (4) identifying and designing an appropriate network of services to be utilized; (5) creating a written contract that includes achievable and measurable goals, time limits, agreed-upon actions, and consequences of failure to fulfill the contract (if any); (6) implementing the plan; (7) monitoring of the plan to determine progress or a need to re-evaluate the contract; (8) evaluating the outcomes of the intervention; (9) terminating the case management relationship; (10) following up on the client after termination to determine if the client has maintained the desired change (Roberts-DeGennaro, 2008). The case manager may also serve as an informal, personal support/contact person or even therapist. As the provision of therapy is an advanced-level intervention, the social worker is bound by the *Code of Ethics* (NASW, 2008) to possess an appropriate degree and training. In contrast to brokers, who may match a client to a single service, case managers take responsibility for assessing, monitoring, and evaluating the coordination of all services required by a client.

For more than three decades, the term case management has been used to describe this overall coordinating function, although many scholars believe that modern generalist practice is actually a form of case management. In more recent times, the component of cost containment has become crucial to case management. Accordingly, contemporary versions of case management have two primary—and often conflicting—purposes: to improve the quality of care through coordination of services, and to control the costs of care. While case management was originally conceived to address integration of system-level services, it has been shown to have become an effective practice approach with a wide array of populations as well as a cost-effective service delivery mechanism. Case management is an accepted strategy for working in family preservation, school attendance and performance, substance abuse treatment, corrections, and health care delivery systems; however, the quality of the services provided and the outcomes for the client systems must be given priority over cost-effectiveness (Rothman, 2009a).

Counselor

The term **counselor** is used in a variety of ways within the helping professions. Within the social work profession, counseling is typically considered to be a specialized clinical social work skill performed by social workers at the graduate level who have advanced training in working in health, mental health, and family service settings. A counselor provides services to individuals, families, groups, and communities that encompass the provision of suggestions and information along with establishing goals (Barker, 2003). Counseling is a term also used to describe volunteers and professionals or paraprofessionals who work in group settings (e.g., camps and residential settings).

While the counseling role can include an array of different activities, the social worker functioning as a counselor typically works with the client system around a specific issue or concern. Dependent on the expertise and training of the practitioner and the needs of the client system, specific approaches and strategies will be utilized. Generally, the counselor's aim is to aid the client system to improve functioning (Hull & Mather, 2006).

Broker

Social workers typically act as **brokers** by linking clients to the services that provide a needed service or resource. Needs may range from instrumental assistance (e.g., food, clothing, and children's toys) to intangible services such as counseling, support groups, and advocacy. Consider the functions and context of brokering, the process of building the necessary networks, and making the match of client to service.

Brokering Functions and Context   Five social work functions of brokering are:

- Assess client needs

- Assess available resources

- Match and initiate referrals to appropriate services

- Link or network services

- Share information

The brokering role can also include modifying resources and creating new resources where none exist. All of these activities can serve to strengthen the client's environment, or context, as well as to support her or his strengths. These activities also overlap, and they reflect much of what was discussed in Chapter 3 regarding assessment of clients and resources, and the fit between them.

One of the early roles associated with the social work profession, the broker role may have less status today than it once had because of the profession's increased interest in psychological and therapeutic roles. Brokering may also seem fairly simple at times. For example, if your client requests assistance with locating used children's furniture, you simply "refer" her or him to the appropriate agency. It is probably somewhat misleading, though, to think of the brokering role as simple, because it requires the worker both to be familiar with the resources and to nurture and maintain a network of and relationships with such resources. In the complex world of contemporary, urban social services, the ability to know one service or resource from the next can itself be a feat. In rural areas, where the service system may be much less comprehensive, with fewer choices, knowing and maintaining effective relationships with the available resources becomes even more important.

Building and Maintaining Networks for Brokering Developing a network will include such activities as making initial and subsequent contacts with appropriate providers in other agencies and organizations, discovering those who will help your clients most effectively, and becoming familiar with eligibility criteria and service elements involved in programs. Effective brokering also involves establishing stable working relationships with people, organizations, and systems that will help your clients. Building an effective working relationship with outside people and systems could involve developing a two-way relationship with network resources, so that you are able to provide referrals that best fit the system of the resource, and able to contribute energy to the relationship in other ways, such as offering to appropriately assist your networks in their service, advocacy, and/or fundraising efforts. For the social worker to build and maintain a network, key elements include reciprocity and open, two-way communication.

To build a network successfully, you must acquire knowledge of the informal aspects of the resource as well as the formal ones. For example, it will be helpful to you to understand the mission statement of a particular community hospice program—the program's goals and methods of service delivery. Other examples include learning that a program has received a large grant for an additional building, that the local university is about to place a field unit there for student training, or that the board of an affiliated organization has approved funding for a development director. Although you will not have access to all informal developments in the services you use, your attention to, and continuous connections with, both formal and informal aspects of the network you maintain will enrich your understanding of your community's resource environment.

Making the Match in Brokering   As discussed in Chapter 3, knowledge and skills are needed to facilitate the matching of clients and services as you maintain an ongoing and continually growing network of contacts. Developing and maintaining a resource network (or "service system linkage") nearly always requires you to use the skills you first learned about in Chapter 3 in connection with clients—that is, looking with planned emptiness and others. When you understand the purpose of the service, as well as the opportunities and challenges of the service, your ability to utilize the service for your client will increase.

Following up on your referrals is important, both to determine if the client is participating in and benefiting from the service and to gain insight into the provider's response to your referral. Remember that the match between clients and services is important from the service's point of view as well as from the client's perspective. When you have taken the time and care to learn about an effective and successful referral to a particular service, you will gain the trust of other providers who will respect your competence and skills. Further, when you develop a genuine understanding of, and appreciation for, the work that others do, you are likely to find your own work gratifying, and perhaps more to the point, you will find "the system" more responsive to your client.

Mediator

Mediation has both a formal and informal dimension in the delivery of human services. Mediation as a professional practice has its own identity and is often more associated with the legal system and public policy than it is with social work practice. There are, in fact, social workers who complete specialized mediation training and become mediators in such areas as divorce and child custody. Most social workers, however, engage in some aspects of mediation fairly frequently, if on a less formal basis. **Mediators**, as outsiders to a dispute, try to: (1) establish common ground between disputing parties; (2) help them understand each other's point of view; and (3) establish that each party has an interest in the relationship's stability past the current area of difference.

Finding Common Ground   Locating the points of agreement in the midst of a dispute is a common skill in social work practice. Assume you are working in a youth agency and have just seen Josh, a 15-year-old who has recently run away from home for the first time. After conversation with him, you understand his challenge to be about the relationship between his mother and her new live-in boyfriend. He is upset and scared and is not certain about the ramifications of being on his own. He dislikes his mother's boyfriend and objects to the curfew and other house rules he imposes. Josh also says he misses his mother's companionship the way it was before "he" entered the scene. When you are satisfied that Josh is safe at home (that he is not being abused in any way), you ask him for permission to schedule a meeting with his mother, her boyfriend, and Josh to explore the issues among them. He somewhat reluctantly agrees.

When his mother enters the youth center, she seems exasperated with her son, but she is also relieved to see him. She begins to cry and hugs him. Her boyfriend remains quiet, but when he catches Josh's eye, he smiles at the boy just slightly.

Walking through It   In exploring the process for one possible avenue of mediation in Josh's family, you might do the following:

- Attempt to establish common ground. In this case Josh's present well-being is the immediate point of common interest. You discover that Josh is 15 years old and is not prepared to support himself physically, financially, or emotionally (or legally in most places). He is scared and concerned about his future. At the same time, however, he is vocal about his freedom and does not want to be bound by all the rules imposed upon him by his mother's new boyfriend. His mother cares for him and wants him to be safe. Her boyfriend wants a peaceful household and likes Josh well enough, although he has no strong connection with him. He cares deeply for Josh's mother.

- Represent yourself genuinely as one who wants to help resolve this issue, trusts the process of working it through, and does not favor any one side.

- Help Josh, his mother, and her boyfriend understand and appreciate one another's points of view. Assume that Josh's mother and her boyfriend may have different perspectives and opinions, and acknowledge all points of view. Facilitate their direct dialogue with one another. The social work skills of planned emptiness and looking from diverse angles will be very beneficial to this interaction.

- Establish with Josh, his mother, and her boyfriend that it is in the interests of all of them to work together during this interaction so that they can come to a resolution regarding Josh's living arrangements and his general safety.

- Help all parties recognize that each will benefit from an ongoing positive relationship in which they can settle differences that go beyond the current dispute. The quality of Josh's future may depend on their ability to work together, as well as the quality of the relationship between Josh's mother and her boyfriend. These are the abiding points of common interest.

This scenario represents just one way in which this situation might play out. You might make other arguments to reach the same goals of finding common ground and identifying solutions. You will notice that no *particular* solution is implied in this process. Josh, his mother, and her boyfriend might agree that Josh should return home, live with another family member, try to survive on his own on a trial basis, or any number of other possibilities. The major point is that the relationship between Josh and his mother (and her boyfriend) is collaborative and that each has a stake in working out a solution that affirms their mutual benefit.

Educator

There are many ways in which social workers function as educators. While the mission and scope of individual practice settings will determine the nature and level of such an activity, some form of education is commonplace in most social work settings. On an interpersonal and concrete level, as an **educator**, you may teach clients about a wide range of topics; for example, you might inform clients about services, new programs, completing an application form, or something as basic as the correct bus to take to travel uptown before noon. You may assure an adolescent client that she is indeed normal when she worries that her moodiness indicates she is not, or you might educate clients about the maximum allowable percentage of income charged for rent in public housing. Much of the direct service aspect of acting as educator relates to helping clients to access resources, as well as to make the behavioral changes they want to make.

Developing Client Skills   On a direct practice level, you, as the social worker, can assist clients in developing the skills they actively seek in particular situations in which they want to change their own participation. The motivation for this kind of change needs to generate from clients' vision for the ways in which their lives may be different, rather than from your opinions about needed improvements. You can assist clients in understanding the steps needed to accomplish that change. For example, if your client, Ramon, feels intimidated by his co-workers or supervisor in his job and wants to increase his assertiveness in the workplace, you might help by demonstrating a more assertive (but respectful) stance in a relevant interchange, and/or role-play or assist him to practice the new behavior. In other settings, you can help older adult clients learn to organize their medications to increase their compliance with medications. You can teach parents strategies for supporting their children through positive feedback. You can model clear communication and gradually assist your client in participating more effectively in problem situations. For example, if you are working with an adolescent who is frequently expelled from school for short periods because of her angry outbursts at teachers, you can work with her on appropriate strategies for expressing herself more effectively without alienating adults. Additionally, you might accompany her to her first meeting with the school principal on her return to classes. You can help her describe her situation and support a more focused, direct, and respectful level of discussion based on her goals. Outside of the meeting you can help her process the session, to include evaluating what went well and what did not go well, and support her ability to negotiate these relationships with some further practice in the future. You may then role-play the next meeting rather than attend yourself to support her goal of self-sufficiency in these types of situations. At the same time, when you use skills with clients, you are modeling skills that they may use on their own in their relationships in the future. In all of these situations the ultimate goal is a more positive sense of strength and agency—a change in clients' thinking about themselves and a greater integration of self and skills into the environment.

Working with the Public   Social workers frequently (more in some settings than others) are called upon to educate larger groups about issues that affect client systems. In some instances, these efforts take on aspects of primary prevention in that they are designed to prevent the development of a problem. For example, you may teach a parenting class or present a session on ways to support racial tolerance in the classroom to a preschool group. Other education efforts may involve providing testimony in a legislative hearing regarding the cultural needs of a group of refugee children or speaking to a community group in response to their concerns about a new group home for discharged clients with psychiatric histories that is to be established in their neighborhood.

Although the activities differ in nature, all of these scenarios involve working in an educator's role. Social work practitioners have a long history of acting as educators when they take on the position of field instructor for students in an academic program leading to a social work degree.

Client Advocate

Advocacy in social work practice is aimed at securing the rights and well-being of clients who are vulnerable or at risk for a negative outcome. The **advocate** may obtain resources, modify existing policies or practices, and promote new policies that will benefit clients. Regardless of the specific activities involved, advocacy represents a struggle over power, and by definition it seeks to obtain and ensure clients' access to resources. This role of defending, championing, or otherwise speaking out for clients is one of the original cornerstones of the profession's commitment, although its intensity has varied somewhat according to the political climate (Haynes & Mickelson, 2006). Although advocacy often focuses on the political or civil rights of clients, as a social worker, you frequently have the opportunity and obligation to advocate in informal, everyday situations when a client is treated disrespectfully or inefficiently, or not provided needed services. Advocacy assumes an active role that is not always comfortable or popular with others.

Many social workers distinguish between **case (or client) advocacy**, defined as advocacy on behalf of an individual client or a single group of clients, and **cause (or class) advocacy**, which is initiated on behalf of a category of clients. **Legislative**

advocacy may be thought of as a specialized version of cause advocacy in which some aspect of the law is addressed. We'll take a brief look at each type.

Case Advocacy   Social workers usually practice case advocacy on an agency or organizational level. For example, if your client has been denied food stamps to which she or he is entitled, you can advocate with the public welfare organization that houses the food stamp service. To be an effective advocate, you will need to know a number of variables, such as eligibility requirements, agency appeal policies, regulations, and power structures, as well as contextual variables such as the way in which the food stamp program fits into the overall welfare organization. You will also want to recognize the situation as one of potential conflict and to enter at the point of least contest so that you do not inspire more resistance than necessary. Therefore, you can address the situation with the social worker who originally denied the food stamps and utilize the grievance process at the agency before taking any other measures, such as involving powerful outside parties in advocacy, calling the media, or organizing a protest.

Cause Advocacy   More political than case advocacy, cause advocacy involves both larger numbers of people and, by definition, a cause that affects them all, either by imposing obstacles to attaining resources or by directly depriving people of these resources. Cause advocacy involves speaking for a large number of people who are not your individual clients and who are not likely to be empowered to participate directly in forming either the goals or the preferred advocacy methods related to the cause. Nevertheless, cause advocacy can be effective when you can partner with other concerned organizations, and can spur change that positively impacts a large number of people. It is also helpful when the issue is very clear and does not impose any solution on people who do not choose it. For example, if your community has no adequate facilities for child care after school, there may be agencies, churches, businesses, or other institutions that are concerned and want to develop a facility for parents in need of such a service. Assuming that you will require funding from local public sources, your coalition of interested partners (who are well organized and well rehearsed) will be in a position to advocate for adequate child care facilities. As in case advocacy, you/your coalition will need to be skillful and to have researched background information regarding the number of children to be served, their needs, the estimated costs of providing the service, the likelihood of participation, the process of getting the issue on the city's agenda, and the benefits to all stakeholders.

Legislative Advocacy   This form of cause advocacy is devoted specifically to adding, amending, changing, or eliminating legislation in order to benefit a large group of clients. For example, when a social worker advocates to lower the legal alcohol limit for driving an automobile from .10 blood alcohol content (BAC) to .08, that is a case of legislative advocacy designed to benefit a large category—drivers and passengers.

There are many other kinds of scenarios in which a large group of people would benefit from some change in legislation, because nearly all entitlement policies have limitations that may present obstacles to your clients. Controversial resources such as family planning and abortion clinics are likely to have more access constraints (such as age limits or pregnancy duration) than do other less disputed services such as food pantries.

A considerable amount of knowledge, insight, and organization are required to change a law, but it is well within the arena of social work practice to initiate or collaborate in such activity. With careful preparation and diligence in appropriate situations, legislative advocacy can produce the desired results. Legislative advocacy usually requires intensive, cooperative work with one or several organizations.

Thoughts about Power and Advocacy   Social work advocacy is frequently related to the social justice dimension of resource allocation; therefore, it is helpful to recall the general assumptions about power. In general, advocates recognize that power is not easily relinquished, not equally distributed, involves conflict, and is necessary to make substantial change. These points may appear harsh if you have not considered power and advocacy within such a context. Familiarity with these concepts can prepare you to enter a more political arena and are beneficial in understanding the social locations of those who have been oppressed and have had little power to exercise in our culture.

Like work with individual clients, advocacy can be a highly rewarding under-taking (Abramowitz, 2005), but can be complex, frustrating, and mysterious. When not well done, it can be costly to clients, as you will recall from the tenants' story in Chapter 4. See Box 5.1 for a list of cautions and strategies regarding advocacy.

Collaborator

Guided by the mission of the social work profession, collaboration is inherent in the daily practice of most social work practitioners. As well as utilizing collaboration skills in developing plans for change with clients, social workers engage in collabora-tive relationships with other professions in a number of different ways. For example, social workers work with health, social service, and legal professionals in the delivery of client services, development of programs and policies, advocacy work, and research. While the terms to describe cooperative practices are sometimes used interchangeably, they do have distinctive connotations. Multidisciplinary practice, for instance, refers to groups of professions working together toward a similar aim, while maintaining their individual interventions (Moxley, 2008). Interdisciplinary practice (also referred to as interprofessional collaboration, collaborative practice, and partnered practice), on the other hand, involves pro-fessionals from different disciplines integrating their professional knowledge to work together toward a common goal. In these situations, social workers engage in **interprofessional collaboration**.

BOX 5.1

Cautions and Strategies Regarding Advocacy

- Enter any situation in which you want to advocate at the point of least contest (Wood & Tully, 2006).
- When clients are directly involved, ensure they genuinely support your efforts and understand the possible repercussions.
- Prepare yourself fully with the knowledge that is relevant to the situation (e.g., eligibility requirements, entitlement limitations, number of people in a given category, history of advocacy on this topic).
- Be clear and specific about your goals; a complaint about a policy means little if there is no solution presented.
- Begin with simple efforts at persuasion; assume first that there has been a mistake or an oversight.
- Be clear when persuasion is not working with the targeted audience and you must enter a new level.
- Assess that new level prior to action: Can you be successful? Are your clients still supportive? Do collaborative partners agree on the next step?
- Use carefully cultivated social work skills in an advocacy effort, including listening, empathy, clarifying, and firmness.
- Use the discourse of collaboration and common ground.
- Seek supervision and consultation. You are as vulnerable to "not seeing" in thinking about cause advocacy as you might be in the most intense interpersonal work.
- When entering into formal processes (e.g., legislative advocacy), become knowledgeable about the technicalities of the legislative process.

Social workers often work in settings in which the primary mission is not the provision of social work services. Known as **host settings**, these include health care facilities and programs, educational institutions, law enforcement or legal systems, military programs, and even financial institutions. While it is essential for social workers working in host settings to understand the philosophies, professional cultures, and language of other professions, social workers will be collaborators in virtually every setting in which they are employed. Known to be effective in enhancing the delivery of services or care, interprofessional collaborations can be complex and, sometimes, frustrating relationships in which to work. Social workers may find that challenges occur in communicating with other professions who have their own professional "jargon," perceived hierarchy of professional influence, and conflicting opinions on approach, roles, implementation, and outcomes related to the work to be completed.

Social workers can utilize their training in collaboration and negotiation with client systems to prepare for becoming effective professional collaborators. Abramson (2009) suggests that social workers can become competent collaborators by learning about the other professions with whom they will be engaged in collaborative relationships, including gaining insights into training, culture, professional ethics and values, language, practice approaches, and priorities. Upon learning about your collaborators' professional socialization experience, you can then seek out common ground on which to begin the process of building a professional collaboration. Taking advantage of opportunities to gain interprofessional competence will serve you well as you move into any area of practice.

PUTTING IT ALL TOGETHER

Thus far, this chapter has explored various aspects of social work practice in action. Specific areas covered include supporting clients' strengths and their environments as well as various actions by workers. Empowerment practice will be utilized as a model for examining the possible points of integration for social work roles within the context of a strengths-based practice approach.

Empowerment Practice

Social work as a profession has been committed to empowering clients for much of its history. Simon (1990), one of the early scholars of empowerment, asserted that, in its purest sense, empowerment cannot be given to someone else because empowerment is not ours to give. Empowerment resides within the individual and can only be encouraged or perhaps released, but not given, by others. Best practices in the application of empowerment theory suggest (Parsons, 2008, p. 124):

- A sociopolitical lens is used to frame situations experienced by the client system.

- Power within the helping relationship is couched within the context of client strengths, self-efficacy, and education as opposed to pathology.

- Informal social networks are integral to the empowerment of the client system.

- Collectivity is key to the intervention with a specific emphasis on support, mutual aid, validation, and promotion of social justice.

The best practice of empowerment-focused social work establishes a clear theoretical connection among individual client strengths and their environment and their capacity to act in a way both to empower themselves and liberate others. This connection in turn supports intervention in multiple and highly interconnected settings as well as recognizes the importance of unleashing or strengthening the client's sense of self and agency. Box 5.2 provides an illustrative case example of an appropriate and sensitive empowerment approach.

The story takes place in a small New England city in the 1970s. Thomas was born with a neurological disorder, cerebral palsy. His family had little idea of how to deal with his severe physical limitations and had three other children to rear as well. His parents cared about him and did what they could to learn ways to support him and his abilities, as well as cope with his disability. He received the standard medical care of the time and was sent to school with his age group.

Early on it was evident that Thomas's body did not reflect his aptitude for schoolwork. He was, in fact, intellectually capable and did exceedingly well in the subjects in which teachers supported him. His family did not understand, however, the ways in which Thomas's socialization was affected by his physical impairments or how he experienced his life. Although he had only a few friends, he attempted, for several years to maintain a positive outlook, even developing an excellent sense of humor. Nevertheless, he continued to feel excluded by peers and adults alike.

COLLIDING WITH THE WORLD

Over time he became hostile with teachers because he had to prove himself over and over again, every time he entered a new grade or school. Teachers and school administrators first assumed that he was unable to do grade-level work. One teacher questioned his very presence in the regular classroom. His pastor at church advised that he seek supported employment through a public vocational program. Everyone seemed to assume he was unable to do, know, or even feel anything. His medical treatment included the excruciating requirement to walk in physical therapy that was promoted in those days. No one noted Thomas's pain or responded to it.

By the time Thomas was an adolescent, his parents sent him to a psychotherapist to learn the reasons for his intense anger. To Thomas, this was yet another insult to someone who had already suffered so many. His therapist told him he needed to "get the chip off his shoulder" and tend to his schoolwork. There would be no money for college—he would have to earn scholarships if he wanted to do more than sit in the living room until he could be matched to a job he did not want.

MEETING MAURA

Finally, Thomas was in need of a new wheelchair. He was directed to a social worker for assistance when his parents could not pay the required deductible. The social worker, Maura, who worked in the primary care office of Thomas's physician, first spent some time getting to know him and hearing what he had to say about the wheelchair. She assisted him in getting the funding for his new chair and continued to ask about his overall experience. He began to talk about his needs to consider his options regarding school, his family, his anger, and his growing sense of estrangement from the world.

Maura helped Thomas by hearing with an openness and reflexivity that assumed he was the expert on his experience. She heard his story, took him seriously, and helped him look at what his disability meant to him by asking him to talk not only about the physical pain but also about the exclusion that he experienced. She helped him look at his resilience in the face of all he had been through. She did not try to challenge his perception of his experience but was completely respectful of it. She asked him to articulate the way he wanted his life to be different in view of his strong capacities. She encouraged him to reflect on his own position and how he might address his goals. As time passed, Maura helped Thomas secure vocational rehabilitation funding for college and validated his, by then, strong commitment to working in human services on disability issues. She also met with Thomas's family to help them understand his choices and the impact these choices would have on the family.

CHANGING DIRECTION

Today, Thomas is studying for a master's degree in disabilities and is preparing for a career in which he can advocate for others with disabilities as well as himself. He is a full participant in school and in the surrounding context of his family, friends, and culture. He is still angry sometimes, but he is not fearful or alone.

Reading this (almost all) true story, you can see how Maura implemented the empowerment focus identified in the chapter: She assists in liberating Thomas's "potent self" and encourages his interpersonal connections. She supports his understanding of his environment and she helps connect him to a direction in which he can address the more political aspects of his experience. Consider now the connections between Thomas's experiences with other social work perspectives.

Social Justice: Maura works diligently to expand Thomas's access to the benefits of his society by helping him to find funding for education. She does not accept the status quo arrangement in which those with private resources are privileged and those without are not. To complete this role, Maura would work toward reallocation of educational funding for all people, not just Thomas.

Human Rights: Thomas's status as a person with a disability is not accepted as a rationale for discrimination in education, nor does his disability preclude the "full development of the personality" (Article 26, United Nations, 1948) through education. Maura recognizes him as a person who has both needs and abilities and the right to fulfill his life as he chooses.

Strengths Perspective: Maura recognizes Thomas's considerable strengths, validates them, and encourages linking their full expression to his goals. She sees him as a whole human being, with many talents to offer, not as a "victim of cerebral palsy."

Critical Social Construction: Maura sees Thomas's disability as a social construction that results from the prevailing collective meaning given to it by our culture. She questions the limitations imposed by that construction, and she believes Thomas can do what he sets out to do. Maura accepts that there are multiple realities and so honors his experience of exclusion and oppression. Because his experience has developed within the context of his social location, on which he is the expert, she makes no attempt to "correct" his understanding. Her effort goes into changing his future experience in order to make it more consistent with how he wants his life arranged.

BOX 5.2

continued

The concept of empowerment has applicability within each of the roles that a social worker assumes when intervening with a client system. As the social worker serves in the roles of case manager, counselor, broker, mediator, education, client advocate, and collaborator, she or he has the opportunity to utilize the concepts of empowerment to carry out the tasks associated with each of these roles. For example, the client working to advocate on behalf of a client system can build the advocacy effort on the strengths of the client, utilize the client's self-efficacy and life experience in the advocacy, and strive to help the client system become empowered to engage in self-advocacy.

Social workers need an array of strategies to initiate and facilitate a strengths-based intervention to empower client systems. For example, while the narrative approach does not provide specific therapeutic skills, the client can be empowered with the social worker's help in constructing, deconstructing, and finally reconstructing their conceptualizations (i.e., stories) that have previously been used to define their lives. The social worker's role is to help the clients determine if they wish to change their perceptions by challenging and broadening their thinking about their lives. As the narrative approach is consistent with the social work values of strengths and collaboration, and the client as the expert on her or his life, the narrative approach can be integrated with other clinical approaches (solution-focused) and cognitive behavioral approaches (Parsons, 2008).

One specific practice behavior that can aid social workers in helping clients to redefine their perceptions of their lives is **motivational interviewing**. Initially developed for practice with clients who are not voluntary, motivational interviewing builds on the client's strengths and her or his right to self-determination to implement a plan for change created by the client her/himself (for more, read Miller & Rollnick, 2002). Currently used in a variety of settings with a range of client situations (e.g., child welfare, substance abuse treatment, and intimate partner violence), motivational interviewing is an evidence-based strategy in which the social worker utilizes the practice skills of empathy and reflective listening (Wahab, 2005). As the expert on her or his life, the client is responsible for articulating her or his story and developing a motivation for initiating life changes. Motivational interviewing is but one of the numerous techniques and skills available to the social work practitioner, but one that is built on a strengths-based, person-centered framework.

STRAIGHT TALK ABOUT INTERVENTIONS: UNEXPECTED EVENTS AND ONGOING EVALUATION

In exploring the various ways to view social work practice, the intervention process may appear to be orderly. If you practice sensitive engagement, careful assessment of both the players and the environment, and planning consistent methods of taking action on behalf of your clients, you might be seduced into thinking that the work will always go smoothly. Such an assumption would be a mistake.

In the real world, not everything goes as planned in spite of the most diligent efforts. Because social work is completely immersed in people's lives, social workers have only limited control over their work with client systems and need to develop an acceptance (or at least tolerance) for the up-and-down nature of working with clients who are living their lives within their environments. In this real world, people get sick, get into accidents, change their minds, get fired and laid off, become disheartened, move, their kids get into trouble, and they experience violence. On the positive side, people also get promoted, find their strengths, find their voices, fall in love, get jobs, read an inspiring book, discover a new friend, and develop insight. All of these factors and many more have the potential to interrupt, postpone, redirect, or even terminate your work together.

In some cases—for example, if the client becomes discouraged or seems simply to lose interest—you will want to inquire about the role you might have played in contributing to these developments. In many cases your responsibility will be to honor, acknowledge, and explore the meaning of the new situation to the client, and reconfigure your work when indicated. It will generally be helpful for you to *expect the unexpected*. Flexibility is one of the most critical of social work attributes.

Just as you have been consistent in evaluating the progress of your work with your client and others involved throughout the engagement and assessment processes, you will want to evaluate the direction of the intervention periodically as well, particularly if there have been substantial changes or unexpected events in the client's life. You may easily get carried away in the plan that you so carefully put together, even when it may no longer fit very well. Checking and re-checking in with the client will serve you well during the intervention process. In that way you can stay connected to your client throughout and sustain a greater likelihood of providing relevant service.

As you recall from Chapter 3, crisis intervention and suicide, are expected, yet unexpected, aspects of social work practice. The social worker's ability to intervene effectively is contingent upon a timely response and accurate assessment. After ensuring during the engagement and assessment phase that the client is safe, the focus during the intervention phase is on empowering the client to resolve the crisis by reconstructing her or his perceptions of strengths, assets, and resources (Eaton & Roberts, 2009). The social worker and the client collaborate to devise a viable plan for addressing the root causes of the crisis and emphasize concrete action strategies and a clear, agreed-upon plan for follow-up and maintenance.

SUPPORTING CLIENTS' STRENGTHS IN TERMINATION AND EVALUATION

"Important things are almost never easy." This statement captures the real work of the termination phase of planned change. Even when all participants in a relationship agree that it is time to move on, ending can be a wrenching process, often punctuated with doubts about whether you have given or done enough, or wishing, in some vague way, to start over. This is a common experience that you have probably had yourself, perhaps when you left home or ended a significant relationship. Endings tend to raise ambivalence: On the one hand they may be sad, while on the other hand they represent a kind of freedom to be on your own, make a new start, and be who you want to be.

The endings between social workers and client systems often reflect these tensions. Some social workers, as well as clients, will be tempted to minimize any significance in saying goodbye and simply "slip out the back." Others will not even want to talk about it, finding it more comfortable just to be gone. Yet others tend to make scrupulous notes with contact information and schedules and agree to call, text, connect on social networking sites, or email each other. Clients may, in fact, demonstrate both positive and negative feelings about their termination process, viewing termination with a sense of accomplishment or as (possibly another) loss in their lives (Fortune, 2009). People tend to develop patterns about endings, and usually these serve to mitigate the loss that inevitably occurs in all significant relationships. The remainder of this chapter will address the processes of ending a professional relationship with your clients. The discussion will focus on both you and your clients' responses to endings. Strategies for evaluation of the practice intervention will be explored on multiple levels. While terminations that occur at the level of the family, group, organization, or community are somewhat unique and will be explored in the following chapters, this discussion will emphasize general issues related to terminating and evaluating the social work relationship with the individual client.

ENDINGS AND TERMINATION

There are considerable variations in the way endings occur in social work practice. Factors that play a role in the ending include age, gender, ethnicity, socioeconomic status, cultural experience, working style, and personality of both the client and the social worker, among other factors. The social location of the work, its purpose, the agency, the perspective used, and the organizational pressures surrounding the work also have an impact. Even within this range, however, general planning is necessary and can be helpful to both the client and the social work in bringing closure to the professional social work intervention.

Planning the Process: Overview

Begin by considering several tasks that relate to endings. These tasks will not apply to all social work relationships and their order does not need to be rigid. Your theoretical orientation and the specifics of the practice situation will guide much of the timing and ordering, but these tasks are common to a wide range of relationships and are consistent with ethical practice. They are:

- Negotiate the timing of the termination.

- Review the agreement for work.

- Process successes and shortcomings.

- Develop and clarify plans for termination and maintenance of change.

- Share responses to ending.

- Respect cultural consistency.

Negotiating the Timing   As termination is a goal that is established at the beginning of the relationship, it should always be before you as you progress through the intervention. In some circumstances your client and you have the opportunity to specify the number of sessions at the beginning of the relationship. The closing date can then be determined during the first meeting. Frequently the same is true of mandated arrangements or managed care situations in which the agency is bound by prearranged guidelines. All of these are, of course, artificial proclamations that the work is done, and they are all externally imposed. In some cases, clients may request an additional number of sessions (as in task-centered models), and workers may petition for an extended number of sessions (as in managed care).

Predetermined boundaries tend to distract from the ideal timing for ending, which is when the worker and client have reached the mutually formulated goals. The point at which the goals have been reached may not be clear, particularly if goals have not been clearly established. Even when goals are put in precise behavioral terms (for example, "the client will contact the school social worker"), there is some risk that the established goals and intervention plans may still not be realized. For example, your client may have unsuccessfully attempted to contact the school social worker, or made contact, but was not able to clearly articulate her message; therefore, meeting the goal technically does not meet the spirit of the issue. Nevertheless, you will need to make a reasoned judgment that the client no longer needs your services. Because you and the client may not necessarily agree on the exact moment when that occurs, in many cases you will need to negotiate the timing and criteria, remembering that you are each subject to your own foibles relating to ending relationships.

There are at least three areas for you to consider in your negotiations regarding the termination of the relationship. The first is your responsibility and relates to preventing an unanticipated ending. In many circumstances you will not have control over the timing, but in others you can anticipate, if not change, the conditions. You have a responsibility to provide full information to the client about the possible nature and timing of termination. For example, a state contract or managed care restrictions may determine an ending date that you think is inappropriate. In such a situation you can at least prepare the client for the possibility that your appeal for more sessions may be denied. Other examples of situations in which you need to be straightforward with clients and make the smoothest transition arrangements you can include a situation in which your agency is about to eliminate services or programs, your position is threatened, or you know you are leaving your job or internship on a particular date.

The second issue relates to maintaining an ongoing dialogue with your client regarding her or his status or progress to determine if your work together is helping, and what needs to happen for the client to know she or he has met the goals. Just as you have ongoing discussion with your client about goals, contracts, and progress, you should also discuss termination throughout your relationship. While the agency or the plan you established with the client may determine the ending point, discussion about termination can and should be integral to the work.

The final issue involves predetermined endings. Knowing that you will have a specified number of meetings with the client provides you with the opportunity to regularly check in with the client to ensure that you both share an understanding of the point at which the work will be completed. Some clients may assume you can or will extend the number of sessions as you prefer, and others might expect if they behave well (especially in mandated sessions) that they will be "dismissed" early. Always be as clear as possible about any limits that are imposed on you for the work and be as open as possible to discussing the meaning of those limits to your client. Even when both sides clearly understand the ending date, either the client or you may still experience difficult ending dynamics.

Reviewing the Agreement for Work   In the process of finishing your work together, you and your client should review the formal contract or informal agreement you made for work. You will want again to negotiate the understanding each of you has about the agreement, as it may have changed in view of your completed work, circumstances in the client's life or your life, or due to the agency's ability to offer services.

Processing Successes and Shortcomings   As you proceeded through the work together, you have discussed and processed the aspects that went well, the things that missed the mark, and any approaches that clearly headed in the wrong direction. This type of assessment should be ongoing and not take place just at the last meeting. Nevertheless, processing a summary of successes at the end is an appropriate strategy to gain perspective on the whole experience and gain insight into the client's view of the work. Sometimes, for example, an experience that seemed difficult at the time, in retrospect, is associated with personal growth. Recall the example from earlier in the chapter of the client with mental illness who had struggled to locate housing. You may have suggested that she was ready to meet with the landlord on her own, which at the time seemed challenging to her. As your work together progressed, however, she may have seen that it was a useful push that helped her to recognize her strengths. Looking through an empowerment lens, this success suggests your client's ability to act on her own needs, and she no longer views herself as a victim, but as a survivor of the power imbalance experienced by people with labels, such as those given to people with mental illness. It is useful for clients and social workers to process successes based on power and human rights definitions.

At this point in the social work relationship, it is not uncommon for some clients to indicate that they have not made as much progress as it seems. The client may point to various criteria to demonstrate her or his own shortcomings or to register some verbal sense of being abandoned. This behavior can be complicated to deal with as it raises the possibility that ending would be premature and possibly harmful. Also possible, however, is that clients choose this means to make known their lack of self-confidence in making their way independently, or their reluctance to leave the relationship. One effective way to address such dynamics is to be transparent about the process and discuss it with the client. Whether or not you offer to continue to work with a client for a longer time is a matter of your professional judgment, your supervisor's judgment, and all the other constraints in the agency or funding sources, such as managed care.

A second possibility is for clients to threaten to leave the relationship early in anticipation of ending. This often seems like an "I'll fire you before you fire me" response to minimize a sense of abandonment and is sometimes called **flight**. In this case, you will want to make every effort to engage the client in the process for at least one more session in which you can address the issue of ending and strive for closure. Clients who pointedly (and physically) avoid the ending steps in the work, in some cases are the ones to benefit most in personal growth by a positive ending process.

The identification of shortcomings in your own work is another area in which you may get an unexpected challenge. When you ask for ideas about those aspects of the intervention that did not unfold as you or the client had hoped or expected, you must be truly open to receiving a critical answer. An account of your shortcomings or those of the process itself can come as a surprise to you, especially if you have not heard such expressions of dissatisfaction along the way. Although hearing critical comments can be difficult, you can choose to learn from them and remain open to the meanings your client has in making them.

Making and Clarifying Plans   Although there are times when the work is clearly finished and the client is ready to move ahead without your assistance, these are certainly not universal. You may determine the best course of action is to make a referral to a different type of service, or transfer your client to another social worker in your agency or to a different agency. For example, you have worked with a client named "Sam" throughout the school year in which you had your practicum at the agency where Sam receives services. As the month of May nears, you realize that it is not likely that he will complete the work he wanted to do before you leave your position. In negotiation with him, you will need to reassess, much as in the earlier phases, where he is in the agreed-to work, where he wants to go from here, and through what arrangement it is mostly likely he can continue his work effectively. You can help to clarify his options and assist him in assessing his own needs at the point in which you must terminate with him. Be aware that this stage represents a potential ending to services, which may either set him back toward reaching his goals or promote a continuation in his growth.

When the decision is made to refer the client to another agency, you will assume the role of broker. As discussed previously, the broker is responsible for establishing a relationship with a network of resources. Regardless of your skill level and the success of your work with the client system, you have the potential to undo any client gains with an inappropriate or ill-conceived referral.

In those cases when the client is ready with some certainty to end professional services, a plan is needed for maintaining the gains and/or continuing further growth in the community. Some clients who no longer have the protective atmosphere of the client–worker relationship may find it difficult to maintain the changes they made without some clear way to reinforce them. You can help by identifying and exploring the situations that are likely to challenge the client's gains and consider strategies for addressing future stresses. You can also help by encouraging the identification of a natural network of support before ending the work, or identifying other community resources that will be available. Consider again the termination with Sam. You and Sam may identify formal (e.g., agencies, services, organizations) and informal (e.g., individuals) resources that are available to him following the termination of his relationship with you. Most clients will have to return to the context in which their struggles arose, so a strategy to cope with that environment can be critical to maintaining the gains. In Sam's case, a "rehearsal" of his response to potential situations that may arise for him may be a strategy that he can rely on when you are no longer a resource for him.

Sharing Responses to Endings This task may be the most sensitive of the dimensions of ending the work. You will need to anticipate, to the extent that you can, the way in which your client will respond and those issues that will require your particular attention. Remember that many clients have endured a series of difficult endings in their lives. For example, they may have experienced relationships that abruptly fell apart without their having any control or understanding of them. They also may have been removed from abusive homes or witnessed violence that resulted in death or separation. The devastation of poverty and social exclusion frequently creates the chaotic climate that leads to turbulence and disconnection. If ending well with your client turns out to be the most positive aspect of your work together, that, in and of itself, will be work well done and could provide the benefit of modeling the healthy ending to a relationship.

Social workers themselves may have experienced similarly chaotic, some-times traumatic, disruptions as clients. It is crucial that social workers know and understand their own history with regard to disengaging from relationships. Many social workers struggle as much as or more than clients in termination, and they need to gain the insights that will allow them to facilitate a professional process that provides a benefit to the client. Many new social workers are surprised to realize how attached they become to a client, and find they are not prepared to respond appropriately to their feelings or the client. This understandable reaction is an issue for supervision. To facilitate this process, the social worker can recall that the relationship is for the clients' well-being, and not for their own well-being.

In the process of discussing feelings about termination, you can let clients know about your ambivalent feeling about the ending: that you feel sad at ending the relationship; but that you have enjoyed knowing them, and that you have confidence that they will meet their own needs effectively in the future. It may be helpful to offer the possibility of future work together if the client needs assistance. It is generally not appropriate to express acute feelings of loss so that clients feel they must help you cope, and it is not appropriate to continue the relationship beyond whatever follow-up arrangements you might make without a new process.

Over the course of a career, many client situations challenge these guidelines. There may be situations, particularly in rural social work practice, that involve the potential for dual relationships. Such situations have less than clear boundaries. In these cases, the social worker can seek dialogue with supervisors and peers and to process the issues for which no simple rule is adequate. The following describes another situation that may challenge these guidelines.

Respecting Cultural Consistency   Just as social workers are ethically bound to honor the cultural dimensions that the client brings to your work together, social workers must also anticipate and attend to the meanings they make of endings. Clients who identify as ethnically different from the dominant culture may have approaches and reactions to endings that are different from that of the social worker. The social worker is, thus, bound to incorporate cultural diversity into the termination process. Termination processes and rituals need to be culturally appropriate (Fortune, 2009). For example, it is not uncommon in some cultural groups for a child's schoolteacher to be invited to a family birthday party. If the client lives in a culture with tightly woven informal ties, a client may view the formal aspects of ending the work and cutting off the relationship as a reflection of your annoyance or rejection.

On the other hand, some clients may find it difficult to share their emotions verbally about ending because their cultural orientation encourages a restrained and private approach to sentiment. It may be more productive to emphasize the return of the client to her or his ethnic community, whose support and nurturance will help to consolidate the gains. This rejoining of the community is viewed as especially critical to communities of color (Lum, 2004). In some situations a client may bring you a gift, a gesture that represents a more comfortable way to express feelings, reflect celebration, and offer a suitable token of closure. In others you may want to maintain a more formal, businesslike relationship similar to the tone maintained throughout the work. Avoid objectifying or stereotyping any client by focusing solely on cultural difference (Diller, 2007). You will need to be mindful of your client as a whole person who brings idiosyncrasies as well as cultural traditions to the social work relationship. The dynamics of endings probably engender more commonalities than differences, and the person sitting across from you saying good-bye is, after all, the same person you have shared the work with all along.

Finally, your own cultural sensibilities about endings will influence the scenario as well. Anticipating your own patterns is helpful, particularly if they are likely to vary from those of your clients in any significant way. As mentioned, endings can evoke difficult feelings for all people, and some of us have developed more sophisticated ways than others to get around them. Even in the social work literature, there is more attention to beginnings than endings. Endings can represent a metaphorical death, and by recognizing your responses to that, you will be able to say goodbye to clients in an effective, positive, and professional way.

STRAIGHT TALK ABOUT TERMINATION AND ENDINGS

The termination processes discussed thus far have assumed conditions in which ending is planned. However, endings often are not planned and are not under your control and your role becomes to negotiate the unexpected. Earlier we explored scenarios in which the client leaves the relationship before you expect. In addition to life-changing events, clients terminate because they do not feel the relationship has been fully established. For example, when the client is not clear about expectations or does not share the social worker's understanding of the purpose, the meetings may seem unfocused and without direction. Social workers identify outcome goals that the client may not find relevant (even when clients "agree" to them). If there is not sufficient clarity about an ending point in the work, the client may not be committed to remaining engaged in the process. In such cases the work may continue, but the client grows discouraged.

There are countless reasons for the work to end prematurely, all of which present the social worker with dilemmas regarding the appropriate response and its meaning to the client system. Without pressuring the client unduly, the most useful strategy is to make contact, if possible, and encourage the client to return to the work, if only to end it in a more purposeful way. This approach conveys respect for the integrity of the work while leaving the client in control of the future of the work. This contact provides an opportunity to explore the dynamics of the relationship, which may provide important information to inform your future work.

In institutional settings in which the client has been transferred to another unit or service, you may want to petition your supervisor for a single meeting so that you can reconnect with your client, if only briefly, to review the work and acknowledge the shift in care. Although institutions tend to organize themselves in terms that meet the staff's, rather than clients', needs, make an effort to prioritize the latter whenever you can. When you have made every effort, either to continue the work with a client or simply to have one session to end your work together, and your client does not respond, you will need to respect the manner of ending she or he has chosen. It is the client's choice at that point, and you, representing the ideal of self-determination, will humbly understand the limits of your influence. You will most likely hope that your client has made a new plan.

An ending that will occur for most social workers at some point in their career is the termination that results from the worker leaving the organization. The already complex process of termination is made more challenging when the social worker informs the client that she or he is leaving the program or organization. When the social work relationship ending is worker-initiated, the client can feel a loss of control, disappointment, and/or anger, both over the ending and the future of her or his intervention (Siebold, 2007). While the social worker and client are best served by following a traditional termination process to the extent possible, another important task is to openly process feelings about the termination. For example, you may say to the client, "You may not have experienced the ending of a formal helping relationship before. What feelings are you having about our work coming to a close?"

FORMAL EVALUATIONS

The term **evaluation** raises anxiety in many practitioners, but most social workers can appreciate the importance of evaluating practice. Evaluation can provide feedback regarding goal achievement, the utility of a particular approach or method, and about the experience of the client in the work (among many other things). Evaluation can be globally focused, behaviorally directed, and process oriented. Evaluations can also reflect on individual progress, group development, and changes in power structures as it recognizes success. In short, evaluation can be exceedingly useful for practitioners when viewed as a tool for development rather than a threat.

The following discussion will highlight issues in evaluation as they increasingly occur in everyday practice. First, preliminary guidelines for the generalist social work practitioner who engages in evaluation procedures will be explored.

Priorities in Evaluation

A longstanding debate continues regarding the types and relevance of various evaluative strategies that are most appropriate for social work practice. As you recall from Chapter 4, some experts maintain that social workers need empirical, evidenced-based practice to practice in our contemporary society. Practice evaluation data can have multiple uses, including being utilized to inform and improve your practice assessment and interventions, incorporated into proposals for funding, and program planning. While there is considerable attention being devoted to the need to justify one's practice, social workers are ethically obligated to maintain their professional commitments and values. Bloom, Fischer, and Orme (2009, p. 15) suggest that, in order to be an evaluation-informed practitioner, one can strive to be a **scientific practitioner**. A scientific practitioner combines the use of evidence and evaluation without compromising the "art and creativity of practice," thus scientific practice includes: (1) incorporating research and evaluation to identify interventions that are known to be effective; (2) systematically monitoring and evaluating one's practice through single-system designs (described below); (3) being committed to ongoing learning to improve practice competencies; (4) approaching social work practice with a goal of problem-solving, investigation, and discovery; and (5) remaining committed to the values and ethics of social work practice (p. 15).

Social work ethics mandates that the provision of service obligations will take precedence over data collection and evaluation efforts. However, in strengthening and enhancing practice, evaluative strategies are an important component of effective practice. Evaluation of practice can provide feedback that is consistent with social work practice requirements, values, and commitment to informed practice.

In the following two sections, two major methods of evaluation will be presented: empirical design processes and reflective assessment. These two evaluation methods serve different purposes, and they can help to balance the overall activity. First, they recognize the contemporary requirement for evidence-based practice, that is, practice guided by empirical, scientific evidence that the intervention has been successful. In addition, they can validate the contemplative, postmodern social worker's inclination to critique the traditional processes of practice and evaluation through focused critical reflection.

Quantitative and Empirical Processes: Evidence-Based Practice

While no substantial overlap exists with research methods in the quantitative processes for evaluating practice, two tools for gathering such evaluative data are discussed: single-subject design and goal attainment scaling (GAS).

Single-Subject Design   Applicable with any theoretically guided intervention, the **single-subject design** (SSD) is a grouping of evaluative procedures based on an intuitive framework for examining changes in one client over time (Fischer & Orme, 2008). Usually, the social worker and client system complete repeated measurements from over the course of their work together. Conversely, a social worker could follow one intervention over a series of clients. Single-system design evaluation plans serve to assess, monitor, and adapt to changes and compare the effectiveness of different interventions (Bloom et al., 2009, pp. 264–265).

In order to administer this design effectively, the client and social worker meet over a period of time to allow for repeated measurements. The social worker and client first agree on the behavior, attitude, or belief to be measured and the way in which this variable will be measured. The behavior(s) selected is one that should reflect(s) the goals of the work. Peripheral concerns, (i.e., if the client arrives on time) are not typically the focus of a single-subject design evaluation. There is no maximum number of attributes that the social worker and client can select, but in general you will want to limit them to a few after considering a wider range (Bloom et al., 2009).

Measurement can be attained by frequency (the number of occurrences) or through a standardized scale that yields a numerical result. The social worker and the client establish a relatively consistent interval for taking measurements throughout the course of the evaluation. For example, if you want to monitor the number of new social contacts your client initiates over time, consider the accumulated frequency over a standard period of time (e.g., every two weeks).

In most cases, the phases of your evaluation begin with a **baseline** (the rate at which or number of times the behavior occurred before the client came to you), intervention, **maintenance** (the period of stabilizing client gains), and follow-up. The measures can then be charted to depict a visual pattern. If a baseline cannot be established because your client needs intervention right away, improvements can still be plotted as they occur during the intervention (for example, after one month, then two months of working together).

If a baseline can be established without withholding the intervention, the differences between no intervention and intervention can be depicted. This provides a bit more evidence that the improvement is a result of your work as it assumes that the baseline measure would continue without your intervention (this is, of course, a big assumption). If the intervention is interrupted (e.g., the client or you go on vacation and no one fills in for you) and the frequency of your client's social initiations is reduced, you can see if restarting your work results in renewed improvement. If it does, the connection between your work and your client's improvement is strengthened, and the possibility that some other event brought on the improvement is reduced. However, such interruptions may not be in the client's best interests, and the course of the work should not be disrupted simply to demonstrate its success. The single-subject design is highly flexible and generally easy to use. Exhibit 5.2 provides an example of an SSD graph.

Goal Attainment Scaling Used in a variety of settings, **goal attainment scaling** (GAS) represents a standardized framework that is customized by inserting individual goals. The first step of the multi-phase process is to identify two to five client goals and develop a scale for each of them based on the quality of the outcome. The following is a useful scale (Bloom et al., 2009):

0 Most unfavorable outcome thought likely.
1 Less than expected success.
2 Expected level of success.
3 More than expected success.
4 Most favorable outcome thought likely.

EXHIBIT 5.2

Simple Single-Subject Design

In this example of the single-subject design model, you can see that during the baseline period, before the work began, the client initiated three, then two, then no new social contacts at intervals of two weeks. During the weeks of service, the numbers increased from two to seven, with a setback at week 8. After the work was over, the client initiated seven, then five, then six, and seven new contacts. This indicates improvement from the baseline period and extends over a four-week period following the work.

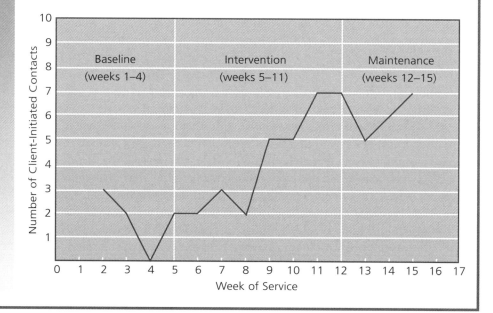

In this model, in a few words, the social worker and client describe the client's condition or status before the intervention on each goal, reflecting position 1 on the scale. The next step is to indicate the way in which deterioration may look at the lowest point (0). Finally, the social worker and client describe the best scenario (4), and they distinguish between levels 2 and 3. For example, if one of your client's goals is to attend parenting classes as part of a plan to regain custody of her children, you may agree on the statements depicted in Exhibit 5.3. Consider that you have also agreed on two additional goals: attending GED classes and maintaining a clean apartment.

Following this process, you and your client can add further precision to measuring goal achievement by assigning a relative weight to each goal reflecting its importance in the individual case situation. As you can see in Exhibit 5.3, the individual weight is 75 for attending parenting classes, 15 for keeping her apartment clean, and 10 for attending GED classes, for a total weight of 100. Your client's

EXHIBIT 5.3

*Quantitative
and Empirical
Processes*

Client: *Clarissa*

Key: ✓ = Beginning level   ✗ = Ending level

Attainment Grade	Task 1: Attend parenting classes	Task 2: Attend GED classes	Task 3: Keep apartment clean
0 Most unfavorable outcome likely	✓ No attendance at parenting classes	No attendance at GED classes	✓ No satisfactory ratings for cleanliness
1 Less than expected success	Attend less than 50% of the time	✓ Attend less than 40% of the time	Receive satisfactory ratings less than 60% of the time
2 Expected level of success	Attend 50–75% of the time	Attend 40–60% of the time	Receive satisfactory ratings 60–80% of the time
3 More than expected success	✗ Attend 76–95% of the time	Attend 61–85% of the time	Receive satisfactory ratings 81–95% of the time
4 Best anticipated success	Attend 96–100% of the time	✗ Attend 86–100% of the time	✗ Receive satisfactory ratings 96–100% of the time

Summary	Task 1	Task 2	Task 3	Total
Percent of goal	75	10	15	100
Change in score	3	3	4	
Total score	225	30	60	315
Possible total score	300	40	60	400
Percent of goal attained	75%	75%	100%	79%

progress is tracked by placing a check mark in the cell that best describes the client's status at the point of entry into the social work relationship (acting as a baseline) and an X indicating the best description at the point of ending. You then calculate the weighted change score by subtracting the beginning score from the ending score and multiplying the difference by the weight.

The next step is to compute the percentage of possible change for each scaled goal. To calculate this percentage, you determine the highest possible mark on the scale and then divide it into the actual weighted change score. Finally, you calculate an overall score by summing all the possible scores for all the goals and dividing that number into the sum of the actual weighted change scores. Although this procedure may seem daunting and overly empirical, it becomes intuitive with practice.

Originally developed for use with individual clients, goal attainment scaling is well suited to a range of social work interventions, including child and adult mental health, families and organizations. GAS has also been shown to be an effective strategy for evaluating interventions targeted at resolving crises (Roberts, 2005). With crisis interventions and GAS both having an emphasis on short-term, structured and specific characteristics, the social worker engaged in crisis intervention work can easily and quickly use GAS to evaluate for both the client and her or himself the process and outcomes of their work together.

Other Forms of Evaluation There are other quantitative measurement scales and other methods of attaining evaluative data that are not always quantitative. This latter group includes such instruments as client satisfaction scales or client evaluations of the agency, the social worker, or both. Although these tools are often considered highly subjective and not particularly rigorous, they can frequently provide both the social worker and the agency with valuable information about the way in which the service was experienced by the client.

Postmodern Views of Evaluation In this world of managed care and increasing calls for evidence-based accountability, effective social workers must be knowledgeable about documenting, evaluating, and accounting for the usefulness of their efforts. Nevertheless, challenges to and criticisms of these methods, based on very different perspectives, do exist and are worth considering. Critics further charge that these models exclude the richer and nuanced contributions of aspects of client situations that are not easily quantified, as well as qualitative research, and overshadow the ethnographic forms of evaluation that question the assumptions of the everyday world.

These approaches have been based on expectation, researcher bias, and a political agenda that most social workers find unhelpful. Even when workers find themselves in a situation in which they must accommodate the system by demonstrating the value of their work through empirical evaluations, they cannot afford to de-emphasize the possibilities of vulnerabilities and opportunities for error in the evaluations themselves. This is a place for a form of bilingualism—that is, you will need to speak the language of contemporary demands, and at the same time keep alert to and keep up with the readings of their critiques.

There are social workers who find these empirical methods somewhat mechanical or lacking in substance and want to examine their work on additional levels. Although the support for evidenced-based practice in quantitative terms is strong in the profession, social workers are not restricted to these evaluative strategies. Social workers can also use the processes of reflection about their practice, as discussed below (see Lawler & Bilson, 2004).

Qualitative and Reflective Processes

Additional ways to view and consider the work of social workers are presented next. Case studies and explorations of compatibility with theoretical perspectives and quality of relationship will be discussed. These methods have the power to expand your thinking and create a different level of consciousness about social work practice. These are not meant to compete with empirical processes but to balance the experience of self-evaluation.

With any of these methods, there are a multitude of questions that could be asked; some are suggested in the discussion. The most useful perspective is to focus your inquiry purposefully on a relatively specific set of dimensions. If you want to take your inquiry further, consider engaging your supervisor as a second reader in a case study or your peers in a conversational group to explore particular issues. Such a focus can constitute a useful framework for ongoing staff meetings and professional development activities, as well.

Case Studies   Like single-system designs, **case studies** involve intensive analysis of one individual, group, or family and depend on accurate, careful, and richly detailed record keeping. A case study typically begins with the engagement of the client and social worker and continues throughout the course of the work. Case studies do not generate empirical data from planned comparisons as they are an accounting of the client's situation while working with you. However, case studies, still in use in contemporary practice, have a long history within the social work profession and provided the basis for the evolution of the formal evaluation process used today (Bloom et al., 2009). While space prohibits the presentation of a case study as they can be lengthy, you are encouraged to review the interactive cases found on the book's companion website for the Sanchez family or Carla Washburn (www.routledgesw.com/cases). As you review the cases and complete the interactive assignments, you can document your thoughts, reactions, and plans in the online notebook. These notes can provide the foundation for a case study. Upon completion of the full planned change effort, you will have ample information to finalize a case study in which you can evaluate the progress and efforts related to the case.

A full case study, though certainly not a new method, can provide you with a rich history for postmodern reflection. For example, in reviewing the initial contact, you might wonder if your sensitivity matched the client's need for validation, consider other ways you could have articulated your purpose, or reflect on the course of your work if you had taken another tack. Or perhaps you thought you were clear about the agency requirements, but looking back on the records, you can see where there might have been some confusion reflected in the language. How might the work have gone if those requirements were truly clear to the client? There are literally hundreds of ways you can reflect on the work that may be helpful, both in supervision and on your own. A record of your observations, what you thought about it, and what the client said—all of these can provide material for analysis later. Case studies are particularly useful in noting your own growth as you learn from the experiences that your clients have in working with you and in turn explore your responses to them.

Explorations of Compatibility with Theoretical Perspectives   Another strategy to evaluate your work is to explore its consistency with the perspectives you want to guide your work. This approach is especially helpful when those perspectives present challenges to you and stretch your thinking.

This book is committed to the four perspectives stressed from the beginning: social justice, human rights, the strengths perspective, and critical social construction. These theoretical frameworks introduce multiple perspectives, therefore they can be translated into broad criteria for evaluating the work you want to do. For example, are you consistently recognizing the strengths of your clients, or do you tend to be pulled into the pathology orientation that dominated much of social work practice throughout our history? Are you alert to social justice concerns when you meet with clients who seem unable to make their way in this culture? Can you truly remain open to the multiple realities that critical social construction emphasizes? Do you rationalize human rights violations because they are so common in our culture?

These considerations can also apply to more specific practice perspectives, such as feminist or narrative lenses. If, for example, you adopt a feminist theory that stresses the importance of power analysis, is your work consistent with that type of analysis? Do you return to a more traditional perspective regarding the issues that your client brings by emphasizing her reluctance to leave an abusive relationship or her lack of self-esteem? Can you keep an analytical structure of gender relations in the forefront rather than falling back into our society's tendency to blame women for occupying a power-down position? Which aspects of feminist theory do you carry out well, and which seem to call for continued growth?

If your framework is narrative, are you completely open to the complexity of the client's story? Do you wish you had been more transparent in your responses to it? Do you recognize your client as expert, or is there a temptation to believe you know better? Which aspects of the perspective are troubling to you? Which seem to come naturally? These considerations, of course, do not yield empirical data; rather, they can help you decide to what degree you can work within the constraints of particular perspectives, and they can help you identify the ways in which you want to grow intellectually and skillfully.

Explorations of Quality of Relationship   The nature of the relationship you develop with your client offers another opportunity for exploration. Is the relationship consistent with your purpose in the work? Was openness a characteristic of the connection early on? Was openness difficult for either you or your client to establish? What can you learn from the client's struggle? What can you learn from your own? What cultural dimensions influenced the development of the relationship, and what was successful in working through those issues (see Maramaldi, Berkman, & Barusch, 2005)?

This might be a situation in which to look at your own idiosyncrasies. For example, do you respond more easily to people most like you? Do you wonder if you encouraged the client's dependence on you? Do you struggle with keeping useful boundaries between you and your client? Are you comfortable with the amount of self-disclosure you engaged in? Are there some kinds of clients that are hard for you to be positive about?

Additional questions that can arise out of this kind of self-examination lead to more generic issues: What is the ideal relationship between client and worker? How does it look? Is it different in one setting from another? Is it likely that all your client relationships will fall into this range of ideal? How does the ideal relationship interface with the client's goal attainment?

STRAIGHT TALK ABOUT EVALUATION AND RECLAIMING OUR KNOWLEDGE

As the discussion on intervention, termination, and evaluation comes to a conclusion, consider the distinctiveness of social work as a profession and consider its greater purposes, as social workers are informed by social justice, human rights, strengths, and the value of multiple realities. This is a profession that lives through a combination of practical orientation and a strong sense of caring. As you struggle to account for yourself and the ways in which you know things, remember social work's legacy of context and care. These are always difficult to measure, and as long as you are pressured to assign numerical indicators, some of your most important contributions could be missed. You will recall from Chapter 1, the term "practice wisdom" was used. Practice wisdom is considered to be the social worker's application of her or his "accumulation of information, assumptions, ideologies, and judgments" (Barker, 2003, p. 334). Identified through the use of reflecting on one's practice experiences, practice wisdom enables the social worker to translate empirical and conceptual knowledge into practice behaviors that are most appropriately suited to the client situation (Chu & Tsui, 2008). Social workers' distinctive knowledge, based on a practice wisdom of person-in-environment, strength and struggle, and heart and grit is the "humble stuff of lived experience and values and flies in the face of most current views about how social workers know what they know" (Weick, 1999, p. 327).

As an empowering practice, then, with real people and real misery as well as real joys, social work will ask other questions about its effectiveness, including:

- Who benefits from this work? If the goals of social work relate to helping clients find empowerment, how are they realized? If a client demonstrates improved capacity to manage a household budget, for example, is there a link to her experience of poverty? Is it identified and challenged? Will she quietly and skillfully manage on close to nothing (and is this progress?), or will the benefit go beyond, to others like her, and to challenge the structure that supports poverty?

- Whose values are most salient? Social work's values are at the heart of the work. Do they dominate the client relationship? How do social workers negotiate differing values among people who do not share theirs? This is one of social work's most challenging dilemmas.

- What changes have occurred in the power structure? Have social workers helped to raise consciousness about oppression and the internalization of it? Have clients joined with others to respond to oppressive imbalances in the structural arrangements of our culture? As work with clients' ends, is some move toward empowerment visibly in progress? (Lee, 2001).

These questions lead us back to the beginning of our exploration of social work practice. As a social worker, you will likely find satisfaction in connecting with clients. You will struggle to meet the demands of their preferred realities and document them for those who require an accounting. You will experience frustrations and successes, answer many questions, and come up with many more than have been raised here. The world will change dramatically and will challenge you with its excitement and danger as well as its incredible potential. You will figure out how to respond to it in ways that are consistent with your values, your social work ethics, your sense of social justice and human rights, and your respect for different views and experience.

Your own story as a social work practitioner will be embedded in the hundreds of stories of your individual clients, groups, and families, the organizations and communities you serve, and in the story of global change. Your choices are legion and your opportunities enormous. In the end, these will return to the story of the profession. You as a member of the next generation of citizen/social workers will author the next chapter.

CONCLUSION

This chapter has looked into several dimensions of the intervention, termination, and evaluation actions that social workers take. The practice setting, theoretical perspectives, and perception of roles influence the ways in which you work to support clients' strengths and to support their environments. The overall fit of your activities with and your beliefs about individuals creates a sound backdrop for expanding your work into other system levels. The following chapters will integrate and extend these same processes to groups, families, organizations, and communities. This will serve both to consolidate the principles and skills in this first part of the book and to take them beyond, across system levels.

In the paradoxical way that some things constantly change while they remain the same, so endings and evaluations continue and evolve. All the same, we will all experience new ways to do things in the future of social work practice. Some of you will work in much more complex settings that integrate public and private sectors through partnerships and alliances that will represent a departure from the agency practice context often discussed here. Some of you will choose more radical forms of practice in which you will challenge the historical and professional legacies you see as unjust or obsolete. Others of you will continue to practice with only incremental changes from the models under which you trained. All of these dimensions of practice will have implications for beginning and ending the social work relationship, for executing and evaluating the work, and for grappling with the obstacles that get in the way of the vision. There are no magic formulas for anticipating all of the implications of change for social work. Your flexibility, integrity, and penchant for the experiential context of your work, as well as your caring for people who struggle, will be your own best guides for your future practice.

MAIN POINTS

- The most pressing client issue in the perspective of the client is the starting point for the intervention. This issue is defined by the context of the client's unique situation and by the actions agreed upon in the assessment and planning phase.

- To support clients' strengths, social workers act in context to normalize and capitalize on those strengths. Social workers engage in responding to feelings, determining their meaning, and supporting diversity.

- To support clients' environments, social workers are accountable to the client system; they should follow the demands of the client task; maximize the potential supports in the client's environments; identify, reinforce, and/or increase the client's repertoire of strategic behaviors; and they apply these principles to themselves.

- Examining traditional social work roles and their assumptions within the context of contemporary social work practice provides another perspective on social work practice in the context of the roles of case manager, counselor, broker, mediator, educator, client advocate, and collaborator.

- Exploring a case situation through the lens of empowerment perspectives demonstrates the work in context and how it fits with the perspectives emphasized in this book.

- The planned ending process with clients consists of several components that can benefit clients by consolidating the gains of the work and the relationship. Social worker and client must have clarity regarding timing, original agreement, successes and failures, and responses to termination. The same basic process for ending work, when flexibly used with different emphases, can be applied to families, groups, organizations, and communities with additional and specific components to consider with groups (to be discussed in Chapters 7, 9, 11, and 13).

- Unplanned endings pose a special challenge to both social workers and clients. Social workers can attempt to reconnect and end the work, but may have to acknowledge the limits of their influence and honor client self-determination.

- Quantitative and empirical evaluation processes are increasingly required in social work practice. Two options for evaluation are the single-subject design and the goal attainment scaling.

- Qualitative and reflective practices also constitute an important method for evaluation and professional growth as they relate to philosophical commitments, theoretical perspectives, and relationship building.

EXERCISES

1. Go to www.routledgesw.com/cases, review the video vignette with Emilia Sanchez and respond to the following questions:
   a. What strengths does she possess?
   b. What thoughts and/or feelings resulted from watching the video that, if verbalized, would not reflect a strengths-based approach?
   c. As the social worker, what are your next steps with Emilia?
   d. Either with a group in or outside of class, develop a strengths-based treatment plan for Emilia.

2. Go to www.routledgesw.com/cases and click on Carla Washburn. Begin by reviewing the engagement and assessment phases. After your review of the first two phases, click on Phase 3: Intervention. Complete each of the tasks identified in the five steps (introduction, goals and needs, client tasks, social worker tasks, timeline, and coalitions).

3. The admissions unit of a psychiatric care facility issues a daily report to all staff on a single sheet of paper that summarizes all the patient admissions, discharges, visits, legal proceedings, and other activities for the preceding 24-hour period. This summary is meant to convey useful information for all staff and it is viewed as helpful to social workers who needed to monitor client status. One of the categories on the form is entitled "body count" and is a tally of the number of patient/residents actually in the hospital at midnight. A social worker from a local community mental health agency was visiting her client who was in the hospital and she heard reference to this sheet. She was horrified at the language of "body count," to which you were by then accustomed.

   a. What do you think is the issue here? Why does it matter? Be as specific as you can.

   b. In what way would you address it? Would such an activity be consistent with your view of a social worker's role?

   c. Develop a plan that includes at least three steps you might take.

   Compare with other students and be prepared to discuss in class or write brief responses to each question to submit.

4. Tammy is a 35-year-old Caucasian female seeking treatment after her release from a 21-day residential drug/alcohol treatment facility. She is referred to your agency by the public child welfare department. As a result of continued substance abuse and an arrest and conviction for driving under the influence with her eight-year-old son, Jared, in the car, physical custody of Jared was granted to Tammy's mother.

   Tammy has a 20-year history of drug and alcohol abuse and she has been diagnosed with Bipolar Disorder. She was recently prescribed medication by the staff psychiatrist at the residential treatment facility. It is a new medication and is not covered by her insurance. She has been non-compliant with medication in the past due to the side effects and her drug/alcohol use. She has had brief periods of sobriety but often relapses after a few weeks. This is the longest she has been sober since the birth of her son eight years earlier.

   Tammy has never been married and has a difficult relationship with her family of origin. Her mother placed her in foster care at the age of eight due to Tammy's behavior. Tammy reports that her mother was physically and emotionally abusive to her and often would leave her with various relatives when her mother found a new boyfriend. Tammy's father is not involved. Tammy has few friends and little contact with her mother. She is angered that her mother has custody of her son. Tammy has been involved with her son's father sporadically for the past nine years. Currently, she names him as a source of support.

Tammy is not currently employed but receives public assistance in the form of Medicaid, disability assistance, and food stamps. She lives with her boyfriend but would like to have her own apartment. She has her high school diploma and is interested in continuing her education.

Partner with other students and complete the following exercises:

a. Using narrative interventions, reconstruct this case from a strengths-based perspective.

b. What roles would you play in helping Tammy?

c. Construct a strengths-based plan of intervention utilizing solution-focused interventions.

d. Share your findings with the class and compare plans of interventions.

5. Reflect on a time in your life when you contemplated making a change. What did you do? Was it successful? What factors led to the success? If not successful, what was missing?

6. Identify an area or behavior in your life that you would like to change (e.g., texting while driving, exercising, budgeting money, or time management). For one week, chart your journey in a journal, and note those factors that are helping you to maintain the change and those that are a negative influence on your efforts to maintain the change. At the end of the week, reflect on your progress or lack thereof. Consider your feelings before the change, during the change, and the results.

7. Write your own life story from a strengths-based perspective.

The Family:
Engagement and Assessment

The social work profession and the family have traveled a long distance together, sometimes in close companionship and sometimes on divergent paths, only to meet once again on the same road. Our profession began in the company of the family and has returned to it once again.

Ann Hartman and Joan Laird, 1983

Key Questions for Chapter 6

(1) What competencies do I need to engage with and assess families? (EPAS 2.1.10(a) & (b))

(2) What are the social work practice behaviors that enable me to effectively engage and assess families? (EPAS 2.1.10(a) & (b))

(3) How can I utilize evidence to practice research-informed practice and practice-informed research to guide the engagement and assessment with families? (EPAS 1.2.6)

(4) How do the perspectives and experiences from my present family and/or family of origin impact my engagement with and assessment of client families?

FAMILY IS THE EARLIEST, MOST BASIC, AND SOME SAY most challenging small group one can experience during a lifetime. It is also probably the most powerful in shaping who we come to be. For some, family means home, safety, and acceptance. For others, family means violence and danger. Some people may feel important and cherished with family or never quite good enough or even useless. Others may feel swallowed up in their family's dysfunction, or may long for, and bask in, the wholeness of unconditional support. Most of us experience a mix of feelings in between these. Family is a complicated enterprise, and many of us harbor some of its tensions on occasion that make us both joyful and troubled. Virtually all members of society have experienced some kind of family, and most have ideas (or dreams) of the qualities that an ideal family could or should possess.

This chapter explores the concept of family—definition, meaning, and place within the contemporary social context—and the process of engagement and assessment with families. Also examined will be several theoretical perspectives for working with traditional and contemporary family structures as well as dynamics, skills, and tools for working with the range of families. Challenges and strategies for finding balance in understanding the impact of families on your clients and yourself are also explored.

FAMILIAR PERSPECTIVES AND SOME ALTERNATIVES

The enormous and rapid changes in social rules in the United States and most Western countries have led many in society to feel that the traditional family has been lost. A traditional vision of the ideal U.S. family portrays a nuclear group consisting of two heterosexual adults and two or perhaps three children. The father supports the family economically, and the mother supports it emotionally. There are clear roles, rules, and jobs that each member undertakes. If the mother also works outside the home, she is still free to participate in the kindergarten car pool, do the laundry, entertain friends, and "be there" for her husband and children. A more contemporary version of the father makes him increasingly sensitive to the feelings and needs of his wife and children, but his work still takes priority. In contrast, the National Association of Social Workers (NASW) (2007a, para. 3) provides a definition of the contemporary family as being "two or more people who assume obligations and responsibilities generally conducive to family life." This inclusive perspective on the concept of family thus embraces parents who are divorced, separated, unmarried, grandparents, gay, lesbian, bisexual, transgender, adoptive, and fostering, along with couples who have no children, partnered couples, and families caring for older adult members. Social workers must have an awareness of the need to utilize practice approaches that recognize the diversity and uniqueness of family constellations (Hull & Mather, 2006). For example, to avoid assumptions and confusion, the social worker is well served to ask the client system to describe and define her or his family unit (Wood & Tully, 2006) rather than make assumptions, based on household composition. Given the changing nature of the family and the fluidity of membership in some families, it is important to ask each member of the family, "Who do you consider to be part of your family?" A follow-up question may then be, "Of these people, who is biologically and/or legally related to you?" For instance, a client's "aunt" may not be a legal or biological family member but is considered by the client to be a part of her or his family.

Those nostalgic for the visions of family in prior eras are appalled at what they see today as a lack of morality in many young families. There is distress about young adults who live together with no permanent commitment. Single women often choose to become parents and do not suffer the social stigma so prevalent only a few generations earlier. Parents who are gay, lesbian, bisexual, and transgender, who earlier had to conceal their sexual identities, are joyfully parenting children, and many are serving as foster and adoptive parents in conjunction with state child protection agencies. Although these developments in our U.S. cultural norms are lamented by some, fear of change may overshadow the research about non-traditional family and parenting arrangements. This issue will be explored in greater detail later in this chapter.

Nonetheless, there are real issues in the surrounding context of the contemporary family that create concerns. The U.S. divorce rate of 52 percent (U.S. Census, 2010b) is closely related to the ever-growing number of children who live in a single parent-headed household with incomes below the poverty level. Numbers of children who live in poverty with a single mother have reached rates of 37 percent, while single father-headed households experience poverty rates of 17 percent (U.S. Census, 2008). Some believe that commitment to the stability and endurance of the most caring sense of family values in some settings seems to have vanished. The number of unmarried teen parents is again on the rise (41.9/1,000 teen females) (Martin et al., 2009), and the percentage of teen parents of color continues to rise (55–83 births/1,000 teen mothers (Martin et al., 2009). The associated legacies of perpetuated poverty, increased family violence, and health and mental health issues, and a sense that two generations—the child and the child's child—have sacrificed much of their potential, provide little hope for the future. Clearly, the change in predominant family compositions has required changes in service delivery, and impacts society. The result of such change has been serious societal issues with which society must grapple.

There are other ways to look at family. In keeping with this book's focus on multiple realities, the experiences of others will be explored that help to expose illusions about the family and present more balanced views. This chapter will discuss the experiences of both traditional and nontraditional families. Consider Box 6.1, which describes the experience of family for countless people who have been **marginalized**, that is, who have lived in the margins of our culture and others.

HISTORICAL ANTECEDENTS FOR FAMILY SOCIAL WORK

The social work profession has a long history of work with families, shaped by the context of the times. In community mental health centers and youth agencies, hospitals and schools, and welfare and child protection efforts, social workers work to strengthen families. Why is there such a concern for the maintenance of the family? What does our culture expect the family to do, and how do we think

BOX 6.1

*Family: Views
from the
Margins*

Rainbow Families of Puget Sound
Copyright: Harry Hu, courtesy of Shutterstock® images

• What we may consider now to be the ideal family has never actually flourished in any culture for any length of time: Children have historically been considered commodities that enhanced the economic status of their fathers, who owned them, and their value was often equated to the amount of work they did. Childhood as a time to be nourished and cherished is a relatively new and narrowly prescribed phenomenon of Western culture and some nations in the East. The United Nations instrument "The Rights of the Child" reflects the need for considering children as genuine people and not possessions. In contrast, in parts of the United States, children are prostitutes, drug dealers, and hired thieves. In much of the world they are all these and also soldiers.

• Ideal conceptions of the family have historically served to restrict and diminish the role of women as categorical caretakers. Many women throughout history have been required to abandon their dreams and have also been seen as property to be exploited. Men, too, are assumed to fit into tightly proscribed roles that may not be compatible with their identities or goals.

• In many families of the past, infant and childhood mortality was high and parents may have died by their early 40s. Such circumstances produced a crisis for remaining family members, resulting in placements with distant relatives, community members, or in orphanage care. The idealistic notion of earlier times places blinders on the realities of disease, early death, and other forms of danger that surely shaped the overall experience of family.

BOX 6.1

continued

- It is still the family, even in contemporary U.S. society, that is the primary force for socialization and nurturing of children and support of the community. As an example, the families of children experiencing mental illnesses still provide most of the care and nurturing of their adult children, in spite of federal and state programs designed to assist them.
- The definition of family as rigidly restricted to biological and legal ties and heterosexual partners or adoption has always marginalized and scapegoated significant numbers of people who have meaningful and productive relationships and who make significant contributions to the community, the socialization of children, and the general economic and social order.
- More contemporary notions of family have liberated both men and women to develop and carry out the roles of child caretaking, economic provision, management, personal development, and health care in a way that does not deny their individual aspirations and talents; the same principles hold for gay, lesbian, bisexual, and transgender families with biological or adopted children.
- Contemporary families have greater biological control over the number and timing of pregnancies and can plan family composition in a way that is consistent with their financial capacities and other internal demands (for example, one partner is in school or another is committed to the care of a parent). Women are now more able to exercise control over their reproduction, and make decisions about their future.

the family should work? Although there are many possible responses to these questions, two particular perspectives are examined that seem to have special relevance for social workers today—the family as a functioning unit and the family as a system.

Family as a Functioning Unit

A concrete way to think about the importance of the family is to explore the societal expectations of the family. The following functions are among those that are typically viewed as critical to the contemporary maintenance of families:

- Provide the material and economic necessities for sustenance and growth.
- Offer members emotional security, respect, safety, and a place for appropriate sexual expression.
- Provide a haven for privacy and rest.
- Assist, protect, and advocate for members who are vulnerable or who have special needs.

- Provide support for members' meaningful connection and contribution to community life.

- Facilitate the transmission of cultural heritage.

- Provide a socially and legally recognized identity.

- Create an environment in which children can be nurtured and socialized.

The responsibilities reflected here emphasize not only the functional roles of individual family members and their needs and identities but also the connection to their communities and the overall societal environment. This compilation is not prescriptive; that is, it does not specify *how* children should be nurtured but allows for individual and cultural interpretation. Rather than seeking individual or family dysfunction, the exploration of these tasks in various areas of family life tends to highlight strengths as well as areas for improvement. In that respect, this set of functions serves as a useful guide for assessing the degree to which societal expectations are met in any particular family.

Family as a System

The social work profession involves itself in interactions among people and between people and the environment and, as a result, the profession adopted systems theory in the 1970s with great enthusiasm. In general, **systems theory** posits that a system involves a series of components that are highly organized and dependent upon each other in an orderly way. In the profession, this conceptualization is applied to the multiple levels of practice (individual, group, family, organization, and community). The systems perspective remains influential in social work theory in spite of a growing number of critiques that suggest it is too rigid and tends to place the worker outside of the work. Nevertheless, systems theory holds continuing authority in many views of structural arrangements, particularly the family. Three elements of systems theory are particularly important:

- Change in one component
- Subsystems and boundaries
- Family norms

Change in One Component   Possibly the most powerful idea in the systems theory for social workers is the proposition that change in one part of the system will affect all other components. Social workers, therefore, seek to learn about various aspects of a client's environment, to include family functioning. For example, the fact that a child's father has just been sent to prison is useful information when exploring reasons for that child having angry outbursts or sullen withdrawals in school. In another example, a mother being physically abused by her intimate partner is likely to have repercussions on her daughter's fragile health. Social workers often find such connections, of one part to another, intuitive and useful. Still, you will want to guard against seeing such a situation as automatically producing one type of response. In systems theory, one set of actions can predict multiple sets of reactions. For example, the child whose father goes to prison may respond by being more attentive to his mother or by working harder in school or in another way that is not at all obvious outside the family.

Subsystems and Boundaries   Another dimension of systems theory that is relevant to social work is the concept of **subsystems**. Subsystems, or components of a system that also have interacting parts, provide a mechanism for organizing relationships and planning ways to engage with them. In systems theory, the individual is considered a subsystem of the family, the family is a subsystem of the community and the community is a subsystem of the culture. A family may also be a subsystem of more than one larger system, or of differing systems, so you must be thoughtful about making unqualified judgments regarding the place that an individual or group occupies within the system. For example, in a blended family, there may be members who consider themselves to be part of the family and community from the previous marriage. Social workers have the opportunity to support and facilitate such healthy transition relationships for client systems.

In thinking about the concept of family, social workers often distinguish between the subsystem of the parents and the subsystem of the children. The relationship between these subsystems is reflected in the types of **boundaries**, or limits that separate the systems that the family constructs. If the children are included in all decisions the family makes, the boundaries are **permeable**, meaning that information and interchange goes easily across them. However, permeable boundaries can be taken to the extreme of **diffuse boundaries**, which means that boundaries are too loose and that parents should assume more decision-making authorities to maintain appropriate boundaries between them and their children.

Appropriate boundaries between the subsystems of parents and children may vary considerably depending on culture, the times, background, and/or the boundaries within which the parents themselves were reared. Can you cite examples in your own family in which these boundaries are similar or different from those of your friends or other extended family members? Further, consider the way in which your experience with your own family might relate to families with whom you will be working.

Family Norms   Most families establish **family norms**, or rules of conduct, that are related to boundaries and subsystems. These can be similar to the norms described in Chapter 7, in application to groups, but have an additional complication in families in that they are often held as sacrosanct and not negotiable. Family norms may also never be articulated, despite the fact that all members of the family are clear about them. This implicit aspect of norms can make them difficult to address and challenge, so much so that family members may not even realize that there are rules; nevertheless, everyone understands the allowable behavior of family members. For example, all the members of a family may understand that no one will enter into a dispute with Dad at the dinner table, or that everyone will say grace, or that all of the children will go out of state to college. Some of these rules apply to everyday boundaries and may simply make some mundane things a lot easier (for example, if a door is closed, one is not to enter without knocking). Other such rules may signal secrets that are taboo or too difficult to talk about or that perpetuate unjust or oppressive situations, such as all the female children know not to find themselves in the same room alone with Grandpa, or no one asks Mom how she got a bruise on her face.

In applying a systems analysis to family norms, a social worker may recognize that interrupting the family's patterns of behavior or relationship by breaking a rule is, in fact, feasible and desirable. For example, a social worker may point out that one of the children spoke out one day about the bruises on Mom's face, which led to the mother talking about the violence and started the process of empowerment and decreased family violence. Yet, this process might also result in violence directed at the child who raised the issue in the first place; therefore, the social worker would not likely encourage a child to take such an action without support and protection. Family norms in such cases are often very powerful and need to be carefully evaluated before any family member is put at risk.

Implications of Family Systems Theory for Generalist Practice

Along with the notion of function, two specific dimensions reflected in family systems theories have influenced generalist social work practice with families. The first is family structure, and the second is intergenerational patterns. In many respects these represent a classic approach to Western ideology of the family and have influenced the responses of many social service policies and agencies. You may discover that these ideas have shaped your thinking also. As a basis for considering family structure and intergenerational patterns, consider the following practice principles for social work assessment and intervention with families that have evolved from a systemic perspective (Logan, Rasheed, & Rasheed, 2008, pp. 184–185):

1.   Family is considered within a "context" that is comprised of multiple systems.

2.   Rooted in the basic systemic foundation, the family "is more than the sum of its individual parts," all of which serves to function as a unique system.

3.   A change within one part of the family system creates change in the entire system.

4. Viewing the family as a unique system provides the practitioner with the opportunity to focus on the issues that present challenges to the entire system.

5. A systemic-focused assessment and intervention provides a view of the family as a complex system.

6. Behaviors are viewed as a product of the multi-faceted system and not the result of one individual or action.

7. A systems perspective that promotes a strengths-based perspective frames the family assessment within the context of the environment in which they live.

8. Family members, particularly those in minority groups, are viewed within the context of their family system as well as the larger societal system.

9. Family function may be impacted by the legal, social, and economic biases and discrimination that affect families with members who are considered to be in cultural, racial, ethnic, religious, or sexual minority groups.

Family Structure   The relationship among the generations of a family, especially between the subsystems of children and parents, constitutes the **family structure**. One of the early scholars in defining models for family interventions, Minuchin (1974) posits that the boundaries between children and parents should be clear and that parents should be in charge of major decisions as they also carry out appropriate caretaking functions. The difficulties that families experience are usually thought to be a result of blurring the boundaries between these two subsystems.

Some family boundaries may be so diffuse that the result is **enmeshment**, which suggests that family members are too close, have few distinctions in role or authority, and enjoy little autonomy or independence (Nichols, 2009). In an enmeshed family, a routine life experience, such as a job change or change in dating relationship by one member of the family creates strong reactions by others in the family. In its worst scenario, enmeshment may result in incest.

On the other hand, if the boundaries between family members are too rigid, the family is thought to be **disengaged**. In this situation, the subsystems are so separated that there is little sense of family identity, and parents are apt to relinquish much of their caretaking role as they pursue their own interests and the children pursue their own. In a disengaged family, a significant job change or a divorce in the family may be barely acknowledged by other family members.

When you read about or work with young people who seem to have little or no effective connections with their families, and have experienced school or legal problems, you may wonder about the boundaries (or lack of) established by the parents and the parents' perception of their own roles. In some respects, you are using this theory when you cite the misplacement or laxness of parental boundaries when children go astray. The work in such cases is to restore clear and appropriate boundaries between children and parents that support parent caretaking and authority. This particular position is reflected in court decisions regarding the delinquency of adolescents and a judge's requirement, for example, that parents receive training on managing their children or that they supervise a child's curfew restriction.

Intergenerational Patterns The identification of **intergenerational patterns** has likewise played an important role in social work practice with families. The term refers to the assertion that families transmit their patterns of relationship from one generation to the next (Papero, 2009). For example, if your adult client, Jane, is so closely connected to her mother that she experiences great anxiety when they are separated and therefore cannot work outside the home, Jane is likely to establish that kind of relationship with her daughter as well. The anxiety generated by any effort to be separate from her mother is contagious and makes it difficult for Jane to think clearly because her feelings are so intense. In this way she becomes dysfunctional, tends to be dominated by feelings, and passes that pattern on to the next generation. This emphasis on feeling in a family sometimes results in constant emotional uproar, frequent violence, major feuds, difficulties with the law, and generalized struggle in accomplishing the basic family functions considered earlier.

Although the whole of intergenerational theory is quite complex, it has influenced attitudes about families. The use of the phrases "welfare families" and "incestuous families" reflects the use of intergenerational theory. These terms reflect the assumption that problematic, emotional patterns and the resulting behavioral consequences (such as violence, inability to focus on work, and substance abuse) appear to be transmitted from generation to generation. Social work then involves breaking cycles, bolstering the strengths, and supporting an appropriate level of autonomy in individual family members. These principles are reflected in many social and educational programs, in which social workers often participate, that are designed to break patterns of economic dependence, substance addiction, lack of educational focus, and build up healthy bonds between family members.

Professionals incorporate a systems orientation when considering crime or drug addiction or school violence among youth and assume the causes to be related to the families involved, whether or not that is a fair assumption. Yet children behave illegally or violent whose parents are caring, hardworking, and doing the best they can. Therefore, the applicability of family systems theory, like any other theory, can be questioned, and does not automatically fit in all situations. The desire to find a rational cause for human behavior sometimes sets in motion the use of methods that have been used before. Also of interest is the eagerness of some to blame child-related problems on the family's behavioral shortcomings or background while not addressing the broader (also systems) aspects of poverty, disenfranchisement, or racism, all of which can significantly impact behavior.

Systems perspectives can be helpful and seem to support logical approaches in assessment, especially of complex arrangements, like the family. These perspectives have a general cultural appeal, and they do not constitute a magic, one-stop answer for conceptualizing about, assessing, or working with families. While systems views have strong currency in today's analyses of social issues, other ways of thinking about them may be relevant. You must be careful not to blame or scapegoat any particular person simply because it seems logical or fits with a possible systemic interpretation of a family situation. As you continue with your social work education and develop your approach to practicing social work with families, you will be exposed to a wide array of philosophical and theoretical frameworks. Your professional obligation is to consider all the available options and determine the approach(es) that is(are) most appropriate for the families you serve.

THE CONTEMPORARY CONTEXT FOR FAMILY WORK

The real-world, real live family of today is only rarely the idealized outdated television version with a stay-at-home mother, fully employed father, and two bright, talented (and usually white) children. Social workers often work with families who were once seen as "other"; that is, they did not fit dominant fantasies of family life. The following sections briefly identify several types of family constellations that have not traditionally been considered mainstream but are a vital part of the contemporary family landscape—grandparents rearing grandchildren; gay, lesbian, bisexual, and transgender parents; single-parent families; families of multiple racial and ethnic heritage; families that include persons with disabilities; blended families, international families, and families with multiple problems—and suggest some specific implications for working with them.

Beyond these types, other current configurations appearing in the literature (and in practice) include adoptive families, foster families, step families, blended families, dual wage earning families, multi-generational families, and, of course, many combinations of these types. In the coming generations, the social work profession will need to expect and remain open to ever-evolving forms of the family. This kind of sociocultural change provides social workers with the opportunity to contribute to a sustained and meaningful impact that will benefit clients across all levels of society.

Grandparents Rearing Grandchildren

In many cultures of the past, grandparents had a significant and ongoing role in the nurturing and socialization of children. Some cultural groups today, typically those who are less mobile or those of strong ethnic identification(s), have maintained those patterns, as consistent with their cultural and instrumental needs. The extended family is an age-old pattern of organization that has been obscured by the mainstream societal changes of the industrialized and "informalized" 20th and

21st centuries. These changes reflect a break with the traditional cultural patterns of their parents and their parents' parents.

In contemporary society, there has been a reemergence of grandparents assuming primary (rather than supportive) parenting roles (Hayslip & Kaminski, 2005), many as a result of family violence, drug addiction, and/or incarceration of their adult children. In fact, over 1.5 million children currently reside with a grandparent and have no parent living in the home (Kreider, 2008). The growing pressures on many child protection agencies have contributed to the increase in parenting grandparents because child protection workers often see biological relatives as preferable to, and more available than, unrelated foster parents. Many grandparents are healthy, active, and potentially able to take on the responsibility of raising their children's children.

Much more is involved, however, than simply being "able." Many grandparents have reached a point in their lives when they can pursue their own interests and dreams that have been put on hold while they worked and reared families. Others may find it exhausting to keep up with young children, who have come from dysfunctional situations and have multiple needs, demands, and activities. Some grandparents take on the unexpected role joyfully and fully, and others are enormously burdened, and sometimes guilt ridden because of their own children's inabilities to parent. They may also be struggling with aging, illness, and their own continued need for employment. In any event, many parenting grandparents, even if eager to care for grandchildren, are likely to want and need significant support from social agencies.

Social workers working with grandparents need to use the major skills and perspectives of generalist practice. Generalist practitioners are trained to recognize the need for and offer several types of support as they sensitize themselves to the complexities of the emotional and instrumental stresses that grandparents experience. Grandparents may need financial support (Fuller-Thomson & Minkler, 2005), counseling, resource coordination, advocacy, policy development (Cox, 2003), and frequent reassurance that they can and do offer their grandchildren a secure and stable home (Bullock, 2005). In some situations, birth parents recovering from substance abuse have visiting privileges or partial child caretaking responsibilities on a preliminary or trial basis. In such cases, there may be considerable tension between grandparents and parents. These and other conflicts may indicate the need for additional assistance from social workers on an ongoing basis.

Gay, Lesbian, Bisexual, and Transgender Parents

Gay, lesbian, bisexual, and transgender persons and couples who are in civil unions may become parents through several different means. The person may be the custodial parent of children from an earlier heterosexual relationship. Some seek artificial insemination and give birth to children. Also, many informal arrangements for parenting still exist, particularly in ethnic communities in which the custom affirms the community's responsibility to raise the child.

A more recent development has supported the adoption or foster care placement of children in state's custody with parents whose sexual orientation is non-heterosexual. The ever increasing pool of children needing a home and the increasing number and type of adoptions being granted has led, just as with grandparents, to less traditional, more creative efforts in placement planning (Barth, 2008). These types of arrangements have been a highly controversial strategy for dealing with child custody arrangements within the child welfare community, as it strikes at the core of the idealized version of the family. Concerns about identity issues for the child, parental adequacy, and the overall mental health of the parents and children have been raised and researched. More than two decades of research on the impact of parental sexual orientation on children's well-being, however, demonstrates no detrimental effect on children's emotional, psychosocial, or behavioral well-being as a result of being reared by non-heterosexual parents (Pawelski et al., 2006).

As prospective parents, gay, lesbian, bisexual, and transgender persons still face obstacles in their pursuit of foster care or adoption and experience institutionalized stigma even at the hands of social workers. Lacking any evidence to the contrary, social workers in both the practice and policy components of the profession should support the efforts of all qualified persons seeking parenthood. Social workers can de-emphasize the search for dysfunction and pathology as they give expression to the strengths and resilience of the parents (see Van Den Bergh & Crisp, 2004). Social workers can also recognize the effects of lingering cultural discrimination directed against non-heterosexuals and draw upon a critical awareness of their own biases regarding the strengths and viability of such people as parents.

Issues that the social work practitioner can be aware of to work effectively with gay, lesbian, bisexual, and transgender parents revolve around sensitivity to the strengths and challenges they face. The strengths perspective may be particularly helpful in working with gay, lesbian, bisexual, and transgender parents. Helping the parents identify not only their own strengths, but the strengths of the system in which they live, can be a informative, and even transformative, strategy for your work together.

Competent practitioners must also engage in reflection regarding their own attitudes, values, and expectations about non-heterosexual parents (Hull & Mather, 2006, p. 218). You must be aware of the challenges they face that are similar to those encountered by heterosexual parents (e.g., parental roles, disciplines, etc.) and those that are different (e.g., lack of legal protections, community supports, etc.). These family arrangements are strengthened by strong social worker emotional and logistical support.

Single Parent Families

While competence in the language that you use is critical in all social work encounters, speaking with and about client systems in a linguistically competent manner is particularly important when working with families. Social workers are ethically bound to develop awareness of appropriate language (oral and written) to be used with the diverse communities with whom they work (NASW, 2009–2012a). Single parent families are a group that is often referred to in ways that are not strengths-based or empowering and can be, in fact, derogatory. A term like "single parent," without the corresponding "double parent," implies that one is normal and does not require description, while the other is "other." As you notice the implications of such terms as "broken family" or "split family," consider how deprecating labels influence initial perceptions and may affect the work that follows. It is easy to lose sight of the strengths and commitment of women or men managing families on their own if the work is prefaced with a sense of deficiency or deviance.

Society and, at times, some social service providers, have historically viewed single parenthood as a blight that necessarily leads to insecure, delinquent, and otherwise unhappy and dysfunctional households. At any point, nearly one-quarter of children live in a household headed by a single parent, particularly if the household head is female, these report lower levels of income than two parent families (Kreider, 2008). However, researchers find no evidence to suggest that children reared in single parent families experience any greater negative outcomes than those reared in two-parent families (Benard, 2006). Moreover, a review of research on single fathers yields findings that indicate that single fathers, who tend to come to single parenting later than single mothers and often do not experience the financial disadvantages that single mothers do, and may approach parenting differently than their female counterparts, are shown to be caring and effective parents to their children (Biblarz & Stacey, 2010).

On the other hand, there is some support in both the literature and practice worlds for recognizing the unique challenges of single parenting, and the way that such parenting impacts both the social work relationship and the parenting functions. Four major issues that frequently arise from divorce or separation are (1) a lack of resources to cope with stress, finances, or other responsibility; (2) unresolved family-of-origin issues often brought on by the single parent's need for assistance from her or his parents, at least temporarily; (3) unresolved divorce or relationship issues, such as anger, grief, or loneliness; and (4) an overburdened older child. Known as a **parentified child**, an older child who is not yet an adult may be pressed into providing excessive household chores or care for another family member. This, in turn, creates concern that the parentified child's own physical and emotional health and well-being is compromised due to the developmentally inappropriate life experiences (Earley & Cushway, 2002).

With the focus of engagement, assessment, and intervention being on the family itself, social work practice with single parent families can utilize the family's strengths to create and stabilize coping skills. Drawing from the work of several family scholars, skills for social work practice with single parent families include (Atwood & Genovese, 2006; Jung, 1996):

- *Joining*, similar to engagement, reflects the social worker's effort to show clients that they are cared about and that the social worker understands them and their struggles.

- *Empowering clients* supports their activities and capacity to address their own issues; and values their uniqueness and skills. In particular, the social worker can aid the parent in clarifying and reinforcing the parental role, while serving in a nurturing and supportive role to the other family members.

- While maintaining a focus on the family, the social worker can *aid the individual members in identifying strengths and resources within the family unit* (e.g., the parent is fully employed with a flexible work schedule to allow for involvement at the children's school), the extended family (e.g., grandparents are committed to helping with childcare), and the community (e.g., the community has active, well-organized after school programming).

- *Involving significant family members* emphasizes collaboration, reduction of stress, and pooled resources.

- *Allocating agency resources* focuses on agency planning, outreach, and networking.

- *Highlighting small changes* emphasizes the strategy of making small shifts that ease overextended schedules and increase energy; such changes can also highlight success and autonomy.

- *Articulating self-efficacy* emphasizes competence, accomplishments, and empowerment for greater control over management of family issues, ideally for all family members.

These knowledge and values related to working with single parent families are consistent with a strengths-based, empowering approach that recognizes both internal and external factors and supports single parents in their ongoing efforts to provide security and nurturance for their children. Further, these knowledge and values can enhance the social worker's efforts to engage and assess the family system by conveying a sense of care and concern for the individual members, identifying and building on the strengths of each member and the unit as a whole, and emphasizing the self-efficacy of the family system.

Families of Multiple Racial and Ethnic Heritages

One of the gifts of an increasingly diverse society, the growth of families with multiple racial and ethnic backgrounds is notable in most U.S. cities and towns. Interracial and interethnic marriages, civil unions, and partnerships appear to be gaining in acceptability since 1967 and are certainly increasing in real numbers (Amato, Booth, Johnson, & Rogers, 2007; U.S. Census Bureau, 2009). Shifting immigration patterns in the United States, globalization, and the breakdown of ethnic barriers in Europe all appear to have an effect on the incidence of racially and ethnically mixed families.

Perhaps few other developments in the everyday life of our communities offer a greater opportunity to view people differently than the growth of families with multiple racial and ethnic heritages. While some members of society will persist in grieving for the purity of "race" (a social and cultural construction by most accounts), others value the contributions of other cultures and challenge the notions associated with racial privilege. It is important, however, not to minimize the negative power of the persistent oppression met by many ethnically diverse families in our culture. In this arena, professionals also need to be educated in this multicultural society regarding our national and cultural history. In this way, social workers can find joy in the richness of diversity and also confront the legacy of oppression and hatred as client families (and perhaps our own families) experience it (Schmitz, Stakeman, & Sisneros, 2001). Flexibility, shared goals, and a willingness to explore and address challenges are critical in working across culturally and ethnically diverse communities. As with all other aspects of individual and family assessment and intervention, race and ethnicity should not solely define the family (Logan et al., 2008). The social work assessment should encompass the many and varied facets of the family's life and the environment in which they live.

One model, "**posture of cultural reciprocity**," proposes an approach for working with diverse families (Kalyanpur & Harry, 1999). This process requires that social workers recognize the cultural aspect of their own personal values as well as those of the social work profession. As depicted in Box 6.2, this posture is achieved in four steps. These principles imply a constructionist understanding of cultural difference and value the distinctions without the value of the social worker's orientation. These principles also provide a useful framework for working with people of other cultures and are consistent with social justice and human rights as they enhance inclusion and reflect a basic assumption of cultural strengths.

Families Including Persons with Disabilities

Social workers work with families in which one or more persons have a physical, cognitive, and/or mental health disability. Grounded in systems theory and currently utilized in developing patient care programs in the provision of health care, **family-centered care** is a "... philosophy of care that permeates all

The steps for achieving a posture of cultural reciprocity include:

BOX 6.2

Working with Diverse Families: Racial and Ethnic Diversity

STEP	EXAMPLE
"Step 1: Identify the cultural values that are embedded in the professional interpretation of a student's [or client's] difficulties or in the recommendation for service."	This would lead to asking why, for example, a culturally different client's behavior is bothersome to you. (Is she late for appointments? Does she interrupt you? Does she respond to you indirectly? How do you interpret her behavior?)
"Step 2: Find out whether the family being served recognizes and values these assumptions and, if not, how their view differs from that of the professional."	For example, you may discover that your client has a different sense of time from yours and that punctuality has little meaning for her. Here you would want to explore how she approaches time, what it means to her, and whether she recognizes your approach to it.
"Step 3: Acknowledge and give explicit respect to any cultural differences identified, and fully explain the cultural basis of the professional assumptions."	This requires you to enter into a dialogue regarding your assumptions and beliefs and how they are different from those of your client. For example, you might recognize and appreciate the less frantic approach to time and deadlines while you explain the need in your agency to abide by a schedule.
"Step 4: Through discussion and collaboration, set about determining the most effective way of adapting professional interpretations or recommendations to the value system of this family."	Work out a solution that respects the nature of the family's values. You might settle on a more flexible appointment time at the end of the day, or agree on a time range, or make outreach visits if that is possible.

Source: Kalyanpur & Harry, 1999, pp. 118–119

interactions between families and healthcare providers. This philosophy places a high value on the contributions made by the family members in relation to their healthcare needs" (Bowden & Greenberg, 2010, p. 5). Family-centered care has evolved into a concept of services being "family-driven." This shift expands the notion of family-centered services and is based on the assumption that the family determines what it needs (Seligman & Darling, 2007, p. 14). This strengths-based approach is a promising method for working with families in many arenas, especially with those who have disabilities. When children have comprehensive and severe health challenges, such as neuro-developmental delays, interdisciplinary teaming is an appropriate response. Social workers can play an important role on such teams that, by their nature, address an array of the many needs of children growing up with serious disabilities. Social workers can also support families in ways that go beyond medical or educational requirements. Social workers also play a key role in working with disabilities experienced across the life span. Social workers thus must also have competency in working with adults who experience developmental, mental or physical health, or cognitive disabilities and their families and support networks.

As one example, when a child with profound disabilities is born, family members usually have to reorganize their everyday lives as well as their long-term dreams. One parent may have to stop working to orchestrate the services and treatments the child needs. The time requirements for involvement with school teams, medical teams, and interprofessional teams, as well as the individual services of a speech therapist, audiologist, occupational therapist, pediatrician, psychologist—the list is sometimes quite long—can turn a family upside down. Siblings are affected, family interactions are affected, and parents often struggle with the emotional ramifications as well as the physical consequences of exhaustion. Social workers can offer support, time management ideas, and help with expanding parents' ability to identify resources. In addition, many families struggle with gaining access to services they are entitled to receive and therefore may need social work advocacy in their negotiation of a complex system.

When working with families that have members with disabilities, social workers may be challenged by societal views of individuals and families that are not strengths-based, but emphasize the individual's deficits. In response, social workers and disability scholars have proposed the following set of beliefs as a foundation for working with such families (Mackelprang, Patchner, DeWeaver, Clute, & Sullivan, 2008, p. 40; Mackelprang & Salsgiver, 1999):

- Persons with disabilities are capable, or potentially capable.

- Disabilities are not equivalent to pathologies and do not require fixing.

- "Disability" is a social construct to which social workers must respond politically.

- Persons with disabilities have the absolute right to control their own lives.

Grounded in a strengths-based perspective, each of the previous statements is critical not only for the social worker to adopt, but equally as important for the person with a disability, the family, and the community in which the individual and family live. Social workers have the opportunity and ethical responsibility to empower clients systems to embrace such a belief system. Disabilities should be viewed within a diversity (or social) model in which societal attitudes, structures, policies, and institutions are seen as responsible for imposing limitations on persons with disabilities. Person-first language is currently in use but "disability identity language" may more appropriately frame the disability as a characteristic of diversity. These ideas imply a social work presence based on advocacy, structural principles, and the skills to work for social justice. Disability work with families is a ripe arena for social work practice and offers practitioners many opportunities. Social workers may engage in significant relationships that focus on empowering the family and the person with a disability to engage in self-determination, self-advocacy, and independence negotiating life transitions with family members, organizations, and themselves (Beaulaurier & Taylor, 2007). Working within a framework of promoting client needs and self-determination, the person with a disability and their family members can be empowered to: (1) expand their range of options and choices; (2) prepare them to be more effective in dealings with professionals, bureaucrats, and agencies that often do not understand nor appreciate their heightened need for self-determination; and (3) mobilize and help groups of people with disabilities to consider policy and program alternatives that can improve their situation (Bueaulaurier & Taylor, 2007, p. 65). Lastly, consider that the social worker often has a dual responsibility when working with the family that includes a member with a disability (Hull & Mather, 2006). In working with both the person with the disability and the other family members, the social worker may have to balance differing and sometimes conflicting needs and goals.

Blended Families

Families are considered to be blended as the result of a number of different circumstances. For U.S. Census purposes, a blended family is considered one in which a parent remarries and the children who reside in the home do not share a biological parent (Kreider, 2008). While this is one possibility for families to be merged, there are other scenarios, including domestic partner relationships, civil unions, and non-related families who co-reside in the same household. Nearly 20 percent of children reside in a living arrangement considered to be a blended family (Kreider, 2008).

While most blended families come together without specifically seeking the services of a helping professional, social workers working with a blended family constellation should be aware of the family history and be sensitive to the dynamics that may occur when two families merge into one. Incorporating information about the blending of multiple families into one household is a critical component of the assessment and intervention process. Family members may not be aware of or able to articulate challenges they are experiencing regarding the "merger" of the two family units. The social worker who can be attuned to the issues that can occur with the consolidation of multiple families can potentially identify the reason the family is struggling.

When working with a blended family, the social worker begins by identifying the strengths of the individual members and the family as a unit. Within the assessment process, the social worker can help the family to identify and discuss the roles of individual members along with boundaries between individual members and the multiple families coming together. It is important to remember that each member of the newly created family unit must be viewed within the context of the system (i.e., original family and new family) in which they exist. There are, however, unique aspects of working with the blended family. Competence in working with blended families requires knowledge of family development and transitions, involvement of noncustodial parents, extended families, and helping families negotiate new and different family roles, boundaries, relationships, and traditions. The social worker can also engage with and assess blended families by aiding them in identifying their individual perspectives on their expectations for the forming of this new unit. Adapted from Shalay and Brownlee (2007, p. 24), the following questions for clients may be helpful to this process:

1.   What do you perceive others think it means to be a family?

2.   How do you think your views of what it means to be family have been shaped by what other people think it means to be a family?

3.   How might ideas about families on TV have influenced how you expected things would be as a family?

4.   If you were a nuclear family what might be different in how you relate to each other?

5.   What do you think expectations about a perfect family encourage you to believe about each other?

6.   How might expectations about what a family should be have influenced what you expect from each other?

International Families

Social work practice with families in contemporary society requires international competency. If you are practicing social work with families in the U.S., your practice will likely involve families who have arrived in the U.S. as immigrants or refugees. If you are a social work practitioner outside the U.S., you must have extensive knowledge of international issues. While working with families in the U.S. or abroad may require a different knowledge base regarding immigration, legal and governmental issues, cultures, and customs, there is a practice skill set that is common to work to all international family social work practice.

To begin to gain competencies in thinking and working internationally, you can strive to learn as much as possible about the family or families with whom you will be working. As with social work practice with individuals who have relocated to the U.S., it is important to be prepared for working with families who are new to their country. Before you meet the client system, assume responsibility for exposing yourself to information about their culture, heritage, relocation history and experience, language, customs and traditions, spiritual practices, and community. While reading about your client's country of origin and culture can be helpful, seek out others who can provide you with personal or professional experiences and guidance. Remember also that the client family can ultimately be your best source of information and insight. Allow yourself to learn from them, especially about them as an individual and unique family. While it is important with all client systems to explore their views regarding working with a helping professional, it is particularly important to understand the perceptions and beliefs about receiving help from the family and those who share their cultural beliefs and traditions.

While there may be characteristics that are common to groups of people who share a country of origin, culture, or traditions, each person within the family and the family itself should be viewed as individual. You may find as many similarities between a family from the U.S. and a family from an African country as between two families from the African country. Learning about the lives of the families that you work with will be an ongoing process that can unfold as you build rapport and trust with the members.

While much of social work practice knowledge and skills you learn is applicable to all families, there are certain competencies that are unique to working with a family that has relocated from their country of origin. First, it is critical to understand the cultural norms of your client family related to the definition of family. Be certain that you have a clear understanding of those persons who are considered to be a member of the family, the relationships of family members to one another, the meaning of those relationships, and any hierarchical traditions that may exist within the family unit. For example, is "family" considered to be the nuclear unit or the larger, extended family? Are persons who are not biologically or legally linked considered to be part of the family? What rules and tasks guide the family members in their daily lives and in making major life decisions such as marriage, parenting, residential arrangements, education, careers, religion/spirituality, and financial priorities?

Regardless of the family's origins, you can utilize a strengths-based approach in completing your assessment and intervention planning. Using the International Family Strengths Model, DeFrain and Asay (2007a, p. 452) suggest that family strengths can be assessed on the basis of: (1) appreciation and affection; (2) positive communication; (3) commitment to the family; (4) enjoyable time together; (5) sense of spiritual well-being; and (6) ability to manage stress and crisis effectively. While these attributes can be applied to families of any ethnic, cultural, or heritage background, they are particularly helpful when considered within the cultural context of the family with whom you are working, as these family dynamics can have different meanings when viewed within the cultural background of the client system.

Building on family strengths can serve as a particularly helpful strategy as families work to adjust to their new country and environment. Parents, for example, may struggle with their children adopting the customs, language, and dress of their culture or older adults may find it challenging to live in a world that is unfamiliar to them. Utilizing the family's strengths can empower the family members to find their place within their new home while maintaining their connections to their heritage. You can help to make the global connections between the world from which the family has come and the one they have entered by pointing out and affirming a family's ability to enjoy being together despite the challenges of adjusting to life in their new country and home.

While the preceding discussion has focused on specific family situations and circumstances, the real world of social work practice means that individuals and families may present with multiple concerns and dilemmas. Known as **multi-barrier families** or families with multiple problems, the challenges may encompass economic, health, behavioral, social, and psychological issues (Hull & Mather, 2006). For example, a grandparent challenged with rearing her adolescent grandson may also be faced with a custody battle with his biological parent. A couple with a child born with a disability may, at the same time, be grappling with the grandmother's dementia. A blended family may be coping with employment layoffs and foreclosure proceedings on their home. The lives of the client systems that social workers work with can be complex and multi-faceted.

Even with multi-barrier families, the social worker's role is to approach each family as a unique system with strengths and individualized needs. Listening to each member of a family unit enables the social worker to gain insight into the perceptions, relationship dynamics, and possibilities held by the individuals within the collective family system. To be a social worker who is competent in working with families, one needs to develop a repertoire of practice behaviors that encompass family-focused knowledge, skills, and values. Prioritizing problem-solving into short and longer-term goals and promoting a supportive and nurturing environment can be a focus for the social worker. The social worker may find that attention must be given to both the internal and external challenges that are confronting the family (Janzen, Harris, Jordan, & Franklin, 2006). For example, an internal challenge faced by a family may be the substance abuse by one of the members. On the other hand, an external challenge may be the family's inability to qualify for subsidized housing or financial assistance. While different practice behaviors may be required to address internal versus external issues, the social worker may find that she or he serves a number of roles (i.e., broker, advocate, counselor, or educator). The remainder of this chapter will highlight a sampling of those practice behaviors needed to work effectively with families.

CONTEMPORARY TRENDS AND SKILLS FOR ENGAGEMENT AND ASSESSMENT WITH FAMILIES

Theoretical perspectives are a reflection of the sociocultural context. Theories can be a response to the theoretical climate that precedes them. As with social work practice with individuals, there is a wide array of theoretical approaches for assessing and intervening with families. "Most practitioners, educators, and researchers tend to practice, teach, and do research based on multiple and interrelated theories" (Logan et al., 2008, p. 177). While three different theoretical perspectives are presented here, you will, through your career, develop the approach that is most consistent with your philosophical and practice perspectives. Each of the frameworks presented here has some components in common and others born in reaction to each other. All correspond in some ways to traditional perspectives and offer an evolving focus. Regardless of the theoretical approach(es) that you use, social work practice with families should encompass goals that are situationally focused, structured, realistic, concrete, and achievable (Logan et al., 2008).

Narrative Theory in Family Engagement and Assessment

Narrative theory is based on a postmodern, constructionist perspective that offers an alternative perspective that enables client systems to make sense of their lives through "stories" or the client system's perception of an individual or a situation. Family interpretations of ongoing events either tend to support the ongoing narrative or refute it. Those stories that are included in the interpretation serve to organize subsequent experience. When there are exceptions, they are often dismissed or forgotten as not representative of the real family. The language used to interpret and describe various family stories is significant and fits into the context of the ongoing experience. The following examples explore the main ideas of an approach based in narrative theory.

The issue that brings the family to the social worker is daughter Liza, who is six years old, the last child, and the only girl in a single parent, male-headed household from an economically affluent neighborhood. Liza has been cast in the role of the family "misfit." Her behavior is oppositional and she is clumsy, speaks disrespectfully, and is disruptive. Any incident involving Liza (e.g., forgetting her pencil or knocking over her milk) becomes just another piece of evidence for the family. Her family members often shake their heads at her behavior, and wonder what to do with someone who is (in their view) oppositional, clumsy, disrespectful, and disruptive. When Liza's first-grade teacher reports to her father that Liza is exceptionally well liked by both her peers and teachers and that she is bright and fun, Liza's father is incredulous. He suspects the teacher has her confused with another student. Or Liza must be faking at school. The *real* Liza, as everyone knows, is oppositional, clumsy, disrespectful, and disruptive, as misfits are inclined to be.

The story that Liza tells about herself is different from that which is perceived by her family. Each story carries the power of the context to perpetuate and expand it, which in turn will influence the way Liza, as the major character, plays her role. If her family persists in maintaining the original perception of Liza, she is likely to respond over time by becoming increasingly rude, failing, or developing truly disruptive conduct. On the other hand, if her family at any point re-authors their perceptions by recognizing the exceptions to their ideas about Liza, her story may unfold quite differently. Everyone has multiple stories, but some have more power, relevance, and a wider audience than others. Liza's alternative story (told by her teacher) has the potential to influence her future in positive and significant ways.

Thickening the Story   Although narrative theory has many components, the exploration in this chapter will include the most relevant concepts for generalist work with families. You may recall, **thickening the story** refers to the social worker's effort to expand "thin" (Morgan, 2000) or **problem-saturated stories** that are one-dimensional perspectives on a truth that client systems created about themselves that may or may not be based in fact (Kelley, 2009). This attempt to create a more complex story may achieve the larger goal of instilling hope that the client system can make positive changes. Liza's first story is a good example of a thin account. She has no redeeming virtues and is simply perceived as an oppositional, clumsy, disrespectful, disruptive misfit. A thickened version of Liza's story reveals her likable personality, talents, and ability to connect with people in spite of, or in addition to, any behaviors that are oppositional, clumsy, disrespectful, and disruptive.

The Smith family provides another example of the value of reframing the story. The Smiths are a family that has experienced considerable challenges in child rearing. One child has been taken into the custody of the state, and now child protection workers are investigating to determine if another child should be removed for reasons of safety. The mother disparagingly claims, in defeat and sarcastic resignation, that her family is "just one of those families." Child welfare workers may likewise view the family as "just one of those families" because various children have been in custody for three generations (as was Ms. Smith).

Rather than assessing the narrowly defined dysfunction of this family, the narrative social worker would search for the exceptions to this story to enrich it and make it more complex. For example, the social worker can ask about Ms. Smith's ability to keep a family together for 10 years in the face of poverty, or to overcome a major childhood health challenge, or survive homelessness. The effort is to expand the narrow failure story so that the family can see itself as having potential, which in turn can support re-authoring the story to reflect the way the family would like it to be. The family then can shape its future to fit the new story. Such an approach can be contrasted with the one taken in the section "Intergenerational Patterns," earlier in the chapter. Through a different lens, it offers the potential for hope through development of the family's resilience and positive attributes.

Externalizing Problems   The notion that problems are external to the family is known as **externalization**. The problem is not the client system itself but is the result of an issue that is separate from the client, thus the focus of the intervention is also then external to the client system (Kelley, 2009). Narrative social workers try to identify and help the family to name the issue that is creating difficulties. By objectifying or personifying it, family members can develop a relationship with the challenge, rather than be consumed by it, and ultimately they may control the challenge.

For example, if a family feels overwhelmed by the demands of a child with disabilities, the resulting "worry" may be externalized. The social worker can then ask about the feelings of being overwhelmed, help family members label their feelings, and support all those times when the family takes control over "the Worry." By separating the issue (or "worry") from the family's identity, the worker can explore with the family ways to defeat their concerns or at least keep them at bay.

Unearthing the Broader Context   One of narrative theory's most relevant contributions to generalist social work practice is a consistent emphasis on the political context of the family. The social worker will be highly sensitized to the danger of reinforcing the oppressive dimensions of a dominant pattern (such as racism) in society. For example, if six-year-old Damion is exhibiting fear that appears to be inordinate regarding school attendance, the social worker will not want to externalize this prematurely as "the school creeps" or "school scares" if in fact Damion is being taunted and bullied because of his color. Using narrative theory, the social worker seeks to identify any political factors that impact the situation with the client, and through a partnership with the client, address those factors that are negatively shaping and impacting the challenge at hand.

Solution-Focused Family Work

Like many contemporary family models, **solution-focused practice** defines the family broadly and does not limit its conception to traditional forms or even require all the members to be present in the meeting with the practitioner, thus de-emphasizing history or underlying pathology (Nichols, 2009). With a focus on brief interventions that narrowly define the arena of specific problems within the context of particular environmental variables, solution-focused family work has been utilized with a wide range of life situations and groups. Solution-focused social workers usually emphasize a cognitive approach, support a collaborative stance with clients, and tend to reject notions that problems serve any unconscious or ulterior motive. Accordingly, solution-focused social workers believe that individuals want to change and assert that any attribution of resistant behavior to families is more about the interpretation of the practitioner than it is about families. The founder of solution-focused therapy, Steve deShazer (1984), early in his work declared resistance "dead" and in turn redefined clients' balking at practitioner directives as their way of educating the social worker about what is needed to help them.

Solution-focused social workers emphasize the future, in which solutions can be used within the specification of clear, concrete, and achievable goals. The self-proclaimed simplicity of this approach, along with its time-limited, highly specific emphasis, has enabled solution-focused work to become an important contemporary model as it generally aspires to short-term, specific, and direct results, thus avoiding costly protracted professional relationships. Long used in community-based programs, solution-focused interventions have shown promise in addressing family and relationship problems, particularly related youth and families (Kim, 2008b; Nowicki & Arbuckle, 2009). The strengths and client perspectives of the approach have made solution-focused practice popular for use in schools settings along with the other components, including portability, adaptability, brief time frame, and the opportunity for small changes to matter and applicability for cultural competence (Kelly, Kim, & Franklin, 2008, p. 8).

In solution-focused work with more than one person, the emphasis is on the relationship, not the individual, and finding and maintaining a common goal (DeJong & Berg, 2008). The assessment process begins with a series of questions to elicit the perceptions of each of the members. The family's responses are then utilized by the social worker and family members to co-construct a plan for intervention (DeJong, 2009). With family groups, the questions, while asked of the individuals present, can focus on the relationships among the members. Questions included in a solution-focused intervention are:

- *Goal-formulation.* Questions aimed at goal-formulation prompt the client system to consider the way in which their situation will be different if the problem that brought them to the social worker is no longer a problem (e.g., "What will be different if the problem is resolved?"). The "miracle" questions are aimed at helping the client system envision life if a miracle occurred that eliminated the presenting problem. In the engagement and assessment phases of work, goal-formulation can serve several purposes: enable the members of the family to communicate their individual goals to one another; focus on the members of the family on a common direction for work; and enable the members to identify and build on individual strengths in pursuit of the agreed-upon goals.

- *Exception-finding.* Critical to the assessment process, questions developed to identify exceptions help client systems recall experiences in which they were successful and provide opportunities for identifying strengths and resources available to incorporate into the intervention.

- *Scaling.* Scaling questions invite the client system to quantify the past and the future within the context of the problem or crisis they are experiencing. The clients are asked to use a scale of 1–10 to rate their belief that a solution will be found for the issue that brought them to see you. During the engagement and assessment phases of the intervention process, scaling questions help to establish the point from which the work will begin and identify current and past successes and areas for future growth.

- *Coping.* Aimed at issues of coping, coping questions strive to connect the client systems to coping strategies that have or could be used. Such questions can serve to engage and invest the client system in the helping process as well as assess the past successes and failures, which may then be utilized to develop the plan of work for the current intervention.

Like narrative proponents, solution-focused social workers concentrate specifically on identifying and bolstering the attempts made by families that have been successful. The goal for solution-focused social work with families is to increase the discussion about solutions and decrease the focus on problems. Client families are asked to remember when their efforts worked, even when they seem like very small incidents occurring rarely. Solution-focused social workers direct their attention to those exceptions and explore the contextual factors that made the exception possible. In this way social workers provide families with the message that they have the strengths to cope, that they have in fact done it successfully before, and that they can do it again (DeJong & Berg, 2008).

Solution-focused practitioners have been credited with promoting a greater emphasis on strengths through their "exception" question that encourages the identification of, and focus on, those strengths that are relevant to the current situation (Weick, Kreider, & Chamberlain, 2009). The "exception" questions allow the client to place strengths within the context of times in which the client was successful.

Environmental Focus   With an ecological orientation, solution-based social work looks to the community as a resource and always seeks to understand the problem in terms of the relationship to the surrounding context.

For example, the social worker assumes that a woman who abandoned her children is embedded within a culture in which she experiences gender discrimination, poverty, unmet mental health challenges, or perhaps racism. These assumptions will be considered as contributing to her current inability to care for children.

All of these considerations are part of the assessment, and a single diagnostic- or strictly pathology-oriented label as a unitary explanation is viewed as inadequate. The overall understanding of the family's difficulty is rooted in their everyday, unique living experience to which they bring their own personalities and idiosyncrasies within the larger context, which also shapes that experience.

BOX 6.3

Contemporary Families May Include Grandparents Rearing Their Grandchildren

Copyright: Monkey Business Images, courtesy of Shutterstock® images

Constructionist and Social Justice Approaches to Family Social Work

The contemporary approaches described in this chapter are complementary and share some constructionist notions that are represented in the client-defined meanings of family, the lack of rigid ideas of so-called normal family development, and the collaborative partnerships built with client systems. Constructionist theories incorporate a critical perspective that reaffirms the long-standing tradition in social workers working with families. Critical social construction suggests the development of a perspective that focuses more directly on constructionist ideas and social justice principles. Narrative and solution-focused concepts also relate to social justice issues in their concerns for the contextual locations that clients experience on a daily basis. In that respect, the approaches are more alike than they are different, and each has a positive contribution to make to contemporary social work practice.

Critical Constructionist Emphasis   Critical constructionist social workers explore the meaning of family within a broad contextual framework. Constructionist descriptions of the family present the social worker with multiple perspectives that can be viewed critically, as such models have implications for social work practice. For example, if you assume a theoretical model in which the family is considered basic for human survival and absolutely sacrosanct, you might view the family, as many did for centuries, as immune from external interference in its internal dynamics, including family violence. If, however, you assume that the meanings (or realities) that client systems make of their lives occur within a larger community, you and the client system can view their situation within the context of the groups to which they belong (e.g., racial, ethnic, socioeconomic, religious, etc.) (DeJong & Berg, 2008). Using the critical constructionist emphasis, the solution-focused intervention then becomes a collaboration between the social worker and the family in which the members of the family explore their realities (i.e., problems, miracles, successes, strengths, and solutions) while incorporating the influence of the multiple groups within which they live their lives (e.g., neighborhood, extended family, schools, job settings, and church) (p. 344).

Social Justice Emphasis   Constructionist theorists call for consideration of both external and internal dimensions of social justice. From an external perspective, social workers will direct their attention to ensuring that all families are granted the rights and privileges of society, not just the idealized families of dominant groups. Diverse families, by ethnicity, sexual orientation, socioeconomic class, or any other difference, should be guaranteed the same access to the benefits of the culture. When they are not, the social worker is called upon to intervene in whatever ways are applicable, including legal advocacy, legislative advocacy, public education, or other forms of social action.

The internal focus requires the worker to look within the family itself for reflection of justice for all family members. Clearly the social worker needs to challenge overt and specific oppressive behaviors such as intimate partner violence and child abuse but also is encouraged to look at family structure, gender dynamics, and roles. Critical constructionist social workers will address these concerns that are external and have clear internal ramifications through such activities as education and advocacy for more just family practices and policies. Such a perspective reflects the continuous and energetic efforts of the social work profession to develop practice models that both confront and support various dimensions of contemporary society.

Generalist Practice Skills Guidelines for Family Engagement and Assessment

While models may differ somewhat, the following list includes family-oriented engagement and assessment practice behaviors that are common to most models:

- Ensure the family is physically as comfortable as possible.

- Work to facilitate a respectful tone throughout the meeting.

- Transmit positive regard or warmth, support, and respect in verbal and non-verbal practice behaviors.

- Engage with and hear from each member of the family, inviting each to share their perception of the family's strengths, areas for concern, and reason for seeking services.

- Ask each family member her or his perception of the family's purpose and goals in coming to see you.

- Agree upon the expectations and focus of the work with the family.

- Recognize your own biases around family forms and norms.

- Observe the family's communication and interrelationship patterns.

- Inquire about, observe and discuss the role and emotional function that each family member fulfills within the family, particularly within the context of intergenerational relationships.

Key to the engagement and assessment process is the thoroughness and pace with which they are completed. Family systems are complex and encompass multiple views and perspectives, thereby creating the need for an assessment process that is unrushed and includes the perspective of each member of the family system (Logan et al., 2008). Family assessment processes are typically determined by the agency. Your agency may or may not utilize a standardized assessment process. If you are in a setting in which a formalized assessment protocol is in place that includes the use of standardized measures, your role is to clarify for the family the purpose and logistics related to the measures to allay potential anxiety and frustration. Specifically, you can clarify the timing, place, and format of the standardized assessment measure, the meaning of the score or outcomes, and the way in which the information will be shared and used (Corcoran, 2009). Family assessment encompasses an array of assessment tools and strategies. The following discussion highlights the use of mapping with families.

Mapping: A Family Assessment and Planning Tool   Competency in assessing and planning for family-focused interventions includes gaining practice behaviors that include knowledge and skills in mapping the family situation. Chapter 4 presented genograms and ecomaps as helpful mapping tools for assessment and planning with individuals. These two tools are also widely used with families and offer many uses for social workers. Genograms and ecomaps are compatible with most models of social work practice with families. For example, everyone in the family may be asked to participate in the genogram, or each member could make her or his own map of the family relational patterns (see Exhibit 6.1). Whether it is a genogram or another mapping activity, the process of collecting the information can provide the social worker with insights into the way in which the family members define membership in the family, perceive the current situation, or interact with one another within the interview and on paper (Minuchin, Colapinto, & Minuchin, 2007).

Genograms are particularly illuminating assessment tools for family social work as they provide a visual depiction of family structure and patterns. Beyond collecting factual information about multiple generations of family members, the

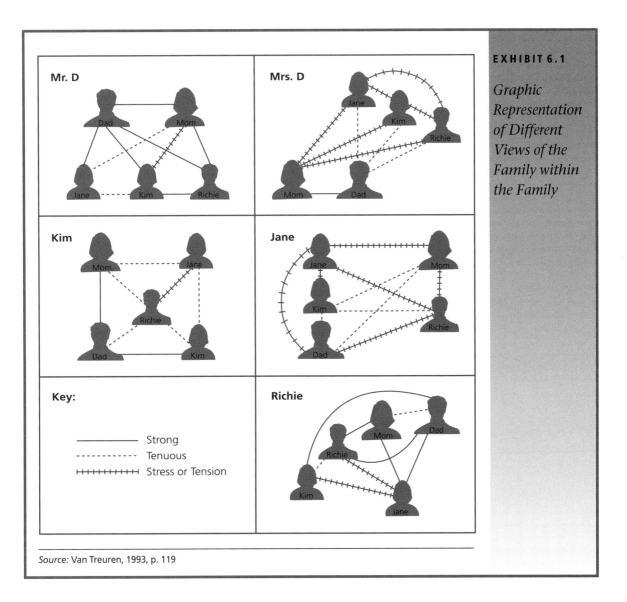

EXHIBIT 6.1

Graphic Representation of Different Views of the Family within the Family

Key:

——————— Strong

- - - - - - - Tenuous

+++++++++++ Stress or Tension

Source: Van Treuren, 1993, p. 119

genogram can serve as an "information net" in which data and insights can be all captured within in an outward and larger context. For example, the presenting problem may be viewed within the larger context of the family's issues, the immediate household may be seen within the context of the extended family and community, the current family situation is a component of the history of similar patterns, nonthreatening questions are perceived in light of painful inquiries, and facts are compared to judgments regarding family patterns and function (McGoldrick, 2009, p. 411).

The Cultural Genogram is a tool with multiple purposes—building rapport, family assessment, and supporting culturally competent practice (McCullough-Chavis & Waites, 2008). Building on the foundation of the genogram, a cultural genogram incorporates the perspective of the client system in areas of culture that impact the family's experience. Culture can encompass, but is not limited to, race, ethnicity, sexual orientation, social and political influences and oppression, socioeconomic status, and religious and spiritual influences. McCullough-Chavis and Waites (2008) outline the role of the social worker in completing a cultural genogram, which is to identify intergenerational patterns and focus on strengths within the context of the larger socio-cultural-political world in which they live.

Ecomaps and other variations that demonstrate relationship patterns can liberate some families from what seems like endless talking, and they usually enjoy developing them and examining the final product. Ecomaps can be used in a visual service evaluation when the goal has been to expand community connections in general or specifically (for example, engaging in more recreational pursuits) or to alter them (such as improving the relationship between the school and the family of a child with disabilities).

Other mapping techniques can prove helpful in social work practice with families. Maps are limited only by imagination. Among the elements they represent are multiple dimensions, the passing of time, interacting components, interpersonal interactions and patterns, levels of intimacy, specific types of connection (such as material or emotional support), and spirituality (Hodge, 2005b). One such map is the **culturagram** which represents a family's experiences in relocating to a new culture (Congress, 2004; 2009). With the increase and diversity of families coming to this country as immigrant or refugees, social workers need culturally competent assessment skills. Targeted specifically for use in engaging and assessing families who have immigrated to this country, the culturagram enables the social worker and family to explore and facilitate empowerment of families from the perspective of their culture. The resulting map illustrates content from inquiries relating to the specifics of the family's experience from immigration to their celebration of values in a new land. A culturagram and the areas for discussion are shown in Exhibit 6.2. This visual and interactive tool helps social workers and families understand the family's internal experiences, recognize differences between and within families and ways in which the family has been successful, and, importantly, areas for planning for potential intervention (Congress, 2009).

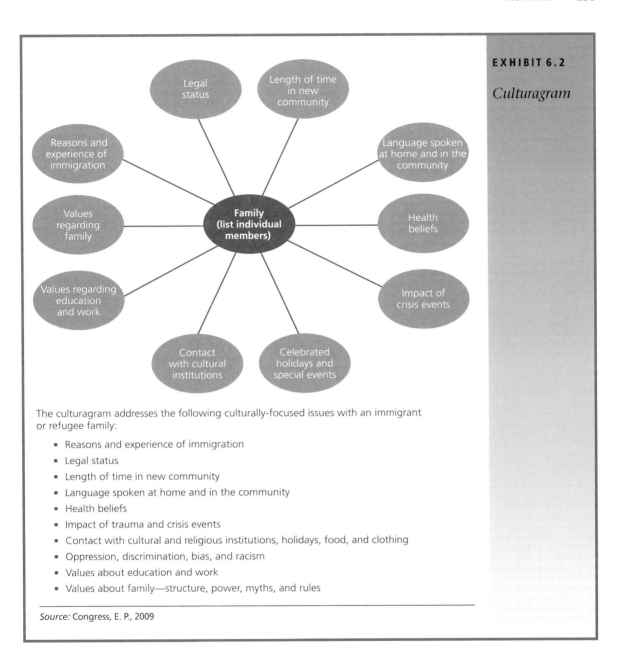

EXHIBIT 6.2

Culturagram

The culturagram addresses the following culturally-focused issues with an immigrant or refugee family:

- Reasons and experience of immigration
- Legal status
- Length of time in new community
- Language spoken at home and in the community
- Health beliefs
- Impact of trauma and crisis events
- Contact with cultural and religious institutions, holidays, food, and clothing
- Oppression, discrimination, bias, and racism
- Values about education and work
- Values about family—structure, power, myths, and rules

Source: Congress, E. P., 2009

More literal maps of physical arrangements such as floor plans in housing situations illustrate concretely the challenges in daily living or the disparities in economic circumstances. For example, a map that shows five children's cots in a tiny bedroom or an older adult on the couch demonstrates a person-in-environment reality that may be difficult to comprehend fully through verbal means. A legend on the map that describes the meaning of all symbols, and a general heading to orient the reader can be used and are especially helpful in any creative or unconventional mapping.

STRAIGHT TALK ABOUT FAMILY SOCIAL WORK PRACTICE

Families are a powerful ingredient in our lives. Families have inspired fierce loyalties, lethal conflicts, abject miseries, and quiet pleasures throughout all of history, and continue to do so today. Whether you view your own family as supportive or toxic or any of the many positions in between, reaching a peace with your own feelings can enhance your work with other families. It is difficult to assess and intervene with the family situations of others if they trigger feelings by their similarity to (or even difference from) your own. Your family concerns need not be perfect or even fully resolved, but your feelings and concerns about your own family situation should not intrude into or influence your work in ways you do not recognize. Such an issue falls into the arena of supervision, and you will benefit from sharing with your supervisor any current struggles you are engaged in with your own family, especially if you are also seeing families in your practice.

Granting that you enjoy a sense of comfort with your own family, you will likely experience situations, at some point, in which your feelings are difficult to manage. Egregious abuse exists in some families, and although contemporary theoretical perspectives can help you temper your responses and recognize that individuals and families do the best they can, the litany of injuries or aggressions emerging in court reports or police accounts or living room conversations can bring on powerful emotions in the most seasoned and balanced social worker. Fortunately, you can use supervision, agency supports, peer connections, and personal strategies for coping with such feelings and reactions. Many social workers utilize the services of professional therapists to process their family challenges and avoid the influence of their family challenges on their professional practice. The most encouraging dimension for social workers today is that the vast majority of families inspire the greatest admiration for their resiliency, spirit, resourcefulness, and agency in the midst of potentially demoralizing circumstances.

Another important "straight talk" item for social work practice with families is the need for accurate and comprehensive documentation. As in social work practice with individuals, documentation is a critical, although more complex, practice behavior. You will recall from Chapter 4 that the components of basic documentation were presented (see Chapter 4 for a review of the guidelines). While these guidelines are applicable to documenting the family interventions, there is the "group" aspect of family work to consider. Recording the assessment and intervention phases of social work practice with families requires the social worker to encompass all members of the family who are participating in the intervention process and to give voice and perspective to the individual contributions. Boxes 6.4

Demographic Data (include all members participating in the assessment and intervention):

- Names, birthdates, and relationship to others
- Contact Information

BOX 6.4

Documentation of a Family Assessment

Family Information:

- Presenting need(s) or concern(s)
- Living situation (e.g., members of household and level of stability)
- Family (composition—parents, siblings, spouse/significant other(s), children, and others (extended family and friends); level of support; and family history of mental illness, as applicable). A genogram and/or ecomap may be a helpful tool to gather and depict this information
- Timeline—significant life events experienced by the family
- Cultural environment (traditions and cultural view of help-seeking)
- Religion/spirituality (statement of beliefs and levels of activity and satisfaction)
- Family strengths and significant events, including trauma (e.g., physical, sexual, and/or emotional abuse or neglect and experience with perpetrator(s))

Individual Family Member Information:

- Individual family member information, including:
  - Educational history of each member (highest level achieved, performance, goals, and challenges)
  - Substance use/abuse (history of addictive behaviors—alcohol, drugs, gambling, sexual, or other)
  - Emotional/behavioral functioning and treatment history
  - Risk factors
  - Physical health
  - Legal status or concerns
  - Financial/employment circumstances (employment status, satisfaction, financial stability, areas of concern or change)

Social and Environmental Information:

- Strengths and concerns regarding physical environment, as applicable (e.g., structure, neighborhood, and community)
- Safety issues (e.g., risks or concerns of and for individual members and social worker)

Summary

- Current providers (including psychiatrist, primary care physician, therapist, caseworker, etc.)
- Community resources being used (including support groups, religious, spiritual, other)
- Family goal(s) for intervention
- Summary of social worker's observations and impressions

Adapted from St. Anthony's Medical Center, St. Louis, Missouri; Missouri Department of Social Services

BOX 6.5

Documentation of a Family Intervention Plan

Intervention Plan:
- Preliminary assessment
- Preliminary plan for intervention and plan for change (to be developed at first visit), including:
  ○ What will each family member do differently?
  ○ How does each family member view themselves accomplishing changes?
  ○ What support and services are needed to accomplish plan for change?
  ○ Who will provide support and services?
  ○ Who will arrange for support and services?
- Interventions and plans for emergency/safety needs
- Other interventions needed
- Needs (include date, identified need, status (active, inactive, deferred, or referred), and reason for deferral or referral)
- Strengths
- Facilitating factors for intervention
- Limitations
- Barriers to intervention
- Other care providers/referrals and purpose (including plan for service coordination)
- Plan for involvement of individual family members, extended family members, significant others and friends
- Review and termination criteria/plan
- Planned frequency and duration of intervention

Adapted from St. Anthony's Medical Center, St. Louis, Missouri; Missouri Department of Social Services

and 6.5 provide guidelines for family-focused information to be included in the documentation of a family assessment and intervention.

CONCLUSION

The contemporary family both supports and challenges the social worker. Social workers engage with the family and its struggles in our culture, thus a goal for the profession is to develop additional and relevant models for working with them that recognize their strengths, agency, and resilience. Education and advocacy for shifts in the structural and political arrangements that exist for families are also required.

As a culture we still value the importance of the family, and social workers can be a part of the solution for creating environments in which families of all kinds are validated and supported.

As the structure and meaning of family itself continue to change, you can stay alert for your own capacities to honor those notions of others. As a form of "group," the family has particular resonance and serves as a grounding point for understanding human collectives. With that dimension in mind, this exploration will move to the intervention, termination, and evaluation of your work with families.

MAIN POINTS

- Historical antecedents for involvement by the social work profession with families, including family function and systems theories, shape the way in which social workers engage with and assess families.

- An idealized, or fantasy, notion of the American family still exists today, but social workers recognize and work with many forms, including grandparents raising grandchildren; gay, lesbian, bisexual, and transgender families; single parent families; families of multiple racial and ethnic heritages; families with persons with disabilities; blended families; and families with multiple problems.

- Several contemporary theoretical perspectives have emerged that are consistent with critical social construction, the strengths perspective, and social justice orientations, including narrative theory, solution-focused work, and constructionist approaches.

- Your practice setting will guide much of your work with families, but the skills and practice behaviors that you have learned for engaging and assessing individuals and groups will be applicable in working with families. Additionally, family-oriented skills and practice behaviors are needed, including engaging the whole family, reframing, and recognizing your own biases around family forms.

- Mapping tools can be helpful in assessing and evaluating the work with families; they can also help to empower families to change.

EXERCISES

1. Go to www.routledgesw.com/cases and review the case file for Roberto Salazar. As the undocumented nephew of Hector and Celia Sanchez, Roberto has consistently earned an income but has also experienced several health challenges. He is currently living with the Sanchez family due to an injury that prevents him from working. He has a number of skills but his current injury and inability to work has him feeling defeated.

   You are the social worker charged with monitoring the status of Hector and Celia's Section 8 housing voucher. While Hector and Celia generally manage their rent payments, they are having difficulty meeting the schedule due to extra expenditures in support of Roberto. Your agency is responsible for controlling expenses and complying with federal regulations. Your supervisor is especially concerned with this aspect of the program.

   On your visit to the Sanchez home, Hector assures you that—even though he knows the landlord can evict him and his family for violating regulations regarding occupancy—Roberto is family and, of course, he and Celia will house and feed him. He remembers his own loneliness when he came to the U.S. and that his uncle helped him. He has no doubt that he can assist Roberto by providing temporary housing and support. Hector explains to you that it is important for immigrants to stick together and support one another, especially family. You are feeling some pressure from the agency to report and help resolve the issue of Roberto's unacceptable presence in the Sanchez home. You are concerned that your supervisor will look unfavorably on you if you allow Roberto to continue to live in the house.

   Respond to the following questions:
   a. How might a family focus differ from an individual focus in this situation?
   b. How will you respond to your Hector? Your supervisor?
   c. How might diversity be a factor in this situation? Compare your responses to those of your peers. Identify and team up with another student whose approach seems similar to yours and develop a unified approach. Brainstorm in class regarding different or creative ways to approach this situation.

2. You are a social worker on an interprofessional team that works with children who have autism, and their families. Three-year-old Jenny is referred to your team. She is the light of her father's life—she is lively, energetic, and bright-eyed. In the last year, she has become quiet, preferring to play by herself, and is less interested in the special outings her father loves to share with her.

   After a series of anxious appointments with the pediatrician, Jenny was referred to a specialist in developmental pediatrics. Many observations and checklists later, Jenny was diagnosed with autism. Her parents, Catherine and Jason, were devastated. Her two-year-old brother, Sammy, was oblivious.

   Over a period of a month, Catherine began to adjust to the diagnosis. She connected with a supportive group of parents coping with autism in children and read all she could about autism. She also spent considerable time with Jenny, playing and coaxing her to interact with her. Jason, however, was notably uninterested in Catherine's activities. He began to refuse to go to Jenny's doctor's appointments. During one argumentative dinner with Catherine, he stated that he did not believe the diagnosis; he thought Jenny was fine, just going through a stage, and accused Catherine of "selling out" her own daughter.

Jenny was referred to the interprofessional team by her pediatrician. Catherine engaged in the process enthusiastically, if painfully. Jason attended the assessment and seemed sullen, participating very little. The team concurs that the family would benefit from your "support work" around the diagnosis. Catherine and Jason agree to meet with you and you speculate this might be your only chance to engage Jason.

Respond to the following questions to compare with your peers.

a. What is your assessment of this family? Identify a theoretical perspective that is most applicable to working with this family. How does your choice of perspective influence your approach to this family? Be specific.

b. Generate a list of three questions or issues that you think are important to address in your first meeting.

c. How might you attempt to engage the family, especially Jason? As you compare responses with your peers, what different (from your own) perspective was most useful to you?

3. Go to www.routledgesw.com/cases and review the case for Carla Washburn. Create a genogram of her family. Explore the connections between Carla and her family members and the ways in which those connections impact her relationships within the family. Address the following:

- What are the strengths of the family?

- What are the issues that have impacted the family?

- How have those issues impacted the various relationships?

- Who has the "power" in the family?

- If you were a social worker working with this family, what issues would take precedent?

4. Create a genogram of your family. Explore the connections within the family and the ways in which those connections impact the relationships within the family, particularly your relationships. Address the following:

- What are the strengths of your family?

- What are the issues that your family has faced?

- How have those issues impacted the various relationships?

- Who has the "power" in the family?

- If you were the social worker working with your family, what issues would take precedence?

- What have you learned about your family from this exercise?

CHAPTER 7

Intervening with Families: Initiation, Termination, and Evaluation

. . . to think larger than one to think larger than two or three or four this is me this is my partner these are my children if we say, these are my people who do we mean? how to declare our bond how to keep each of us warm we are in danger how to face it and not crack

Melanie Kaye/Kantrowitz, in *We Speak in Code: Poems & Other Writings*, 1980

Key Questions for Chapter 7

(1) What competencies do I need to intervene with families? (EPAS 2.1.10(c))

(2) What are the social work practice behaviors that enable me to effectively intervene with families? (EPAS 2.1.10(c))

(3) How can I engage in research-informed practice and practice-informed research to guide the processes of intervention, termination, and evaluation with families? (EPAS 1.2.6)

(4) What potential ethical dilemmas might I expect to occur in intervening with families? (EPAS 2.1.2)

SOCIAL WORKERS HAVE A LONGSTANDING HISTORY OF intervening in family situations and crises. Dating to the era of Mary Richmond and the Charity Organization Society and Jane Addams and the Settlement House movements, social workers have focused on intervening with families to enhance their functioning (Logan et al., 2008). Just as social work practitioners respond to societal changes, social workers have also adapted their practice behaviors, including knowledge, skills, and values, to the developmental stages of families or changing structure of families. While families are generally self-sufficient in meeting their ongoing financial, emotional, and caregiving needs, when they seek help outside the family, they require a response from the helping professions that is developed for that family's unique needs and differs from the intervention that may be negotiated with an individual client or another family (Briar-Lawson & Naccarato, 2008). Thus, **family social work** interventions require competencies to address the complexities of the contemporary family, which may include challenges involving culture, racial and ethnic diversity, financial and legal challenges, and intergenerational relationships and dynamics. Different from family therapy, family social work is an approach based on generalist social work skills for intervening with families who are at-risk for a negative outcome as family social work assumes the intervention is family-centered, and support can be provided in the home or in the office and in times of crisis (Collins, Jordan, & Coleman, 2010). Family social work practice interventions may be focused on: (1) reinforcing family strengths to prepare families for long-term change, such as a member arriving, leaving, needing care, or dying; (2) providing additional support to family therapy so families will maintain effective family functioning; and/or (3) creating concrete changes in family functioning to sustain effective and satisfying daily routines independent of formal helpers (Collins et al., 2010, p. 3).

Essential to the planning of an effective intervention with families is the engagement and assessment that you have completed. Building on the assessment that focused on the family's strengths and self-determined needs, the intervention process is an opportunity to collaborate with the family to facilitate growth and change. With its emphasis on brief, efficacious interventions, managed care has influenced contemporary social work practice with families by focusing the social worker clearly, systematically, and succinctly on identifying and assessing the problem or concerns, developing and implementing an intervention plan, and terminating the working relationship (Jordan & Franklin, 2009, p. 429). This chapter will highlight theoretical frameworks and practice behaviors that will be helpful to you as you embark on working with families.

THEORETICAL APPROACHES TO INTERVENING WITH FAMILIES

Just as with social work practice interventions with individuals, family intervention is a planned change process in which the social worker and client system work together to implement the steps to reach the goals established in the assessment and planning process. Research has shown that families, even those who endure intense or chronic stressors, can be resilient (Benard, 2008). An array of theoretical conceptualizations provide the underpinning for the array of approaches to social work practice with families, including systems, ecosystems, family life cycle, cultural and social diversity, strengths-based, and empowerment (Logan et al., 2008, p. 184). The social worker who is well grounded in theoretical approaches to working with families can select the approach(es) and techniques that is(are) best suited for the social worker's practice philosophy and the needs of the client family. In an effort to best serve the families with whom they work, practitioners "often use a combination of family techniques from different models rather than adhering to one particular approach. Integrationism [i.e., blending models and techniques], technical eclecticism [i.e., using different techniques] and the use of common factors are the preferred ways that most practitioners work" (Franklin, Jordan, & Hopson, 2009, p. 434). As a practitioner, you will recognize that theories each have their own limitations within the context of the client family's ethnic, cultural, familial traditions and your scope of practice as a social worker (Hull & Mather, 2006). However, the family intervention models that are most effective typically share certain elements, including education, opportunities to practice and model new behaviors and skills, and multi-faceted intervention plans (Franklin et al., 2009). As an ethical and culturally competent social work practitioner, you are responsible for gaining the training necessary to utilize the evidence on available family models and select and implement that approach or combination of approaches that you believe will be most effective for your client system.

Created by Hull and Mather (2006), Exhibit 7.1 depicts a framework for approaching family intervention from a multidimensional perspective. As shown in the exhibit, the process of developing a family intervention begins with viewing the family within their environment, followed by the selection of a relevant theoretical approach, and concludes with the creation of an intervention utilizing appropriate techniques.

Following is a discussion that explores theoretical approaches utilizing the strengths and empowerment, narrative, and solution-focused perspectives. In keeping with the overall approach of this book, the theoretical perspectives presented here will be within the postmodern grouping of frameworks. Derived from a social constructionist philosophy, working with families to grow and change by aiding them in identifying and building on strengths, reconstructing their life experiences, and developing new realities are approaches explored here. While postmodern

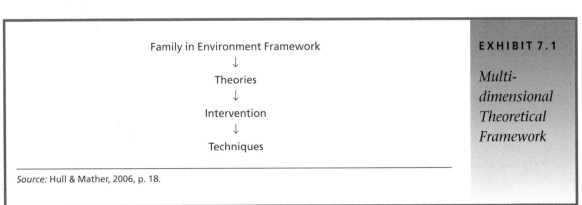

Family in Environment Framework
↓
Theories
↓
Intervention
↓
Techniques

EXHIBIT 7.1

Multi-dimensional Theoretical Framework

Source: Hull & Mather, 2006, p. 18.

approaches may be perceived as counter to traditional systemic approaches, Logan and colleagues (2008) posit that, in fact, the two complement one another. Systems theories help the practitioner to view and frame the family within the context of environment, while the postmodern constructs help the social worker to view the family within the context of the meaning of the presenting issues that are provided by the family.

Strengths and Empowerment Perspectives and Family Interventions

Having completed an assessment and planning process that identifies the strengths on which the family can build, an intervention in the strengths tradition strives to not only enhance the family's assets but to empower the family to develop new coping and resiliency strategies for the current situations as well as the future. From a strengths perspective, challenges are viewed as opportunities and possibilities (Saleebey, 2009). An intervention that is grounded in a strengths perspective is one that strives to build capacity and assets and focus on solutions (Briar-Lawson & Naccarato, 2008). For example, an intervention that emanates from the traditional deficit-based perspective will view the family as the source of its problems (e.g., poor parenting, dysfunctional relationships, or irreparable problems). A strengths-based intervention seeks to identify the family's assets (e.g., the parents are committed to rearing healthy, productive children and the family has remained together in the face of adversity) and capacities and focus on solutions (e.g., the family is willing to work on the challenges that brought them to a social worker).

In the face of the complexities of "being" a family in contemporary society, practitioners may find it easier when developing an intervention plan with a family to focus on the problems that exist within the family, rather than the strengths. Asking the family members, for instance, to describe the characteristics of a healthy, strong family can lead to a discussion of those characteristics that are shared by their own family. To address the family's current situation, it is important to understand their views on strengths and to incorporate those strengths into the planning and intervention process (DeFrain & Asay, 2007b). Engaging in an exploration of those actions that the family members can take individually and collectively has the potential to result in an altered and different perspective for the family (and possibly the social worker, as well). Gaining insight into interacting in a new way with one another and the environment can be an empowering experience for the family.

Grounded in a commitment to build on family strengths, empowerment-oriented practice has applicability for use in family interventions. Having been developed over the past several decades from a concept to practice principles and methods, empowerment-oriented interventions extend beyond intentions to encapsulate the principles and actions (Parsons, 2008, p. 124). Particularly helpful for families in crisis, especially those who have experienced a history of crises, empowerment-driven interventions can aid the social worker in helping the family to create solutions for the challenges being experienced. An empowerment approach utilizes seven principles of practice (Wise, 2005):

1. **Build on strengths and resources and diminish oppressive factors** As noted, the strengths that can be utilized in addressing the challenges must first be identified by the family. The family then reviews existing and potential resources and begins the mobilization of those resources. Oppressive factors or barriers to growth and change may lessen as family members perceive options and possibilities. Strategizing with the family about ways in which oppressive factors may be confronted, ameliorated, or minimized can also be empowering. A first step, however, may be for family members to confront the oppressive factors that may be perceived to exist *within* the family.

2. **Multicultural respect** A vast concept, multicultural respect requires attention to a wide and growing array of phenomena that may be relevant for the family with whom you are working, including race, ethnicity, gender, age, socioeconomic status, religious/spiritual beliefs, sexual orientation, differing ability, language, and developmental phases. The family may be impacted in multiple areas. The role of the social worker in helping the family create an intervention is to ensure awareness by all members of their perceptions and experiences in these areas and to help the family understand the meaning and impact and confront stereotypes and barriers.

3. **Recognize needs at the personal, interpersonal, and community levels of empowerment** While families may well know their needs, they may have difficulty, particularly during a crisis, articulating those needs to one another or the social worker. A successful empowerment-focused intervention relies on the social worker to help the family create solutions that are directly linked to the needs that have been voiced. Regular individual and group check-ins are necessary to ensure that the needs have been accurately and thoroughly voiced and are being addressed through the plan that was developed for the intervention. Needs can and do change and the social worker can help the family to recognize that fact and maintain a realistic approach to success.

4. **With sufficient resources, family can empower themselves** Upon identifying and mobilizing resources, the social worker can facilitate action by the family members. The social worker does not have the ability to complete the work for the family, but can, however, monitor and interpret the family's use (or lack) of the resources.

5. **Support is needed from each other, from other families, and from the community** Receiving support from within the family and outside the family can be the impetus that the family needs to reach their agreed-upon goals and

solutions. The role of the social worker may be to normalize experiences, provide information, and connect the family to one another and others.

6.   **Establish and maintain a "power WITH" relationship** Power can serve as an asset and a barrier in a family intervention. Being able to convey to the family that each member has power, the family has power, and the social worker has power and, most importantly, this power can be shared for the purposes of achieving the goals of the intervention. Interventions should not rely on the "power" of any one or sub-group of the family-social worker partnership, but should be shared in a collaboration utilizing the strengths, assets, and resources that each person or sub-group brings to the intervention.

7.   **Use cooperative roles that support and assist family members** Implementation of the intervention requires that each member assume a variety of roles over the course of the relationship. Such roles may include co-consultant, co-collaborator, guide, co-teachers/learner, co-investigator, and co-creator (pp. 86–88). The social worker is in a position to point out ways in which the family members can utilize their knowledge and skills.

To bring these principles to life, consider the situation being faced by the Murray family, a three generation family living together in the same house. William (55-year-old high school teacher) and Georgia (50-year-old occupational therapist) Murray have been married 27 years and have three children: Elle, a 25-year-old unemployed licensed practical nurse, recently returned to her parents' home with her two children ages four and two years, following a divorce; Stephen, 21, who lives at home, works part time, and attends a local university; and Samantha, 16, who is a high school junior. Recently, William's mother, Edna, 76, moved into the house. Edna suffers from Alzheimer's disease. After a recent car accident, the family determines that Edna is no longer able to safely live in an independent living situation. The arrival of Elle and her children and Edna resulted in Stephen and Samantha having to give up their bedrooms. A makeshift bedroom has been created for Samantha in the basement and Stephen is sleeping on the fold-out couch in the den. While the crisis that brings the Murray family to your agency is Samantha's arrest for driving under the influence of alcohol and subsequent suspension from school, it is immediately evident that this is a family in crisis in several additional areas: Edna's illness and increasing need for care; Elle's adjustment to divorce and single parenting; displacement and lack of privacy for Stephen and Samantha; and the stress experienced by William and Georgia in supporting the family.

Utilizing strengths and empowerment-based perspectives, how can this family be supported through this challenging period in their lives? Consider first the strengths and resources that exist. William and Georgia have a longstanding marriage; are employed; have opened their home to their daughter, her children, and William's mother; and are willing to provide care for these family members. The family can be a resource for itself but an important intervention strategy is to ascertain from each member their perception of the issues and any factors that are barriers to resolution of the issues. Samantha, for example, may view her grand-mother as the problem as Edna has taken her room and her parents' time and resources, leading her to argue constantly with her parents and spend as much time away from home as possible. Helping the family to articulate their needs within a multiculturally respectful way is the next step in creating alternatives with the fam-ily. For example, providing information about Alzheimer's disease and its course may help the family better understand and accept Edna's behavior and needs. The social worker can enlist ideas from each family member about ways in which the family can support one another and offering suggestions for accessing resources outside the family (e.g., caregiver support group, respite care, substance abuse treatment, and employment support program).

Collaborating with the family to access and mobilize resources can not only provide a model for them to utilize but can engage them in an alternative to their present incapacitation. Examples of collaborating with the family include: (1) Capitalizing on Elle's professional expertise as an LPN, the family can apply for a family caregiver program in which a family member can be paid to care for an older adult. Elle can contribute financially to the family, care for her grandmother and her children, and work toward rebuilding her life; (2) Co-investigating with Stephen options for utilizing his experience as a camp counselor to apply for a live-in resident assistant position on campus can provide him with the much needed space and privacy; and (3) Samantha's substance use and arrest has effectively gotten her parents' attention. Guiding the family to consider the various responses and treatment options can enable them to make choices together and learn from one another to co-create a new way of being a family. While the social worker may guide the family members toward resources, the members would be encouraged to handle as many of the logistics of accessing and utilizing the resources as possible.

Narrative Theory and Family Interventions

Sharing a number of the components for intervention that are encompassed within strengths and empowerment approaches, a narrative approach to intervening with families also incorporates strengths, viewing the family as experts on the family unit, and collaboration between the social worker and the family. In hearing each family member's perceptions of the family and the problems that brought them to a social worker, the family members are able to identify the meaning of the problem and discover alternatives to those meanings that will aid in changing the family's interactions (Kelley, 2009). As with the narrative approach to working with individuals, the problems confronting the family are assessed through respectful listening, the perceptions are reflected upon and deconstructed, then reconstructed by challenging perceived truths. Through the reconstruction process, the family members in collaboration with the social worker are able to create an intervention plan that enables them to arrive at unique outcomes that have meaning and viability within their family unit.

Implementation of an intervention based in a narrative approach is the culmination of the family–social worker partnership. A narrative approach provides the social worker with a variety of strategies that will optimize the family's strengths to expand their perceptions of themselves and their problems and to create a new vision of themselves that breaks from the view previously held by them. Within the discovery process, the family has the opportunity to envision a future in which the current problem persists or a future in which the problem is altered through their actions.

Returning to the Murray family, their crisis could be framed utilizing a narrative approach, as with an empowerment approach, by the social worker listening to each member share her or his views on the family situation. As you can imagine, the perceptions of the Murray family are likely to be quite different. William and Georgia may share that they are doing their best to provide for all the members of the family and they feel betrayed by Samantha's arrest and suspension. Samantha (as earlier) may believe her parents have given more to other members than they have to her, particularly her grandmother. Despite struggling with cognitive impairment, Edna may feel she is a burden to her family but feels powerless to change the situation. Elle likely also feels guilt for being unable to support her children and herself. Stephen is feeling pressured to hold down a job and maintain his grades and scholarship so that he can move out of the house, thus relieving some family stress. After reaching a consensus with the family regarding the desired outcomes, the social worker can begin deconstructing and reconstructing the family's perceptions by externalizing the problems (i.e., focusing the family on the issue not the person). Should the family, for example, choose to focus on stabilizing the situation with Edna's care, the social worker can externalize Edna's behaviors as being her cognitive impairment and not within her control. The social worker can then help the family to envision life if they take no steps to improve their perceptions of Edna's situation as well as life that includes them understanding the disease course, coping strategies, care and respite options, and ways to interact with her to honor her and value the remaining time with her. While reconstruction of Alzheimer's disease will not alter the course of the disease, the quality of life for Edna and her family can be enhanced through challenging the problem-saturated perceptions that were previously held. Edna will be viewed as an honored member of the family, not as a burden.

Solution-Focused Family Interventions

Like other family-focused interventions that are derived from postmodern thought, solution-focused family interventions also emphasize strengths and empowerment, client self-determination, and collaborating with the social workers to construct new realities by mobilizing assets and resources. Solution-focused interventions differ from other similar approaches in the use of several specific techniques involving questions that are intended to move the client system from crisis to solution through the co-construction of solutions that alter the present situation (De Jong, 2009).

With an emphasis on the relationships and competence, family solution-focused interventions incorporate explorations of the skills, strengths, and competence of clients in a way that is consistent with many postmodern approaches. This focal point serves to solidify the social worker-client relationship as a collaboration focused on building on past successes (De Jong & Berg, 2008). The assumptions inherent in their ecological orientation encourage social workers to look to environmental, structural supports for solutions rather than to internal dynamics for pathology. Social workers do not disregard individual responsibility for behaviors such as those that occur in child abuse or intimate partner violence, but these are viewed as evidence that the client's external resources and skills are underused (Christiensen, Todahl, & Barrett, 1999). For instance, family violence may occur when a family is experiencing stress but not utilizing resources outside the family (e.g., social, health, mental health, or financial aid services). Thus, the assumption that individuals and families can grow and change and ultimately be responsible is sustained.

You will recall from Chapter 6 that a series of questions are used for assessment and planning of the solution-focused intervention. Upon completion of the assessment, the social worker and the client system develop a plan for change. Once the plan is underway, the social worker checks in with the members to monitor progress through the use of "what's better?" questions. The scaling questions that were included in the assessment phase can become a part of the intervention as well. Within the context of the intervention, scaling questions can be utilized to review previously discussed solutions and exceptions and highlight changes as they are made (Nichols, 2009). The use of "what's better" and scaling questions enable the family and the social worker to reflect on changes that have occurred and to compare perspectives.

Additional techniques for completing the solution-focused intervention include: (1) providing compliments to emphasize strategies that have been successful and (2) taking a break within an interaction to provide feedback—recapping the work of the family and social worker and providing suggestions for future work (i.e., "homework" that focuses on observing successes, engaging in new tasks, and predicting desired changes) (Nichols, 2009, pp. 273–274).

Returning to the Murray family once again, consider the intervention from a solution-focused perspective. During the assessment and planning phase, you questioned each of the members regarding their perceptions of life in their household. Imagine William and Georgia's responses to goal-formulation or miracle questions. They will likely talk about having imagined a near "empty-nest" household with their two older children living on their own and Samantha about to head off to college. Samantha's response to the "miracle" question might likely involve her grandmother not living with the family, not facing legal issues related to her driving under the influence arrest, and her school suspension. Elle's "miracle" might include employment, a supportive partner and a home of her own. Stephen's miracle may involve a room of his own. Edna may wish desperately to have her memories back and to return to independent living.

Given the diverse array of goals that may be expressed by each of the family members, helping the Murray family to connect with a realistic set of goals can be a complicated process. Highlighting the fact that the family members care for one another is a technique to foster goodwill and strive for finding common ground on which the members can agree (De Jong & Berg, 2008). In working with the Murray family, reminding them of their commitment to and concern for one another can be a regular part of the intervention. Imagine that the agreed-upon goal is to find a solution to the overcrowded housing situation. Your role can be to work with the family to develop concrete and achievable short- and long-term solutions, check in regularly with "what's better?" questions, and terminate when the family and you agree the goals have been achieved.

Regardless of the theoretical approach that guides your work with families, your social work values and ethical standards will provide the foundation on which you will develop interventions to be implemented with families. Ensuring that the client system's rights to self-determination, strengths, and diversity are honored is the priority for your intervention with families. Emphasizing the practice behaviors to enable you to become a practitioner who is competent in social work practice with families will be the focus of the following discussion.

CONTEMPORARY TRENDS AND SKILLS FOR INTERVENING WITH FAMILIES

Families are comprised of individuals and are a form of a group, and as such, benefit from the careful use of the same practice behaviors that assist individuals and groups to engage in their work together with you. Interventions with families are likely to vary according to your practice setting and the constraints of your agency. For example, if you are a member of the intake unit of a child protection team, your intervention with the family will probably differ from that of your colleague who works in a community mental health agency. The theoretical lens through which you are working will also influence the way you intervene with family members. You may develop an intervention plan from a systems focus, or you may work with family members to build an intervention plan based on their perceptions of ways in which you might help them, as in solution-focused work. In any situation, your intervention begins with an invitation to the family to tell their story, but your agency mission and purpose and your own theoretical biases will influence the intervention approaches you take.

Social work practice interventions with families shares many similarities with individually focused interventions. Recall from Chapter 5 the discussion on roles that a social worker may have in working with individuals (e.g., case manager, counselor, broker, mediator, educator, client advocate, and collaborator). Each of these roles is applicable for working with families with some unique features that are noteworthy, particularly in light of the setting in which the intervention may occur. Family-focused social work practice can take place in a wide array of settings, including child welfare, mental health centers, schools, health care facilities, and community centers, to name a few. For example, the social worker working with a family in a child welfare setting may engage in all the roles, but emphasize case management and brokering activities in particular as the focus of the work in on reunification of the family unit. In a health care setting, the social worker's emphasis may be on education and advocacy, for instance. With families, it is important to consider all the members' perspectives, recognize relationship dynamics, and the strengths-based intervention goals that will optimize family functioning.

As with practice with individuals, the setting in which you practice and your philosophical and theoretical approach will frame your intervention activities. While model-specific practice behaviors have been previously discussed, there are additional general practice skills that transcend the continuum of practice approaches. Building on the practice behaviors utilized in the phases of family engagement and assessment, the following strengths-based skills for intervening with families can be helpful (Benard, 2006, p. 214; Hull & Mather, 2006):

Identify the issues and concerns, use active listening to enable the family members to tell their story and reflect on the information shared by the family members.

- Acknowledge the pain.
- Look for strengths.
- Ask questions about survival, support, periods of time that were positive for the family, interests, dreams, goals, and pride.
- Point out strengths.
- Link strengths to the goals and dreams of the family members (both group and individual).
- Find opportunities for family/members to be contribute to the intervention by helping to educate other members and serve as helping agents in achieving the family's agreed-upon goals.
- Use brainstorming for solutions as a strategy to help the family to view the situation and themselves differently.

Written homework assignments, task designation, and teaching are strategies that can be helpful but must be appropriate to the family's situation, their investment in the process, and the framework you are using in the intervention. Return for a moment to the Murray family scenario and consider the above list of practice behaviors. In order to mobilize the family into working toward crisis resolution, you can begin by asking each member her or his priorities for change. From those verbalizations, it is likely that you will glean the pain, strengths, goals, and dreams felt by each of the family members. You may choose to engage the family in brainstorming strategies they can use to address each of the areas of concern or assign the family homework in which they put their ideas on paper for addressing the concerns. An alternative may be to ask the family to have a family conference and bring their ideas back to the next meeting with you. Once the family has developed a range of possible ways to address their prioritized concerns, consider asking them to have a discussion in which specific tasks are identified and assigned. Be sure to explore the possibility that the expertise for problem-solving resides within the family and individual members can function as teachers and guides.

In addition to the individual and group skills, reframing, perspectival (or circular) questions, family group conferencing, motivational interviewing, and re-enactments (i.e., role-playing or rehearsals) are a sampling of practice strategies with good applicability in many family situations when carefully used. Previously discussed in Chapter 6 as an assessment tool, mapping will be highlighted as a strategy to be incorporated into the intervention process.

Reframing

An approach used frequently in social work with families, as well as individuals, groups, communities and in organizations, **reframing** is a practice skill in which the social worker conceives of and describes a situation in different terms. Reframing can be particularly helpful in family conversations in which one member makes an incendiary statement to or about another family member, which sometimes occurs in conversations with the social worker. Carefully used, reframing can assist both recipient and "sender" to view the situation with diminished uproar so they can begin to listen to each other. Focused on strengths and positive alternatives, reframing must be appropriately timed to have a meaningful impact. To have a significant effect, the social worker must stay carefully attuned to the family members' dialogues to identify opportunities for reframing as they occur (Minuchin et al., 2007).

For example, a 15-year-old boy, who sees his mother as an autocratic barrier to his enjoyment because she will not allow him to go out with friends who drive, says, "There is no person on the face of this earth who is more controlling and overprotective than my mother. She is just like Hitler! She keeps me locked up in the prisoners' camp." You may suggest that the teen's mother cares so much for him that she fears he will be hurt in an automobile accident or in some other way if he goes out with his friends.

When reframing, offer a plausible alternative that does not resonate as a "gimmick" or "Pollyanna" type of effort to diffuse strong feelings and, accordingly, will be heard by the parties involved. The danger lies in interpreting the thoughts or feelings of another person without directly having been told. In the example of the 15-year-old teen and his mother, it is quite likely that the mother is not intentionally attempting to torture her son (and that she truly worries about his going out with friends who drive), but he may or may not be able to "hear" her sentiment as reframed. Another reframing effort may be more effective depending on the nature of the relationship and the people involved. Developing the content of such interpretations requires judgment and skill; use reframing cautiously and only when conditions are relatively straightforward. How can reframing be utilized with the Murray family? Instead of focusing on the upheaval created by Edna, Elle, and Elle's children moving into the house, consider emphasizing the strong family commitments and caring environment that is created for members who are in need of support.

Perspectival Questions

Mentioned in connection with individuals in Chapter 5 and with group work practice in Chapter 9, perspectival questions can be effective in family social work. By seeking the perspective of another family member, you can help clarify the feelings and meanings of one member's view of another. If the family is experiencing stress because the eldest son is leaving home, you may ask the teenage daughter, "What do you think your mother will do to prepare for Johnny's leaving?" Or you may ask the mother, "What will your daughter miss most about Johnny?"

The responses to these questions can communicate ideas and feelings that no one in the family has openly or previously recognized. Such assistance in communication is relevant when family members assume they know all they need to about the responses of other family members as a result of long-term, "stuck" patterns of argument or difference or "saving face." As in the use of reframing, perspectival questioning is a strategy to be used carefully and only when you are confident that you can respond appropriately to any statement. The daughter in the example just provided may respond with, "Mother will sew name tags in Johnny's underwear so he won't lose it in the dorm laundry room at college," or, alternatively, she may say, "Mother will no doubt start to drink again." The same element of the unexpected that can create new ways of thinking for families can also throw a curve ball to the unwary or unprepared social worker. Utilizing perspectival questions with the Murray family could potentially yield some illuminating insights. Consider, for example, the new perspective that could be uncovered if Edna were asked about the support that her son and daughter-in-law have provided to Elle and her children and her response was that they should not have invited Elle and the children to move into their house. The social worker who incorporates perspectival questions must be prepared for the unexpected.

Family Group Conferencing

A strategy for use with families, family group conferencing (FGC) is an empowerment-focused intervention aimed at creating or strengthening a network of support for families as they are experiencing a crisis or transition. Originally developed for work with families in which children were at risk for abuse or neglect, this practice strategy has been extended to other family situations, including families with older adults experiencing life changes. Usually an activity that occurs after the assessment and planning phases, the family conference is a collaborative effort that includes the social worker, family (including extended family members), and members of the family's community who are existing or potential resources for the family (Wise, 2005).

Convened by the social worker who functions as a coordinator, the conference goal is to gather the family members together with persons who are connected to the family for the purpose of making decisions. The social worker confers individually with each potential participant prior to the conference to ensure that each agrees to be actively involved in the process of decision-making and action steps. During the conference itself, the desired outcomes are determined by the participants themselves with the strengths and areas for concerns being included in the planning process (Brody & Gadling-Cole, 2008). Once a plan is established, the group adjourns and may reconvene after a period of time has elapsed in which the plan is implemented to discuss progress or re-negotiate the plan.

Return for a moment to the Murray family. If you were to convene a family group conference with the Murrays, consider those persons you would invite to participate and the reasons for inviting those persons. What would you anticipate the goals being that could provide the Murrays with a much needed support network and stronger coping skills? What are their strengths? How might they benefit individually and collectively from participation in a family group conference? What is your role? While answers to these questions can only be speculative, you can utilize this exercise to begin to see yourself in the role of a family practitioner.

Motivational Interviewing

As you recall from Chapter 5, motivational interviewing (MI) has been introduced for use with a variety of clients, including those who are nonvoluntary, experiencing substance abuse, or intimate partner violence (Wahab, 2005). Using the five principles of MI—expressing empathy, developing discrepancy, avoiding argumentation, rolling with resistance, and supporting self-efficacy—to promote behavior change, MI is particularly well-suited for situations in which the client systems is uncertain about making the change and/or the time in limited (Miller & Rollnick, 2002; Wagner, 2008).

Motivational interviewing has also been shown to have applicability for social work with families. Miller and Rollnick (2002) offer strategies for engaging in motivational interviewing with families with adolescents. Utilizing the FRAMES strategy, the social worker can conduct a Family Check-up that provides the social worker and the family with the opportunity to: (1) give personal Feedback; (2) place Responsibility for change with the individuals; (3) Advise one another on change; (4) empathetically provide a Menu of change options; (5) provide Empathy; and (6) reinforce Self-efficacy (Miller & Rollnick, 2002, p. 326). Motivational interviewing provides another opportunity for you, as a social worker, to engage in a collaborative partnership with the client family aimed at providing the opportunity for change. If you opted to employ motivational interviewing with the Murray family, you may begin by providing feedback to them based on the perceptions they have shared with you regarding the various crises that are occurring within the family. They also have the opportunity to provide feedback to one another. Following feedback being shared, you can empathetically reiterate that the family members are the experts about themselves and it is within their power and responsibility to initiate and implement change. Strive to create an environment in which the family is empowered to view themselves as having the capacity to respond to their crises with resilience and efficacy.

Re-enactments

Participation in experiential activities can provide insights and alternatives for families who are experiencing a crisis or challenging transition. Re-enactments can be completed in the form of role-plays or rehearsals. Re-enacting a particularly challenging interaction and then role-playing or rehearsing the scenario with alternative behaviors can be a powerful experience mechanism for the family to "try on" new ways of being a family. Viewed as a safe way to share feelings and rehearse, role-plays can be carried out in a variety of settings, for a range of situations, and re-visited as the work progresses. Considerations for developing role-played activities include (Hull & Mather, 2006, pp. 163–164): (1) purpose and parameters are to be discussed; (2) members can play themselves or other members of the family; (3) members should play the roles accurately and consider their feelings as they move through the rehearsal; (4) the role-play can be stopped so members can discuss, reflect, and change interactions; and (5) the role-play should be de-briefed so alternatives can be explored. A re-enactment may be an ideal activity in which to engage the Murray family. Once the family has identified the issues that are their highest priority to address, you can help them to "rehearse" the change strategies they have brainstormed through an experiential exercise. With the multiple generations, issues, and priorities that exist within the Murray family, role-playing can enable the family to work on individual issues and relationships. Imagine a role-play in which William and Georgia share with Samantha their feelings and concerns regarding her life choices and decision-making. More importantly, envision a dialogue between Samantha and her parents that any one of the three may stop so they may regroup, change course, or ask for input. Such a rehearsal may enable the family to change a pattern of interactions.

Mapping as an Intervention

Mapping strategies have been examined primarily within the context of assessment. They do, however, have a place within the intervention process itself. If not completed during the assessment phase, mapping can be incorporated into the intervention phase of work. During the intervention, mapping in the form of genogram, in particular, can be used for clarifying family patterns, framing and detoxifying family issues, and in developing the intervention plans (McGoldrick et al., 2008). Utilizing the patterns and unhealthy family issues to identify and facilitate change plans can be a liberating experience for the family members. McGoldrick and colleagues (2008) promote the use of genograms as an intervention strategy to empower clients through changing existing relationships. Being able to see the historical patterns of loss, relationships (healthy and unhealthy), physical and mental health issues, substance uses and abuses, responses to stress and crisis, and cultural traditions can illuminate for family members the options they have for change. Genograms can also provide family members with an opportunity to engage in intergenerational dialogue in ways they may not have been able to do previously. Consider the Murray family, for instance. Providing the family members with the opportunity to engage in dialogue with Edna could provide them with family history they had not previously known as well as have meaningful time with her before her memory fades away. The social worker can incorporate the genogram into the development of the intervention by asking members to identify strengths on which they can build in relationships and cultural traditions (McCullough-Chavis & Waites, 2008). They may also be able to identify patterns of substance abuse, trouble with the law, or other troubling patterns that can inform their present collective and individual work.

Ecomaps and culturagrams are also assessment tools that can be integrated into the intervention. Utilizing the baseline ecomap or culturagram as a strategy for monitoring change throughout the intervention provides the family and the social worker with a visual depiction of the work they are doing. Updating the ecomap or culturagram can indicate those areas in which progress is being made or not made and the barriers preventing success. New maps can be constructed as a means for ritualizing a successful outcome.

As with social work practice with individuals, intervening with family units requires the social worker to complete comprehensive and ongoing assessments from which flexible, individualized interventions can be created through collaboration with the family. The outcome of a successful intervention is, of course, the termination. Our focus will now turn to the phases of terminating and evaluating the family intervention.

ENDING WORK WITH FAMILY CONSTELLATIONS

The general principles for ending the work of social work interventions apply to all levels and areas of practice. The need for culturally sensitive practice plays out in individuals, families, groups, communities, and organizations. Just as you need to explore the meaning of endings with individual client systems, so you do for families. This discussion assumes a cumulative recognition of the important areas for ending the work, based on considerations covered so far, and a flexible application with greater emphasis on some principles than others according to context. With those principles in mind, we will look to some specific variations as additional perspectives.

In voluntary family work, endings tend to occur when the family is satisfied that they achieved the hoped-for goals that brought them to your organization. In some circumstances, the restrictions of third party insurers or managed care companies may mandate an earlier end point. With a lessened focus on the relationship with the social worker than exists in individual work, the emphasis often falls on examining the ways the family wanted the dynamics of their relationship or their relationship with outside entities to be different, and the extent to which they have been successful. There is also likely to be some focus on translating the gains into future situations that the family can anticipate so that responses can be predicted. For example, if a family is struggling with the decision to allow an adolescent son freedom to develop a unique identity when he has a history of legal altercations, it will be useful for the family to consider ways in which they will manage that issue when he leaves home for college or when the next sibling reaches an age to declare herself or himself a separate person. These positions are all consistent with the principles of review and exploration highlighted earlier in Chapter 5 regarding terminating with individuals.

To take a different perspective, the following discussion will identify brief responses to ending work with families from the perspectives of the previously discussed theoretical frameworks, strengths and empowerment, narrative, and solution-focused approaches. These approaches strive to minimize the difficulty of endings. In general, they propose a naturalized and comfortable process that is flexible and controlled by clients whenever possible.

Endings with Strength and Empowerment

Viewing each family as unique, both the individuals and the unit as a whole, means that the social worker's role is to help each person to articulate her or his feelings about the work coming to a close (Wise, 2005). The family members, individually and as a group, can benefit from the opportunity to talk about feelings and insights about the strengths that each individual and the group brought to the intervention. These insights can reinforce the successes that have been accomplished through the intervention and enable the members to acknowledge the ending. Keeping in mind

the original goal (i.e., the family's desire to improve their situation for the better), the social worker and the family can focus on the future and the ways in which the changes can be sustained. If the goals that were hoped for were not achieved, but the relationship is terminating nonetheless, the termination phase can focus on lessons learned that can be taken forward into the future.

Just as assessment and intervention with families is approached from a strengths perspective, so too is the termination process. Building on the strengths that were identified in the assessment process and those identified or created during the intervention phase, the strengths- and empowerment-oriented social worker can focus the termination process on strengths as well. The existing and new strengths can become the basis for the family to sustain the changes they have made. Together, the social worker and the family can review the family's strengths. The social worker can then ask the family to consider the way in which they can apply these strengths to future situations. Those strengths can also be used as coping skills when and if the family encounters new challenges. For example, the social worker may ask the family members, "How can ending our work together help you to achieve your goals?" (Wise, 2005, p. 215). To further probe, you may opt to ask the family members to speculate on their motivation and ability to continue working on their goals even after the formal intervention has ended.

Endings in Narrative-Focused Work

In narrative work as with other approaches, there is a similar emphasis on normalizing the point at which the family decides to end. Narrative social workers often punctuate the ending of their work by working with families to develop rituals or ceremonies in which the family invites an audience to witness the changes they have made and to rejoice in their achievements. Public acknowledgment of the family's successes not only celebrates them but also provides a structure for their supportive maintenance when the work is over (Morgan, 2000). This focus, like solution-focused work, represents a departure from traditional views of endings while acknowledging the same concerns regarding the maintenance of gains. The reduced emphasis on stages with specific boundaries in both these approaches, as compared to more structured approaches marks a shifting pattern in which the view of the client as expert is primary.

Endings in Solution-Focused Work

Solution-focused work emphasizes ending almost from the beginning. As a short-term intervention approach, a solution-focused approach stresses the view that the clients have abilities to manage their lives competently. As this approach is built on the premise that change can occur within a brief, time-limited period, an early question asked by the social worker may be, "What [number] do you need to be in order not to come and talk to me anymore?" (De Jong, 2009). This question refers to the number from 1 to 10, on a scaling question, that reflects the degree of well-being that the client reports experiencing. In this approach, a family's concerns about needing further work are honored, and they determine the number and content of further sessions. There is very little emphasis on the relationship between the social worker and the family because "not coming to talk to me anymore" is seen as the preferred reality and a natural and comfortable conclusion to a problem for which the family is already likely to have the solution. In this sense, then, ending is seen as success almost by definition.

Termination, as well as follow-up (i.e., checking in with the family, inviting the family to return for follow-up session, or making referrals) when possible, is as equally as important to the planned change process as any other stage of the social work relationship with families. Bringing the intervention to a close can serve as an opportunity for the social worker and family to engage in: (1) a recital (i.e., review of the work); (2) creating an awareness of changes made; (3) consolidating gains (i.e., changes, successes, and achieved goals); (4) providing feedback to the social worker; and (5) preparing the family for handling challenges that arise in the future (Collins et al., 2010, p. 385).

Evaluation of Social Work Practice with Families

As with evaluation at other levels of social work practice, evaluation of family interventions is intended to help you as the practitioner and your organization determine if the intervention has been complete and is effective. By gathering information from the family members at the beginning of the working relationship, evaluation of family interventions also enables the social worker to identify the changes that were or were not made and reasons that the intervention was or was not effective (Hull & Mather, 2006). If you have utilized evidence-based practice approaches, your evaluation can provide insights and contributions to the fund of knowledge for your future applications of the practice approaches in your own practice and that of your agency. While evaluation of your interventions with individuals can yield similar information about your practice, it is critical that you do not assume that evaluation of family interventions can be completed with the same evaluative strategies. Just as families are unique so, too, are evaluations of family interventions.

The ongoing evaluation of the family work that social workers do is often largely contingent on, and defined by, the context and goals of the original contact. For example, if you are working with a family in child or adult protective services, the first goal may be imposed externally as the continued safety of a child(ren) or adult. There may be other goals, such as the parents' improved skills in managing a family, meeting the health needs of a particular child or adult, or providing appropriate care for an older adult. Goals in cases such as these, in most cases, are documented in written goals, and you will want to pay attention to them along the way, just as you do in other forms of practice.

The focus of evaluation in social work interventions with families is, of course, on the family unit itself and not the individuals within the family. An examination of the family's ability to have new behaviors and coping skills, realistic attitudes, and new information and learning will promote enhanced well-being for the entire family (Wise, 2005). For example, if you and the family are able to determine that the power has shifted among and between the family members, this could be indicative of an effective family intervention. Family evaluations may focus not only on the outcomes of the intervention for the family that were based on the goals established during the assessment and planning phases, but on the relationship with the social worker and the agency as well.

Strengths-Based Measures for Families   While family-focused intervention evaluations differ from evaluations of individual and group practice, the evaluative strategies described in Chapter 5 can provide a basis for developing plans for evaluation of family interventions. Ensuring that the focus of the evaluation is on the family and not the individual members, strategies such as single-system design, goal attainment scaling, and case studies, can be effective evaluation tools. There has been an array of evaluation measurements developed specifically for use with families. While the scope of this book cannot address the vast number of selections that are available for evaluating your practice with families, the following discussion will briefly explore the selection of measures that are grounded in a strengths-based perspective.

Several instruments are designed to be used in strengths-based practice with families and also to allow social workers to document their service effectiveness (Early, 2001). Standardized evaluative tools are increasingly important as agencies and practitioners are held accountable for measurement of outcomes by funders, boards of directors, client advocacy organizations, and the social work profession itself. Additionally, practice evaluation instruments can be helpful in maintaining the social worker's focus. Some of the instruments emerged as strengths-based emphases were introduced in the 1980s and remain useful tools today because they measure family perceptions and assets. With the advent of evidence-based practice, there has been an increase in the number of standardized family assessment measures from which to select. While your agency or you will select the evaluative strategy that is most appropriate to your setting and the families that you serve, the following is a small representative list of valid and reliable strengths and empowerment-focused evaluation measures that may be of help to you as you consider evaluating your practice:

- *The Caregiver Well-Being Scale* (Berg-Weger, Rubio, & Tebb, 2000; Tebb, 1995): A strengths-based clinical measure to help family caregivers or adults or children identify the strengths and areas for change in their caregiving experience, this scale is applicable for families caring for adults and/or children. See Exhibit 7.2 for an example.

Caregiver Well-Being Scale

EXHIBIT 7.2

*Strengths-
Based
Measures for
Families*

I. ACTIVITIES

Below are listed a number of activities that each of us do or someone does for us. Thinking over the past three months, indicate to what extent you think each activity has been met by circling the appropriate number on the scale provided below. You do not have to be the one doing the activity. You are being asked to rate the extent to which each activity has been taken care of in a timely way.

   1. Rarely   2. Occasionally   3. Sometimes   4. Frequently   5. Usually

1. Buying food	1	2	3	4	5
2. Taking care of personal daily activities (meals, hygiene, laundry)	1	2	3	4	5
3. Attending to medical needs	1	2	3	4	5
4. Keeping up with home maintenance activities (lawn, cleaning, house repairs, etc.)	1	2	3	4	5
5. Participating in events at church and/or in the community	1	2	3	4	5
6. Taking time to have fun with friends and/or family	1	2	3	4	5
7. Treating or reward yourself	1	2	3	4	5
8. Making plans for your financial future	1	2	3	4	5

II. NEEDS

Below are listed a number of needs we all have. For each need listed, think about your life over the past three months. During this period of time, indicate to what extent you think each need has been met by circling the appropriate number on the scale provided below.

   1. Rarely   2. Occasionally   3. Sometimes   4. Frequently   5. Usually

1. Eating a well-balanced diet	1	2	3	4	5
2. Getting enough sleep	1	2	3	4	5
3. Receiving appropriate health care	1	2	3	4	5
4. Having adequate shelter	1	2	3	4	5
5. Expressing love	1	2	3	4	5
6. Expressing anger	1	2	3	4	5
7. Feeling good about yourself	1	2	3	4	5
8. Feeling secure about your financial future	1	2	3	4	5

Source: Berg-Weger, Rubio, & Tebb, 2000

- *The Parent Empowerment Survey* (see Dunst, Trivette, & Deal, 2003): Designed to measure parental perceptions of control over life event (see Herbert, Gagnon, Rennick, & O'Loughlin, 2009 for review of empowerment measures).

- *The Family Support Scale* (see Dunst et al., 2003): Measures what is helpful to families. See Exhibit 7.3 for an example.

- *The Family Strengths Profile* (see Dunst et al., 2003): Designed to chronicle family functioning, the profile provides a qualitative format for identifying and assessing family strengths and type of resources needed. Exhibit 7.4 provides an example of this measure.

- *The Family Resource Scale* (see Dunst et al., 2003): Measures the adequacy of resources in households with young children and emphasizes success in meeting needs, while it also identifies needs.

- *The Family Functioning Style Scale* (see Dunst et al., 2003): Measures family values, coping strategies, family commitments, and resource mobilization. Families indicate to what degree various statements are "like my family."

- *The Family Empowerment Scale* (Koren, DeChillo, & Friesen, 1992): Measures family empowerment on three levels: family, service system, and community/political.

- *The Behavioral and Emotional Rating Scale: A Strengths-Based Approach to Assessment* (Epstein & Sharma, 1998). This scale focuses on children to determine the presence of behavioral or emotional conditions.

In strengths- and empowerment-oriented measurements, the phenomenon of self-report is seen as an asset. Self-report can complement the traditionally oriented, scientific measurements in which the goal of objectivity is thought to conflict with the biases in self-report. Bias is inherent within self-reported information as the individual is the sole source and may be unable to maintain objectivity. The strengths perspective supports the expertise of individuals and families about their own lives, experience, and aspiration, thereby making self-report a natural and theoretically consistent method of data collection.

The empirical procedures in these scales are just a few among many. Some of these are flexible and with social worker creativity, they can meet a wide variety of situations, result in a credible judgment as to effectiveness, and serve as inspiring affirmation for client families. Utilizing both quantitative and qualitative evaluative strategies can provide the social worker and the profession with a comprehensive picture of the intervention. Remember, as well, that all evaluative measures have their limitations. Drawing conclusions regarding the impact of the change may not be possible as change may have occurred separately from the intervention (Hull & Mather, 2006). Further, just because the goals of the intervention were not achieved

EXHIBIT 7.3

Strengths-Based Measures for Families

Family Support Scale

Name_____ Date _____

Listed below are people and groups that oftentimes are helpful to members of a family raising a young child. This questionnaire asks you to indicate how helpful each source is to your family.

    Please circle the response that best describes how helpful the sources have been to your family during the past three to six months. If a source of help has not been available to your family during this period of time, circle the NA (Not Available)

How helpful has each of the following been to you in terms of raising your child(ren):	Not Available	Not at All Helpful	Sometimes Helpful	Generally Helpful	Very Helpful	Extremely Helpful
1. My parents	NA	1	2	3	4	5
2. My spouse or partner's parents	NA	1	2	3	4	5
3. My relatives/kin	NA	1	2	3	4	5
4. My spouse or partner's relatives/kin	NA	1	2	3	4	5
5. Spouse or partner	NA	1	2	3	4	5
6. My friends	NA	1	2	3	4	5
7. My spouse or partner's friends	NA	1	2	3	4	5
8. My own children	NA	1	2	3	4	5
9. Other parents	NA	1	2	3	4	5
10. Co-workers	NA	1	2	3	4	5
11. Parent groups	NA	1	2	3	4	5
12. Social groups/clubs	NA	1	2	3	4	5
13. Church members/minister	NA	1	2	3	4	5
14. My family or child's physician	NA	1	2	3	4	5
15. Early childhood intervention program	NA	1	2	3	4	5
16. School/day-care center	NA	1	2	3	4	5
17. Professional helpers (social workers, therapists, teachers, etc.)	NA	1	2	3	4	5
18. Professional agencies (public health, social services, mental health, etc.)	NA	1	2	3	4	5
19. _____	NA	1	2	3	4	5
20. _____	NA	1	2	3	4	5

Source: Dunst, Trivette, & Deal, 2003, pp. 155–157

EXHIBIT 7. 4

Family Strengths Profile

Recording Form

Family Name _____   Interviewer _____

INSTRUCTIONS
The Family Strengths Profile provides a way of recording family behaviors and noting the particular strengths and resources that the behaviors reflect. Space is provided down the left-hand column of the recording form for listing behavior exemplars. For each behavior listed, the interviewer simply checks which particular qualities are characterized by the family behavior. (Space is also provided to record other qualities not listed.) The interviewer also notes whether the behavior is viewed as a way of mobilizing intrafamily or extrafamily resources, or both. A completed matrix provides a graphic display of a family's unique functioning style.

FAMILY MEMBER	DATE OF BIRTH	AGE	RELATIONSHIP

FAMILY BEHAVIOR	Commitment	Appreciation	Time	Sense of Purpose	Congruence	Communication	Role Expectations	Coping Strategies	Problem Solving	Positivism	Flexibility	Balance			TYPE OF RESOURCE Intrafamily	Extrafamily

NOTES

Source: Dunst, Trivette, & Deal, 1988

does not mean that positive or meaningful change did not occur. While practice evaluations can be immensely helpful tools, they must be viewed within a context for family, yourself as a practitioner, and your agency.

Consider also your own role with the family and reflect on the viability of your relationship with the family. Reflection is typically a more introspective and interactive process. Some questions you can ask yourself and members of the family are: Does each member feel valued as if she or he can contribute to the work? Are there issues regarding the family's culture? Does the family still agree with the direction of the work? How is the work changing their experience? Checking in with families, through a dialogic process, to make sure they feel heard, understood, and are invested in the work you are doing with them is just as important as it is with other levels of practice. Be certain as well to remain attuned to non-articulated feedback from the family members. Lack of follow through with assignments or commitments and nonverbal gestures can be indicators of the family members' feelings about the intervention (Hull & Mather, 2006).

STRAIGHT TALK ABOUT FAMILY INTERVENTION, TERMINATION, AND EVALUATION

While social work practice with families is a complex enterprise, the intervention, termination and evaluation processes have the potential to include the unexpected. Your responsibility thus is to expect the unexpected. The members of a family have individual relationships, networks, and influences outside the family; therefore, the work that is accomplished within the intervention may be positively or negatively impacted by those external persons or groups. Within the family unit, the members may establish alliances that can also serve to strengthen or, in some cases, undermine the work within the intervention. Staying attuned to the family members' descriptions of their activities, relationships, and pressures may aid you in identifying those potential unanticipated occurrences within the intervention.

Just as with terminations with individuals, ending the work with families can be emotional, particularly if the family members have developed a positive relationship with the social worker. The social worker may even be viewed as a member of the family; therefore, termination can elicit powerful reactions from the family. Sensitivity to the family's cultural norms and feelings is important for both the social worker and the family (Logan et al., 2008). Terminations can also elicit negative responses from some members of the family. As a result, members may refuse to participate or display such emotions as anger, denial, anxiety, or even regression as the termination approaches (Fortune, 2009). As the social worker, you may find yourself juggling a variety of different responses from family members to the ending of the family intervention. Addressing the individual and collective reactions to termination, while building on the strengths and gains of the intervention, can serve as an intervention in and of itself. Empowering the family to handle a change (perceived possibly as another loss) can be a meaningful new experience for the family as they can provide support to one another, model new behaviors, and mobilize strengths and resources developed during the intervention.

Evaluations of family interventions may also yield unexpected results. As you complete the evaluative process, you may have anticipated a particular outcome based on the work you have completed together. If, for instance, you completed a pre- and post-intervention evaluation and the members of the family provide responses different from those you expected, you may be surprised at the family members' perceptions. Such occurrences can provide you with the opportunity to explore with the family their responses so you may gain insight into differing interpretations.

CONCLUSION

Facilitating an intervention with a family from engagement through termination and evaluation can be an immensely rewarding professional accomplishment for you and transformative for the family members individually and as a unit. As highlighted in this and the previous chapter, working with families requires the social worker to develop a repertoire of practice behaviors that include theoretical frameworks and skills to optimize family strengths and create and mobilize needed resources. This chapter further explored the integration of several theoretical approaches into social work practice with families and provided examples of ways in which the approaches can be applied to family situations.

MAIN POINTS

- Social workers have an array of theoretical perspectives to choose from to guide and frame interventions with families. The social worker's training, philosophical and value system, and agency orientation will provide the primary influence for selection.

- Approaches for developing intervention plans with family groups highlighted in this chapter include strengths, empowerment, solution-focused, and narrative perspectives. While each shares similarities with the others, each has characteristics that make it unique.

- While specific practice behaviors are included within the various models of family intervention, there are basic skills for working with families that are found in most of the models: collaboration, utilizing strengths, and supporting each member of the family in having a voice in the development of the intervention and termination.

- Both your own and your clients' families can impact your work with families. Ongoing evaluation includes not only documenting achievement of externally imposed goals but also determining whether your role and relationship with the family are working.

- Endings with families require thoughtful considerations regarding the relationships formed in the work, the theoretical perspectives used, and the practical, contextual dimensions of the work.

- The evaluation of families may emphasize an empirical process and/or a qualitative one. Standardized tools may be helpful in the evaluation process of family social work. In some family models, the emphasis is on the family's qualitative satisfaction with the outcome of the work; postmodern views of evaluation question the emphasis on standardized, scientific, and quantitative measures and remind social workers of their susceptibility to bias even when their work is supported by numbers.

EXERCISES

1. Go to www.routledgesw.com/cases and review the case file for Carmen Sanchez. Address Critical Thinking Questions 1, 2, and 3. For Critical Thinking Question 2, identify at least one article in each of the two areas that concern Carmen: the impact on families of children with special health needs and outcomes of children in different types of families.

   Gather into groups with four to five of your classmates and develop a potential work plan for the family, based on your answers to the Critical Thinking Questions, focusing on the following areas:
   a. Identify the areas of potential challenge.
   b. Develop strategies for working with the entire Sanchez family around these challenges.
   c. Develop a plan to insure Carmen's maximum participation in the process.
2. Go to www.routledgesw.com/cases and review the case file for Carla Washburn. While Carla does not have the traditional family network, she does have a support system of persons to whom she is connected. Strategize about ways in which you might integrate each of the members of her support network into your intervention with Carla, identifying the strengths and potential contributions each can make. You may wish to review the case files and ecomap to develop your plan.
3. Go to wwww.routledgesw.com/cases and review the case file for Riverton. While the Riverton case initially appears to be a case focused on a neighborhood and

a community, each community is comprised of individuals and families. In your role as the social worker who has just moved into the Riverton community, consider the Williams family (not described in the case file). Joyce is a 48-year-old single mother who lives with her two children, 18-year-old Amanda and 17-year-old Jason, and her mother, 77-year-old Nina. Joyce divorced her husband as a result of his chronic alcoholism and she is worried about Jason as she knows he regularly drinks and uses marijuana. She has come to your agency and asked for your help with Jason. In light of the alcohol and drug issues that are occurring in the neighborhood, she feels powerless to handle the situation alone. She cannot afford to move out of the neighborhood as the house is owned by her mother and Joyce is unable to work full-time due to the caregiving responsibilities she has for her mother. Utilizing your knowledge of the Riverton community, its resources and current culture, develop a strategy for engaging, assessing, and intervening with the Williams family.

4. As a social work practitioner at a community mental health center, you serve primarily individual and family client systems. You have recently been called by a family and will conduct an intake appointment later on today. You have the following information about the family:

- The father, self identified as African American, made the appointment.

- The family includes the mother, father, their two adolescent sons, and the father's parents who share the home with the family.

- The elder son is of most concern to the family, having expressed suicidal thoughts and recent but increasing withdrawal from school, family, and community life. Last year this son was a well-known school athlete and this year is not active in any school or athletic activities.

- The parents suspect that alcohol or other drug use is involved in the family.

- Both sons are reluctant to attend the appointment but will because their father has indicated they will.

- Mother will "go along."

In your preparation for this appointment, you consider several dimensions of the work that appear below. In small groups, discuss these and explore the questions. Report back to the entire class.

a. You are not African American but are of Jewish heritage, which is relatively rare in the town. You know there are cultural differences between this family and you but believe you can bridge those to some extent because you consider yourself different culturally as well. What might you need to consider in your own assumptions?

b. What model of family social work (of those in the chapter) do you believe will provide the most useful base? Discuss the reasons for this selection.

c. What specific information will be important to first clarify?

d. What specific approaches will be most important here with this particular family?

e. How would you begin your intervention with this family? What practice behaviors will you use? What might you actually say? (Give an example.)

CHAPTER 8

Social Work Practice with Groups: Engagement, Assessment, and Planning

Alone we can do so little. Together we can do so much.

Helen Keller

Key Questions for Chapter 8

(1) What competencies do I need to engage with and assess client systems at the group level of social work practice? (EPAS 2.1.10(a & b))

(2) How can I utilize evidence to practice research-informed practice and practice-informed research to guide the engagement and assessment practice behaviors with groups? (EPAS 2.1.6)

(3) What are the potential ethical issues that may occur in social work practice with groups, particularly in the early phases of the group's development? (EPAS 2.1.2)

(4) What knowledge and skills do I need for culturally competent group-level engagement and assessment practice? (EPAS 2.1.4)

NONE OF US LIVES WITHOUT SOCIAL CONNECTIONS. Many of us spend much of our lives negotiating our closeness to family, neighbors, friends, associates, and colleagues. Regardless of the ways in which the connections are experienced, virtually everyone has relationships to small collectives of other people or groups. In this context, *group* refers to the natural or planned associations that evolve through common interest (e.g., supporting the local Little League), state of being (e.g., having a child with a disability), or task (e.g., working together at a place of employment). The degree to which persons are connected to groups of others is contingent not only on one's individual needs for affiliation but also on cultural norms, social arrangements, and social location (e.g., faith traditions, children's school, or neighborhood of residence). Within social work practice, **group work** is considered to be a "goal-directed activity that brings together people for a common purpose or goal" (Toseland & Horton, 2008, p. 298).

This chapter addresses the nature of groups, briefly reviews the history of group work in social work practice, and explores a variety of dimensions related to types and purposes of groups that you may encounter within your social work practice. Along with Chapter 9, in this chapter you will explore the purpose of groups and the relationship of groups to other areas of social work practice and practice behaviors for approaching the various aspects of the process of group work from engagement and assessment through intervention, termination, and evaluation.

GROUPS: THE SOURCE OF COMMUNITY

The social dimension of social work implies that people need and want to relate to others within the context of a "community." Yet the ways in which to meet this need are not always clear to social work professionals or the clients they serve. In contemporary U.S. culture, there is a pervasive emphasis on independence, mobility, and pursuit of success. Employment opportunities far away, upward mobility, and pressures to achieve professionally, socially, and economically influence most people and have developed new definitions and parameters for community. Such influences are not necessarily negative, but they can take a heavy toll on one's sense of connection and linkages (i.e., community) to stable, consistent groups on which they can depend over time.

A brief review of the advertisement section of any major newspaper provides support for this need to have a connection with others. The number of announcements for therapy groups, support groups, community groups, and educational groups suggests that, as a culture, people are looking for a way to relate to others that is outside of themselves. In other words, people seek out groups with whom to form a community. What do artificially created group experiences (i.e., those group experiences developed as a service) offer to people? Such groups provide a sense of belonging or community, a chance for reality testing, a source of mutual aid, and a means of empowerment (Reid, 2009, p. 433). By implication, these dimensions of social group work seem to afford people the means to participate in significant experiences that may be lacking in the natural contexts of their everyday lives.

Group as a Natural Orientation

Beyond individual idiosyncrasy, the influence of culture has an important impact on the amount and type of connections people seek. "People relations" (Diller, 2007, p. 68) is one of the cultural paradigms that distinguish one cultural group from another. European-Americans are more apt to be individual in their social relationships as contrasted with the collateral focus of many cultures whose members are persons of other racial and ethnic heritage. The degree to which a culture embraces individualism over collective demands varies greatly. Cultural paradigms within some groups that place more emphasis on group or familial connection than on independence and the encouragement of individuation can create conflicts among group members and between members and the group leader or facilitator (Ringel, 2005). The social worker facilitating the group must be culturally astute and aware of the cultural backgrounds of the group participants, and the cultural influences that affect group dynamics.

Implications of Cultural and Global Connections for Social Work Practice   As the cultural emphases of our society focus more on self-determination than co-operation, the social work professional may observe and perhaps question the impact of social connections through group interventions. As a social worker, you can make a commitment to self-determination (a hallmark of social work practice) and still know that it is not understood the same way in all cultural groups. The postmodern, reflective thinker will notice that in some circumstances, these concepts are empowering but they can also be perceived as oppressive.

An increasingly global perspective on social work practice adds support for increasing sensitivity in this area. In 1996, the NASW *Code of Ethics* was amended to include an international perspective in the statement "social workers should promote conditions that encourage respect for cultural and social diversity within the United States and globally" (Standard 6.04©). This addition to the *Code of Ethics* indicated an increasing global consciousness, a perspective that has become well integrated in social work practice in the 21st century.

Most practicing helping professionals can benefit from exploring the degree to which their own orientation to achievement, independence, and competition as cultural variants is not compatible with the cooperation and collaboration that clients from other cultures may value more highly. Regardless of your own cultural heritage, take care not to privilege your position as normal just because it is the one with which you are most familiar. You may be well served in some instances, but impeded in your effectiveness in others. For instance, independence, as an ideal, can create obstacles in working cross-culturally with clients who do not share an understanding or enthusiasm for its relevance in their lives. As an example, if you encounter a child, Joey, in a school setting, who appears to lack an eager, competitive spirit, who seldom raises his hand when a teacher asks a question, and who always defers to others, you may attribute a deficit of one kind or another to him.

You may find him slow, shy, or lethargic, and you may see him as dependent, or even as depressed or developmentally delayed. Joey may simply be reflecting the cultural imperative to cooperate, to prioritize the communications of others, and to behave demurely in the company of people who are older and who have authority.

The nature of "groupness" is complex and variable according to social location. While all persons need and seek social connections, this phenomenon is tempered and shaped by cultural expectations related to family and community, customs, propriety, loyalty, authority, individualism, and the way in which these factors fit together. Although Western values of competitiveness and individualism have been responsible for much of the accomplishments and power of U.S. culture, these values have the potential to create disconnection, isolation, and detachment as well as a fertile environment for the design of constructed groups, particularly in the human services. The social work profession has responded to and continues to be vigilant about this need throughout a long history of social work group practice.

Historical and Contemporary Contexts for Group Work

Like other legacies in social work, the early roots of social work practice with groups derive from England and the Industrial Revolution. The political and economic context of this time period resulted in disrupted lives and broken social connections of countless children and families. The time was ripe for the development of group social work. A brief history provides a glimpse at the role of groups in social work practice (Alissi, 2009; Furman, Rowan, & Bender, 2009; Reid, 1997).

Group work developed in the United States in the 19th century in the midst of professional and political tensions. Inspired by religious and philanthropic organizations, the concept of bringing people together in small groups became a popular strategy for helping clients within community-based settings (e.g., YMCA/ YWCA, Boy/Girl Scouts, and faith-based community centers). The early approach focused on individuals and their need for change. In contrast, another group of helping professionals of the time utilized group efforts focused instead on social reform with a humanitarian impulse and believed that social change was the critical ingredient in making a positive difference in people's lives. These reformers were more likely to see the group (rather than the individual) as the medium for that form of intervention. You will notice here some reverberations from the social control/ social change tension discussed in Chapter 1. In addition, group work was not yet firmly a part of social work practice. This segment of the group movement were often partisan Socialists, concerned with political action and identified with several types of social services, among which social work was only one.

By the end of the 19th century, the Progressive Era added fuel to the growth of group work. Settlement houses, community organizations, and self-help groups sprang up in response to the influx of immigrants and the dramatic needs of the teeming urban environment. These organizations stressed group methods (e.g., language classes, cooking groups, recreation, the arts, and youth services) and were aimed at the social justice issues of inclusion and acculturation. They were designed to maximize the ability of newly arrived residents to achieve their desired quality of life through access to society's assets. Still, group work was not clearly identified with social work.

Throughout the 1930s, group work continued to have less status than social casework in the minds of many professionals. This perception was due, in part, to the fact that recently developed curricula in schools of social work had been aimed at individual casework, a result of the pervasiveness of Freud's influence. Group work had by then a strong association with recreational activities (e.g., sponsoring dances or creating arts and crafts with children). Such activities were not held in as great esteem as the more clinically focused casework. When group work had developed a greater affinity to social work, practitioners proposed their own association, which emphatically declared itself a part of social work, but as a discrete unit, using distinctive methods within the practice of social work with groups.

In the 1950s, group work expanded its venue from the community into hospitals and psychiatric facilities and introduced **therapeutic group work** or **treatment groups**. These therapeutically focused groups were designed to heal or help people change. This shift altered the nature of the formerly community-based model by adopting a more professional stance. Through the process, group work began to impede on the boundaries of casework, and the distinctions between the two began to blur somewhat.

Three classic models for group practice—the **social goals model**, the **reciprocal model**, and the **remedial model**—emerged during the period of the late 1950s through the 1970s. They reflect, however, much of the work that came before them, as well as after, since theory is ideally embedded in the context of previous theory. These particular perspectives are still used in contemporary social work practice with groups in various current contexts and will be discussed in detail later in this chapter and in Chapter 9. See Exhibit 8.1 for a brief description of the origin and aim of these three classic models.

By the 1970s, the **Council on Social Work Education (CSWE)**, the accrediting body for social work education in the United States, required all schools of social work to adopt a generalist focus throughout undergraduate programs and for the first half of master's programs. With an aim toward integrating all practice methods across levels, the generalist focus requirement served to de-emphasize the distinctive role of group work as a method and, many believe, to forsake its soul. Most school curricula already emphasized casework, and with the CSWE mandate, there was little incentive to develop more group work courses. The result was that many social work students did not complete coursework that focused specifically and comprehensively on social work practice with groups. Nevertheless, a strong core of social workers committed to the power of social work with groups is vital, and the Association for the Advancement of Social Work with Groups (AASWG) was founded in 1979. First issued in 1999 and revised in 2006, the AASWG established *Standards for Social Work Practice with Groups*, a guide for effective practice with groups that is

MODEL TYPE	MAJOR FOCUS	SOCIAL WORKER ROLE	EXAMPLE	ORIGINAL AUTHORS	**EXHIBIT 8.1**
Social Goals	Democratic values, social conscience, responsibility, and action; uses strengths of members.	Fosters social consciousness and serves as model for democratic values.	School groups that promote student affiliation and contributions to student governance.	Pappel and Rothman, 1962	*Classic Models for Social Group Work, 1950s to 1970s*
Reciprocal	Interaction in an attempt to fulfill mutual affiliation goals; mutual aid.	Serves as mediator between each member and the group as a whole; finds common ground.	Adolescent children of incarcerated parents developing coping skills.	Schwartz, 1961	
Remedial	Prevention and rehabilitation aimed at behavior change and reinforcing individual behaviors.	Works both in the group and outside of it to ameliorate conditions in environments; acts as motivator.	Discharge group in mental health settings to increase patient capacity to negotiate community.	Vinter, 1974	

widely used in contemporary social work practice. Available at www.aaswg.org, the second edition of the *Standards* provides practitioners with guidelines and practice perspectives for gaining knowledge, tasks, and skills for use in group work that include: core values and knowledge; phases of the group process (pre-group planning, beginning, middle, and ending); and ethical considerations.

The climate of social work practice today offers practitioners a unique opportunity to work with groups in ways that will help to meet the needs individuals have for genuine connection and social action in our challenging culture. In that respect, the value of social work practice with groups will be on a focus that emphasizes the group as a whole. A group-focused orientation is one of the characteristics that distinguish social work group practice from psychology or mental health counseling groups. In group work, the social worker's effort is on the development of the group, and while individual well-being is one goal, it is achieved through the interactions and structures of the group.

DIMENSIONS OF SOCIAL WORK PRACTICE WITH GROUPS

For the purpose of this discussion, a social work group intervention refers to a small, face-to-face gathering of people who come together for a particular purpose. The major dimension of a group experience is the interdependence among person, group, and social environment. Like many aspects of social work practice, the concept of group work can be delineated in several ways to represent distinctions. Types, forms, and functions of groups will be explored in the following section.

Types, Forms, and Functions of Groups

The major division at the most basic level in social work groups is between formed, or constructed, groups and unconstituted, natural groups. **Natural groups** occur in the context of socialization and are not organized from the outside. These may be based on spontaneous friendships, common interests, or common social location, such as living in the sophomore wing of a college dormitory. Families are the original natural group. Natural groups usually do not have formal sponsorship or agency affiliation, but social workers may have occasion to work with them (particularly families). Social workers and their agencies can also provide support to these naturally formed groups in a variety of ways (e.g., offer meeting space, access to office equipment, or staff consultation).

Social workers are more likely to facilitate **formed groups**, which are organized by an institution or organization, such as a school or hospital, agency, or community center. Formed groups can be divided between three models: **task groups**, designed to accomplish a specific purpose; the previously described **social action or goals groups**, focused on advocating for social justice; and **client groups**, geared toward personal change. These models can be further delineated as follows:

1. Task groups include task forces, committees and commissions, legislative bodies, staff meetings, interprofessional teams, case conferences and staffing, and social action groups. The task group is aimed at facilitating a change that is external to the group with a focus on a specified purpose, policy development, completing a product or a plan, or creating a mechanism for collaborative decision-making (Strand et al., 2009, p. 42). The social worker can function as a convener, member, chair/leader, facilitator, or a combination of these roles. The social worker in the leadership role is responsible for initiating and monitoring the meeting and progress toward the stated goals and objectives, managing the group interactions and maintaining focus (Furman et al., 2009). Task groups are explored in more detail in Chapter 10. You may also visit http://www.routledgesw.com/ to learn about a task group that functions in the community of Riverton to oversee the activities and growth of the community.

2. Social action or goals groups are a form of a task group that includes groups that are created for the purpose of addressing a social issue that is considered to be oppressive or unjust or to empower a group of individuals for strengthening the community (Toseland & Horton, 2008). The social action approach has a number of strengths, including (a) the collective effort of a group of people can be more powerful than that of the individual; (b) the social worker is not the expert leader, but a facilitator for the group; (c) groups can help to harness the individual capacity to create social change; (d) professionals and group members work in partnership; (e) the agenda is determined by the group members; and (f) groups can create a safe environment for the individual and collective exploration of issues of oppression, discrimination, and disadvantage (Fleming, 2009, pp. 275–276). As with task groups overall, the social worker can function in a variety or combination of roles. As an example, the parents of the Riverton community come together to address their growing concerns about alcohol abuse among the youth in their neighborhoods.

3. Client treatment groups may be aimed at support, education, growth, therapy, socialization, empowerment, and remediation. Client groups can be formed for two purposes:

    a. **Reciprocal groups**, also referred to as support, mutual aid and mutual-sharing groups, form to enable members who share a common experience to provide support and mutual aid to one another. With an emphasis on self-help and not specifically on therapeutic intervention, reciprocal groups can range from informal to highly structured to psychoeducational (blending of mutual support and educational focus). Reciprocal groups provide members with an opportunity to experience "shared empathy," which is the experience that brings members together and provides the potential for cohesion and mutual problem-solving (Furman et al., 2009, p. 63). Finding others who share similar life experiences can be validating and affirming for group members as well as provide opportunities to share valuable insights and coping strategies.

    This model for group work intervention has wide applicability, particularly among adults who face a new or unanticipated struggle and can benefit from education as well as group support. **Psychoeducational groups** focus on the education of group members regarding a psychological condition. One approach has been especially helpful to parents of young adult children experiencing mental illness. Frequently, the individual develops new symptoms in their early 20s and their parents may not have been touched by mental illness before. Local community mental health agencies often offer group sessions to the families to help them learn more about mental illnesses, what to expect in terms of their children's behavior and symptoms, how they can best provide support, and how they can cope with their own grief. These groups have been particularly effective and were started in the mental health arena by the National Alliance for the Mentally Ill (NAMI). Psychoeducational groups usually incorporate considerable factual information, but also rely on a supportive and accepting attitude both by worker/facilitators and other group members. Groups can be structured, with a curriculum and lessons in sequence, or freer in form. In some locations, parents who originally attended these groups have become group facilitators themselves, generally with training and technical support from the local agency.

Social work involvement in reciprocal groups can range from initiator to facilitator to "silent" support person. The social worker role will be related primarily to the origins of the group (i.e., a larger role if social worker-initiated and a lesser role if member-initiated). In the case of a psychoeducationally focused group, the social worker may have a more formalized role based on possessing a particular knowledge or skill expertise. An example of a psychoeducational group is a grief support group for children living in the Riverton community who have lost a family member to alcohol or drug abuse.

An example of a **support group** in contemporary life is the HIV/AIDS support group. The proliferation of HIV/AIDS in the past 25 years has engendered strong feelings in nearly everyone. Social workers are frequently in the position of working with persons who either have HIV/AIDS, live with someone who has HIV/AIDS, or love someone who has HIV/AIDS. The associated stigma and isolation for some of the men and women living with HIV/AIDS is as devastating as the disease. This makes support a critical component, and the support group can offer a chance to share feelings, combat loneliness, gain information, exchange resources, and normalize the overall experience. Similar issues arise for families and other loved ones of someone with HIV/AIDS and social workers may facilitate groups for them as well. Social workers need to understand the effects, symptoms, and issues that people with or touched by HIV/AIDS experience. HIV/AIDS can invoke volatile emotions, therefore it is particularly important for facilitators to acknowledge and understand their own reactions and biases regarding the disease and those living with it.

b. **Remedial groups** are developed for the purpose of changing behavior, restoring functioning, or promoting coping strategies of the individual members who join the group voluntarily or involuntarily (Toseland & Horton, 2008). The social work role is typically that of facilitator or leader, as clinical knowledge and skills are paramount for the functioning of the group. Returning to the Riverton community as an example, a remedial group may be formed at a mental health center or hospital to provide psychotherapy for substance-abusing clients.

In most cases, the group's major purpose and form is usually emphasized in its title. Many groups, however, have more than one purpose, and the types are not mutually exclusive since there is potential overlap. Groups may also be distinguished by the role of the social worker. In treatment or psychotherapy groups, the social worker may use methods consistent with counseling and interpretation, while in educational groups the focus may be on teaching and processing. Task groups are likely to direct the social worker's focus on facilitation, as she or he assists the group in taking action to address an undertaking. Along with phases of the group intervention, social worker and member roles and activities are further depicted in Boxes 8.1–8.3.

	BOX 8.1
PHASE I: BEGINNING Background: Concerned about the use and abuse of alcohol among their adolescent children, a group of parents in the Riverton community approach a local community service agency to ask for help in addressing this problem. Later phases of the group's work will be highlighted in Chapter 9. Note: While the stages of group interventions are not linear and may, in fact, overlap, the following depicts a possible approach to responding to the identified need.	*Riverton Against Youth Drinking ("RAYD"): An Example of Social Goals/Action Group*

PRE-GROUP PLANNING AND ENGAGEMENT	ASSESSMENT
Meet with parent groups to gather information	Determine individual and group members "agendas"
Identify current and potential stakeholders who are/may be invested in the issue	Conduct community assessment, including needs, assets, and resources (see Chapter 10 for further information on community assessment)
Identify interests of group members	
Research evidence for approaches for facilitating social goals group on this topic	Gather and analyze data from assessment; identify and prioritize options for intervention
Determine general focus/goal of launching an intervention	Re-determine/confirm focus of intervention
Identify role for agency and social worker	Finalize plan for intervention, including objectives, tasks, activities, persons/groups responsible, timeframe, and plans for evaluation and sustainability
Arrange first meeting and logistics, including time, location, refreshments, etc.	
Develop agenda for first meeting	Re-clarify agency and social worker roles and responsibilities
	Revisit needs
	Make plans for continued assessment

BOX 8.2

Riverton Children's Grief Support Group: An Example of Reciprocal Group

PHASE I: BEGINNING

Background: A social worker in a local community service agency has become aware of a number of children of Riverton who have lost a parent to alcohol and substance-related deaths. The social worker takes steps toward offering a support group to the community that includes to an educational focus. Later phases of the group's work will be highlighted in Chapter 9.

Note: While the stages of group interventions are not linear and may, in fact, overlap, the following depicts a possible approach to responding to the identified need.

PRE-GROUP PLANNING AND ENGAGEMENT	ENGAGEMENT AND ASSESSMENT
Gather information to support the need and appropriateness of this group intervention	**Pre-Group** Prior to first meeting, meet individually with parents/guardians and separately with children to assess interest in and appropriateness (i.e., "fit") for psychoeducational support group
Analyze data and confirm plans to move forward with forming group	
Research evidence for approaches for facilitating reciprocal group with children	
Determine group components: • Composition of group (number, age, range, and gender) • Recruitment strategies • Format (open or closed) • Time frame (time-limited or ongoing)	**First Session** Introduce self and ask members to introduce themselves Orient members to group, including review of purpose, goals, rules, norms, format, time frame, intervention plan, termination, evaluation, and confidentiality
Determine and implement appropriate recruitment strategies	Assess individual member goals, function, and interaction with other members
Conduct screening interview with potential members (see note in Assessment regarding group membership)	Assess group cohesiveness Continue to assess individual and group needs (for support and education), interests, strengths, and "agendas"
Invite group members (including obtaining written permission from legal guardians)	
Determine roles of agency, social work facilitator, children, and legal guardians	Monitor and assess social worker role Administer pre-group measurements to be utilized in the evaluation process

The first decision that you must make is to determine if a group experience will meet the needs you have identified. While group interventions can be powerful and have the potential to address a number of individual, community, or societal needs, you must assess the situation at hand to discern if a group approach is, in fact, going

<table>
<tr><td colspan="2">

PHASE I: BEGINNING

Background: A new social worker at the Riverton Mental Health Center has recently assumed leadership for a clinical intervention group for persons with dual diagnoses (i.e., substance abuse and mental illness) who receive outpatient services at the agency. The group is diverse in membership, including mixed genders, range of ages, and mandated and voluntary members. Membership turnover is dependent on members' "graduation" from the treatment program; therefore, the group often has entering and exiting members. Two new members have been referred to the group. This will be the first time new members have been referred since the social worker took over responsibility for the group. Later phases of the group's work will be highlighted in Chapter 9.

Note: While the stages of group interventions are not linear and may, in fact, overlap, the following depicts a possible approach to responding to the identified need.

</td><td>

BOX 8.3

Riverton Mental Health Center Group for Persons with Dual Diagnosis: An Example of Remedial Group

</td></tr>
</table>

PRE-GROUP PLANNING AND ENGAGEMENT	ENGAGEMENT AND ASSESSMENT
Obtain information on potential new members from referral sources and agency records, as appropriate	First Session Facilitate introduction of new members to group and review group expectations, norms, and rules
Research evidence on incorporating new members into an existing group	Assess individual member goals, interests, and "fit" with group
Determine structure for admission, including criteria and process	Assess member reactions to new group members
Meet with potential new members to screen for potential "fit" with group purpose, goals, and other members	Assess group cohesion
Invite new members to first session, introduce self, and provide orientation (e.g., composition, goals, expectations, norms, and rules)	Monitor/assess progress of other members

to be the most effective way of responding to the concern. In addition to bringing people together who have a common life experience, concern, or need, a group effort can promote an environment for creativity and problem-solving, influence individual thoughts and behaviors, and provide a convenient strategy for delivery of services to a large group of clients who present with similar issues (Garvin & Galinsky, 2008). While all of these can be valid reasons for launching a group intervention, consider if the potential gains to be achieved for the group as individuals and a collective are optimally efficacious and efficient. Recognizing that the individual's work is completed within the context of the group's fluid and interactive (and sometimes conflictual) dynamic, ask yourself if your desire to establish a group is meeting the client system's needs or your needs to efficiently serve a larger group of clients, meet your agency's revenue goals, mount an advocacy effort, or a combination of reasons.

Group Work Logistics

Social work groups may occur in community agencies, schools, community mental health centers, medical practices, public assistance offices, job training centers, residential care settings, church or faith facilities, or any other setting in which participants come together. The physical location may be a setting that group members already use (such as a school), or it may be a local community facility that makes itself available to such activities (a community hospital housing a grief and loss group, for example). Many residential settings such as prisons or mental health facilities also host social work groups, and these may be restricted to residents, their significant others, or may include a mix, such as a group for about-to-be-released prisoners and their partners.

Social work groups may differ on other variables such as the number of group meetings or the way in which they are organized. A group may meet for a fixed number of sessions or it may be ongoing, with changing membership over time. Some groups are structured as **closed groups** in which the membership and number of sessions are fixed. Many others are **open groups**, which allow new members to join at any time (or occasionally only at fixed times, such as after the third and sixth sessions).

Being a voluntary or mandated group is another important distinction. In mandated situations, the social worker may have different expectations (not always realized) of member investment, and the influence of the mandating institution (such as the court) is likely to be greater relative to voluntary groups. Many scenarios in involuntary treatment employ groups as the method of choice. For example, recall the innovative practice in the family group decision-making model in Chapter 7, which involved a child protection violation and used a large group of community and extended family members. More traditional models also use groups for working with clients challenged by intimate partner violence, parenting issues, and substance abuse. Group work focuses particularly on interrelatedness and extension to the "outside" world, thus creating opportunities to engage involuntary clients in a process from which they can benefit long after the treatment period.

Three important areas for social work group practice include process (how people do what they do), linking (making connections with other people and situations), and inclusion (involving everyone present) (Thomas & Caplan, 1999). These areas are especially applicable for mandated groups as they focus on connecting members through the group process. Some of the skills necessary for successful group work are validating experience, clarifying, paraphrasing, linking one member's response to another's, collaborating, developing group rituals, role-playing, setting tasks, and processing body language (Thomas & Caplan, 1999). These skills draw upon a combination of individual and extended group work skills that can facilitate the work of connection.

THEORETICAL APPROACHES TO ENGAGEMENT AND ASSESSMENT WITH GROUPS

Just as with social work practice with individuals and families, developing competencies for engaging and assessing in groups practice begins with identifying a theoretical stance from which you will work. In keeping with the commitment of this text to the strengths-based perspective, the following discussion will be grounded in the premise that social work practice with groups is approached from the concept that all members have strengths on which the goals and objectives can be built. As Kurland (2007) notes, "the very act of forming a group is a statement of our belief that every member of the group has something to offer the others, something to give to others, not just to get from them" (p. 12).

Since all groups create and function as a system, most theoretical frameworks for group practice can be considered as deriving from the systemic perspective (Garvin & Galinsky, 2008). Thus, you can apply the knowledge you have gained regarding systems theory with individuals and families to your work with groups. Specifically, groups can then be viewed as being fluid, dynamic interactions between a set of individuals who develop interdependence on one another. When the group composition is altered (e.g., a member joins or exits), the dynamics and interpersonal interactions of the group subsequently change as well. A systemic perspective suggests that the work of each phase of the group process "coalesces into a meaningful whole" (Manor, 2008, p. 101). Building on the conceptualization that social work group practice is guided by both systemic and strengths-based frameworks, the following discussion will highlight the previously explored areas of narrative and solution-focused perspectives within the context of a social work group experience.

Narrative Approach in Group Engagement and Assessment

Similar to social work practice with individuals and families, incorporating a narrative approach into social work practice with groups begins with viewing the client system (i.e., the group) as a collaborator. With a group, the number of potential collaborations is significantly increased as the social worker can collaborate with each individual member and the group and the group members can collaborate with one another. Having a group of individuals who share common experiences can further aid in the process of engaging the client to elicit her or his story, then challenging the client's perspective, and partnering to reconstruct a new story/reality. Members can benefit from not only sharing and reconstructing their own narrative, but listening and contributing to the reconstruction of the stories of other group members.

The narrative framework places an emphasis on client strengths and empowerment that enables the client to be the viewed as the expert on her or his life (Kelley, 2008). Within the context of assessment in group practice, group members can work together with one another and the social worker to identify members' strengths and help members externalize or separate themselves from the problems for the purposes of assessment and planning for change. As with social work practice with individuals and families, narrative theory has been integrated with other theoretical and practice approaches. Utilizing a narrative approach blended with a solution-focused approach within a group intervention will be explored in the following section.

Solution-Focused Approach in Group Engagement and Assessment

Experiencing an increase in its application to group practice, the solution-focused approach is particularly well-suited for social work practice with groups for a number of reasons. You will recall from earlier discussions on the utilization of the solution-focused approach with individuals and families the emphasis on brief, targeted interventions. When considered for use in the group experience, a solution-focused approach "encourages more purposeful interaction among group members" (De Jong & Berg, 2008, p. 275). With its grounding in strengths-based perspective and emphasis on problem-solving, a solution-focused approach can quickly focus the members on the issues that brought them to the group, aid them in collaborating on the development of a plan for change, and activate the planned change—all with the input and support of other group members and the social work facilitator.

Group interventions are often intentionally time-limited due to the nature of the work (e.g., mandated groups or psychoeducationally focused groups), financial or agency resources, or characteristics of the group members (e.g., children or adolescents). In engaging potential group members, the social worker can emphasize the time-limited and targeted, future-oriented nature of a solution-focused group. This orientation clearly sets the stage from the engagement phase that your work together will be purposeful, occur within a specified time period (ideally 6 to 12 meetings), and emphasize concrete, achievable outcomes. Such an approach is likely to appeal to many potential group members who may be reticent about joining a group. Solution-focused strategies have been shown to be particularly helpful with children and youth in addressing bullying behaviors (Young, 2008) and clients mandated for intervention (e.g., prison inmates and offenders of intimate partner violence) (Uken, Lee, & Sebold, 2008; Walker, 2008).

While the applicability of a solution-focused approach is apparent from the engagement phase of the group intervention, the assessment phase of solution-focused group work promotes particularly helpful techniques. Introducing assessment through the use of the standard series of solution-focused questions highlights previous successes, strengths, and resources while focusing the client (and the group) on specific and viable solutions. For example, returning to the group of Riverton residents who share the loss of a significant person to substance abuse, the social worker can begin the assessment phase by asking individual members the "miracle" question (i.e., "How would your life be if you were no longer acutely grieving the loss of your loved one?"). Continuing on with the assessment, the group member can be asked to recall a time when they were successful coping with a challenge or crisis in their lives. While the social worker recognizes that grief is not easily resolved, she or he can guide the group members to consider alternative strategies for coping with their loss. The benefit of using such an approach in the group setting is that group members can share ideas and strategies, help to identify strengths in themselves and others, and provide support and nurturance to one another.

As noted previously, solution-focused approaches can be effectively integrated with other intervention approaches. For example, incorporating strategies from the strengths- and narrative-based schools of thought can serve to enhance the impact of the intervention (Kelley, 2008). All three approaches emphasize engagements and assessments focused on the assets and resources of each person with an ultimate goal of mobilization for empowerment and change. Narrative-focused techniques can be utilized to elicit the stories of the group members and to develop alternative and unique change outcomes for the individual and the group.

Clearly, there are a number and array of effective theoretical or philosophical frameworks available for your work with groups. Regardless of the orientation(s) to which you subscribe, remember that your client in group work is, in fact, the group itself and the group experience can be a powerful one for both you and the group members.

CONTEMPORARY TRENDS AND SKILLS FOR THE BEGINNING PHASES OF GROUP WORK: ENGAGEMENT AND ASSESSMENT

As with social work practice with individuals and families, pre-planning, engagement and assessment and planning are critical to the implementation of an effective social work intervention with a group. These areas of work coincide with the phases of the group intervention—planning, beginning, middle, and ending phases. Along with pre-group formation planning, engaging and assessment, group logistics and process will be discussed here. While group practice skills are not unique, but built on the skills and knowledge that you have gained for working with individuals and families, the purposes for which they are used are unique to practicing with groups (Ephross & Greif, 2009, p. 681).

Pre-group Planning

A successful social work group intervention requires significant planning prior to the first meeting. There are many considerations that you, as the social worker, should address before engaging in the process of developing a group in social work practice. As the practitioner, consider eight specific areas before organizing a group. Each of the areas should be considered within the context of the agency, your supervisor's preferences, and the larger social environment. These nine areas (adapted from Kurland & Salmon, 1998, p. 24) provide a useful guide:

- Need

- Purpose

- Composition, eligibility, and appropriateness

- Structure

- Content

- Agency context

- Social context

- Pre-group contact

- Contacting prospective group members

These areas of consideration are interrelated, and decisions in one category may influence decisions in another. While there is room for a variety of approaches in group work practice, the considerations here do not presuppose certain answers. They are simply areas to which you can give thought, as they are likely to be the source of unexpected obstruction later if ignored in the beginning. See Exhibit 8.2 for schematic drawings relating to pre-planning models.

Need To determine if a need exists for creating a group experience, you may begin by identifying the major and relevant issues that confront the population from which you will draw members. To accomplish the step, you want to know your clients well and be aware of the needs as perceived by potential members. Establishing a vital, functioning group is dependent on having an understanding of members' lives and struggles and being able to focus on some aspect of their lives that is important to them. For example, if you work with several young mothers who live in poverty, consider the direct dimension of that battle (e.g., managing a meager household budget, taking an assertive stand with landlords, or meeting children's needs) rather than offering a group whose activity is based on an issue that is not relevant for the members (e.g., needlework skills). On the other hand, needlework skills may be very appealing to women who have little outlet for

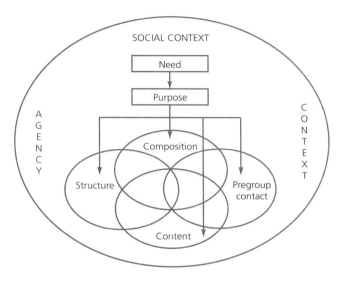

Pregroup Planning Model
(for use when group composition *is not* predetermined)

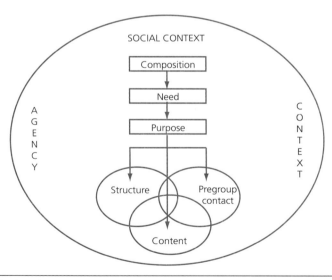

Pregroup Planning Model
(for use when group composition *is* predetermined)

Source: Kurland & Salmon, 1998, p. 209

EXHIBIT 8.2

*Pre-group
Planning
Models*

creativity or companionship and seldom feel as if they accomplish much through the day. The point is to know your clients' needs and respond to them in a way that is consistent with your agency's purpose. Sources of data that may prove helpful include a community needs assessment, agency service statistics, and interviews with staff and clients.

Purpose   Consider both collective and individual objectives: What hopes will the group as a whole have? What expectations will individuals have? Ask yourself, what is the function of the group, and what will your role be? The focus may be on, for example, counseling, teaching, or facilitating social action. Consider ways in which member interaction will contribute to the purpose of the group.

Composition, Eligibility, and Appropriateness   The number of members and their characteristics, such as gender, age, experience, skill, beliefs, and values, serve as the group's composition. The major area of consideration in determining the composition of a group is the degree of homogeneity or heterogeneity that will be preferable and conducive to the group achieving the desired outcomes. In general, scholars agree that some common characteristic or situation optimally provides a unifying focus, but there should also be some difference to sustain interest and the potential for growth through exposure to different ideas. Frequently a particular condition, such as living with cancer, can bridge many differences on other dimensions, such as age or ethnic background, but these aspects should be evaluated carefully in each situation.

In addition to individual descriptive variables, behavioral characteristics are also important. The group has the potential to be more successful if members have a compatible (among each other) interpersonal style, level of verbal development, and understanding of the potential for groups. This does not mean the same level, but ideally the variation should not be so great as to present overwhelming obstacles. Different types of groups will vary on the balance of these components—for example, similar ages in children's groups would probably be more important than in most adult groups.

The need and purpose of the group intervention will help to determine the eligibility criteria and type of members that are appropriate for the group. As you are exploring the potential for forming a group, take into consideration the impact of the focus of the group and the ability of members to connect to one another. For example, consider these questions. Will caregivers of spouses with Alzheimer's disease have issues that are similar or different from caregivers of adult children with a developmental disability? Will persons who are in recovery from an addiction be eligible to remain in the group if they are found to be engaging in the addiction? Staying focused on the intended goals of the group intervention will aid you in answering these questions and creating a group of persons who will hopefully be of help to one another.

Structure   Determine if a group will be open or closed and if there will be any "trade-offs" for your particular group. What is the agency's position on this question? What are the challenges to you with either form? What type of group will best address the short- and long-term needs of the members?

Structure also refers to the logistical arrangements of the group: location, frequency of sessions, time of meetings, and duration. Other practical questions to be answered include: What type or size of room will be optimal? Will members require transportation or child care? Will a fee be charged? How will confidentiality be maintained? How much coordination within the agency will be required?

Content   Developing the content of a group intervention often occurs through a process of examining the purpose of the group, the members' needs, and agency and personnel resources. The activities or other means used to accomplish the group's purpose may require special equipment or educational or art materials. Consider the agenda and content of the meetings. Who will be responsible for making arrangements for the group, establishing timelines, creating an agenda, and developing a group purpose? If the group will use discussion, will the content facilitate interaction among members?

Agency Context   Consider the ways in which the agency will affect the group and the ways in which the group will affect the agency. Specifically, do the agency personnel endorse group work for the population served, and is group work consistent with the agency's mission and emphasis? Do not assume support without confirming it. Your group is likely to have repercussions for others. For example, a children's group is often rather noisy and may be viewed as disruptive by other staff and clients. The support staff may inherit increased administrative responsibilities with the addition of group work to the agency's repertoire of service. Individual social workers may feel possessive of their clients and may be reticent to refer current clients to a group experience. It is to your advantage to address these and other concerns as directly as possible prior to offering a group experience.

Social Context   Finally, consider social and cultural influences that may influence the group's bonding and functioning. Will the group compete with other community services? Are there appropriate resources for members after the group? Do the cultural contexts of the members support group participation? If you want to facilitate a group for adolescent girls, you will want to consider whether their families will approve of that kind of activity.

Pre-group Contact   Prior to a first meeting, consider these issues related to contact with potential group members: How will members be recruited or referred? What promotion will be required and how will promotion be conducted? Will individual pre-group screening interviews be conducted to determine if an individual is appropriate for the group? How will members be prepared for the group experience?

How will they be oriented to ensure maximum participation? While each group and each potential member is unique, developing a plan to address these questions can enable you to assemble a group composed of members with whom you are familiar and who are already oriented to the purpose, structure, and format of the group they may be joining.

Contacting Prospective Group Members   There are many ways to build up the membership of a prospective group and to connect with potential group work clients, including outreach and on-site service referral. **Outreach** is a method for contacting persons in their homes and communities to inform them of services and information about which they may not have been aware (Barker, 2003). Reaching out to potential group members may be accomplished through connections with other professionals in the community (e.g., school guidance counselor). Other times, outreach may require a more concerted coordination campaign (e.g., advertising and individual contacts), particularly if potential clients fear discrimination or barriers to eligibility.

Contacting prospective group members directly through **on-site service referral** is a frequently useful way to connect with potential members. You may, for example, recruit members from your caseload of individual clients, or you might ask your colleagues for referrals after you have established their support of your effort. Postings and announcements are helpful, but they must be paired with personal contact, such as another staff member's enthusiastic recommendation, to be effective.

In nearly all scenarios, a pre-group interview is ideal. First, it allows you to get an in-depth sense of the potential member and her or his "fit" with the goals and purpose of the group and if she or he is an appropriate member. A pre-group meeting also provides an opportunity to assess the potential dynamic components in relation to other members of the group. At least as important, it provides the opportunity for the prospective group member to air any anxieties and develop a sense of this new experience, to ask questions, and to make a more empowered choice about joining the group. A pre-group meeting also is a time to raise questions or concerns regarding fees or associated costs of joining the group. Finally, you can recognize this contact with group members as a form of engagement, assessment, and planning that carries with it all of the requirements in the way of knowledge and skills that engagement and assessment and planning with individuals entails.

Engagement

Overlapping with the important pre-group planning phase, engagement is the beginning phase of the group intervention. The *Standards for Social Work Practice with Groups* (AASWG, 2006, pp. 10–17) provides practice behavior guidelines for the practitioner working in the engagement or beginning phase of the group work intervention, including such pre-group activities as:

- Identify member aspirations and needs as perceived by the member, agency, and yourself.

- Clarify member goals and expectations along with the person's feelings about joining the group.

Following the pre-group phase of work, practice behaviors needed for continuing the engagement and assessment of group members include:

- Develop contracts for explication of individual and group goals, tasks, and activities for the duration of the group and beyond.

- Following your own introduction and clarification of your role in the group, invite each member to introduce themselves and share their reasons and hopes for joining the group.

- In collaboration with the group members, develop a clear statement of purpose, rules and norms, and roles that incorporates the individual and group member and agency goals, needs, and perceptions.

- Develop, as appropriate, content, activities, and resources that are relevant for the group purpose.

- Promote group cohesion among members and between the members and you by establishing rapport with each member and the group as a whole by highlighting common interests and goals, direct interactions, and potential linkages to one another and you.

- In cooperation with the group members, establish the work plan for the group for the rest of the beginning phase as well as the remainder of the group planned time together (or for the individual's time in the group if the group is open-ended and not time-limited).

- Awareness and overt recognition of the unique characteristics of each group member, including but not limited to cultural and ethnic heritage, age, gender, sexual orientation, presenting concerns, and noting that each person brings strengths to the group process.

A first session ideally begins with you, as the social worker, and members sharing their expectations of the group. Be transparent about what you (you alone or with a co-facilitator) hope to accomplish. Likewise, members are encouraged to talk about their perceptions of their roles. Confidentiality is often one of the first dimensions discussed, and, as you can imagine, unless all members feel safe in revealing their struggles and feelings, it is not likely that many will participate fully.

Establishing **norms**, or expected rules of conduct, creates a productive group climate and requires active participation from members so the social worker is not in the position of dictating regulations for the group. The actual norms for the group will depend on the type of group. For example, a socialization group for seven-year-old boys in residential treatment may include "no hitting" as the major expectation. "No shouting" might be applicable to an anger management group, or "celebrating holidays" to a single parents' group. Some groups also discourage contact between members outside of the group, because it may dilute the group process, and others encourage it, because it fosters translation of group benefits into the "real world." The primary emphasis here is to facilitate group members' involvement through a relatively clear set of behavioral expectations that in turn will increase their comfort in being in the group and will encourage their maximum participation. If, for example, group members have differing cultural heritages, and some members interpret lateness as disrespectful while others view it as culturally appropriate or simply flexible, the social worker may opt to explore timeliness as an area for negotiation. Knowing the membership can help you anticipate particular issues that may affect group process. All of these early negotiations with group members serve, like the interview, as important opportunities for both engagement and ongoing assessment.

The engagement phase can be challenging for both the social worker and the group members. The social worker is striving to engage with each individual member and the group as a whole as well as promoting cohesion among the members themselves *and* establishing the group structure and format *and* keeping the group on task and target for the previously stated goals. Creating an environment that is safe, comfortable, and perceived as supportive is essential to the members' ability to establish rapport and engagement with the process and you as the facilitator (Furman et al., 2009). Achieving the desired level of engagement with and among group members can then empower the members to begin sharing with and supporting one another, thus alleviating the full responsibility for leadership from the social worker. Also challenging is the engagement of new members or facilitators who join an established group. The social work facilitator is responsible for engaging the new member and encouraging the group to do the same or if she or he is the new member, reaching out to the members. Attrition is a particular concern if members do not feel engaged in the first meeting. Members who are in a group voluntarily but who do not feel connected to the group or the facilitator may feel reticence about returning to the group.

The beginning phases of group work can present challenges for group members as well. Despite your best efforts to orient members to the purpose, structure, and format of the group, members may still be uncertain or even resistant about participating in the group, their role in the group, perceptions of others about them (as well as their perceptions of others), and concern that the group will not meet their individual needs (Yalom & Leszcz, 2005). Being attentive to individual reactions and responses is a skill to be utilized by the social worker to ensure that individuals are not "lost" or deterred from investing in the group experience.

Assessment and Planning

As with social work practice with individuals and families, the transition from one phase of work to another is often not linear or clearly delineated. Just as engagement can be an ongoing process, assessment and planning may also be revisited throughout the duration of the group experience. Assessment and planning both logically and naturally occur as potential members are being recruited and screened for membership and again as the group is forming and collaborating on the development of individual and group contracts. The need for assessment and planning can recur throughout the life of the group as individual and group goals change and evolve, as members arrive and depart, and unanticipated events influence group interactions (e.g., conflict, change of facilitator, or termination).

Within the context of group practice, assessment is a strategy for determining if the issues and characteristics presented by the group member are consistent with those of other members as well as a tool for monitoring individual and group progress toward goals. Recall the earlier example of the group for Riverton children who had lost a family member to substance abuse. As the facilitator of this group, you may have to determine if an individual who has lost a close friend is an appropriate candidate for membership in this group.

Assessment can also be employed to measure such group-related issues as cohesiveness or group facilitator skills (Macgowan, 2009b). Upon determining the area of assessment that you want to measure, you can opt for assessment by using standardized measures, observation, group member self-reports, or feedback from an external source (e.g., person or video-/audio-recording).

Planning within the assessment phase of group work often requires attentiveness and flexibility. While most group facilitators spend considerable time and effort in the pre-group planning phase and in developing an agenda or plan for each group session, the experienced group practitioner can attest to the need to be able and willing to adjust quickly and creatively to a need to shift plans. Regardless of the type of group you are facilitating, it likely that a member(s) will present for any given meeting with an issue, crisis, request, or behavior that will need to take precedence over the plans that you prepared for that session. While you will want to be responsive to the needs of the individual(s), you must strive to balance the needs of the group. You may be able to set aside your plans for that session to devote time to the individual, but use caution to ensure that the other members or agenda items are not sacrificed in the process.

As noted, flexibility is an essential aspect of the social work practice with groups, particularly the beginning stages of group work. Despite the need for adaptability, the social worker may find that the engagement and assessment processes of most group experiences will include comparable and expected areas of emphasis. Utilizing the descriptions of groups developed by and with residents of Riverton described earlier in this chapter, Boxes 8.1, 8.2, and 8.3 provide for examples of the beginning phases—pre-group planning, engagement, and assessment—of group processes implementing the social goals/action, reciprocal, and remedial models.

STRAIGHT TALK ABOUT GROUP ENGAGEMENT AND ASSESSMENT

For many students and new workers, learning to trust the group process and to maintain a stance of **facilitator** (not necessarily "leader" and certainly not "runner of") can be a challenging aspect of facilitating groups. Learning to share the control of the relationship(s), to share the helping role with group members, and to allow the group its own unique path in developing what it will come to be are important practice skills. Such a position, however, can by definition create challenges for the social worker. A tolerance for relinquishing control will place you in good stead. Despite your best efforts to refrain from controlling the group, it is important to recognize that you will, in fact, influence and shape the norms of the group simply due to your role as a facilitator/convener (Yalom & Leszcz, 2005). Fortunately, most social workers agree that those early anxieties regarding control and its management abate substantially with experience.

Surprisingly, many workers fail to attend thoroughly to the logistics, or the detailed mechanics, of group preparation and implementation. While you consider the philosophical dimensions of launching a group intervention, also make sure there are enough chairs, the meeting is not scheduled on a religious holiday, and all members have transportation to the group. Ensure, for example, that the group for male perpetrators of violence does not meet at the same time and place as the group for their survivors. Consider competition with other known schedules, so that the parenting group does not conflict with the mothers' and children's group. While it is not possible to avoid all conflicts or awkwardness, giving thought to as many of these aspects as you can is worth the effort.

Particularly important to the engagement and assessment phases of group work is "tuning in" to the messages and communication being conveyed to you by group members and others connected to the group process (Shulman, 2009b). "Tuning in" requires you to have awareness of and empathy for the thoughts, feelings, and reactions that are held by you, group members, and others (e.g., family, staff, or referral sources). For example, if you are facilitating a group for Riverton residents concerned about the use of alcohol and drugs by local teens, it is crucial that you "tune in" to your own experiences and feelings related to substance use and abuse and the origins and meanings of the statements being made by the Riverton residents. "Tuning in" is important for your ability to work with any population as it will enable you to determine if you have biases, unresolved personal concerns, or conflicted values that may prevent you from objectively and empathetically serve a client system.

An issue related to attending to logistical details and "tuning in" is documentation of the group experience. While documenting the process of the group experience presents a unique set of challenges, it need not be an overwhelming or complex task. Documentation of any group experience serves a range of purposes, including (1) insights into the positive and challenging events that occurred during the group session; (2) recording gains and potential future challenges; (3) negative interactions among group members; (4) interpretation of behaviors and interactions (including cohesion, process, norms, new directions, and gaps); (5) the termination and evaluation process; and (6) accountability for billing, planning, and referral sources (Yalom & Leszcz, 2005). Typically, two separate records of the group experiences are maintained. A "group" record includes information on attendance, general themes, cohesion, interactions, and plans, while documentation in the individual group members' record includes only information regarding that client and her or his goals, needs, etc. In order to protect individual client confidentiality, the names of other group members should not be included in the individual client document. Box 8.4 provides sample items of documentation that may be included for a client-oriented group session and Box 8.5 includes a list of questions the social worker can ask the client to determine if she or he is appropriate for membership in the group.

While documenting the work of non-client groups—social goals/action and task groups—may include some of the information found in a client group (e.g., attendance, themes, and plans), the focus is more typically directed toward creating a record of actions, decisions, and plans. Often compiled in the form of minutes or notes, documenting group process and outcomes for social action/goals or task groups emphasizes the work being completed as opposed to the interactions among the group members. See Exhibits 8.3 and 8.4 for templates that you can use to record the work of a non-client group. Exhibit 8.3 provides a template for a matrix-style record, while Exhibit 8.4 provides an outline for a narrative-style document.

The early phases of a group experience can bring unique and possibly unexpected challenges for the social worker. Four examples of challenges specific to a group experience include: (1) perceived goal incompatibility; (2) member turnover; (3) delayed results; and (4) sub-groupings (Yalom & Leszcz, 2005, pp. 298–299). Somewhat interrelated, each of these situations relates to group member expectations and dynamics. Group members may struggle to view the group process as being helpful to them, particularly when compared to an individual helping relationship or in an immediate time frame, thus they may then leave the group. Group members often find that the common experiences they share extend beyond the group and lead to alliances within the group session and/or socializing outside the group. While not necessarily negative, such relationships can be disruptive to the group process.

Regardless of the challenge that may present itself to you as a group facilitator or leader, maintaining a transparent, open, and equitable style will best serve both the group and your own sense of competence. Gaining as much group experience as

BOX 8.4

Information to Include in a Group Assessment/ Intervention Plan

AGENCY/ORGANIZATION NAME
GROUP NAME

Demographic Data:

- Name
- Contact information
- Legal status and needs
- Group participation needs (e.g., child or adult care needs, transportation, etc.)
- Presenting concerns as they relate to the group purpose or focus
- Current living situation (level of stability, support, and safety)
- Social environment (level of activity, satisfaction, and relationships with others)
- Cultural environment (client satisfaction and view on helping-seeking; and cultural view of help-seeking, particularly in the group environment)
- Religion/spirituality (statement of beliefs and levels of activity and satisfaction)
- Military experience (branch, time in service, discharge status, coping with experience, and view of experience)
- Childhood (supportive, strengths, and significant events, including trauma)
- Family (composition—parents, siblings, spouse/significant other(s), children, and others; level of support; and family history of mental illness)
- Sexual history (activity level, orientation, satisfaction, and concerns)
- Trauma history (physical, sexual, and/or emotional abuse or neglect and experience with perpetrator(s))
- Financial/employment circumstances (employment status, satisfaction, financial stability, areas of concern or change)
- Educational history (highest level achieved, performance, goals, and challenges)
- Substance use/abuse (history of addictive behaviors—alcohol, drugs, gambling, sexual, or other)

History of Emotional/Behavioral Functioning:

For each of the following areas, gather information regarding: current status (current, previous, or denies history); description of behavior; onset and duration; and frequency

- Self-mutilation
- Hallucinations
- Delusions or paranoia
- Mood swings
- Recurrent or intrusive recollections of past events
- Lack of interest or pleasure
- Feelings of sadness, hopelessness, isolation, or withdrawal
- Decreased concentration, energy, or motivation
- Anxiety
- Crying spells

BOX 8.4

continued

- Appetite changes
- Sleep changes
- Inability to function at school or work
- Inability to control thoughts or behaviors (impulses)
- Irritability or agitation
- Reckless behavior, fighting, or fire setting
- Stealing, shoplifting, or lying
- Cruelty to animals
- Aggression

Past and Current Behavioral Health Treatment History (i.e., individual, family, and/or other group experiences):
- Date(s)
- Program or facility
- Provider
- Response to treatment

Mental Status Exam:
- Attention (rate on scale of: good, fair, easily distracted, or highly distractible; and describe behavior)
- Affect (rate on scale of: appropriate, labile, expansive, constrictive, or blunted; and describe behavior)
- Mood (rate on scale of: normal, depressed, anxious, or euphoric; and describe behavior)
- Appearance (rate on scale of: well groomed, disheveled, bizarre, or inappropriate; and describe behavior)
- Motor activity (rate on scale of: calm, hyperactive, agitated, tremors, tics, or muscle spasms; and describe behavior)
- Thought process (rate on scale of: intact, circumstantial, tangential, flight of ideas, or loose associations; and describe behavior)
- Thought content (note: normal, grandiose, phobic, reality, organization, worthless, obsessive, compulsion, guilt, delusional, paranoid, ideas of reference, and hallucinations; and describe behavior)
- Memory (note: normal, recent (good or impaired), past (good or impaired); and describe behavior)
- Intellect (note: normal, above, below, or poor abstraction; and describe behavior)
- Orientation (note: person, place, situation, and time; and describe behavior)
- Judgment and insight (rate on scale of: good, fair, or poor; and describe behavior)
- Current providers (including psychiatrist, primary care physician, therapist, caseworker, etc.)

BOX 8.4

continued

- Community resources being used (including support groups, religious, spiritual, other)
- Client goal(s) for treatment
- Summary—including social worker's assessment of client "fit" with the group (see Box 8.5 for assessment questions).

Adapted from St. Anthony's Medical Center, St. Louis, Missouri; Women's Support and Community Services, St. Louis, Missouri

BOX 8.5

Screening Questions for Group Assessment

A component of the assessment process for a group intervention is to determine a client's appropriateness for membership in a group. This phase of assessment can also help to ensure emotional and physical safety for all group members. The following list of general questions can aid in evaluating client appropriateness and safety:

- How does the client respond to opinions, thoughts, and insights that differ from her or his own?
- When the client becomes angry or upset, what is her or his reaction and thought process?
- Is the client able to express her or his emotions in an appropriate way and to assume responsibility for the emotion?
- How are the client's emotional responses triggered?
- What is the developmental age of the client? Is the client able to cope with negative emotions and thoughts at an appropriate developmental level with other group members?
- Does the client demonstrate:
  - impulse control challenges?
  - appropriate boundaries?
  - self-awareness?
  - self-destructive behaviors?
  - potential to monopolize or disrupt the group?
  - ability to respond to social cues?
  - sensitivity toward others?
  - potential for personal growth?
  - appropriate group interaction behaviors?
  - difficulty making decisions?
- Is the client's behavior potentially going to limit group participation or benefit?
- If the client is currently experiencing a crisis, will the benefits of the group outweigh risks?

Adapted from Women's Support and Community Services, St. Louis, Missouri

AGENCY/ORGANIZATION NAME
GROUP NAME

Date

Present:

Absent:

Minutes submitted by:

ISSUE	DISCUSSION	FOLLOW-UP/RECOMMENDATIONS	PERSON(S) RESPONSIBLE
Call to Order			
Minutes			
Announcements			
Old Business			
New Business			
Adjournment			
Future Meetings			

EXHIBIT 8.3

Task Group Documentation Template

Agency/Organization Name
Group Name
Date

In attendance:

Absent:

1. Call meeting to order
2. Review meeting agenda
3. Review minutes from previous meeting
4. Announcements
5. Old business
6. New business
7. Adjournment and next steps

Respectfully submitted,

Note taker's name and title

EXHIBIT 8.4

Task Group Documentation Template

possible, particularly facilitator or leadership experience, throughout your social work education can also serve to prepare you for being a contributing member and capable leader in your social work career.

CONCLUSION

In emphasizing the importance of relational components in our lives, first as people and then as social work practitioners, this chapter advocates for social work practitioners to mediate the culturally imposed isolation of many citizens through the use of purposeful groups. Currently there are many exciting adventures into group work in the service of contemporary theoretical perspectives, social justice, and diversity that could not be reported here. Scenarios relating to cultural inclusion, gender and disability, collaboration, and spirituality in models that emphasize process over stages and story over problem all point to the empowering direction that social group work is taking as it returns to its place in the history of the profession. Group work has renewed and significant potential for the future and particular relevance for the social justice, diversity, and human rights connections that give social work its meaning.

The focus will now turn to the next phases of social work practice with groups. Building on the pre-planning, engagement, and assessment work that has been completed, the social worker–facilitated group moves into the intervention or middle phase of work followed by the termination and evaluation (or ending) phases of the group experience.

MAIN POINTS

- All persons are members of groups that provide meaning and critical human connections. Western philosophy tends to underemphasize the gifts and power of group connection.

- Group work in the social work profession has been a controversial topic but remains a vital part of practice that lends itself especially to social justice, diversity, and human rights perspectives.

- Organizing a group requires careful planning and continuous consideration for the value of the group as a whole.

- Traditional theoretical models for group work include the task group, social action or goals model, the reciprocal model, and the remedial model.

- Social work group practice can be approached using a variety of theoretical frameworks. The approaches highlighted in this chapter include: strengths and empowerment, narrative-focused, and solution-focused perspectives.

- Engaging and assessing group members individually and collectively constitutes the beginning phase of group formation.

- While primarily completed during the beginning phases of group work, engagement and assessment can be ongoing aspects of the group experience. The fluid and evolving nature of group work can result in changing membership and leadership, new and unexpected issues, and interpersonal dynamics and conflicts that can all influence the course of the early (and later) stages of the group intervention.

EXERCISES

1. Go to www.routledgesw.com/cases and review Carla Washburn's video vignette and complete the following:
   a. Summarize the group's activities as they are depicted in the vignettes.
   b. Document the group practice behaviors that the social worker, Shannon, is utilizing.
   c. Identify any challenges you anticipate that may occur in completing a group-level intervention with the members of this group.
   d. Brainstorm about the next steps that you would initiate as the social worker facilitating this group.
2. Review the Carla Washburn video vignette and explore options for facilitating this group using a range of different approaches, including:
   a. Psychoeducational group
   b. Reciprocal group
   c. Remedial group
   After you have considered strategies for facilitating the group using the three different models, respond to the following questions:
   a. How does each group differ in its focus?
   b. How does the social work role differ in each group?
   c. What engagement skills did the social worker utilize?
   d. Utilizing the case vignette as an example, role-play the group as a one of each of the following: (1) psychoeducational, (2) reciprocal, (3) remedial
3. As a skilled individual and group practice social worker at a local community health center, you have several young clients who have been diagnosed with attention deficit hyperactivity disorder (ADHD). The clients are Hispanic children who range in age from six to eight years of age. Although you usually meet with the children individually, you notice that when their parents pick them up from appointments, some of the parents appear sad about their children, while others appear frustrated or angry. The children themselves seem somewhat isolated and all are experiencing social, academic, and behavioral problems in school.

Assume that you have the time, interest, and agency support to offer a group. Choose one of the following interventions from the list below that you think will be the most helpful:

a. A play/social skills group for the children.

b. A support group for the parents.

c. A psychoeducational group for the parents.

d. An empowerment group for the children.

Be prepared to provide a rationale for your choice to your classmates. How might one choice intersect with another? Compare with peers.

4. You work for a child welfare organization and are facilitating a support group for adolescent females who have recently given birth and are preparing to return to their high schools. Some of the babies are being partially cared for by their grandparents, and some have been adopted through the agency. Some of the group members have concerns about returning to school and others are eager to get back into a "normal" social life again. Most members are participating well, although one member, Janine, has said almost nothing in the three meetings that have already occurred. All the members of the group are African American. You are a white, female student, 23 years old.

At the beginning of the fourth meeting, the mood of the entire group seems contentious. After brief preliminary pleasantries and a restatement of the agenda for this session (hoping that would bring everyone on board), you realize that Janine is quietly crying in the corner. At the same time, two of the other members start calling your name angrily, competing for your attention. They tell you they are annoyed at the group, at the plan for today, at the agency, and at Janine who is sitting there acting like a "baby."

Respond to the following:

a. Identify two skills from the chapter that you would use and provide an example of the way in which you would perform the skills.

b. Provide a rationale for your selection of these particular skills. What are the expected results from the use of the skills?

c. Which of the models described in this chapter offers the best explanation for the group dynamics?

5. Attend a mutual aid group in the community and write a reflection about your experience, including:

a. Describe the group type, purpose, and structure.

b. Identify group leader and member roles.

c. Reflect on your previous experiences as a group member. What role do you often play? Why? Do you want to do things differently?

6. In small groups of three or four, create your own social action group.

a. Identify an issue that is of mutual interest to group members.

b. Determine the roles for each member.

c. Develop a plan of action for the group.

Prepare as a presentation for the class.

Social Work Practice with Groups: Intervention, Termination, and Evaluation

I found myself slipping into that self trashing thing, man, you know, putting myself down, thinking and saying I'm a dumb broad, ugly and worthless, just like J. used to tell me. But they got on me, those awesome women! They told me I was breaking the friggin' rules! Me! Breaking the rules, and then I remembered what they meant. We're not doing that stuff in this group. The end. Not okay. They are really the most awesome! What would I be without them?

Marcy (of the Debbie, Joan, Marcy, and Kate Battered Women's Group)

Key Questions for Chapter 9

(1) What competencies do I need to intervene, terminate, and evaluate with client systems at the group level of social work practice? (EPAS 2.1.10(c & d))

(2) How can I utilize evidence to practice research-informed practice and practice-informed research to guide the evaluation of a group I am facilitating? (EPAS 2.1.6)

(3) What is the appropriate response for a social worker leading a group if one group member violates the confidentiality of another member of the group? (EPAS 2.1.2)

(4) What is distinction between the appropriate social worker role in facilitating an intervention with a self-help support group and a therapy group? (EPAS 2.1.3)

THE EFFICACY OF SOCIAL WORK PRACTICE INTERVENTIONS, terminations, and evaluations with groups, like those with individuals and families, are linked to the engagement and assessment from which they evolve. Considered the middle and ending phases of work, interventions are identified as the period of the group experience in which the "majority of the work of the groups gets accomplished" and endings are "the time to consolidate the work of the group" (Toseland & Horton, 2008, p. 302). As with the other aspects of group work, interventions, terminations, and evaluations are multi-faceted as the dual focus is on both the individual as well as the group. Such complexity requires the social worker to possess a specialized skill to implement the intervention and facilitate the termination and evaluation processes.

To complete the exploration of social work practice with groups, this chapter provides a continuation of the group experience from the development of the intervention process through the termination and evaluation phases. Also included in the discussion is a focus on theoretical frameworks for group interventions and models of group intervention that are guided and informed by the perspectives followed by an overview of the social work practice behaviors needed for intervening with groups. Social worker and group member roles are reviewed. The chapter will continue with a look at the final phase of the group intervention—termination and evaluation. To set the stage for delving into the middle and ending stages of group work practice, consider first the interface of such key issues as social justice, diversity, and human rights.

INTERFACE: SOCIAL JUSTICE, DIVERSITY, AND HUMAN RIGHTS

Social work with groups is a natural setting for practitioners who are particularly committed to social justice, diversity, and/or human rights concerns. As discussed elsewhere in this book, much of social injustice is rooted in exclusion—from resources, opportunities, respect, supports, and so on. This kind of exclusion is especially evident in the experiences of those considered "other" or different. Even in the current culture, that can mean persons with disabilities, persons of color, groups living in poverty, older adults, persons who are gay, lesbian, bisexual, or transgendered; unfortunately the list is very long (see Greif & Ephross, 2005). An ongoing debate within group work practice is the social worker's response to issues of diversity within the group intervention. Are group interventions more effective if the group is heterogeneous or homogenous? While there is no one or simple response to that question, the consensus of scholars is that the appropriate response can be found within the research that has been conducted on group interventions (i.e., identifying evidence to support those interventions that are most effective with a heterogeneous versus a homogenous group structure (Toseland & Horton, 2008)). Diverse groups are reflections of the world in which most people live, but not all individuals may feel comfortable or safe taking personal risks with persons who are different from them in the areas that brought them to the group. In addition to consulting the research on group diversity, social workers can also benefit by examining their own views (including their own "isms") on the groups they will be bringing together for a group intervention (Toseland & Horton, 2008).

Group work practice brings people together in meaningful ways that connect them and can serve as a forum for increasing understanding, appreciation, and respect for others. In short, group membership can reduce the effects of exclusion and the injustices associated with it. There is potential in social work practice with groups to identify, establish, articulate, and mediate the rights, as well as needs, of group members within the microcosm of the group. This can be an important and empowering experience for many people who may have rarely (or never) understood their own social contexts in terms that affirmed their rights as human beings (Kurland et al., 2004). This arena—human rights and social work with groups—holds great promise for the integration of human rights practice into the profession.

THEORETICAL APPROACHES TO INTERVENING WITH GROUPS

Just as there are many theoretical models for social work intervention with individuals and families, there is also a full legacy of theory related to group interventions, processes, skills, and ending points. Subscribing to a specific theoretical perspective can influence the group intervention in terms of guiding the formation of the group, define roles, and impact group dynamics (Macgowan, 2008).

In this section, the examination of the previously discussed theory-driven approaches to group practice will be continued with an emphasis on intervention. Following an overview of theoretical applications, several classic, contemporary and developmental models will be explored. Later, the focus will shift to group work intervention skills, examples of current groups, and finally, consideration of contemporary innovations in group work.

Strengths and Empowerment Perspectives on Group Intervention

As you recall from Chapter 8, this book is grounded in the premise that social work practice with groups should be approached from the position that all group members bring strengths to the group. A strengths-based perspective integrates easily with other theoretically driven intervention approaches. Within the intervention itself, the social worker can utilize the strengths for a range of purposes. Strengths identified by an individual group member can be utilized to affirm and motivate the individual's change process, to enable the individual strengths to serve as models for other group members, and to identify and integrate the individual members' strengths into strengths for the group.

One of the theoretical models that can be utilized to incorporate a strengths perspective into a group intervention is empowerment. With origins in an ecological perspective and aimed at addressing social injustices, an empowerment-focused group intervention emphasizes reciprocal connections with members' environments (Hudson, 2009, p. 48). Within this context, empowerment as a principle generally incorporates three major areas of concern: (1) the personal, including attitudes, values, and beliefs; (2) the interpersonal, including knowledge, skills, and networks; and (3) the sociopolitical, including individual and collective action (East, Manning, & Parsons, 2002). These components are well suited to illumination in **empowerment groups** because membership itself can support the personal and interpersonal dimensions of empowerment as well as the critical analysis of the political environment and participation in change efforts. This means that group members are empowered from the earliest planning and participate in such processes as the identification of needs, as discussed earlier (Breton, 2004).

With an emphasis on negotiating a change between the group members and their environment, the role of the social worker is to collaborate with the members to mediate between the members and the entities or issues within their environment that creates oppression or injustice (Hudson, 2009). For example, the social worker is thus viewed as a "co-activist" working along with the group to achieve the desired goals. Such an approach can be utilized in multiple types of group interventions, including social goals/action and reciprocal mutual aid groups.

Recall the situation in Chapter 1 of Georgia, who experienced intimate partner violence and joined an empowerment group with other women who had been in violent relationships. This group supported Georgia's personal needs for esteem and dignity, offered her the opportunity to expand her interpersonal skills and connections, and opened the door to analyze and take action in the wider context of societal institutions that both sustain and challenge the status quo (see Donaldson, 2004). The quote that appears at the beginning of this chapter provides a glimpse into a similar experience in the personal and interpersonal realms as experienced by Marcy's revelations.

Narrative Theory and Group Interventions

Building on a strengths- and empowerment-focused engagement and assessment process, a narrative approach in intervening with groups continues to emphasize not only the collaboration between the client and social worker, but the collaboration among group members as well. A narratively oriented group intervention requires the social worker and members to listen to the voices of each member and aid in the deconstruction and reconstruction of the individual or group story. In the case of a mutual aid or therapy group, the stories will be individual, but in a social goals/action group, the "story" may be the group's story. The reshaping of the individual or group perceptions are then transformed into an intervention plan aimed at achieving the unique outcome desired by the individual or group member(s). The group members can then contribute to individual or group change process by brainstorming and processing the members' motivations, options, and behaviors.

One of the hallmarks of the narrative approach is the use of witness groups and community supports. Both strategies have particular relevance for the group intervention. Witness groups are persons called together by the social worker to serve as "witnesses" to discussions between the social worker and the client and/or among the group members. In the case of a group intervention, the witness group is already in place to serve in this capacity. Known as the outside-witness group, these persons provide feedback to the social worker and individual group member based on the dialogue they have just heard (Morgan, 2000). Such feedback can include questions, observations, and interpretations. The individual receiving the feedback then has the opportunity to ask questions and respond. This process aids in the development of an alternative approach to the client's current dilemma or concern.

The strategy of using "insider" knowledge (i.e., hearing from others with similar life experiences) has long been used within the narrative approach. This practice strategy is well suited for use with a group intervention, particularly if the group members have, in fact, shared life experiences and they are at different phases of their experiences. As noted in Chapter 8, narrative approaches are also well suited for application with other theoretical frameworks. The discussion will now shift to incorporating a solution-focused approach into the group intervention.

Solution-Focused Group Interventions

Solution-focused interventions with groups share similarities with solution-focused interventions with both individual and family work, but have particular commonalities with family interventions. While a group of family members and a group of unrelated persons may be of similar size, have a common area of concern, and identify similar goals, the dynamics of interpersonal interactions will likely differ. Family members have a history together, while the members of a group intervention do not typically have a prior relationship that shares the intensity, commitment, or future orientation that a family group has. Nonetheless, much of the knowledge and skills that you can attain for working with families can be applied to a solution-focused group intervention with a formed group.

To set the stage for implementing a group intervention from the solution-focused perspective, return to the work accomplished during the individual client engagement and assessment phases of group work. During the beginning phases of group work, you collaborated with the client system through a series of questions to identify desired new realities and available strengths and resources that can be mobilized to achieve the clients' goals for change (De Jong, 2009). For the intervention plan, you can continue to build on the questions that were utilized in the assessment phase by asking the clients to consider again the "miracle," "exceptions," and "scaling" questions to solidify the plan for change. While the questions are posed to individual group members, the entire group is a resource for development of a plan for change. Not only can the members contribute to the development, implementation, and evaluation of individual change plans, they can continue to be a resource throughout the change process through their own questions, observations, and experiences. Once the plan is developed and underway, questions again can be incorporated to monitor the members' progress by checking in with the group member to determine if change has occurred (i.e., "what's better?") and if the area of concern has improved.

As noted throughout the discussions of solution-focused interventions with individuals, families, and groups, this approach is used in conjunction with other approaches (e.g., narrative therapy and cognitive behavioral approaches) to enhance the effectiveness and accountability of interventions. De Jong and Berg (2008) suggest that implementing a solution-focused intervention with a group is often attempted after gaining competence with the approach at the individual and family levels of work. In practice, it may be easier and have more positive outcomes to begin utilizing this approach with individual or small family client systems before attempting to manage a larger scale group intervention with which you are not yet comfortable or proficient. Along with combining theoretical frameworks, group interventions can been guided by a range of theoretical perspectives and implemented via various models. Of particular relevance to this discussion is the examination of two developmental models presented in the following section.

Developmental Models

One of the classic theoretical perspectives on group work, the **developmental model,** is defined by the apparent nature of group evolution. The assumption in developmental models is that the group changes and grows in somewhat predictable ways during its course. This assumption does not mean the group goes through a rigid progression but rather a series of ripening relationships in which members are perhaps ambivalent about joining at the beginning, then jockey for position within the membership, grow closer together through the work of the group, establish differences from one another, and finally separate at the group's ending. This perspective reflects the idea of stages or phases and has been extremely influential in contemporary group work. Developmental models are still the norm in many practice contexts and are frequently very useful in alerting the worker to possible dynamics, gauging what is happening, and thinking about how to intervene. Two different models—the Boston Model and the relational model—are examined here.

Boston Model   First developed at Boston University's School of Social Work, the **Boston Model** (Garland, Jones, & Kolodny, 1965) has remained a prominent feature in social work education and particularly in practice. The Boston Model outlines five stages of group development: preaffiliation, power and control, intimacy, differentiation, and separation.

- During **preaffiliations** members may feel some ambivalence or reservations about joining the group as well as excitement and eagerness. For example, the individual joining a support group for persons diagnosed with an illness may be eager to connect with others who have a similar experience, while at the time wonder if she or he will find others who share experiences, fears, and needs.

- In the **power and control** stage, members vie with each other and with the social worker for influence and status within the group. Continuing with the support group for the newly diagnosed person, members who are further along in their illness, treatment, or recovery may perceive themselves as having more status and influence within the group than those members who are recently diagnosed.

- **Intimacy** occurs when the members become closely connected, having worked through their power issues; they may seem more homogeneous than at any other time in the group. Having processed the issues of power and control, the support group for persons diagnosed with an illness can begin to bond around their common life experiences. Members will often share coping strategies and develop relationships outside of the group sessions in which they are available during times of crisis.

- During **differentiation** members feel they are safe enough to express and value the differences among each other and the worker; the homogeneity of the former phase matures into a respect for difference. Returning to the illness support group, members may gain enough comfort with one another that they can confront one another on such issues as difference of opinion, coping behaviors, or lack of compliance. Such confrontation can occur successfully only when members have reached a point of mutual respect for one another.

- In the final stage, **separation**, members begin to withdraw from the group in anticipation of its ending. Members of an illness support group may separate as they finish treatment, recover, or learn the illness is terminal.

Although the authors propose a general progression through these stages, there is no assumption that progress will occur as a rigidly linear sequence. There are likely to be points in the life of a group in which one or more members seem to loop back to the behavior common to a previous stage or tend to jump ahead to another one. See Exhibit 9.1 to learn how the developmental stages have been applied to three different group populations. Also worthy of note is the fact that these phases of group process are not typically thought to be applicable for working with a task group. However, the stages of work may, in fact, be relevant for working with tasks groups as they form, bond, and progress through similar relationship-building stages as client groups.

There are also several take-offs on this stage scheme in the current literature in which the stages divide slightly differently, and some have additional substages. The

EXHIBIT 9.1 *Three Models* *for Stages of* *Group* *Development* *Based on the* *Boston Model* *Prototype*		BOSTON PROTOTYPE	FEMINIST	FEMALE ADOLESCENT FOSTER CARE GROUP	OLDER INSTITUTIONALIZED PERSONS: FLOOR GROUP
		Garland, Jones *& Kolodny,* *1965*	*Schiller, 1995,* *1997*	*Lee & Berman-* *Rossi, 1999*	*Berman-Rossi &* *Kelly, 1997*

	Stage 1	Preaffiliation	Preaffiliation	Preaffiliation:
				• Approach-
				   Avoidance
				• Power and
				   Control
					Approach-
					Avoidance

	Stage 2	Power and Control	Establishment of a Relational Base	Intimacy and Flight	Intimacy
	Stage 3	Intimacy	Mutuality and Interpersonal Empathy	Differentiation	Power and Control 1: Challenging the Institution
	Stage 4	Differentiation	Challenge and Change	Termination	Power and Control 2: Challenging the Worker
	Stage 5	Termination	Termination		Differentiation & Empowerment

Adapted from Berman-Rossi & Kelly, 2003

group population also influences the degree to which members progress through the phases and the way in which they progress. For example, in an adaptation applied to older institutionalized persons in a group, Kelly and Berman-Rossi (1999) found that separate stages emerged in which the members first challenged the institution and then challenged the worker. In an empowerment-oriented group (Lee & Berman-Rossi, 1999), adolescent girls in foster care demonstrated an impulse to take flight rather then enter the intimacy stage (not surprising, given their family history of chaos and separation). While this well known and used model for stage development in groups has its critics, the discussion will now shift to a variant, the relational model.

Relational Model   This model derives from feminist theorists and practitioners who have objected to the exclusion of women in developmental theory building. For example, many feminists challenge Erik Erikson's famous male-normed psychosocial sequence of life stages on grounds that he has stereotyped girls as being concerned with "inner space" and boys with "outer space." Some feminists believe the intimacy stage, a clearly relational dimension, actually precedes the identity stage in girls, which reverses Erikson's order. Nearly three decades ago, Carol Gilligan suggested that the identity and intimacy stages are intertwined in girls (1982).

The feminist orientation to the importance of relational aspects of development offers a different emphasis for women and girls and appears in group work models as well. Although the **relational model** incorporates stage development, the model also proposes that women go through stages that are different from those of the Boston Model. The second and third stages reflect the emphasis on relationship that is established before the conflict, or challenge, stage. The original model is posed as follows (Schiller 1995; 1997):

- *Preaffiliation:* Members experience ambivalence about joining.

- *Establishment of a relational base:* Members build strong, affective connections with others.

- *Mutuality and interpersonal empathy:* The connections deepen into a commitment to mutual aid.

- *Challenge and change:* Differences are recognized, and the connections may change in nature.

- *Termination:* Members conclude their work and separate.

This model has solid utility in feminist groups or in groups working with women as it supports one of the more carefully considered gender constructions relating to women's development and theory (Lesser et al., 2004); that is, the importance of established relationship and relational patterns as a precursor to engagement in challenge.

Bringing the discussion of theoretical frameworks applicable to group interventions to a close again serves as a reminder that there are numerous and valid theories and perspectives that can be used to guide group interventions. Each social worker contemplating group leadership must determine for her or himself the theoretical perspective that is most compatible with her or his philosophy and professional and personal value systems given the agency structures and guidelines and funding sources. Along with comfort level, the practitioner must develop competency in the approach(es) selected. Regardless of the theory one opts to employ, demonstrating competency through practice behaviors is essential as outlined in the following discussion.

CONTEMPORARY TRENDS AND SKILLS FOR THE MIDDLE PHASE OF GROUP WORK: INTERVENTION

The middle phase of the formed group experience is the time for the social worker, the client, and the entire group to implement the planned change. Having completed the work of the beginning phase, the social worker and the group move into a pattern of interaction in which cohesion, unity, integration, trust, and communication are all enhanced (Macgowan, 2008, p. 284). The primary function of the middle, or intervention, phase of group work is to implement the plan of action. The *Standards for Social Work Practice with Groups* (AASWG, 2006) provides guidelines for organizing this phase of work and identifying skills needed:

1.   Support progress toward individual and group goals—having established both individual and group goals in the assessment phase, the members can plan and implement the action steps needed to accomplish the goals. The social worker must be attentive to the need for goals to be re-negotiated during this phase of work.

2.   Attend to group dynamics and processes—the social worker must be vigilant in her or his ongoing observations of group dynamics and processes. As group members become familiar with one another, they may feel more confident in confronting one another, which can create conflict within the group. Moreover, the social worker must be mindful of alliances that form within the group and outside the group and the impact of those relationships on individual and group functioning.

3.   Identify and access resources within and outside the group—as the work phase progresses, the social worker should have knowledge of and access to resources that may be helpful to the individual members of the group or the entire group itself.

4.   Have knowledge, skills, and other resources of group work, group members, and sources outside the group—the social worker may find that she or he encounters situations, dynamics, and needs (e.g., group member conflicts, non-compliance with rules, or needs unable to be met by a group experience) within the intervention phase that require additional knowledge, skills, or resources that can be gained through researching the literature, consulting with colleagues, and even conferring with the group members themselves.

5.   Use evidence-based practice techniques in facilitating the group—the social worker is responsible for familiarizing herself or himself with the research and scholarship that is available for the type and structure of the group intervention being implemented.

Examining the literature for evidenced-based resources for intervening with groups who are members of specific populations or communities can also yield useful information for your own group practice or you can incorporate it into a legacy of best practice information for future groups at your agency or organization. Having both quantitative and qualitative evidence to support the "best available" practices is known as **evidence-based group work** (EBGW) (Macgowan, 2009a, pp. 132–133). Using rigor, impact, and applicability as the criteria for determining the strength of the evidence, EBGW enhances practice and policy accountability, enables social workers to improve practice competencies utilizing empirically validated tools and research outcomes, and ultimately bolsters the desired efficacy of the group intervention. Crafting an evidence-based approach to implementing and evaluating a group intervention should include attention to: (1) the way in which client needs and strengths were assessed; (2) identification of desired outcomes; (3) risks involved in various approaches; (4) compliance with the intervention plan; (5) client responses to intervention; (6) assessment of outcomes; and (7) distinction between individual and group outcomes (Meier & Comer, 2005, pp. 417–425).

While the group format and the social worker's role can vary during this phase of work, there is a set of practice behaviors that are needed for facilitating the "work" phase of group practice. Two examples of innovative approaches to group intervention will provide an introduction to an overview of social work skills for group intervention.

Social Work Group Interventions

The long history of the social work profession using the group as a means to carry out the profession's values and concerns has been highlighted in this and the previous chapter along with the four types of groups within which social work practitioners often facilitate the intervention: task groups; social action/goals groups; reciprocal groups (including psychoeducational groups and support groups); and remedial groups. These social work groups often overlap in outcomes. For example, the support group educates, the psychoeducational group empowers, the social goals group supports, and all deal with some aspect of social justice, diversity, or human rights, as each issue and population represents some dimension of exclusion, which in turn leads to unmet needs and violation of rights (see Goodman, 2004).

At the same time that group work has many traditional approaches in full use today, it also reflects, as does the profession as a whole, the sociocultural context of the times. Accordingly, several innovations in working with groups reflect current theoretical, political, and social issues. Two contemporary issues that the profession has addressed through group work models are intimate partner violence, with constructionist groups, and new approaches to corrections or crime restitution, through restorative justice groups. Each of these will be discussed as an example of a constructivist approach to group intervention.

Each of the efforts described here represents a vital, responsive attempt to counter the negative effects of a contemporary societal issue, and each demonstrates creativity and courage. Note that these are living works in progress and as such may not be proven effective, and many conclude with recommendations to improve the experience. Although they are based on recognized social work perspectives and guided by research inquiries, they will no doubt evolve and be fine tuned as they undergo evaluation procedures to gauge effectiveness and pinpoint the need for change. They take risks in forging new territory and reflect group work's solid potential in groundbreaking efforts.

Constructionist Groups for Women Experiencing Intimate Partner Violence A **constructionist group** is a social work group intervention that is facilitated from a social constructionist perspective. This approach requires the facilitator to recognize that reality is created through shared meanings and offers members the opportunity to develop new understandings of themselves through the group process. A constructionist group intervention embodies feminist and narrative theories as well as the postmodern notion of the way in which a person develops a new and preferred **representation of the self**, or a new view of her or his own worth and identity. In this feminist group, the members accomplish their new representations of the self by resisting and protesting the male violence they have experienced. The work of the group includes three processes: (1) revealing and undermining the oppressive discourse relating to women experiencing violence, which is a *political* process; (2) identifying and detailing the protest that women actually use in response to violence, the recognition of which reflects *change*; and (3) reconstructing the identities of participants based on the protest. This last process is celebrated in an empowering **"definitional ceremony"** (Wood & Roche, 2001a, p. 17), which allows the women to present to an audience of people important to them their new understandings of self.

To illustrate, the social worker in this group points out the common themes of the women's conversation relating to the violence they have experienced. For example, some women adopt a socially imposed understanding, which incorporates shame and guilt when male partners perpetrate violence on them. They believe that their own shortcomings cause violence against them and that they are responsible for changing their behaviors in exchange for safety. After a period of time in which the social worker expresses support for the woman, the social worker can then help to counter that thinking by asking perspectival questions that help to break the logic of self-deprecation (for example, "What would your sister say about the way Mike treats you?" "What did the court say about this?"). Such questioning over time encourages a focus on multiple realities by helping women see that others would not think they "deserved" violence or "had it coming," or should "just put up with it."

At this point the social worker seeks descriptions from the women in the group regarding their actual responses, that is, the ways they have resisted and protested. Protest may be in the form of simply not accepting the negative statements made by the batterer, or it may be considerably more confrontational, such as obtaining a restraining order. Some protests may be viewed as passive (giving older bread and milk to an abusive partner while saving fresher food for a child). These incidences of protest, however they are expressed, begin to form the basis for a new understanding of the self as a person of agency who can make real and meaningful life changes.

Group members ask where a woman got her ideas for the protest or the courage to carry it out, and they also consider what the protest says about her. These explorations challenge the woman's identity as helpless and worthless as they lead to a new view. The social worker and other group members then anchor this new more positive representation through reinforcement. The members do this by seeking to enrich the story through the woman's further detailed description, and finally they celebrate her new identity as she sees it through a definitional ceremony to be created collectively by the woman, the group members, and the social worker. Through an emphasis on process rather than group stages, this group is committed to helping the women in its membership discover the other side of their survivorship and become who they want to be.

New models like this one, based on narrative ideas of the story and constructionist ideas of self, are highly useful in political contexts in which contemporary views on gender and power relationships are highlighted. They are especially applicable in domestic or sexual violence centers as well as in some community mental health centers.

Restorative Justice Groups for Combating Crime   In another response to a contemporary phenomenon, in this case the climate of punishment and stricter approaches to criminal offenders, social workers have been among those advocating for a different strategy. Seeing the criminal justice system as bogged down in practices that neither heal nor rehabilitate, scholars and practitioners have developed an approach thought to be both more relevant and responsive to the issues of offenders as well as survivors (see Van Wormer, 2004). A loosely associated collection of strategies called **restorative justice groups** focus on crime as an interpersonal conflict that has repercussions on the victim, offender, and community at large. The emphasis is more on the harm done to the relationships of those hurt, and their restoration (see, for example, Boyes-Watson, 2005), than on the violation of the law (Lovell, Helfgott, & Lawrence, 2002). The involvement of the community as an invested party in the occurrence of crime represents an important focus. It is the community that loses when its members are engaged in crime through damage to property and relationships and the community that gains when they return with relationships restored.

Based on an actual series of groups conducted at the Washington State Reformatory, the purpose of the groups was to address (1) offender accountability, (2) the rights of victims, and (3) citizen involvement in the justice process in a way that balanced all three. The major work of the three groups was accomplished through the story of each participant's personal crime experience. Each week one victim, one offender, and one community member shared their personal accounts. Such storytelling increases understanding, validates experience, reduces isolation, and increases the vision for change. Group participants then determined how offenders could respond to the needs of individual victims and what needed to be done to restore the harm done.

The group progress and process variables of these groups were seen as largely consistent with classic models of developmental group work theory (that is, there was initial anxiety and a stage of conflict, followed by greater connectedness) but were also influenced by individual members so that each of the three group meetings reflected different stages of development. A number of additional obstacles to the development of group unity were noted, such as the emphasis on crime, the large number of participants, the fragility of participants, problematic group dynamics at times, safety concerns, confidentiality issues, and the implications of diversity, among others. This emphasis on an alternative strategy to respond to crime that heals and helps people reconnect with each other holds encouraging promise in a society struggling with the alienation of both victims and perpetrators. A recent addition to this concept is the enactment of Neighborhood Activity Boards. In many communities, groups of volunteers come together to meet with first-time, non-violent offenders and those persons victimized by the criminal activity to discuss the impact of the crime. The offender is typically required to complete community service along with participating in the impact panel.

Social Work Skills for Group Interventions

While all theoretical models require skills, and group work interventions may seem different from one-to-one models in social work settings, many of the same generalist practice roles and skills of individual and family interventions are not only applicable but vital to group work interventions. When working to maintain a group-centered focus during the intervention, you will find that listening, supporting, empathizing, and more all have as important a place in group work as they do in work with individuals. While these skills are critical for group intervention, additional skills include the following list adapted from the authors' practice experience as well as AASWG (2006) and Middleman and Wood (1990, pp. 96–102):

Leadership

- Maintaining a "**thinking group**" posture assumes an orientation in which you, as the social worker, consider the group-as-a-whole first and individual members second. This concentration on the whole can require a paradigm shift from thinking of the individual exclusively. For example, you may avoid a prolonged exchange with a single group member as that focus hinders the group's communication.

- **Scanning** is a strategy for visually maintaining all members—the "group version of the attending skill."

- **Balanced leadership** can challenge social workers who believe they must have control of the group and its agenda or it will explode or become chaotic. In actuality, if the social worker allows the group to evolve without close attention to process, it *can* become chaotic, members may be emotionally hurt, or the group fragments and loses its meaning for the members. The social worker's ability to effectively facilitate is dependent on many factors: group connection, functioning, and the presence of internal, or **indigenous leadership**; that is, leadership that evolves within the membership.

Generally, the social worker is more directive in the early stages of groups, in groups with lower-functioning members, in groups with little indigenous leadership, and in task-oriented groups. As the group progresses, the social worker role is to retreat and encourage growth in group ownership of the activity. The key here for any social worker is to recognize group needs and to be flexible with respect to the degree of direct leadership used. The overall goal for group workers is typically to reduce their activity to as little as possible while maintaining a safe environment and encouraging members to be in charge of their own group.

- Maintaining **cohesiveness**, or connectedness, means sustaining a sense of "we" through language, encouragement of rituals (for example, marking the beginning and end of each meeting in a specific way), and recording the group's progress. These skills contribute to group members' spirit and facilitate a sense of belonging to something significant. Development and recording (through a chart on the wall, for example) of group agreed-upon norms or customs contributes to a sense of connection, as well.

- Assisting group members in making progress toward goals through support, programmatic activities, addressing obstacles, assessing progress, and re-contracting for goal achievement, as needed.

- Promoting development of mutual aid; may involve re-review of group norms and values and conflict resolution.

- Reviewing and reiterating definitions and rules related to confidentiality with the group, particularly related to sharing information about other group members outside of the group meetings.

Communication

- The patterns of communication used in a group intervention must be chosen carefully. If you respond only to the members who speak up, there is likely to be a subset of members who are marginalized and excluded. On the other hand, if you always go around the group, member by member, some members will feel pressed to contribute, and all will feel a certain amount of routinization. A more effective approach is to encourage a respectful balance so that all members can have their opportunity to speak without any one member dominating. Alternatively, you may choose to invite participation by all members (especially those members who remain quiet) and ask if others in the group think or feel the way this (currently speaking) member does. Remind members periodically of the group's commitment by verbalizing the norms that the membership agreed upon, and emphasize the group's accomplishments and history when appropriate.

- A challenging group work intervention skill is **redirection**, or redirecting questions and concerns away from you back to the group or to individual members. For example, some members will continue to address you over time as the source of authority for the group. Given the power dynamic that many group members may have experienced as clients in other services, such behaviors are not unexpected. By the same token, some members may complain about other members through a third party (often you). In both these situations, the social worker can redirect the message. In the first scenario, you turn the question back to the group. For example, a member asks if visitors can attend a group meeting. That issue has not been previously addressed, so you submit the question to the full membership: "How do others see this question?" or "How do you as a group want to handle this?" Within this response you may also want to invite quieter members to participate while softening the messages of the louder voices. In the second scenario, you may simply say, "Why don't you tell Bernice that?" or "I don't think you need my help in talking to Kate about that." The goal is to facilitate direct, constructive, communication within the group and the environment that supports it.

- Establishing both consensus and difference occurs when you invite agreement and disagreement on issues (e.g., the visitor issue). Registering dissent in a group who approve something heartily, particularly for a person who has not been highly vocal, can be challenging. Early and strong feelings of connectedness and strong group bonds can make that dissent even harder. Later, as the group matures, expressions of difference should be less troublesome to members, but continue to support difference and encourage others' capacities to respond.

- **Exercising silence** can be challenging. If the facilitator is talking, members cannot. The group should engage in most of the interchange and frequently can be supported in achieving that by the social worker's well-placed silence, which allows the communication patterns of members to develop.

Problem Solving

- **Connecting progress to goals** Summarizing progress, identifying options, prioritizing decisions, mediating conflicts, confronting lack of progress and group interactions, and weighing potential outcomes are skills and activities that a social worker employs in problem-solving during the intervention phase of group work. On occasion, the social worker may have to negotiate an amended contract with the individual members or the entire group. The social worker may also identify the next areas for discussion at future group meetings.

- **Locating resources to benefit group members** involves the mutual identification of resources for group members and accentuating inclusion of natural assets (e.g., friends, family, or neighbors) into the helping network that may also include services, and emphasizing the connections between the group and the community. By making this a joint discussion with and among members early in the process, your expectation is conveyed that the group has both the ability and the responsibility to deal constructively with its own issues. As resources outside the group are identified, the potential network expands for all members and supports the interdependence between members, groups, and the environment.

- **Making use of group process and problem solving** The tension between the needs of individual group members and those of the group as a whole reflects the major substance of social work practice with groups. The negotiation of differences and the creative enrichment that is possible from the process are the greatest values of the effort. The goal then becomes the reconciliation of difference through a genuine compromise that benefits both the individual and the group. One of the group's clearest responsibilities is to establish an acceptable expression and appreciation for difference. Consider an example, described in a social worker's notes of the eighth meeting of a socialization group of 12-year-old girls, who were referred by their school as having a "rocky time" both at home and in adjusting to middle school life.

The girls were bustling around preparing crepe paper streamers and searching for birthday candles, giggling, joking about how old Lila was really going to be. Some said she was probably going to be 60 or so, judging by how glum she had seemed last week about the party they were planning. Lila was late, and when she finally showed up, she looked more miserable than ever. Finally, she blurted out, "I HATE BIRTHDAYS!!" in a voice very unlike her usual somber tones. The other girls were horrified and silent for a moment—almost unheard of in this group. Lila started to cry. Finally, she choked out the story: Her mother had died the night before her birthday two years ago, and she didn't know how to tell anybody in the group that before. The very word "birthday" was a terrible reminder. She didn't want to celebrate.

The girls seemed to feel sorry, they liked Lila, but they also really wanted to celebrate birthdays in this group. It was an important ritual for them. I confess I didn't have a clue what to do, as their facilitator. After a moment, Betsy, whose grandmother came from France, cheerfully volunteered, "Well, let's be tres francais in this group and say we're celebrating our anniversaries! That's what the French call them, the anniversary of birth!" The others responded loudly, hoping their ritual was rescued from certain demise. Lila was silent. She looked up. Finally she almost smiled and said, "I think that would work." And that was that. The group took on a "French theme" ever after and was the only group of 12-year-olds I ever knew that celebrated their anniversaries!

Management of Group Function and Process   Inherent in all effective social work interventions is the social worker's ability to interact competently with the client systems. Encompassed within those interactions is an awareness of the spectrum of potential roles that are represented by both the social worker and the group members. Social worker roles with groups have been highlighted throughout this and the previous chapter, but will be summarized here followed by an overview of the roles displayed by group members that social workers in group practice may encounter.

Social Worker Roles   While the social worker's primary role in the intervention phase of group work is to provide leadership for the group intervention, this role often encompasses a range of roles and skills in order to be effective. The type, format, and goals of the group may determine the role that the social worker will play. The social work group practitioner may find her or himself needing to function in one or more of the following roles (Furman et al., 2009; Collins & Lazzari, 2009, pp. 299–302; Reid, 2002, pp. 435–436):

- Serving as a **facilitator** requires the social worker to invite sharing and participation, reframe and link issues, and maintaining group boundaries and rules to promote appropriate interactions. The facilitative role requires the social worker to be a skilled listener as well. In a task group, the role of the facilitator may include setting the agenda, maintaining the group's focus on the tasks, and providing documentation of the meeting.

- The social worker in the **synthesizer** role summarizes the group members' discussions, identifies themes and patterns, and connects content from one session to the next to promote continuity and substantive discussion.

- **Norm setting** is demonstrated when the social work provides information regarding appropriate group member behavior through role modeling and direct feedback. For example, the social worker establishes appropriate group interaction by encouraging the use of direct interactions, use of "I" statements, appropriate challenges, and concrete examples, and helping to set the rules at the beginning of the group.

- Social workers functioning as **educators** or teachers within a group setting find themselves providing factual information and content specific to the goals of the group.

- As with social work practice with individuals and families, social workers may **collaborate** with another professional. In group work, co-leadership is often an effective strategy in group intervention that involves equal commitment, motivation, and vision and builds on the strengths that each of the leaders brings to the intervention.

Group Member Roles Group members bring their unique characteristics and traits to the group experience regardless of the type of group or its purpose. These qualities can be experienced by the social worker as both strengths and challenges. Ideally, group members will be open to new information, growth, and change and will be willing and able to actively participate in the group process (Furman et al., 2009). While such characteristics and qualities as these are obvious strengths, even challenging behaviors can be reframed and utilized for positive individual and group outcomes. The social worker can set the stage for appropriate group member interactions by incorporating expectations for appropriate group interactions and responses into the beginning phases of the group intervention, but may still have to work with the personality characteristics that are likely to emerge within the group process.

There are some group member roles that commonly emerge within a group intervention. As individual personalities emerge, they will influence and interact with the dynamics of the group itself (much like the dynamics of the family interaction). The competent group practitioner can thus begin to anticipate these roles and behaviors and, having previously considered these possibilities, be prepared with an appropriate response. Caution must be exercised, however, to ensure that you do not generalize or stereotype the group member behaviors, but respond to each as the unique individuals they are. Four of the potentially challenging group member roles and possible social worker responses that you can expect include the following (adapted from Furman et al., 2009; Yalom & Leszcz, 2005, pp. 391–405):

- The "silent" group member is challenging as it is difficult to determine if the individual is not speaking because she or he is not engaged or is uncomfortable or intimidated and thus not able to benefit from the group experience. While it is possible to experience vicarious gains without active engagement, the social worker typically strives to bring the reticent group member into active participation. Inviting the individual to participate, noting non-verbal gestures, and speaking with the member outside of the group about her or his silence are all strategies for promoting participation.

Should these strategies result in continued lack of participation, the social worker has the option to allow the individual to continue in the group being silent or to develop an alternative intervention outside the group for the individual.

- Equally as challenging for a group leader is the "monopolizer" who is perceived as talking too much. In this role, the group member may attempt to offer her or his opinion on virtually every statement made by others or may spend an inordinate amount of time describing her or his own situation or needs. While understanding the reasons for this person's behavior is important for changing the behavior, the impact on the group process and members can be negative. As with the "silent" group member, the social worker can address the monopolizing behavior within the group her or himself or encourage the group to address the behavior, work with the monopolizer outside the group to address the reasons she or he feels compelled to speak so frequently, or develop an alternative intervention strategy.

- The group member who appears to reject help/ideas can be viewed as both a challenge and a resource. As a challenge, the "help-rejecting" or complaining group member is likely to have a negative influence on the group dynamics and be unable to experience actual change or growth. As a resource, the negative perspective can be utilized by the other group members to see the potential possibilities (if only as a reaction to the negativity). The social worker can respond, not to encourage the individual, but to maintain a focus on concrete feedback and the group process and can encourage the group to respond to this member as well.

- The "caregiver" is the group member who strives to take care of others, including the group facilitator. Not surprisingly, the caregiver often neglects to attend to her or his own needs, but utilizes others as a way to avoid addressing individual challenges. The social worker can respond to the caregiver by acknowledging her or his history of altruistic caregiving, praising the caregiver for her or his willingness to now take care of her or his own needs, and incorporating gentle confrontation when the caregiver attempts to care for others as a way to impede personal progress.

As the discussion of the intervention or middle phase of the group work process comes to a close and the exploration shifts to the termination and evaluation phases of group work, a review of those skills needed for competently intervening with groups may be helpful. In general, the social worker engaged in the intervention phase of social work practice with groups should be knowledgeable and skilled in group leadership (e.g., logistics and time management), facilitating group communication and group dynamics, problem-solving and progress toward group and individual goals, and management of group functions.

CONTEMPORARY TRENDS AND SKILLS FOR THE ENDING PHASE OF GROUP WORK: TERMINATION AND EVALUATION

Although all of the concepts explored in terminating (i.e., ending) and evaluating social work with individuals and families can be applied to most clients in any constellation, there are some additional considerations and dynamics that often occur in social work practice with groups. As in social work terminations and evaluations with individuals and families, the intensity of the phases of ending a group and evaluating the work is related to the type and function of its purpose. The following sections present a discussion of the final phase of social work practice with groups, including termination and evaluation.

Social Work Group Endings

Social work practice with groups comes to an end in a variety of ways with a range of member responses and interactions. Terminations may occur when individual members opt to leave the group, the group had a pre-determined time limit, or the leader leaves the group (Furman et al., 2009). Regardless of the reason for the group's termination, endings have the potential to evoke emotional responses from the members; therefore, the social worker's role in termination is to "help members examine their accomplishments, review their experience together, and prepare for the future .... and express and integrate positive and negative emotion" (Garvin & Galinsky, 2008, pp. 291–292). Group members may experience such positive emotions as success and elation and/or such negative emotions as loss, threat, rejection, abandonment, or anger—all of which may relate both to experiences from the group and their own lives (Furman et al., 2009). For example, members of an educational group are likely to experience fewer highly emotional responses than those of a treatment group. A group that has met only six times will probably not have the level of investment in the group process as a group that has met for three years. Addressing members' responses is a part of the social worker's responsibility in helping the group to arrive at its endings. In any event, ending with groups is often a complex endeavor as you deal with endings on three different levels:

- The relationship between group members and the social worker.
- The relationships among the group members.
- The structure of the group itself.

A practitioner needs to consider the termination phase of group work from the theoretical framework from which the group intervention originates. The discussion that follows will explore endings from the perspectives of the theoretical frameworks that have previously been discussed for group practice interventions.

Endings in Group Work with Strengths and Empowerment   Continuing with the integration of strengths and empowerment concepts into the termination phase can enable the individual members and the group itself to review the progress made toward the previously identified goals and develop strategies for sustainability of the changes. In the case of social work groups with clients, the social worker can invite each member to review and reflect on her or his individual experience in the group, including strengths brought to the group process, status in the beginning, middle, and endings phases of work, change experienced, and plans for maintaining the change(s) while utilizing the strengths brought to the group and those created or mobilized during the group experience. Having individual members engaged in this process provides an opportunity for the social worker and other group members to contribute to this process. Other group members can also take advantage of their fellow group members' reflections for their own review and sustainability processes.

A strengths-based perspective can further enable the social worker and the group members to reflect on the group strengths that have evolved as the group moved through the various phases of the group process. The social worker can utilize the group ending as an opportunity to provide feedback on the changes observed in the group's engagement, cohesion, and work. The group members can also be invited to reflect on their experience being part of a strengths-focused group experience. Such a reflection can serve to empower the group members and the social worker to integrate the power of the group process.

In situations in which the individual or group goals are not realized, the formal ending of a task, social action, or client-oriented group can still be oriented toward a strengths perspective. One strategy is to engage in an exercise in which the members review the strengths that existed at the outset of the group, those strengths gained or mobilized during the group, and those strengths that can be carried on by the members after the group is terminated. While the members (and the social worker) may be dismayed by the perceived failure of not achieving the desired goals, strategizing about ways in which the members can continue to work toward achieving the goals can, in fact, be empowering.

Endings in Narrative-Focused Group Work   With an emphasis on strengths, termination of a narrative-focused group lends itself well to the use of a ritual or ceremonial activity as well as the public acknowledgement of growth and change. Group members can continue as collaborators with one another and the social worker to plan a celebration to recognize the ending of the group's formal phase of work together. This "definitional" ceremony can serve to acknowledge the achievement of goals and the next phase of the individual and group members' growth experience as well as helping individuals to reclaim or redefine themselves (Morgan, 2000, p. 121).

As with individual and family work endings, public testimonials are a part of the termination process (Morgan, 2000). Utilizing the group members to listen to individual testimonials and provide feedback can serve to empower the members' changes and to solidify plans for maintaining change beyond the formalized group experience. A process similar to that used with individuals can be employed with groups, with the group members serving as the outsider-witness persons. The definitional ceremony begins with the social worker and group members listening as the individual group member re-authors her or his work in the group. The witnesses then reflect back to the individual the re-authored story, the individual member responds to the feedback, and the entire group engages in discussion about the process. This process can be helpful both as a tool for recognizing individual and group strengths and goal attainment and to evaluate the process of change.

Endings in Solution-Focused Group Work   Termination of the solution-focused group intervention can be viewed as the achievement of the initial and overall goal for the work of the group. From the outset, solution-focused group interventions are aimed at identifying the issues and planning and activating a planned change effort centered on achievable solutions. In the case of a group intervention, the other group members provide a structure for vetting the issues as well as the solutions. You will recall that solution-focused interventions are grounded in the ongoing use of a series of questions to elicit strengths, thoughts and feelings regarding change, and developing plans for change. The questioning technique can be carried into the termination phase as well with the individual members being queried regarding the progress made via the use of scaling questions (e.g., "On a scale of 1 to 10, where were you when you began this group? Where are you now? Where do you need to be in order to leave this group and maintain the change?") (De Jong, 2009). The group members can be integrated into the individual member's response by providing their own observations of her or his change process. Shifting the emphasis from the present to the future can also empower the individual and group members to perceive themselves as separate from the group and the social worker leading the group, thus enabling them to view themselves as empowered to implement and maintain the desired changes.

Regardless of the theoretical perspective employed for the group intervention, a number of competencies are needed for effectively bringing an intervention to an end. As with all aspects of the social work intervention, groups are comprised of unique individuals and situations and the social worker must be attune to those unique aspects within the termination phase of work. However, there are a set of termination-related skills that will be commonplace within your group practice experiences.

Skills for Social Work Group Terminations

Just as the other phases of the group intervention have a primary function and requisite skill set, so too does the termination phase. With an emphasis on consolidating the work, the social worker focuses on bringing closure for the individual group member, the group itself, and for her or himself (AASWG, 2006; Toseland & Horton, 2008). As a result of the complexity and intensity of group endings, even those that are planned, social workers need a skill set that is reflective of the unique features of the group intervention.

The social worker should recognize and attend to all the meanings that evolve (Kurland & Salmon, 1998). Let us look at each of these levels.

Ending the Relationship between Group Members and Social Worker A more extensive examination of the ending of the relationship between group members and the social worker is warranted, as this ending, more than the other two, has implications for the social worker. In this final phase of any type of group (i.e., task or client group), the social worker has several specific responsibilities with respect to the entire group, including (AASWG, 2006; Furman et al., 2009; Kurland & Salmon, 1998; Toseland & Horton, 2008):

- Prepare members for ending.

- Assess progress toward achievement of group goals.

- Help stabilize member and group gains.

- Anticipate and elicit individual and group responses to ending.

- Plan timing and content to maximize the sessions/meetings left.

- Help group members express their ambivalence about the group's ending and address individual and group reactions and behaviors to individual or group accomplishments.

- Share observations of progress and confidence in members' abilities to function successfully without the group or in the case of a task group, continue working toward identified goals (may be helpful to identify any obstacles to success and needed connections to resources outside the group).

- Support members' efforts to begin the process of separating from the group and identify strategies for implementing change and applying new knowledge.

- Develop awareness of ways in which individual and group change will impact systems external to the group.

- Help members connect their experiences in the group to life experiences in the future.

- Develop awareness of your own feelings regarding ending and reflect on and share feelings with the group.

- Elicit feedback from the group members about the group process.

The social worker's task is to help the group end positively and help members' achievements translate into the "real world" outside the group. The social worker also has to monitor her or his own responses; after all, she or he has invested a great deal of effort in facilitating an effective experience, and the more successful it is, the more difficult the end may be. Recalling the overall purpose of the group and focusing on the specifics of the process can help balance the response between task and emotion.

There are also a number of typical group behaviors at ending that may be directed either at the social worker or the group as a whole. These include (1) denial (or simply "forgetting" that the group is ending, (2) **clustering**, moving toward more connection rather than less, (3) **regression**—either claiming verbally, or acting out in behavioral terms, that the group is not ready to end, (4) withdrawal or passivity related to active participation, (5) rebellion, or (6) flight—leaving the group before it ends (Furman et al., 2009; Reid, 1997).

The responses to ending are similar to those that occur in intervening with individuals and families. The fact that they may be multiplied by the number of people in the group can make them feel quite momentous to you as the social worker. For example, when an entire collective of 13-year-old girls makes it clear, through sudden and orchestrated hostility to you, that they do not want the experience to end, you can certainly feel the power of the group. In this case, just as in individual or family work, you can view the group's reaction as a function of the process (and perhaps of the success of the group), rather than focused personal assault.

Social worker skills that are particularly useful in ending work with groups include (Middleman & Wood, 1990):

- *Thinking group:* As always, in group work, this skill keeps the social worker focused on the processes of the entire group and the priority of its development as an entity rather than on individual members.

- *Summarizing:* Completing a review of group decisions and actions is a useful strategy for ending group work as achievements can be clarified and noted.

- *Voicing group achievements:* The social worker and group members can acknowledge the group's successes and validate the members' hard work.

- *Preserving group history and continuity:* This skill involves emphasizing the entity of the group in its social location and linking its history to the members' futures. In the process of ending, the social worker can focus on the group's continuity as translation to the world outside of the group.

Ending the Relationships among Group Members   In this aspect of ending, members may exhibit individualized versions of denial or flight as well as variations of these. Some members may not attend meetings that are specifically dedicated to ending activities. Others may attend but refuse to enter any group interactivity about endings, or they may simply resign themselves to rejection. Individuals may become increasingly short-tempered and impatient with specific other members, as if to negate the importance of their relationship and to render ending insignificant or even a relief. This behavior can occur among members who have worked the hardest at making connections with one other.

In other situations, individual members will question their ability to maintain the changes they have made without the assistance of the group and the social worker. These members will sometimes lobby for individual sessions with the worker or a reconstituted "mini group" in which only a few members of the original group would attend. In addition, some individuals may initiate more intense relationships with other group members outside the confines of the group meetings, as if to negate the need for the group. The most helpful thing you can do is articulate your observations regarding group dynamics. Staying focused on thinking group, rather than on the individuals, can be challenging, but it is part of negotiating a successful ending.

Ending the Group Itself This ending is at once philosophical and technical. On the philosophical level, reflect on your own feelings about ending this unit of work and this group of unique characters. How will it contribute to your professional growth? What could you have done differently? How will members benefit from it? If the group has been difficult, you may struggle with feelings of inadequacy or a sense of work left undone. When there is an overall sense of the group's having gone well, you may feel exhilarated by a sense of accomplishment, of having crossed a particular hurdle, or of entering into the realm of the skilled. When you consider a metaphor for your experience, would it be death? Divorce? Disengagement? A required course? Graduation?

On a much more practical side, you will need to close out the records of participation, complete the evaluation process (addressed shortly), and terminate the logistical arrangements such as space and place. Finally, you will need to honor follow-up commitments and ensure that any referrals or transfers are made successfully.

As an example of the issues that can arise when terminating with a group, consider the following group scenario:

A community-based agency that serves new immigrants offers a group for high school-aged students focused on the students' transitions from their country of origin to their newly adopted country. The group has a secondary purpose: providing an opportunity for the students to practice their English skills in a safe environment. The group composition is mixed gender and ethnicity. The social worker who is charged with facilitating this group has developed her cultural competency through her commitment to learn as much as she can about the students' heritage and traditions, language, the rules and norms for gender interactions, and faith traditions. She personally conducts an interview with each student who is referred to the group and her or his parents/family/guardians so she can be familiar with the individual student's needs and goals for joining the group.

The current group of students has developed into a cohesive group, particularly around the issues of being "Americanized" as they are enthusiastically adopting the customs of teens in their new country. The group members also share similar struggles with their parents who are distressed that their children are abandoning their heritages. The social worker has become aware of a potential dilemma. The time-limited group is scheduled to come to an end but the social worker has been approached by a number of the parents who have asked her to continue the group for the purpose of reconnecting the teens to their ethnic and cultural roots. While the teens enjoy the group, they have already planned their "graduation" celebration and appear ready to move on with life outside the group. The social worker is conflicted—she empathizes with the parents' concerns but believes the group should terminate as planned. What options or alternatives might the social worker consider in order to meet the needs of both groups?

In sum, endings can and should be a time for reflection and celebration. Equally important for all social workers in group practice, but particularly critical for those in the early stages of their career, is reviewing the group process as it has impacted your personal and professional growth. This exploration will now come to its own ending with a discussion of the process of evaluating the group intervention as experienced by the group members and the social worker.

Evaluation of Social Work Practice with Groups

Evaluation of social work practice with groups serves the same purpose as evaluating practice with individuals and families; that is, to examine the work, the process, and the social worker's skills. Specifically, an evaluation of a social work group intervention is aimed at reviewing the progress and reflecting on the process (Furman et al., 2009). While there are similarities in the evaluations of individual, family, and group interventions, there are also differences. Unlike family interventions that focus exclusively on the unit and individual intervention evaluations that focus solely on the individual, the evaluation of a group intervention encompasses both the individual and the group thus moving evaluation to a level of complexity not typically found with individual and family evaluations.

As noted previously, groups are comprised of a number of individuals who arrive at the group with individual goals, personalities, needs, and expectations. Oftentimes, evaluative strategies must be considered within the context of a large, diverse group of individuals who perceive their experience differently from one another. An evaluation of any group intervention must be framed within the context of the purpose, type, structure, and format of the group. To further heighten the complexity of group evaluation, the social worker must work within the agency or organizational structure in which the group is conducted. Having to address multiple needs with a group of individuals thus requires the social work group practitioner to have a clear and thoughtful approach to evaluation of the group intervention *prior* to the first meeting of the group.

Regardless of the method(s) used to evaluate the group intervention, it is important for all persons involved in the intervention to participate in the evaluative process (Garvin & Galinsky, 2008). An array of strategies is available for accomplishing the goals for this phase of the group intervention and will be highlighted here (Bloom, Fischer, & Orme, 2009; Furman et al., 2009; Garvin & Galinsky, 2008):

- Review individual and group member accomplishments within the group with an emphasis on preparing for the future, sustaining change, and ensuring the inclusion of support systems to reduce risk for failure.

- Gather group members' impressions of the group experience and the activities/programming. Data can be collected publically as part of the group process (within the group or written evaluations) or anonymously (in writing), using caution to avoid "satisfaction-only" surveys.

- Administer pre- and post-group measures of behaviors, attitudes, and function. Consider the use of previously validated and standardized measures that have been administered on groups comparable to the group intervention you are evaluating. Such measures will provide you with evidence-supported data from which to interpret your findings. While standardized measures of the individual are appropriate for use in group interventions, consider also the use of standardized measurements developed specifically for group interventions (e.g., Group Engagement Measure (Macgowan, 1997)).

- Through direct observation by the social worker, document behaviors and changes in individual group members and the group. Data can be gathered quantitatively and/or qualitatively.

- Complete a self-evaluation, including exploration into such areas as: meeting group member needs, development of appropriate structure and interventions, and assessment of own performance as a social work practitioner.

- Solicit direct observation and feedback by other professionals.

In addition to the type(s) of evaluative strategies for examining group interventions that are described here, consider utilizing the data that you gather and analyze to develop evaluation tools that can be used for future groups (Garvin & Galinsky, 2008). For example, you and other group facilitators may find it helpful to have a menu of strategies for monitoring group progress or a manual for conducting a group intervention.

In the practice of social work intervention, termination, and evaluation services with groups, the social worker will find that each group will develop its own personality, thus making each group experience unique. There are, however, aspects of each phase of the process that you will find are often replicated when you are providing leadership to a group. Recall from Chapter 8 the examination of the engagement and assessment phases of three group models (social goals/action, reciprocal, and remedial models) comprised of parents from the Riverton community. Returning to the Riverton example, Boxes 9.1, 9.2, and 9.3 depict the intervention, termination, and evaluation phases from the perspectives of the three models.

PHASES II and III: MIDDLE AND ENDING WORK

BOX 9.1

Riverton Against Youth Drinking ("RAYD"): An Example of Social Goals/ Action Group

Background: Concerned about the use and abuse of alcohol among their adolescent children, a group of parents in the Riverton community approach a local community service agency to ask for help in addressing this problem.

Work thus far: Stakeholders and their interests and goals have been identified. The social worker's role has been agreed upon. A community needs assessment has been conducted, including strengths, resources, needs, and priorities. A plan for intervention, termination, and evaluation has been established and will focus on developing and mounting a public education campaign to raise awareness about the issue of teen drinking.

Note: While the stages of group interventions are not linear and may, in fact, overlap, the following depicts a possible approach to responding to the identified need.

INTERVENTION	TERMINATION	EVALUATION
Identify community partners who will support the education campaign and help with dissemination	Terminate intervention	Conduct evaluation
		Analyze data gathered from evaluation effort
Confirm the plan, time frame, and resources for intervention, termination, and evaluation continue to be viable		Implement plan for sustainability
		Document findings
Launch the intervention Monitor progress, particularly dissemination and relationships with community partners		
Adapt the intervention, as needed		
Revisit plan for evaluation and sustainability		

BOX 9.2

Riverton Children's Grief Support Group: An Example of Reciprocal Group

PHASES II and III: MIDDLE AND ENDING WORK

Background: A social worker in a local community service agency has become aware of a number of children of Riverton who have lost a parent to alcohol and substance-related deaths. The social worker takes steps toward offering to the community a support group that includes to an educational focus.

Work thus far: Based on the social worker's assessment of community need and interest, group members were recruited, screened, and invited to join the group. A first session was planned and has been held, at which time group rules and norms were determined collaboratively by the social worker and the group members. Individual group goals and needs were shared. The social worker's role as a facilitator/educator was established.

Note: While the stages of group interventions are not linear and may, in fact, overlap, the following depicts a possible approach to responding to the identified need.

INTERVENTION	TERMINATION	EVALUATION
Social worker begins each session by reviewing group rules and norms and conducting member check-in	Begin termination as planned	*Individual* Determine if goals were met (informal or formal)
Social worker engages in ongoing assessment of individual member needs, group interactions, and group cohesiveness	Check in with each group member regarding feelings regarding the termination of the group and the process	Administer post-group collection of data
Social worker has developed a repertoire of agency and community resources available to suggest as needed	Invite each member to talk about individual gains and continuing needs	*Group* Determine if group goals were met (informal or formal)
Revisit group needs and adapt intervention and educational programming plans as appropriate	Discuss plans for sustaining change and any perceived obstacles to maintenance	Ask members to provide feedback regarding satisfaction with the group process
Share information, as agreed upon prior to group initiation, with legal guardians	Provide resources as needed to help members sustain change	Document findings
Monitor individual and group progress and adapt as needed	Conduct termination ritual or celebration	
Regularly revisit time frame and plans for termination and evaluation		
Invite suggestions from group members regarding plans for recognizing group termination		

PHASES II and III: MIDDLE AND ENDING WORK

Background: A new social worker at the Riverton Mental Health Center has recently assumed leadership for a clinical intervention group for persons with dual diagnoses (i.e., substance abuse and mental illness) who receive outpatient services at the agency. The group is diverse in membership, including mixed genders, range of ages, and mandated and voluntary members. Membership turnover is dependent on members' "graduation" from the treatment program; therefore, the group often has entering and exiting members. Two new members have been referred to the group. This will be the first time new members have been referred since the social worker took over responsibility for the group.

Work thus far: The social worker has gathered information on eligibility criteria for group membership and integrating new members into an ongoing group. The social worker has met with the two persons who have been referred and determined they would be appropriate for inclusion. The two members have been oriented and attended their first meeting. During this session, the social worker introduced the new members to the group, revisited group rules and norms, and assessed the individual goals and needs and group cohesion.

Note: While the stages of group interventions are not linear and may, in fact, overlap, the following depicts a possible approach to responding to the identified need.

INTERVENTION	TERMINATION	EVALUATION
At the beginning of each session, social worker reminds members of group rules and norms	Ongoing as membership is open	Complete formal evaluation as required by agency
Social worker conducts check in by asking members to share with the group the events/actions since the last session	Determine termination ritual appropriate to an open-ended group	Obtain information from existing members regarding achievement of goals and experiences with group format and process (e.g., open vs. closed and time-limited format) and social worker leadership
Social worker assesses individual member needs and goals, and monitors progress towards goals (critical as each person may potentially be at a different point in their progress)	Prepare existing and remaining members for termination	
	Check in with members regarding their feelings about termination	Document findings
Social worker assesses group cohesion		
Members with longer membership serve as guides/mentors for newer members		

STRAIGHT TALK ABOUT GROUP INTERVENTION, TERMINATION, AND EVALUATION

The social worker's overall role and purpose in social work practice with groups is to encourage and release the strengths of the group. The concern for individual well-being and growth is augmented by the social factors of the group, one member to another. Consistent with trusting the group process, the social worker should strive to avoid overinvestment in the centrality or power that may attribute to her or his role. The goal, after all, is for the group to gain its voice and develop its strength, even as individual members continue to grow. You will not be able to take credit, even in your own mind, for all of the potential successes in your group. In exchange, you will have the privilege of experiencing and respecting the power of group connection and the autonomy it ultimately can exercise as it liberates the power of its members.

The emphasis on the group does not mean that your own role in the group's functioning and outcome is any less important. You are responsible for the safety of each member in the group and for ensuring the group processes its own activity. Accordingly, your role is to evaluate group process and functioning on an ongoing basis, just as you do in other forms of social work practice interventions. This will vary according to the nature of your group purpose, goals, and format. For example, if you are working in a task group, monitoring progress in completing the group's project will be the focus of the intervention and evaluation processes. If you facilitate a group for school-aged children, attention must be given to assure that an appropriate developmental level is used. Other forms of evaluation that are especially useful come from members: Is the group meeting their social and affiliation needs? Do they continue to feel safe in it? Is it a helpful forum to address the issues they want to deal with? As always, consider the work of evaluation as an ongoing process.

CONCLUSION

In emphasizing the importance of relational components in our lives, first as people and then as social work practitioners, this chapter has presented social work practice with groups in the role of mediating a range of social and emotional issues, including isolation, oppression, and life crises. Currently there are many exciting adventures into social work practice with groups that build upon contemporary theoretical perspectives, social justice, and diversity. Scenarios relating to cultural inclusion, gender and disability, collaboration, and spirituality in models that emphasize process over stages and story over problem all point to the empowering direction that social group work is taking in the history of the profession. Social work practice with groups offers significant potential for the future and is particularly relevant for the social justice, diversity, and human rights connections that give social work its meaning.

MAIN POINTS

- Effective social work practice interventions with groups provide an interface for social justice, diversity, and human rights.

- Middle-phase (intervention) and ending phase (termination) strategies were approached from the perspectives of strengths and empowerment, narrative- and solution-focused approaches.

- Developmental models, such as the Boston Model and others based on it, have provided a widely used theoretical perspective on group development. Many applications of, and departures from, this model can be found in the contemporary practice environment.

- Social workers working with groups hone their skills for intervening with individuals and must develop some additional skills for group intervention in the areas of group leadership, community, problem-solving, and management of group functioning.

- Contemporary examples of innovative, evidence-based group practice models, such as constructionist groups and restorative justice groups, help to provide vision and possibility for responding to current cultural and social issues as they unfold.

- Termination occurs in three distinct areas of group practice interventions: between the group members and the social worker, among the group members, and the group itself.

- While evaluation of group practice shares some commonalities with evaluation of individual and family interventions, evaluating group interventions is more complex as examination of the individual members of the group and the group itself is both required.

EXERCISES

1. Go to www.routledgesw.com/cases and review Carla Washburn's video vignette and consider the roles each member plays for the following activities and questions:
   a. Gather into groups. Starting the group session from the conclusion of the video vignette, role-play the next session. What happens next? Process the group session with the class.

    b. Round robin: Each student takes the opportunity to role-play the social worker. Change roles when the "social worker" is not sure how to proceed with the group. Debrief about the experiences and practice behaviors demonstrated for each role-play. What were strengths and areas for growth for each student as a facilitator?

    c. Select a member of the group and discuss her or his role in the group process.

    d. Identify the social worker's strengths as a group facilitator along with those practice behaviors that may be improved.

2. Termination of a group intervention can be challenging. Returning to the grief support group depicted in the Carla Washburn video vignette, role-play the final session. Consider the following:

    a. What is the most important role the social worker plays at this stage of the group process?

    b. What practice behaviors are critical for the termination phase of a group intervention?

    c. Brainstorm strategies for responding to the array of possible member reactions to the ending of the group experience.

3. At the conclusion of a group intervention, the evaluation of the effectiveness of your interventions is critical. Research various evaluation tools and complete the following for the grief support group in which Carla Washburn is a member:

    a. Create a satisfaction survey.

    b. Create a pre-test/post-test.

    c. Create a six-month evaluation tool.

4. Go to www.routledgesw.com/cases and view the Riverton video vignette that depicts a group meeting of the Riverton Neighborhood Association. Upon viewing the video, respond to the following:

    a. What model of group intervention is being conducted in this vignette?

    b. Identify practice behaviors and skills covered in this chapter that the group facilitator is demonstrating in the meeting.

    c. Compare and contrast group facilitation skills needed for a group such as the Riverton Neighborhood Association and a client-focused group.

Social Work Practice with Communities: Engagement and Assessment

Change will not come if we wait for some other person or some other time. We are the ones we've been waiting for. We are the change that we seek.

Barack Obama, Feb. 5, 2008

Key Questions for Chapter 10

(1) What competencies do I need to engage and assess communities? (EPAS 2.1.10(a & b))

(2) What are the social work practice behaviors that enable me to effectively engage and assess communities? (EPAS 2.1.10(a & b))

(3) How can I utilize evidence to practice research-informed practice and practice-informed research to guide the engagement and assessment with communities? (EPAS 2.1.6)

(4) How can I apply critical thinking to engagement and assessment with communities? (EPAS 2.1.3)

(5) How can I apply social work values and ethics to community engagement and assessment? (EPAS 2.1.2)

COMMUNITY PROVIDES THE PLACE IN WHICH PEOPLE FIND identity and meaning for their lives in their various roles as individuals, parents, children, partners, friends, and professionals. **Community** is the structure, both tangible and metaphoric, that supports interaction and connectedness among people over time. The characteristic of the community in which people grow, live, and develop can have important implications for the resources and opportunities available to the individuals who inhabit the community. Communities are the central context of social work practice with all types of client systems; therefore, community practice is an important aspect of generalist social work practice.

This chapter examines the concept of community and your relationship to it as a practitioner. This chapter will explore the types of community and function through which community is given meaning, and consider methods of inquiry into its study, including community analysis, community needs assessment, and community asset mapping. Finally, the need for and avenues to a global perspective is considered.

FAMILIAR PERSPECTIVES AND SOME ALTERNATIVES

Contemporary research and literature about community often discuss the loss of community in U.S. society (Putnam, 2000). There are many forces working against connections within communities located in a specific place, to include technology that allows individuals to share interests and build bonds with people all over the globe, and the individualistic character of U.S. culture, which provides less social reinforcement for community involvement than in other cultures. Globalization is a force that may also work against developing strong place-based community connections, as corporations and financial capital shift quickly from place to place to find the most profitable locations for business, and workers move to places to find optimal employment opportunities. The human service system has reflected the societal value of individualism in its emphasis on the individual and family and the perpetual pursuit of self-fulfillment. The inclusion of encouraging individual and family clients to build and invest in local communities within human services is yet under-developed.

Although individuals are influenced by many forces that facilitate individualism, the power of community forces, such as education, housing, health, amenities such as recreational opportunities, local businesses, and employment opportunities are important to community residents. Local relationships, experiences, resources, and opportunities continue to play an important role in the daily lives of people, and local residents invest time, energy, and resources into creating community resources and opportunities that will positively impact their quality of life. For example, local residents and business owners work hard to maintain and increase property values and decrease crime in their neighborhood. Similarly, residents will strive to prevent the location of hazardous environmental materials in their neighborhood, and to garner resources to increase the quality of public education in their community. Clearly, there are challenges, issues, and incentives for residents to take action on behalf of a community. The idea of **interdependence**—the idea that individuals are dependent on one another—resonates in practice models with individuals, families, and groups that emphasize health and recovery based on both professional and peer support.

Community Practice and Generalist Practice

Promoting community involvement is important for social workers who primarily work at the community level, as well as for those who work at the individual, family, and group level. Communities play a critical role in clients' lives because communities comprise the environment within which individuals live their lives, and are the formal conduit through which resources, formal and informal systems, and political, social, and economic forces shape individuals, families, and neighborhoods. Communities therefore shape experiences and influence the ability of social workers to affect the outcomes of their work with client systems. Even when social workers never go outside of the traditional one-to-one social work relationship, the success of their efforts depends in large part on the nature and responsiveness of the clients' communities. For example, a client who is young and low-income with two children seeking shelter is impacted by the community's overall capacity to provide decent, affordable housing for single persons who receive public assistance. If this client seeks your assistance to locate housing, you need knowledge of the resources for shelter, transitional housing, and low-income housing available in her community, as well as resources to combat discrimination if the client suspects that she is denied housing illegally (such as rental housing that is not available to her because the landlord will not rent to single mothers with children who receive public assistance). Other considerations about her housing choices may include other resources, such as employment, schools, child care, the quality and quantity of after-school programs, and the existence of a community center, as well as dangers in the community, to include the rate of crime, presence of former partners that pose safety concerns and presence of specific gangs in the area. To practice competently, social workers need knowledge of community resources, as well as skills to address challenges related to such resources, the entity(ies) that make(s) decisions about resources, the individuals or bodies that possess decision-making power about resources and ways to advocate for resources for clients. Social workers also need knowledge about the various dimensions of a community to be an effective catalyst to change communities. Skills working with individuals, groups, families, and organizations are vital to community practice, and skills working with communities are important to every other type of client system.

Working with communities includes mastery of a wide variety of social work competencies and practice behaviors (CSWE, 2008). For example, social workers must be able to respond to the contexts that shape practice (EPAS 2.1.9) by being proactive and engaging in community work that will seek to prevent problems and unnecessary challenges from occurring. As in work with other client systems, social workers also utilize ethical principles (EPAS 2.1.2), critical thinking (EPAS 2.1.3), and practice culturally competent practice (EPAS 2.1.4) in community practice. A major outcome of community practice is the advancement of human rights and economic justice (EPAS 2.1.5), the use of research-informed practice (EPAS 2.1.6) and the use of evidence-based practice. Lastly, the use of the change process (i.e., engagement, assessment, intervention, termination, and evaluation) is utilized in practice with all types of clients, including community. This chapter will explore many of these competencies, and discuss the practice behaviors associated with them. To begin, types of communities, the nature of community functions and ways to understand a community are discussed. These topics assist with mastery of the competencies related to responding to contexts that shape practice (EPAS 2.1.9), and critical thinking (EPAS 2.1.3).

DEFINITIONS AND TYPES OF COMMUNITY

Several types of community are discussed in the social work literature. This section describes three types that are often described: communities of locality, communities of identity, and personal communities (Fellin, 2000).

Communities of Locality

Communities can be understood as geographic entities, such as a town, city, small neighborhood, or college dormitory. **Communities of locality** are structures of connectedness based on a physical location. Communities of locality may have clear, physical boundaries, such as a river, mountain, gate, or wall, or a legally defined boundary, while other communities of locality may only have boundaries that are agreed upon by **stakeholders**, or those who have an interest in community affairs, such as neighborhood leaders. These boundaries may provide safety and security for community members, but may also be experienced as a means of exclusivity for others. The degree to which community residents perceive themselves as community members will depend on many dimensions, but access to the community's benefits is among the most influential. Those residents of a community who do not access community benefits, such as a community center, the public library, and other resources, may not feel personally affiliated with their community of residence. Large communities of locality, such as New York, are likely to have many communities within the larger community. Communities of locality of all sizes can be diverse: For example, Jackson Heights New York, with 175,000 residents in the borough of Queens, is one of the most diverse communities in the U.S., with 138 languages spoken in the community (Samways, 2008).

Communities of Identity

Groups that share a common interest, concern, or identity share a similar sense of belonging, and can also be considered a community. **Communities of identity** relate more to affiliations than a location, such as a student community, an Asian community, a lesbian community, a veterans' community, or a skateboard community. As in communities of locality, people will differ on the meaning of and extent of affiliation with a community of identity and their affiliation with a particular type of community of identity may change over time. For example, the Jewish community may play a significant role for a lifetime for some, and have less significance for others throughout their lives. In another example, the community of those who skateboard may be very important for several years, and fade in importance after adolescence. Some social workers have a particular interest in specific communities of identity for their entire careers, such as women who experience intimate partner violence. Social workers may develop interest in a particular community of identity based on their personal experiences, or early professional experiences. People can find a powerful sense of connection and commitment in their community of identity.

Personal Communities

Many persons are part of more than one type of community. For example, you may have affiliation with the community in which you live, a worship community, an online community of gamers, a community of yoga teachers, your dorm, and the community of undergraduate students. A **personal community** consists of a collection of both locality and identity communities, and often serves to provide meaning to one's identity. These unique arrangements of place and non-place communities are networks within which one interacts, and serve to integrate personal and professional lives. Social workers may be interested in the personal community of the clients they serve because personal communities provide socialization and resources, such as helping networks (formal and informal), that may be helpful for clients facing a crisis or challenges. Personal communities can also provide cross-cultural dimensions that aid in a wider world view.

COMMUNITY FUNCTIONS

A traditional view of community includes the idea that community performs certain necessary functions for its residents or members, including the following (Streeter, 2008; Warren, 1978):

- Production, distribution, and consumption of goods and services. This may include the basic needs of food, clothing, shelter, medical care, and employment. People must also have adequate wages to access the goods and services.

- Transmission of knowledge, social values, customs, and behavior patterns of residents or members. This socialization process guides the perceptions and attitudes of residents about their view of themselves, others, and their rights and responsibilities. Both formal institutions, such as schools and faith communities, as well as informal institutions, such as friends and peer groups, can be involved in this function.

- Social control to maintain conformity to community norms. Laws, rules, and regulations, enforced by formal governmental entities such as police and court systems, as well as informal systems of enforcement, such as schools, families, peers, and organized neighborhood watch, serve to reinforce community standards. Patterns of service provision that regulate access to resources, (e.g., eligibility guidelines for local food pantries), also serve as a mechanism of social control.

- Social participation through formal and informal groups. Interaction with others through groups, associations, and organizations provides social outlets, and the way to build natural helping and support networks. People are engaged in social participation when they are involved in sports leagues, volunteer, vote, attend Parent Teacher Association (PTA) meetings and attend local music festivals.

- Mutual support. Families, friends, neighbors, and volunteers provide aid and support one another, and assist individuals and families to solve problems independent of professionals. Due to the complexity of modern society, this function is often supplemented by the work of human service professionals, such as social workers.

UNDERSTANDING A COMMUNITY

Given the complex nature of communities, possessing an understanding of the many ways that a community can be understood and examined is imperative for moving into the change process of engagement, assessment, intervention, and termination and evaluation. We will examine communities as a social system, an ecological system, as a center for power and conflict, and from two contemporary perspectives: strengths, empowerment and resiliency, and postmodern.

Community as a Social System

Communities can be viewed as a social system through the lens of general systems theory. General systems theory offers a helpful framework with which to analyze and understand communities. General systems theory posits that a system, such as a community, is composed of multiple intersecting components that relate to one other, and are also part of larger systems, such as a larger community. Communities are part of subsystems that perform specialized functions for the larger system, or community as a whole. Through community assessments (discussed below), social workers can critically assess the extent to which subsystems, such as the function of mutual support, or the business subsystem within a community, meet the needs of the community, and advocate for a higher level of functioning of a subsystem, if needed (Netting, Kettner, & McMurtry, 2008; Streeter, 2008).

Community as an Ecological System

Viewing community from the ecosystems perspective emphasizes the interdependence of people and their environment in our understanding of communities. The spatial organization of community resources, the relationship of these resources to one another and to groups of people, and the corresponding social and economic consequences is a meaningful view of community. For example, the physical feature of a major road or highway bisecting a community can have implications for the social organization and economics of the community. The physical aspect of a major road bisecting a community can result in some businesses with many customers, and some businesses going out of business because of few customers. The social organization implications of the road can include the ways in which individuals and groups interact (or do not interact) with one other. Other concepts related to the ecosystems perspective that may be helpful include the topic of competition, which may occur between communities for resources, or within a community between groups. For example, competition for land is common in many communities, as some groups want to develop land for residences and businesses, others would like to keep land available for the public uses of parks, community centers and hiking trails, while others may advocate for keeping land devoted to family-based agriculture. The dominance of communities (i.e., political or economic) over one another or of one group over another within a community often results in differential access to resources, and has consequences for the dynamics of social interaction within a community. Dominance of a group can translate to access to better schools, employment, health care facilities, and public services such as police and fire protection. The ecological system perspective can help in understanding a hierarchical, uneven power structure of a community. Other related concepts of segregation (i.e., the isolation of groups within a community), centralization (i.e., concentration of resources in one part of a community), and succession (i.e., the movement of groups of people into and out of areas of a community) also aid in analyzing communities (Netting et al., 2008; Streeter, 2008). These concepts help to analyze and explain the ways in which populations move and settle in various areas of communities, and resource availability in areas of communities.

Center for Power and Conflict

Communities are settings in which political and social dynamics and conflict are powerful forces. Opportunities and constraints for community members are often significantly impacted by power. Often, the interests of one segment of a community clash with the interests of another segment, and a struggle can emerge (Streeter, 2008).

Three distinct theories assist in our understanding of the community as a setting for power and conflict. They are described here (Hardina, 2002):

Power Dependency Theory This theory focuses on the dynamics associated with dependent relationships of communities to their sources of resources. Communities may be dependent on external forces that provide needed resources, which can dramatically affect the dynamics of the communities. For example, community dependency on a funder with close ties to a large retail chain may influence their decisions about promoting small, locally-owned businesses in the community.

Conflict Theory Using this theory, social workers view the community as divided into influential and non-influential groups that compete for limited resources. Other important assumptions of this theory include the assumption that the influential group has power over the non-influential group, and that dimensions of diversity play a central role in oppression.

Resource Mobilization Theory This theory aids in understanding the conditions needed to promote change in community practice. Large scale community change can more easily occur when groups that are excluded from a decision making process, create a collective identity, and protest their exclusion as a group. Groups also need to create an appealing message to attract people to join the group, and create an inclusive structure.

Taken together, these theories inform the social work profession's thinking about the community as a setting in which power and control are forces to be recognized. Groups within a community vie for power and control to implement change that will benefit their interests, even if the change may oppress others within the community. This perspective can aid social workers in understanding that change can occur within communities from rational planning and collaborative efforts, as well as from confrontation, efforts to build power, and negotiation. Dimensions of diversity, such as race, socio-economic status, and ethnicity, as well as the factor of interests, such as area of the community, residential or business, and other interests, can be driving factors in community conflicts. Viewing the community as a center for power and conflict can help social workers assess the community power structure, understand the reasons and the process for community decision-making, and their roles in community processes. Social workers may also use this lens to learn more about ways in which marginalized groups are oppressed in communities, as well as the ways in which power is maintained by powerful forces in communities (Netting et al., 2008; Streeter, 2008).

Contemporary Perspectives for Community Practice

In this section, two contemporary perspectives in understanding and assessing communities will be discussed. The strengths, empowerment and resiliency perspectives will be examined, as will the postmodern perspectives.

Strengths, Empowerment, and Resiliency Perspectives   As previously mentioned, the strengths perspective, originally presented by Dennis Saleebey (2009) focuses on identifying possibilities and assets of individuals and communities, rather than deficits and problems. The application of the strengths perspective to communities that have few resources can be challenging. Identifying strengths in such communities can lead to empowerment, or assisting communities to recognize the resources they possess and help to develop power to effect change. The recognition of resources can lead to resiliency, or the potential of problem-solving. For example, communities with large plots of vacant land and boarded up homes may be challenged to think about the land and homes as valuable, with the potential use of the land for community gardens, greenhouses for small businesses, or other uses. Community strengths also include the skills and talents of the residents. Later in this chapter, community asset mapping, a tool to use in community assessment, will be discussed as a means to implement the strengths, empowerment and resiliency perspectives (Netting et al., 2008; Ohmer & DeMasi, 2009; Pennell, Noponen, & Weil, 2005).

Community in a Postmodern Perspective   The postmodern perspective assumes that knowledge is socially constructed, and multiple "truths" exist, depending on the perspective taken. Postmodern approaches, including social construction and critical social construction approaches, invite examination of the cultural assumptions that underlie many of the arrangements of power and politics, and these approaches tend to be critical of assumptions or theories that claim absolute or authoritative truth. Social workers using this perspective are interested in the assumptions and explanations about the current state of affairs and causes of perceived problems in the community, as well as examining situations from multiple perspectives. For example, social workers, using the postmodern perspective, would be interested in learning about different perspectives and assumptions surrounding the presence of undocumented immigrants in a community to learn about the various viewpoints. Also of interest are cultural symbols and norms that are being used in a community, such as the ways in which the social structures of specific populations are organized, and the cultural symbols used to signify the structure (Reed, 2008).

The traditional and contemporary perspectives on community aid in understanding communities as setting in which different lenses can be used to understand the dynamics and decision-making processes in communities. The perspectives also help us to understand the sources of and barriers to change in ways that inform engagement, assessment, intervention, and termination and evaluation with communities. Next discussed are the skills for engagement and assessment, to include comprehensive community-based analysis, community needs assessment, and community-based participatory research. Also discussed in this next section are the trends that impact these stages of the helping process.

ENGAGEMENT AND ASSESSMENT OF COMMUNITIES

Engagement of Communities

Engagement, the first step in the change process, occurs through myriad ways with communities. When working with individuals, families, groups, and organizations in communities, many of the skills of engagement and assessment discussed in previous chapters are helpful. The active listening skills, among others, are as useful in working in community practice as they are with individuals, families, and groups and organizations. Engagement with community work involves working with all other client systems, on behalf of entire communities.

Social workers begin to work with communities through involvement in challenges and opportunities as the primary focus. For example, social workers may work for such community-based services as an education program attached to a local public school, and discover the lack of available employment for community residents. Alternatively, social workers employed by a local or state correctional system may learn about a grant opportunity to prevent juvenile crime, and engage the local community to plan and write a grant to benefit the local community. Social workers may also engage in community practice through their work with a **population**. A social worker in a care facility for older adults may learn about the lack of respite services available for family care providers. The social worker may help the care providers organize themselves to approach a potential funder, such as local, state, or federal legislators, or local foundation, to advocate for funding for respite care. Lastly, social workers also engage with communities based primarily on **setting**. For example, a social worker who is employed by an elementary school may learn about hazardous waste materials being dumped into a neighborhood, endangering the health of the children of the community. The social worker may work to engage local leaders of the community to conduct community-wide meetings and/or communicate with the appropriate decision-makers and work toward a resolution to protect the health of the children. There are many ways that social workers become engaged with communities, either formally through employment or a volunteer role at the community level, or by involvement through a challenge/opportunity, population or setting about which they learned through their primary professional roles with micro or mezzo client systems (Netting et al., 2008).

Assessment Process

The assessment process often occurs simultaneous to the engagement process, and can consist of several different types of techniques. The following discussion will explore comprehensive community-based analysis and a community needs assessment as two community assessment techniques. Community asset mapping will also be discussed as a strengths-based technique of community assessment.

Comprehensive Community-Based Analysis

Social workers in a variety of settings and with a range of job descriptions need an understanding of the overall community in which they serve client systems, as well as an understanding of the population of a community and the primary challenges faced by a community. Understanding communities involves learning about aspects and functioning of a community. Developing an accurate knowledge base about a community can lead to more effective assessments and interventions with individuals, groups, families, organizations, and communities. An overall understanding of a community includes learning about the following major community domains (Chaskin, Venkatsh, Vidal, & Brown, 2001; Sherraden, 1993):

Physical Setting   The physical setting of a community includes the geography (e.g., presence of water or flat or hilly land), main geographical boundaries and natural barriers, and the degree to which communities are integrated or isolated from surrounding neighborhoods. For example, is the community near a downtown area? Do the streets dead-end or go through to other communities?

History   The history of a community includes the identity of the population(s) that originally settled the community, time period of settlement and the major historical events that shaped the community. Additionally, you might also consider the ways in which the architecture and layout of the community reflects early inhabitants, and whether the community history impacts the current dynamics of community functioning.

Demographics of the Population   Knowledge about the current population of the community, as well as the well-defined and informal subpopulations with distinct cultures within the community, is very important.

Economic System   The economic system includes employment for community residents, types, number and industry of community large businesses, the presence of small, locally owned businesses, the presence of stores that residents can utilize for their basic needs, such as grocery stores and co-ops, farmer's markets, clothing stores, and hardware stores, the rate of employment in the community and type of transportation available to community residents.

Political System   An awareness of the political system provides helpful information about key decision-makers within and for the community. Learning about all types of elected officials with decision-making authority about the community will help to obtain a more complete understanding of the community. Also seek information about the level of political activity (for example, by looking for bumper stickers and yard signs). Additionally, information about the degree to which the business community is organized into a business association and involved in politics is also helpful information. You also might inquire about the degree to which human service systems are involved in the local political system?

Social Characteristics   Questions to consider regarding the social characteristics include: What are the characteristics of residents in terms of social class, race, ethnicity, age, and other dimensions of diversity? Is the community known as friendly or unfriendly to new residents and visitors? Are there many places of worship? What size are the congregations and which denominations are present? Are there formal or informal meeting places besides places of worship (i.e., coffee shops, meeting halls, clubs, associations, etc.?) What is the condition of the parks or recreational areas? What are the housing conditions of the neighborhood in terms of upkeep, quality, and the proportion of rental versus family owned? Does it vary by section? Is housing for sale? Is the for-sale housing dispersed or clustered? Is there evidence of construction and home repair? Are there strong institutions in the community related to social needs?

Human Service System   The human service system includes education and human services of all types. Questions to consider include the following: What kinds of public and private schools are located in the community? What is their educational quality, physical condition, and funding sources? What kinds of voluntary agencies are located in the community? How available are services to residents? How well organized are the organizations within the community? Are there strong or weak networks among the professionals in the community? Are external resources brought into the community and distributed to residents?

Values, Beliefs, Traditions   While observing and building relationships to learn about values, beliefs, and traditions, consider the following questions: What do community residents value? Are there differences based on race, ethnicity, and sections of the community or another dimension of diversity? Do members of the community celebrate specific traditions that may be unique to that community, or to a sub-population of the community?

Evidence of Oppression and Discrimination   Using a social justice perspective to learn about communities requires a concern with oppression and discrimination within the community, and/or from other communities. Questions to consider include: Is there a history of oppression and discrimination in the community (such as separate recreational facilities, housing patterns that suggest discrimination, and/ or school enrollment and quality patterns that suggest discrimination)? Are there current patterns of discrimination and oppression?

Learning about these aspects of a particular community will assist you to discover its unique characteristics, including strengths, challenges, history, and concerns of the residents. The answers to these questions could be utilized by creating a formal document for an organization or community, or could be utilized informally. The methods by which you can learn about the overall functioning of a community are similar to the methods of a needs assessment, which are discussed in the following section.

Another way to study a community is to narrow the focus to a particular community of identity or population and to assess the degree to which the social services system meets their needs. This process, called a **needs assessment**, is sharply focused to consider the gap between needs and resources, informs the planning process for specific social work community interventions, and can be considered more practical than comprehensive studies. Ideally, gaining overall knowledge about a community through a community analysis and gaining more focused knowledge through a needs assessment are integrated processes, rather than constituting an either/or choice.

Community Needs Assessment

Many social workers begin to learn about a community through the focus of the predominant population they are serving, or because of a specific community challenge faced in social work service delivery, such as poor quality housing, gangs, or truancy. A needs assessment is a formal process for identifying unmet community needs, placing needs in order of priorities and planning to target resources to solve problems. The overall process of a community needs assessment can be compared to a research project. As with a research project, the purpose of a needs assessment may be shaped by the goals of the sponsor of the study. For example, a social service organization may want more information about the needs of the older adult population in a community, but may not be as interested as you are, as a researcher, in examining the growing lesbian-gay-bisexual-transgender (LGBT) older adult population. This difference of interest may require a negotiation about the needs assessment process, tools, data sources, and reporting. Regardless of the sponsor, the needs assessment should be conducted using six recommended steps, which are to (1) review the evidence; (2) assess local knowledge; (3) select study methods; (4) conduct the study; (5) process and study the data; and (6) report the findings (Mulroy, 2008, p. 386). The research process should be guided by the principles of evidence-based practice, as discussed here.

Using Evidence-Based Practice in Community Practice   Using the steps of **evidence-based practice**, social workers begin with a review of the relevant research literature about similar communities and theories of change to guide the development of the design of the needs assessment. The next step is to clarify the unit of analysis for the study, whether that is a specific population, a geographic area or a particular challenge, such as homelessness, or a combination of units. Consultation with community members and other interested parties, and the sponsor, about the current evidence, local knowledge, research design, study methods, analysis, and the structure of the report can help to achieve the highest quality needs assessment (Mulroy, 2008).

Research methods used for a comprehensive community analysis can also be used for a comprehensive needs assessment or a needs assessment that is focused on a particular population or challenge. An understanding of each of these approaches can inform the determination of the most appropriate method(s) for a particular situation through engaging in evidence-based practice. Methods of gathering data about a community discussed below include observation, use of **census** and administrative data, interviews with key informants, focus groups, community forums, and survey data (Chow & Crowe, 2005; Royse, Staton-Tindall, Badger, & Webster, 2009). The use of maps to visually display data and community asset mapping are also discussed.

Community Needs Assessment Process   Social workers are involved in community needs assessments for a variety of reasons, to include seeking new resources and support for a program, targeting a program to best meet community needs, or simply getting to know the community to better serve individuals, families, and groups. Funders considering a request for program funding will often require justification for the proposed program or services, which may include demonstration of community need. A community assessment may also be used to modify policy, such as in a situation where an organization, due to increased demand, was considering changing their eligibility policy for their food pantry to the population with the highest unmet need, be that women with children, runaway youth, or women who have experienced intimate partner violence. Organizations may wish to improve services to a particular group of clients, and undertake a needs assessment to learn about, for example, the unmet needs for single men in the community. Finally, social workers may also be involved in a needs assessment to establish or strengthen partnerships. For instance, a homeless shelter may be encountering children on an increasing basis who are medically fragile. The staff of an organization may conduct a community needs assessment to collect the data about the health needs of homeless and near-homeless children, to have the information needed to approach local health providers to develop a service partnership.

There are many potential sources of data, either primary or secondary, or quantitative or qualitative, for a community needs assessment. Discussed next are the following kids of data: observation, service statistics and previous studies, census data, administrative data, other data, interview, focus groups community forums, and survey data. Several of them, as well as guidelines for making decisions about methods, are discussed below (Mulroy, 2008; Netting et al., 2008; North Central Regional Center for Rural Development, Iowa State University, n.d.).

Sources of Data

Observation   The purpose of observation is to collect information about the community processes and events as they occur. Communities can be observed as a nonparticipant, where the observer simply witnesses, but does not engage in events, and as a participant in activities. Observation can be achieved through physically walking around and/or attending events within the community, to include the city hall, coffee shops, community centers, busy parks, commercial strips, fairs and markets, and schools. Data gathered through this method includes notes about observations, items in local newspapers, pamphlets that describe community resources, local maps, local directories, and historical markers. Observers also attend popular community events, such as free concerts, plays and/or political rallies to notice aspects of community life, such as ethnic composition, geographical divisions, and apparent patterns of community life. For example, an observer may detect the presence or absence of late-night street activity, the number of older adults visible in a community, the number of children playing outside during school hours, and the number of young people hanging out on the streets during the day.

Participant Observation   occurs when an observer joins in community events and interacts with local residents. For example, a participant observer could eat at local establishments and interact with patrons and staff, while remaining in a learning mode by asking questions. During the interaction, a participant observer takes the perspective of a respectful learner and avoids taking the stance of an expert or a change agent. Other aspects to notice include interpersonal relationships, patterns and styles of residents relating to one another, and relationship of residents to the space in the community.

Service Statistics and Previous Studies   Data from local human service organizations may be helpful for the needs assessment. Such data can include rate of utilization of services, types of services provided, waiting list information, and case-load data, as well as data from other types of organizations (such as businesses, faith communities, neighborhood groups, youth organizations, and others). This information may be available through a variety of sources, such as annual reports issued by organizations, public data available on the internet from organizations or community collaborations, through a contact person at an organization, or from an elected official who represents the community or an appointed official. Similarly, previous studies about the origins of community problems may be helpful, such as studies from the public health department or community organizations.

Use of Census Data   The U.S. Census Bureau conducts a national **census** every 10 years, and gathers extensive demographic information about people living throughout the nation. The Census Bureau also collects some data annually through the American Community Survey from a sample of residents. Census data can be accessed through a variety of databases and websites, some of which are very user friendly, and can be accessed at small geographic levels within broader communities.

Administrative Data   is data publically available through school districts, public assistance offices, child welfare offices, public health agencies, and police departments. Administrative data can be helpful in understanding community issues concerning a wide variety of issues, to include local academic performance, truancy, child abuse, rate and prevalence of sexually transmitted disease, teen pregnancy, crime, and other issues. These data are typically available at the zip code level, and may be **social indicator** data, or serve as a proxy for other kinds of information, such as the number of young people who drop out of high school because of the demands of parenting, that is not directly collected by any institution or organization.

Other Data   may include data available from human service organizations about their clients served, and/or community-level data on populations or issues. These data may be publically available, or could be made available on request to social workers. These organizations may collect data to ensure that their services are meeting the community needs that are the highest priority, or due to funder requirements. The data may be collected community-wide, or may just be a sample. See Box 10.1 for ideas for sources of census and administrative data.

Mapping of Data   The use of geographic information systems (GIS) technologies is enhancing the usefulness of data that is attached to a specific geographic location. Using GIS, census, and other types of data may be visually mapped to combine relevant data onto one map. GIS is computer technology that utilizes **geocoding** of data that are mapped spatially, and allows researchers to identify spatial patterns among challenges and resources (Chow & Crowe, 2005). For example, as Exhibit 10.1 demonstrates, mapping both probable subprime loans and foreclosures on the same map can add to the depth and complexity of a needs analysis, and provide even more useful data. This map can inform a discussion of a local task force working on foreclosure prevention about the possible relationship of subprime home mortgage loans and the rate of foreclosure in St. Louis City Missouri. GIS also offers the possibility of adding more layers of data, such as race and ethnicity to this map, so that a possible relationship of race, subprime home mortgage loan, and foreclosure could also be studied.

BOX 10.1

Sample of Sources for Census and Administrative Data

National Center for Health Statistics (http://www.cdc.gov/nchswww/fault.htm)	This site's links lead to information such as descriptions of recent health surveys and data collections on vital statistics. This link was developed and managed by the Centers for Disease Control and Prevention.
Bureau of Labor Statistics (http://stats.bls.gov/)	The Bureau of Labor Statistics, updated by the Department of Labor, provides FTP links for downloading raw data on Local Area Unemployment statistics and Geographical Profiles.
County and City Data Books http://www.census.gov/statab/www/ccdb.html	County and City Book, from the U.S. Census Bureau, provides information about individual cities and counties in the U.S.
FedStats (http://www.fedstats.gov/)	This site includes a listing for approximately 100 federal agencies (e.g., National Center for Health Statistics) with links to information on statistics, and other resources.
U.S. Census Bureau (http://www.census.gov/)	The most up-to-date information from the Census Bureau is available from this site. To gather information about a site, you can use "QuickFacts," and select your state.
Bureau of Justice Statistics (http://bjs.ojp.usdoj.gov/)	This site contains information on crime, criminal offenders, victims of crime, and the operation of justice systems at all levels of government.
Statistical Abstract (http://www.census.gov/compendia/statab/)	This site includes provides a summary of statistics on the social, political, and economic organization of the United States.

Source: http://libguides.slu.edu/content.php?pid=41724&sid=419380

Interviews with Key Informants   Although any person with some level of knowledge can be an informant, cultivating relationships with **key informants** who can act as guides to the inner workings of community life may be most useful. Key informants are carefully selected individuals who have expertise in a given area, or

EXHIBIT 10.1

GIS Map of St Louis City Foreclosures and Probable Subprime Loans

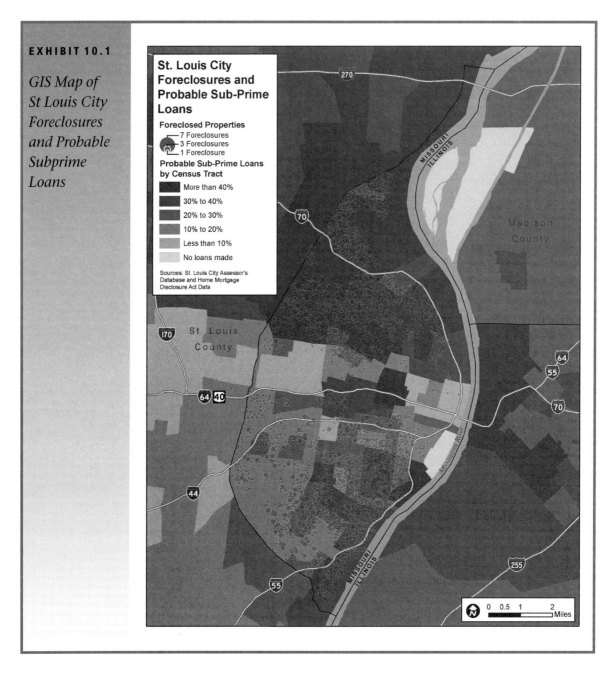

have formal or informal influence in an issue or with a population of interest. These may be formal leaders, (e.g., mayors, business association chairs, executive directors of organizations, clergy members, or alderman/city council people), or informal leaders, (e.g., longtime citizens' advocates, volunteers for the community association, or gang leaders).

If you are seeking information about systemic and political barriers to solving community problems, select key informants who have extensive history with the community, population, or issue studied. Choosing key informants who are well informed about the institutions involved in shaping the community, population and/or challenge, both past and present, is also helpful. This person can provide information about both the day-to-day dynamics and the past and present forces that impact the dynamics. If you are just seeking key informants to learn the lived reality of community life, you may want to consider someone who does not necessarily have the qualities mentioned here, but who has a helpful perspective to provide to the data collection, such as a longtime resident or matriarch of a family who has been in the community for several generations. This type of key informant may be able to share about residents' lived community experience, values and beliefs, and/or oppression, and discrimination. To locate key informants, begin by approaching leaders of community meetings, leaders of community organizations, and those quoted in local news sources, to include websites and newspapers. Your first key informants may direct you to other people you might contact for an interview. Box 10.2 provides a structure for a key informant interview and examples of questions to ask key informants. The questions relate to informants personal views and their sense of significant community facts, relationships, and dynamics.

Focus Groups   A moderated discussion among a group of people who share a common characteristic, or a **focus group**, is another method of collecting data about a community. The common characteristic could be participants in the same program, living in the same community, or caregiving for an older adult. Questions asked in focus groups can include questions about the most important issues, the reasons that something is a challenge, how a challenge exists in a community, and questions about attitudes, beliefs, and opinions. Due to the ease of facilitation, focus groups are an inexpensive, flexible, and efficient way to collect data. The open discussion among participants provides a venue for people to build their thoughts and ideas off the comments from others.

Community Forum   Public meetings in which information is exchanged and debated, and strategies considered and critiqued are **community forums**. In these forums, community residents can be educated about an issue, and state their preferences and/or present their demands. Forums can be organized to introduce an idea for solving a problem or debating an issue. Participants can range from all community residents to a select number of persons, based on specific criteria. The format usually consists of a formal presentation and a general session or breakout sessions to facilitate a higher level of interaction. Careful facilitation is needed to ensure that everyone feels welcome to participate, and that a small minority of participants do not dominate the discussion.

BOX 10.2

Guide to Key Informant Interviews

General Guidelines

Prepare a few general questions prior to conducting the interview, based on your previous research about the community.

The format should be flexible to allow for more depth on some questions, depending on the answers.

Prepare for a 30–40 minute interview, with the flexibility for a longer interview if allowed by the key informant

Prepare for the interview ahead of time by educating yourself with available data from census and administrative data, prior needs assessments, observation, and/or other available data.

Interview Format

Display the interview skills discussed in Chapter 3, such as empathy, genuineness, warmth, and others.

At the beginning of the interview, develop rapport by engaging the key informant, define the purpose of the interview, agree on the time allotted for the interview, and provide the format to the key informant (such as the number and topics of the questions, the issue of confidentiality, etc.) and information about what will be done with the data. If taping, obtain consent for taping the interview.

At the end, consider offering an open-ended question for the key informant to share any other pertinent information about which you might not have asked, or they might not have remembered to tell you.

Questions

Consider funneling the questions (i.e., moving from general questions to specific).

Avoid using jargon, and double-barreled, leading, long, and negative questions.

Ask about strengths of the community, as well as challenges.

Ask about internal structure of the community (i.e., organizations, decision-makers), as well as the external structure

Sample Questions for Key Informants

Tell me a little bit about your history with the community. Why have you chosen this community in which to live/work/volunteer?

What are the advantages to living/working/volunteering in this community? What are the main challenges?

What are the organized groups in this community? How do these groups relate to one another?

Who is significantly involved in community affairs in this community? Which groups, if any, do they belong to? Are they elected or appointed to any official positions? Who are key decision-makers in this community? Who influences them?

Who has been involved in efforts to make changes to or advocate for the community?

What were those efforts? What were the results of those efforts?

What groups or types of individuals are not served by the community? In what ways?

What groups or individuals are not involved in community affairs? What might explain the lack of engagement?

Survey Data   **Surveys** are a common method of collecting data for community practice. Survey data is often used to gauge attitudes, beliefs, and opinions about an issue, or a proposal. Surveys should be widely disseminated, be clear, easy to complete and consist mostly of closed ended questions so the survey can be given quickly to a large number of people via door-to-door, face-to-face in public spaces, or over the web, telephone, or through the use of other technology. Surveys can deliver information about specific needs within a community or population that even census data and administrative data cannot provide. Surveys can provide information about the availability and accessibility of services, and can identify unmet needs or gaps in services. Depending on the amount of resources available, the survey can be created or one could be purchased that has been tested in the past. Small targeted surveys involve collecting data from a small group within a larger group or community without trying to generalize the finding to the larger population. Small surveys may be given to certain types or groups of residents, business owners, organizations, and service providers. For example, data on the impacts of use of methamphetamine in a community could be obtained by surveying those involved with this issue (e.g., treatment providers, physicians, social workers, clergy, health providers, lawyers and judges, and others directly involved).

Determining Your Assessment Approach

There are several important considerations for designing a community needs assessment. Key principles to guide the design of a community needs assessment include (Mulroy, 2008):

1. *Value participation from diverse constituencies*—Seek multiple perspectives on the community and experiences in the community, particularly those that may be previously overlooked and undervalued, such as disadvantaged and oppressed populations. While gathering data from diverse constituencies may be challenging, you will need to carefully consider the way in which you can fairly report on dissenting opinions in your final report.

2. *Use multiple methods*—Both quantitative and qualitative methods offer unique types of data for the project. Using both types provides the most informative community needs assessment.

3. *Encourage civic participation and technical elements*—Encourage participation by key stakeholders and/or members of the community in the design and selection of technical elements, such as the selection of survey questions, focus group participants and key stakeholders, as well as for the collection and analysis of data and formulating recommendations, if appropriate. Participation by stakeholders and/or community residents will help to ensure that the data gathered is relevant, and may be useful to efforts to better the community.

4.   *Keep the assessment realistic*—Community stakeholders and agency staff want usable knowledge as evidence for local community and agency decision-making, and community improvement. Lengthy assessments and overly long documents may not be helpful.

5.   *Value strengths and asset-building*—Along with needs, note strengths and assets of the community. Institutional resources, such as churches, locally owned businesses, nonprofit organizations, schools, financial institutions, networks of organizations, and individuals can all be considered strengths. Asset building programs, such as those that encourage savings, employment, small businesses, local investment of resources, and other types of assets are intended to increase the individual and collective assets of a community. Local control of resources serves to empower residents and strengthen the community.

The purpose, desired impact, and potential uses of the assessment and resources must be major considerations about your methods (North Central Regional Center for Rural Development, n.d.; Royse et al., 2009). Questions to consider include:

- What do you/your sponsor hope to learn?

- How will the information be used?

- Can existing data provide the needed information?

- Can you combine existing data with newly gathered data?

- What resources do you have for the project?

The purpose of the assessment will help to shape the specific data you collect. For example, if you are conducting a needs assessment about financial services for low-income residents in a community, you might ask a key stakeholder, "When you think about the residents using financial institutions in this community, what services do they need that currently do not exist locally?" or "What type of institutions, if any, would be more beneficial to local residents?"

If your project is viewed as controversial, or you anticipate a skeptical or even a hostile response to the findings, plan the most rigorous data collection you can afford on the budget you have been given. Political issues surface in a needs assessment, because the data may be used to convince decision-makers to approve and/or fund a program or service, modify or end a program or service, or to recognize a previously unrecognized challenge in the community. Assessments can challenge the status quo in communities, and therefore be contentious. Including specific influential individuals and organizations in the assessment may help the findings to be seen as more credible. Other individuals and organizations have less credibility in a community, and data from them may cast doubt on your findings.

Major considerations for an assessment will be financial resources and time. For example, social workers interested in creating a new financial education program for local youth may have few resources to conduct a needs assessment, and little time before a proposal is due. However, a new city council member may ask their social work staff member to provide a more comprehensive community assessment, and provide adequate resources and time to carry out a longer, more involved assessment. If you have little of both funds and time, consider using data that is publically available, including those data available from government sources, United Way in the local area, nonprofit organizations, and perhaps including a focus group and/or a community forum. If you have more time and/or resources, you may add small targeted surveys, key informant interviews, and/or larger surveys. Exhibit 10.2 provides information about the way in which the time frame,

TIME FRAME	FINANCES	EXPERTISE	POSSIBLE DESIGN	
6 months to 1 year (or even longer) to complete a needs assessment	Financial support—grants or other significant funding in excess of $1500 to complete the needs assessment*	Expertise-needs assessment researchers are primarily research and/or evaluation staff with some experience in needs assessment*	• Probability surveys; personal interviews	**EXHIBIT 10.2** *Considerations for Needs Assessment Designs*
3–6 months to complete a needs assessment	Some financial support—small grants or funding ($500–1500) to complete the needs assessment	Some expertise-needs assessment researchers are primarily staff with some experience in research of evaluation	• Small targeted surveys	
Less than 3 months to complete a needs assessment	Limited financial support—small grants or funding ($500 or less) to complete the needs assessment	Limited expertise-needs assessment researchers are primarily agency staff or students who have other commitments and limited research or statistical expertise	• Focus group • Community forum • Unobtrusive measures including secondary data collection from agency files	

Resources (vertical label, left)   *Scientific Rigor* (vertical label, right)

* Note: In needs assessment projects that are funded by larger grants, a professional organization may be used
(Reference: Royse, Staton-Tindall, Badger, & Webster (2009))

budget, expertise, and possible designs are interrelated factors in designing a community needs assessment.

In sum, key considerations about needs assessments, the scope of the type of information you need, intended use of the data, political considerations, and funding and time resources available for either type of assessment will shape the methods used for the assessment. For examples of community needs assessments, see Box 10.3.

Assessing Specific Population Needs and Social Problems

Social workers often work with populations of community members who are vulnerable, at risk, or otherwise in need of particular services, to include runaway (or "throwaway") youth, older adults, persons with HIV/AIDS and their families, persons with disabilities, families who are working poor, and formerly hospitalized psychiatric patients. Likewise, social workers often work to alleviate issues in the community. Creating or continually modifying services to effectively and efficiently meet the needs of specific populations or targeted at a specific issue is critically important, and can help ensure the success of long-term funding sources. Needs assessments are often focused on a particular population or about a particular social problem. Both a general needs assessment and one targeted to a specific population or community challenge utilizes the same process and data collection methods as a general needs assessment.

Understanding the needs of a particular population or about a particular challenge can be achieved through a community needs assessment focused on a specific population or challenge. The goal of this type of needs assessment is to learn about the community from the perspective of a specific population or about the particular challenge. In the process of a community needs assessment, social workers work toward understanding the history and characteristics of a population or challenge and profile the specific challenges associated with the population or challenge. For the needs assessment focused on a population, the perspective

---

BOX 10.3

*Examples of
Needs
Assessments*

Federal Reserve System and Brookings Institution (http://www.frbsf.org/cpreport/)
This report is a 2006 report of case studies from communities across the U.S.

American Public Health Association
(http://apha.confex.com/apha/138am/webprogram/Paper219081.html)
This is a 2010 report of a needs assessment of homeless individuals in King County, Washington.

Vermont Housing Finance Agency
(http://www.vhfa.org/documents/hna2010/01-highlights.pdf)
This is a 2010 report about housing needs in the state of Vermont.

of the population about the community and patterns of resource availability, among other things, is important to identify in the process. When learning about community characteristics, information about community strengths, issues and problems from the perspective of a specific population is important. Learning about differences between groups in the community is important, such as the dominant values of each and methods of oppression and discrimination by dominant group(s) in communities towards other populations. For needs assessments focused both on populations and community challenges, learning about the power structure of the community, while learning about other aspects of the structure of the community, is helpful. Questions about resource distribution and decision-making processes can help uncover these dynamics (Netting et al., 2008). For example, if a social worker is learning about the needs of a Filipino population within a city, asking key informants about the relationship of Filipino leaders to leaders of the wider community may be helpful in learning about power, dominance, and oppression. If the needs assessment is focused on a particular community challenge, such as homelessness, key informants can be asked about the history of the location of the shelters in the community, the history behind the funding patterns for homeless services, and/or the relationship of key providers to political decision-makers in the community. Box 10.4 provides an example of a needs assessment focused around a particular community challenge.

Mapping Community Assets

Social workers using a strengths-based approach to working with communities seek to learn about and identify the people, institutions, and organizations in the community, as well as those who work on behalf of a community, in the assessment process. Social workers must possess knowledge of the resources available to work on local issues to using a strengths-based approach to effectively address the challenges that face communities. The key to this approach is the idea that collectively, the resources available within the community offer the capacity to address local issues. Asset mapping prepares the way for an intervention that focuses on effectiveness, interdependencies within a community, and seeks to empower people through identifying ways that people can contribute to a community change effort (Kretzmann & McKnight, 1993). Like individual, family, and group assessments, the information gathered in the process can be useful in planning a community intervention.

The community mapping process is the first stage of an asset-based community intervention, generally called the asset-based community development approach. This approach was first developed by Kretzmann and McKnight (1993), and is spearheaded by the Asset-Based Community Development Institute at Northwestern University (available at http://www.abcdinstitute.org/). Using a strengths-based approach, the first activity of community practice is to inventory, "map," the assets of a community, which includes members of the community, both those that

BOX 10.4 *Case Study—* *Community* *Practice and* *Child Welfare*	A social worker working in child welfare services in a smaller community can engage in community practice in a variety of ways. One social worker in child welfare was working in a community within a county characterized by a higher-than-average rate of poverty, substance abuse, and criminal justice violations. A substantial number of children in the county endure prolonged childhood sexual abuse. These children are first placed in foster care, but many are removed shortly thereafter and placed in residential facilities because their acute emotional disruptions are reflected in dangerous or out-of-control behaviors. However, residential care is more costly than placement in a foster home, and has implications for both the current quality of life and for the future community integration of the children.

Due to the behaviors displayed by the children who have been abused in your caseload and those of your peers, the social worker forms a working group, composed of caseworkers, supervisors, foster parents, former foster children, and allies in other organizations, to complete a needs assessment. The group reviews previous needs assessments of foster children in that community, as well as U.S. Census data, public health data, juvenile court data, educational data and other administrative data, and decides to complete a needs assessment with a survey. The survey is given to all foster parents, and those providing any services to foster children, including teachers. The survey is designed to elicit strengths, resources, and stressors.

The plan is, as a group, to analyze the data, and integrate the survey data with previous data and studies, and issue a report to the child welfare supervisor for the county. Additionally, the group will ask that the needs assessment, which will include recommendations, be shared with other local decision-makers, to include politicians, in an effort to change policy and possibly raise funds for additional services, if needed.

currently participate in community affairs and those who do not, as well as institutions, and formal and informal organizations. Conducting an inventory of the assets of individual people includes the identification of abilities, talents, gifts, and capacities of community members. For example, community members may have home repair, child/older adult care, craft, music, and other types of skills that are underutilized. Exhibit 10.3 provides an example of the topics included in an individual capacity inventory. After asking people questions on these topics, individuals would then be asked to prioritize their skills, about their involvement in community activities, their interests in starting a small business, and their current business activities. Formal and informal organizations and associations that exist within the community are also mapped, to include economic, education, political, religious, kinship, and associations. Associations can include many types of formal and informal organizations and groups, such as self-help groups that assist with addictions, youth groups, environmental groups, and charitable groups. Institutions can

CATEGORY	EXAMPLE OF SKILLS
Health	Caring for older adult or person with a mental illness
Office	Typing, writing letters, telephone skills
Construction and Repair	Painting, roof repair, tuckpointing, demolition
Maintenance	Washing windows, mowing lawns, gardening
Food	Catering, bartending, baking, washing dishes
Child Care	Caring for children, assisting with field trips
Transportation	Driving a taxi, truck, or ambulance, hauling
Operating Equipment and Repairing Machinery	Repairing electronics, using a forklift
Supervision	Completing forms, planning work for others
Sales	Operating a cash register, selling services
Music	Singing, playing an instrument
Security	Guarding property, installing security systems
Other	Sewing, upholstering, managing property

EXHIBIT 10.3

Capacity Inventory for Individuals

Adapted from John P. Kretzmann & John L. McKnight (1993). *Building communities from the inside out: A path toward finding and mobilizing a community's assets.* Evanston, IL: Center for Urban Affairs and Policy Research.

include parks, libraries, schools of all types, law enforcement, hospitals, and other health care resources (Beaulieu, n.d; Kretzman & McKnight, 1993). Exhibits 10.4 and 10.5 provide examples of community asset mapping tools for associations/ organizations and institutions. There are several helpful tools available from the internet, including one available from the Southern Rural Development Center at Mississippi State University available at: http://srdc.msstate.edu/publications/227/ 227_asset_mapping.pdf.

The process of mapping assets will vary, depending on your needs, sponsor, and resources. While some circumstances may lend themselves to a thorough mapping process in a relatively short period of time, in other circumstances, the mapping process may take a year or longer. Like a community needs assessment, the process of asset mapping is an assessment process that provides a foundation for a community intervention, yet is also a process that may continue while an intervention is underway as well. Chapter 11 will discuss the next steps for utilizing the community mapping data for an intervention. Discussed next are skills for community-based participatory research.

EXHIBIT 10.4

Capacity Inventory for Associations/ Organizations —Abbreviated List

TYPES	EXAMPLES OF TYPES
Artistic	Artists Coalition
Business	Business Association
Charitable Groups and Drives	Red Cross, United Way
Church Groups	Service, Prayer, Youth, Women's and Men's, Choir
Civic	Lions, Rotary
Collectors Groups	Stamps, Antiques
Ethnic Associations	League of Americans of Ukrainian Descent
Health and Fitness	Basketball League
Interest	Antique car owners, Book clubs
Local Media	Local cable TV, local community radio
Mutual Support	Le Leche League, Alcoholics Anonymous
Neighborhood	Block Group, Community Development Corporation
Outdoor	Biking, Hiking, Rollerblading
Political	Ward Democratic Party
School	Parent-Teacher Association
Service	Habitat for Humanity

Adapted from John P. Kretzmann & John L. McKnight (1993). *Building communities from the inside out: A path toward finding and mobilizing a community's assets.* Evanston, IL: Center for Urban Affairs and Policy Research.

EXHIBIT 10.5

Capacity Inventory for Local Institutions— Sample

TYPES	EXAMPLES OF CAPACITIES WITHIN TYPES
Parks	Personnel, Space/Facilities, Materials/Equipment
Libraries	Expertise, Materials, Fundraising Resources
Schools	Personnel, Space/Facilities, Students, Financial
Police	Personnel, Authority, Financial
Hospitals/Health Care Facilities	Expertise, Financial
Local Government	Expertise, Space/Facilities, Financial

Adapted from John P. Kretzmann & John L. McKnight (1993). *Building communities from the inside out: A path toward finding and mobilizing a community's assets.* Evanston, IL: Center for Urban Affairs and Policy Research.

SKILLS FOR COMMUNITY-BASED PARTICIPATORY RESEARCH

The community analysis and needs assessment process offers valuable opportunities to engage in community-based participatory research. This research methodology involves the engagement of a wide group of persons with interest in the community and/or the research, or stakeholders. The involvement of community members, representatives of organizations, elected officials, and/or other researchers in the research process enhances the possibility for the research to be informed by and respond to the experiences and needs of the community.

The participatory research method is guided by the following key principles (Sohng, 2008):

- Seek to identify and work with communities as a whole as well as to strengthen the social bonds of community through the engagement of people within the community.

- Use a strengths-based approach by identifying, building on and promoting strengths and assets, as well as social structures and processes that promote community involvement in community decision-making.

- Seek collaborative involvement with partners in all phases of the research with particular attention to the knowledge possessed by members of the community, sharing information and resources among all involved, and an equitable decision-making process among the partners.

- Structure the process so the members of the community and community groups have the power and ability to act on the research findings.

- Seek to promote and develop the capacity of local people and organizations to create and sustain any change that may occur as a result of the research process and outcomes.

Participatory research can be utilized when conducting a wide variety of research tools and techniques. The research process itself is a mechanism through which the well-being of communities can be enhanced through the inclusion of community members and organizations in all phases of the research, to include the research question. The promotion of the community and community process through the research process increases the likelihood that the data and analysis will accurately reflect needs, and that action can be taken to follow up the identification of the needs by the community.

A key point lies in its recognition of and respect for the centrality of the community experience to people who are experts on their community. In this way it is consistent with critical social construction, acknowledging the multiple realities that are brought to bear in any community context. Participatory action-research offers community members an opportunity to take their power back and use their needs to drive the transformation of their lives.

CONTEMPORARY TRENDS IMPACTING COMMUNITY PRACTICE

Twenty-first century community social work practice work is undertaken with a context of specific opportunities and challenges. Social workers often work within communities of people with low incomes, and these communities are faced with unique challenges in optimizing recent political, economic, and social trends. Some of the major trends and the corresponding challenges to social workers, are discussed here (Mondros & Staples, 2008; Mulroy, Nelson, & Gour, 2005; Ohmer & DeMasi, 2009; Weil & Gamble, 2005).

- *The **devolution**, or decentralization, of control of many federally funded programs and policies to states*. States have increasingly relied on nonprofit and for-profit organizations to deliver social services. This decentralization has increased the importance of communities and neighborhoods in designing, providing input to, and actually delivering services. For example, some federal block grants for child welfare have placed the allocation of funds under state or local control, which offers opportunities for community participation. Social workers are frequently in a position to contribute to these discussions through their work with state and local agencies, public hearings on regulations, and legislative testimony. Unfortunately, this change has also been accompanied by declining resources for low-income communities.

- *The increasingly multicultural composition of society*. The foreign-born population in the U.S. has grown tremendously, and is estimated to be nearly 40 million, the largest group of whom is Latinos (U.S. Census Bureau, 2010a). This increase in foreign-born populations in communities offers the opportunity for social workers to advocate for greater inclusion, participation, and social justice through increased attention to community issues that impact these populations, such as immigration, bilingual education, health care, and other related topics.

- *The increasing inequality in the fabric of our social, racial, and ethnic relations*. Social workers will continue to play a central role in working with and advocating for a more responsive community for all citizens. For example, the differential access to technology, especially computers, and the internet, is a significant barrier for many individuals and communities, particularly those that are low income.

- *The widening venues for community practice.* Social workers have increased opportunities to work with different types of communities, including those that organize around identity (or shared experiences), geography, and faith. For example, social workers may work with an online community of people with a similar medical diagnosis, a planning group for HIV/AIDS prevention funding, a specific neighborhood, or with people of various faiths.

- *The increasing integration of community practice ideas and strategies into other models of practice.* For example, elements of community practice are increasingly viewed as a part of work with individuals, families, and groups. Newer practices in services for children and families and older adults increasingly use community-based service practice models. For example, the use of Assertive Community Treatment, a community-based, intensive wrap-around case management program, is an intervention gaining increased usage for individuals with severe mental illness (Killaspy et al., 2006).

- *The decline of democratic participation and civic engagement.* Putnam (2000) documents the decline of social capital, including networks, norms, and trust that facilitates collective action. The degree to which citizens engage in public life affects community practice, including identity and shared values in a community. Social workers can work to energize and mobilize a diverse array of groups to be engaged in public life within their communities.

Having discussed the trends impacting community practice in the U.S., the next section will focus on the world as a community. This discussion will broaden the topic of community practice, and set the stage for Chapter 11, in which community intervention, termination, and evaluation will be explored.

THE WORLD AS A COMMUNITY

Ease of travel, communication, and economic interdependence impact on social work practice in the U.S. and will certainly grow in influence in coming decades. In this section, **global interdependence** is discussed (the connectedness of all nations), and the implications for domestic community social work practice are explored.

Global Interdependence: Implications for U.S. Practice

Global interdependence influences social work practice in the U.S. in an array of areas. Most of these have to do with political, social, and technological events. Four influences are described here (Healy, 2008):

- Due to the increased migration of peoples in all parts of the world, culturally competent skills and an understanding of the social problems associated with refugee status and transborder issues are important for social workers in most U.S. communities today. Migration occurs as a result of international events and political forces.

- Social workers seek information from multiple sources, rather than from just Western sources, about meeting the social challenges that are similar in many places, such as homelessness, poverty, violence, street children, HIV/AIDS, unemployment, increasing longevity, runaway contagious disease, and growing divisions between the "haves" and "have-nots." Mutual inquiries and information sharing will be increasingly relevant as these conditions are addressed on a worldwide basis.

- Social workers are more engaged in the actions of other countries. The actions of one country influence the social and economic well-being of others, as well as the world's overall social health, and social work involvement is imperative. For example, people all over the world are affected by natural disasters, the world economy, and nuclear accidents.

- Social workers seek new ways of using advanced technologies to advance universal human rights. The potential for using technology to share agendas and materials, and to collaborate toward meeting basic human needs, is virtually endless.

Approaches for a Global Community

A global perspective is growing in importance in community social work practice. The following points may be helpful in developing a global perspective and expanding your thinking as a global citizen (adapted from Ramanathan & Link, 1999, pp. 225–230).

1. *Making a personal review of global awareness:* Developing a global awareness first requires an awareness of your present orientation. For example, how often do you think about economic and/or social conditions in other countries? Do you know where your clothing and shoes are made and under what conditions?

2. *Expanding knowledge of social work practice in a range of countries:* Another factor in expanding your awareness is considering learning about and being aware of your opinion of social work practices in other countries. Practices in other countries can inform your practice in your location. Do you consider yourself the expert and other countries' approaches as secondary or inferior? Awareness of this issue is vitally important to your approach.

3. *Understanding "cultural competence" and respect for language:* Understanding the dynamics of culture and its implications for access to power and resources

can lead to highly effective relationships in social work practice. For example, think about the degree to which you understand the ideas of other cultures other than your own, the degree to which your language is respectful about other cultures, and if you avoid assuming your culture is the worldwide norm.

4. *Analyzing global policy instruments built upon consensus:* An understanding of global policy statements that apply to issues of concern to social workers provides an understanding of the foundation upon which social work practice is built. Relevant documents include the 2008 UN Convention on the Rights of Persons with Disabilities, among many others (Stevenson, 2010).

5. *Becoming historically aware:* Understanding the historical context of U.S. policies is essential for the development of a global perspective. For example, an understanding of the contribution of U.S. policies to the economic situations of other countries can assist in a broader understanding of immigration patterns in the U.S.

6. *Becoming aware of privilege*: An appreciation of the privilege associated with economic power can assist in the development of a global perspective. For example, awareness of your technological privilege, and issues of distributive justice, energy resources, and other dimensions related to the distribution of resources and the ethics associated with it can be illuminating.

7. *Reviewing values and ethics:* The ability to understand the global application of the NASW *Code of Ethics* is key to a global perspective. For instance, do you respect the dignity of all the peoples of the earth, rather than the dignity of people in the U.S.? Do you reflect a preoccupation with material goods? How do you reconcile this focus with the fact that global resources are finite and inequitably distributed?

8. *Evaluating local variations and uniqueness:* As a social worker, you are obliged to balance the tension between upholding universal principles that will strengthen the profession and valuing individual and local expressions of uniqueness. The goal of social work practice is not to make everything the same, but to promote a "unified purpose" (Ramanathan & Link, 1999, p. 230).

STRAIGHT TALK ABOUT COMMUNITY PRACTICE

In addition to these forces and trends, **globalization** has led to deindustrialization and the outsourcing of traditional "blue collar" as well as "white collar" jobs. In particular, the loss of well-paying manufacturing jobs to lower-wage markets has increased the difficulty with which low-income populations can access well-paying jobs with little formal education and training. The corresponding economic insecurity has resulted in weaker local institutions, such as churches, schools, and businesses. **Areas of concentrated poverty** have left increasing numbers of poor communities isolated, making it difficult for families in those communities to take advantage of mainstream social and economic opportunities. For example, it may be more difficult for persons in low-income communities to access available living-wage job opportunities if the jobs are located far from the community and if transportation options are limited.

A related trend is the **gentrification** of metropolitan areas with rapidly growing populations. Gentrification occurs when low-income communities experience a physical renovation that results in increased property values, and decreasing affordability. Property owners wishing to take advantage of increasing property values may convert their properties into high-cost housing, which can force low-income families to seek housing elsewhere and change the social fabric of the community (Ohmer & DeMasi, 2009). These issues reflect many of the major dimensions of contemporary society that challenge all human service professions, and they also present unique and exciting opportunities for the renewal of vibrant community practice.

CONCLUSION

This chapter has introduced community as an important concept that provides the place in which individuals and groups find identity and meaning for their lives in their various roles. Most important for social workers, community is a practice arena that impacts all areas of practice, and social workers in a wide variety of settings will benefit from a working knowledge of community practice. Community is the structure that supports interaction and connectedness among people over time, and can be understood using a wide range of theories and perspectives. The characteristic of the community in which people grow, live, and develop has important implications for the resources and opportunities available to community residents. Communities are the central context of social work practice with all types of client systems; therefore, community practice is an important aspect of generalist social work practice. Having considered community engagement, assessment, and the global community, we will now examine community intervention strategies, termination, and evaluation processes.

MAIN POINTS

- Communities play a critical role in the lives of workers and clients, even in traditional individual, family, and group practice.

- There are multiple definitions, types, and functions of community, to include the use of tradition and postmodern approaches to the community.

- Community engagement and assessment involves many skills and practice behaviors, including community analysis, needs assessment, community asset mapping, and community-based participatory research.

- Various factors, including the population and/or problem focus, aid in the determination of the assessment approach.

- Contemporary trends and globalization are changing community social work practice.

- Developing a global perspective is imperative to contemporary community engagement and assessment.

- Understanding the traditional and contemporary perspectives helps to view community through many different lenses.

- Skills of engagement, assessment, and intervention in community social work build on those relevant for social work practice with individuals, families, and groups. In addition, you will find the skills of participatory action-research useful as an ethnographic approach to your work.

EXERCISES

1. Go to www.routledgesw.com/cases, and click on the Riverton case (click on "Start This Case"). Familiarize yourself with the Riverton Town Map (under "Explore This Town" case study tool), the Sociogram (case study tool) and the Interaction Matrix (case study tool). Answer the critical thinking questions on the Riverton case. Additionally, what other players would you add to the interaction matrix?

2. After completing Exercise #1, consider the following case. In your position as social worker at the Alvadora Community Mental Health Center, you have observed that there are some strained connections between the center's staff and the Hispanic community served. You would like to learn more about the Hispanic community to both become more culturally competent, and learn more about the needs of the community. You decide to explore the idea of a community analysis.

   a. Define the type of community you would be studying.

   b. Discuss the approach that you might take to conduct a community analysis. What type of information would you seek? Who would you involve? With whom might you talk?

3. After completing Exercises #1 and #2, you decide to conduct a community needs assessment. Using the material in Chapter 10, create a plan for a community

needs assessment of the Hispanic population in Riverton, to include the sources of data and assessment approach that you plan to use.

4. Go to www.routledgesw.com/cases and become familiar with the Sanchez family. Review the material in the chapter that discusses the world as a global community. Using the Sanchez family as a focal point, identify and describe the ways in which the Sanchez family context in particular is shaped by each of the four dimensions of global interdependence. Add any other ways you think would make an impact.

5. The Chapter 10 section "Approaches for a Global Community" discusses points that could be helpful in creating a global perspective for social work practice. Focusing again on the Sanchez family, apply four of the eight points in the chapter to work with the Sanchez family. In your application, focus your discussion on the ways in which you can accomplish each of the tasks to create a global perspective toward the larger goal of being a culturally competent social worker.

6. Select a community of which you are a member. Reflect on an issue that your community faces. What is the issue? How might you conduct a community analysis of your community? How might you conduct a needs assessment of your community? Create a thorough plan for each.

7. Select a community within which you are a member. Using the "Create Your Own Ecomap" template, create a sociogram of your community.

Social Work Practice with Communities: Intervention, Termination, and Evaluation

Passion begins with a burden and a split-second moment when you understand something like never before. That burden is on those who know. Those who don't know are at peace. Those of us who do know get disturbed and are forced to take action.

Wangari Maathai

Key Questions for Chapter 11

(1) How can I prepare for action with all client systems? (EPAS 2.1.10(a))

(2) What are the key interpersonal skills and techniques that I need to know to work with communities? (EPAS 2.1.10(a))

(3) How can I utilize evidence to practice research-informed practice and practice-informed research to guide the intervention, termination, and evaluation with communities? (EPAS 2.1.6)

(4) How can I apply critical thinking to intervention, termination, and evaluation with communities? (EPAS 2.1.3)

(5) How can I apply social work values and ethics to community intervention, termination, and evaluation? (EPAS 2.1.2)

LIKE PRACTICE WITH INDIVIDUALS, FAMILIES AND GROUPS, the second phase of social work practice with communities is linked to the engagement and assessment from which they evolve. Intervention, termination, and evaluation are considered the middle and ending phases of work with all client system levels. Community practice is a broad term that includes grassroots community organizing, community development, and human service planning and coordination (Weil & Gamble, 2009). Community intervention utilizes a blending of various approaches, and is based on the community assessment. The general aim of community practice is to create institutions and communities that are responsive to human needs. As the central focus is on the community, community-level interventions, terminations, and evaluations are multi-faceted, with a dual focus on individual, family, and group change. Such complexity requires the social worker to possess specialized skills to implement the intervention and facilitate the termination and evaluation processes.

To complete the exploration of social work practice with communities, this chapter explores the continuation of community practice from the development of the intervention plan through the termination and evaluation phases. Included in the discussion is a focus on practice models for community interventions that are guided and informed by theoretical perspectives. An overview of the social work practice behaviors needed for intervening with communities will be provided. The chapter will continue with a look at the final phase of community practice—the termination and evaluation processes. The exploration will begin with a discussion of the most recognized models for community intervention: planning/policy, community capacity development, and social advocacy, as well as the ways in which they are mixed in practice (Rothman, 2008).

SOCIAL WORK THEORY AND MODELS FOR COMMUNITY INTERVENTION

As discussed in Chapter 10, theory informs community social work practice by providing a lens through which communities can be understood and analyzed. For example, the strengths approach can be applied to communities, in general, through the identification of assets and possibilities within a community, including individuals. The empowerment approach can be achieved through the realization that a community has the capacity to build on strengths (Netting et al., 2008).

Community intervention is guided community practice models, which are primarily based in the concepts and language of systems, ecological and power, and change and politics theories (Netting et al., 2008, p. 159). As seen in Exhibit 11.1, systems theory helps to recognize that planned community change reverberates throughout a community, and affects units within and outside of a community. The community intervention chosen, therefore, must account for the possibility that any community change may affect a broader constituency than those intended. Ecological theory informs community interventions through its focus on competition for limited resources, which can affect the relationship among units within

THEORIES	CONTRIBUTIONS TO COMMUNITY PRACTICE	
Social Systems	Reveals that changes in one community unit will impact other units	**EXHIBIT 11.1**
	Indicates that changes in subunits also influence the larger community	*Summary of*
	Allows comparisons between the functioning of different communities	*Contributions*
Ecology	Sheds light on relationship among community units	*of Theories to*
	Recognizes that community groups are competing for limited resources, with survival of those in power	*Community*
	Recognizes that groups without power must adapt to community norms	*Practice*
	Acknowledges the influences of the interconnections and mutual shaping of physical and social structures	
Power, Change, and Politics	Reveals the influence of external sources of resources on local communities	
	Views the community as divided into "haves" and "have-nots"	
	Focuses heavily on the "isms"	
	Acknowledges the role of power in all interpersonal transactions	

Source: Netting, Kettner, & McMurtry, 2008, p. 160

a community or between communities. Community intervention can be planned that accounts for competition and limited resources. Power, change, and politics theories shed light on the influence of external sources on local communities. Using these theories, community intervention can be planned that utilizes this influence to focus on growing the power and control that a community possesses over internal affairs and in relationships with other persons and institutions that possess power.

As discussed in Chapter 10, the data produced by the community assessment process is the basis for community change efforts, which are often a blend of various approaches. The three models most commonly used in the literature are Rothman's (2008) three models of community practice: planning/policy, community capacity development, and social advocacy. These three models, explained here, have several common elements (Rothman, 2008; Weil & Gamble, 2009):

- the formulation of a change goal

- roles for staff

- leaders and members

- a process of selecting issues to work on

- a target of the change effort

- assessment of resources needed to produce change

- an understanding of the role of organizations in the change process

Planning/Policy

The planning/policy model of community intervention is based on the use of data and logic to achieve community change. This model of intervention focuses on the rational process of using experts to assist in the process of studying problems and applying rational planning techniques. Social workers using social planning also consider political considerations and advocacy in the process of the intervention, but the primary emphasis is on rational planning.

The planning/policy model is implemented in a range of practice situations. For example, the use of data is prioritized when social workers are involved in comprehensive planning, such as working with city officials to create a plan for homeless shelters, or prison facilities for the community, where data, such as U.S. Census data, local government data, or data generated by local nonprofits, is the primary consideration for making decisions. Statistics, computer modeling, and forecasting techniques are often utilized with this model (Rothman, 2008; Weil & Gamble, 2009).

Community Capacity Development

The focus of community capacity development is to develop local community collective ability to accomplish change. Therefore, this model focuses on the process of building relationships and skills toward solving local problems in a cooperative manner. Consensus by the participants is highly valued as the decision-making process for this model. Community capacity development is consistent with the strengths-based approaches of community asset mapping (discussed later in this chapter).

The emphasis of the community capacity development model is on building competency of community members and for the community as a whole through self-help and local problem solving. Common themes to this approach include empowerment, solidarity (e.g., achieving harmonious interrelationships among diverse persons), participation in civic action within a democratic process, and the development of leadership among local leaders. For example, neighborhood associations and clubs may work to educate themselves on ways to address a trash-dumping problem, or settlement houses may assist to organize local citizens and leaders to offer summer activities for youth to prevent violence and crime. The work of the U.S. Peace Corps, in which international volunteers work with local communities to create a project or increase capacity in an ongoing community effort, is another example of the community capacity development model. For example, a Peace Corps voiunteer may work with the local schools to develop their capacity to improve the hygiene facilities in the schools, and lower the rate of illness and disease among the school-age children. To do this, a volunteer could work with a local committee involved with the school and help them to raise money, prioritize needs, make plans, contact experts within or outside of the community, and carry out other tasks needed for the project (Rothman, 2008; Weil & Gamble, 2009).

Social Advocacy

This model is based in conflict, power dependency, and resource mobilization theories of power and politics (discussed in Chapter 10). This model is both process- and task-oriented. The focus is the effort to shift power relationships and resources to affect institutional change. Pressure is applied to a target(s) (e.g., persons and/or institutions), that has created or exacerbated a problem. Empowerment is achieved when beneficiaries feel a sense of mastery in influencing community decision-making.

A helpful example of the social advocacy model is the work of the organization Greenpeace. To seek solutions to environmental dilemmas, Greenpeace conducts nonviolent confrontations with decision-makers and those who may influence decision-makers. The goal of their nonviolent actions is to promote public dialogue about environmental issues and to pressure decision-makers (Greenpeace, n.d.). Other social advocacy activities include protests, strikes, picket lines, and other militant pressure tactics (Rothman, 2008; Weil & Gamble, 2009).

Box 11.1 provides a case example and applies each type of model to the example.

Blending Models

While the models were presented in a "pure" form, the models are often blended in a variety of ways in practice, as described here (Rothman, 2008; Weil & Gamble, 2009). While the same blend occurs more than once, the first model mentioned indicates the emphasis of the blended approach:

Planning/Policy Can Be Utilized with Community Capacity Development   with the use of citizen input into a planning process that is data driven. For example, the St. Louis, Missouri Mental Health Board (hereafter referred to as "Board") periodically completes a needs assessment focused on mental health services for the City of St. Louis, in order to identify the areas of largest unmet needs. The Board then creates a plan to allocate funding for the next several years to best meet those needs. In the process, the Board receives feedback from mental health providers and consumers about the plan. In this way, the two models are mixed through the strong

The south side of a large Midwestern city is a low-income community populated mostly by Latino and African-American populations. The other parts of the city are mainly populated with White, non-Latino middle and high income families. The south side of the city has a history of oppression, including poorer quality schools and less public funding for roads and other infrastructure. In addition, there is a past history of discrimination against minority families in mortgage lending, which led to a very high rate of rental housing rather than home ownership. There have been several efforts over the past half-century by real estate developers to redevelop the residential and commercial parts of the community, with little success.

In the past two years, a real estate developer has been buying up abandoned property in the area, and is now requesting public funding (in addition to bank loans) to redevelop a large area of the community. Community groups and local political leaders have not been asked for their input or feedback on the redevelopment plans.

Using the **Planning/Policy** model, the community group or local political leader would request that the city planners generate data or utilize previously existing data to create a redevelopment plan for the community.

Using the **Community Capacity Development** model, one or more of the community groups from the affected area would begin a process of developing their ability to create a community redevelopment plan that they could present to real estate developers and/or city officials.

Using the **Social Advocacy** model, one or more of the community groups from the affected area would utilize pressure tactics on a targeted decision-maker to affect the outcome of a decision about public funding for the project, such as specific city elected or appointed officials.

reliance on data (Planning/Policy) and the use of citizen and provider input into the planning process (Community Capacity Development) (Rothman, 2008).

Planning/Policy Can Be Utilized with Social Advocacy   by emphasizing the use of data and logic in policy advocacy efforts. For instance, the Board can utilize the needs assessment and funding allocation plans to advocate for policy changes at the local, state, and/or national levels via intensive education and lobby efforts toward improves services for those with mental health challenges. In this manner, the Board is utilizing data (Planning/Policy) and advocacy efforts (Social Advocacy) to implement community change (Rothman, 2008).

Community Capacity Development Can Be Combined with Planning/Policy   (with an emphasis on the Capacity Development) by utilizing institutions that primarily exist to assist communities to increase their development. For example, based on the results of a needs assessment, the Mental Health Board could work with mental health providers based on neighborhoods in their efforts to strengthen the response of local communities to mental health needs of residents by developing local leaders, and emphasizing a local problem-solving process for working with individuals with chronic mental health needs. In a second example, Community Development Corporations (CDCs) are resident-driven organizations that exist in many communities to provide assistance to the community. This assistance can include the facilitation of housing stock improvements, or the support of the businesses and commercial real estate efforts, and involvement in child care, community centers, and other components in the community. The CDCs are governed by a board consisting of residents, business owners, and/or local government officials. The CDCs can use data-informed approaches to improve communities, such as create small business assistance programs, create cooperatives, or rehabilitate affordable housing in the community (Garkovich, 2011). In the approach for both examples, the emphasis on developing the capacity of local communities (Capacity Development) with the use of data and logic (Planning/Policy) is emphasized to make decisions about the focus of community change efforts (Rothman, 2008).

Community Capacity Development Can Be Combined with Social Advocacy to encourage networks of community stakeholders to utilize pressure on decision-makers for the betterment of the community. This mixed approach can be utilized by all types of communities, on a wide variety of targets, for policy and practice decisions. For example, a neighborhood group may learn about the plans for a casino to be located in their community, and decide to fight against it by lobbying key decision-makers, delivering petitions, and/or picketing the local government. A self-help group may decide to engage in an online advocacy effort to advocate for civil rights for lesbian, gay, bisexual, transgender, and questioning (LGBTQ) persons in their community that may include a sit-in at the office of a local elected official to ask for their support. This mixed approach emphasizes the utilization of community capacity (Community Capacity Development) with the use of social advocacy techniques, in situations where this mix will maximize the possibility for community change (Rothman, 2008).

Social Advocacy Can Be Mixed with Planning/Policy to utilize data and logic to support advocacy efforts. This blending can best describe the efforts of many of the prominent social workers in the history of the profession, such as Jane Addams, John Dewey, Margaret Sanger, and others. These pioneers based the arguments used in their advocacy techniques about child labor, housing codes, food and drug safety, and other issues in data and logical arguments. Today, "think-tanks" such as the New America Foundation and others provide well-researched factual reports used by social advocacy groups to press for change. Therefore, the mix of tactics that bring pressure to bear on decision-makers (Social Advocacy) and data and logic

(Planning/Policy) is most closely aligned with the roots of the profession (Rothman, 2008).

Social Advocacy Can Be Combined with Community Capacity Development   to create strong networks of persons engaged in advocacy, which is also structured to focus on developing leadership, empowering participants, and building solidarity. This mixture can most readily be seen in long-term social advocacy efforts, such as the gay rights movement, the environmental movement, the women's rights movement and others. In this combination, the use of pressure tactics and techniques (Social Advocacy) and the development of the skills and knowledge of community members (Community Capacity Development) are utilized to create long-term aptitude for community intervention (Rothman, 2008).

These models, both in pure and mixed forms, offer ways in which to analyze and describe community interventions. While the framework is helpful, the possibilities of mixing are endless. The mixtures described above can be altered by having a smaller or larger degree of the secondary model in the mix. For example, many faith-based organizations focus on Community Capacity Development through an emphasis on programming for empowerment, leadership development, and solidarity through self-help group work, and engage in only a small amount of Social Advocacy (Rothman, 2008). While there are several other conceptual frameworks for community interventions that provide helpful practice models (see for example, Weil & Gamble, 2005), these models presented provide a starting point for many types of community intervention. Having discussed the models of community intervention, next highlighted is the middle phase of community work, with a discussion of various intervention strategies, and skills needed for intervention.

CONTEMPORARY TRENDS AND SKILLS FOR THE MIDDLE PHASE OF COMMUNITY WORK: INTERVENTION

Community intervention consists of action to improve community conditions and quality of life for the residents or members. The discussion will focus on the intervention strategies of community social and economic development, community organizing, and community asset mapping. Conducting meetings and participating in decision-making are important skills for community practice, and will also be discussed.

Community Social and Economic Development

Community social and economic development (hereafter referred to as "community development") is a community intervention method that seeks to maximize human potential by improving the physical and social fabric of communities by utilizing a dual focus on social relationships and the environment (Rubin & Rubin, 2008). Community development focused on social development prioritizes relationship building, education, motivation for self-help, and leadership development, toward the goal of strengthening democracy at the local community level by encouraging local participation in community efforts, and can include efforts to revitalize institutions. Community development focused on economics includes economic development, affordable housing, employment services, and other activities. Often community social development and community economic development efforts are simultaneous and interdependent, and can be viewed as a continuum.

Community development, also called "locality development" and "community building," is an often ambiguous term with a wide variety of definitions, and can include professions from many fields, to include business, sociology, anthropology, psychology, and others (Gamble & Hoff, 2005). Community development work most closely aligns with the Community Capacity Development model discussed earlier, as the focus is on creating a higher level of ability of local communities to solve problems and effectively work with institutions, rather than engage in Social Advocacy or Planning/Policy work. However, community development work also can utilize a mix of models, depending on the needs at the time.

The assumptions that drive community development include (Cnaan & Rothman, 2008, pp. 247–248):

- People may need to become aware of a common problem and create a desire to act to solve problems.

- A diverse group of people across various dimensions of diversity (i.e., race, ethnicity, socio-economic status, etc.) adds value and authenticity to the efforts, and ensures that the interests of more than one group of people are served.

- Local self-determination is valued and fostered by democratic decision-making and participatory democracy.

- Empowerment, or the capacity to solve problems by working with the authorities and institutions that affect their lives, is a central goal of community development.

- The primary constituents of the community development social worker are the community members and community organizations, rather than those with more power.

- Planned change is preferred to inaction that allows current conditions to continue.

Community Development Skills The most common practice skills utilized are analysis of community issues, facilitating the increase of communication among community members, educating, forming groups, seeking consensus, encouraging group discussion, and focusing to solve concerns and problems common to the group (Cnaan & Rothman, 2008).

Clearly, group work, covered extensively in Chapters 8 and 9, is a major part of community development work. To ensure success, community development social workers must employ task group work skills, to include leadership, communication, problem-solving, and management of group function and processes. As discussed in Chapter 9, an important skill is the promotion of indigenous leadership within the group work involved in community development, which involves the ability to extend leadership activities and responsibilities as widely as possible among persons involved with the work. An example of a leadership skill that social workers may use, or teach to indigenous leaders, is the facilitation of effective task meeting. Exhibit 11.2 provides an overview of the tasks involved in effective meetings. These tasks can be disseminated among individuals involved in meetings or handled by a small group, as a way to learn and exercise leadership skills.

Another task group skill utilized by social workers is related to group decision-making. Learning and using decision-making processes in task group work that promotes full participation by all persons involved is an important group process skill. Decision-making for groups can be handled in a variety of ways, to include the use of **parliamentary procedure**, or **Robert's Rules of Order**, and **consensus decision-making**. Box 11.2 provides an overview of Robert's Rules of Order, and Box 11.3 provides an overview of consensus decision-making. Both types of decision-making processes are commonly used in task groups, depending on the context of the work. Social workers need familiarity with decision-making processes to fully participate as a individual, and to assist others to participate.

Recruitment of new participants is an ongoing and important community development skill. Participants involved in community development work are often volunteers, and recruitment of new volunteers is important to the success of the long-term goals. The most effective techniques for recruitment of participants include focusing efforts on those persons who are most likely to join, utilizing a well-formed recruiting message, using multiple recruitment methods, providing an orientation for new participants, and facilitating easy access to joining activities (Cnaan & Rothman, 2008).

Community Development Programs   Community economic development (CESD) approaches focus on utilizing economic approaches toward the development of low-income people and neighborhoods (Robinson & Green, 2011). Programs that fall into this approach include (Robinson & Green, 2011; Rubin & Rubin, 2008):

- Individual Development Accounts (IDAs). IDAs are matched saving accounts for low-income employed persons who meet income guidelines. IDA programs involved financial education and case management. IDA funds can be spent on approved assets, such as a home, home repair, starting or expanding a small business, or secondary education;

STAGE	ELEMENT	NOTES
Preparation	Goals	Develop goal(s) for each meeting.
	Site	Establish a meeting site that is familiar, accessible, perceived as safe, and has parking.
	Date/Timing	Set a date and time that is convenient for the majority of (would-be) participants.
	Facilitator	The facilitator is involved in setting the agenda.
	Agenda	Include the speaker's name in each agenda item, information about the item, and a time limit. Discuss easy items first, followed by hard, followed by moderate decisions.
	Food	Offer food at various times, unless disruptive.
	Recruitment/ Turnout	Provide oral and written meeting announcements, and remind people a few days prior to the meeting.
	Meeting Roles	Assign roles ahead of time, including facilitator, note taker, timekeeper, presenters, and greeter.
	Room Arrangements and Logistics	Set up chairs, AV equipment, flipchart, sign-in table, food/drink, and microphone.
	Background Materials	Prepare background materials about pending decisions and preliminary proposals to discuss.
Meeting	Timeliness	Begin and end the meeting on time.
	Welcome, Introductions	Begin with a warm welcome and introductions to set a positive tone, regardless of the turnout.
	Agenda	Review the agenda with the group, and make changes as needed.
	Meeting Rules	Explain any rules utilized, including decision-making rules.
	Discussion	Encourage discussion of various viewpoints; encourage all to speak by drawing out quieter people, limiting those who dominate, and encouraging respect for viewpoints; summarize; and bring closure to discussion.
	Focus	Bring the group back to the agenda if discussion wanders.
	Ending	Summarize meeting results, decisions, and follow-up needed. Thank people for attending.
Follow-up	Notes	Prepare and disseminate meeting notes quickly.
	Thank People	Contact people, especially new people, to thank them for their contribution to the meeting, to encourage follow-up on commitments for action, and to encourage them to attend the next meeting.

EXHIBIT 11.2

Elements of Effective Meetings

Adapted from Bobo, Kendall, & Max, 2010, and Minieri & Getsos, 2007

BOX 11.2

Utilizing Robert's Rules of Order

Many formal groups, such as Boards of Directors, committees, and policy-making groups, use some form of a formal decision-making process. The use of *parliamentary procedure*, or *Robert's Rules of Order*, is often used because it is well known, helps to maintain order and allows actions to be taken in an expedient and consistent manner. Although the process can be quite complex, some groups utilize the general rules without learning the minutia. Understanding the major concepts of parliamentary procedure is a critical skill for facilitating and participating in a meeting.

Robert's Rules of Order provide a structured, democratic (majority rules) mechanism whereby formal groups can engage in efficient and fair decision-making. The following are major elements of the process:

- The use of a *motion* to introduce a proposal. Any idea for consideration of a group must be introduced as a motion (i.e., "I move that . . ."). Only one motion can be considered at a time.

- The *seconding* of a motion to move a proposal forward for discussion. A motion cannot move forward in the process unless someone other than the person who made the motion "seconds" the motion (i.e., "I second the motion"). Without a second, a motion dies, and is not discussed.

- The use of *debate/discussion* to enable participants to present perspectives and ask questions about a motion. After a motion is made and seconded, the facilitator can open discussion about the motion, and questions can be asked of the author of the motion.

- *Amendments* to reflect revisions to an original motion based on the debate/discussion. During the discussion, one or more participants may offer an amendment to clarify or narrow the motion. This amendment must be voted on before the original motion is voted on. A majority vote is required to pass an amendment.

- *Majority rules* (i.e., a minimum of 51 percent of members agreeing) to establish a motion as a decision.

Adapted from Rozakis, 1996

- employment training and placement;

- support of small and home-based businesses;

- financial education and credit building;

- services to help low-income families purchase a home;

- assistance for families to file their federal and state taxes and receive the Earned Income Tax Credit (EITC), which is a refundable tax credit for working, low income families; and

Real change, at the individual, family, group, community, or organizational level, comes from persons who are personally committed to a decision or direction in which they fully participated. Consensus decision-making, or a cooperative process in which all members develop and agree to support a decision that is in the best interests of the whole group, can be effective in situations in which the following conditions are present:

BOX 11.3

Utilizing Consensus for Decision-making

- Participants feel a genuine stake in the decision.
- Participants share a common purpose and values.
- Participants trust each other.
- Participants are willing to put the best interests of the group over personal preferences.
- Participants can share their ideas and opinions freely, without fear of ridicule.
- Enough time is available for the process.
- Participants can engage in active listening and consider different points of view.

After meeting preparation work, the process includes:

- Exploring the issue toward the goal of developing an informed, shared understanding of the facts and the issue.
- Establishing decision criteria, including such factors as interests/needs that must be met, resource constraints, and possible ramifications of decisions.
- Developing and discussing a written preliminary proposal.
- Testing for consensus by asking participants whether they can live with the proposal (original or amended), whether it meets the decision criteria, and whether it is the best decision possible.
- Reaching agreement by restating the proposed decision and ensuring that participants can support the implementation of the proposal.

Adapted from Dressler, 2006

- human-rights work (i.e., Fair Housing, civil rights, environmental justice, disability, and sexual orientation discrimination).

There are many examples of community social and economic development work. Youth development work often involves leadership development and relationship skills, as well as job training and employment placement services (Chaskin, 2010; Wheeler & Thomas, 2011). Domestic violence services can include education, financial education, and credit building, as well as IDAs services (Redevelopment Opportunities for Women, n.d.). Building community partnerships for school-based services, such as physical and mental health services, counseling, mentoring, and other programs, provides an example of community development work focused primarily on social development (Poole, 2009). Work with immigrants and refugees can include community development work, including financial literacy; assistance for small business owners to start, expand, and strengthen their business; lending for small businesses; micro business loans through a peer lending program; as well as case management, translation, education and other services (International Institute St. Louis, 2010). Some community development efforts are focused solely on the physical environments of communities, such as the production of affordable housing, commercial space development in low income communities, and/or the redevelopment of entire streets.

Asset-Based Community Development

Community asset mapping as an assessment process was discussed in Chapter 10. The community data that were gathered as part of the assessment process can be utilized for community intervention in a variety of ways. After collecting the data, the next step is to group all of the data into categories, such as capabilities of individuals, including those marginalized within the community, associations, local institutions, physical assets of the communities, and (potential) leaders. As a social worker, building your relationship with all of these types of assets, as well as relationships between these types of assets, is a key ingredient in a community change effort. Building strong networks among these assets will serve to strengthen the social fabric of the community, and build capacity as a whole community. For example, a social worker may be involved in establishing a network of social service providers, representatives of educational institutions, and business leaders in communities to work on local community challenges. Social workers may need to identify the self-interest of the various groups when recruiting them to become ivolved, such as mentioning to local businesses that strengthening their ties to organizations serving local youth also involves the possibility of expanding their pool of future labor. These efforts can benefit the community through increased self-reliance.

As relationships are built, the ability of the community to solve problems locally increases, and local competence is increased. Social workers prompt associations and institutions to increase their contributions to community efforts. For example, social workers can facilitate and support the development of local media sources by associations and institutions, such as websites, local newspapers, and radio stations, to facilitate the flow of information that can be utilized toward other purposes. Additionally, the process of community asset development may involve community-wide convening to develop a local vision and strategies to implement the visions. Community planning processes can be sponsored by faith communities (such as churches or synagogues) or faith networks (such as a ministerial alliance), or associations (such as clubs or groups) or institutions (such as a local school district or large employer). After a planning process, outside resources can be sought, if needed, to carry out a community plan. Bringing in outside resources, such as foundations, government actors and others, after a plan is created ensures that community plans are truly resident-driven (Kretzmann & McKnight, 1993).

In addition to community development work, community social work practice interventions also includes community organizing. Having considered community development, the discussion now turns to community organizing as a stand-alone community intervention and one that can be integrated with community development.

Community Organizing

Community organizing is a practice skill that entails mobilizing people and resources to advocate for change to improve the quality of life in marginalized communities (Rubin & Rubin, 2005). Community organizing skills can be utilized within any of the three models of community practice mentioned earlier (planning/policy, community capacity development, and social advocacy). The target of community organizing efforts varies widely, and can include local, state, and federal government officials, legislators, private landlords, corporate CEOs, and officials of the World Trade Organization.

While community organizing efforts are typically focused on a particular change effort, such as passing a local ballot issue about sales tax, the form that community organizing takes can vary widely. Community organization actions can include accepting and working with the existing power relationships, or "consensus organizing," and challenging the existing power relationship, or "direct action organizing." Exhibit 11.3 describes the continuum of services as framed by the degree to which the existing power relationships within a community are accepted.

The left side of the exhibit depicts *consensus organizing*. Consensus organizing involves developing strong relationships and partnerships among and between community members and stakeholders, and with persons and institutions that are external to the community and hold power that can facilitate community change.

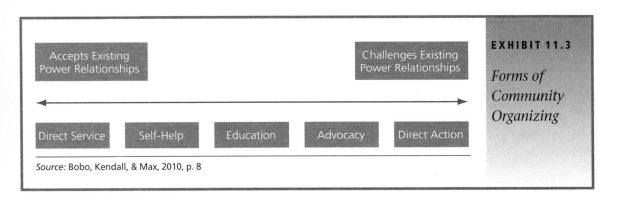

EXHIBIT 11.3

Forms of Community Organizing

Source: Bobo, Kendall, & Max, 2010, p. 8

BOX 11.4

Assumptions of the Consensus Organizing Approach

- Ordinary people can and should be involved with creating sustainable community change.
- Identify and build on community strengths and assets, rather than deficits.
- Potential leaders are everywhere, and often need recognition and support to thrive.
- The organizer must be a selfless promoter of others.
- The organizer must seek to achieve self-interest for residents and external partners.
- Powerful people and institutions want to assist with community change.

Adapted from Ohmer & DeMasi, 2009

External powers can include government officials, landlords who own rental property in the community, and/or private business owners. Engaging in consensus community organizing brings together community participants and utilizes the power structure as a partner in the change effort. Box 11.4 provides assumptions of the consensus organizing approach.

The right side of Exhibit 11.3 represents direct action community organizing, or *conflict organizing*. This form of community organizing assumes that a disadvantaged population must be organized to made demands on a target for equal treatment/ resources, with the larger goal of gaining power and changing the structure of power. With conflict organizing, the power structure is not utilized as a partner, but more as a target of action (Ohmer & DeMasi, 2009). The targets of conflict organizing are those with power in the community to make change, such as landlords and government officials, the same persons and institutions with which consensus organizers seek to create partnerships.

Community Organizing Skills   For community organizing along the continuum, the three essential elements for community organizing are empowering individuals, building and strengthening community bonds, and building progressive organizations (Rubin & Rubin, 2008). Empowering individuals occurs in a number of ways, to include: (1) encouraging participation; (2) arranging tasks so individuals experience success and build their confidence to engage in public affairs; (3) organizing tasks so individuals' involvement is meaningful and builds leadership skills; and (4) recognizing and supporting their efforts (Minieri & Getsos, 2007). Building progressive organizations involves working to build an organization whose mission is to promote social equity and which is governed by a participatory democracy process (Rubin & Rubin, 2008), such as Robert's Rules of Order or consensus.

Building bonds among people occurs through developing a shared sense of community through the organizing process. When individuals work together on a common goal through such processes as determining common community issues, analyzing the issues, selecting issues on which to work, developing and implementing strategies, and engaging in evaluation, social networks and bonds are created (Rubin & Rubin, 2008). The process of community organizing across the continuum begins with building relationships with individuals, followed by facilitating the identification of common challenges with a core group of involved people. While recruitment of individuals occurs continually, the core group works to enact change, even one of a small magnitude (Ohmer & DeMasi, 2009).

The ultimate desired outcomes of community organizing efforts frame many aspects of community practice. For example, for conflict organizing, altering the balance of power so that resources are more equitably distributed is the final desired outcome, while at the other end of the continuum, strong partnerships between community residents and external power sources that result in tangible resources is the desired outcome (Ohmer & DeMasi, 2009). This difference effects the emphasis or importance of specific skills, such as the degree to which a social worker can analyze the power of a target or choose issues on which to work (conflict organizing) or build relationships with external resources and broker relationships between community groups and institutions (consensus organizing) (Bobo, Kendall, & Max, 2010; Ohmer & DeMasis, 2009).

A Generalist Approach to Community Intervention

Depending on the context of the community intervention, generalist social work practitioners often integrate aspects of community organizing and community development activities in their community practice. For example, in many communities, a shared identity, bonds between residents, the skills for public discourse, the ability to determine priorities among many challenges, the skills to work together on common challenges, and leadership skills are elements that must be developed for community change efforts to be possible. Social workers can play an important role in facilitating the development of these prerequisites. Social workers who work primarily with individuals, families, and groups have opportunities to support the development of these skills, and to encourage persons to participate in community efforts. These skills provide the foundation for collective action at the community level.

There are many ways that social workers can help build the capacity of individuals to engage in community interventions. At the interpersonal level, social workers emphasize collaboration with their clients to optimize individuals' rights, strengths, and capabilities. Social workers discuss power and control with their clients, to increase client awareness of these dynamics in their everyday life, as well as in community activities. Social workers can regard clients as citizens, consumers, and partners in change efforts, and use dialogue to raise client awareness about the sociopolitical realities. As first suggested by educator Paulo Freire (1973), social workers educate clients about the social conditions, patterns of resource distribution, oppression, and other social and environmental factors that contribute to their situation using respectful discussion and questioning. Social workers help persons to become prepared and supported while engaging in collective action. Research indicates that the activities that develop personal and political skills are among the most effective community intervention activities that social workers undertake (Ohmer & Korr, 2006). Social workers also engage in social planning efforts by participating in proposals for action by elected officials or human service planning councils. As part of that process, social workers can carefully create opportunities for participation by community participants, so their participation is meaningful and effective, rather than a token effort to involve "residents." For example, social workers invite community residents to testify at public hearings about proposals to close schools in their neighborhood, and help prepare them for the testimony. Social workers also seek resident involvement in neighborhood committees, and work to ensure that residents can voice their opinions, participate fully in decision-making and assist to implement decisions. Social workers also make connections between disparate situations, so that the needs of individuals are connected to broader efforts and wider structures. For example, if a social worker encounters a resident whose child has lead poisoning, the social worker may be able to link this "case" to a broader "cause" of a community problem with lead poisoning due to the old housing stock in the neighborhood and the reluctance of landlords to remediate the lead in their units. Social workers also invite residents to participate in community-wide efforts to alleviate and prevent the problem, such as lead paint screenings in schools, and programs to assist tenants to test for lead paint in their apartments.

GLOBAL APPROACHES FOR COMMUNITY SOCIAL WORK PRACTICE

While all types of social work practice methods, including casework, group work, and family work, are utilized around the world, community social work practice offers unique contributions as an intervention method. Social workers are concerned about poverty and social issues that they encounter in every country, yet large differences in the scope and severity of social issues exist. While poverty and social issues encountered on a small scale can be addressed through individual, family, and group social work interventions, and a social welfare approach through offering governmental income and/or health assistance, widespread poverty and disasters in countries without a social safety net often requires a community practice approach (Healy, 2008). Exhibit 11.4 provides an overview of strategies to link local social work practice with global social work practice, particularly focused on community practice. While any of the models described in this chapter may be appropriate, given a specific community context, described next will be specific application of community development and community organizing using global approaches and in other countries.

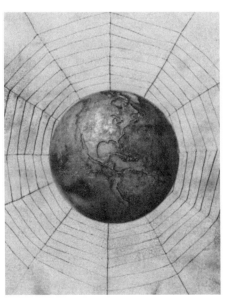

The global local web

EXHIBIT 11.4

Priorities for Social Work Practice Linking the Global and the Local

- Concentrating on community development as a focus for practice, and the incorporation of community development approaches in all social work practice.

- Extending the practice of policy advocacy to international forums.

- Developing techniques to enable the disadvantaged and oppressed to find a voice not merely in national forums but also globally, in international solidarity.

- Making effective use of the new technologies to link both workers and community groups globally.

- Including global forces as a critical component of problem analysis and consciousness raising.

- Social work roles and positions in international nongovernmental organizations (NGOs) and United Nations (UN) agencies.

- Incorporating a strong human rights analysis alongside more traditional social work needs-based practice.

- Seeking opportunities for social workers to develop internationalist understandings through such things as exchange programs and international courses in schools of social work.

- Developing further analysis and research about the link between the global and the local across social work knowledge, values, and skills.

Source: Ife, 2000, pp. 62–63

International Social Work Community Development

As with domestic social work community development practice, the spectrum of social and economic development activities is broad, and has many actors. Some large international organizations (e.g., the United Nations Development Programme, World Health Organization, World Bank, International Monetary Fund), as well as national players, such as U.S. Agency for International Development (U.S.-AID) and the U.S. Peace Corps, play important roles in community development work in developed and developing countries through funding, facilitation, oversight, and management of community development projects and programs.

These organizations facilitate and plan the creation of large-scale physical projects, such as the building of dams, small business loans, credit guarantees, and the provision of primary health care, among other activities. Non-governmental organizations, such as the International Red Cross, CARE, Catholic Relief Services, and Save the Children, also focus on development projects that are self-sustaining and have long-reaching positive effects on communities. Examples include forming local cooperatives, introducing farming techniques, preventive health care projects, and local sanitation projects (e.g., digging wells and building latrines) (Healy, 2008).

The goal of community development projects is to be self-sustaining by the community. Local-level development, in which the responsibility for the work is at the local community level, is increasingly utilized (Cox & Pawar, 2006). Local-level development requires that strategies are planned and implemented with and by the persons experiencing the problem or need. The local-level approach requires social workers to focus on the development of relationships with community members, groups and institutions, so that development projects are truly locally determined and directed (Healy, 2008). Box 11.5 provides an overview of key strategies and programs for local-level community development. Boxes 11.6 and Box 11.7 provide case examples of international community development work that implements several of the strategies and programs.

Globalization and Community Organizing in Social Work Practice

Similarities exist between community organizing efforts at the international level and efforts in the U.S. For example, regardless of the setting or context, empowering individuals, building and strengthening community bonds, and building progressive organizations, are appropriate community organizing goals. Community organizing skills are similar, as the focus is on a particular change effort.

Community organizing efforts, both in the U.S and abroad, are closely related to global issues. For example, international migration of workers from the Global South to the Global North has created large numbers of workers, some who are not documented, vulnerable to abuses and exploitation by their employers due to a tenuous legal status, and desperate to generate income to support themselves and their families in their home countries. A worldwide effort has ensued to combine the efforts of labor organizing and community organizing to build the power of immigrant workers to raise wages and improve working conditions. These efforts mostly use direct action, or conflict, organizing strategies, and activities to gain changes in public policy (Hanley & Shragge, 2009). Other global community organizing efforts are focused on domestic violence experienced by immigrants (Kasvin & Tashayeva, 2004), child welfare issues related to deportation of immigrants, and a host of other issues that are interrelated in the global interconnections of systems.

Community social work practice, just like social work practice with other systems levels, has the ending phase of termination and evaluation. The next

- *Basic literacy courses.* Teachers can be recruited from local communities and trained to provide basic literacy instruction that conforms to local culture, socioeconomic realities and response to the desires of the local population.

- *Primary school education.* Primary school education is a key element to further development. Social workers can provide support to children seeking an education, and can work with the local community to provide resources needed.

- *Basic health care.* Staff can be recruited from local communities and trained to provide basic health care. Social workers can be involved in education about basic hygiene, immunizations, and disease prevention efforts.

- *Adult education, basic training, and capacity building of individuals.* If desired by the community, social workers can facilitate adult basic education or training in such fields as agriculture, forestry, or marketing for small businesses.

- *Awareness-raising and empowerment.* Through informal or formal dialogue, social workers can assist individuals, families, groups, and communities to understand their life situation of oppression, exclusion, poverty, drug addiction, and others. This realization includes an understanding of the forces that have led to and reinforce the present situation. This realization can lead to change efforts.

- *Local income-generation programs.* Social workers can be involved in education or facilitation of programs that lead to higher income generation at the individual, family or community level. Such programs can lead to better farming methods, increased number of or profitability of small businesses, or large community-wide industries, such as a food processing plant.

- *Credit schemes and people's banks.* To overcome the inability of community members to access financial credit through formal institutions, social workers can be involved in local level, small lending programs (for example, see Box 11.6).

- *Community-based self-help programs.* Social workers can assist to facilitate a planned response by the community to a community need, such as developing a local program to assist the disabled, mentally ill, or AIDS orphans.

- *Leadership development.* Social workers can support existing leaders, as well as train new leaders.

- *Local organization and institution promotion and capacity building.* Social workers may be involved in assisting to create or promote local institutions, such as those that oversee education or community recreation.

- *Linking local organizations to government agencies and international structures.* Social workers can provide the information, support, and connections between local organizations and external resources.

- *Comprehensive community development programs.* Social workers can assist to facilitate the integration of development efforts to create a holistic effort.

BOX 11.5

Key Strategies and Programs for Local Level Development

Source: Cox & Pawar, 2006, pp. 143–159

<table>
<tr>
<td>

BOX 11.6

International Community Development Case Example— Grameen Bank

</td>
<td>

An effort to assist one Bangladesh woman by loaning her 27 U.S. dollars has evolved into a world-wide movement to assist the poor to escape dire poverty by providing micro-credit. Many poor small business owners lack the money to purchase needed raw goods or supplies for their business, and they are dependent on high-cost credit from money-lenders. The Grameen (which means "village") Bank was founded on the idea that small loans with reasonable terms would make a large difference in the lives of the poor. The bank began as a very small effort in 1983, and now has over 2,500 branches in 78,000 villages in Bangladesh, with a loan repayment rate of 98.6 percent.

The bank offers loans without collateral requirements, a credit history, or any legal instruments. The bank makes loans to a self-made group of five friends, rather than an individual. When one wants to take out a loan, the other group members must approve. Members of the group provide encouragement, support, and practical assistance to one another. The groups from each village attend weekly meetings in their village, in which loan repayments are collected, loan applications are accepted, and activities are undertaken to foster community bonds and provide education about important topics. Positive social pressure by the group structure has facilitated high repayment rate of the small loans. The Grameen Bank borrowers also commit to "The Sixteen Decisions," a list of values and activities that foster healthy living, communal action, and education for children.

For his efforts, Muhammad Yunus and the Grameen Bank won the 2006 Nobel Peace Prize.

</td>
</tr>
</table>

<table>
<tr>
<td>

BOX 11.7

International Community Development Case Example— Project Restore

</td>
<td>

Project Restore (PR) is a humanitarian development and relief agency that supports, rehabilitates, and enhances the quality of life and well-being of individuals and communities across the world. By focusing on four key issues, Project Restore promotes self-sustainable, prosperous communities in the U.S. and around the world. The four areas of focus are clean water, education, hunger, and healthcare.

Specifically, PR is currently engaged in community development in a village in Uganda, Africa. The first step in the development process was the identification of the develop-ment priorities of the village by the village council (i.e., village leaders). The village council identified the needs, the plan for meeting those needs, their contribution to the development plan, and their request for PR. Projects that have been completed or that are still ongoing include the preparation, purchase, and placement of several water harvesting tanks, the repair of several wells, the distribution of mosquito nets, the purchase and distribution of livestock to produce milk and offspring to sell for food for school lunches, and a matched savings account program for the children in secondary school to help pay for their supplies and tuition. Medical supplies are also furnished to the local clinic.

</td>
</tr>
</table>

section will consider trends that impact this phase, as well as the skills needed to professionally master the ending phase of social work community practice.

CONTEMPORARY TRENDS AND SKILLS FOR THE ENDING PHASE OF COMMUNITY SOCIAL WORK: TERMINATION AND EVALUATION

Community social work practitioners join with the community in change efforts, and facilitate the leadership of the efforts by the community members. Often, community practice efforts are the result of months and even years (or decades) of work, and consist of many smaller change efforts. For example, social workers may engage in community development and community efforts with the community to rid the community of child lead poisoning. This overarching change effort can involve efforts to change policy at the local level about rental housing, work with landlords to remediate lead paint, the promotion of local school screening for child lead poisoning, and work with the local public health clinic to create an outreach program to prevent lead poisoning and reach persons potentially affected. Each of these may have involved lengthy efforts.

Achieving goal implementation of community change efforts, whether smaller efforts within larger goals, or the larger goal itself, is the catalyst for turning to the next phase of the change effort, termination and evaluation.

Community Social Work Practice Endings

Termination in community social work practice can be more complex than termination with other client systems, due to the potential involvement of many players and institutions in the process. The termination phase in community practice is often termination of the social worker from the community (if moving on to other responsibilities), of the social worker's sponsoring organization from a community change effort (if the organization can no longer participate for some reason), or termination of persons or institutions from community change efforts, which may continue without them. Termination of one change effort can also occur when the community has prioritized other needs, such as a situation where the community is grappling with a natural disaster. For example, a social worker may terminate with a community lead prevention and remediation effort if lead poisoning levels drop dramatically, and/or if local leadership is effectively working on the issue and the assistance of the social worker is no longer needed.

As in terminations with other client systems, endings have the potential to evoke emotional responses from the participants. Building relationships is a key element to all types of community practice; therefore, the social worker's role in termination is to "help [participants] examine their accomplishments, review their experience together, and prepare for the future" (Garvin & Galinsky, 2008, pp. 291–292). Social workers may also facilitate the expression and integration of positive and negative emotion, which can includes such feelings as elation and joy about successes achieved and/or such negative emotions as disappointment, rejection, abandonment, or anger, depending on the circumstances of the termination. While participants in community practice efforts are likely to experience fewer highly emotional responses than those of individual, family or group work, social workers must be attuned to the possibility of emotional reactions to the termination (of all types mentioned above).

Endings in Community Practice Utilizing Strengths and Empowerment   The use of the strengths and empowerment approaches leads the social worker to facilitate the community process of reviewing the progress made toward the previously identified goals and developing strategies for sustainability of the changes. In the case of social work community practice, the social worker can invite each participant to review and reflect on her or his individual experience in the change effort, including strengths brought to the process, any change that they personally experienced, and plans for contributing to the maintenance of the change(s). Having individual members engaged in this process can provide closure for all involved. Like group work practice, participants can also utilize the reflections of the other participants to examine their own growth processes.

As community social work practice often involves the use of task groups, many elements of and skills needed for the termination process of group work can apply. For example, using a strengths-based perspective, the social worker can assist the group in reflecting on the group strengths that have evolved as the group engaged in community change efforts. The social worker can utilize the group ending as an opportunity to provide feedback on the individual, group, and community changes observed.

In situations in which the community goals are not realized, the termination process can still employ a strengths perspective. The participants can review the community and group strengths that existed at the outset of their efforts, those strengths gained or mobilized during the process, and those strengths that can be carried on by the participants after the formal change effort has ended. While the members (and the social worker) may be dismayed by the perceived failure of not achieving the desired goals, strategizing about ways in which the participants can continue to work toward achieving the goals can, in fact, be empowering.

Like termination with individuals, families, and groups, a key element of the termination process is a focus on sustaining the gains achieved, such as community bonding, leadership skills, civic engagement, and/or the continuation and growth of community networks and community programs. Regardless of the circumstances of the termination, a focus on community strengths and positive outcomes of the intervention can serve to sustain efforts by energizing community members and institutions to continue their efforts. If the termination occurs because the goal of the community intervention was achieved, the community can build on their successes, and begin the assessment, intervention, and evaluation process anew. However, sustaining the gains from the intervention may involve many persons and institutions, particularly if the social worker (and his/her sponsoring organization) supplied many resources for the intervention. New actors, such as new community participants or institutions, may need to become involved to continue with the community change efforts if professional social work resources will not be available. For example, using the example presented in the previous section, if the social worker involved in the change efforts related to lead paint worked for the school district and the social worker was transferred to a different school and needed to terminate from the efforts, the social worker would transfer responsibilities to another leader in the effort, such as a co-worker, parent, local development organization staff member, other community resident, or a group of professionals involved in the effort, so that the change effort could continue. If the local leadership was not sufficiently developed to maintain the community change effort, the effort would discontinue.

Evaluation of Social Work Practice with Communities

Similar to evaluation with individuals, families, and groups, evaluation of social work community practice interventions can assess the process along the way, the extent to which the goals were achieved, and the social worker's skills in the intervention phase. Just as the community change effort was a collaborative process with the community, so too is the evaluation process a collaborative effort. Community participation is important throughout the change effort for empowerment of participants, and during the evaluation process, collaboration as an equal partner in this process leads to an ownership of the information. The evaluation process seeks to determine the value of something, and differs from monitoring the intervention (Netting et al., 2008).

The evaluation process begins as an element of the intervention design, and requires social workers and community members first to determine: (1) if both the process and outcomes will be evaluated; (2) the ways in which the process and outcomes will be evaluated; and (3) the means by which data will be collected as the basis for the evaluation. Evaluation of community change efforts may include both an examination of the personal and interpersonal levels, as well as the community level. Evaluation of the community effort may include an evaluation of the group work involved, which is covered extensively in Chapter 9. Preferably, the evaluation process will include both qualitative and quantitative data to provide information about the process of community change, as well as progress on the desired outcomes at the personal, interpersonal, and community levels. Methods may include pre- and post-measures of community functioning, to include the use of validated and standardized measures, direct observation by the social worker to document change, use of publically available data (i.e., U.S. Census data and others), and feedback from other professionals.

An example of a community evaluation process is an evaluation of a community development effort in Perth, Western Australia. The aim of the evaluation was to assess the quality of life in a community that had experienced community development initiatives as compared to a nearby community that had not experienced the initiatives. The residents rated the quality of their lives and communities using the Australian Unity Wellbeing Index to measure individual and neighborhood well-being. Additionally, the well-being of the residents was compared to national averages (Blunsdon & Davern, 2007). In another example, semi-structured interviews and observations were used to evaluate the extent to which an initiative to involve parents in the planning and decisions about delivery methods of a community child development program was successful (MacNeill, 2009).

STRAIGHT TALK ABOUT COMMUNITY INTERVENTION, TERMINATION, AND EVALUATION

Community social work practice, including the intervention, termination, and evaluation phases, offers many rewards and challenges. One challenging aspect of some types of community social work practice is long hours at salaries less than those in individual, family, and group practice. Further, community social work practice can involve working during the day with professionals in organizations and institutions, and in the evenings and on weekends with community participants. Efforts to change institutions, policies, and practices can take a long time, and there may be many setbacks along the way. Tangible rewards and successes for the work may be few and far between, which can lead to burnout (Rubin & Rubin, 2008).

The rewards include the personal satisfaction of working to change environments to better meet the needs of persons, and provide opportunities for the empowerment of individuals and communities. Many community practitioners appreciate the ability to partner with individuals, families, and groups to better their lives, while avoiding the view of persons as "clients," which can include the use of diagnostic labels, treatment plans, and a primarily individualistic perspective. Through community practice, people are involved in decision-making about aspects that affect their lives, sometimes for the first time. Helping people gain their voices and working toward large-scale social change is work toward social justice. The variety of tasks completed, the joy of successes, and the wide autonomy and flexibility of the tasks involved are other factors that draw and keep social workers in community practice (Rubin & Rubin, 2008).

Community practitioners must have energy for long-term work, and be able to see value in the process and effort involved, rather than just the outcomes. The occasional victories, even short-term or small, must provide the drive to sustain community practitioners. The community practitioner must often work diligently on short-term or immediate goals, while keeping the larger, systemic, institutional change in focus, and celebrate small gains.

CONCLUSION

This chapter has presented the range of social work community practice as an important client system level for generalist practitioners. Engagement in community practice offers social workers the opportunity to impact the environment for persons by influencing the community in which people live to create institutions and communities that are truly responsive to the human needs of all community members. Community interventions, terminations, and evaluations are complex, with a primary focus on the community, and a secondary focus on individual change. Community practice includes developing leaders, facilitating bonding among community residents, and other personal and interpersonal work that is important as a foundation for community change, and are important interventions in and of themselves. Such complexity requires the social worker to possess skills with various client systems to implement the community intervention and facilitate the termination and evaluation processes.

MAIN POINTS

- Community intervention uses guided community practice models, which are primarily based in the concepts and language of systems, ecological and power, change, and politics theories.

- The three models most commonly used are Rothman's (2008) three models of community practice: planning/policy; community capacity development; and social advocacy. These models can be blended to best match the context of the community change effort.

- The intervention strategies of community social and economic development, community organizing, and community asset mapping are aimed at improving community conditions and the quality of life for the community residents or members.

- Community social work practice, including community development and community organizing, offers unique contributions as an intervention method both domestically and around the globe.

- Termination in community practice can be more complex than termination with other client systems, due to the potential involvement of many players and institutions in the process.

- Evaluation of social work community practice functions to assess the process along the way, the extent to which the goals were achieved, and the social worker's skills in the intervention phase.

EXERCISES

1. Go to www.routledgesw.com/cases and review the video of the Alverez neighborhood association meeting. In groups, begin a role-play where the video ends and continue the discussion. Did the Chair of the committee vote? If not, what may have occurred? If the committee delays their vote, what additional information might be helpful to the decision-making process? Summarize the points of view. Which arguments are most persuasive? How might you vote if you were on the committee? How would you like to see this end? Compare your preferences with classmates.

2. After completing Exercise #1, discuss the following questions with your classmates. What other information would you need to make a decision? If you were the facilitator, what might you have done differently as the Chair? What elements of Robert's Rules of Order were used in the Alverez video? What elements were not used? How might other elements have been used? How might that have changed the course of actions in the video?

3. Go to www.routledgesw.com/cases, and become familiar with the Riverton case file, especially the "Your History" section. Choose either the planning/policy, community capacity development, or social advocacy models of community intervention described in Chapter 11 and describe a possible community intervention for Riverton to address the concerns about the coal-fired power plant. Describe a community intervention using a second model, and compare and contrast the intervention with the first intervention. What are some key differences?

4. Choose a social issue that is important to you. Assume the role of a community developer. How would you address the issue using community development skills and techniques?

5. Choose a social issue that is important to you. Assume the role of a community organizer. How would you address the issue using community organizing skills and techniques?

6. Go to www.routledgesw.com/cases and become familiar with the Riverton case file. You would like to begin to address community concerns and issues using a community social and economic development approach. What issues could you address? How would you address the issues using a community social and economic development approach?

7. Go to www.routledgesw.com/cases and become familiar with the Riverton case file. With many types of community interventions, recruiting allies from a diversity of groups adds to the strength of the intervention. Describe how you would recruit from various populations within Riverton to participate in a community intervention.

CHAPTER 12

Social Work Practice with Organizations: Engagement, Assessment, and Planning

"Why study organizations?" There are two answers to this question. The first answer is obvious. Organizations surround us. We are born in them and usually die in them. Our life space in between is filled with them. They are just about impossible to escape. They are as inevitable as death and taxes . . . the second answer to the question . . . is . . . organizations have outcomes.

Richard Hall, 1991

Key Questions for Chapter 12

(1) What competencies do I need to engage and assess organizations? (EPAS 2.1.10(a & b))

(2) What are the social work practice behaviors that enable me to effectively engage and assess organizations? (EPAS 2.1.10(a & b))

(3) How can I utilize evidence to practice research-informed practice and practice-informed research to guide the engagement and assessment with organizations? (EPAS 2.1.6)

(4) How can I apply critical thinking to engagement and assessment with organizations? (EPAS 2.1.3)

(5) How can I apply social work values and ethics to engagement with and assessment of organizations? (EPAS 2.1.2)

INFLUENCING ORGANIZATIONS OFFERS THE PROSPECT OF improving services for current and future clients. Social workers may think of organizations as small, supportive structures that help to organize the maze of work, or as large bureaucracies that are unresponsive to individual efforts. *Organizations* can be defined as "formally structured arrangements of people, tools, and resources brought together to achieve predetermined objectives through institutionalized strategies" (Barker, 2003). Social workers work in many types and sizes of organizations, and utilize their knowledge of organizations to promote the best interest of their client systems. Knowledge of organizations is imperative to professional practice. Although there has been considerable growth in the number of social workers choosing independent practice settings (Whitaker & Arrington, 2008), the majority today work in agency settings.

This chapter focuses on the general nature of organizations and social work agencies, particularly as experienced by social work practitioners. Theoretical perspectives on and dimensions of organizations will be explored. Also discussed will be the engagement and assessment process with organizations. The discussion emphasizes the social worker's interface with organizations, and the ways in which organization functions shape professional practice. The chapter will also look at the skills needed for organizational engagement and assessment, and will close with a discussion about types of organizations.

UNDERSTANDING ORGANIZATIONS

Organizations carry out multifaceted tasks to address individual, family, group, and community needs. Organizations, like other client systems, can be understood through the lens of various theories, models, and perspectives. Prior to moving into the change process, a theoretical understanding of organizations can assist social workers in the process of engagement, assessment, intervention, and termination and evaluation. In this next section, organizations will be described as a social system, as well as from the integration of contemporary theories of organizations.

Organization as a Social System

As mentioned in earlier chapters, general systems theory posits that a system, such as an organization, is composed of multiple intersecting components that relate to one other, and are also part of larger systems, such as the community at large and society. Organizations, therefore, acquire resources from their environments and return products or services to their environment. Understanding organizations includes the notion that organizations exchange resources with their environments (Brueggemann, 2005). In the organizational assessment process, which is described later in this chapter, social workers can critically assess the extent to which subsystems, such as funders, other organizations, or networks of organizations, meet the needs of the organization and advocate for a higher level of functioning of a subsystem.

Contemporary Theories and Organizations

Organizational and management theory has a history that dates back to the late 1800s. Like earlier theories, contemporary theories about organizations, such as power and politics, organizational culture, quality-oriented management, and evidence-based management, help to analyze organizations and understand their structure and operations. In understanding organizations, theories of today emphasize the following: (1) the role of culture in helping to understand the ways in which groups of persons affiliated with organizations define and pursue collective organizational goals; (2) the idea of quality has become the benchmark in the design of organizational structures (such as administrative relationships), processes (such as decision-making processes), and the evaluation of success as an organization. In this respect, the process of the work of the organization is as important as the outcomes of the programs and services that are delivered to clients; and (3) there is no one correct approach to structuring organizations. Many aspects of an organization, including size, mission, clients, staff qualifications, and other factors, are important to consider when structuring an organizations and developing a style of management (Netting et al., 2008).

Dimensions of Organizations

Social and human service organizations differ widely along a number of dimensions. These differences affect service delivery to clients, as well as the employee experience. Three dimensions of difference between organizations are of particular interest: (1) purpose of the organization; (2) structure of governance; and (3) the internal power relations.

Purpose

The stated purpose of an organization provides the rationale for the organization's existence, as well as the agency's general goals and activities. While organizational objectives and activities provide information about the means by which the organization works toward the general goals, the stated purpose describes the concerns of the organization in broad terms. A brief review of three types of purposes follows, with a human-service example. The three purposes are: (1) to fill a public mandate; (2) to provide a particular service; and (3) to foster social change in regard to an ideological concern.

Organizations Sanctioned by Law   The law sanctions organizations in several ways. First, organizations sanctioned by federal and state law ("public organizations") provide mandated social services that are widely recognized by the public. For example, adult protection services, available in all 50 states, are usually housed within a large and visible state organization. Social workers representing these organizations are expected to act in the best interests of older adults who cannot protect themselves against abuse, neglect, or exploitation, carry out the activities of daily living, or manage their own affairs. Public organizations are directly account-able to the public, as they derive the vast majority of their funding through tax revenue (i.e., federal, state, county, or local government funds). Secondly, most social services are offered through nonprofit organizations designated as 501(c)3 organizations by the U.S. Internal Revenue Service (IRS). Nonprofit organizations are sanctioned by the law to meet specified public needs. Designated nonprofit organizations are exempt from paying taxes on organizational income, and donors are allowed to deduct contributions from their individual taxes (Holland, 2008).

Organizations with Service Goals   Organizations with specific service goals develop as a result of an agreed upon need or concern. For example, youth who have or are at risk of dropping out of school are often visible in local communities in such locations as among homeless populations and those loitering along certain com-mercial areas. Adolescent high school drop-outs are a high risk population for poverty, health concerns, and criminal activity. Organizations providing youth services provide myriad services, to include prevention services to help youth avoid dropping out, assist adolescent drop-outs in acquiring tangible resources, and provide legal assistance and referrals to substance abuse treatment. Service goals are an important type of purpose, as they define the work of the organization and the social need or concern addressed by the organization.

Organizations Arising from Social Movements   Some grassroots organizations, which are organizations started by ordinary citizens rather than professionals, arise in response to ideological positions regarding particular social problems. The early development of shelters for women who are battered by partners or spouses is an example of a **social movement**, a political effort designed to change some aspect of society. A social movement is led by citizens whose commitments and energies are channeled into a political movement, and organizations were created to implement the long-term work of the social movement. As the organizations are created, profes-sionals, such as social workers, are employed by the organizations. Frequently, the founders, professionals, and volunteers of such organizations are indigenous to the movement, which means they have personally experienced the oppression that is the focus of the organization. Professionals and volunteers often have extraordinary commitment to the mission of the organization.

Structures of Governance

The way in which an organization is governed is another variable in the structure of an organization. Organizational structure, much like family structure, refers to the way in which various members, tasks, and units relate to one another. The structure shapes the rules, or norms, of the organization. Some of the rules or norms are explicit, such as personnel policies, and others are implicit, such as the best ways to influence the decision of an administrator. These rules or norms may be communicated openly to employees and volunteers, while others may be communicated through nonverbal communication and interpretation of decisions. In the next section, three kinds of organizational structures will be explored as representative of those found in many contemporary agencies: bureaucracies, project teams, and functional structures.

Bureaucracies Many human service organizations, including state and local government organizations and nonprofits, are structured as a bureaucracy; therefore, social workers benefit from knowledge about the structure of their employing organization.

German sociologist Max Weber invented the term **bureaucracy** as a conceptual type, rather than a reality, of structure. The following 10 points describe the characteristics of a bureaucracy (Weber, 1947, as cited in Netting et al., 2008):

- Each position in the organization has a limited area of authority and responsibility.

- Control and responsibility are concentrated at the top of a clear hierarchy.

- The activities of the organization are documented in a central system of records.

- The organization employs highly specialized workers based on expert training.

- Staff demands require full-time commitment, and each position represents a career.

- Activities are coordinated through clearly outlined rules.

- The relationships among workers are characterized by impersonality.

- Recruitment is based on ability and relevant, technical knowledge.

- The private and public lives of the organization's members are distinct.

- Promotions in the organization are made by seniority and/or achievement.

Several aspects of these characteristics of bureaucracy have been incorporated into the organizational experiences of many professionals, even those in smaller organizations. For example, the notion that recruitment is based on ability, rather than a relationship with other staff members, is a widely accepted idea of fairness in employment practices. On the other hand, the top-down, hierarchical authority or the impersonality of relationships among members is often an aspect of bureaucracies with which employees are challenged. The organizations that most often display the characteristics of bureaucracies are those embedded in large systems, such as local, state, or federal government; therefore, older adult/child protection, public health and mental health, and corrections, are fields in which bureaucratic approaches tend to be most common.

Project Teams   In a sharp contract with bureaucracy, **project teams** consist of a group of persons who collectively work on organizational challenges or opportunities through committee or task force structures (Brueggemann, 2005). Project teams are a flexible way to accomplish work tasks, as the committees may exercise their best collective judgment in decision-making, and the group has minimal hierarchy. Often such groups are challenged in their efforts to maintain this structure longer than a limited time for a variety of reasons, such as the growth of the group, and/or the resources dedicated for the effort become subject to more careful accountability and additional structure may be imposed from higher authority.

For example, a group of women and men concerned about intimate partner violence may utilize a project team approach to develop and operate an organization dedicated to providing services for survivors of intimate partner violence. The intended services include a domestic violence shelter, therapy, and violence prevention programming. Team members may structure the organization of the shelter staff so that everyone shares the tasks of managing the agency's physical space, and identical salaries are paid to everyone. The project team structure has many positive aspects; however, the structure may be challenged by those with concerns relating to the appropriateness of some duties for those staff with higher degrees (i.e., the appropriateness of a person with a master's degree answering phones or vacuuming the shelter office). The project team approach can be challenged as organizations hire new workers who demand a competitive salary, or as their budget grows from sources that require a hierarchal structure.

Functional Structures   When an agency becomes too large for a single person to administer the details of all the programs or an organization, a layer of administrative personnel will be added. These administrative additions are usually divided literally by function or area of responsibility; thus the name **functional structures**. In a community development agency, for example, the executive director may appoint an experienced social worker as the program director of the youth services department, and another social worker as the program director of the affordable housing development unit. In this situation, the two midlevel administrative leaders would be equals, and may form a management team that works directly with the executive director in larger administrative functions and decisions. Frequently, these administrative roles are added to already existing direct service roles. For example, the program director of the youth services programs would retain responsibility for actually implementing one of the programs. As the agency grows larger, the program directors may not provide the direct services due to the heavy demands of the supervisory and administrative activities.

Internal Power Relations

Organizations have arrangements of power that are overt, such as the hierarchical arrangements of personnel. Organizations also have power arrangements that are subtle and are unique to the organization. Chapter 3 discusses several sources of power for social workers, including agency, expert knowledge, interpersonal, and legitimate power. The following discussion considers the view of authority as "consensual power" (Netting et al., 2008, p. 219), or power that is non-coercive and derives from content. In the next section, authority based on tradition, charisma, and rational/legal principles is discussed. Rather than being imposed on persons, these sources of power are derived from authority given by persons to someone.

Traditional Authority   Authority attributed by title or ancestry, such as a king or a pope might claim, is **traditional authority**. This type of authority is most often seen in the U.S. as based on family relationships and history or inheritance. For example, CEOs of large corporations are often related to other powerful people, such as former presidents or other CEOs, and are frequently members of the original family who started the business. Such authority is seen infrequently in human service agencies, but is viewed on occasion.

Charismatic Authority   This type of authority is considered an unstable but present dynamic in U.S. organizations. As contrasted to traditional authority, the **charismatic authority** model suggests that a captivating personality (rather than heritage, ideas, skills, or commitments) is the variable required to gain power by consensus. This form of authority is often displayed in state and national elections when, for example, entertainers and celebrities run for and win public office without previous political experience. Such authority is often present with founders of human service agencies who are successful at the necessary start-up tasks of garnering supporters, raising funds, recruiting an initial board of directors, and others tasks that involve persuasion.

Rational/Legal Authority   This authority is based on ability to achieve outcomes and, like charismatic authority, is persuasive rather than coercive. An example of a person with **rational/legal authority** is an agency staff member who is an expert in program development and program evaluation. A staff member with a particular expertise and a track record of accomplishments in the area of expertise is likely to be persuasive in an appeal to initiate new programs. Large human service agencies, particularly bureaucracies, often contain staff members with rational/legal authority because the staff is able to specialize and develop expertise. Staff in smaller organizations can also develop rational/legal authority, depending on their backgrounds, interests, opportunities, and agency needs.

   In social work practice, these forms of authority can exist on a continuum (i.e., from non-influential to very influential) and/or co-mingle. For example, human service organizations may have an executive director who was the founder and began the position with a great deal of charismatic authority, and developed rational/legal authority while in the position by developing expertise as an administrator. Another executive director may have initially had mainly traditional authority due to a connection with a powerful family member in human services and/or also has or developed charismatic authority due to strong persuasion skills.

Intersections among Dimensions of Organizations

Thus far, the discussion has focused on several dimensions of organizations that influence practice and the social worker's experience. These dimensions, purpose, structures of governance, and internal power relations, often intersect in practice, and some dimensions are likely to be associated with other dimensions. For example, a domestic violence shelter, whose purpose reflects a social movement and ideological position, is more likely to adopt a project team rather than a bureaucratic structure. With feminist organizational roots, a domestic violence shelter is also more likely to be subject to charismatic or rational/legal authority, as social workers with strong interpersonal skills may tend to take on leadership roles even without the authority that comes with a formal position of authority.

Understanding the possibilities of interconnections among these dimensions aid to understand the nature of organizations and develop a framework for examining their distinctions and impact on social workers. Ultimately, understanding possible interconnections can assist in discerning the combination of dimensions that best fit the talents and work styles of workers. For example, some social workers learn that an organization structure characterized by project team approach and rational/legal authority is the best fit for them. Gaining knowledge about agency dimensions also helps to recognize the ways in which agencies in various environments can most effectively and efficiently help client systems reach their goals.

Social Work Practice in Host Settings

Many social workers practice in **host settings**, such as hospitals, residential care facilities, public and private schools, and correctional facilities. Host settings are those organizations in which social workers provide social services as a secondary activity. The following are some examples: (1) the primary service in a school is education, yet social workers provide services to augment and support the educational goals; (2) various programs maintained by the court system, aimed at diversion or advocacy, often include social workers; and (3) housing programs and many disability projects employ social workers to support the main goal of the organization. A number of organizational aspects to this arrangement may provide unique opportunities, as well as challenges for the social worker. Next, two opportunities and challenges are discussed: being a guest in a host setting, and being a member of an interprofessional team.

Guest Status   Expectations and privilege accompany a **guest status** for a social worker practicing within a host setting. Professionals of other disciplines in the setting may not understand the scope of the social work role, and have inaccurate expectations—too high or too low—of the social worker. At the same time, social workers may experience the privilege of working with other professionals on a team that is able to accomplish more than a social worker could independently. The experience of social worker Diane can illustrate the point.

Diane is a recent BSW graduate hired to facilitate discharges in a residential psychiatric treatment center that has a positive reputation in the community. A staff psychiatrist serves as medical director, and the executive director has a degree in public health. Diane is the first social worker ever employed by the center. The nurses and nurse aids had responsibility for discharge work until the number and pace of discharges outgrew their capacity to conduct discharge planning along with their other nursing duties.

Diane is warmly welcomed by staff, who hope that she will fill an acute organizational need. Diane is hopeful that she will gain new competencies and practice behaviors because she will be exposed to different perspectives and practices regarding treatment strategies, medication, and ethics. She knows that she will have the opportunity to observe firsthand the work of the psychiatrist, the public health administrator, nurses, and others, and learn about the ways in which different professional perspectives can assist clients.

While much of the above hopes were realized, Diane also discovers that she does not have a role in decision-making about discharges; rather, the other staff expect her to simply carry out the instructions she is given. The exclusion from the decision-making process occurs because she is viewed as extraneous to the discharge (medical) decisions, rather than for any personal reason. Further, Diane is ambivalent about the possibility of notifying officials about the lack of professional, dignified treatment of some staff toward patients that she has noticed. Due to her exclusion from decision-making, Diane feels undervalued, and more as a guest than a valued team member.

While she understands that the center is primarily a medical facility and medical issues take priority over other concerns, she also understands the potential value of her involvement in decision-making about discharge. She knows she has much more to contribute than she is currently allowed, and wishes to create the possibility of articulating her possible contributions in a way that will facilitate the staff's appreciation and growth, rather than engendering their resistance and resentment. Specifically, she knows that she needs to educate the staff about the complexities of discharge planning (for example, the need for day programming, employment, training, housing, emotional support, family support, and income support), and the possible contributions that she could make to addressing these complexities within the decision-making process about the timing of discharge, and the appropriate placement for patients. In the future, she may also want to address several practices that are inconsistent with socially just and respectful treatment.

Clearly, a guest status within an organization brings unique challenges for social workers. Social workers who have a guest status must exhibit effective practice behaviors concerning the education of other professions about the roles and responsibilities of social workers. Building credibility and networks of support within host organizations, a keen sense of timing, and displaying diplomacy are key skills in this process. On the other hand, social workers in host settings must also advocate for themselves and their professional obligations for client services.

Interprofessional Teams   Projects and programs that include members of several professions (e.g., medicine, public health, public administration, and social work) create **interprofessional teams**. These teams can provide an enriching and exciting atmosphere in which to practice social work. Although the social work profession emphasizes a holistic view of client systems, social workers join many helping professionals in delivering services in a fragmented fashion. Many families seeking the assistance of social workers are also involved with other helping professionals, such as vocational counselors, non-social work therapists, psychologists, income maintenance specialists, physicians—including psychiatrists—and community support workers.

In an interprofessional setting, all professions carry equal power and share decision-making responsibilities—the value is in the total contribution of an integrated approach. In order to be effective, each profession must value the contribution of others. Social workers need competent collaborative practice behaviors when working with other professionals, including conflict mediation skills. A truly interprofessional setting is challenging to implement in practice. For example, in many medically oriented interprofessional teams, physicians are dominant and appear to have a privileged standpoint. Additionally, the socialization of many professions can encourage narrow views to bias the perspective of the chosen profession over other perspectives. Nevertheless, even with such challenges, interprofessional settings offer vast opportunities to wrestle with the challenges of providing an integrated, highly skilled approach in the best interests of clients, as well as to explore the internal dynamics of teaming through the lens of multiple realities.

ENGAGEMENT AND ASSESSMENT OF ORGANIZATIONS

The previous discussion focused on understanding organizations through the use of theory and general organizational dimensions, and made several applications to human service agencies. The next section spotlights the process of engagement and assessment of organizations, including the sources of data and information for the assessment. Engagement and assessment set the stage for the organizational change process of intervention, termination, and evaluation. The section closes with a discussion about integrating the information gleaned in the assessment.

Engagement of Organizations

Engagement of an organization first involves the perception of the organization as a client system. An organization is comprised of many individuals and systems, yet the social worker must view the entire organization as a client system in order to participate in the change process with an organization. This first step in the change process utilizes many of the skills needed for engagement with individuals, families, groups, and communities; namely, the active listening skills and research, evaluation, and analyzing skills discussed in previous chapters. Engagement with organizations work involves working directly with all client system levels, within the perspective of the organization.

Social workers can engage organizations for the change process as an employee, volunteer, interested citizen, or as a consultant, although most often the change process occurs with employing organizations. Social workers often see the need for organizational change, so the organization can operate more efficiently and effectively, provide a higher quality of services, and/or to better address human needs. For example, social workers who work for a school system may identify the need to make a change in the schools, and begin to engage other social workers, teachers, principals, administrators, committees, and task groups across the school district and even across districts to address a specific organizational need. Social workers may also engage organizations as part of advocacy efforts. For example, social workers may engage with individuals and groups within the public agency that serves older adults in their state in an attempt to influence their organizational practices to better address older client needs by making organizational changes. Social workers engage with a community of organizations, such as a network of homeless shelters, to work for organizational changes across many organizations, such as to coordinate data management systems to better meet the needs of clients who are homeless, are struggling with substance abuse, and have a chronic mental illness. In all these cases, engagement skills used with other client systems are necessary.

Assessment of Organizations

The overall assessment of organizations involves both a review of the internal environment of the organization, or the internal mechanisms within organizations, and the external environment with which the organization receives and provides resources, such as funders, accreditation organizations, suppliers of goods and services, clients, other organizations, and others. The following assessment framework, which is based on and an integration of previous frameworks, may be helpful in the assessment task (Gitterman & Germain, 2008b; Netting et. al., 2008;

Miley, O'Melia, & DeBois, 2011), and are more fully described in the following section:

Internal Assessment

- Legal basis, mission, by-laws, and history

- Administrative structure and management style

- Program structure, programs, and services

- Organizational culture (i.e., physical surroundings, public relations, language, procedures, social justice/diversity)

- Personnel policies and procedures

- Resources (i.e., financial, technological, personnel)

External Assessment

- Relationship with funders and potential funders

- Relationship with clients

- Relationship with organizations in network (i.e., referrals and coalitions)

- Relationships with political figures

Assessment of an organization, similar to assessment with all client systems, involves gathering data. Like community assessment, data can be gathered through observation, written documents, key informant interviews, publically available data, service statistics, previous organizational assessment (partial or full), administrative data, other data, and focus groups. Depending on the size of the organization to be assessed, a public forum and survey data may also be appropriate ways to gather data (Gitterman & Germain, 2008b; Netting et al., 2008; Miley et al., 2011).

Organizations often create documents that may be helpful in the assessment process. Documents that may contain needed information and data include organizational charts, policy and personnel manuals, procedure manuals, job descriptions, meeting minutes, and annual reports from within organizations, as well as information from media sources and annual reports and reports from other organizations.

Elements of an Internal Assessment

The internal structures and dynamics of an organization affect many aspects of service delivery of the organization, as well as the employee experience (Freund, 2005). The following section discusses those elements of an organization that can be considered as part of an organizational assessment.

Legal Basis   Organizations must be recognized by the law to legitimately operate. The **legal basis** for public organizations exists in a statute or executive order, while a private organization has a legal basis in the articles of incorporation. These documents authorize an organization to officially exist, and define the parameters for their operations.

Mission Statement   Most nonprofit organizations create a **mission statement**, which is a concise, broad statement of the purpose of the organization that describes a shared vision. While the statement is too broad to provide many details, identified in the statement are the client system needs the organization strives to meet, the population served, and the intended client system outcomes. The details about programs, services, organizational structure, and other specifics are outlined in other documents. The mission statement provides a rationale for the existence of the organization, and does not change as easily as programs and services can change. Revising a mission statement is needed if an organization perceives a mismatch between the mission statement and current client system needs and organization activities. For example, many child welfare agencies were founded in the early 20th century as orphanages, and needed to revisit their mission statements in light of the focus in child welfare on home-based placements. Box 12.1 provides an example of a mission statement.

By-laws   The way in which a nonprofit organization governs itself is described in the **by-laws**. By-laws are legal documents that describe the basic structure and abilities of the board of directors, such as the composition of the board, terms of the members, permanent committees, voting rights, and other matters that concern governance. The by-laws are typically brief, and the rules about them vary from state to state.

History   Like other client systems, organizations create history that defines and impacts the future of the organization. Important aspects of history include the founding of the organization, major funders, influential staff members and administrators, accomplishments, and challenging periods.

Our mission is to enhance the quality of life of older adults, children, and families in the regional area by serving their basic needs by providing: (1) Access to education, counseling and health services; (2) Recreation and social program; (3) Daily nutritional meals.

BOX 12.1

Mission Statement, Longview Community Center

Administrative Structure and Management Style   The structure of the administration of an organization is often reflected in an organizational chart that depicts the units of the organization, and their relationship to one another. The management style of the organization is reflected in the way in which work is allocated, decisions are made, the nature of the supervision of employees and the way in which conflict is handled, among other items. Some elements of the management style will be included in written documents, while others can be learned from the experience of staff members.

Structure of Programs, Services, and Activities   Human service organizations provide programs and services and/or carry out activities to meet overall organizational goals and objectives. An assessment process would include a review of official documents where these are described, and review the extent to which the programs, services, and activities are consistent with the overall mission, goals, and objectives of the organization, as well as are based on evidence-based practice.

Organizational Culture   Organizational culture consists of many factors, including history, philosophy, styles of communication, patterns of decision-making, expectations, collective preferred personal styles of social workers, myths, behaviors, and formal and informal rules. Culture is also shaped by the purpose, structure of governance and internal power relations. While not reflected in the mission statement or any one official document, the organizational culture is, nevertheless, an important element that shapes aspects of the work of the agency, and the experience of employees. For example, the extent to which social workers are expected to work overtime without financial compensation or earned time off, or if practicum students take shifts of being "on call," both represent the types of issues that are shaped by organizational culture. Exhibit 12.1 provides to review some of the facets of your own organizational style.

   While the concept of organizational culture is intangible and imprecise, culture is an important dynamic of any organization. In the next section, additional dimensions that shape services will be discussed, including the legal basis, mission statement, by-laws, physical surroundings, public relations, procedures, and social justice/diversity factors.

Physical Surroundings   The internal **physical surroundings** of an organization and the location of the organization can provide some information about the culture of the organization. An organization with dark, messy physical surroundings and/or having little privacy for client interactions could be an organization with a culture that places less priority on the potential impact of physical surroundings on client outcomes than an organization with bright lighting, clean surrounding and plenty of space for private interviews. To best serve their clients, many human service agencies are located near the homes of their clients, often in low- and middle-income communities. While few social workers are employed by organizations that

Using the key below, rate yourself on the items listed here to review your organizational style. Add other items you think are important. Be prepared to discuss this survey in class and to apply it to your field placement. What obstacles do you encounter in fulfilling these points?

EXHIBIT 12.1

Rate Your Organizational Style

☐ I offer positive feedback to my colleagues for behaviors that contribute to effective services.

☐ I involve my colleagues in seeking changes in policies and programs to improve the quality of services.

☐ I value learning about my colleagues' points of view. For example, I seek feedback that will help me to enhance my competencies and practice behaviors. When I have a complaint, I discuss it with the person directly involved.

☐ I involve others in arranging opportunities to discuss practice/policy issues/topics.

☐ I communicate congratulations to others regarding professional or personal events/accomplishments.

☐ I come prepared for all types of meetings.

☐ I make positive contributions at meetings.

☐ I refrain from idle gossip at work.

☐ I make more positive than negative comments at work.

☐ _____

☐ _____

Key: **0** (not at all) **1** (a little) **2** (a fair amount) **3** (a great deal) **4** (best that could be)

Adapted from Gambrill, E., 2006

are housed in luxurious surroundings and/or in expensive neighborhoods, the physical atmosphere and location of an organization reflects and impacts aspects of organizational culture (Weeks, 2004). While the meaning of physical surroundings can be over-interpreted, the organizational environment is an important area for exploration relative to organizational culture.

Public Relations   Organizations reflect their culture in their **public relations** activities and products (Brueggemann, 2005). Public relations is the practice of managing communication between an organization and the public. Organizations seek to gain support from a positive communication both from the public at large, as well as from specific groups, such as funders, politicians, client populations, and even employees. Organizations can use a variety of mediums to manage their public information and image, to include websites, social media, blogs, printed materials, print newspaper articles and commentaries, and face-to-face encounters. The communication between organizations and others provides clues about the culture of the organization.

Language   The **language** used in agency settings includes the actual words used, as well as the tone, range of sentiment, and degree of empathy and respect expressed by the words. In previous chapters, postmodern ideas regarding the role of language and the way persons create and sustain meanings based on language was discussed. Using postmodernism concepts, language both reflects and shapes the thoughts and feelings expressed. Therefore, the language used in organizations reflects and shapes the self-perceptions of the social workers, their work, and their clients. Social workers' use of disrespectful language toward and about client systems violates the *Code of Ethics* (NASW, 2008), displays a violation of the core commitment to respect people and treat them with dignity, and can affect other social workers through a culture of disrespect. While some organizations may attempt to justify pejorative language patterns by stating that staff members need to "blow off steam," the lack of respectful, strengths-based language can have a powerful, detrimental impact on organizational culture.

Procedures   A simple **procedure**, such as the manner in which a new client is greeted, asked to be seated, invited to an office from the waiting room, or given paperwork to be completed, makes a strong impact on the quality of the experience of becoming a client and maintaining that status. Social workers must be respectful and sensitive about the explanation of the procedures concerning such matters as confidentiality, fees, appointment times, and negotiations in scheduling appointments. These aspects of working with clients are relevant as a social worker's expression of respect for individual, couple, family, and group clients, but also as clearly understood agency policy. Exhibit 12.2 provides an opportunity to assess client and employee treatment regarding procedures at an organization familiar to you.

Complete the following assessment utilizing an organization with which you are familiar.

1. Persons seeking services from my agency are more likely to experience:

_____a poorly maintained waiting room

_____a warm and well-furnished waiting room

_____a place to sign in and be told to take a seat

_____a courteous and personal greeting

_____having their name called out and being told to "follow me" to the office

_____being personally met and invited to "follow me" to the office

_____nonverbal cues from the staff that they are a bother

_____nonverbal cues that suggest we are glad they are here

_____treatment that says "you are another case"

_____treatment that says "you are a person"

2. Persons seeking services in my agency are more likely to be:

_____treated as problems that need to be solved

_____treated as partners in a mutual process of deciding how to proceed

_____given treatment based on the medical model

_____provided treatment based on a competency model

_____seen as problems

_____seen as people with issues and needs

_____seen as needing an expert

_____seen as the expert

3. Employees within my setting are more likely to experience:

_____getting written memos about new changes

_____being asked for input about new changes

_____an expectation of independent work without much support

_____being supported in their roles

_____wishing for another job

_____joy in coming to work

_____feeling like their consumers are not important to the agency

_____feeling their consumers are important to the agency

_____feeling like they are a drain to the community

_____feeling like they are a resource to the community

_____feeling unimportant to the agency

_____feeling important to the agency

_____lack of respect for other employees

_____respect for other employees

4. My experience with the organizational culture is that:

_____respect for human diversity is ignored

_____respect for human diversity is valued

_____membership in the community is blocked to those who are different

_____membership in the community is open to all

_____social services are at best tolerated

_____social services are willingly supported

Adapted from Locke, Garrison, & Winship, 1998, pp. 278–279

EXHIBIT 12.2

Dignity Assessment and Human Services Guide

Social Justice/Diversity Factors   Aspects of social work practice that affirm social justice and support diversity can be nurtured and sustained across all client system levels, including organizations. Unless organizations promote social justice through policies and practices, clients may find their social workers to be "nice people" but feel victimized by unjust organizational practices. To fully promote social justice, organizations may arrange the internal administrative practices of the agency to reflect diversity and social justice concerns. For example, posters, magazines, and signs in the waiting area can reflect multiple languages and cultures to convey a welcoming atmosphere for clients from diverse backgrounds. Activities and services that clearly take into account cultural values, such as food at events that reflect ethnic food traditions and restrictions send a message. Activities and services can also honor history of groups, and/or reflect histories of oppression for specific populations. Just as ethnically dominant white middle-class social workers struggle to become competent in working with other cultures, so must organizations assess their culture competency and the extent to which the organization works toward social justice goals. Exhibit 12.3 addresses some of the assumptions that underlie organizational practices and approaches that are critical to address in the process toward culture competency.

EXHIBIT 12.3

Basic Assumptions across Systems or Agencies for Cultural Competence

Validating client experience

Organizations that are culturally competent display the following characteristics

- Respect the unique, culturally defined needs of various client populations.
- Acknowledge culture as a predominant force in shaping behaviors, values, and institutions.

- View natural systems (i.e., family, community, faith communities, healers) as the primary mechanism of support for minority populations.
- Start with the "family" as defined by each culture, as the primary and preferred point of intervention.
- Acknowledge that minority people are served in varying degrees by the natural system.
- Recognize that the concepts of "family," "community," etc., are different from various cultures and even for subgroups within cultures.
- Believe that diversity within cultures is as important as diversity between cultures.
- Function with the awareness that the dignity of the person is not guaranteed unless the dignity of his/her people is preserved.
- Display understanding that minority clients are usually best served by persons who are part of or have knowledge about their culture.
- Acknowledge and accept that cultural differences exist and have an impact on service delivery.
- Treat clients in the context of their minority status, which creates unique mental health issues for minority individuals, including issues related to self-esteem, identity formation, isolation, and role assumptions.
- Advocate for effective services on the basis that the absence of cultural competence in any part of the organization compromises the cultural competency of the entire organization.
- Respect the family as indispensable to understanding the individual, because the family provides the context within which the person functions and is the primary support network of its members.
- Recognize that the thought patterns of non-Western peoples, though different, are equally valid and influence the ways in which clients view problems and solutions.
- Respect cultural preferences that value process rather than product, and harmony or balance within one's life rather than achievement.
- Acknowledge that when working with minority clients, process is as important as product.
- Recognize that taking the best of the Western and non-Western worlds enhances the capacity of all.
- Recognize that minority people have to at least be bicultural, which in turn creates its own set of mental health issues such as identity conflicts resulting from assimilation.
- Function with the knowledge that some behaviors are the expression of adjustments to being different.
- Understand when values of minority groups are in conflict with dominant society values.

EXHIBIT 12.3

continued

Adapted from Cross, Bazron, Dennis, & Isaacs, 1989

Personnel Policies and Procedures   Staff members are important resources for organizational operations. The size and legal basis of an organization are important factors in the extent to which organizations create formal policies and procedures; small, newly created nonprofit organizations have relatively simple and concise policies and procedures, while larger, public organizations often have highly formal, complex policies and procedures. Nevertheless, the development of written policies and procedures, including a plan for recruitment, selection, development, evaluation, and termination, is important. Some organizations also develop plans to enhance staff diversity.

Resources (i.e., Financial, Technical, and Personnel)   Other types of resources are also important to organizations. For example, the adequacy of the financial resources of organizations can be viewed through annual and monthly budgets, where income and liabilities are documented. Technical resources include the facilities and equipment of the organization, such as the office space, computers, software, and cellular phones. Personnel resources include the capacity of current staff. All of these types of resources are important to assess as part of an overall organizational assessment.

Elements of an External Assessment

The external environment of organizations consists of many players. The assessment process focused on the external environment reviews the individuals, groups, organizations, and policies that impact operations. The external environment can offer opportunities and challenges for organizations, and maintaining a focus on relationships with external players is an important organizational activity. For assessment purposes, the use of a **sociogram**, whereby relationships between external players and the organization are visually depicted, can be helpful in integrating and displaying the external environment. The following section discusses those elements external to an organization that can be considered as part of an organizational assessment.

Relationship with Funders and Potential Funders   An assessment process should uncover the sources of agency funding, as well as the nature of the relationship between the organization and each funding source. For example, the assessment process would seek to uncover the amount and percentage of the overall budget received from each funding source. The funding sources could include government appropriations and contracts, donations, investment income, fees, fundraising events and activities, and profit-making activities. A source of funding that constitutes nearly half or more of the organization's overall budget indicates a strong relationship. Organizations that rely on a diverse source of funds have increased program and staff flexibility compared to those that rely on fewer sources.

Relationship with Clients   Human service organizations rarely have the resources to serve all persons who live in their service area; therefore, organizations create client eligibility requirements for programs and services. An assessment in this area may include examination of the method of recruiting and determining client eligibility, the manner in which clients are treated who are not eligible for services, the degree to which clients are mandated to receive services, and which organizations are sources of referrals.

Relationship with Organizations in Network (i.e., Referrals and Coalitions)   Constructive, professional relationships with other organizations is imperative to a positive community perception of the organization. Organizations that deliver similar services often have motivation to work together to meet community needs, yet often compete for funding from similar sources. Therefore, strong positive relationships between similar organizations can generate positive benefits for the community through stronger service delivery, collective advocacy efforts, and in other ways, yet can be challenging due to the element of competition for resources. An assessment of this aspect would uncover the nature of the relationship with similar and referring organizations, and those with whom the organization networks.

Relationships with Political Figures   Elected and appointed officials often carry a great deal of influence over public opinion about and resources for organizations. An assessment would investigate the key political and appointed figures for an organization, and describe the nature of the relationship of the organization's administration to these.

ORGANIZATIONAL ENGAGEMENT AND ASSESSMENT AND GENERALIST PRACTICE

While administrators of organizations have an official role that includes organizational responsibilities, and therefore are naturally involved in the organizational change process, social workers in direct practice with individuals, families, groups, and communities, including generalist practitioners, must also be involved with the organizational change process. Both generalist practitioners and administrators are bound by the NASW *Code of Ethics* (NASW, 2008) Section 3.09 to work to improve services, carry out their ethical obligations even if employer structures are challenging, and act to eliminate discrimination in organizations.

What does the ethical obligation to participate in organizational change mean for social workers who are not administrators? Social workers must always learn about as many aspects as possible of an organization with which they are affiliated— either as an employee, board member, volunteer, or consultant. Many organizational problems emerge through the experiences of clients or members of the community, and defining and documenting client or community member problems is a powerful way to make a strong case for organizational change. Working to engage others in identifying and documenting client problems for which the organization contributes or fails to assist in alleviating the problem is also important (Gitterman & Germain, 2008b). As discussed in Chapter 13, successful organizational change efforts often involve many individuals and groups.

Organizational engagement and assessment involve many of the same competencies and practice behaviors utilized with other client systems. Discussed in the next section are those skills needed to effectively begin the organizational change process.

SKILLS FOR ENGAGEMENT AND ASSESSMENT WITH ORGANIZATIONS

In addition to the skills previously mentioned in this chapter, including active listening, research and analysis, group facilitation, and documentation skills, integration of the data gathered in the assessment process must occur to provide direction to the next phases of the change process. A particular skill helpful to the assessment process for organizations as well as communities is a **force-field analysis** (FFA) (Bar-Gal & Schmid, 1992; Pippard & Bjorklund, 2004), first proposed by Kurt Lewin (1951). The FFA is a mechanism to gather and sort all of the information and data gathered in the assessment process, and provide the basis for a plan for an intervention, as will be discussed in Chapter 13.

An FFA is a method of identifying and assessing the forces that impact a decision about an issue by organizing the assessment data. To begin, a social worker would identify the forces that could impact the outcomes of change efforts, meaning constraints that work to prevent a change and advantages that will help overcome resistance to change. The forces could include influential individuals who could shape the opinion of others or who are decision-makers; organizations, committees and task forces; groups; and political parties. The technique enables a social worker to make a decision about whether to move forward with a change process, and if so, to create a plan based on an evaluation of the forces working for and against a proposed change (Bar-Gal & Schmid, 1992).

For example, the school social worker mentioned earlier has documented that gay, lesbian, bisexual, transgendered, and questioning (GLBTQ) students experience a higher number of social and academic problems in middle and high school than other students. The social worker has completed an organizational assessment, and would like to synthesize the information to determine whether and how to move forward. Working with a group of students that self-identify as GLBTQ, the social worker would like to engage in a change process to provide more comprehensive services to this population across the school district. After engaging and assessing the organization, the GLBTQ work group conducted an FFA to determine

SUPPORTING FORCES	NEUTRAL FORCES	OPPOSING FORCES	
Student leaders	Principal Association	Four influential teachers	**EXHIBIT 12.4**
Student government	School counselors	Parent Association	*Force Field*
All high school principals	Local TV and radio station	Two student groups/clubs	*Analysis,*
American Civil Liberties Union	Chair of the School Board	Three School Board members	*Assessment of Forces*
Three School Board members		All middle school principals	*Impacting*
Local activists			*GLBTQ Initiative*

whether to proceed in the change process, and to assist in developing an intervention plan.

As seen in Exhibit 12.4, there are many forces that support an initiative to provide more comprehensive support services to GLBTQ teens, to include student leaders, student government, and the high school principals. Those neutral forces, to include the principal association, the school counselors and others, are those that could support or oppose a change process, and do not yet have an opinion about the possibility. Through lobbying and education, these neutral forces could become supporters, and therefore, may become the focus of such efforts in the intervention phase. The forces that are opposed to the proposed concept of providing support services, including several influential teachers, the parent association and others, would work against a change process. As other forces are discovered, they could be added to the analysis. The FFA is one tool to assist the LGBTQ work group in making a decision whether to proceed with their efforts, and in making an intervention plan.

The advantage of an FFA are numerous—the individuals, groups, and coalitions relevant to the issue are identified, as well as the driving and restraining forces most likely to effect the change effort. The strength of each force is assessed and ranked, and the amenability to change of each force is ranked as high, low, or uncertain. A plan for change is then created based on the information contained in the FFA. The FFA is a simple technique that can be used with groups of all sizes as a group decision-making tool that fosters creativity and critical thinking. The social worker must demonstrate keen group facilitation skills to avoid a focus on forces against change at expense of forces for change, to avoid the domination of a minority of the group, and to encourage the group to be specific (Pippard & Bjorklund, 2004).

STRAIGHT TALK ABOUT PRACTICE WITHIN ORGANIZATIONS

The type of organization in which a social worker is employed offers distinct professional rewards, opportunities, and challenges. Expectations and experiences differ from organizational setting to setting, and work style preferences that fit one type of organization may not be a match at another organization or type of organization. The following discussion will highlight several of the different types of social service organizations.

Although working for public organizations brings challenges, there are advantages unique to employment with public agencies. Compared to working within the private (i.e., nonprofit and for-profit) sector, needed services can be offered to clients with less consideration given to cost effectiveness, because there are fewer demands for demonstrated outcomes than in nonprofit and for-profit organizations. In stable economic times, social workers within public agencies enjoy relative predictability and job security, with highly structured job levels and raise structures (McInnis-Dittrich, 1994). Some social workers in public organizations earn higher salaries than in the nonprofit sector (Whitaker, Weismiller, & Clark, 2006). Many clients served in public organizations are those without many alternatives; therefore, social workers within these agencies are implementing the historical preference of social work for working on behalf of the poor. Lastly, social workers in public organizations gain invaluable experience with a wide range of client issues and with clients with complex problems.

The number of social workers working in for-profit social service agencies, such as private practices and for-profit health care systems, has grown in recent years (Whitaker & Arrington, 2008). In contrast to public and nonprofit organizations, for-profit (or proprietary) agencies seek to produce a financial profit for their owners or shareholders. Social workers in residential care facilities, medical and psychiatric hospitals, long-term care for persons with disabilities, home health services, health maintenance organizations, substance abuse treatment centers, and child welfare services may be in for-profit settings.

Depending on the type of services provided, social workers in for-profit organizations may enjoy a more comfortable physical setting, more resources, use of cutting-edge interventions and treatment modalities, higher expectations of efficiency and effectiveness than in other settings, and higher salaries than in public and nonprofit organizations. In some for-profit settings, a wide socioeconomic diversity of clients may seek services. Social workers may also enjoy the opportunities to advocate for the primary goal of client-centered human services to meet community needs, rather than a profit (Kong, 2007).

Most social service organizations are nonprofit (Holland, 2008). Advantages to working for a nonprofit organization are numerous, and include the following: (1) social workers generally have little need to advocate internally to maintain the historical commitment to serving the poor (Netting et al., 2008); (2) the funding base is often a diverse mixture of sources, to include grants, contracts, memberships, fee for service, investment, donations, and events. Social work employees may enjoy more autonomy, flexibility, and creativity in service delivery due to the multitude of funding sources; and (3) social workers in faith-based nonprofit organization can implement their religious traditions and beliefs in their employment setting.

While there are other types of organizations beyond public, for-profit, and 501(c)3 nonprofit organizations (i.e., hybrid nonprofit and social enterprises, whereby nonprofit organizations engage in commercial activity (Cooney, 2006), other classifications of 501(c)), these three are the central types of organizations that employ social workers. While generalities may be helpful, each setting offers a unique working environment. Prestige, an important element to social worker commitment and job satisfaction (Carmeli & Freund, 2009), can be found in many different settings. Social workers who explore types of organizations may gain more insight about the best fit for their preferred work style and career aspirations.

CONCLUSION

This chapter has introduced organizations as an important arena for the social work change process. Social workers in direct practice and their supervisors are uniquely informed about the impact of organizational operations on client systems. Social workers may best be able to identify unmet client system needs, and initiate a change process designed to meet the best interests of the client system—whether that be an individual, family, group, or community. Social workers, therefore, have a mandate to engage persons from within the organization and external to the organization, and learn about both the internal and external environments of organizations to competency lead and participate in organizational change processes. In addition to engagement, this chapter focused on the assessment process to provide the foundation knowledge needed to initiate the change process. Organizations are an important context of generalist social work practice with all types of client systems. Chapter 13 will focus on organization intervention strategies, termination, and evaluation processes.

MAIN POINTS

- Social workers work in many types of and sizes of organizations, and utilize their knowledge to promote the best interests of their client systems.

- Organizations, like other client systems, can be understood through the lens of various theories, models and perspectives, including systems theories and contemporary organizational and management theories.

- Three dimensions of difference between organizations are of particular interest: (1) purpose of the organization; (2) structure of governance; and (3) internal power relations.

- Social workers also practice in host settings, which are those organizations in which social workers provide social services as a secondary activity.

- Social workers can engage organizations for the change process in a range of roles to provide a higher quality of services and/or to better address human needs.

- The overall assessment of organizations involves both a review of the internal environment of the organization, and the external environment.

- The NASW *Code of Ethics* provides direction to both generalist and specialist social workers to work to improve services, carry out their ethical obligations in the work place, and to act to eliminate discrimination in organizations.

- A skill helpful to the assessment process for organizations is a force-field analysis, a tool to sort assessment information and data gathered in the assessment process and aid in the decision-making process about the change process.

- The type of organization in which a social worker is employed offers distinct professional rewards, opportunities, and challenges.

EXERCISES

1. Imagine you were hired as a social worker approximately three months ago at a community center that serves the Sanchez family. As you have settled into your job responsibilities, you notice some tensions within the agency. Several social workers are grumbling at "the way things are around here."

   As you consider the reasons for your feelings of being unsettled, you decide to gather information about the organization to gain a better understanding of the dynamics. Referring back to the chapter, discuss ways in which you might obtain knowledge about each factor, and how each factor could influence the experience of staff members (one paragraph for each): purpose, structure of governance, and internal power relations.

2. After you gather information about the organization, you still are not sure about the dynamics that have led you to feel unsettled, and co-workers to grumble. You decide to learn more about the agency, but are not quite ready to undertake a full organizational assessment. You decide to start your mini-assessment by focusing on culture. Using the concepts described in the chapter, describe the elements of culture that exist in the center, and how you would go about learning them, to

include the types of individuals you might interview, the documents you would seek, the groups you would access, and any other source of information you might utilize. Justify your choices.

3. Log onto www.routledgesw.com/cases. Review the Riverton case file (i.e., Your History and Your Concerns). View the community sociogram, and note all of the organizations and their relationships to one another. Develop a sociogram for an organization with which you are familiar.

4. Using the Riverton case (at www.routledgesw.com/cases), answer the Critical Thinking Question #2.

5. Using the Riverton case (at www.routledgesw.com/cases), answer the Critical Thinking Question #3 by assuming that the organization is the client. What would be your next steps after deciding that an organization in the community is the client? Which organization (use the sociogram and/or town map to review the possibilities)?

6. Choose an organization with which you are familiar. Familiarize yourself with the elements of an organizational assessment, as discussed in Chapter 12. Interview a person familiar with the organization to gather as much information as possible related to the internal and external elements of an organizational assessment. As part of the interview, ask whether the organization has completed an organizational assessment in the past, and whether there are any written documents that describe the assessment that you could review. Report on your interview in class.

CHAPTER 13

Social Work Practice with Organizations: Intervention, Termination, and Evaluation

The time when you need to do something is when no one else is willing to do it, when people are saying it can't be done.

Mary Frances Berry

Key Questions for Chapter 13

(1) How can I prepare for action with all client systems? (EPAS 2.1.10(a))

(2) What are the key interpersonal skills and techniques that I need to know to work with organizations? (EPAS 2.1.10(a))

(3) How can I utilize evidence to practice research-informed practice and practice-informed research to guide the intervention, termination, and evaluation with organizations? (EPAS 2.1.6)

(4) How can I apply critical thinking to intervention, termination, and evaluation with organizations? (EPAS 2.1.3)

(5) How can I apply social work values and ethics to intervention, termination, and evaluation with organizations? (EPAS 2.1.2)

CONSIDER THE FOLLOWING SITUATIONS:
Toby, a tenth-grader, left the social worker's office commenting that he wished that other kids would just "leave him alone," and that he wished he "knew other kids like him." Toby, who shared with the social worker that he thinks he is

gay, was the third student that week to say similar things to the social worker, who is struggling with a response to the needs of lesbian, gay, bisexual, transgendered, and questioning (LGBTQ) students. The social worker has seen these students struggle with bullying, less social integration, and poor school performance, which they often state is due to a lack of acceptance by teachers, administrators, and peers.

Carrie, a social work case manager at a mental health service organization, is at the end at her rope. Four of the clients on her caseload, who are dual diagnosed with a chronic mental illness and a substance abuse issue, have become homeless this month due to the lack of affordable rental housing in the community. The few units that are available are owned by landlords who will not rent to clients of the organization.

These are examples of situations that may prompt organizational change that occurs as a result of client needs not adequately being met by the agency, the institution, or community. Organizational change can range in size from large (i.e., changing the decision-making process within the organization), to small (i.e., changing eligibility for one program, or the working hours for staff members), and from short-term (i.e., creating a short-term project) to long-term (i.e., creating new programs). Large scale change within organizations can change the nature and mission of organizations, such as a legal merger with another organization. However, small scale change can also make an important difference to the client systems and community served, such as offering a new program that allows homeless individuals who have a chronic mental illness and also abuse substances to live in supportive housing while the clients work to reduce and eliminate substances from their lives. Both types of changes involve utilizing the change process of engagement, assessment, intervention, termination, and evaluation.

As discussed in Chapter 12, the impetus for organizational change can emerge from many sources, including administrators, direct practice staff, stakeholders, and persons external to an organization (Frey, 1990). Social workers' concerns for an aspect of service, whether ineffective, wasteful, or in some other way troubling, may be the most accessible route to effect change. As front line staff, social workers are often the first to notice that clients experience difficulty with organizational practices, and they can voice their concerns as part of the engagement and assessment process, and participate in the next parts of the change process. This chapter will focus on the change process from the perspective of direct service social work staff members.

After completing the engagement and assessment process outlined in Chapter 12, the social worker, with allies who have formed a "change work group," must carefully consider possible solutions, develop a change proposal (i.e., intervention) to pursue, select an intervention strategy, and if successful, possibly be involved in the implementation of the intervention, as well as its termination and evaluation. Organizations are entities that change in much the same way individuals change. Organizations structured as bureaucracies, like persons with a rigid personality, tend to change slowly; and organizations with a long history can resist change because staff feel that "we have always done things this way," and change may be a great deal of effort. Organizations with a more open, flexible structure, like persons who are flexible, tend to make purposeful changes easily. Working with a change work group, social workers must carefully choose the intervention strategy to best match the organization, the change proposed, and the context of the change, based on the assessment process.

This chapter will examine ideas social workers, working with change work groups, can use for effecting change within organizations to change policies, programs, projects, and practices of organizations. Based on the engagement and assessment phase of the change process, the next three steps, intervention, termination, and evaluation, can help organizations to become more responsive to the client systems served, to include individuals, families, groups, and communities. First discussed are approaches, perspectives, and models for interventions with organizations. In the next section, a framework for organizational change is provided. The challenges and methods for implementing the organizational change are explored, followed by a discussion of termination and evaluation of change in organizations. The chapter ends with an overview of the challenge of maintaining a hopeful stance with clients regarding organizational change.

APPROACHES, PERSPECTIVES, AND MODELS FOR INTERVENTIONS WITH ORGANIZATIONS

Approaches, perspectives, and models that are grounded in theory can assist to describe the organizations, which can inform the change process for organizations. In the following section, the organization is described as a self-learner, relative to a systems approach, a social ecology approach, the power and politics model, postmodernist approaches, and a social constructionist approach. Each approach is described in the following section and the implications for the social worker are discussed.

Self-Learning Model

Gambrill (2006) describes the **self-learning model** as a contemporary organizational climate that emphasizes the ability of organizations to self-correct when needed. The increasing emphasis on accountability and accessibility to clients, increasing use of information technology, and a limited resource pool, lead to the ability of the organization to improve the quality of its decisions and develop new knowledge. This model maintains that organizations seek and use corrective feedback from internal and external sources by ongoing monitoring and solicitation of feedback from client systems that provide information about their experiences with services, and other stakeholders who provide information about the external environment of the organization. This model also assumes a rational process in which all members of an organization agree on the mission, goals, and objectives of the organization, and will work collaboratively to achieve them. Although no organization perfectly implements its mission, goals, and objectives, the self-learning model has widespread applicability in small, well-focused organizations with clear goals and values. Smaller organizations rely on common ground, the wisdom and creativity of staff, and the capacity of groups to develop positive directions.

This model is closely related to the ecosystems perspective, described fully in Chapter 1 as a perspective focused on the fit between the environment and a human system. As mentioned in Chapter 1, the ecosystems perspective can relate to all client systems, including work within organizations to create more responsive policies and programs (Gitterman & Germain, 2008a). The model is also related to the social ecology approach in which the organization is assumed to be continually interacting with and adapting to its environment. An organization must continue to adjust and adapt to environmental changes in order to survive and prosper. With the social ecology approach, change efforts may emanate from changes that occur in the external environment, which has rendered some part of the organization in need of a change. For example, when economic conditions force many families to seek social work services, different policies and procedures may be needed to adequately serve the larger number of clients with a higher level of needs. Social workers need to continually keep abreast of changes to the environment of the organization (e.g., new funding sources, a change in an area of social policy, new political support for an idea about human services), and help the organization strategize to make needed changes (Hasenfeld, 2000).

Social workers within organizations that are using the self-learning model contribute to an organizational culture focused on receiving feedback from the internal and external environment, learning, and seeking knowledge about ways to improve their functioning and programs/services. This model of change may be seen in organizations that are involved in networks of organizations, have close relationships with their funders, and/or have a highly developed internal evaluation and feedback systems.

Systems Model

The **systems model** recognizes the organization as a system composed of many individuals, subsystems, rules, roles, and processes operating within the wider environment. Using a systems approach, change in one part of the organization can create changes in other parts of the organization. This model asserts that efforts involved in organizational maintenance and survival need to be balanced with specific achievement goals. For example, job stress, staff disagreements, and social and emotional needs of employees need to be addressed because, unaddressed, these issues have potential to divert workers from their commitments. Change efforts in this model are more likely to include attending to such organization maintenance functions as clarification of goals, improving morale, and emphasizing better communication among employees.

The systems model is represented in such activities as agency retreats, training sessions, and requests for consultation regarding staff relations or in redefining agency direction (Campbell, 2000). In an important respect, this approach recognizes the impact of human service work by acknowledging the stresses that accompany working within organizations, and recognizing the necessity to attend to the human side of the professionals who constitute the organization and engage in the work.

Power and Politics Model

Assuming that the organization is essentially a political body, the **power and politics model** emphasizes competition for resources, personal advancement, and inter- and intrapower struggles. The model asserts that the primary path to change requires strategic access to decision-makers and/or the persons who have the greatest power and primary influence over decision-makers. Using this model, a common tactic is to work to convince influential persons that the proposed change is both in the organization's and their personal best interest. Use of pressure from outside sources, such as media sources, is also viewed as a potential strategy to gain the support of influential persons (Pfeffer, 1992). This model is related to the critical social construction approach, first introduced in Chapter 1, as a postmodern approach. The approach is based in a contemporary analysis of power, which recognizes that any social group can shape its beliefs to its own benefit at the expense of other groups (Hartman, 1994). The analysis of power includes questioning the power relationships between decision makers and others, which can lead to the use of the power and politics model of organizational change.

The power and politics model can most easily be adapted to large bureaucratic organizations, where change can be more difficult. However, the ideas in this model are adaptable to any size organization. The model reflects the reality of conflict over resources and power that can emerge in change efforts, and the necessity of consideration of the role that politics and power play in change efforts.

Postmodern Approaches

As discussed in Chapter 1, in a postmodern view of change, actions, interactions, and patterns of relationships play an important role in the change process. Interaction patterns between persons and between units become stable, dominate, and occur repeatedly in a dynamic process, and the language used in organizations can serve to reinforce the patterns and processes (Hasenfeld, 2000).

Recognizing the power of language, the process of social meaning making, and the potential for taking part in reshaping their world, social workers can engage with persons, groups, units, and committees within bureaucratic organizations to influence the development of individual and organizational approaches. There is nothing inevitable about the structures and processes that shape and guide institutions or practice—persons have created them and have the ability to change them. Changes to improve the organization's functioning can occur through understanding the language, symbols, relationships, and dialogues that structure the organization, and using dialogue to explore the perceptions, values, ideologies, ideas of reality, and assumptions held by staff members, stakeholders, and decision-makers for the organization (Hasenfeld, 2000). While not an easy or quick process for change, the importance of dialogue and language in the change process cannot be overstated.

Social Constructionist Approach

A social constructionist approach to organizational change emphasizes the impact that social processes, such as dialogue, have on the perception of social reality, which impacts the prospects for change. Therefore, dialogue about a problem experienced by an organization has an impact on the perception of problems, and can be one of the most effective tools in building support for a change proposal. Dialogue that is continuous, patient, and respectful can positively impact the view of staff about the change proposal, which can serve to break down structural barriers to organizational change.

Organizations rarely utilize only one approach or model in change efforts, and often a mixture is utilized. These approaches and models offer a lens through which change efforts can be viewed, and offer ideas to social workers involved in an organizational change effort. In the next section, an exploration of a framework for intervention with organizations will be discussed, including the recruitment of allies into a "change work group," the selection of a feasible solution(s), the selection of a change strategy, implementing the change strategy (i.e. intervention), terminating the change effort, and evaluating the change effort as well as any resulting program or project.

FRAMEWORK FOR ORGANIZATIONAL CHANGE

Gathering Allies and Creating a Change Work Group

Similar to change efforts with other client systems, promoting a change within organizations can be challenging. The ability to successfully complete a change effort as an individual effort is rare. Therefore, a team effort, whether through an informal or formal, structured group, adds credibility and power to a change effort, as well as allowing for shared work. Even if the engagement and assessment process began through the work of one person, social workers will want to identify supporters and allies while engaged in these processes to potentially assist with the change process. The degree to which persons will join the work and be supportive will vary, from mildly supportive to those who will actively work as part of a change work group for an organizational change. Those who are supportive may change the degree to which they are helpful and encouraging throughout the process, with some persons beginning as mildly supportive, and at some periods, actively joining the work, while others that may begin as active members of a change work group may lessen their work responsibilities at certain times. The key is to continually recruit allies and change work group members throughout the change process, so that even if membership of the group changes, a change work group is always in place to support the change effort. While some change processes are short term, many are long term and require a great deal of energy, so allies are essential to the sustainability of many interventions (Packard, 2009).

In the ally recruitment process, social workers must raise the concerns discovered in the assessment process with staff and administrators in staff and committee meetings, and in discussions with individuals. When trying to garner support for a change proposal from other colleagues, social workers will want to be as specific as possible regarding the concern, and use client examples when feasible. Statements about problems that are in clear, behavioral, and values-oriented terms are the most effective. In these discussions, the client problems must be translated into potential solutions in which the organization can participate. For example, if you think the problem is that LGBTQ adolescents in a school district need additional social and administrative support, the social worker must first consider various solutions in which the organization can participate. Can each individual school in the district partner with the local mental health center to provide education about sexuality and gender to all students? Should the partnership provide in-school or in-home family therapy related to sexuality and adolescents? Should the partnership provide individual therapy? Should the school district provide services without organizational partners, either in-school or in-home? Should the school district engage the parent-teacher association in their efforts? Rather than provide therapy, should the school refer LGBTQ students to private therapists? Or should the school provide services more quietly, so as not to arouse opposition, by providing, but not widely marketing, support services through the counseling department? This translation of problem into potential solutions will help others understand and have input into potential solutions. After recruiting allies into a change work group and establishing the manner in which they will work together, to include group leadership, decision-making, and other decisions regarding the operation of a task group (see Chapter 9), the group must generate possible solutions and select a specific solution to address the problem, which is discussed in the next section.

Considerations for the Development of Feasible Solutions for Organizational Change

The change work group, including the social worker, must ultimately develop a potential solution to the identified problem(s) that is acceptable to the decision-maker(s) and that addresses the identified client system problem to the best of the organization's ability, based on the information gathered and analyzed in the engagement and assessment process. The identified solution will be discussed hereafter as a "change proposal," which varies in shape, such as a formal, written document for more in-depth change proposals, or an idea presented orally for smaller change proposals. Decision-makers for change proposals related to organizations can be colleagues (who may be able to make decisions about small changes related to organizational practices, such as changing the way the telephone is answered or email is sent), administrators, the executive director or director, members of the board of directors, legislative bodies, or funders of the organization. Additionally, the change work group must also select a feasible solution that is based in evidence-based practice (as first defined and discussed in Chapter 4). There are several important *considerations* to the process of selecting feasible solutions to the identified problem, including the following:

1.   Depending on the scope of the problem and potential solutions, the change work group must account for *resistance to change*, as discussed in Chapter 12 (Frey, 1990). According to systems theory, all organizations seek to maintain the status quo, or stability. **Inertia** can impede change by preserving a stable state that actively works against change. Change work groups must expect some opposition to the very idea of change, regardless of the type of change proposed or the specifics of the change proposal, because change takes energy away from other pursuits (Gambrill, 2006).

2.   The amount of organizational *effort* and *risk* involved in a change process must be considered (Frey, 1990). Those change processes that will require considerable time, energy, and/or risk to the organization are those that involve in-depth change, and will involve a high level of challenge to the change work group. If, for example, an organization has spent significant resources on a program, the process for ending that program may take a long time. In another example, a change proposal that involves implementing activities that are new to the organization may be perceived as highly risky to the financial stability and reputation of the organization. A high level of effort and risk inherent in a change proposal typically translates to a high level of challenge for the change proposal.

3.   The change process may encounter *competition* for resources and attention from other change processes. The assessment process should have uncovered any other change process occurring within the organization, as well as any

plans that are designed to structure future change efforts. For example, organizations often create **strategic plans**, which are comprehensive, formal plans for the future direction of the organization. These plans often involve incremental, highly focused modifications to current operations that are projected to contribute to a preferred result for the organization (Austin & Solomon, 2009). A change process that is occurring in another part of the organization can impact a change proposal if the organization does not have enough resources to consider more than one change proposal and/or implement a change proposal at a time.

4. The organization must be readied for change in term of possessing the *ability*, experiencing a *need* for change, and the change proposal must be a *match with the mission and values* of the organization (Frey, 1990). The engagement and assessment process, depending on the methods used, may have made administrators and staff aware of a possible problem, potential solutions, and the possibility of an organizational change effort. If not, staff members and administrators must become aware of the problem, become dissatisfied with the current situation, and perceive that a proposed solution will alleviate the problem. In sum, the organizational system that supports the current structure that creates or exacerbates the problem must become weakened.

5. The *perceived advantages and disadvantages* to the organization, including staff members, must be considered (Frey, 1990). For example, if potential solutions will involve additional work for a particular staff member or group of staff, the person(s) or unit(s) involved should be consulted prior to the selection of the solution so the impact of the proposal on any person(s) or unit(s) can be taken in consideration. The process of gathering input from the person(s) or unit(s) may shape the change proposal itself or strengthen the support for the proposed solution, as their suggestions and concerns can be considered and possibly addressed in the solution chosen, as well as the change strategy (discussed later in this chapter). The process of consultation with person(s) or unit(s) may garner their support for the potential solution. If possible, the work of implementing a solution to a problem should be shared as widely as possible.

6. Gathering *history* on the organization's efforts of making policy or program changes will provide helpful context to future change efforts. For example, did prior change efforts induce staff disgruntlement or staff support? Were changes perceived as coming from the top down (i.e., imposed from administrators) or from the bottom up (i.e., suggested by staff)? Long-term staff members may be helpful sources of historical information.

7. In discussions with other staff members about potential solutions, the change work group should also gather an initial impression about change ideas, and the degree to which they are *understandable*, and likely be met with apathy,

resistance, or support. The change work group must learn about formal and informal groupings of staff members and charismatic leaders within the organization, and account for the sentiment of such "subgroups" and leaders in the change proposal.

8.   Prior to the development of a particular change proposal, the change work group must engage in *evidence-based practice* by researching the identified problem and potential solutions using evidence-based literature (Johnson & Austin, 2006). This information must be integrated with the expertise of the change work group, and the values, experiences, and expressed wishes of the client system.

9.   The *timing* of a proposed solution can significantly impact the receptivity that the proposal receives. For example, the time in which one administrator is leaving an organization and a new administrator is arriving is one in which a window of opportunity may exist for some change proposals. The change work group may take advantage of this period in which there may be a vacuum of administrative power by taking action to propose changes to organizational practices (to possibly include a change that was not acceptable to the outgoing administrator) such as a policy change to allow staff and/or clients to participate on the committee that screens and interview candidates for administrative positions, or changes to the decision-making process so that there is increased participation by staff members and clients. The time between administrators is an ideal time for exploring organizational changes.

These important considerations speak to the need for a comprehensive process to determining a specific solution, or intervention, to address a problem. Some considerations may be more important than others, and there may be important considerations that are specific to a particular organization. Developing a specific change proposal to pursue involves thinking through such considerations. The creation of a specific change proposal may also be impacted by the chosen change strategy (discussed later in this chapter). Additionally, the change proposal may evolve as information learned in the remainder of the process may influence the contents of the change proposal. One element of a change proposal is the form, the options for which are discussed in the next section.

Change Proposal Form   The change proposal may be in the form of a policy, program, project, personnel, or practice, or some combination (Kettner, 2002; Netting et al., 2008). The **policy** approach involves a formal statement regarding the direction for a course of action. A policy change often involves the decision of persons with high decision-making authority, such as administrators, elected officials, or a board of directors, that involves large-scale change to create new or amend existing policy. For example, a change work group in a school system that is striving to create improved services to LGBTQ students in the school district may determine that the most effective change strategy is to work toward a harassment policy that would include harassment based on sexual orientation.

A **program** solution involves the creation of or change to ". . . structured activities, [which are] designed to achieve a set of goals and objectives" (Netting et al., 2008, p. 329). Programs are designed to provide services to a client system, and are long-term activities. These are often high-profile aspects of an organization, because client systems interact with, and know organizations for, their programs. For example, a program approach to the perceived unmet needs of LGBTQ adolescents in the school system would be to create an education program about sexual orientation for all students. **Projects** are similar to programs, but are typically smaller, more flexible, can be adapted to changing needs relatively easily, and are not permanent. A demonstration project, a short-term test of an idea, can be a less controversial way of implementing change. For example, the education program described above could be implemented for a specific time period, such as a semester, with the possibility of extension of the program in the spring semester, and the possibility of changing the program in the first semester, as needed. A change in **personnel** can address different types of problems in programs and projects. Staff members within organizations may lack the specific competencies or practice behaviors to effectively work within programs or projects, and a personnel approach is needed. A personnel approach can include additional education, internships, change in responsibilities for staff, or complete change of staff. Changes that involve personnel must be undertaken carefully, with a thorough examination to determine if such a change will better serve the client system (rather than simply change office dynamics). Using the example of the unmet needs of the LGBTQ adolescents, the proposed solution may be to educate teachers to become more supportive of LGBTQ adolescents in the school. Lastly, a change for an organization can involve a **practice**, or the way in which organizations implement basic functions, which may or may not be formally described in written documents. For example, a sub-set of counselors or teachers may become the unofficial resource and support persons for LGBTQ adolescents in each school, so LGBTQ adolescents have supportive adults in each school (Netting et al., 2008). Box 13.1 provides a summary of these approaches. Exhibit 13.1 provides a case example of an organization that implemented these approaches to change.

Selecting an Organizational Change Strategy

Thus far, the social worker has completed the engagement and assessment process, gathered allies, and created a change work group. Together with the change work group, the social worker has taken many factors into consideration when developing a proposed solution, including evidence-based practice, and made a decision about a specific change proposal, or intervention, to pursue that entails a change in the organization. The next step in the process is to determine the strategy for making a change. A **strategy** is an overall approach to a change effort. In contrast, a **tactic**

APPROACH	DEFINITION	
Policy	A formally adopted statement that reflects goals and strategies or agreements on a settled course of action.	**BOX 13.1**
Program	Prearranged sets of activities designed to achieve a set of goals and objectives.	*Approaches to Organiza-tional Change*
Project	Similar to programs, but have a time-limited existence and are more flexible so that they can be adapted to the needs of a changing environment.	
Personnel	Persons who are in interaction within the change arena.	
Practice	The way in which organizations or individuals go about doing business. Practices are less formalized than policies and may be specific to persons or groups.	

Source: Netting, Kettner, & McMurtry, 2008, p. 331

The local mental health organization has a long-standing program for the chronically mentally ill who also have a substance abuse problem, or "dual diagnosed" clients. In recent years, the social work case managers have noticed increasing difficulty locating affordable, decent rental housing for clients in the dual diagnosed program. The social work case managers have convened a change work group, and they are considering a variety of change approaches, including the following:

A **policy** change—The change work group may approach the administration and the board of directors to change organizational policy, so the organization can move from only providing social services to an organization that also owns and manages affordable, supportive housing for clients.

A **program** change—The change work group may propose to the administration that the organization seek to partner with local private landlords to provide the intensive, on-site case management and supportive services needed to maintain a stable living environment through a live-in care provider. The organization will guarantee that the rent and utilities will be paid on time, and that the apartment will be kept clean. The live-in care provider will be the first-responder for any problems in the building that involve the client.

A **project** change—This change would be the same as the program change (described earlier), but would involve a six-month trial period. During the trial period, the social worker who is overseeing the project reports weekly to the administrator, who then reports on the project monthly to the board of directors. Ongoing adjustments will be made to the project as needed. If the project is deemed successful, the board of directors may consider creating a long-term program.

A **personnel** change—Using this approach, social workers will be trained to become trainers to the family members of clients about being live-in case providers to their family member with chronic mental health challenges. The trained live-in family members will allow clients to live with their families, and alleviate the need for rental housing.

A **practice** change—Using a practice approach, social workers will learn different approaches for assisting clients to live together in their current rental housing, so that at least two clients can live in each apartment. This will have the effect of housing more clients with the same number of rental units.

EXHIBIT 13.1

A Dearth of Affordable Rental Housing: A Case Example of Approaches to Change refers to specific actions, or skills, taken to implement a strategy (Brager & Holloway, 1978). This section will include discussion of strategies, while the next section focuses on tactics, or specific skills, needed to implement strategies.

Change Strategies   There are three basic strategies for organizational change: collaborative, campaign, or conflict (Brager & Holloway, 1978). A **collaborative** change is one in which the change work group and the decision-maker(s) *agree that some type of change in the organization is required*, and co-operation is needed to create a joint effort to create change in the organization. The change work group and the decision-maker(s) need to create a partnership to communicate, plan, and co-ordinate and share tasks to implement a change. All parties involved agree that a change is needed, therefore, the decisions involved include the approach (i.e., whether a policy, program, project, personnel, or practice), ways in which the resources needed can be obtained, and other implementation decisions. Using this strategy involves the determination that there is little opposition to a change, and the change can best be carried out through a collaborative strategy. For example, if the change work group and the school principal and administrators agree that LGBTQ adolescents need support and that the school should and can assume a role in creating additional support, the change work group and administrators could partner in a joint collaborative change effort to determine the form that the support would take (e.g., further education of teachers, support groups, and/or education of the students) and in the implementation of the change.

A **campaign** strategy is used when *communication can occur* between the decision-makers and the change work group, but there is *no agreement that a change is needed*. The key to this strategy is the willingness of the decision-makers to listen to arguments on behalf of a change proposal. The decision-makers may need additional information or persuasion. For example, if the change work group and the school principal and administrators do not agree that LGBTQ adolescents need additional support from the school, the change work group could choose a campaign strategy of providing additional information, developing persuasive arguments, and arranging regular communication about this topic with the principal and administrators.

The third strategy, **conflict**, can be used when *the decision-makers are opposed to a change, and are unwilling to communicate with the change work group*. Due to the lack of communication, the change work group is unable to educate or persuade the decision-makers through organizational processes, and is only able to influence the decision-makers through a public conversation. This change strategy involves efforts to draw support from a wider group of supporters, and often involves public conflict. The conflict strategy often involves heated and/or passionate discussion that includes negative reactions, and is therefore not typically used as a first change option. For example, if the school principal and administrators do not agree that the school can take a role in providing additional support for the LGBTQ adolescents, and are unwilling to communicate with the change work group about the topic, the

RELATIONSHIP OF DECISION-MAKERS AND CHANGE WORK GROUP	TACTICS	**BOX 13.2**

Collaboration
Decision-makers and change work group agree (or are easily convinced to agree) that change is needed, and resources must be allocated for a change.
	1. Implementation
	2. Capacity Building
	  a. Participation
	  b. Empowerment
		Strategies and Tactical Behaviors

Campaign
Decision-makers are willing to communicate with the change work group, but do not agree that a change is needed or that resources are needed for a change.
	1 Education
	2. Persuasion
	  a. Co-optation
	  b. Lobbying
	3. Mass Media Appeal	

Contest Decision-makers oppose change and/or allocation of resources and are unwilling to communicate with the change work group.	1. Bargaining and Negotiation 2. Group Actions	

Adapted from Netting, Kettner, & McMurtry, 2008, p. 350

change work group could choose to take a conflict strategy. The group may decide to organize a march or rally to apply additional pressure to the decision-makers to begin communicating with the group. Box 13.2 provides an overview of Change Strategies and Tactics.

Contemporary Tactics and Skills for Interventions with Organizations

The skills needed for interventions with organizations are built on the skills for intervention covered in previous chapters (i.e., relationship skills in Chapter 3, intervention skills with individuals, families, groups, and communities in Chapters 3–12). In addition to basic intervention skills, social workers need specific skills for working with change processes in organizations. The following tactics, or skills, are organized by the strategy with which they are most commonly associated. The terms tactics and skills are used interchangeably in the following section.

For collaborative change strategies:
Implementation Skills Implementation skills are those that involve solving problems and making decisions about logistics. Examples include engaging in research about an issue, developing written materials relating to the change proposal (e.g., written proposals, fact sheets), creating and facilitating task groups and workshops, and communicating with interested parties and decision-makers (Schneider & Lester, 2001).

Capacity Building   Building the capacity of client systems has two components: (1) participation, or involving members of the client system in the change process; and (2) empowerment of clients through participation in the effort. These capacity building efforts, both a process and an outcome, can improve the ability of client systems to remove real or perceived barriers to participation in change processes, and increase the likelihood of client systems participating in future change processes.

To elaborate on the example provided earlier for collaborative change strategies in the situation of the principal and administrators agreeing that LGBTQ adolescents in the school needed additional support and that the school could take a role in providing additional support, these collaborative change skills could be utilized to create a new program. The change work group can utilize supporters and friends of LGBTQ students and LGBTQ students themselves to provide assistance with every aspect of the program, to include researching, analyzing, and creating program ideas, facilitating groups, educating other students and education personnel about their unmet needs, and other tasks. Involving the LGBTQ students and student supporters in such effort can increase their competence in these skills, and potentially enable them to teach them to others in a manner appropriate to their stage of life development.

For campaign change strategy:

Education   Education involves communication skills, that may include in-person meetings with individuals and groups, formal and informal presentations, written materials, and education materials designed for persons and groups influential with decision makers. The goal of such efforts is to present a variety of types of information to impact the perception, knowledge, attitude, and/or opinions of decision-makers through information.

Persuasion   Convincing others to accept and support a particular view of an issue is the goal of persuasion. Skillful communication that appeals to the reasoning of the decision-makers is an essential part of persuasion. The change work group must discern the information or incentives that would be important to the decision-maker, and make every effort to appeal to these. Additionally, choosing persons with credibility with the decision-makers to communicate with the decision-makers also helps make persuasive argument. One form of persuasion is **co-optation**, defined as ". . . minimizing anticipated opposition by including those who would be opposed to a change effort in the change effort" (Netting et al., 2008, p. 354). Including the opposition in the change effort can neutralize the opposition because the opposition was part of designing the change effort, and may be able to advance an interest through it. **Lobbying** is the use of persuasion with targeted decision-makers who are neutral or opposed to the change effort (Schneider & Lester, 2001).

Mass Media Appeals   This skill refers to the use of all types of media to influence public opinion, as well as the opinion of decision-makers, either directly or indirectly. Involved in this skill is the development and shaping of news-worthy stories that will affect viewer opinion in the hoped-for direction.

In the example of the unmet needs of LGBTQ adolescents in the school setting, these campaign skills can be applied if the change work group and school principals are able to communicate about the need for additional support, but the principals did not agree that additional support was needed and/or that the school could take a role in providing additional support. The change work group can be involved in education efforts with the principal through such efforts as holding meetings, presenting factual information about LGBTQ adolescents and the challenges they face, providing statistics on the number of LGBTQ adolescents in the community, and submitting op-ed articles and letters to the editor to the local newspaper. The change work group can also engage in a variety of persuasive efforts, such as appealing to the motives and interests of the decision-makers by describing the potential of increased academic performance and decreased fighting by LGBTQ adolescents, and increased tolerance for diversity throughout the school as a result of the implementation of a new program. The change work group can also utilize co-optation by inviting the principal or another administrator to be part of the change work group (or an advisory committee to the change work group), or engage in lobbying the principal and other administrators who are neutral or in opposition to the idea of the school providing additional support. As part of the lobbying effort, the change work group can also utilize websites, blogs, and social media, as well as print media, to influence the opinion of other students, staff, parents, and district administrators about the unmet needs of LGBTQ adolescents in the hope that these populations will be persuaded to attempt to influence the opinion of the principal.

For contest change strategy:

Bargaining and Negotiation   Discussing a change proposal, with the possibility of both the decision-maker and the change work group making compromises to their preferred change proposal, involves bargaining and negotiation skills. The use of bargaining and negotiation skills often occurs when both the decision-maker and the change work group understand the position of one another, understand the change proposal, and there is a sense of urgency on both sides about settling the matter. Rather than confrontation, at the core of this skill is the assumption that both sides use persuasive arguments about their position on a change proposal, and that both give and receive accommodation to their preferences in the process of a final decision. This process may involve a third party acting in the role of a mediator (Schneider & Lester, 2001).

Group Actions   Group actions include many activities designed to increase political pressure on decision-makers. These confrontational tactics cover a wide range of legal and illegal activities, including rallies, demonstrations, marches, picketing, sit-ins, vigils, blockages, strikes, slow-downs, boycotts, class action lawsuits, and civil disobedience. Several of these actions require the involvement of attorneys and other professionals, while others are possible with a skilled social worker, change work group, and/or a large group of supporters (Schneider & Lester, 2001).

Ethic and Change Tactics   The choice of tactics utilized for a change effort is influenced by a number of factors, to include the type of relationship between the decision-maker(s) and the change work group, the degree to which the sides agree on the goal, the extent of the communication, as well as social work ethics. Actions taken, particularly group actions that can involve confrontation, should be undertaken after careful thought and consideration, as well as preparation of the client systems involved for any possible negative consequences, such as negative publicity, fines, lost wages, or physical injury. As mentioned, when there is a moderate amount of agreement and communication between the parties, more co-operative tactics should first be attempted prior to campaign tactics, and conflict-oriented tactics are often the last set of tactics used (Brager & Holloway, 1978). The *Code of Ethics* (NASW, 2008) should always be used as a guide for ethical decision-making.

Returning to the example of the unmet needs of LGBTQ adolescents in a school setting, if the change work group attempts tactics associated with collaborative and campaign strategies without any success, the next set of tactics utilized may be those of the contest strategy. Ultimately, the change work group wants the principal to implement a new program, and the principal has rejected the idea and is unwilling to formally communicate further about the change proposal.

In response, the change work group may consider several different actions in terms of perceived effectiveness, best estimate of any negative consequences of each, and their comfort level with each. Inevitably, the change work group may decide to organize and implement a march to raise the visibility of the unmet needs. The march can be on public property in front of the school, and occur before or after school hours, so no school or district rules will be violated. This choice of a tactic involves several skills needed by the social worker, to include utilizing the research-based evidence about social action in general, and marches in particular, and empowerment work with LGBTQ adolescents in academic settings, and integrating the research findings with the professional and client experience and preferences. The social worker may also seek to involve external organizations involved with advocacy and diversity issues for additional guidance and support. If this, or any subsequent actions, successfully persuades the principal and administrators to begin formally communicating again with the change work group, bargaining and negotiation between the principal and the change work group may produce a satisfactory outcome, such as a modified version of a program to be used for one year, as a project, with evaluation occurring throughout and at the end of the year. Exhibit 13.2 provides a case example of the use of strategies and tactics.

The social work case managers of a local mental health organization who work with clients who have dual diagnoses and are experiencing challenges in locating affordable rental housing have convened a change work group. The goal of the change work group is to pursue a policy change, so the organization can develop and manage affordable rental housing. The decision makers in this situation are the board of directors, which includes the Executive Director. The work change group is considering a variety of change approaches, including the following:

The change work group may first attempt **collaborative change strategies** with the decision makers. If all agree that a policy change is needed so the organization can develop and manage affordable rental housing for clients, the work will involve implementation skills. The social worker and change work group may be involved in such activities as locating and presenting data regarding affordable housing development and management, creating written materials relating the policy change, creating and facilitating a task groups (which includes clients), and communicating with other housing developers and managers interested parties and decision makers. Other tactics used are capacity building. The social worker, with the change work group, would ensure that clients would be involved in the change process, to possibly include participating in the change work group itself or selected activities. This involvement can be considered empowerment work with the clients, in that the social workers involved with each participating client can work to build client skills related to organizational change tasks (e.g., participating in task groups and public speaking), and client self-image.

The change work group may decide to begin with **campaign change strategies**, if collaborative change strategies are unsuccessful, or if decision-makers will communicate with the change work group, but do not agree that a policy change is needed. The work change group can utilize education skills, to include conducting in-person meetings with individuals on the board of directors and others who can influence board members, such as long-term employees. The group can also provide formal presentations at the board meetings, as well as create educational materials for these meetings. In addition to education efforts using facts, the work change group must also utilize persuasion to convince the board of directors to accept and support a policy change. The work group attempts to appeal to the interests of board members, to include better meeting the needs of clients, as well as potentially raising new revenue for the organization, and increasing the status of the organization among peer organizations. The change work group carefully chooses persons with credibility to communicate with the board members, to include clients, former clients, and long-time employees. The change work group may also utilize cooptation if they invited a member of the board of director to join the change work group in determining the exact direction and wording of the policy change proposal. Change work group members may also lobby board members about the policy change.

The change work group may decide, after unsuccessfully attempting a campaign change strategy, to utilize a **contest change strategy**. After careful thought and deliberation, the change work group may utilize a group action to raise the pressure on the members of the board of directors. For example, the change work group may decide to organize a rally, march, or a vigil, along with other similar service providers who are experiencing the same challenges with affordable rental housing. The publicity materials specifically request that organizations respond to the need for affordable rental housing for the chronically mentally ill. If board members feel there is some urgency in settling the situation, the change work group may engage in **bargaining and negotiation** with the board of directors. In this process, the two sides may agree on a policy change for the organization that looks similar to, but is the same as, the original policy change sought by the change work group.

EXHIBIT 13.2

A Dearth of Affordable Housing: Strategies and Tactics

Similar to change efforts with other client systems and levels of practice, not all change efforts are successful. Change work groups may need to change strategies or tactics, and the end result of the change process may differ from the original proposals. A proposed program may be a short-term, small project, a policy change may differ from the original intention, and an attempt to create a project may require a policy change. Some change efforts are not successful at all, and the status quo is maintained. At this point, the social worker, along with the change work group, must reassess the situation to determine next steps. The change effort may benefit from starting over at the engagement and assessment phase to determine if the identified unmet need may still be as urgent, or other data needs to be collected. Alternatively, the change effort may need to begin anew at the intervention stage, where the decision to pursue an intervention, the type of intervention, and/or the change strategy may need revisiting. An evaluation of the process to date is in order to determine if different directions may yield more successful results, toward the goal of better meeting the needs of the client system. Overall, advocates for change at all client system levels benefit from persistence of efforts, as many factors may be impacting the possibility of change, to include factors external to the organization, such as a poor economy. Many change efforts take a long time, even years, before success is realized (Schenider & Lester, 2001). If the change process has been successful thus far, the next step is to implement the change process within the organization, discussed in the next section.

IMPLEMENTING ORGANIZATIONAL CHANGE

If the change work group has been successful in its work to create an organizational change, the next step is to implement the organizational change. At this point, the change effort converts to administrative functions, such as implementing a new or modified policy, program, project, personnel, or practice change. A change in one element of the organization, such as a new policy, can often impact change in another area, such as a new program, project, or even another policy change. For example, a policy change that affects the members of a committee that screens and interviews candidates for administrative positions will result in practice changes, so that clients will now be recruited for the committee, and educated about organizational personnel procedures, interviewing techniques, and written evaluation process for interviews. Those changes that involve policy, program, or project most significantly impact organizations, and those that impact personnel and practices, while important, may not represent an in-depth change to the organization. The following discussion will apply to the implementation of a new or modified program or project, to include developing goals, objectives, and evaluation criteria, and the possible use of a Gantt chart to guide the time frame of activities. Implementing a new or modified program or project involves similar components, and will be discussed together.

Implementation Structure

Successful programs and projects need elements of structure to guide the implementation, and for evaluation purposes, although the elements for a project may be less elaborate than those for a program due to the short-term nature of a project. The elements of a program include goals and objectives, timelines, eligibility criteria, rules and procedures, an evaluation plan, and a management information system (Hardina, Middleton, Montana, & Simpson, 2007). **Goals** are broad statements related to an ideal state for a target, such as population or community, while **objectives** are steps toward reaching the goals. Objectives can relate to an outcome, or a specific task, or a process, or the means to completing a task. A **timeline** spells out in detail the activities that will carry out the goal and objectives, with specific deadlines in place. The **eligibility criteria** define the group of clients who can participate in the program, while the **rules and procedures** provide the structure for the day-to-day functioning of the program, such as the roles that individuals will play, the decision-making process, the responsibilities for each person involved, and the process for delivering the program. The **evaluation plan** provides the details about the instruments and/or data to be collected on a specific timetable, and the identity of those that will collect, analyze, and report on the program data. The **management information system** is the process for collecting program data, and is often a type of software or internet-based application.

For example, if the change work group focused on the unmet needs of LGBTQ adolescents is successful in promoting a new program within the school to better educate, support, and nurture LGBTQ students, the next step is to create the elements of a program. The change work group, the school social worker, and/or administrators can create program goals and objectives, and corresponding evaluation criteria, such as the following (Hardina et al., 2008):

Program Goal: To enhance the academic and social functioning of LGBTQ students and their supporters in Jefferson High School.

Outcome Objective: By December 2012, at least one support group and three sexual orientation educational sessions will be offered to students.

Evaluation Criteria: Number of support groups and educational sessions offered.

Process Objective: By November 30, 2012, recruit at least 10 students for an LGBTQ support group through one-to-one contact and advertising in the school.

Evaluation Criteria: Number of students recruited, number of in-person recruiting contacts made, amount of school newspaper coverage.

Process Objective: By October 2012, create outlines of two different curricula related to sexual orientation education for consideration by the administration.

Evaluation Criteria: Number of existing curricula reviewed, number of curricular outlines created.

EXHIBIT 13.3	ACTIVITY	SEPT	OCT	NOV	DEC
Gantt Chart, LGBTQ Support Group and Sexual Orientation Education	Produce recruitment materials and begin recruiting for support group	X			
	Locate and review at least three sexual orientation education curricular materials	X			
	Create at least two outlines of a sexual orientation education curricular		X		
	Recruit five students		X		
	Recruit five additional students			X	
	Facilitate one weekly support group.			X	X
	Conduct one education session			X	
	Conduct two education sessions				X

Adapted from Hardina et al., 2008, p. 154

Gantt Chart

An important component of planning program implementation is specifying activities that will implement objectives and a time frame for each of them so that actions can be undertaken in a logical, sequential order. The specification of activities and a corresponding timeframe can be viewed in a **Gantt chart**, as displayed in Exhibit 13.3 (Hardina et al., 2008). A Gantt chart provides a visual display of the activities that must be undertaken and the time frame for the completion of each activity, which can be helpful in both implementing a program, and evaluating the success of the implementation (discussed later in this chapter). The Gantt chart depicts a sample of the activities to be completed for implementation of an LGBTQ support group and sexual orientation education sessions.

For the implementation process, in addition to the activities in the Gantt chart, client eligibility criteria, program rules and procedures, and a management information system will be created to track the program participants, as well as overall evaluation criteria for the program.

Challenges to Implementation

Due to the complexity of organizations, implementation of a change effort can be fraught with difficulty. The organization may be facing challenges imposed by external constraints, such as a scarcity of available funding for the change proposal.

The challenges faced by social workers who are attempting to implement a change can include the following (Brager & Holloway, 1978):

Change Participant Affects Although the change process has been successfully approved and authorized, those staff members involved in actually implementing the change may significantly impact the implementation. Change proposals often encounter resistance from staff members with a different perspective or philosophy than the change work group, or who simply have a personal conflict with a member of the change work group. Staff members may oppose the change for a variety of reasons, to include a different worldview about the potential for change in persons and organization, a distrust of non-experts (or experts), or a fear of conflict, among other reasons. If the staff member was opposed to the change initially, the staff member may covertly express her or his opposition through inaction or subversion, may simply incorrectly implement the change due to a lack of understanding or skill, or may decide to implement the change with her or his unique style such that the original intent is not realized.

Generality of the Change Changes that are major in scope, such as policy changes, can be worded too generally; therefore, the implementation of the change may suffer from distortion from the original intent as the staff member implementing the change may not understand or be competent to implement the change according to the original intent.

Organizational Supports Change proposals may be adopted with low levels of commitment by the decision-makers, and the implementation consequently may suffer from inadequate financial, planning, implementation, and other types of resources. A partial implementation of a change proposal may mean that the change is unsuccessful, when a complete implementation may have resulted in a highly successful implementation. The perspective of a decision-maker about change may be affected by external relationships with other organizations, as with a change in policy, programs, or projects, which may be perceived as creating or exacerbating competition with other organizations or creating unnecessary duplication of the programming of other organizations, at a time when the administrator is trying to create a stronger relationship with another organization. In short, support for the implementation by the organization's decision-makers can be affected by many factors other than the merits of the change proposal.

TERMINATION AND EVALUATION OF CHANGE IN ORGANIZATIONS

The next phase in the change process, termination, can apply to the change process and/or termination from the client system of the organization. Most social workers engaged in a change effort from within an organization will continue to participate in the work of the organization as an employee or a volunteer. In a sense, many organizations experience continual change processes, as the organization seeks to maintain programs and services that are relevant to client system needs.

If the change process has been unsuccessful, the change work group may decide to begin anew at the assessment phase to gather more information and consider different possible unmet needs as the basis for a new intervention effort. The group may also decide to pursue a change effort based on the same unmet need, but with a different change proposal and/or a different strategy for change. Alternatively, the change work group may decide to abandon intervention efforts for now and disband. In this case, termination by the change work group from the change process may occur until the next unmet need is identified, when the change process can begin anew (with possibly a different change work group).

If the change process has been successful, the end of the change effort may occur when the change proposal has been approved by the decision-makers, or after the policy, program or project change has occurred, and an evaluation has determined that the change has successfully impacted the organization. The change work group may be disbanded either after the approval or implementation and evaluation (or may stay together and begin the next organizational change effort).

When the change work group is disbanded, similar with other client systems, the termination may evoke an emotional response from participants, and group termination processes may be helpful (see Chapter 9). Change work groups are one type of task group, and members may have built relationships with one another. Just as in groups used for other purposes, the role of the social worker in termination is to help the group members examine and celebrate their experiences and accomplishments, and discuss the ways in which their shared experiences and skills utilized may be useful to the participants in the future (Garvin & Galinsky, 2008). Social workers may also facilitate the expression and integration of positive and negative emotion, depending on the circumstances of the termination. While change work group members are likely to experience fewer emotional responses than those of other client systems, social workers must always be attuned to the possibility of emotional reactions.

Evaluation of Social Work Practice with Organizations

Similar to evaluation with social work practice with individuals, families, groups, and communities, evaluation of social work practice with organizations is an important part of the change process. The evaluation process of a change effort with an organization can be focused on the change process itself, as well as the result of the change process (i.e., the new or changed policy, program, or project that resulted from the change process). The evaluation of both the change efforts and evaluation of policies, programs, and projects have similar components, discussed in the next section.

Evaluation of an advocacy effort or of a program or project begins with a decision regarding the measurable objectives. Such decisions are usually made at the beginning of a change effort. The evaluation process begins as an element of the change effort, and requires a decision: (1) if both the process and outcomes will be evaluated; (2) the ways in which the process and outcomes will be evaluated; and (3) the means by which data will be collected as the basis for the evaluation. The goal of the evaluation process is to determine the *value* of something, which differs from simply monitoring an intervention (Netting et al., 2008).

Types of Evaluation   For both the change process and the implementation of programs and projects, there are three types of evaluation that can be used to assess the objectives: (1) process, (2) outcome, or (3) impact evaluation. A **process evaluation** focuses on the *degree to which the effort operated well*. For example, did the change work group have a sufficient number of persons for the work involved? What methods were used to recruit persons to the change work group? If evaluating a program, a process evaluation could focus on whether sufficient resources were available for the program, the ways in which decisions were made as a group, or whether there was sufficient and timely communication between staff members implementing a program. An **outcome evaluation** focuses on *information about specific results* that the effort achieved. Questions to be answered may include, did the work group successfully arrange meetings with decision makers? Create educational materials? Were there any policy changes? Were new programs or projects created as a result of policy changes?

An outcome evaluation for a program focuses on the results of program efforts. For example, did support groups meet? Were educational trainings held? The objectives for the program should be reviewed, and success in their achievement should be noted. An **impact evaluation** reviews the *impact of the efforts*, such as individual or community-level behavioral changes (Edwards & Yankey, 2006). For example, in relation to advocacy efforts, is there a new decision-making process in the organization that is more participatory? In relation to a new program, are LGBTQ adolescents achieving at higher academic levels as a result? Have clients experienced behavioral changes as a result of a new policy, program, or project? Have specific changes occurred in the community, such as decreased suicides or increased involvement in community programs?

Structure of Evaluation   The structure of evaluation involves four specific concepts: inputs, activities, outputs, and outcomes. **Inputs** are those resources necessary to implement a change effort or a program. Inputs can include funding, equipment, staff, time, expertise, and other resources needed for the effort or program. **Activities** are those actions that organizations take to produce change. Activities can include attending meetings, creating flyers, interviewing clients, and conducting assessments. **Outputs** are products that emerge from the activities. Outputs are often measured by a number (e.g., number of clients served by a program, flyers produced, or hours worked). **Outcomes** are the benefits gained or changes that have occurred as a result of the activities. Outcomes may relate to behavior, skill, knowledge, attitudes, values, condition, or other attribute. In essence, the outcomes are the impact made by the change effort or program (Dudley, 2009).

Logic Model A **logic model** is a graphic depiction of the relationship of inputs, activities, outputs, and outcomes. Logic models provide a way to demonstrate the links between resources, efforts, accomplishments, and the impacts of change efforts and programs (Dudley, 2009). Exhibit 13.4 provides an example of a logic model used for a program of rental housing for dual-diagnosed clients.

In this example, funding is needed to purchase and/or renovate an apartment building (*input*), so that clients can be housed with a trained, supportive roommate and provided with intensive case management (*activities*). These activities may result in clients being housed in a decent, affordable unit, leading a more stable life, and being compliant with their medication (*output*), so that fewer clients would be homeless and/or incarcerated (*outcome*). This logic model can be useful in making a persuasive argument to a decision-maker who is interested in decreasing the number of dual diagnosed clients who are hospitalized or incarcerated. Other decision-makers may be interested in other outcomes, such as lowering levels of homelessness among persons who are dual diagnosed in the community to improve the relationship between the police force and the organization. Logic models provide a rational connection between inputs, activities, outputs, and outcomes, and are often used in evaluating change efforts, programs, and projects (Dudley, 2009).

Information and Data Sources Developing and maintaining an adequate system for tracking specific information and data about change efforts, as well as programs

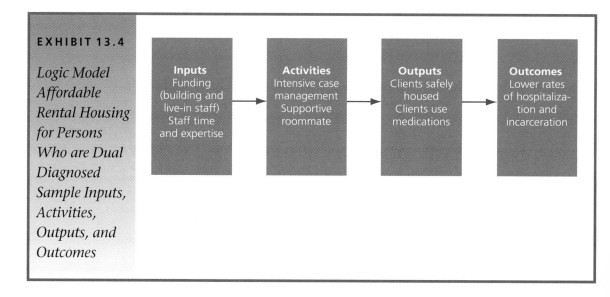

EXHIBIT 13.4

Logic Model Affordable Rental Housing for Persons Who are Dual Diagnosed Sample Inputs, Activities, Outputs, and Outcomes

Inputs
Funding (building and live-in staff)
Staff time and expertise

Activities
Intensive case management
Supportive roommate

Outputs
Clients safely housed
Clients use medications

Outcomes
Lower rates of hospitalization and incarceration

and projects, is the backbone to the evaluation process. Information (hard copy and/or electronic) that may be helpful includes the following (Schneider & Lester, 2001):

- Minutes of meetings, logs of activities, sign-in sheets

- Information noting time spent on activities, appointments, assessments, client progress, activities in need of completing, and accomplishments

- Client system evaluation materials, to include standardized measures

- Organization strategic plans, mission, value statements, goals, objectives, and timelines

- Media coverage

- Funding sources, amounts, responsibilities, and required communications

- Information about key individuals to change efforts or programs/projects

- Government organizations related to the change effort and/or programs/projects

- Previous internal and external evaluations of advocacy efforts and programs/projects

- Records about previous internal and external advocacy efforts

As with evaluations of community change efforts, the evaluation process ideally includes qualitative and quantitative data to provide information about the process and outcomes of organizational change. Methods may include pre- and post-measures of organizational and/or community functioning, to include the use of validated and standardized measures, direct observation, use of publically available data (i.e., U.S. Census data and others), and feedback from other professionals.

Roles in Evaluation   Generalist social work practitioners commonly contribute in several ways to the evaluation efforts. Social workers can lead and/or assist with evaluation efforts by assisting to maintain organizational records, submitting data for an analysis, participating in interviews and/or focus groups, or creating questions to be used in the evaluation process. Participation on evaluation teams and committees provides a way for social workers to learn about and direct the evaluation efforts, and some social workers function in the role of researchers to collect, analyze, and report on quantitative and qualitative data. Organizations benefit from well-designed and executed evaluation efforts.

STRAIGHT TALK ABOUT ORGANIZATIONAL LIFE

This chapter has highlighted both the challenging and the exhilarating aspects of social work practice in an organizational setting. Social workers can be tempted to view the organization as a source of challenges in practice. Sometimes organizations can be perceived as posing confounding or complex barriers to the helping process due to policies, procedures, and practice requirements.

In much the same way that some persons blame their families for their challenges, some social workers point to the organization as the source of the problem when work becomes challenging or proves more difficult than expected. Shifting responsibility for challenges to organizations relieves the burden of responsibility from the social worker for a role in those organizational challenges. Social workers may not always fully understand the practice constraints inherent in organizations (such as constraints on practice by funders or regulators), and may find it easier to adopt a cynicism that eases their sense of responsibility. A related problem can occur if the social worker joins with the clients to collude about the problems of the organization as the source of the clients' challenges. In doing so, the social worker may feel temporarily relieved by engaging the client in her or his desperation with the organizational system. However, such collusion can convey a sense of hopelessness to the client, when the social worker's goal may be to convey a sense of hopefulness about the client's situation. In its most extreme implication, a hopeless stance may promote a generalized, scornful distrust of all helping efforts. The client may generalize that all helping efforts are ineptly carried out by social workers who are helpless and caught in troubled organizational structures that fail to implement their mission statements. Social workers, at times, must identify problematic agency policies or obstacles to clients. An element of empowerment practice is creating an alliance with clients, or a joint effort designed to promote more effective responses to clients. However, social workers must be able to convey an overall hopeful message to clients about their interaction with an organization.

At the same time, social workers must invest in a thorough engagement and assessment process prior to engaging in change efforts within and for an organization. For example, social workers need to understand the dynamics of bureaucracies and the slow nature of change within bureaucracies before engaging in a change effort. Social workers are sometimes discouraged by seasoned professionals in their efforts to create change because efforts will result in no effect, or to wait until credibility is built through time and experience at the organization so that those facilitating change are not likely to be censured or fired.

Social workers who facilitate organizational change efforts must be well informed, and have completed the earlier phases of the change process, knowing that every change effort will encounter resistance. In addition to having an understanding of the organization, social workers must also understand their own strengths and weaknesses, and enlist allies to assist with the effort. However, a social worker who does not address any problematic organizational policy or practice due to fear of criticism or loss of employment is likely to have a difficult time in a social work career. Social work practice requires principled, thoughtful, and respectful risks across all settings to fully implement the work of the profession.

CONCLUSION

Organizations are structures that shape and facilitate social work practice. The change process in organizations provides an opportunity to make significant changes to provide improved services to client systems. While the change process can be lengthy and complex, the process provides the opportunity to make changes that positively impact a large number of persons, to include entire communities. Most organizations undergo at least modest change on a regular basis due to changes in many factors, such as funding, relationships, personnel, accreditation requirements, or accountability requirements, and staff members are in a unique position to implement the change process based on feedback and critical thinking about client system needs as experienced by staff working directly with clients. While organizations can seem vague and too complex to change, understanding and impacting organizations is important to social work practitioners on all levels because of the significant impact on clients and practitioners. Taking an active role in shaping the organization is a significant aspect to generalist social work practice.

MAIN POINTS

- The approach of an organizational change effort will be impacted by the results of the engagement and assessment process, as well as the approach, perspective, or model utilized.

- The organizational change effort is facilitated by using a framework.

- Gathering supporters and allies into a change work group, considering important factors when choosing a change proposal, and selecting an organizational change strategy are vital steps in the intervention.

- Social workers consider social work ethics when choosing specific tactics to utilize for the change process.

- The implementation of an organizational change is facilitated by a structure, as well as consideration of challenges to implementation that can impede the implementation.

- Termination of a change effort can occur after a change proposal has been successful or after the implementation of the change.

458 THE PRACTICE OF GENERALIST SOCIAL WORK

- The evaluation phase can include evaluation of the change effort as well as evaluation of the change, such as a program or a project.

- Social workers should exercise caution about identifying organizational challenges with client systems, and only do so while maintaining a hopeful stance about the ability of the organization to assist the client system.

EXERCISES

1. Review Exhibit 13.1. Create a different policy, program, project, personnel, or practice approach to the case provided.
2. Review Exhibit 13.1. Create an approach to change that mixes these approaches.
3. You are a social worker at an organization that provides treatment for adolescents who have alcohol and drug addiction issues. Yesterday, you suggested that the organization extend the service hours of the organization into the evenings and weekends so that the families of the clients would have greater access to meet with the staff, participate in treatment planning, and provide additional face-to-face support for their children. The staff was enthusiastic about the idea, and you agreed to the director's request that you compose a written proposal to be discussed at the next staff meeting.

   In your weekly meeting with your supervisor, you learn that she is upset with you. In your discussion, she is curt and states that you may not have taken into account the increased amount of work that extended service hours would entail. She states that increased service hours will have a negative impact on her life in terms of her social life and time with family members, and cost the agency additional funds. Considering the material discussed in Chapter 13, discuss the factors that may have led to this encounter in terms of creating a change proposal. Discuss possible next steps for this change process.

4. Go to www.routledgesw.com/cases and become familiar with the Carla Washburn case, to include reviewing her client history, concerns, and goals. Explore the town map, and determine those organizations that may be able to assist Carla with her concerns and goals. Choose one of the organizations and consider the way(s) in which the organization may be able to assist Carla with one or more of her concerns and/or goals. Imagine that you are employed by the organization, and the assistance needed for Carla is currently not offered by the organization. Using the material from Chapter 13, describe:

   - The type of approach, perspective, or model with which you most closely identify.

   - The way in which you would go about creating a change work group.

   - Two to three possible solutions to Carla's concern or goal with which the organization could assist.

- Two to three considerations that are important to consider in deciding on the change proposal.

5. Go to www.routledgesw.com/cases and become familiar with the Riverton case, to include the history, concerns, and goals, as well as the town map and the interaction matrix. Imagine that you decide to work to find a solution to the problem of public intoxication by working with the organizations in the community as a "non-employee."

    Which organizations would you approach to develop a community-wide response to this problem? What kind of changes might be needed in those organizations to better meet the unmet needs of the clients in the community? What steps might you take to facilitate the development of a change work group in these organizations? What might be some feasible solutions that organizations could implement through a partnership?

REFERENCES

Abramowitz, M. (2005). The largely untold story of welfare reform and the human services. *Social Work, 50,* 2, 175–186.

Abramson, J. (2009). Interdisciplinary team practice. In A.R. Roberts, *Social workers' desk reference* (2nd ed.) (pp. 44–50). New York: Oxford Press.

Alissi, A.S. (2009). United States. In A. Gitterman & R. Salmon, *Encyclopedia of social work with groups* (pp. 6–12). New York: Routledge.

Amato, P.R., Booth, A., Johnson, D.R., & Rogers, S.J. (2007). *Alone together: How marriage in America is changing.* Cambridge, MA: Harvard University Press.

Anderson, K.M., Cowger, C.D., & Snively, C.A. (2009). Assessing strengths. Identifying acts of resistance to violence and oppression. In D. Saleebey (Ed.) *The strengths perspective in social work practice* (5th ed.) (pp. 181–200). Boston: Allyn & Bacon.

Arrington, P. (2008). *Stress at work: How do social workers cope? NASW Membership Workforce Study.* Washington, DC: National Association of Social Workers.

Association for the Advancement of Social Work with Groups, Inc. (AASWG) (2006). *Standards for social work practice with groups* (2nd ed.). Alexandria, VA: AASWG, Inc.

Atwood, J.D. & Genovese, F. (2006). *Therapy with single parents. A social constructionist approach.* New York: The Haworth Press.

Austin, M.J. & Solomon, J.R. (2009). Managing the planning process. In R.J. Patti (Ed.) *The handbook of human services management* (pp. 321–337). Thousand Oaks, CA: Sage Publications.

Bar-Gal, D. & Schmid, H. (1992). Assessing prospects for organizational change: The uses of a Force Field Analysis. In G. Brager & S. Holloway (Eds.) *Organizational change and development in human service organizations* (pp. 15–28). Binghamton, NY: Haworth Press.

Barker, R.L. (2003). *The social work dictionary* (5th ed.). Washington, DC: NASW Press.

Barsky, A.E. (2010). *Ethics and values in social work.* New York: Oxford University Press.

Barth, R.P. (2008). Adoption. In T. Mizrahi & L.E. Davis, *Encyclopedia of social work* (20th ed.) (pp. 1:33–44). Washington, DC and New York: NASW Press and Oxford University Press.

Beaulaurier, R.L. & Taylor, S.H. (2007). Social work practice with people with disabilities in the era of disability rights. In A.E. Dell Orto & P.W. Power, *The psychological and social impact of illness and disability* (5th ed.) (pp. 53–74). New York: Springer Publishing.

Beaulieu, L.J. (n.d.). *Mapping the assets of your community: A key component for building local capacity.* Southern Rural Development Center, Mississippi State University. Retrieved June 23, 2010 from: http://srdc.msstate.edu/publications/227/227_asset_mapping.pdf

Beck, J. (2005). *Cognitive therapy for challenging problems: What to do when the basics don't work.* New York: Guilford Press.

Benard, B. (2008). Using strengths-based practice to tap into the resilience of families. In D. Saleebey, *The strengths perspective in social work practice* (5th ed.) (pp. 197–220). Boston: Allyn & Bacon.

Berg-Weger, M., Rubio, D.M., & Tebb, S. (2000). The caregiver well-being scale revisited. *Health and Social Work, 25*(4), 255–263.

Berman-Rossi, T. & Kelly, T.B. (2003). *Group composition, diversity, the skills of the social worker, and group development.* Presented at the Council for Social Work Education, Annual Meeting, Atlanta, February.

Biblarz, T.J. & Stacey, J. (2010). How does the gender of parents matter? *Journal of Marriage and Family, 72,* 3–22.

Bloom, M., Fischer, J., & Orme, J.G. (2009). *Evaluating practice: Guidelines for the accountable professional* (6th ed.). Boston: Allyn & Bacon.

Blunsdon, B. & Davern, M. (2007). Measuring wellness through interdisciplinary community development: Linking the physical, economic and social environment. *Journal of Community Practice, 15*(1/2), 217–238.

Bobo, K., Kendall, J., & Max, S. (2010). *Organizing for social change.* Santa Ana, CA: The Forum Press.

Bowden, V.R. & Greenberg, C.S. (2010). *Children and their families: The continuum of care.* Philadelphia: Wolters Kluwer/Lippincott Williams and Wilkins.

Bowlby, J. (1969). *Attachment and loss: Vol. 1, Attachment.* New York: Basic Books.

Boyes-Watson, C. (2005). Seeds of change: Using peacemaking circles to build a village for every child. *Child Welfare, 84*(2), 191–208.

Brager, G. & Halloway, S. (1978). *Changing human service organizations: Politics and practice.* New York: The Free Press.

Breton, M. (2004). An empowerment perspective. In C.D. Garvin, L.M. Gutierrez, & M.J. Galinsky (Eds.) *Handbook of social work with groups* (pp. 58–75). New York: Guilford Press.

Briar-Lawson, K. & Naccarato, T. (2008). Family Services. In T. Mizrahi & L.E. Davis, *Encyclopedia of social work* (20th ed.) (pp. 2:206–212). Washington, DC and New York: NASW Press and Oxford University Press.

Briskman, L. & Noble, C. (1999). Social work ethics: Embracing diversity? In J. Fook & B. Pease (Eds.) *Transforming social work practice: Postmodern critical perspectives* (pp. 57–69). London: Routledge.

Brody, K. & Gadling-Cole, C. (2008). Family group conferencing with African-American families. In C. Waites (Ed.) *Social work practice with African American families: An intergenerational perspective.* New York: Routledge.

Brueggemann, W. G. (2005). *The practice of macro social work.* Belmont, CA: Thomson Higher Education.

Bullock, K. (2005). Grandfathers and the impact of raising grandchildren. *Journal of Sociology & Social Welfare, 32*(1), 43–59.

Burry, C. (2002). Working with potentially violent clients in their homes: What child welfare professionals need to know. *Clinical Supervisor, 21*(1), 145–153.

Campbell, D. (2000). *The socially constructed organization.* London: Karnac Books.

Carmeli, A. & Freund, A. (2009). Linking perceived external prestige and intentions to leave the organization: The mediating role of job satisfaction. *Journal of Social Service Research, 35*(3), 236–250.

Carter, L. & Matthieu, M. (2010). *Developing skills in the evidence based practice process.* St. Louis, MO: Washington University in St. Louis. Presented March 12, 2010.

Chaskin, R.J. (2010). The Chicago School: A context for youth intervention, research and development. In R.J. Chaskin (Ed.) *Youth gangs and community intervention: Research, practice, and evidence* (pp. 3–23). New York: Columbia University Press.

Chaskin, R., Venkatsh, S., Vidal, A., & Brown, P. (2001). *Building community capacity.* New York: Aldine de Gruyter.

Chow, J.C. & Crowe, K. (2005). Community-based research and methods in community practice. In M. Weil (Ed.) *Handbook of community practice* (pp. 604–619). Thousand Oaks, CA; Sage.

Christiensen, D.N., Todahl, J., & Barrett, W.C. (1999). *Solution-based casework: An introduction to clinical and case management skills in casework practice.* New York: De Gruyter.

Chu, W.C.K. & Tsui, M. (2008). The nature of practice wisdom in social work revisited. *International Social Work, 51*(1), 47–54.

Clowes, L. (2005). *Crossing cultures in systems of care.* Presented at the 1st New England LEND Conference, Burlington, VT.

Cnaan, R. A. & Rothman, J. (2008). Capacity development and the building of community. In J. Rothman, J. Erlich, & J. Tropman (Eds.) *Strategies of community intervention* (7th ed.) (pp. 243–262). Peosta, Iowa: Eddie Bowers Publishing Co., Inc.

Collins, D., Jordan, C., & Coleman, H. (2010). *An introduction to family social work*. Itasca, IL: Peacock.

Collins, K.S. & Lazzari, M.M. (2009). Co-leadership. In A. Gitterman & R. Salmon, *Encyclopedia of social work with groups* (pp. 299–302). New York: Routledge.

Congress, E.P. (2004). Cultural and ethical issues in working with culturally diverse patients and their families: The use of the culturagram to promote cultural competent practice in health care settings. In A. Metteri, T. Krôger, A. Pohjola, & P. Rauhala (Eds.) *Social work visions from around the globe* (pp. 249–262). Binghampton, NY: Haworth.

Congress, E.P. (2009). The culturagram. In A.R. Roberts, *Social workers' desk reference* (2nd ed.) (pp. 969–975). New York: Oxford Press.

Cooney, K. (2006). The institutional and technical structuring of nonprofit ventures: Case study of a U.S. hybrid organization caught between two fields. *Voluntas: International Journal of Voluntary and Nonprofit Organizations*, *17*(2), 143–161.

Corcoran, J. (2009). Using standardized tests and instruments in family assessments. In A.R. Roberts, *Social workers' desk reference* (2nd ed.) (pp. 390–394). New York: Oxford Press.

Council on Social Work Education. (2008). *Educational policy and accreditation standards*. Washington, DC: Author.

Cox, C.B. (2003). Designing interventions for grandparent caregivers: The need for an ecological perspective for practice. *Families in Society*, *84*(1), 127–134.

Cox, D. & Pawar, M. (2006). *International social work: Issues, strategies, and programs*. Thousand Oaks, CA: Sage Publications, Inc.

Cross, T.L., Bazron, B.J., Dennis, K.W., & Isaacs, M.R. (1989). *Toward a culturally competent system of care*. Washington, DC: Georgetown University Development Center.

DeFrain, J. & Asay, S.M. (2007a). Epilogue: A strengths-based conceptual framework for understanding families world-wide. In J. DeFrain & S.M. Asay, *Strong families around the world: Strengths-based research and perspectives* (pp. 447–466). New York: Haworth Press, Inc.

DeFrain, J. & Asay, S.M. (2007b). Family strengths and challenges in the USA. In J. DeFrain & S.M. Asay,

Strong families around the world: Strengths-based research and perspectives (pp. 281–307). New York: Haworth Press, Inc.

De Jong, P. (2008). Interviewing. In T. Mizrahi & L.E. Davis, *Encyclopedia of social work* (20th ed.) (pp. 2:539–542). Washington, DC and New York: NASW Press and Oxford University Press.

De Jong, P. (2009). Solution-focused therapy. In A.R. Roberts, *Social workers' desk reference* (2nd ed.) (pp. 253–258). New York: Oxford Press.

De Jong, P., & Berg, I.K. (2008). *Interviewing for solutions* (3rd ed.). Belmont, CA: Thomson Brooks/Cole.

deShazer, S. (1984). The death of resistance. *Family Process*, *23*, 11–21.

Diller, J. (2007). *Cultural diversity: A primer for the human services* (3rd ed.). Belmont, CA: Thomson/Brooks/Cole.

Dolgoff, R., Loewenberg, F. M., & Harrington, D. (2009). *Ethical decisions for social work practice* (8th ed.). Itasca, IL: F. E. Peacock.

Dombo, E.A. (2005). Rape: When professional values place vulnerable clients at risk. In J.C. Rothman, *From the front lines: Student cases in social work ethics* (2nd ed.) (pp. 177–187). Boston: Allyn & Bacon.

Donaldson, L.P. (2004). Toward validating the therapeutic benefits of empowerment-oriented social action groups. *Social Work with Groups*, *27*(2), 159–175.

Dressler, L. (2006). *Consensus through conversation*. San Francisco, CA: Berrett-Koehler Publishers, Inc.

Dudley, J. R. (2009). *Social work evaluation: Enhancing what we do*. Chicago, IL: Lyceum Books, Inc.

Dunst, C.J., Trivette, C.M., & Deal, A.G. (2003). *Enabling and empowering families: Principles and guidelines for practice*. Newton: MA: Brookline Books.

Earley, L. & Cushway, D. (2002). The parentified child. *Clinical Child Psychology & Psychiatry*, *7*(2), 163–178.

Early, T.J. (2001). Measures for practice with families from a strengths perspective. *Families in Society*, *82*(3), 225–232.

East, J.F., Manning, S.F., & Parsons, R.J. (2002). Social work empowerment agenda and group work: A workshop. In S. Henry, J. East, & C. Schmitz (Eds.)

Social work with groups: Mining the gold (pp. 41–53). New York: Haworth Press.

Eaton, Y.M. & Roberts, A.R. (2009). Frontline crisis intervention. Step-by-step practice guidelines with case applications. In A.R. Roberts, *Social workers' desk reference* (2nd ed.) (pp.207–215). New York: Oxford Press.

Edwards, R.L. & Yankey, J.A. (2006). *Effectively managing nonprofit organizations.* Washington DC: NASW Press.

Ephross, P.H. & Greif, G.L. (2009). Group process and group work techniques. In A.R. Roberts, *Social workers' desk reference* (2nd ed.) (pp.679–685). New York: Oxford Press.

Epstein, M.H. & Sharma, J. (1998). Behavioral and emotional rating scale: A strengths-based approach to assessment. Austin, TX: PRO-ED.

Fellin, P. (2000). *The community and the social worker* (2nd ed.). Itasca, IL: F.E. Peacock.

Finn, J.L. & Jacobson, M. (2003). Just practice: Steps toward a new social work paradigm. *Journal of Social Work Education, 39*(1), 57–78.

Fischer, J. & Orme, J.G. (2008). Single-System Designs. In T. Mizrahi & L.E. Davis, *Encyclopedia of social work* (20th ed.) (pp. 4:32–34). Washington, DC and New York: NASW Press and Oxford University Press.

Fleming, J. (2009). Social action. In A. Gitterman & R. Salmon, *Encyclopedia of social work with groups* (pp. 275–277). New York: Routledge.

Fortune, A.E. (2009). Terminating with clients. In A.R. Roberts, *Social workers' desk reference* (2nd ed.) (pp. 627–631). New York: Oxford Press.

Franklin, C., Jordan, C., & Hopson, L.M. (2009). Effective couple and family treatment. In A.R. Roberts, *Social workers' desk reference* (2nd ed.) (pp. 433–442). New York: Oxford Press.

Freedenthal, S. (2008). Suicide. In T. Mizrahi & L.E. Davis, *Encyclopedia of social work* (20th ed.) (pp. 4:181–186). Washington, DC and New York: NASW Press and Oxford University Press.

Freire, P. (1973). *Education for critical consciousness.* New York: Seabury Press.

Freund, A. (2005). Work attitudes of social workers across three sectors of welfare organizations: Public, for profit, and third sector. *Journal of Social Service Review, 31*(3), 69–92.

Frey, B.A. (1990). A framework for promoting organizational change. *Families in Society, 71*(3), 142–147.

Fuller-Thomson, E. & Minkler, M. (2005). American Indian/Alaskan Native grandparents raising grandchildren: Findings from the Census 2000 Supplementary Survey. *Social Work, 50*(2), 131–139.

Furman, R., Rowan, D., & Bender, K. (2009). *An experiential approach to group work.* Chicago, IL: Lyceum Books, Inc.

Gamble, D.N. & Hoff, M.D. (2005). Sustainable community development. In M. Weil (Ed.) *The handbook of community practice* (pp. 169–188). Thousand Oaks, CA: Sage Publications.

Gambrill, E. (2006). *Social work practice: A critical thinkers guide.* New York: Oxford University Press.

Garkovich, L.E. (2011). A historical view of community development. In J.W. Robinson, Jr. & G.P. Green (Eds.) *Introduction to community development* (pp. 11–34). Los Angeles, CA: Sage Publications, Inc.

Garland, J., Jones, H., & Kolodny, R. (1965). A model for stages of development in social work groups. In S. Bernstein (Ed.) *Explorations in group work: Essays in theory and practice* (pp. 12–53). Boston: Boston University School of Social Work.

Garvin, C. (2009). Developing goals. In A.R. Roberts, *Social workers' desk reference* (2nd ed.) (pp. 521–526). New York: Oxford Press.

Garvin, C.D. & Galinsky, M.J. (2008). Groups. In T. Mizrahi & L.E. Davis, *Encyclopedia of social work* (20th ed.) (pp. 2:287–298). Washington, DC and New York: NASW Press and Oxford University Press.

Gil, D.G. (1998). Foreword to J. Wronka, *Human rights and social policy in the 21st century* (Rev. ed.) (pp. xiii–xiv). Lanhan, MD: University Press of America.

Gilligan, C. (1982). *In a different voice.* Cambridge, MA: Harvard University Press.

Gitterman, A. & Germain, C.B. (2008a). Ecological framework. In T. Mizrahi & L.E. Davis, *Encyclopedia of social work* (20th ed.) (pp. 2:97–102). Washington, DC and New York: NASW Press and Oxford University Press.

Gitterman A. & Germain, C.B. (2008b). *The life model of social work practice: Advances in theory and practice* (3rd ed.). New York: Columbia Press.

Goodman, H. (2004). Elderly parents of adults with severe mental illness: Group work interventions. *Journal of Gerontological Social Work, 44*(1/2), 173–188.

Grant, D. (2008). Clinical social work. In R. Mizrahi & L.E. Davis (Eds.) *Encyclopedia of Social Work. National Association of Social Workers and Oxford University Press, Inc.* Encyclopedia of Social Work: (e-reference edition). Oxford University Press. Retrieved April 1, 2010 from: http://www.oxfordnaswsocialwork.com/entry?entry=t203.e63

Greenpeace. (n.d.). *About us.* Retrieved July 7, 2010 from: http://www.greenpeace.org/usa/about

Greif, G. & Ephross, P.H. (Eds.). (2005). *Group work with populations at risk* (2nd ed.). New York: Oxford University Press.

Hall, R.H. (1991). *Organization: Structures, processes, and outcomes* (5th ed.). Englewood Cliffs, NJ: Prentice-Hall.

Hanley, J. & Shragge, E. (2009). Organizing for immigrant rights. *Journal of Community Practice, 17*(1), 184–206.

Hardina, D. (2002). *Analytical skills for community organization practice.* New York: Columbia University Press.

Hardina, D., Middleton, J., Montana, S., & Simpson, R. A. (2007). *An empowering approach to managing social service organizations.* New York: Springer Publishing Company.

Hartman, A. (1994). *Reflection & controversy: Essays on social work.* Washington, DC: NASW Press.

Hartman, A. & Laird, J. (1983). *Family-centered social work practice.* New York: Free Press.

Hasenfeld, Y. (2000). Social welfare administration and organizational theory. In R. J. Patti (Ed.) *The handbook of social welfare management* (pp. 89–112). Thousand Oaks, CA: Sage Publications.

Haynes, K.S. (1998). The one-hundred year debate: Social reform versus individual treatment. *Social Work, 43*(6), 501–511.

Haynes, K.S. & Mickelson, J.S. (2006). *Affecting change* (6th ed.). Boston: Pearson/Allyn & Bacon.

Hayslip, Jr., B. & Kaminski, P.L. (2005). Grandparents raising their grandchildren. A review of the literature and suggestions for practice. *The Gerontologist, 45*(2), 262–269.

Healy, L. (2008). *International social work: Professional practice in an interdependent world.* New York: Oxford University Press.

Healy, L.M. & Hokenstad, T.M.C. (2008). International social work. In T. Mizrahi & L.E. Davis, *Encyclopedia of social work* (20th ed.) (pp. 2:482–488). Washington, DC and New York: NASW Press and Oxford University Press.

Herbert, R.J., Gagnon, A.J., Rennick, J.E., & O'Loughlin, J.L. (2009). A systematic review of questionnaires measuring health-related empowerment. *Research and Theory for Nursing Practice: An International Journal, 23*(2), 107–132.

Hodge, D.R. (2005a). Social work and the House of Islam: Orienting practitioners to the beliefs and values of Muslims in the United States. *Social Work, 50*, 2, 162–173.

Hodge, D.R. (2005b). Spiritual life maps: A client centered pictorial instrument for spiritual assessment, planning, and intervention. *Social Work, 50*(1), 77–87.

Holland, T. (2008). Organizations and governance. In T. Mizrahi & L. E. Davis (Eds.) *Encyclopedia of Social Work* (pp. 3:329–333). Washington DC: NASW Press and Oxford University Press.

Hopson, L.M. & Wodarski, J.S. (2009). Guidelines and uses of rapid assessment instruments in managed care settings. In A.R. Roberts, *Social workers' desk reference* (2nd ed.) (pp. 400–405). New York: Oxford Press.

Hudson, R.E. (2009). Empowerment model. In A. Gitterman & R. Salmon (Eds.) *Encyclopedia of social work with groups* (pp. 47–50). New York: Routledge.

Hull, G.H. & Mather, J. (2006). *Understanding generalist practice with families.* Belmont, CA: Thomson Brooks/Cole.

Ife, J. (2000). Localized needs and a globalized economy. Social work and globalization (Special Issue), *Canadian Social Work, 2*(1), 50–64.

"Indicators for the Achievement of the NASW Standards for Cultural Competence in Social Work Practice" (2008). In T. Mizrahi & L.E. Davis (Eds.) *Encyclopedia of social work.* National

Association of Social Workers and Oxford University Press, Inc. (e-reference edition). Available at: http://www.oxford-naswsocialwork.com/entry?entry=t203.e427

International Federation of Social Workers and the International Association of Schools of Social Work (IFSW & IASSW). (2004). *Ethics in social work: Statement of principles*. Retrieved July 16, 2010 from: http://www.ifsw.org/f38000032.html

International Institute St. Louis. (2010). *Homepage*. Retrieved July 11, 2010 from: http://www.iistl.org/index.html.

Janzen, C., Harris, O., Jordan, C., & Franklin, C. (2006). *Family treatment: Evidence-based practice with populations at risk*. Belmont, CA: Thomson Brooks/Cole.

Jayartne, S., Croxton, T.A., & Mattison, D. (2004). A national survey of violence in the practice of social work. *Families in Society, 85*(4), 445–453.

Jenson, J.M. & Howard, M.O. (2008). Evidence-based practice. In T. Mizrahi & L.E. Davis, *Encyclopedia of social work* (20th ed.) (pp. 2:158–165). Washington, DC and New York: NASW Press and Oxford University Press.

Johnson, M. & Austin, M. J. (2006). Evidence-based practice in the social services: Implications for organizational change. *Journal of Evidence-Based Social Work, 5*(1/2), 239–269.

Jordan, C. (2008). Assessment. In T. Mizrahi & L.E. Davis, *Encyclopedia of social work* (20th ed.) (pp. 1:178–180). Washington, DC and New York: NASW Press and Oxford University Press.

Jordan, C. & Franklin, C. (2009). Treatment planning with families: An evidence-based approach. In A.R. Roberts, *Social workers' desk reference* (2nd ed.) (pp. 429–432). New York: Oxford Press.

Jung, M. (1996). Family-centered practice with single parent families. *Families in Society, 77*(9), 583–590.

Kagle, J.D. (2008). Recording. In T. Mizrahi & L.E. Davis, *Encyclopedia of social work* (20th ed.) (pp. 3:497–498). Washington, DC and New York: NASW Press and Oxford University Press.

Kagle, J.D. & Kopels, S. (2008). *Social work records* (3rd ed.). Long Grove, IL: Waveland Press, Inc.

Klyanpur, M., & Harry, B. (1999). *Culture in special education*. Baltimore: Paul H. Brookes.

Kaplinsky, R. (2005). *Globalization, poverty, and inequality: Between a rock and a hard place*. Cambridge, UK: Polity Press.

Kasvin, N. & Tashayeva, A. (2004). Community organizing to address domestic violence in immigrant populations in the U.S.A. *Journal of Religion and Abuse, 6*(3/4), 109–112.

Kelley, P. (2008). Narratives. In T. Mizrahi & L.E. Davis, *Encyclopedia of social work* (20th ed.) (pp. 3:291–292). Washington, DC and New York: NASW Press and Oxford University Press.

Kelley, P. (2009). Narrative therapy. In A.R. Roberts, *Social workers' desk reference* (2nd ed.) (pp. 273–277). New York: Oxford Press.

Kelly, M.S., Kim, J.S., & Franklin, C. (2008). *Solution-focused brief therapy in schools. A 360-degree view of research and practice*. New York: Oxford University Press.

Kelly, T.B. & Berman-Rossi, T. (1999). Advancing stages of group development theory: The case of institutionalized older persons. *Social Work with Groups, 22*(2/3), 119–138.

Kettner, P.M. (2002). *Achieving excellence in the management of human service organizations*. Boston: Allyn & Bacon.

Khinduka, S. K. (2008). Globalization. In T. Mizrahi & L.E. Davis, *Encyclopedia of social work* (20th ed.) (pp. 2:275–279). Washington, DC and New York: NASW Press and Oxford University Press.

Killaspy, H., Bebbington, P., Blizard, R., Johnson, S., Nolan, F., Pilling, S., & King, M. (2006). The REACT study: Randomized evaluation of assertive community treatment in north London. *British Medical Journal, 332*, 815–820.

Kim, J.S. (2008a). Strengths perspective. In T. Mizrahi & L.E. Davis, *Encyclopedia of social work* (20th ed.) (pp. 4:177–181). Washington, DC and New York: NASW Press and Oxford University Press.

Kim, J.S. (2008b). Examining the effectiveness of solution-focused brief therapy: A meta-analysis. *Research on Social Work Practice, 18*, 107–116.

Kisthardt, W.E. (2002). The strengths perspective in interpersonal helping: Purpose, principles, and function. In D. Saleebey (Ed.) *The strengths perspective in social work practice* (3rd ed.). Boston: Allyn & Bacon.

Kondrat, M.E. (2002). Actor-centered social work: Revisioning "person-in-environment" through a critical theory lens. *Social Work, 47*(4), 435–448.

Kong, E. (2007). The development of strategic management in the non-profit context: Intellectual capital in the social service non-profit organization. *International Journal of Management Reviews, 10*(3), 281–299.

Koren, P.E., DeChillo, N., & Friesen, B.J. (1992). Measuring empowerment in families whose children have emotional disabilities: A brief questionnaire. *Rehabilitation Psychology, 37*, 305–310.

Kreider, R.M. (2008). *Living arrangements of children: 2004.* Current Population Reports, P70–114. Washington, DC: U.S. Census Bureau.

Kretzmann, J.P. & McKnight, J.L. (1993). *Building communities from the inside out: A path toward finding and mobilizing a community's assets.* Evanston, IL: Center for Urban Affairs and Policy Research.

Krumer-Nevo, M. (2005). Reading a poor woman's life: Issues and dilemmas. *Affilia: Journal of Women & Social Work, 20*(1), 87–102.

Kurland, R. (2007). Debunking the "blood theory" of social work with groups: Groups workers *are* made and not born. *Social Work with Groups, 31*(1), 11–24.

Kurland, R. & Salmon, R. (1998). *Teaching a methods course in social work with groups.* Alexandria, VA: Council on Social Work Education.

Kurland, R., Salmon, R., Bitel, M., Goodman, H., Ludwig, K., Newmann, E.W., & Sullivan, N. (2004). The survival of social group work: A call to action. *Social Work with Groups, 27*(1), 3–16.

Lawler, J., & Bilson, A. (2004). Towards a more reflexive research aware practice: The influence and potential of professional and team culture. *Social Work & Social Sciences Review, 11*(1), 52–69.

Lee, J.A.B. (2001). *The empowerment approach to social work practice* (2nd ed.). New York: Columbia University Press.

Lee, J.A.B. & Berman-Rossi, T. (1999). Empowering adolescent girls in foster care: A short-term group record. In C. W. LeCroy (Ed.) *Case studies in social work practice* (2nd ed.). Pacific Grove, CA: Brooks/Cole.

Lee, M.Y. (2009). Using the miracle question and scaling technique in clinical practice. In A.R. Roberts, *Social workers' desk reference* (2nd ed.) (pp. 594–600). New York: Oxford Press.

Lee, M.Y. & Greene, G.J. (2009). Using social constructivism in social work practice. In A.R. Roberts, *Social workers' desk reference* (2nd ed.) (pp. 294–299). New York: Oxford Press.

Lesser, J.G., O'Neill, M.R., Burke, K.W., Scanlon, P., Hollis, K., & Miller, R. (2004). Women supporting women: A mutual aid group fosters new connections among women in midlife. *Social Work with Groups, 27*(1), 75–88.

Lewin, K. (1951). *Field theory in social science.* New York: Harper and Row.

Locke, B., Garrison, R., & Winship, J. (1998). *Generalist social work practice: Context, story, and partnerships.* Pacific Grove, CA: Brooks/Cole.

Logan, S.L.M., Rasheed, M.N., & Rasheed, J.M. (2008). Family. In T. Mizrahi & L.E. Davis, *Encyclopedia of social work* (20th ed.) (pp. 2:175–182). Washington, DC and New York: NASW Press and Oxford University Press.

Lovell, M.L., Helfgott, J.B., & Lawrence, C. (2002). Citizens, victims, and offenders restoring justice: A prison-based group work program bridging the divide. In S. Henry, J. East, & C. Schmitz (Eds.) *Social work with groups: Mining the gold* (pp. 75–88). New York: Haworth Press.

Lowery, C.T. & Mattaini, M. (2001). Shared power in social work: A Native American perspective of change. In H.E. Briggs & K. Corcoran (Eds.) *Social work practice: Treating common client problems* (pp. 109–124). Chicago: Lyceum Books.

Lum, D. (2004). *Social work practice and people of color: A process stage approach* (5th ed.). Belmont, CA: Thomson Brooks/Cole.

Lum, D. (2008). Culturally competent practice. In T. Mizrahi & L.E. Davis, *Encyclopedia of social work* (20th ed.) (pp. 2:497–502). Washington, DC and New York: NASW Press and Oxford University Press.

Mackelprang, R., Patchner, L. S., DeWeaver, K.L., Clute, M.A., & Sullivan, W.P. (2008). Disability. In T. Mizrahi & L.E. Davis, *Encyclopedia of social work* (20th ed.) (pp. 2:36–43). Washington, DC and New York: NASW Press and Oxford University Press.

Mackelprang, R. & Salsgiver, R. (1999). *Disability: A diversity model approach in human service practice.* Pacific Grove, CA: Brooks/Cole.

MacNeill, V. (2009). Forming partnerships with parents from a community development perspective: Lessons learnt from Sure Start. *Health and Social Care in the Community, 17*(6), 659–665.

Macgowan, M.J. (1997). A measure of engagement for social group work: The Groupwork engagement measure (GEM). *Journal of Social Service Research, 23,* 17–37.

Macgowan, M.J. (2008). Group dynamics. In T. Mizrahi & L.E. Davis, *Encyclopedia of social work* (20th ed.) (pp. 2:279–287). Washington, DC and New York: NASW Press and Oxford University Press.

Macgowan, M.J. (2009a). Evidence-based group work. In A. Gitterman & R. Salmon (Eds.) *Encyclopedia of social work with groups* (pp. 131–136). New York: Routledge.

Macgowan, M.J. (2009b). Measurement. In A. Gitterman & R. Salmon (Eds.) *Encyclopedia of social work with groups* (pp. 142–147). New York: Routledge.

Manor, O. (2008). Systemic approach. In A. Gitterman & R. Salmon (Eds.) *Encyclopedia of social work with groups* (pp. 99–101). New York: Routledge.

Maramaldi, P., Berkman, B., & Barusch, A. (2005). Assessment and the ubiquity of culture: Threats to validity in measures of health-related quality of life. *Health & Social Work, 30*(1), 27–36.

Martin, J.A., Hamilton, B.E., Sutton, P.D., Ventura, S.J., Menacker, F., Kirmeyer, S., & Mathews, T.J. (2009). Births: Final data for 2006. *National Vital Statistics Report, 57*(7), 1–102.

McCullough-Chavis, A. & Waites, C. (2008). Genograms with African American families: Considering cultural context. In C. Waites (Ed.) *Social work practice with African-American families: An intergenerational perspective* (pp. 35–54). New York: Routledge.

McGoldrick, M. (2009). Using genograms to map family patterns. In A.R. Roberts, *Social workers' desk reference* (2nd ed.) (pp. 409–423). New York: Oxford Press.

McGoldrick, M., Gerson, R., & Petry, S. (2008). *Genograms assessment and intervention* (3rd ed.). New York: W.W. Norton & Company.

McInnis-Dittrich, K. (1994). *Integrating social welfare policy and social work practice.* Pacific Grove, CA: Brooks/Cole.

McNutt, J. & Floersch, J. (2008). Social work practice. In T. Mizrahi & L.E. Davis (Eds.) *Encyclopedia of social work.* National Association of Social Workers and Oxford University Press, Inc. (e-reference edition). Available from: http://www.oxford-naswsocialwork.com/entry?entry=t203.e375-s2

Meier, A. & Comer, E. (2005). Using evidence-based practice and intervention research with treatment groups for populations at risk. In G.L. Greif & P.H. Ephross (Eds.) *Group work with populations at risk* (2nd ed.) (pp. 413–439). New York: Oxford University Press.

Meyer, C. (1993). *Assessment in social work practice.* New York: Columbia University Press.

Middleman, R.R. & Wood, G.G. (1990). *Skills for direct practice in social work.* New York: Columbia University Press.

Miley, K.K., O'Melia, M.O., & DuBois, B. (2011). *Generalist social work practice.* Boston: Pearson Allyn & Bacon.

Miller, W. & Rollnick, S. (2002). *Motivational interviewing: Preparing people for change* (2nd ed.). New York: The Guilford Press.

Minieri, J. & Getsos, P. (2007). *Tools for radical democracy.* San Francisco, CA: Jossey Bass.

Minuchin, S. (1974). *Families & family therapy.* Cambridge, MA: Harvard University Press.

Minuchin, P., Colapinto, J., & Minuchin, S. (2007). *Working with families of the poor* (2nd ed.). New York: The Guilford Press.

Mondros, J. & Staples, L. (2008). Community organization. In T. Mizrahi & L. E. Davis (Eds.) *Encyclopedia of social work* (pp.1:387–398). Washington DC and New York: NASW Press and Oxford University Press.

Morgan, A. (2000). *What is narrative therapy?* Adelaide, South Australia: Dulwich Centre Publications.

Moxley, D. (2008). Interdisciplinarity. In T. Mizrahi & L.E. Davis, *Encyclopedia of social work* (20th ed.) Washington, DC and New York: NASW Press and Oxford University Press. (e-reference edition). Accessed August 17, 2010 from: http://

www.oxford-naswsocialwork.com/entry?entry=
t203.e200

Mulroy, E. (2008). Community needs assessment. In
T. Mizrahi & L. E. Davis (Eds.) *Encyclopedia of social
work* (pp. 1:385–387). Washington DC and New
York: NASW Press and Oxford University Press.

Mulroy, E.A., Nelson, K.E., & Gour, D. (2005). Community building and family-centered service collaborative. In M. Weil (Ed.) *Handbook of community
practice* (pp. 460–474). Thousand Oaks, CA: Sage
Publications.

National Association of Social Workers. (2007a).
Children and families. Retrieved March 14, 2010
from: http://www.socialworkers.org/pressroom/
swm2004/toolkit/pressReleases/children.asp

National Association of Social Workers. (2007b). *Indica-
tors for the achievement of the NASW Standards for
Cultural Competence in Social Work Practice.*
Washington, DC: NASW.

National Association of Social Workers (NASW). (2008).
Code of ethics. Washington, DC: NASW.

National Association of Social Workers. (2009–2012a).
Cultural and linguistic competence in the social
work profession. *Social work speaks: National
Association of Social Workers policy statements 2009–
2012.* Washington, DC: NASW Press.

National Association of Social Workers. (2009–2012b).
Professional self-care and social work. *Social work
speaks: National Association of Social Workers policy
statements 2009–2012.* Washington, DC: NASW
Press.

Netting, F. E., Kettner, P. M., & McMurtry, S. L. (2008).
Social work macro practice. Boston: Pearson Allyn
& Bacon.

Newhill, C.E. (1995). Client violence toward social
workers: A practice and policy concern. *Social
Work, 40,* 631–636.

Nichols, M.P. (2009). *The essentials of family therapy*
(4th ed.). Boston: Allyn & Bacon.

Nissly, J.A., Barak, M.E.M., & Levin, A. (2005). Stress,
social support, and worker's intentions to leave
their jobs in public child welfare. *Administration in
Social Work, 29*(1), 79–100.

North Central Regional Center for Rural Development,
Iowa State University. (n.d.). *Community assessment.* Des Moines, IA: Author.

Nowicki, J. & Arbuckle, L. (2009). The social worker as
family counselor in a nonprofit community-based
agency. In A.R. Roberts, *Social workers' desk reference*
(2nd ed.) (pp. 45–53). New York: Oxford Press.

Ohmer, M.L. & Korr, W.S. (2006). The effectiveness of
community practice interventions: A review of the
literature. *Research on Social Work Practice, 16*(2),
132–145.

Ohmer, M.L. & DeMasi, K. (2009). *Consensus
organizing: A community development workbook.*
Thousand Oaks, CA: Sage Publications, Inc.

Packard, T. (2009). Leadership and performance in
human services organizations. In R. J. Patti (Ed.)
The handbook of social welfare management
(pp. 143–164). Thousand Oaks, CA: Sage
Publications.

Papero, D.V. (2009). Bowen family systems theory. In
A.R. Roberts, *Social workers' desk reference* (2nd ed.)
(pp. 447–452). New York: Oxford Press.

Parsons, R.J. (2008). Empowerment practice. In
T. Mizrahi & L.E. Davis, *Encyclopedia of social work*
(20th ed.) (pp. 2:123–126). Washington, DC and
New York: NASW Press and Oxford University
Press.

Pawelski, J.G., Perrin, E.C., Foy, J.M., Allen, C.E.,
Crawford, J.E., Del Monte, M. Kaufman, M., Klein,
J.D., Smith, K., Springer, S. Tanner, J.L., & Vickers,
D.L. (2006). The effects of marriage, civil union,
and domestic partnership laws on health and well-
being of children. *Pediatrics, 118,* 349–364.

Payne, M. & Askeland, G. A. (2008). *Globalization
and international social work: Postmodern change
and challenge.* Burlington VT: Ashgate Publishing
Company.

Pennell, J., Noponen, H., & Weil, M. (2005).
Empowerment research. In M. Weil (Ed.) *Handbook
of community practice* (pp. 620–635). Thousand
Oaks, CA: Sage Publications.

Pfeffer, J. (1992). *Managing with power and politics: Influence in organizations.* Boston, MA: Harvard Business
School Press.

Pippard, J.L. & Bjorklund, R.W. (2004). Identifying
essential techniques for social work community
practice. *Journal of Community Practice, 11*(4),
101–116.

Polack, R.L. (2004). Social justice and the global economy: New challenges for social work in the 21st century. *Social Work, 49*(2), 281–290.

Poole, D.L. (2009). Community partnerships for school-based services. In A. Roberts (Ed.) *Social workers desk reference* (pp. 907–912). New York: Oxford University Press.

Potocky, M. (2008). Immigrants and refugees. In T. Mizrahi & L.E. Davis, *Encyclopedia of social work* (20th ed.) (pp. 3:441–445). Washington, DC and New York: NASW Press and Oxford University Press.

Putnam, R.D. (2000). *Bowling alone: The collapse and revival of American community*. New York: Simon & Schuster.

Ramanathan, C.S. & Link, R.J. (1999). *All our futures: Principles and resources for social work practice in a global era*. Belmont, CA: Brooks/Cole.

Randall, A.C. & DeAngelis, D. (2008). Licensing. In T. Mizrahi & L.E. Davis, *Encyclopedia of social work* (20th ed.) (pp. 3:87–91). Washington, DC and New York: NASW Press and Oxford University Press.

Rapp, C.A. & Goscha, R.J. (2006). *The strengths model: Case management with people with psychiatric disabilities*. New York: Oxford University Press.

Rawls, J. (1971). *A theory of justice*. Cambridge, MA: Harvard University Press.

Reamer, F.G. (1983). The concept of paternalism in social work. *Social Service Review, 57*(2), 254–271.

Reamer, F.G. (2003). Boundary issues in social work: Managing dual relationships. *Social Work, 48*(1), 121–133.

Reamer, F.G. (2005). Ethical and legal standards in social work: Consistency and conflict. *Families in Society, 86*(2), 163–169.

Reamer, F.G. (2006). *Social work values and ethics* (3rd ed.) New York: Columbia University Press.

Reamer, F.G. (2008). Ethics and values. In T. Mizrahi & L.E. Davis (Eds.) *Encyclopedia of social work* (pp. 2:143–151). Washington DC: NASW Press.

Redevelopment Opportunities for Women. (n.d.). *Programs*. Retrieved July 11, 2010 from: http://www.row-stl.org/Content/Programs.aspx

Reed, B. G. (2008). Theorizing in community practice. In M. Weil (Ed.) *Handbook of community practice* (pp. 84–102). Thousand Oaks, CA; Sage.

Reichert, E. (2003). *Social work and human rights: A foundation for policy and practice*. New York: Columbia University Press.

Reid, K.E. (1997). *Social work practice with groups: A clinical perspective* (2nd ed.). Pacific Grove, CA: Brooks/Cole.

Reid, K.E. (2002). Clinical social work with groups. In A.R. Roberts, *Social workers' desk reference* (1st ed.) (pp. 442–436). New York: Oxford Press.

Reid, K.E. (2009). Clinical social work with groups. In A.R. Roberts, *Social workers' desk reference* (2nd ed.) (pp. 432–436). New York: Oxford Press.

Ringel, S. (2005). Group work with Asian-American immigrants: A cross-cultural perspective. In G.L. Greif & P.H. Ephross, *Group work with populations at risk* (2nd ed.) (pp. 181–194). New York: Oxford University Press.

Roberts, A.R. (2005). Bridging the past and present to the future of crisis intervention and crisis management. In *Crisis intervention handbook: Assessment, treatment and research* (3rd ed.) (pp. 3–34). New York: Oxford University Press.

Roberts, A.R. (2008). Crisis interventions. In T. Mizrahi & L.E. Davis, *Encyclopedia of social work* (20th ed.) (pp. 1:484–491). Washington, DC and New York: NASW Press and Oxford University Press.

Roberts-DeGennaro, M. (2008). Case management. In T. Mizrahi & L.E. Davis, *Encyclopedia of social work* (20th ed.) (pp. 1:222–227). Washington, DC and New York: NASW Press and Oxford University Press.

Robinson, J.W. & Green, G.P. (2011) *Introduction to community development: Theory, practice, and service-learning*. Thousand Oaks, CA: Sage.

Rogers, C. (1957). The necessary and sufficient conditions of therapeutic personality change. *Journal of Consulting Psychology, 22*, 95–103.

Roosevelt, E. (1958). Presentation of *In your hands: A guide for community action for the tenth anniversary of the Universal Declaration of Human Rights* [online]. Available: www.udhr.org/history/inyour.htm

Rothman, J. (2008). Multi modes of community intervention. In J. Rothman, J. Erlich, & J. Tropman (Eds.) *Strategies of community intervention* (7th ed.) (pp. 141–170). Peosta, Iowa: Eddie Bowers Publishing Co., Inc.

Rothman, J.C. (2009a). An overview of case management. In A.R. Roberts, *Social workers' desk reference* (2nd ed.) (pp. 751–755). New York: Oxford Press.

Rothman, J.C. (2009b). Developing therapeutic contracts with clients. In A.R. Roberts, *Social workers' desk reference* (2nd ed.) (pp. 514–520). New York: Oxford Press.

Royse, D., Staton-Tindall, M., Badger, K., & Webster, J.M. (2009). *Needs assessment*. New York: Oxford University Press.

Rozakis, L. (1996). *New Roberts Rules of Order*. New York: Smithmark Reference.

Rubin, H.J. & Rubin, I.S. (2005). The practice of community organizing. In M. Weil's (Ed.) *The handbook of community practice* (pp.189–203) Thousand Oaks, CA: Sage Publications.

Rubin, H.J. & Rubin, I.S. (2008). *Community organizing and development*. Boston: Pearson Allyn & Bacon

Saleebey, D. (2009). *The strengths perspective in social work practice* (5th ed.). Boston: Allyn & Bacon.

Samways, M. (2008, Sept 19–25). Most diverse: Jackson Heights. *Time Out, New York*. Retrieved June 24, 2010 from: http://newyork.timeout.com/articles/features/60591/new-yorks-most-diverse-neighborhood.

Schiller, L.Y. (1995). Stages of development in women's groups: A relational model. In R. Kurland & R. Salmon (Eds.) *Group work practice in a troubled society: Problems and opportunities* (pp. 117–138). New York: The Haworth Press.

Schiller, L.Y. (1997). Rethinking stages of group development in women's groups: Implications for practice. *Social Work with Groups, 20*(3), 3–19.

Schmitz, C., Stakeman, C., & Sisneros, J. (2001). Educating professionals for practice in a multicultural society: Understanding oppression and valuing diversity. *Families in Society, 82*(6), 612–622.

Schneider, R. L. & Lester, L. (2001). *Social work advocacy*. Belmont, CA: Brooks/Cole.

Schultz, D. (2004). Cultural competence in psycho-social and psychiatric care: A critical perspective with reference to research and clinical experiences in California, US and in Germany. In A. Metteri, T. Krôger, A. Pohjola, & P. Rauhala (Eds.), *Social work visions from around the globe* (pp. 231–247). Binghamton, NY: Haworth.

Seligman, M. & Darling, R.B. (2007). *Ordinary families, special children: A systems approach to childhood disability* (3rd ed.). New York: The Guilford Press.

Shalay, N. & Brownlee, K. (2007). Narrative family therapy with blended families. *Journal of Family Psychotherapy, 18*(2), 17–30.

Shebib, B. (2003). *Choices*. New York: Allyn and Bacon.

Sherraden, M. (1993). Community studies in the baccalaureate social work curriculum. *Journal of Teaching in Social Work, 7*(1), 75–88.

Shields, G. & Kiser, J. (2003). Violence and aggression directed toward human service workers: An exploratory study. *Families in Society, 84*(1), 13–20.

Shulman. L. (2009a). Developing successful therapeutic relationships. In A.R. Roberts (Ed.) *Social worker's desk reference* (pp. 573–577). New York, NY: Oxford University Press.

Shulman, L. (2009b). Group work phases of helping: Preliminary phase. In A. Gitterman & R. Salmon (Eds.) *Encyclopedia of social work with groups* (pp. 109–111). New York: Routledge.

Siebold, C. (2007). Everytime we say goodbye: Forced termination revisited, a commentary. *Clinical Social Work Journal, 35*(2), 91–95.

Simmons, C.S., Diaz, L., Jackson, V., & Takahashi, R. (2008). NASW Cultural Competence Indicators: A new tool for the social work profession. *Journal of Ethnic and Cultural Diversity in Social Work, 17*(1), 4–20.

Simon, B. (1990). Re-thinking empowerment. *Journal of Progressive Human Services. 1*(1), 29.

Smith, B.D. (2005). Job retention in child welfare: Effects of perceived organizational support, supervisor support, and intrinsic job value. *Children and Youth Services Review, 27*(2), 153–169.

Sohng, W. S. L. (2008). Community-based participatory research. In T. Mizrahi & L. E. Davis (Eds.) *Encyclopedia of social work* (pp. 1:368–370). Washington DC and New York: NASW Press and Oxford University Press.

Sowers, K.M. & Rowe, W.S. (2009). International perspectives on social work practice. In A.R. Roberts (Ed.) *Social workers' desk reference* (2nd ed.) (pp. 863–868). New York: Oxford University Press.

Specht, H. (1990). Social work and the popular psychotherapies. *Social Service Review, 64*, 345–357.

Steger, M. B. (2003). *Globalization: A very short introduction*. New York: Oxford University Press.

Stevenson, M. (2010). Flexible and responsive research: Developing rights-based emancipatory disability research methodology in collaboration with young adults with Downs Syndrome. *Australian Social Work, 63*(1), 35–50.

Stiglitz, J. E. (2002). Information and the change in the paradigm in economics. *The American Economic Review, 92*(3), 460–501.

Strand, V., Carten, A., Connolly, D., Gelman, S.R., & Vaughn, P.B. (2009). A cross system initiative supporting child welfare workforce professionalization and stabilization. A task group in action. In C.S. Cohen, M.H. Phillips, & M. Hanson (Eds.) *Strength and diversity in social work with groups* (pp. 41–53). New York: Routledge.

Streeter, C. (2008). Community: Practice interventions. In T. Mizrahi & L. E. Davis (Eds.) *Encyclopedia of social work* (pp. 1:355–368). Washington DC and New York: NASW Press and Oxford University Press.

Strom-Gottfried, K.J. (2000). Ensuring ethical practice: An examination of NASW Code violations, 1986–97. *Social Work, 45*(3), 251–261.

Strom-Gottfried, K.J. (2003). Managing risk through ethical practice: Ethical dilemmas in rural social work. Presentation at the National Association of Social Workers Vermont chapter, Essex, VT.

Strom-Gottfried, K.J. (2008). *The ethics of practice with minors*. Chicago, IL: Lyceum Books, Inc.

Sulmasy, D. P. (2002). The biopsychosocial-spiritual model for the care of patients at the end of life. *The Gerontologist, 42*(3), 24–33.

Swenson, C.R. (1998). Clinical social work's contribution to a social justice perspective. *Social Work, 43*(6), 527–537.

Swigonski, M.E. (1996). Challenging privilege through Africentric social work practice. *Social Work, 4*(2), 153–161.

Tebb, S.C. (1995). An aid to empowerment: A caregiver well-being scale. *Health and Social Work, 20*(2), 87–92.

Terrazas, A. & Batalova, J. (2009). *Frequently requested statistics on immigrants and immigration in the United States*. Available at: http://www.migration information.org/USfocus/display.cfm?ID=747#1.

Thomas, H. & Caplan T. (1999). Spinning the group process wheel: Effective facilitation techniques for motivating involuntary client groups. *Social Work with Groups, 21*(4), 3–21.

Thyer, B.A. (2009). Evidence-based practice, science, and social work. An overview. In A.R. Roberts, *Social workers' desk reference* (2nd ed.) (pp. 1115–1119). New York: Oxford Press.

Toseland, R.W. & Horton, H. (2008). Group work. In T. Mizrahi & L.E. Davis, *Encyclopedia of social work* (20th ed.) (pp. 2:298–308). Washington, DC and New York: NASW Press and Oxford University Press.

Uken, A., Lee, M.Y., & Sebold, J. (2008). The Plumas Project: Solution-focused treatment of domestic violence offenders. In P. De Jong & I.K. Berg, *Interviewing for solutions* (3rd ed.) (pp. 313–323). Belmont, CA : Thomson Brooks/Cole.

United Nations. (1987). *Human rights—Questions and answers*. United Nations Department of Public Information, New York: Author.

United Nations, Department of Economic and Social Affairs. (2005). *Auditing for social change*. New York: Author.

U.S. Census Bureau. (2008). Living arrangements of children: 2004. Available at: http://www.census.gov/prod/2008pubs/p70–114.pdf.

U.S. Census Bureau. (2009). *America's Families and Living Arrangements: 2009*. Current Population Reports. Washington, D.C. Government Printing Office.

U.S. Census Bureau. (2010a). Race and Hispanic origin of the foreign-born in the United States, 2007. Retrieved July 6, 2010 from: www.census.gov/prod/2010pubs/acs-11.pdf

U.S. Census Bureau. (2010b). Valentine's Day 2010: February 14. Available at: http://www.census.gov/newsroom/releases/pdf/cb10-ff02.pdf

Van Den Bergh, N. & Crisp, C. (2004). Defining culturally competent practice with sexual minorities: Implications for social work education and practice. *Journal of Social Work Education, 40*(2), 221–238.

Van Soest, D. (2008). Oppression. In T. Mizrahi & L.E. Davis, *Encyclopedia of social work* (20th ed.) (pp. 3:322–324). Washington, DC and New York: NASW Press and Oxford University Press.

Van Treuren, R.R. (1993). Self-perception in family systems: A diagrammatic technique. In C. Meyer, *Assessment in social work practice* (p. 119). New York: Columbia University Press.

Van Wormer, K. (2004). Restorative justice: A model for personal and social empowerment. *Journal of Religion & Spirituality in Social Work, 23*(4), 103–120.

Vodde, R. & Gallant, J.P. (2002). Bridging the gap between micro and macro practice: Large-scale change and a unified model of narrative deconstructive practice. *Journal of Teaching in Social Work, 38*(3), 439–458.

Vodde, R. & Giddings, M.M. (1997). The propriety of affiliation with clients beyond the professional role: Nonsexual dual relationships. *Arete, 22*(1), 58–70.

Wagner, E.F. (2008). Motivational interviewing. In T. Mizrahi & L.E. Davis, *Encyclopedia of social work* (20th ed.) (pp. 3:273–276). Washington, DC and New York: NASW Press and Oxford University Press.

Wahab, S. (2005). Motivational interviewing and social work practice. *Journal of Social Work, 5*(1), 45–60.

Walker, L. (2008). Implementation of solution-focused skills in a Hawai'i prison. In P. De Jong & I.K. Berg, *Interviewing for solutions* (3rd ed.) (pp. 302–308). Belmont, CA: Thomson Brooks/Cole.

Walz, T. & Ritchie, H. (2000). Gandhian principles in social work practice: Ethics revisited. *Social Work, 45*(3), 213–222.

Warren, R.L. (1978). *The community in America*. Chicago: Rand McNally.

Weeks, W. (2004). Creating attractive services which citizens want to attend. *Australian Social Work, 57*(4), 319–330.

Weick, A. (1999). Guilty knowledge. *Families in Society, 80*(4), 327–332.

Weick, A., Kreider, J., & Chamberlain, R. (2009). Key dimensions of the strengths perspective in case management, clinical practice, and community practice. In D. Saleebey (Ed.) *The strengths perspective in social work practice* (5th ed.) (pp. 108–121). Boston: Allyn & Bacon.

Weil, M. & Gamble, D.N. (2009). Community practice model for the twenty-first century. In A. Roberts (Ed.) *Social workers' desk reference* (pp. 882–892). New York: Oxford University Press, Inc.

Weil, M. & Gamble, D. J. (2005). Evolution, models and the changing context of community practice. In M. Weil (Ed.) *Handbook of community practice* (pp. 117–149). Thousand Oaks, CA; Sage.

Wharton, T.C. (2008). Compassion fatigue: Being an ethical social worker. *The New Social Worker, 15*(1), 4–7.

Wheeler, W. & Thomas, A. M. (2011). Engaging youth in community development. In J.W. Robinson Jr. & G.P. Green (Eds.) *Introduction to community development: Theory, practice and service-learning* (pp. 209–227). Los Angeles, CA: Sage Publications.

Whitaker, T. & Arrington, P. (2008). *Social workers at work. NASW Membership Workforce Study*. Washington, DC: National Association of Social Workers.

Whitaker, T., Weismiller, T., & Clark, E. (2006). *Assuring the sufficiency of frontline workforce: A national study of licensed social workers*. Washington, DC: NASW

Wise, J.B. (2005). *Empowerment practice with families in distress*. New York: Columbia University Press.

Witkin, S.L. (2000). Ethics-R-Us. *Social Work, 45*(3), 197–212.

Wood, G.G. & Roche, S.E. (2001a). Representing selves, reconstructing lives: Feminist group work with women survivors of male violence. *Social Work with Groups, 23*(4), 5–23.

Wood, G.G. & Tully, C.T. (2006). *The structural approach to direct practice in social work: A social constructionist Perspective* (3rd ed.). New York: Columbia University Press.

World Commission on the Social Dimension of Globalization. (2004). *A fair globalization: Creating opportunities for all*. Retrieved from: http://www.ilo.org/public/english/wcsdg/docs/report.pdf.

Yalom, I.D. & Leszcz, M. (2005). *The theory and practice of group psychotherapy* (5th ed.). New York: Basic Books.

Young, S. (2008). Solutions for bullying in primary schools. In P. De Jong & I.K. Berg, *Interviewing for solutions* (3rd ed.) (pp. 293–302). Belmont, CA: Thomson Brooks/Cole.

CREDITS

Box 2.1: From *Ethics in social work: Statement of principles.* Copyright 2004, the International Federation of Social Workers and the International Association of Schools of Social Work (IFSW & IASSW). Reprinted with permission.

Box 2.2: From *Ethical decisions for social work practice* (8th ed.), by R. Dolgoff, F.M. Loewenberg and D. Harrington. Copyright 2009, F.E. Peacock. Reprinted with permission.

Exhibit 2.3: From *The propriety of affiliation with clients beyond the professional role: Nonsexual dual relationships,* Arete, 22(1), by R. Vodde and M.M. Giddings. Copyright 1997. Reprinted with permission.

Box 3.1: From *Skills for direct practice in social work,* by R.R. Middleman and G.G. Wood. Copyright 1990, Columbia University Press. Reprinted with permission.

Box 4.1: From *Assessing strengths. Identifying acts of resistance to violence and oppression,* by K.M. Anderson, C.D. Cowger and C.A. Snively. In *The strengths perspective in social work practice* (5th ed.), by D. Saleebey (Ed.). Copyright Allyn & Bacon, 2009.

Box 4.2: From *Assessing strengths. Identifying acts of resistance to violence and oppression,* by K.M. Anderson, C.D. Cowger and C.A. Snively. In *The strengths perspective in social work practice* (5th ed.), by D. Saleebey (Ed.). Copyright Allyn & Bacon, 2009.

Box 4.3: Adapted from *The strengths perspective in social work practice* (5th ed.), by D. Saleebey. Copyright 2009, Allyn & Bacon.

Box 4.5: Adapted from St. Anthony's Medical Center, St. Louis, Missouri. Reprinted with permission.

Box 4.6: Adapted from St. Anthony's Medical Center, St. Louis, Missouri. Reprinted with permission.

Box 4.7: Adapted from St. Anthony's Medical Center, St. Louis, Missouri. Reprinted with permission.

Box 4.8: From P. De Jong. In *Encyclopedia of social work* (20th ed.), by T. Mizrahi and L.E. Davis. Copyright 2008, NASW Press and Oxford University Press. Reprinted with permission.

Exhibit 5.1: Adapted from *The structural approach to direct practice in social work: A social constructionist perspective* (3rd ed.), by G.G. Wood and C.T. Tully. Copyright 2006, Columbia University Press. Reprinted with permission.

Exhibit 6.1: From *Self-perception in family systems: A diagrammatic technique,* by R.R. Van Treuren. In *Assessment in social work practice,* by C. Meyer. Copyright 1993, Columbia University Press. Reprinted with permission.

Exhibit 6.2: From *The Culturagram,* by E.P. Congress. In *Social workers' desk reference* (2nd ed.), by A.R. Roberts. Copyright 2009, Oxford Press. Reprinted with permission.

Box 6.2: From *Culture in special education,* by M. Kalyanpur and B. Harry. Copyright 1999, Paul H. Brookes. Reprinted with permission.

Box 6.4: Adapted from St. Anthony's Medical Center, St. Louis, Missouri. Reprinted with permission.

Box 6.5: Adapted from St. Anthony's Medical Center, St. Louis, Missouri. Reprinted with permission.

Exhibit 7.1: From *Understanding generalist practice with families,* by G.H. Hull and J. Mather. Copyright 2006, Thomson Brooks/Cole. Reprinted with permission.

Exhibit 7.2: From *The caregiver well-being scale revisited,* Health and Social Work, 25(4), by M. Berg-Weger, D.M. Rubio and S. Tebb. Copyright 2000. Reprinted with permission.

Exhibit 7.3: From *Enabling and empowering families: Principles and guidelines for practice,* by C.J. Dunst, C.M. Trivette and A.G. Deal. Copyright 2003, Brookline Books. Reprinted with permission.

Exhibit 7.4: From *Enabling and empowering families: Principles and guidelines for practice,* by C.J. Dunst, C.M. Trivette, and A.G. Deal. Copyright 2003, Brookline Books. Reprinted with permission.

GLOSSARY / INDEX

AASWG. *See* Association for the Advancement of Social Group Work

Abramson, J., 176–177

abuse
assessment documentation, 237
community practice, 364
confidentiality issues, 88–89
critical constructionist perspective, 231
duty to report, 46–47
emotional responses to, 236
ethical dilemmas, 50–51
refocusing the client, 164
Roman Catholic Church, 49
social work values, 35
societal interests, 54
strengths perspective, 26

acceptance, 16

accompaniment means to accompany a client in the performance of a task, 79

accountability, 159–160, 199–200, 432
Code of Ethics, 37
evaluation, 10
legal issues, 48

accreditation, 9

activities are those actions that organizations take to produce change, 453, 454

Addams, Jane, 243, 381

adjustment, 16–17

administrative data, 354, 355

administrative structure, 416

administrative tasks, 130–131, 408

adolescents, 3, 42
motivational interviewing, 257
nonvoluntary clients, 137
school drop-outs, 406

adoption
cultural competence, 110
gay, lesbian, bisexual and transgender parents, 207, 215
legal issues, 48

adult education, 395

adult protection services, 47, 405–406

advanced social work practice, 2–3

advocacy, 3, 88, 173–175
cautions and strategies, 176
community organizing, 389
community practice, 377, 379–382, 393
critical constructionist perspective, 231
cultural competence, 421
engagement skills, 413
family social work, 253
shared power, 17, 81
social action, 127

advocate in social work practice is a practitioner who works toward securing the rights and well-being of clients, 3, 166–167, 173–175, 180

affirmative action, 87

African Americans, 82, 83

agency, 14

agency perspective
assessment, 130–135
group work, 291

agency resources, 81, 217

agency work, 35

alcohol
parental addiction to, 129
Riverton Against Youth Drinking, 281, 333

American Association of Social Workers, 36

Anderson, K.M., 104

anger, 142, 143, 147, 178

areas of concentrated poverty are economically disadvantaged communities that are relatively isolated from mainstream social and economic opportunities for families and communities, 372

Asay, S.M., 223

Assertive Community Treatment, 369

assessment focuses on the analysis of the major area for work; the aspects of the client environment that can offer support for a solution; the client knowledge, skills, and values that can be applied to

the situation; and ways in which the client can
    meet her or his goals, 8, 21. *See also* **evaluation**
agency perspective, 130–135
attachment theory, 100–101
blended families, 222
brief history of, 98
brokering role, 168
case management, 167
client perspective, 135–146
cognitive theory, 101
community, 344–345, 349–366, 373
    diversity in, 108–112
    evidence, 106–108
family social work, 210–211, 218, 232, 236–238, 244,
    251, 258
goal-formulation, 228
group work, 281–283, 286–287, 295–296, 297–300,
    303, 309
history-taking, 99
honest responding, 118–120
individual work, 96–153
mapping skills, 120–123, 166
narrative theory, 103–105, 112–114
organizations, 404, 413–423, 424–425, 428, 456
preferred reality, 115–116
psychoanalytic theory, 100
reflective, 190, 195–197, 200
resources, 123–126
scaling questions, 229
social worker perspective, 146–150
solution-focused approach, 105–106, 114–115
strengths perspective, 102–103, 104, 112
suicide, 145–146
support for client's goals, 116–118
violence, 140–144
assets, 347, 360, 363–365, 388
Association for the Advancement of Social Group Work
    (AASWG), 276–277, 318
attachment theory, developed by John Bowlby, asserts
    that early bonding occurs between a mother and
    infant and subsequently plays a critical role in the
    child's future capacity to provide and sustain
    opportunities for his or her own children, 100–101
attending is maintaining attentiveness expressed
    through appropriate verbal following, eye contact,
    mindful but relaxed posture, and disciplined
    attention, 65
attitudes, 29, 86. *See also* **values**
Australia, 43, 400
authority, 409–410

autonomy, 23–24
    dual relationships, 54
    ethical principle screen, 50

balanced leadership is the appropriate level of control
    maintained by a group social worker that allows
    the group freedom for growth and ownership
    while keeping the group healthy and helpful for all
    members, 319
bargaining skills, 445, 447
Barker, R.L., 64, 65, 76–77, 167, 197, 404
baseline is the measurement of the client's behavior
    taken prior to the initiation of the intervention,
    and thus it establishes the difference between no
    intervention and intervention related to a selected
    goal or goals, 191, 192, 258
Behavioral and Emotional Rating Scale, 264
behavioral functioning, 133, 298–299
Berg, I.K., 286, 310
Berman-Rossi, T., 312
Berry, Mary Frances, 430
biases, 21–22, 64, 232, 269
bicultural code of practice is to practice using the
    recognition that more than one culture merits
    recognition, 43–44
biopsychosocial knowledge, 4
bisexuals
    diversity codes, 43
    exclusion, 306
    family social work, 205, 207, 214–215
    school problems, 424–425, 431, 436, 439–440,
        442–443, 444–446, 449–450
    social advocacy, 381
blended families, 209, 221–222
Bloom, M., 190
Boston Model is the name given to a particular
    theoretical developmental model for social group
    work originated by researchers at Boston
    University, 310–312
boundaries are limits or dividers that separate
    subsystems within a system or a system from the
    outside world, 209, 211–212. *See also* professional
    boundaries
Bowden, V.R., 218–219
Bowlby, John, 100–101
brainstorming, 253, 254, 308
Briskman, L., 43
broker is a social worker who links clients to existing
    services through referral and connection, 3,
    168–170, 186, 253

Brownlee, K., 222

bureaucracy is a conceptual type of organization in which a clear hierarchy, rules, expectations, relationships, and job description define the social worker's participation, 407–408, 431, 434, 456

burnout is a nontechnical term used to describe workers who feel apathy or anger as a result of job related stress and frustration and can be found among social workers who have more responsibility than control, 146, 151–152, 400

by-laws are legal documents that describe the basic structure and abilities of a board of directors, such as the composition of the board, terms of the members, permanent committees, and voting rights, 415

campaign is a strategy in which a group utilizes open communication channels to persuade decisionmakers to make a change, 442, 443, 444–445, 447

capacity building, 444

capacity development, 377, 378–382, 383

capacity inventories, 364, 365, 366

Caregiver Well-Being Scale, 262, 263

caring, 27

case (or client) advocacy is social work advocacy designed to influence a particular client's outcomes, 3, 173, 174, 253. *See also* advocacy

case management is the assessment, coordination, and monitoring of services on behalf of clients with multiple service needs, and is focused on issues and the identification of resources, 81, 167–168

case managers coordinate client services and monitor their effectiveness across systems and are concerned with controlling the cost of services, 3, 167–168, 253

case studies involve intensive analysis of one individual, group, or family and depend on accurate, careful, and richly detailed record keeping, 195–196, 262

casework is the type of practice used by professional social workers in which psychosocial, behavioral, and systems concepts are translated into skills designed to help individuals and families solve intrapsychic, interpersonal, socioeconomic, and environmental problems through direct face-to-face relationships, 6, 111, 276

cause (or class) advocacy is social work advocacy

designed to influence a class or group outcomes, 173–174

CDCs. *See* Community Development Corporations

celebration, 79

census is an official enumeration of the population, 354, 355, 378, 399, 455

CEUs. *See* continuing education units

change

acceptance versus change tension in social work, 16

community development, 383

community organizing, 389–390, 391

community practice, 341–342, 346, 377, 378, 397, 398–399

developing client's skills, 172–173

family social work, 244, 261

group work, 278, 309–310, 327, 328

miracle questions, 115

motivational interviewing, 257

organizational, 413, 423–424, 431–457

relational model, 313

resistance to, 431–432, 437, 451

single parent families, 217

strengths perspective, 26

systems theory, 208–209

change proposals, 437–439, 451

change questions, 113

change work groups, 431, 435–436, 437–439, 442–443, 444, 446–448, 452

charismatic authority is authority gained by the power of personality or persuasiveness, 409, 410

child protection, 46–47, 100, 139, 214, 252

child welfare, 364, 368, 394

civic engagement, 369

clarifying is directly asking for client feedback to clarify a point, 69–70

client-directed resources are services that the client or client system chooses and obtains with assistance, 81

client groups are groups comprised of individual clients in which clients are motivated toward personal change, 6–7, 21, 278, 279–280, 297

clinical work is the professional application of social work theory and methods to the treatment and prevention of psychosocial dysfunction, disability, or impairment, including emotional and mental disorder, 11–12, 13, 14

closed groups are groups with a fixed membership and time period for the duration of the group; contrast to open groups, 284, 291

closed questions, 70–71

clothing, 66, 67

clustering is a process in which some group members gravitate toward more connection as a response to the group's ending phase, 329

Code of Ethics (NASW), 2, 5–6, 36, 37–38, 45, 149
  adherence to, 41–43
  cultural diversity, 274
  disrespectful language, 418
  dual relationships, 52
  evaluation, 9
  global application, 371
  as guide for ethical decision-making, 446
  individual conduct, 57
  legal issues, 48
  litigation, 57
  organizations, 423, 428
  self-determination, 55
  social equity, 13
  social justice, 25, 86
  social worker qualifications, 167
  well-being of clients, 56

cognition is knowledge acquired through a process that includes thoughts, intuitions, perceptions, and reasoning, 101

cognitive behavioral approaches, 180

cognitive theory, associated with Aaron Beck, asserts that thoughts largely shape moods and behaviors and likewise that changing thoughts can influence moods and behaviors, 101

cohesiveness is the members' sense of connectedness or belonging to the group in group social work practice, 319

collaboration is the procedure in which two or more professionals work together to serve a given client (individual, family, group, community, or population)
  assessment, 98
  collaborator role, 175–177, 253, 323
  community practice, 367, 391, 399
  crisis intervention, 181
  empowerment approach, 247, 249
  family social work, 258
  group work, 285, 308, 323
  narrative theory, 103, 249–250, 285
  single parent families, 217
  solution-focused approach, 250–251
  strengths perspective, 26–27

collaborative refers to a co-operative strategy to create change in an organization, 442, 443–444, 447

communication. *See also* dialogue; listening skills
  campaign strategies, 444
  dialogue skills, 65–67
  empathic, 72–73, 142
  engagement with client, 8
  group work, 319–320
  honest and open, 5
  interviewing skills, 67–73
  nonverbal, 66, 67, 68, 77
  pitfalls, 73–74
  public relations, 418
  "talking in the idiom of the other", 80

communities of identity are those communities based on a common identification rather than location, as the community of women social work students; contrast to community of locality, 342–343, 369

communities of locality are communities defined by place or governing structure, as an area of a state; contrast to communities of identity, 342

community is the structure, both tangible and metaphoric, that supports connectedness to others over time, 273, 372–373. *See also* **community practice**
  assessment, 349–366
  definition of, 339
  engagement, 348
  functions, 343–344
  participatory research, 367–368
  shared sense of, 390–391
  strengths perspective, 27
  support from the, 162
  types of, 342–343
  understanding, 344–348
  world as a community, 369–371

community asset mapping, 347, 378, 388

community capacity development, 377, 378–382, 383

community development, 382–389, 393–394, 395, 396, 400

Community Development Corporations (CDCs), 381

community forums are public meetings in which information is exchanged and debated, and strategies considered and critiqued, 357, 361

community needs assessment, 351–363, 364

community organizing, 389–391, 394

community practice is an area of social work that emphasizes working closely with citizens' groups, cultural and multicultural groups, and human service organizations to improve life options and opportunities in communities and to press for the expansion of civil and human rights, political

equity and distributive justice, 7, 339–374, 375–402
assessment, 349–366
contemporary trends, 368–369
engagement, 348
evaluation, 90, 399–400
generalist approach, 391–392
global approaches, 392–396
models of, 377–382, 401
participatory research, 367–368
postmodern perspective, 347
relationship skills, 62
social justice, 25
strengths perspective, 347
termination, 397–399, 401
types of community, 342–343
community social and economic development, 382–389
community support, 309
compassion fatigue is emotional distress experienced as the result of serving in a helping role, 146, 151–152
competencies, 4–10. *See also* **skills**
client's, 156–157
community practice, 341
scientific practice, 190
competition, 345, 437–438
complaints, 10, 57
comprehensive community-based analysis, 349–351
confidentiality is an ethical mandate that requires social workers to prevent client-related information from becoming disclosed to unauthorized persons, 43, 88–89, 92
ethical dilemmas, 49, 51
ethical principle screen, 50
group work, 293, 297, 319
legal issues, 48
conflict (or contest) is a strategy in which a change work group is only able to influence the decision-makers through a public conversation because the decision-makers are opposed to a change and are unwilling to communicate with the group, 442–443, 445–446, 447
conflict, community, 345–346
conflict organizing, 390, 391
conflict theory, 346, 379
confrontation, 119, 164
"consensual power", 409
consensus decision-making is a co-operative process in which all members develop and agree to support

a decision that is considered to be in the best interests of the whole group, 320, 378, 384, 387
consensus organizing, 389–390, 391
constructionist group is a group facilitated from a social constructionist perspective, that recognizes that reality is created through shared meanings, 316–317
contextualizing is placing clients' issues into the perspective of the wider community, society and/or global context in order to discourage them from blaming themselves for their problems, and encouraging them to take environmental and structural roots of their challenges, 78
continuing education units (CEUs), 10–11
contracting refers to the process by which the client and the social worker agree to the plan for change, areas of responsibility, and priorities in a formal or informal or written or verbal format, 118
co-optation is the minimizing of anticipated opposition by including those who would be opposed to a change effort in the change effort, 444
coping questions, 229
corrections
case management, 168
group work, 315, 317–318
cost containment, 167–168
Council on Social Work Education (CSWE) is the accrediting body for social work education programs in the US
competencies, 4
evaluation, 9
evidence-based practice, 106
generalist focus, 276
counselor, in social work, is typically considered to be a specialized clinical skill performed by social workers who have advanced training in health, mental health, and family service settings, 3, 168, 253
cover terms are expressions and phrases that carry more meaning than the literal meaning of the term, such as the term "welfare mother", 110
Cowger, C.D., 104
creativity, 41
credit schemes, 395
crime
group work, 315, 317–318
intergenerational patterns, 212
rape, 55
social work values, 36

crisis intervention, 144–145, 181
    family social work, 248
    goal attainment scaling, 194
critical reflection, 190
critical social construction is that form of social
    construction that particularly focuses on a critical
    analysis, 30, 32, 155, 179
    evaluation of intervention's compatibility with,
    196
    family social work, 230, 231
    participatory research, 367
    power politics model, 434
critical thinking, 41, 58
    community practice, 341
    force-field analysis, 425
CSWE. *See* **Council on Social Work Education**
culturagram is a mapping technique used to represent
    and assess a family's transition to a new culture,
    234–235, 258
cultural competence refers to the process by which
    individuals and systems respond respectfully and
    effectively to people of all cultures, languages,
    classes, races, ethnic backgrounds, religions, and
    other diversity factors in a manner that recognizes,
    affirms, and values the worth of individuals,
    families, and communities, and protects and
    preserves the dignity of each, 5, 370–371
    assessment issues, 108, 109–110, 111–112
    community practice, 341
    group work, 330–331
    organizations, 420–421
    self-knowledge, 21
cultural consistency, 187–188
cultural exclusion, 86, 87
Cultural Genogram, 234
culture. *See also* cultural competence
    accompaniment, 79
    assumptions, 7
    biases, 22
    bicultural code of practice, 43–44
    community practice, 347
    group work, 274–275, 294
    individualism versus collectivism, 274
    international families, 222–224
    knowledge of, 5
    multicultural respect, 247
    organizational, 405, 416, 418, 419
    posture of cultural reciprocity, 218, 219
    U.S., 18–19
    warmth, 64

data collection, 353–362, 399, 454–455
De Jong, P., 75, 260, 286, 310
decentralization, 368
decision-making
    context, 41
    ethical change tactics, 446
    ethical dilemmas, 49–56, 57–58
    family group conferencing, 256
    force-field analysis, 425
    groups, 384, 386
    guest status of social workers, 411–412
    influences on practice decisions, 22
    organizational change, 437, 442, 453
deconstruction refers to the analysis of a written text,
    idea, or belief in order to discover how it came to
    be prevalent, how it reflects the context in which it
    arose, and whose ideas had power in its formation,
    14, 28–29, 250
deconstruction questions, 114
definitional ceremony is a celebration, used in
    narrative work, in which the person seeking
    consultation has finished her or his work and
    celebrates the achievement by inviting significant
    witnesses and important people to define the
    changes made, 316, 326, 327
DeFrain, J., 223
demographic data
    community assessment, 349
    family social work, 237
    group work, 298
    individual work, 132–133
denial, 329
dependence, 54, 79
deShazer, Steve, 227–228
developmental models are theoretical perspectives in
    generalist practice relating to groups, which assert
    that social work groups evolve in predictable
    patterns in more or less sequential phases,
    310–313, 318, 337
developmental socialization is a term used by Harry
    Specht in which a worker both assists clients to
    make the most of their environments by providing
    support, information, and opportunities and
    confronts the obstacles that interfere with clients'
    efforts; contrast to resocialization, 12–13
devolution is the relegation of power by a central
    authority to local governing units, 368
Dewey, John, 381
diagnosis, 98, 130–131
"dialogic process", 41

dialogue is a process of open communication in which both or all parties participate through listening as well as speaking in an effort to arrive at a mutual understanding, 75, 91
 assessment, 98, 151
 communication pitfalls, 73–74
 ethical practice, 41
 family social work, 258
 honest, 139
 human rights perspective, 25
 interviewing skills, 67–73
 mediator role, 171
 organizational change, 435
 specific skills, 65–67
 termination, 184

differentiation refers to a developmental stage in group work practice, according to the Boston Model, in which members feel safely accepted and can therefore establish differences from other group members, 311, 312

diffuse boundaries is a term used in family social work practice in which the separation between subsystems, (eg, parent subsystem and child subsystem) is weak, with few clear understandings as to differential roles or responsibilities of either, 209

dignity, 65, 419
 cultural competence, 5, 421
 globalization, 20
 IFSW *Statement of Principles*, 39, 40
 unconditional positive regard, 65

direct, closed questions are used to encourage the client to provide factual information in a concise manner, and can be helpful in gaining specifics about behaviors, such as frequency, duration, and intensity, 70–71

direct work or practice is social work on a face-to-face level with individuals, small groups, or families who participate in the work, 11

disability, 306, 410
 confidentiality issues, 88
 deconstruction, 28–29
 empowerment practice, 178–179
 family social work, 218–221, 227
 transportation of disabled children, 160–161
 UN Convention, 371

disclosure, 50

discovery-oriented questions are designed to invite the client to communicate her or his purposes in communicating with you and to express goals for the relationship, 67

discretion, 53

discrimination, 86, 87, 161
 community assessment, 350–351, 363
 family social work, 211
 gay, lesbian, bisexual and transgender parents, 215
 group work, 279
 IFSW *Statement of Principles*, 40
 organizations, 423

disengagement is a term used in systemic family work to describe families in which boundaries between members are so rigid that members have little connection with each other, 211

dispute resolution, 170–172

distance, minimization of, 18

diversity, 42–44
 assessment, 108–112
 communication skills, 67
 communities of locality, 342
 community conflicts, 346
 community development, 383
 community practice, 368
 critical constructionist perspective, 231
 cultural competence, 421
 family social work, 204, 213, 218, 239, 252
 group work, 302, 306–307, 315, 336–337
 IFSW *Statement of Principles*, 40
 NASW *Code of Ethics*, 274
 organizations, 420
 supporting, 159

divorce, 205

documentation
 change proposal form, 439–440
 family social work, 236–238
 group work, 297–301
 individual work, 131–135, 136
 organizational assessment, 414

domestic violence, 3, 15, 208–209
 community development, 387
 critical constructionist perspective, 231
 family norms, 210
 genograms, 165
 global community organizing, 394
 group work, 284, 308, 315, 316–317
 intergenerational patterns, 212
 involuntary clients, 139–140
 narrative theory, 103–105
 project teams, 408, 410
 societal interests, 54
 solution-focused approach, 251

dress, 66, 67

dual relationships are relationships between social workers and clients that exist in addition to and are distinct from their professional contacts, 52–54, 187

duty to protect is the ethical obligation of social workers and other professionals to protect people from serious, foreseeable, and imminent harm, 47–48

duty to report is the obligation of social workers and other professionals to report evidence of child abuse and neglect and cases of exploitation of vulnerable adults to governmental agencies, 46–47

duty to warn is the obligation of social workers and other professionals to disclose clients' future intentions to do harm to a specific person or specified organization as mandated by legislation and court judgments, 47

ecomap is a mapping tool that represents the client's ecological relationships through the strengths, type, and ,nature of connections to community institutions, people, or processes
  family social work, 233, 234, 258
  individual work, 122–123, 124, 165–166
economic development, 382–389
economic system, 349
ecosystems (ecological) perspective, 24, 32
  community, 345, 376–377
  self-learning model, 433
Educational Policy and Accreditation Standards (EPAS), 4, 13, 106
educator is one of the roles social workers perform when they teach clients skills or inform the public about social work—related issues or populations, 3
  family social work, 253
  group work, 323
  individual work, 166–167, 172–173
eligibility criteria define the group of clients who can participate in a program, 449, 450
emotions
  change work groups, 452
  cognitive theory, 101
  community practice endings, 398
  empathic communication, 72–73
  family social work, 236, 267
  group work endings, 325
  planning and, 128–129
empathic communication is the capacity to accurately perceive a client's feelings and subjective experiences and to grasp the meanings they have for the client, 72–73, 142

empathy is the act of perceiving, understanding, experiencing, and responding to the emotional state and ideas of another person, 64–65, 68, 72–73, 142
  group work, 279, 318
  motivational interviewing, 180, 256, 257
  reflection of empathy, 158
  relational model, 313
empirical evaluation processes, 190–195, 200
empowerment is a specific approach in generalist practice that combines both individual growth and support with social action and political activity in the environment, 14, 177–180, 185, 198, 200
  alliance with clients, 456
  assessment, 98
  capacity building, 444
  community capacity development, 378, 382
  community development, 383
  community organizing, 390
  community practice, 347, 363, 376, 398
  disabled clients, 220–221
  family social work, 246–249, 259–260, 268
  group work, 307–308, 326
  legitimate power, 82
  local-level development, 395
  narrative theory, 103
  single parent families, 217
  social advocacy, 379
  solution-focused approach, 105
empowerment group refers to a face-to-face social work practice group in which the primary goal of the work is to cultivate the skills and power of its members, 3, 308
engagement is building a relationship among the social worker, the client, and the client system's environment, 7–8, 61–95
  communication pitfalls, 73–74
  community, 348, 367, 373
  confidentiality issues, 88–89, 92
  core relationship qualities, 64–65, 75, 91
  dialogue skills, 65–67
  family social work, 232, 239, 244
  goal-formulation, 228
  group work, 281–283, 286, 287, 292–294, 296, 303, 309
  interviewing skills, 67–73
  involuntary clients, 137–139
  listening skills, 62–64, 91
  logistics and activities, 79–80
  ongoing evaluation, 90–91

organizations, 412–413, 424–425, 427, 428, 456
overall purpose, 75–76, 91
power issues, 80–85, 92
privacy issues, 89–90, 92
scaling questions, 229
skills and methods, 77–79
social justice and human rights, 85–88, 92
transparency, 75
enmeshment is a term used in systemic family work to describe families whose members are so close that they have few distinctions in role or authority and enjoy little autonomy or independence, 211
environment, 159–166
ecosystems perspective, 24
group work, 308
self-learning model, 433
solution-focused approach, 229, 251
EPAS. *See* Educational Policy and Accreditation Standards
equality, 50
equity, 13, 24
Erikson, Erik, 313
esteem questions, 113
ethical dilemma is a dilemma that occurs when a person holds two or more values that compete with each other. An ethical dilemma exists when no clear single response satisfies all considerations in a situation, 49–56, 57–58
examples, 52–56
models for resolution of, 51–52
ethical principle screen assists in the decision-making process by highlighting the relative significance of values and the likely results of particular decisions, 50–51
ethics are a system of moral principles and perceptions of right versus wrong and the resulting philosophy of conduct that is practiced by an individual, group, profession, or culture, 5, 35–60. *See also* *Code of Ethics*
brief history of, 36–37
community practice, 341
confrontation, 119
context, 41
diagnosis, 131
diversity, 42–44
global application, 371
law and, 45–49, 58
litigation, 57–58
organizational change, 446, 457
risk taking and creativity, 41–43

scientific practice, 190
suicide, 145–146
sustaining ethical practice, 149–150
thoughtful practice in a postmodern world, 57
eugenics, 28–29
evaluation refers to strategies that systematically examine the effectiveness of social work practice, 9–10. *See also* **assessment**
case management, 167
community practice, 399–400
family social work, 261–267, 268, 269
goal attainment scaling, 191–194
group work, 331–335, 336, 337
individual work, 90–91, 181, 189–197, 200
organizational change, 452–455, 458
postmodern views of, 194–195
priorities in, 189–190
qualitative and reflective processes, 190, 195–197
single-subject design, 190–191, 192
evaluation plan provides the details about the instruments and/or data to be collected on a specific timetable, and the identity of those that will collect, analyze, and report on the program data, 449
evaluative questions, 114
evidence-based group work is a model for group work that emphasizes the importance of and utilizes interventions backed by empirical, scientific evidence proving its effectiveness, 315
evidence-based practice is an approach asserting the importance of empirical, scientific evidence that an intervention has been successful and is likely to be successful in the future, 9
assessment, 106–108
community needs assessment, 351, 352
community practice, 341
crisis intervention, 144
evaluation, 189–195, 261
group work, 314–315
organizational change, 439
exception questions
family social work, 228, 229
group work, 309
individual work, 113, 114, 115, 158
excessive questioning, 74
exclusion, 86, 178–179, 186, 306, 307
exercising silence is the social worker's well-placed silence in the group setting, which allows the communication patterns of members to develop, 320

expert knowledge is that knowledge attained through education, training, and practice and demonstrated in professional credentials, 17, 81

exploitation, 53, 54, 88–89

extended family, 213–214, 223

externalization is a process used in narrative interventions in which the problem of the consulting person is separated from, or put outside of, the person so that it is ,not a constituent part of that person, 114, 157, 227, 250

eye contact, 66, 68

facilitator is a social worker who makes change possible through the process of establishing a safe environment in which clients' own strengths and capacities for growth, connection, and development can be released; frequently applied to social work groups in which she or he helps the group find its own unique path to development, 296, 322

Family Empowerment Scale, 264

Family Functioning Style Scale, 264

family group conferencing (FGC), 256

family norms are the rules of conduct established within a family system that may be implicit or explicit, 209–210, 232

family preservation, 168

Family Resource Scale, 264

family social work is an intervention facilitated by a professional social worker with a group of family members who are considered to be a single unit of attention. This approach focuses on the whole system of individuals and interpersonal and communication patterns, 6

  blended families, 209, 221–222

  critical constructionist approach, 230, 231

  disability, 218–221, 227

  engagement and assessment, 203–242

  evaluation, 261–267, 268, 269

  family as a functioning unit, 207–208

  family group conferencing, 256

  gay, lesbian, bisexual and transgender parents, 214–215

  grandparents raising grandchildren, 213–214

  intergenerational patterns, 210, 212–213

  international families, 222–224

  intervention, 243–258, 267, 268–269

  mapping, 232–236, 258

  motivational interviewing, 256–257

  multiple racial and ethnic heritages, 218

  narrative theory, 225–227, 249–250, 260

  perspectival questions, 255

  re-enactments, 257–258

  reframing, 254–255

  single parent families, 216–217

  social justice approach, 230–231

  solution-focused approach, 227–229, 250–252, 260–261

  strengths and empowerment perspectives, 246–249, 259–260, 262–266

  systems theory, 208–213

  termination, 259–261, 267–268, 269

Family Strengths Profile, 264, 266

family structure is the system that organizes and governs relationships among the generations of a family, especially between the subsystems of children and parents, 210, 211–212

  assessment documentation, 132

  ecomaps, 123, 124

  genograms, 121–122, 233, 234

Family Support Scale, 264, 265

family therapy, 14, 244

family-centered care is a model of service provision to families in which professionals value and prioritize family goals, support family control over interventions, and recognize family expertise regarding what its members want and need, 218–220

feedback

  family social work, 261, 267

  group work, 326, 328

  motivational interviewing, 257

  ongoing evaluation, 90

  reinforcement, 79

  self-learning model, 432, 433

  solution-focused approach, 105

  witness groups, 309

feminist approaches, 18, 410

  constructionist groups, 316

  evaluation of intervention's compatibility with, 196

  group development, 312, 313

FFA. *See* **force-field analysis**

FGC. *See* family group conferencing

Fischer, J., 190

flexibility, 21, 181, 295

flight is a term for a person's inclination to leave a relationship before it is formally ended by another person or process, 185

focus group is a method of collecting data about a community through moderated discussion among a group of people who share a common characteristic, 357, 361

following responses give clients immediate feedback that their message has been heard and understood, which are conveyed through paraphrasing, summarizing, conveying empathy, and showing attentiveness, 69

follow-up
  case management, 167
  family social work, 261
  group work, 330
  single-subject evaluation design, 191

force-field analysis (FFA) is a mechanism used to gather and sort information and data gathered in the assessment process, and provide the basis for an intervention plan, 424–425, 428

formal resources are programs, services, or institutions that have been established in response to need; contrast to informal services, 123–124, 186

formative research is research conducted about the implementation of interventions, 10

formed or constructed groups are groups that do not occur ,naturally but which are created by a worker or agency, 278

for-profit organizations, 426

foster care
  community practice, 364
  gay, lesbian, bisexual and transgender parents, 215
  group development, 312
  planning, 8–9

"Frames of Reference", 160

FRAMES strategy, 257

Franklin, C., 245

free trade policies, 20

freedom, 50

Freire, Paulo, 391

Freud, Sigmund, 23, 100, 276

functional structures describe a form of organizational governance defined by the activities that social workers complete, 408

funding, 352, 361, 422, 426–427

fundraising, 3

Galinsky, M.J., 325, 397

Gambrill, E., 432–433

Gandhi, Mahatma, 57

Gantt chart provides a visual display of the activities that must be undertaken and the time frame for the completion of each activity, 450

Garland, J., 312

Garvin, C.D., 325, 397

GAS. *See* **goal attainment scaling**

gay people
  diversity codes, 43
  exclusion, 306
  family social work, 205, 207, 214–215
  school problems, 424–425, 430–431, 436, 439–440, 442–443, 444–446, 449–450
  social advocacy, 381

genogram is a mapping device that reproduces the family tree, or pedigree, and usually represents three generations and may emphasize particular processes such as common employment patterns, health status, educational achievement, and relationship types
  family social work, 233–234, 258
  individual work, 121–122, 165

gentrification is the social phenomenon in which homes in low-income communities are converted to more expensive dwellings for affluent families, which has the effect of raising the property values, rents, and tax rates of all homes in the community and excluding less-affluent people from the community, 372

genuineness is the act of expressing sincerity and honesty, 65

geocoding is the process of creating map features from addresses, places, names, or similar information, 354

Germain, C.B., 13

Giddings, M.M., 53, 54

gifts, 187

Gilligan, Carol, 313

Gitterman, A., 13

global community practice, 369–371, 392–396

global individual practice, 111–112

global interdependence is the interconnections between all nations of the world, 369–370

Global South is a less pejorative term used to describe countries that have been called "third world," "underdeveloped," or "developing," and generally refers to countries located in the southern hemisphere, 19, 394, 396

globalization refers to the collective processes that have made the world a single community through the effects of economic enterprise, media technology, and travel, 19–21, 340, 371–372, 394

goal attainment scaling (GAS) is a standard evaluation framework that measures the degree to which individual goals are met, individual weights are assigned client problems, and outcome scores are estimated, obtained, and averaged across all problems of one client or all clients in one program, 191–194, 262

goal-formulation, 228

goals are broad statements related to an ideal state for a target, such as population or community
adjustment and challenge, 16
advocacy, 176
assessment, 8, 97, 99
case management, 167
community organizing, 394
community practice, 397, 398, 400
contracting, 118
developing client's skills, 173
family social work, 224, 248, 260, 261, 262, 264–267
group work, 308, 309, 314, 319, 321, 326–327, 328
honest responding, 118–119
implementation of change, 449
ongoing evaluation, 90–91
organizations, 405, 406, 433
planning, 128, 129
preferred reality, 115
realistic, 120
self-care, 148
setting, 117–118
solution-focused approach, 30, 105, 228, 252
strengths perspective, 27, 102
support for client's, 116–118
termination, 183
Goethe, Johann Wolfgang von, 35
Goscha, R.J., 77, 78, 79
Grameen Bank, 396
grandparents, 213–214
grassroots organizations, 406
Greenberg, C.S., 218–219
Greenpeace, 379
group conferencing, 256

group work is a classic goal-focused social work practice method that emphasizes a common purpose, 6–7, 272–304
assessment and planning, 295–296, 297–300, 303
community development, 384
developmental models, 310–313, 337
engagement, 292–294
evaluation, 331–335, 336, 337
group member roles, 323–324
historical and contemporary contexts for, 275–277
intervention, 305–324, 336–337
logistics, 284–285, 296

narrative theory, 285–286, 287, 308–309, 326–327
pre-group planning, 288–292
privacy issues, 89–90
skills for intervention, 318–324
social worker roles, 322–323
solution-focused approach, 286–287, 309–310, 327
strengths and empowerment perspectives, 307–308, 326
termination, 325–331, 333–335, 337
types, forms and function of groups, 278–284

groups are natural or planned associations that evolve through common interest, state of being, or task, 6–7, 273
change work groups, 431, 435–436, 437–439, 442–443, 444, 446–448, 452
definition of, 272–273
as natural orientation, 274
project teams, 408, 410
types, forms and function, 278–284

guest status is the position of a social worker practicing within a host setting that conveys distinct expectations and privileges, 411–412

Hall, Richard, 403
harm
assessment documentation, 135
confidentiality issues, 88
dual relationships, 53
ethical principle screen, 50–51
prevention of, 5
Hartman, Ann, 203
Hayes, Resa, 61
health care, 395
history-taking
community, 349
family social work, 237
group work, 298–299
individual work, 62, 99, 133–134
organizations, 415, 438
HIV/AIDS
global nature of, 19
globalization policies, 20
social work values, 36
support groups, 280
home visits, 143
homelessness, 10, 19, 36, 363
homework, 251, 253–254
honest responding, 118–120
honesty, 65, 125–126, 139
hopelessness, 456

Hopson, L.M., 245
Horton, H., 306
host setting is the organizational practice
    environment (eg, hospitals, schools, or substance
    abuse agencies), in which social work is not the
    major profession but rather is a guest, 176,
    410–412, 428
housing, 63, 341, 410
    client's competencies, 156, 157
    community development, 388
    community practice models, 380
    logic model, 454
    organizational change, 441, 447
    social action, 127
Howard, M.O., 106
Hull, G.H., 245
human rights are those inherent rights that people
    must have and to which all people are entitled, 3,
    25–26, 30, 32
    assessment, 97
    community development, 387
    community practice, 341
    disabled clients, 179
    engagement with clients, 85–88, 92
    ethical practice, 37
    evaluation of intervention's compatibility with, 196
    global community practice, 393
    globalization, 19, 20–21
    group work, 302, 306–307, 315, 337
    IFSW *Statement of Principles*, 39, 40
    posture of cultural reciprocity, 218
    of social workers, 149
    universal, 370
human service system, 350
human worth, 5, 65
humor, 77

IDAs. *See* individual development accounts
identity
    communities of, 342–343, 369
    constructionist groups, 316, 317
Ife, J., 25
IFSW. *See* International Federation of Social Workers
illness, 26
immigrants, 20, 369–370
    assessment, 111
    community development, 388
    community organizing, 394
    culturagrams, 234–235
    group work, 275–276, 330–331

international families, 222–224
impact evaluation reviews the impact of the efforts,
    such as individual or community-level behavioral
    changes, 453
impartiality, 53
implementation skills, 443
"incestuous families", 212
income-generation programs, 395
independence, 274
indigenous leadership occurs when a member or
    members of a social group exert leadership from
    within that group, 319, 384
indirect questions are questions phrased as sentences,
    rather than questions, 71–72
Individual Development Accounts (IDAs), 384, 387
individual exclusion, 87
individual work is the professional application of
    social work theory and methods to the treatment
    and prevention of psychosocial dysfunction,
    disability, or impairment, including emotional
    and mental disorder, 6
    assessment and planning, 96–153
    engagement, 61–95
    evaluation, 90–91, 181, 189–197, 200
    intervention, 154–181, 199–200
    involuntary clients, 139–140
    termination, 181–189, 200
individualism, 274, 275, 340
inequality
    community practice, 368
    violence and, 141
inertia according to systems theory, is the tendency of
    organizations to seek to maintain the status quo, or
    stability, by working actively against change, 437
inferred empathy, 72
informal resources are those resources that exist
    naturally in individuals, families, organizations,
    and communities that may benefit people seeking
    services; contrast to formal services, 124–125,
    169–170, 186
information provision, 163, 183–184
information sharing, 370
inputs are those resources necessary to implement a
    change effort or a program, 453, 454
institutional settings
    group work, 284, 312
    termination, 188–189
intangible resources are non-concrete resources, such
    as individual counseling and education groups, 81
interdependence occurs when people depend on one

another for the goods, services, relationships, social, and spiritual dimensions required to function, 340

interdisciplinary practice, 175, 220

intergenerational patterns refer to the assertion that families transmit their patterns of relationship from one generation to the next, 210, 212–213

internalization of oppression is the process by which individuals come to believe that the external judgments are valid, thus resulting in a devaluing of one's self, 128, 151

international community development, 393–394, 396

international families, 222–224

International Family Strengths Model, 223

International Federation of Social Workers (IFSW), 38–39, 40

international financial institutions, 19–20

international social work describes work with international organizations using social work methods or personnel, social work co-operation among countries, and transfer among countries of methods or knowledge about social work, 7

interpersonal power is the personal attribute characterized by the ability to build strong relationships, develop rapport, and persuade people, 81–82

interpretation, 165, 227

interprofessional collaboration refers to situations when professionals from different disciplines integrate their professional knowledge to work together toward a common goal, 175–177, 412

interprofessional team is an organized group of people, each trained in different professional disciplines, working together to resolve a common problem or achieve common goals, 220, 411, 412

intervention is the joint activity of the client system and the social worker that will enable the client and the practitioner to accomplish the goals decided upon in the assessment, 9
   client's environment, 159–166
   community practice, 376–397, 400–401
   diversity, 159
   documentation, 136, 236–238
   empowerment practice, 177–180
   family social work, 243–258, 267, 268–269
   group work, 305–324, 336–337
   individual work, 154–181, 199–200
   narrative, 157–158
   organizations, 432–451, 457
   solution-focused approach, 158

strengths perspective, 155–157, 158

termination, 181–189

traditional social work roles, 166–177

unexpected events, 180–181

interviewing, 67–73, 75, 91
   communication pitfalls, 73–74
   community needs assessment, 355–357, 358, 361
   involuntary clients, 138
   motivational interviewing, 180, 256–257

intimacy refers to a developmental stage in group practice, according to the Boston Model and those models deriving from it, in which members feel emotional closeness, 311, 312, 313

invitational empathy, 72

involuntary clients receive services but do not seek them on their own; contrast to mandated and ,nonvoluntary
   group work, 284
   individual work, 136–140, 144, 151

involuntary hospitalization, 55, 56

irrelevant questions are questions that do not relate to the topic at hand, 74

jargon is verbal shortcuts or profession-specific language that can be confusing to clients, 73

Jenson, J.M., 106

joining, 217

Jones, H., 312

Jordan, C., 245

judgement, 99–100, 108, 164

Kagle, J.D., 131

Kaye, Melanie, 243

Kelley, P., 103

Kelly, T.B., 312

key informants are persons informed about a community who provide important information to researchers studying that community, 355–357, 358

Khinduka, S.K., 20

Kiser, J., 141–142

knowledge is comprised of facts, resource findings, and institutional and cultural awareness, 4–5, 13, 21
   community, 360, 367
   cultural competence, 109
   expert, 17, 81
   global awareness, 370
   group work, 314
   information provision to clients, 163

organizations, 404
practice wisdom, 197–198
Kolodny, R., 312
Kondrat, M.E., 14
Kopels, S., 131
Kretzmann, J.P., 363
Kurland, R., 285

Laird, Joan, 203
language includes the actual words used, as well as the tone, range of sentiment, and degree of empathy and respect expressed by the words that are used in agency settings
cover terms, 110
involuntary clients, 138
non-English speakers, 159–160
organizations, 418
person-first, 221
respect for, 370–371
solution-focused approach, 105
law
confidentiality issues, 88–89
ethics and the, 45–49, 58
involuntary clients, 139
organizational assessment, 415
leadership
community capacity development, 378
community development, 384
group work, 318–319
local-level development, 395
leading questions are questions that manipulate client systems to choose the preferred answer, 73
"least contest" approach, 161, 176
Lee, J.A.B., 312
legal basis provides authorization for an organization to officially exist, and defines the parameters for the operations, 415, 422
legal issues
confidentiality issues, 88–89
ethics, 45–49, 58
involuntary clients, 139
organizational assessment, 415
legislative advocacy is cause-focused advocacy that aims to add, delete, implement, or alter legislation, 88, 173–175, 176
legitimate power refers to legal power to perform actions to control the behavior of others, 82
lesbians
diversity codes, 43
exclusion, 306

family social work, 205, 207, 214–215
school problems, 424–425, 431, 436, 439–440, 442–443, 444–446, 449–450
social advocacy, 381
Lewin, Kurt, 424
licensure, 10–11, 13, 45
life, protection of, 50, 51, 146
listening skills, 62–64, 91
active listening, 253, 348
crisis intervention, 144
group work, 318
motivational interviewing, 180
narrative theory, 250
literacy courses, 395
litigation, 47–48, 57–58, 88
lobbying is the use of persuasion with targeted decision-makers who are neutral or opposed to the change effort, 444
local-level development, 394, 395
location, 79–80, 284
Logan, S.L.M., 225, 246
logic model is a graphic depiction of the relationship of inputs, activities, outputs, and outcomes, which provides a way to demonstrate the links between resources, efforts, accomplishments, and the impacts of change efforts and programs, 454
logistics
group work, 284–285, 291, 296
implementation skills, 443
individual work, 79–80
lying, 55

Maathai, Wangari, 375
macro practice, 12
maintenance is the time period utilized in evaluation that follows the intervention in order to determine whether gains made during the intervention are sustained, 191, 192
managed care organizations (MCOs), 130
management information system is the process for collecting program data, and is often a type of software or internet-based application, 449, 450
management style, 416
mandated clients are clients who are ordered by a court to obtain services
group work, 284, 286
individual work, 136–137, 138–139, 140, 144, 151
Maori people, 43, 44
mapping is a technique in which complex phenomena

are represented visually to enable a perceptual
rather than linguistical presentation
community asset mapping, 347, 363–365, 378, 388
community needs assessment, 354, 356
family social work, 232–236, 239, 258
individual work, 120–123, 151, 165–166
marginalized persons are those who live on the
periphery of society or are denied full participation
in social processes due to stigmatization, 205, 207,
320, 346, 389
mass media appeals, 444–445
Mather, J., 245
McCullough-Chavis, A., 234
McGoldrick, M., 258
McKnight, J.L., 363
MCOs. *See* managed care organizations
meaning questions, 113, 114
media, 388, 434, 444–445
mediator is a person who helps two or more opposing
parties recognize their common investment in
resolving their differences, 3, 170–172, 253
Medicaid, 81, 130
meetings, 384, 385
mental health issues
affordable housing, 441, 447
Assertive Community Treatment, 369
assessment documentation, 134, 299–300
children, 207
community practice, 379–381
cultural competence, 421
employee safety, 141
group work, 279–280, 283
involuntary clients, 139–140
self-determination, 56
stigma, 78
mentoring, 3
metaphors, 80
Meyer, Carol, 96, 97
Middleman, R.R., 80, 318
migration, 369–370, 394. *See also* immigrants
Miller, W., 257
"minimax" principle, 162
Minuchin, S., 211
miracle questions
family social work, 228, 251–252
group work, 287, 309
individual work, 115, 158
mirroring is verbal reflection of the client's talents and
capabilities so that the client can see himself or
herself from a strengths perspective, 77

misconduct, 57
mission statement is a concise, broad statement of the
purpose of the organization that describes a shared
vision, 2, 169, 415
Morgan, A., 75
motivational interviewing is an evidence-based
strategy in which empathy and reflective listening
are used to aid the client in sharing her or his story
and developing a plan for intervention, 180,
256–257
multi-barrier families are those families whose
challenges may encompass economic, health,
behavioral, social, and psychological issues, 224
multiculturalism
community practice, 368
multicultural respect, 247
multidisciplinary practice, 175
multiple questions is asking two or more questions at
the same time, 74

NAMI. *See* National Alliance of the Mentally Ill
narrative theory is a practice perspective that puts the
client's story at the center of the work in an effort
to rewrite that story in the way that the client
prefers and guides practitioners to utilize "stories"
to understand the lived experience of clients, 14,
29–30
assessment, 103–105, 112–114
empowerment practice, 180
evaluation of intervention's compatibility with,
196–197
family social work, 225–227, 249–250, 260
group work, 285–286, 287, 308–309, 326–327
intervention, 157–158
NASW. *See* National Association of Social Work
National Alliance of the Mentally Ill (NAMI), 280
National Association of Social Work (NASW), 2. *See also*
Code of Ethics
cultural competence, 109
definition of the family, 204
employee safety, 141, 142
sanctions, 45
social justice, 25
Native Americans, 18
natural groups are those associations of people that
occur without professional intervention, such as
families, friendship groups, and common interest
groups, 278
needs
community needs assessment, 351–363, 364

family social work, 247, 249
human rights perspective, 25
pre-group planning, 288–290
needs assessment is a focused inquiry into the extent
    to which a service system is meeting the needs of a
    specific population, 351–363, 364
neglect
    confidentiality issues, 88–89
    duty to report, 46–47
    global nature of, 19
    societal interests, 54
negligence, 57
negotiation skills, 445, 447
neighborhood committees, 392
Netting, F.E., 440, 444
networks, 124–125, 169–170, 388
New Zealand, 43, 44
Newhill, C.E., 141
NGOs. *See* ,non-governmental organizations
Noble, C., 43
nonclinical work usually refers to work that addresses
    environmental supports of individuals or groups of
    individuals, 11–12, 13, 14
non-discrimination, 44
non-governmental organizations (NGOs), 393, 394
nonprofit organizations, 406, 426–427
nonverbal communication, 66, 67, 68, 77
nonvoluntary clients are clients who are coerced or
    pressured into receiving social services, 137, 151
norm setting is demonstrated when the social worker
    provides information regarding appropriate group
    member behavior through role modeling and
    direct feedback, 322–323
norms are rules or agreements about conduct that are
    usually explicit in social work groups
    community, 344, 347
    cultural, 223
    family, 209–210, 232
    group work, 293–294, 319, 320, 322–323
    organizational, 406–407

Obama, Barack, 339
objectives are steps toward reaching the goals and can
    relate to an outcome, or a specific task, or a process,
    or the means to completing a task, 449, 453
observation, 332, 353, 399, 455
older people
    confidentiality issues, 88
    duty to report, 47
omission, 149

on-site service referral is a method of recruitment for a
    group in which potential members are generated
    from the social worker's caseload or from other
    social workers' caseloads on the same site, 292
open groups are groups in which members may join at
    any time that are usually ongoing rather than time
    limited, 284, 291
open-ended questions are questions designed to
    encourage the client to reveal specific information
    concisely and factually, without opinion,
    embellishment, or detail, 71
opening space questions, 114
oppression, 42, 45, 161
    community assessment, 350–351, 363
    empowerment approach, 247
    families of multiple racial and ethnic heritages, 218
    group work, 279
    internalization of, 128, 151
    planning, 128
organizational culture, 405, 416, 418, 419
organizational exclusion, 87
organizations, 403–429, 430–459
    assessment, 412, 413–423, 424–425, 428, 456
    contemporary theories, 405
    definition of, 404
    dimensions of, 405
    engagement, 412–413, 424–425, 427, 428, 456
    evaluation, 452–455, 458
    framework for change, 435–448
    host settings, 410–412
    implementation of change, 448–451, 457
    interconnections between dimensions, 410
    postmodern approaches, 434–435
    power politics model, 434
    power relations, 409–410
    purpose of, 405–406
    self-learning model, 432–433
    social constructionist approach, 435
    as social systems, 404
    structures of governance, 406–408, 410
    systems model, 433–434
    termination, 451–452, 457
    types of, 426–427, 428
Orme, J.G., 190
outcome evaluation focuses on information about
    specific results that the effort achieved, 453
outcomes are the benefits gained or changes that have
    occurred as a result of the activities, 454
outputs are products that emerge from the activities,
    453–454

outreach is a method of recruitment for a group in which potential members are identified from inside or outside the agency, 292

outsourcing is a phenomenon of globalized economics in which U.S. companies shift jobs formerly held by U.S. workers to countries in which much cheaper labor can be located, 19

overall purpose is the general reason or intention of an effort
group work, 290, 293
individual work, 75–76, 91, 164

painful events, 146–147

paraphrasing is the expression of an idea of the relevant points of the immediate past statement of the client in your own words, 69

Parent Empowerment Survey, 264

parentified child is a term used in family work when a child is required to take on adult tasks of taking care of the home or younger siblings because the parent is not available, 216

parenting. *See also* **family social work**
attachment theory, 100–101
case vignette, 82–85
confidentiality issues, 89
confrontation, 119
goals, 116–117
group work, 284
information provision, 163
resource assessment, 125

parliamentary procedure is a structured, democratic (majority rules) mechanism whereby formal groups can engage in efficient and fair decision-making, 384, 386

participant observation, 353

participation
capacity building, 444
community capacity development, 378
community development, 383
community needs assessment, 359
community organizing, 390
community practice, 344, 392, 399
exclusion from, 86, 87
group work, 293–294, 320, 323–324, 332
right to, 40

participatory research, 367–368, 373

partner violence, 3, 15, 208–209
community development, 387
critical constructionist perspective, 231
family norms, 210

genograms, 165
global community organizing, 394
group work, 284, 308, 315, 316–317
intergenerational patterns, 212
involuntary clients, 139–140
narrative theory, 103–105
project teams, 408, 410
societal interests, 54
solution-focused approach, 251

partnerships
community needs assessment, 352
community organizing, 390, 391

paternalism is the process of interfering with clients' self-determination because the social worker believes she or he has a better understanding than the client of the actions that are in the clients' best interests, 55–56

pathology, 76

Peace Corps, 378–379, 393

permeable boundaries are boundaries through which information and interchange pass relatively easily; similar to diffuse boundaries, 209

personal community is the collective of all communities to which an individual belongs and include communities of locality and identity, 343

personal triggers, 146, 147

personnel are persons in communities and organizations who are in interaction with one other, 422, 440, 441, 448

perspectival questions, 113, 255

perspective is a view, or lens, generally less structured than a theory, through which the world can be observed and interpreted, 23. *See also* **theoretical perspective**

persuasion, 444

physical health, 146, 148

physical surroundings are the atmosphere of an organization that reflects and impacts aspects of organizational culture, 416–418

planning is the practical preparation for carrying out an intervention and involves arranging and scheduling the choice of activities that generated from the assessment process, 8–9
case management, 167
community practice, 377, 378, 379–382, 392
crisis intervention, 144–145
documentation, 136, 238
family social work, 244, 246, 256
group work, 281–283, 287, 295–296, 309–310
individual work, 126–129

strategic plans, 438
suicide risk, 145
termination, 182–188
police, 143
policy is represented by a formally adopted statement that reflects goals and strategies or agreements on a settled course of action
community needs assessment, 352
community practice, 378
global, 371
IFSW *Statement of Principles*, 40
organizational change, 439, 441, 448
policy practice is social work practice that is designed to improve institutional responses; initiate, remove, or change laws; or otherwise affect social structures that affect people's lives, 12, 126, 127
politics
cause advocacy, 174
community, 350, 360, 377
family social work, 227
organizational relationships, 423
population is the number of people of a specified class or group in a specified space or geographic region, 348, 349, 362–363
possibility questions, 113
postmodernism is a contemporary perspective that questions the way in which knowledge is attained and valued, and distinguishes belief from truth, 27–30, 32
community practice, 347
ethical practice, 57, 58
evaluation, 194–195
family social work, 245–246
language use, 418
organizational change, 434–435
preferred reality, 115
posture of cultural reciprocity is a model for working with diverse families developed by special educators that offers a useful guide for social work practice, 218, 219
poverty
areas of concentrated, 372
chaotic climate created by, 186
community practice, 392
exclusion, 306
global nature of, 19
globalization policies, 20
impact on children's behavior, 212
self-knowledge, 21–22
single parent families, 205

strengths perspective, 76
structural exclusion, 87
violence and, 141
power, 80–85, 92
advocacy, 173, 175
case vignette, 82–85
community, 345–346, 363, 377, 389–390, 391
critical social construction, 30
dual relationships, 54
empowerment practice, 177
family social work, 248
involuntary clients, 140
minimization of distance, 18
organizations, 409–410
shared, 17, 81, 148
sources of, 81–82
power and control refers to a developmental stage in social group work practice in which members vie for control among themselves and between members and the worker, 311, 312
power dependency theory, 346, 379
power politics model describes a theoretical perspective used to depict organizational change that emphasizes competition for resources, personal advancement, and inter- and intra-power struggles and asserts that the primary path to change requires strategic access to the persons who have the greatest power and primary influence, 434
practice is the way in which organizations implement basic functions, 440, 441, 448
practice, social work, 2–3
family social work, 253
group work, 292–294, 305–338
host settings, 410–412
practice framework, 7–10
practice wisdom, 4, 197–198
preaffiliation refers to a developmental stage in group practice, according to the Boston Model, in which members are ambivalent about joining a group, 310–311, 312, 313
preference questions, 114
preferred reality is a term reflecting the client's desire for creating a different reality that is consistent with her or his dreams and goals, 115–116, 139, 261
prejudice, 86
primary education, 395
privacy, 50, 55, 89–90, 92
private organizations, 426

privilege, in the context of culture and diversity, is a phenomenon in which unearned advantages are enjoyed by members of a particular dominant group simply by virtue of membership in it, 30, 371

problem solving, 321–322, 388, 443

problem-saturated story is a term used in narrative and solution-focused practice to refer to an excessive emphasis on problems, to the exclusion of other dimensions, in the stories of those people coming for help, 226

procedures are the processes through which the agency members interact with client systems that impact the experience of the client system, 418, 449, 450

process evaluation focuses on the degree to which an effort functioned optimally, 453

professional boundaries, 53, 57, 88, 187

professionalism, 13

program is a prearranged set of activities designed to achieve a set of goals and objectives, 440, 441, 448

Project Restore (PR), 396

project teams consist of a group of persons who collectively work on organizational challenges or opportunities through committee or task force structures, 408, 410

projects are prearranged sets of activities designed to achieve a set of goals and objectives, and are timelimited in existence and flexible, 440, 441, 448

pseudopaternalism, 56

psychoanalytic theory is a classic theory, primarily associated with Sigmund Freud, that maintains that unconscious processes direct human behavior, 23, 100

psychoeducational group is a group focused on educating members regarding psychological processes or principles and supporting their common experiences, 3, 279–280, 315

psychosocial history, 62, 99

psychotherapy, 12, 13

public, working with the, 173

public organizations, 405–406, 426

public relations is the practice of managing communication between an organization and the public, 418

Putnam, R.D., 369

qualifications, 10

quality of life, 50

questions, 67, 70–72, 253

communication pitfalls, 73–74

discovering strengths, 112, 113

focus groups, 357

group work, 309, 327

key informants, 357, 358

narrative theory, 114, 157

perspectival, 255

screening for group assessment, 300

solution-focused approach, 114–115, 158, 228–229, 251–252

race

exclusion, 306

families of multiple racial and ethnic heritages, 218

teenage parents, 205

racism

case vignette, 83

ethical dilemmas, 49

exclusion, 86, 87

impact on children's behavior, 212

institutionalized, 28

violence and, 141

RAIs. *See* rapid assessment instruments

rape, 55

rapid assessment instruments (RAIs), 130

Rapp, C.A., 77, 78, 79

rational/legal authority is the authority in an organizational setting that is derived from the ability to achieve and persuade; it usually results from careful study of an issue as well as experience, 409, 410

Reamer, F.G., 51, 52, 53, 55

re-authoring, 114, 157, 327

reciprocal groups are groups designed to provide instrumental and/or emotional supports to persons living a shared experience. Also referred to as support, mutual aid, and mutual-sharing groups, 279–280, 282, 315, 334

reciprocal model is a classic model of social work groups in which the primary focus is the members' interactive and supportive relationships with each other; also known as interactional model, 276, 277

redirection is a group work skill in which the social worker directs the communication away from herself or himself and toward the appropriate group member or members, 320

re-enactments, 257–258

referrals

brokering role, 168, 169, 170, 186

group work, 292

reflective assessment, 190, 195–197, 200
reflective practice, 58, 267
refocusing is a practice skill in which the worker returns the client to the original purpose of their work and the priority of their goals, 163–164
reframing is a practice skill in which the worker conceives of and describes a situation in different terms, context, and with a different judgment than the client uses, 102, 226, 254–255
refugees, 20, 161–162
  assessment, 111
  community development, 388
  culturagrams, 234–235
  global community practice, 369–370
  international families, 222
regression is used to describe a literal "going back" to earlier stages; in group work it may occur in order to avoid ending; may be expressed verbally or behaviorally, 329
reinforcement is a process that strengthens the tendency of a response to recur, 79, 114
relational model is a feminist model for individual or group practice in which the emphasis is on the relatedness of the person to others rather than on individual achievement or separation from others, 313
relationships, 61–95. *See also* **engagement**
  brokering role, 169
  bureaucracies, 407
  community, 353, 388, 397
  core relationship qualities, 64–65, 75, 91
  exploration of quality of, 197
  group work, 314, 325, 329–330
  organizational, 422–423
  termination, 181–189
remedial groups are developed for the purpose of changing behavior, restoring function, or promoting coping strategies of the individual members who join the group voluntarily or involuntarily, 280–281, 283, 315, 335
remedial model is a classic model for group work practice in which the emphasis is on healing or changing individual members who have deviated from societal expectations, 276, 277
reparenting, 23
representation of self is a social constructionist term to describe one's perceptual picture of the totality of oneself, 316
resiliency is the human capacity to cope with crises, stressors, and normal experiences in an emotionally and physically healthy manner, 76–77, 92, 102
  community practice, 347
resocialization is a term used to describe an intervention to assist people in dealing with their feelings and inner perceptions that are primarily related to the "self"; thought to be more relevant to psychology than social work, 12–13
resource mobilization theory, 346, 379
resources
  agency, 81
  assessment of, 123–126, 151
  brokering role, 169–170
  client's environment, 161
  community, 341, 345, 346, 360, 376–377
  developing, 88
  dual relationships, 54
  empowerment approach, 247, 249
  group work, 314, 321
  IFSW *Statement of Principles*, 40
  organizations, 404, 422
  single parent families, 217
  solution-focused approach, 250–251
  strengths perspective, 27, 102, 103
  termination planning, 186
respect, 5
restorative justice groups focus on crime as an interpersonal conflict that has repercussions for the victim, offender, and community at large; they emphasize the harm done to the relationships of those involved rather than the violation of the law, 315, 317–318
Richie, H., 57
Richmond, Mary, 13, 98, 243
risk, suicide, 135, 145–146
risk management is the identification, assessment, and prioritization of risks, 37, 57–58
risk taking, 41–43
Riverton Against Youth Drinking (RAYD), 281, 333
Riverton Children's Grief Support Group, 282, 334
Riverton Mental Health Center Group for Persons with Dual Diagnosis, 283, 335
Roberts, A.R., 144–145
Robert's Rules of Order, 384, 386, 390
Rogers, Carl, 64
role-playing, 257–258
Rollnick, S., 257
Roman Catholic Church, 49
Roosevelt, Eleanor, 154
Rothman, J., 377, 401

rules and procedures are the set of laws and processes that provide the structure for the day-to-day functioning of the program, 449, 450

rural areas
brokering role, 169
dual relationships, 53, 187

safety issues, 141–144
Saleebey, D., 26, 102, 112, 120, 156, 347
sanctions, 45
Sanger, Margaret, 381
scaling questions
family social work, 228–229, 251, 260–261
group work, 309, 327
individual work, 115, 158
scanning is a social work group practice skill in which the social worker uses visual contact with all group members to monitor their affect, participation, and non-verbal communication, 319
Schiller, L.Y., 312
school drop-outs, 406
school-based services, 172, 387–388, 410, 413
case management, 168
LGBTQ students, 424–425, 436, 439–440, 442–443, 444–446, 449–450
scientific practitioner combines the use of evidence and evaluation without compromising the art and creativity of practice, 190
secondary trauma, also known as "vicarious trauma," is the sense of trauma experienced by those close to the victim of trauma, such as a family member, helping professional, or bystander near the trauma site, 146, 151–152
self-blame, 162
self-care, 146, 147–149, 152
self-determination is an ethical principle that recognizes the rights and needs of clients to be free to make their own decisions, 23–24, 55–56, 274
community development, 383
disabled clients, 221
dual relationships, 53
family social work, 252
IFSW *Statement of Principles*, 40
miracle questions, 115
motivational interviewing, 180
solution-focused approach, 250
strengths perspective, 103
suicide, 145–146
termination, 189, 200
self-disclosure occurs when the social worker reveals feelings, values, and personal information to clients, 78–79
self-efficacy
empowerment practice, 177, 180
motivational interviewing, 256, 257
single parent families, 217
self-evaluation, 105, 158, 332
self-harm, 71
self-help
community organizing, 389
group work, 279
local-level development, 395
self-knowledge, 2, 21–22, 109
self-learning model is a theoretical perspective that emphasizes the ability of organizations to selfcorrect as needed, 432–433
self-report, 264
separation refers to a developmental stage in social group work practice, according to the Boston Model, in which the group disbands and the members separate from each other and from the social worker, 311
service statistics, 353
setting is the context or place in which the social worker engages in community practice, 348, 349
setting goals refers to the process in which the client and the social worker establish clear behavior outcomes of their work together, 117–118
sexism, 83, 86
sexual abuse. *See* abuse
sexual orientation. *See* gay people; lesbians
sexual relationships with clients, 52
Shalay, N., 222
shared power is the idea that the individual is considered to be an expert on her or his life, culture, dreams, experience, and goals, 17, 81, 148
Shields, G., 141–142
shortcomings, identification of, 185
silence, 67–68, 73, 320
Simon, B., 177
single parenthood, 205, 216–217
single-subject design is a conceptual framework for evaluating and graphically representing changes in one client over time, 190–191, 192, 262
skills are the implementation of the knowledge, theoretical perspectives, and values the social worker brings to her or his work with client systems, 4, 6, 13, 21, 91
assessment and planning, 112–123
assessment of resources, 123–126

community development, 383–384
community organizing, 389, 390–391
community practice, 341
developing client's, 172–173
dialogue, 65–67
environment-sensitive, 162–166
family social work, 268–269
group work, 284–285, 314, 318–324, 327–331, 337
interviewing, 67–73
mapping, 120–123
organizational engagement and assessment, 413, 424–425
organizational interventions, 443–446
strengths perspective, 77–79, 158
termination, 327–331
smoking, 35
Snively, C.A., 104
social action is a method of community organization generally aimed at shifting power structures in order to change institutional responses and often involves conflict or social tensions, 126, 127
social action or goals groups are groups in which the primary focus is advocating for social justice, 278, 279, 281, 297, 308, 315, 333
social advocacy, 377, 379–382
social capital, 369
social change, 15, 16
community practice, 400
group work, 275, 279
social construction is a postmodern perspective that proposes that reality is created through shared meanings or beliefs that develop in social interaction and are perpetuated through language, 14, 27–28, 30–31, 32. *See also* **critical social construction**
disabled clients, 179
family social work, 230, 231, 245
organizational change, 435
posture of cultural reciprocity, 218
social control, 15, 344
social ecology approach, 433
social exclusion, 86, 87, 186
social goals model is an early classic model of group practice in which the emphasis is on democratic values, social conscience and responsibility, and the strengths of group members to participate productively, 276, 277
social histories, 99
social justice is the means by which societies allocate their resources, which consist of material goods

and social benefits, rights, and protections, 13–14, 15, 24–25, 32, 158
adherence to ethical codes, 42
adjustment and challenge, 16
advocacy, 175
assessment, 97
community practice, 400
disabled clients, 179, 221
empowerment practice, 177
engagement with clients, 85–88, 92
evaluation of intervention's compatibility with, 196
family social work, 230–231
Gandhian principles, 57
globalization, 19, 20
group work, 275–276, 302, 306–307, 315, 336–337
IFSW *Statement of Principles*, 39, 40
narrative theory, 103
organizations, 420
posture of cultural reciprocity, 218
social workers, 149
violence, 141
social location refers to the time, place, and prevailing ideas or discourse that influence standards, particularly about what is considered "right" Social movement is a political effort designed to change an aspect of society, 28, 29
social model of disability, 221
social movement is a political effort designed to change an aspect of society, 406
social networks, 124–125, 177
social work
competencies, 4–10
definition of, 39
licensure, 10–11
practice of, 2–3
purpose of, 2
tensions in, 11–19, 32
theoretical perspectives, 23–31
traditional roles, 166–177, 200, 253
socialization
community, 343–344
developmental, 12–13
family, 207, 208, 213
groups, 278
society, responsibility to, 54–55
socioeconomic class, 21–22
sociogram is a diagram or graphic presentation whereby relationships between external entities and the organization are visually depicted, 422

solidarity
  bicultural code of practice, 44
  community capacity development, 378, 382
  IFSW *Statement of Principles*, 40
  international, 393
solution-focused practice is a specific therapeutic
    perspective that emphasizes brief interventions,
    narrowly defined specific problem areas, and
    cognitive support in identifying explicit solutions
    to pressing problems, 30, 105–106, 114–115
  crisis intervention, 144, 145
  critical constructionist emphasis, 231
  family social work, 227–229, 250–252, 260–261
  group work, 286–287, 309–310, 327
  intervention, 158
Specht, Harvey, 12–13
spirituality, 5, 110, 148
stakeholders are those who have an interest in
    community affairs, such as neighborhood leaders,
    342, 359, 360
standardized assessment, 232, 262, 269, 295, 332
standards, ethical, 37, 38
Standards for Social Work Practice with Groups, 276–277,
    292–293, 314
Statement of Principles (IFSW), 39, 40
stigma, 78
story development questions, 114
strategic plans are comprehensive, formal plans for
    the future direction of the organization, 438
strategy is an overall approach to a change effort,
    440–443
strengths perspective is an orientation that
    emphasizes client system resources, capabilities,
    support systems, and motivations to meet
    challenges and overcome adversity to achieve
    wellbeing, 18, 26–27, 30, 31, 32, 92
  assessment, 98, 102–103, 104, 112
  client's goals and dreams, 120
  community needs assessment, 360
  community practice, 347, 363, 367, 376, 398
  crisis intervention, 145
  cultural competence, 108, 109, 111
  dialogue skills, 65
  disabled clients, 179
  empowerment practice, 177, 180
  evaluation of intervention's compatibility with, 196
  evaluation tools, 262–266
  exception questions, 229
  family social work, 211, 246–249, 253, 259–260,
    262–266

family-centered care, 219–220
  gay, lesbian, bisexual and transgender parents, 215
  group work, 285, 287, 307–308, 326
  IFSW *Statement of Principles*, 40
  international families, 223–224
  intervention, 155–157, 158, 199
  logistics and activities, 79–80
  respectful stance, 76
  shared power, 148
  single parent families, 217
  skills and methods, 77–79
Strom-Gottfried, K.J., 51–52, 57
structural exclusion, 87
substance abuse, 18, 42
  assessment documentation, 133, 298
  case management, 168
  grandparents raising grandchildren, 214
  group work, 284
  intergenerational patterns, 212
  nonvoluntary clients, 137
subsystems are a dimension of systems theory; they are
    a way of organizing relationships and engaging
    with them, 209, 211, 344–345
suicide, 36, 181
  ethical dilemmas, 49
  risk assessment, 135, 145–146
summarizing is a way to confirm an understanding the
    client's message and address assumptions, 70, 329
summative research is research conducted to learn
    about the outcome, or effect, of interventions, 10
supervision, 10, 152
  advocacy, 176
  ethical decision-making, 57–58
  social worker's own family issues, 236
  sustaining ethical practice, 149–150
  tips for effective, 150
support
  client's environment, 161
  community, 344
  empowerment practice, 177
  family social work, 244, 247–248
  grandparents raising grandchildren, 214
  networks of, 31, 148
  termination planning, 186
support groups, 280, 311, 315. *See also* **reciprocal
    groups**
support questions, 113
survey is a systematic fact-gathering procedure in
    which a specific series of questions is asked,
    through written or oral questionnaires, of a

representative sample of the group being studied or of the entire population, 359, 361, 364

survival questions, 113

Swenson, C.R., 13

synthesizer is a role for a social worker in group work in which one summarizes the group members' discussions, identifies themes and patterns, and connects content from one session to the next to promote continuity and substantive discussion, 322

systems model is an approach that recognizes the organization as a system composed of many individuals, subsystems, rules, roles, and processes operating within the wider environment, 433–434

systems theory asserts that each system involves a series of components that are highly organized and dependent upon each other in an orderly way, 24

community, 344–345, 376, 377

family social work, 208–213, 246

group work, 285

organizations, 404, 433–434, 437

tactics are specific actions, or skills, taken to implement a strategy, 440–442, 443–446, 447, 457

"talking in the idiom of the other", 80

tangible resources are material resources, such as clothing or money for emergency housing, 81

Tarasoff, Tatiana, 47–48

task groups are groups in which the main focus is completion of a specified undertaking or assignment, 278, 281, 315, 336

community practice, 384, 398

documentation, 297, 301

implementation skills, 443

tax credits, 386

teenage pregnancy, 46–47, 96, 97, 205

tensions in social work, 11–19

termination is the process of ending contact with client systems, 9

case management, 167

community practice, 397–399, 401

cultural consistency, 187–188

family social work, 259–261, 267–268, 269

group work, 311, 312, 325–331, 333–335, 337

individual work, 181–189, 200

negotiation of the timing, 183–184

organizational change, 451–452, 457

plans, 185–186

relational model, 313

review of agreement for work, 184

shared responses to, 186–187

successes and shortcomings, 184–185

testimonials, 326–327

theoretical perspective is a lens, based on some components of theory, through which practice is interpreted; it is sometimes used interchangeably with theory and perspective, 8, 9, 23–31

assessment, 99–108, 151

community practice, 347–348

ecosystems perspective, 24, 32

evaluation of intervention's compatibility with, 196–197

family social work, 225–231, 239, 244–252, 268

group work, 285–287, 302, 307–313

human rights perspective, 25–26, 30, 32

postmodern perspective, 27–30, 32

social justice perspective, 24–25, 32

sociocultural context, 225

strengths perspective, 26–27, 30, 31, 32

theory is an explanation of some event or phenomenon, usually having clear principles and propositions that provide a framework for prediction and applicability, 23, 106, 376, 405

therapeutic group work. *See* **treatment group**

therapy, 12, 13, 167

thickening the story is a narrative principle in which the social worker encourages the client system to describe life stories in increasingly complex terms that recognize both effective and ineffective components, 103, 226

"think tanks", 381

thinking group is the group worker's emphasis on the group as a collective entity and subject of practice, 318, 329

timeline spells out in detail the activities that will carry out the goal and objectives, with specific deadlines in place, 449

Toseland, R.W., 306

traditional authority is the authority gained through status that emphasizes traditional power arrangements, such as queen or president, 409, 410

training, 245

transgender people

diversity codes, 43

exclusion, 306

family social work, 205, 207, 214–215

school problems, 424–425, 431, 436, 439–440, 442–443, 444–446, 449–450

social advocacy, 381

transparency refers to social workers' communication about the intention of their involvement, 75, 88, 140

trauma
assessment documentation, 133, 237, 298
crisis intervention, 144
migrants, 111
secondary, 146, 151–152
strengths perspective, 26

treatment group is social group work in which the emphasis is on healing or initiating change, 276, 281

trust, 7, 68
building, 77
confidentiality issues, 89
honesty, 126
migrants, 111
self-disclosure, 78

truthfulness, 50

Tully, C.T., 159

"tuning in", 296

two-component model of assessment, 102, 104

unconditional positive regard is the expression of acceptance and non-judgmentalness of client systems, regardless of whether a social worker approves or accepts individual or collective client system actions, 65

unexpected events, 180–181

United Nations (UN), 25, 206, 371, 393

values are strongly held beliefs about preferred conditions of life, 4, 5–6, 13, 21, 36, 198
biases, 22
community assessment, 350
culturagrams, 234–235
cultural competence, 421
ethical dilemmas, 49
global application, 371
NASW *Code of Ethics*, 37–38

perspectives, 23
posture of cultural reciprocity, 218, 219
scientific practice, 190
supervision, 149–150
theoretical perspectives, 23
value conflicts, 49

verbal communication, 65, 66, 67, 77, 80

violence, 140–144, 151. *See also* partner violence
duty to protect, 47–48
global nature of, 19
globalization policies, 20
self-blame, 162
societal interests, 54

vision, 112, 115–116, 120, 151

Vodde, R., 53, 54

volunteers, 378–379

vulnerability, 53, 54

Waites, C., 234

Walz, T., 57

warmth is a non-possessive caring, or an expression of caring and concern without expectations for the individual or relationship, 64, 232

Weber, Max, 407

Weick, A., 198

"welfare families", 212

well-being, 56, 400

Witkin, S.L., 41

witness groups, 309

women
constructionist groups, 316–317
family roles, 206
rape, 55
relational model, 313
reproductive control, 207

Wood, G.G., 80, 159, 318

World Trade Organization (WTO), 19–20, 389

youth development, 387

Yunus, Muhammad, 396